Portfolio Management
Study Sessions 9–12

CFA® PROGRAM CURRICULUM • VOLUME 4

LEVEL III
2010

Custom Publishing

New York   Boston   San Francisco
London   Toronto   Sydney   Tokyo   Singapore   Madrid
Mexico City   Munich   Paris   Cape Town   Hong Kong   Montreal

**Pearson
Custom Publishing**
is a division of

www.pearsonhighered.com

ISBN 10: 0-558-16032-8
ISBN 13: 978-0-558-16032-6

CONTENTS

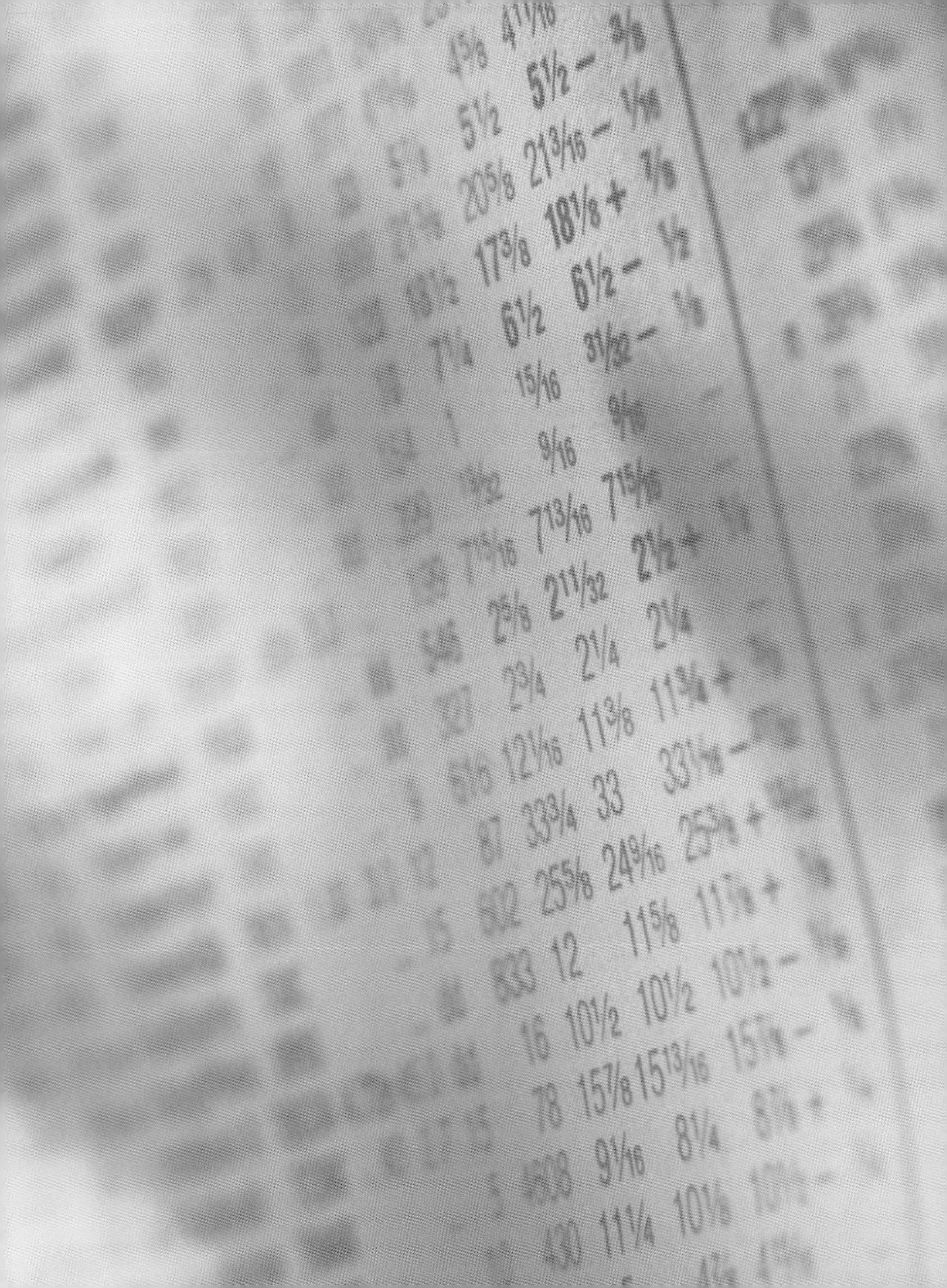

4⅝ 41 1/16

5⅝ 5½ — ⅜

5½ 5½

20⅝ 21 3/16 — 1/16

17⅜ 18⅛ + ⅞

18½ 18⅛ +

6½ 6½ — ⅛

7¼ 3 1/32 —

15/16

9/16 9/16

13/32 7 15/16

7 15/16 7 13/16 7 15/16

2⅝ 2 11/32 2½ +

2¾ 2¼ 2¼

5⅛ 12 1/16 11⅜ 11¾ +

87 33¾ 33 33⅛ —

602 25⅝ 24 9/16 25⅝ +

833 12 11⅝ 11⅞ +

16 10½ 10½ 10½ —

78 15⅞ 15 13/16 15⅛ —

4508 9 1/16 8¼ 8¼ +

430 11¼ 10⅛

HOW TO USE THE CFA PROGRAM CURRICULUM

Congratulations on passing Level II of the Chartered Financial Analyst (CFA®) Program. This exciting and rewarding program of study reflects your desire to become a serious investment professional. You are participating in a program noted for its high ethical standards and the breadth of knowledge, skills, and abilities it develops. Your commitment to the CFA Program should be educationally and professionally rewarding.

The credential you seek is respected around the world as a mark of accomplishment and dedication. Each level of the program represents a distinct achievement in professional development. Successful completion of the program is rewarded with membership in a prestigious global community of investment professionals. CFA charterholders are dedicated to life-long learning and maintaining currency with the ever-changing dynamics of a challenging profession.

The CFA examination measures your degree of mastery of the assigned CFA Program curriculum. Effective study and preparation based on that curriculum are keys to your success on the examination.

Curriculum Development

The CFA Program curriculum is grounded in the practice of the investment profession. Utilizing a collaborative website, CFA Institute performs a continuous practice analysis with investment professionals around the world to determine the knowledge, skills, and abilities that are relevant to the profession. Regional panels and targeted surveys are also conducted annually to verify and reinforce the continuous feedback. The practice analysis process ultimately defines the Candidate Body of Knowledge (CBOK™) an inventory of knowledge and responsibilities expected of the investment management professional at the level of a new CFA charterholder. The process also determines how much emphasis each of the major topic areas receives on the CFA examinations.

A committee made up of practicing charterholders, in conjunction with CFA Institute staff, designs the CFA Program curriculum to deliver the CBOK to candidates. The examinations, also written by practicing charterholders, are designed to allow you to demonstrate your mastery of the CBOK as set forth in the CFA Program curriculum. As you structure your personal study program, you should emphasize mastery of the CBOK and the practical application of that knowledge. For more information on the practice analysis, CBOK, and development of the CFA Program curriculum, please visit www.cfainstitute.org/toolkit.

Organization

The Level III CFA Program curriculum is organized into two topic areas. Each topic area begins with a brief statement of the material and the depth of knowledge expected.

Each topic area is then divided into one or more study sessions. These study sessions—18 sessions in the Level III curriculum—should form the basic structure of your reading and preparation.

Each study session includes a statement of its structure and objective, and is further divided into specific reading assignments. The outline on the inside front cover of each volume illustrates the organization of these 18 study sessions.

The reading assignments are the basis for all examination questions, and are selected or developed specifically to teach the CBOK. These readings are drawn from CFA Program-commissioned content, textbook chapters, professional journal articles, research analyst reports, and cases. Many readings include problems and solutions as well as appendices to help you learn.

Reading-specific Learning Outcome Statements (LOS) are listed in the pages introducing each study session as well as at the beginning of each reading. These LOS indicate what you should be able to accomplish after studying the reading. We encourage you to review how to properly use LOS, and the descriptions of commonly used LOS "command words," at www.cfainstitute.org/toolkit. The command words signal the depth of learning you are expected to achieve from the reading. You should use the LOS to guide and focus your study, as each examination question is based on an assigned reading and one or more LOS. However, the readings provide context for the LOS and enable you to apply a principle or concept in a variety of scenarios. The candidate is responsible for the entirety of all of the required material in a study session, the assigned readings as well as the end-of-reading questions and problems.

Features of the Curriculum

▶ **Required vs. Optional Segments** - You should read all of the pages for an assigned reading. In some cases, however, we have reprinted an entire chapter or article and marked those parts of the reading that are not required as "optional." The CFA examination is based only on the required segments, and the optional segments are included only when they might help you to better understand the required segments (by seeing the required material in its full context). When an optional segment begins, you will see an icon and a solid vertical bar in the outside margin that will continue until the optional segment ends, accompanied by another icon. *Unless the material is specifically marked as optional, you should assume it is required.* Keep in mind that the optional material is provided strictly for your convenience and will not be tested. You should rely on the required segments and the reading-specific LOS in preparing for the examination.

▶ **Problems/Solutions** - *All questions and problems in the readings as well as their solutions (which are provided directly following the problems) are required material.* When appropriate, we have included problems within and after the readings to demonstrate practical application and reinforce your understanding of the concepts presented. The questions and problems are designed to help you learn these concepts and may serve as a basis for exam questions. Many of the questions are adapted from past CFA examinations.

For your benefit, we have also made available the last three years' LIII essay questions and solutions. Please visit www.cfainstitute.org/toolkit to review these resources.

▶ **Margins** - The wide margins in each volume provide space for your note-taking.

▶ **Two-Color Format** - To enrich the visual appeal and clarity of the exhibits, tables, and text, the curriculum is printed in a two-color format.

▶ **Six-Volume Structure** - For portability of the curriculum, the material is spread over six volumes.

▶ **Glossary and Index** - For your convenience, we have printed a comprehensive glossary and index in each volume. Throughout the curriculum, a **bolded blue** word in a reading denotes a term defined in the glossary.

▶ **Source Material** - The authorship, publisher, and copyright owners are given for each reading for your reference. We recommend that you use this CFA Institute curriculum rather than the original source materials because the curriculum may include only selected pages from outside readings, updated sections within the readings, and may have problems and solutions tailored to the CFA Program.

▶ **LOS Self-Check** - We have inserted checkboxes next to each LOS that you can use to track your progress in mastering the concepts in each reading.

Designing Your Personal Study Program

Create a Schedule - An orderly, systematic approach to examination preparation is critical. You should dedicate a consistent block of time every week to reading and studying. Complete all reading assignments and the associated problems and solutions in each study session. Review the LOS both before and after you study each reading to ensure that you have mastered the applicable content and can demonstrate the knowledge, skill, or ability described by the LOS and the assigned reading. Use the new LOS self-check to track your progress and highlight areas of weakness for later review.

You will receive periodic e-mail communications that contain important study tips and preparation strategies. Be sure to read these carefully.

CFA Institute estimates that you will need to devote a minimum of 10–15 hours per week for 18 weeks to study the assigned readings. Allow a minimum of one week for each study session, and plan to complete them all at least 30–45 days prior to the examination. This schedule will allow you to spend the final four to six weeks before the examination reviewing the assigned material and taking online sample and mock examinations.

At CFA Institute, we believe that candidates need to commit to a *minimum* of 270–300 hours reading and reviewing the curriculum and end-of-reading questions and problems. Many candidates have also incorporated the online sample examinations into their preparations during the final weeks before the exam. This recommendation, however, may substantially underestimate the hours needed for appropriate examination preparation depending on your individual circumstances, relevant experience, and academic background. You will undoubtedly adjust your study time to conform to your own strengths and weaknesses, and your educational and professional background.

You will probably spend more time on some study sessions than on others, but on average you should plan on devoting 15 hours per study session. You should allow ample time for both in-depth study of all topic areas and additional concentration on those topic areas for which you feel least prepared.

Candidate Preparation Toolkit - We have created the online toolkit to provide a single comprehensive location with resources and guidance for candidate preparation. In addition to in-depth information on study program planning, the CFA Program curriculum, and the online sample and mock examinations, the toolkit also contains curriculum errata, printable study session outlines, sample examination questions, and more. Errata that we have identified in the curriculum are corrected and listed periodically in the errata listing in the toolkit. We encourage you to use the toolkit as your central preparation resource during your tenure as a candidate. Visit the toolkit at www.cfainstitute.org/toolkit.

Online Sample Examinations - As part of your study of the assigned curriculum, use the CFA Institute online sample examinations to assess your exam preparation as you progress toward the end of your study. After each question, you will receive immediate feedback noting the correct response and indicating the relevant assigned reading, so you'll be able to identify areas of weakness for further study. The 120-minute sample examinations reflect the question formats, topics, and level of difficulty of the actual CFA examinations. Aggregate data indicate that the CFA examination pass rate was higher among candidates who took one or more online sample examinations than among candidates who did not take the online sample examinations. For more information on the online sample examinations, please visit www.cfainstitute.org/toolkit.

Online Mock Examinations - In response to candidate requests, CFA Institute has developed mock examinations that mimic the actual CFA examinations not only in question format and level of difficulty, but also in length. The three-hour online mock exams simulate the morning and afternoon sessions of the actual CFA exam, and are intended to be taken after you complete your study of the full curriculum, so you can test your understanding of the CBOK and your readiness for the exam. To further differentiate, feedback is provided at the end of the exam, rather than after each question as with the sample exams. CFA Institute recommends that you take these mock exams at the final stage of your preparation toward the actual CFA examination. For more information on the online mock examinations, please visit www.cfainstitute.org/toolkit.

Tools to Measure Your Comprehension of the Curriculum

With the addition of the online mock exams, CFA Institute now provides three distinct ways you can practice for the actual CFA exam. The full descriptions are above, but below is a brief summary of each:

End-of-Reading Questions and Problems - These are found at the end of each reading in the printed curriculum, and should be used to test your understanding of the concepts.

Online Sample Exams - Typically available two months before the CFA exam, online sample exams are designed to assess your exam preparation, and can help you target areas of weakness for further study.

Online Mock Exams - In contrast to the sample exams, mock exams are not available until closer to the actual exam date itself. Mock exams are designed to replicate the exam day experience, and should be taken near the end of your study period to prepare for exam day.

Preparatory Providers - After you enroll in the CFA Program, you may receive numerous solicitations for preparatory courses and review materials. Although preparatory courses and notes may be helpful to some candidates, you should view these resources as *supplements* to the assigned CFA Program curriculum. The CFA examinations reference only the CFA Institute assigned curriculum—no preparatory course or review course materials are consulted or referenced. Before you decide on a supplementary prep course, do some research. Determine the experience and expertise of the instructors, the accuracy and currency of their content, the delivery method for their materials, and the provider's claims of success. Most importantly, make sure the provider is in compliance with the CFA Institute Prep Provider Guidelines Program. Three years of prep course products can be a significant investment, so make sure you're getting a sufficient return. Just remember, there are no shortcuts to success on the CFA examinations. Prep products can enhance your learning experience, but the CFA curriculum is the key to success. For more information on the Prep Provider Guidelines Program, visit www.cfainstitute.org/cfaprog/resources/prepcourse.html.

SUMMARY

Every question on the CFA examination is based on specific pages in the required readings and on one or more LOS. Frequently, an examination question is also tied to a specific example highlighted within a reading or to a specific end-of-reading question and/or problem and its solution. To make effective use of the curriculum, please remember these key points:

1. All pages printed in the Custom Curriculum are required reading for the examination except for occasional sections marked as optional. You may read optional pages as background, but you will not be tested on them.

2. All questions, problems, and their solutions - printed at the end of readings - are required study material for the examination.

3. You should make appropriate use of the CFA Candidate Toolkit, the online sample/mock examinations, and preparatory courses and review materials.

4. You should schedule and commit sufficient study time to cover the 18 study sessions, review the materials, and take sample/mock examinations.

5. **Note:** Some of the concepts in the study sessions may be superseded by updated rulings and/or pronouncements issued after a reading was published. Candidates are expected to be familiar with the overall analytical framework contained in the assigned readings. Candidates are not responsible for changes that occur after the material was written.

Feedback

At CFA Institute, we are committed to delivering a comprehensive and rigorous curriculum for the development of competent, ethically grounded investment professionals. We rely on candidate and member feedback as we work to incorporate content, design, and packaging improvements. You can be assured that we will continue to listen to your suggestions. Please send any comments or feedback to curriculum@cfainstitute.org. Ongoing improvements in the curriculum will help you prepare for success on the upcoming examinations, and for a lifetime of learning as a serious investment professional.

$4\frac{5}{8}$ $4\frac{11}{16}$ $-\frac{3}{8}$

$5\frac{1}{2}$ $-$

$5\frac{1}{2}$ $21\frac{3}{16}$ $-\frac{1}{8}$

$20\frac{5}{8}$ $18\frac{1}{8}$ $+\frac{7}{8}$

$17\frac{3}{8}$

$6\frac{1}{2}$ $6\frac{1}{2}$ $-\frac{1}{2}$

$7\frac{1}{4}$ $3\frac{1}{32}$ $-$

$\frac{15}{16}$ $\frac{5}{8}$

$\frac{9}{16}$

$7\frac{13}{16}$ $7\frac{15}{8}$

$7\frac{1}{16}$

$2\frac{5}{8}$ $2\frac{11}{32}$ $2\frac{1}{2}$ $+$

$2\frac{3}{4}$ $2\frac{1}{4}$ $2\frac{1}{4}$

$12\frac{1}{16}$ $11\frac{3}{8}$ $11\frac{1}{4}$ $+$

87 $33\frac{3}{4}$ 33 $33\frac{1}{16}$ $-$

602 $25\frac{5}{8}$ $24\frac{9}{16}$ $25\frac{3}{8}$ $+$

633 12 $11\frac{5}{8}$ $11\frac{7}{8}$ $+$

16 $10\frac{1}{2}$ $10\frac{1}{2}$ $10\frac{1}{2}$ $-$

78 $15\frac{7}{8}$ $15\frac{13}{16}$ $15\frac{7}{8}$ $-$

508 $9\frac{1}{16}$ $8\frac{1}{4}$ $8\frac{1}{2}$ $+$

430 $11\frac{1}{4}$ $10\frac{1}{8}$

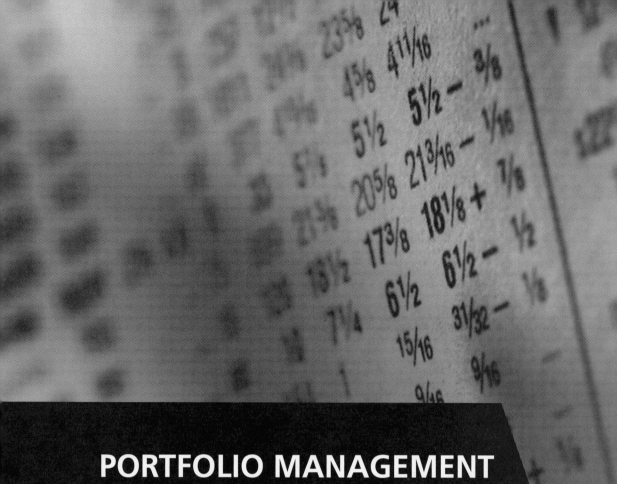

PORTFOLIO MANAGEMENT

STUDY SESSIONS

This volume includes Study Sessions 9–12.

TOPIC LEVEL LEARNING OUTCOME

The candidate should be able to construct an appropriate investment policy statement and asset allocation; formulate strategies for managing, monitoring, and rebalancing the investment portfolio; and interpret performance relative to benchmarks and present investment returns in a manner consistent with Global Investment Performance Standards (GIPS®).

STUDY SESSION 9
MANAGEMENT OF PASSIVE AND ACTIVE FIXED-INCOME PORTFOLIOS

The fixed-income market is one of the largest and fastest-growing segments of the global financial marketplace. Government and private debt currently constitute close to half of the wealth in international financial markets.

The basic features of the investment management process are the same for a fixed-income portfolio as for any other type of portfolio. Risk, return, and investment constraints are considered first. As part of this first step, however, an appropriate benchmark must also be selected based on the needs of the investor. For investors taking an asset-only approach, the benchmark is typically a bond market index, with success measured by the portfolio's relative investment return. For investors with a liability-based approach, success is measured in terms of the portfolio's ability to meet a set of investor-specific liabilities. The first reading addresses these primary elements of managing fixed-income portfolios and introduces specific portfolio management strategies. The second reading introduces additional relative-value methodologies.

READING ASSIGNMENTS

Reading 28   Fixed-Income Portfolio Management—Part I
Managing Investment Portfolios: A Dynamic Process, Third Edition, John L. Maginn, CFA, Donald L. Tuttle, CFA, Jerald E. Pinto, CFA, and Dennis W. McLeavey, CFA, editors

Reading 29   Relative-Value Methodologies for Global Credit Bond Portfolio Management
Fixed Income Readings for the Chartered Financial Analyst®️ Program, Second Edition, Frank J. Fabozzi, CFA, editor

$4\frac{5}{8}$ $4\frac{11}{16}$ $-\frac{3}{8}$

$5\frac{1}{2}$ $5\frac{1}{2}$ $-\frac{3}{8}$

$20\frac{5}{8}$ $21\frac{13}{16}$ $-\frac{1}{4}$

$17\frac{3}{8}$ $18\frac{1}{8}$ $+\frac{7}{8}$

$18\frac{1}{2}$ $6\frac{1}{2}$ $6\frac{1}{2}$ $-\frac{1}{2}$

$7\frac{1}{4}$ $3\frac{1}{32}$ $-$

$\frac{15}{16}$

$\frac{9}{16}$ $\frac{9}{16}$

$\frac{19}{32}$ $7\frac{13}{16}$ $7\frac{15}{16}$

$7\frac{15}{16}$ $2\frac{11}{32}$ $2\frac{1}{2}$ $+$

$2\frac{5}{8}$ $2\frac{1}{4}$ $2\frac{1}{4}$

$2\frac{3}{4}$ $11\frac{3}{8}$ $11\frac{3}{4}$ $+$

$12\frac{1}{16}$ 33 $33\frac{1}{16}$ $-$

87 $33\frac{3}{4}$ $24\frac{9}{16}$ $25\frac{3}{8}$ $+$

602 $25\frac{5}{8}$ $11\frac{5}{8}$ $11\frac{7}{8}$ $+$

833 12 $10\frac{1}{2}$ $10\frac{1}{2}$ $-$

16 $10\frac{1}{2}$ $15\frac{13}{16}$ $15\frac{7}{8}$ $-$

78 $15\frac{7}{8}$ $8\frac{1}{4}$ $8\frac{1}{8}$ $+$

4508 $9\frac{1}{16}$ $10\frac{1}{8}$

430 $11\frac{1}{4}$

FIXED-INCOME PORTFOLIO MANAGEMENT—PART I

by H. Gifford Fong and Larry D. Guin, CFA

LEARNING OUTCOMES

The candidate should be able to:	Mastery
a. compare and contrast, with respect to investment objectives, the use of liabilities as a benchmark and the use of a bond index as a benchmark;	☐
b. compare and contrast pure bond indexing, enhanced indexing, and active investing with respect to the objectives, techniques, advantages, and disadvantages of each;	☐
c. discuss the criteria for selecting a benchmark bond index and justify the selection of a specific index when given a description of an investor's risk aversion, income needs, and liabilities;	☐
d. review and justify the means, such as matching duration and key rate durations, by which an enhanced indexer may seek to align the risk exposures of the portfolio with those of the benchmark bond index;	☐
e. contrast and illustrate the use of total return analysis and scenario analysis to assess the risk and return characteristics of a proposed trade;	☐
f. design a bond immunization strategy that will ensure funding of a predetermined liability and evaluate the strategy under various interest rate scenarios;	☐
g. demonstrate the process of rebalancing a portfolio to reestablish a desired dollar duration;	☐
h. explain the importance of spread duration;	☐
i. discuss the extensions that have been made to classical immunization theory, including the introduction of contingent immunization;	☐
j. critique the risks associated with managing a portfolio against a liability structure, including interest rate risk, contingent claim risk, and cap risk;	☐
k. compare and contrast immunization strategies for a single liability, multiple liabilities, and general cash flows;	☐
l. compare and contrast risk minimization with return maximization in immunized portfolios;	☐

Managing Investment Portfolios: A Dynamic Process, Third Edition, John L. Maginn, CFA, Donald L. Tuttle, CFA, Jerald E. Pinto, CFA, and Dennis W. McLeavey, CFA, editors. Copyright © 2007 by CFA Institute. Reprinted with permission.

m. demonstrate the use of cash flow matching to fund a fixed set of future liabilities and contrast the advantages and disadvantages of cash flow matching to those of immunization strategies. ☐

1 INTRODUCTION

Over the past 25 years, fixed-income portfolio management has moved from a sleepy backwater of the investment arena to the cutting edge of investment thought. Once, managers in the field concentrated on earning an acceptable yield to maturity and used a few relatively simple measures to control risk in the portfolio. Today, the portfolio manager has a stunning array of new tools at his disposal, capable of measuring and explaining the smallest variations in desired performance while simultaneously controlling risk with a variety of quantitative tools. This reading examines the results of that revolution in fixed-income portfolio management.

It is not our purpose to examine in great detail the analytical "tools of the trade"; these techniques are covered extensively elsewhere. Our focus is broader and emphasizes the effective construction of a fixed-income portfolio and related risk issues. The fixed-income portfolio management process and the major themes in managing the fixed-income portion of a portfolio receive the emphasis in this reading.

The reading begins with a short review in Section 2 of the framework used for managing fixed-income portfolios. A fixed-income portfolio manager may manage funds against a bond market index or against the client's liabilities. In the former approach, the chief concern is performance relative to the selected bond index; in the latter, it is performance in funding the payment of liabilities. Managing funds against a bond market index is covered in Section 3 while management against liabilities (asset/liability management or ALM) is covered in Section 4. The final section summarizes the reading.

2 A FRAMEWORK FOR FIXED-INCOME PORTFOLIO MANAGEMENT

To make our discussion easier to follow, let us revisit the four activities in the investment management process:

1. setting the investment objectives (with related constraints);
2. developing and implementing a portfolio strategy;
3. monitoring the portfolio; and
4. adjusting the portfolio.

These four steps as they apply to fixed-income portfolio management are shown in Exhibit 1. For ease of illustration, Exhibit 1 breaks the second activity

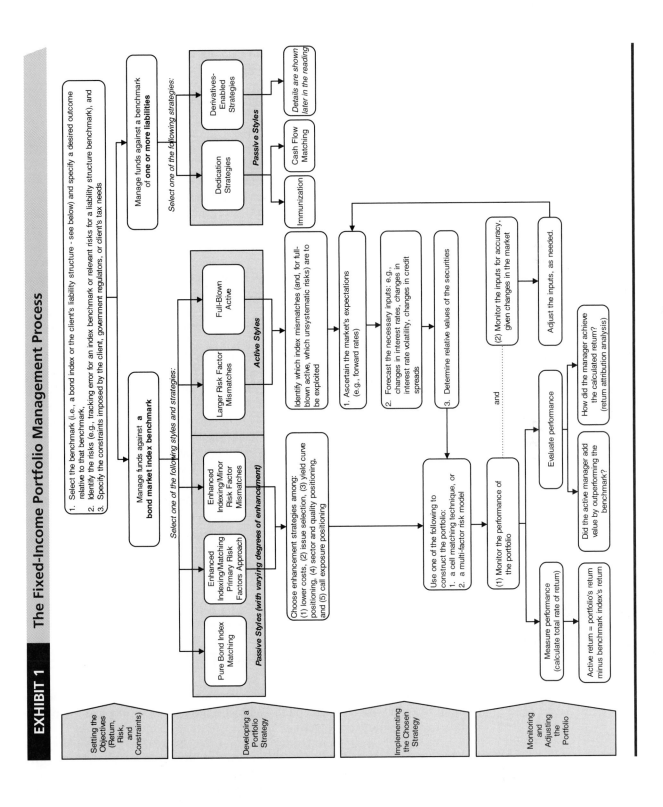

EXHIBIT 1   The Fixed-Income Portfolio Management Process

(developing and implementing a portfolio strategy) into its individual parts and combines the third and fourth activities (monitoring and adjusting the portfolio).

As can be seen in Exhibit 1, the basic features of the investment management process are the same for a fixed-income portfolio as for any other type of investment. Risk, return, and constraints are considered first. If the client is a taxable investor, portfolio analysis must be done on an after-tax basis and considerations of the tax-efficient placement of fixed-income assets come to the fore. For any type of client, the fixed-income portfolio manager must agree with the client on an appropriate benchmark, based on the needs of the client as expressed in the investment policy statement or the investor's mandate to the portfolio manager.

Broadly, there are two types of investor based on investment objectives. The first type of investor does not have liability matching as a specific objective. For example, a bond mutual fund has a great deal of freedom in how to invest its funds because it does not have a set of liabilities that requires a cash flow stream to satisfy them. The fund receives money from investors and provides professional expertise in investing this money for them, but the fund is not guaranteeing investors a certain rate of return. An investor (and manager) not focused on liability matching will typically select a specific bond market index as the benchmark for the portfolio; the portfolio's objective is to either match or exceed the rate of return on that index. In other words, the bond market index serves as the benchmark for the portfolio. This approach is sometimes referred to as investing on a benchmark-relative basis. However, the investor taking this approach will generally evaluate the risk of bond holdings not only in relation to the benchmark index but also in relation to the contribution to the risk of the overall (multi-asset-class) portfolio.

The second type of investor has a liability (or set of liabilities) that needs to be met. For example, some investors create a liability by borrowing money at a stated rate of interest, thereby leveraging the portfolio. Other investors have a liability as a result of legal promises that have been made, such as the payouts under a defined-benefit pension plan. Some investors may have quasi-liabilities represented by their retirement needs, and these can be treated as liabilities in the context of portfolio management. The investor with liabilities will measure success by whether the portfolio generates the funds necessary to pay out the cash outflows associated with the liabilities. In other words, meeting the liabilities is the investment objective; as such, it also becomes the benchmark for the portfolio.

Later we will examine in detail managing funds to ensure that the investor's liabilities are met. But for now, let us concentrate on managing the portfolio against a bond market index.

3 MANAGING FUNDS AGAINST A BOND MARKET INDEX

This section addresses fixed-income portfolio management from the perspective of an investor who has no liabilities and who has chosen to manage the portfolio's funds against a bond market index (as shown in Exhibit 1).

A passive management strategy assumes that the market's expectations are essentially correct or, more precisely, that the manager has no reason to disagree with these expectations—perhaps because the manager has no particular expertise in forecasting. By setting the portfolio's risk profile (e.g., interest rate sensitivity and credit quality) identical to the benchmark's risk profile and pursuing a passive strategy, the manager is quite willing to accept an average risk level (as defined by the benchmark's and portfolio's risk profile) and an average rate of return (as measured by the benchmark's and portfolio's return). Under a passive strategy, the manager does not have to make independent forecasts and the portfolio should very closely track the benchmark index.

An active management strategy essentially relies on the manager's forecasting ability. Active managers believe that they possess superior skills in interest rate forecasting, credit valuation, or in some other area that can be used to exploit opportunities in the market. The portfolio's return should increase if the manager's forecasts of the future path of the factors that influence fixed-income returns (e.g., changes in interest rates or credit spreads) are more accurate than those reflected in the current prices of fixed-income securities. The manager can create small mismatches (enhancement) or large mismatches (full-blown active management) relative to the benchmark to take advantage of this expertise.

When the major decision to manage funds against a benchmark index has been made, the next step is to select one or more appropriate investment strategies. Strategies can be grouped along a spectrum, as explained in the next section.

3.1 Classification of Strategies

Volpert (2000, pp. 85–88) provided an excellent classification of the types of fixed-income strategies relevant to this discussion.[1] Exhibit 1, in the shaded group of boxes next to "developing a portfolio strategy" shows these five types of strategies based on a scale that ranges from totally passive to full-blown active management. The types can be explained as follows:

1. *Pure bond indexing* (or *full replication approach*). The goal here is to produce a portfolio that is a perfect match to the benchmark portfolio. The pure bond indexing approach attempts to duplicate the index by owning all the bonds in the index in the same percentage as the index. Full replication is typically very difficult and expensive to implement in the case of bond indices. Many issues in a typical bond index (particularly the non-Treasuries) are quite illiquid and very infrequently traded. For this reason, full replication of a bond index is rarely attempted because of the difficulty, inefficiency, and high cost of implementation.

2. *Enhanced indexing by matching primary risk factors.*[2] This management style uses a sampling approach in an attempt to match the primary index risk factors and achieve a higher return than under full replication. **Primary risk factors** are typically major influences on the pricing of bonds, such as changes in the level of interest rates, twists in the yield curve, and changes in the spread between Treasuries and non-Treasuries.

   A. By investing in a sample of bonds rather than the whole index, the manager reduces the construction and maintenance costs of the portfolio. Although a sampling approach will usually track the index less closely than full replication, this disadvantage is expected to be more than offset by the lower expenses.

---

[1] Note that the terms "investment style" and "investment strategy" are often used interchangeably in the investment community. In this reading, we use the term "style" as the more general term (i.e., either active or passive). An investment style may encompass many different types of strategies, which are implementation techniques or methodologies for achieving the portfolio's objective.

[2] Factor matching is considered an implementation choice for indexing by some other authorities.

> **B.** By matching the primary risk factors, the portfolio is affected by broad market-moving events (e.g., changing interest rate levels, twists in the yield curve, spread changes) to the same degree as the benchmark index. The portfolio manager may try to enhance the portfolio's return using bonds that are perceived to be undervalued, for example.

3. *Enhanced indexing by small risk factor mismatches.*[3] While matching duration (interest rate sensitivity), this style allows the manager to tilt the portfolio in favor of any of the other risk factors. The manager may try to marginally increase the return by pursuing relative value in certain sectors, quality, term structure, and so on. The mismatches are small and are intended to simply enhance the portfolio's return enough to overcome the difference in administrative costs between the portfolio and the index.

4. *Active management by larger risk factor mismatches.* The difference between this style and enhanced indexing is one of degree. This style involves the readiness to make deliberately larger mismatches on the primary risk factors than in Type 3—definitely active management. The portfolio manager is now actively pursuing opportunities in the market to increase the return. The manager may overweight A rated bonds relative to AA/Aaa rated bonds, overweight corporates versus Treasuries, position the portfolio to take advantage of an anticipated twist in the yield curve, or adjust the portfolio's duration slightly away from the benchmark index's duration to take advantage of a perceived opportunity. The objective of the manager is to produce sufficient returns to overcome this style's additional transaction costs while controlling risk.

5. *Full-blown active management.* Full-blown active management involves the possibility of aggressive mismatches on duration, sector weights, and other factors.

The following sections offer further information and comments on these types of management.

3.2 Indexing (Pure and Enhanced)

We begin by asking the obvious question: "Why should an investor consider investing in an indexed portfolio?" Actually, several reasons exist for bond indexing.

▶ Indexed portfolios have lower fees than actively managed accounts. Advisory fees on an indexed portfolio may be only a few basis points, whereas the advisory fees charged by active managers typically range from 15 to 50 bps. Nonadvisory fees, such as custodial fees, are also much lower for indexed portfolios.

▶ Outperforming a broadly based market index on a consistent basis is a difficult task, particularly when one has to overcome the higher fees and costs associated with active management.

▶ Broadly based bond index portfolios provide excellent diversification. The most popular U.S. bond market indices each have a minimum of 5,000 issues and a market value measured in the trillions of dollars. The indices contain a wide array of maturities, sectors, and qualities.[4] The diversification inherent in an indexed portfolio results in a lower risk for a given level of return than other less diversified portfolios.

---

[3] "Small" here is used to refer to the size of the mismatch and not the level of risk.

[4] "Qualities" refers to the default risk of the bonds. This can be measured by the bonds' rating, for example, Standard & Poor's/Moody's Investor Services AAA/Aaa, AA/Aa, A, BBB/Baa, and so on.

3.2.1 Selection of a Benchmark Bond Index: General Considerations

Once the decision has been made to index, important follow-up questions remain: "Which benchmark index should I choose?" "Should the benchmark index have a short duration or a long duration?" "Is the benchmark index's credit quality appropriate for the role that the bond portfolio will play in my overall portfolio?" At the risk of oversimplifying, you should choose the index containing characteristics that match closely with the desired characteristics of your portfolio. The choice depends heavily on three factors:

1. *Market value risk.* The market value risk of the portfolio and benchmark index should be comparable. Given a normal upward-sloping yield curve, a bond portfolio's yield to maturity increases as the maturity of the portfolio increases. Does this mean that the total return is greater on a long portfolio than on a short one? Not necessarily. According to the expectations theory of term structure, a rising yield curve means that investors believe interest rates will likely increase in the future. Because a long duration portfolio is more sensitive to changes in interest rates, a long portfolio will likely fall more in price than a short one. In other words, as the maturity and duration of a portfolio increase, the market risk increases. For investors who are risk averse, the short-term or intermediate-term index may be more appropriate as a benchmark index than the long index.

2. *Income risk.* The portfolio and benchmark should provide comparable assured income streams. Many investors (e.g., foundations and retirees) prefer portfolios that generate a high level of income while conserving principal. Investing in a long portfolio can lock in a dependable income stream over a long period of time and does not subject the income stream to the vagaries of fluctuating interest rates. If stability and dependability of income are the primary needs of the investor, then the long portfolio is the least risky and the short portfolio is the most risky.

3. *Credit risk.* The average credit risk of the benchmark index should be appropriate for the indexed portfolio's role in the investor's overall portfolio and satisfy any constraints placed on credit quality in the investor's investment policy statement. The diversification among issuers in the benchmark index should also be satisfactory to the investor.

4. *Liability framework risk.* This risk should be minimized. In general, it is prudent to match the investment characteristics (e.g., duration) of assets and liabilities, if liabilities play any role. The choice of an appropriate benchmark index should reflect the nature of the liabilities: Investors with long-term liabilities should select a long index.[5] Of course, bond investors that have no liabilities have much more latitude in the choice of a benchmark because of the lack of this restriction.

For the taxable investor, returns and risk need to be evaluated on an after-tax basis. For example, in the United States, where there are active markets in tax-exempt bonds, a taxable investor would compare the anticipated return on taxable and tax-exempt benchmark bond indices on a net-of-taxes basis.[6] In some countries, different tax rates apply to the income and capital gains components of bond returns. Furthermore, if a taxable investor can hold the bond portfolio within a taxable or a tax-deferred account, the investor can effectively

---

[5] Management of a portfolio against liabilities is covered in detail in Section 4.

[6] Tax-exempt bonds are bonds whose interest payments are in whole or in part exempt from taxation; they are typically issued by governmental or certain government-sponsored entities.

view the benchmark index as having one set of return–risk characteristics in a taxable account and another set in a tax-deferred account. This perspective can be helpful in a joint optimization of the asset allocation and asset location decisions. (The asset location decision is the decision concerning the account(s) in which to hold assets.)

Example 1 illustrates the selection of a benchmark index. As the indices mentioned in the example illustrate, index publishers segment in the fixed-income universe in distinctive ways. Major classification criteria include broad issuer sector (e.g., corporate, government), maturity sector (e.g., short term, intermediate, long-term), and credit quality (e.g., investment grade and high yield).

EXAMPLE 1

Illustrations of Benchmark Selection

Trustworthy Management Company specializes in managing fixed-income investments on an indexed basis. Some of the indices they consider as possible benchmarks are as follows:

Merrill Lynch 1–3 Year Corporate Bond Index

Lehman Brothers Corporate High-Yield Bond Index*

Lehman Brothers Corporate Intermediate Bond Index

Merrill Lynch Long-Term Corporate Bond Index

All of the above include U.S. corporate debt, and all except Lehman Brothers Corporate High-Yield Bond Index include only debt issues rated investment grade, which means they are rated Baa or higher. The duration of the Merrill Lynch 1–3 Year Corporate Bond Index is short, the duration of the two Lehman Brothers indices is medium, and the duration of the Merrill Lynch Long-Term Corporate Bond Index is long.

Of the above, which index(es) would be suitable as a benchmark for the portfolios of the following clients?

1. A highly risk-averse investor who is sensitive to fluctuations in portfolio value.
2. An educational endowment with a long investment horizon.
3. A life insurer that is relying on the fixed-income portfolio being managed by the Trustworthy Management Company to meet short-term claims.

Solution to 1: Because the investor is quite risk averse, an index with a short or intermediate duration would be appropriate to limit market value risk. Of the short and intermediate duration indices listed above, the Lehman Brothers Corporate High-Yield Bond Index is not suitable because it invests in less-than-investment-grade bonds. Accordingly, either the Merrill Lynch 1–3 Year Corporate Bond Index or the Lehman Brothers Corporate Intermediate Bond Index could be selected as the benchmark.

* Barclays has acquired Lehman Brothers and will maintain the family of Lehman Brothers indices and the associated index calculation, publication, and analytical infrastructure and tools.

Solution to 2: Given the endowment's long-term horizon, the Merrill Lynch Long-Term Corporate Bond Index, which has the longest duration of the indices given, is an appropriate benchmark.

Solution to 3: For a company issuing life insurance policies, the timing of outlay (liabilities) is uncertain. However, because the insurer is relying on the portfolio to meet short-term liabilities, stability of market value is a concern, and the insurer would desire a portfolio with a low level of market risk. Therefore, Merrill Lynch 1–3 Year Corporate Bond Index, a short duration index, is an appropriate benchmark.

To build an indexed portfolio, the manager begins by selecting a broadly diversified bond market index that will serve as the benchmark for the portfolio. Fortunately, a wide variety of these are available. A well-constructed bond market index will have the same exposure to risks as a portfolio that contains available fixed-income securities trading in the marketplace. The index may contain only a sample of all the marketplace's bonds; but if the characteristics and risk exposure are the same, the index will match the performance of the larger portfolio made up of all bonds.

However, although the bond market index may serve as a realistic benchmark portfolio, it is not a real portfolio. It exists only on paper or, more accurately, in a computer system somewhere. Therefore, a portfolio manager cannot invest directly in the index. The manager must construct her own portfolio that mimics (closely tracks) the characteristics of the index (and the market). That is, as Exhibit 2 illustrates, the bond market index is constructed to mimic the overall market and the manager's portfolio is constructed to mimic the bond market index. In this way, the manager's portfolio will also mimic the overall market.

EXHIBIT 2	Indexing

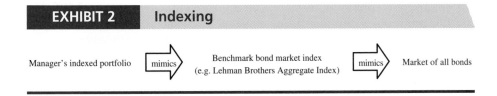

Manager's indexed portfolio → mimics → Benchmark bond market index (e.g. Lehman Brothers Aggregate Index) → mimics → Market of all bonds

3.2.2 Risk in Detail: Risk Profiles

The identification and measurement of risk factors plays a role both in benchmark selection and in a major benchmark construction.

The major source of risk for most bonds relates to the **yield curve** (the relationship between interest rates and time to maturity). Yield curve changes include 1) a parallel shift in the yield curve (an equal shift in the interest rate at all maturities), 2) a **twist** of the yield curve (movement in contrary directions of interest rates at two maturities), and 3) other curvature changes of the yield curve. Among the three, the first component (yield curve shift) typically accounts for about 90 percent of the change in value of a bond.

In assessing bond market indices as potential benchmark candidates, the manager must examine each index's **risk profile**, which is a detailed tabulation of the index's risk exposures. After all, if the portfolio manager is going to create (and invest in) a portfolio that mimics the benchmark index, the portfolio needs to contain the same exposures to various risks as the benchmark index. The manager needs to know: "How sensitive is the benchmark's return to changes in the level of interest rates (**interest rate risk**), changes in the shape of the yield curve (**yield curve risk**), changes in the spread between Treasuries and non-Treasuries (**spread risk**), and various other risks?" Bonds are subject to a wide variety of risks, as illustrated in Exhibit 3.

Having obtained a clear grasp of the chosen benchmark's risk exposures, the portfolio manager can then use the risk profile in constructing an effective indexed portfolio. A completely effective indexed portfolio will have the exact same risk profile as the selected benchmark. The portfolio manager may use various techniques, perhaps in combination, to align the portfolio's risk exposures with those of the benchmark index.

A **cell-matching technique** (also known as **stratified sampling**) divides the benchmark index into cells that represent qualities that should reflect the risk factors of the index. The manager then selects bonds (i.e., sample bonds) from those in each cell to represent the entire cell taking account of the cell's relative importance in the benchmark index. The total dollar amount selected from this cell may be based on that cell's percentage of the total. For example, if the A rated corporates make up 4 percent of the entire index, then A rated bonds will be sampled and added until they represent 4 percent of the manager's portfolio.

A **multifactor model technique** makes use of a set of factors that drive bond returns.[7] Generally, portfolio managers will focus on the most important or primary risk factors. These measures are described below, accompanied by practical comments.[8]

1. *Duration.* An index's **effective duration** measures the sensitivity of the index's price to a relatively small parallel shift in interest rates (i.e., interest rate risk). (For *large* parallel changes in interest rates, a convexity adjustment is used to improve the accuracy of the index's estimated price change. A **convexity adjustment** is an estimate of the change in price that is not explained by duration.) The manager's indexed portfolio will attempt to match the duration of the benchmark index as a way of ensuring that the exposure is the same in both portfolios. Because parallel shifts in the yield curve are relatively rare, duration by itself is inadequate to capture the full effect of changes in interest rates.

2. *Key rate duration and present value distribution of cash flows.* Nonparallel shifts in the yield curve (i.e., yield curve risk), such as an increase in slope or a twist in the curve, can be captured by two separate measures. **Key rate duration** is one established method for measuring the effect of shifts in key points along the yield curve. In this method, we hold the spot rates constant for all points along the yield curve but one. By changing the spot rate for that key maturity, we are able to measure a portfolio's sensitivity to a change

---

[7] For a more complete coverage of how multi-factor risk models are used in portfolio construction, see Fabozzi (2004b, Chapter 3).

[8] This discussion draws heavily from Volpert (2000).

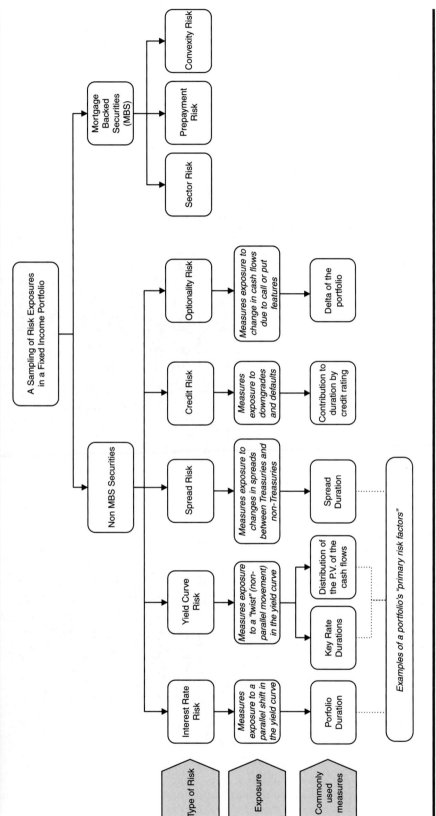

EXHIBIT 3 Typical Fixed-Income Portfolio Risk Exposures

A Sampling of Risk Exposures in a Fixed Income Portfolio

Non MBS Securities

Mortgage Backed Securities (MBS)

Interest Rate Risk — Measures exposure to a parallel shift in the yield curve — Porfolio Duration

Yield Curve Risk — Measures exposure to a "twist" (non-parallel movement) in the yield curve — Key Rate Durations / Distribution of the P.V. of the cash flows

Spread Risk — Measures exposure to changes in spreads between Treasuries and non-Treasuries — Spread Duration

Credit Risk — Measures exposure to downgrades and defaults — Contribution to duration by credit rating

Optionality Risk — Measures exposure to change in cash flows due to call or put features — Delta of the portfolio

Sector Risk

Prepayment Risk

Convexity Risk

Examples of a portfolio's "primary risk factors"

Type of Risk

Exposure

Commonly used measures

in that maturity. This sensitivity is called the **rate duration**. We repeat the process for other key points (e.g., 3 years, 7 years, 10 years, 15 years) and measure their sensitivities as well. Simulations of twists in the yield curve can then be conducted to see how the portfolio would react to these changes. Key rate durations are particularly useful for determining the relative attractiveness of various portfolio strategies, such as bullet strategies with maturities focused at one point on the yield curve versus barbell strategies where maturities are concentrated at two extremes. These strategies react differently to nonparallel changes in the yield curve.

Another popular indexing method is to match the portfolio's present value distribution of cash flows to that of the benchmark. Dividing future time into a set of non-overlapping time periods, the **present value distribution of cash flows** is a list that associates with each time period the fraction of the portfolio's duration that is attributable to cash flows falling in that time period. The calculation involves the following steps:

A. The portfolio's creator will project the cash flow for each issue in the index for specific periods (usually six-month intervals). Total cash flow for each period is calculated by adding the cash flows for all the issues. The present value of each period's cash flow is then computed and a total present value is obtained by adding the individual periods' present values. (Note that the total present value is the market value of the index.)

B. Each period's present value is then divided by the total present value to arrive at a percentage for each period. For example, the first six-month period's present value might be 3.0 percent of the total present value of cash flows, the second six-month period's present value might be 3.8 percent of the total present value, and so forth.

C. Next, we calculate the contribution of each period's cash flows to portfolio duration. Because each cash flow is effectively a zero-coupon payment, the time period is the duration of the cash flow. By multiplying the time period times the period's percentage of the total present value, we obtain the duration contribution of each period's cash flows. For example, if we show each six-month period as a fractional part of the year (0.5, 1.0, 1.5, 2.0, etc.), the first period's contribution to duration would be 0.5×3.0 percent, or 0.015. The second period's contribution would be 1.0×3.8 percent, or 0.038. We would continue for each period in the series.

D. Finally, we add each period's contribution to duration (0.015 + 0.038 + . . .) and obtain a total (3.28, for example) that represents the bond index's contribution to duration. We then divide each of the individual period's contribution to duration by the total. The resulting distribution might look as follows:

> period 1 = 0.46 percent
>
> period 2 = 1.16 percent
>
> period 3 = 3.20 percent
>
> . . . , etc.

> It is this distribution that the indexer will try to duplicate. If this distribution is duplicated, nonparallel yield curve shifts and "twists" in the curve will have the same effect on the portfolio and the benchmark portfolio.

3. *Sector and quality percent.* To ensure that the bond market index's yield is replicated by the portfolio, the manager will match the percentage weight in the various sectors and qualities of the benchmark index.

4. *Sector duration contribution.* A portfolio's return is obviously affected by the duration of each sector's bonds in the portfolio. For an indexed portfolio, the portfolio must achieve the same duration exposure to each sector as the benchmark index. The goal is to ensure that a change in sector spreads has the same impact on both the portfolio and the index.

    The manager can achieve this by matching the amount of the index duration that comes from the various sectors, i.e., the sector duration contribution.

5. *Quality spread duration contribution.* The risk that a bond's price will change as a result of spread changes (e.g., between corporates and Treasuries) is known as spread risk. A measure that describes how a non-Treasury security's price will change as a result of the widening or narrowing of the spread is **spread duration**. Changes in the spread between qualities of bonds will also affect the rate of return. The easiest way to ensure that the indexed portfolio closely tracks the benchmark is to match the amount of the index duration that comes from the various quality categories.

6. *Sector/coupon/maturity cell weights.* Because duration only captures the effect of small interest rate changes on an index's value, convexity is often used to improve the accuracy of the estimated price change, particularly where the change in rates is large. However, some bonds (such as mortgage-backed securities) may exhibit negative convexity, making the index's exposure to call risk difficult to replicate. A manager can attempt to match the convexity of the index, but such matching is rarely attempted because to stay matched can lead to excessively high transactions costs. (Callable securities tend to be very illiquid and expensive to trade.)

    A more feasible method of matching the call exposure is to match the sector, coupon, and maturity weights of the callable sectors. As rates change, the changes in call exposure of the portfolio will be matched to the index.

7. *Issuer exposure.* Event risk is the final risk that needs to be controlled. If a manager attempts to replicate the index with too few securities, event risk takes on greater importance.

The degree of success of an indexer in mimicking the returns on a benchmark is measured by tracking risk.

3.2.3 Tracking Risk

Tracking risk (also known as tracking error) is a measure of the variability with which a portfolio's return tracks the return of a benchmark index. More specifically, tracking risk is defined as the standard deviation of the portfolio's active return, where the active return for each period is defined as

Active return = Portfolio's return − Benchmark index's return

Therefore,

Tracking risk = Standard deviation of the active returns

EXAMPLE 2

EXHIBIT 4		Calculating Tracking Risk		
Period Return (1)	Portfolio Return (2)	Benchmark Return (3)	Active Return (AR) (4)	(AR – Avg. AR)^2 (5)
1	12.80%	12.60%	0.200%	0.00012%[9]
2	6.80	6.50	0.300	0.00044
3	0.80	1.20	−0.400	0.00240
4	−4.60	−5.00	0.400	0.00096
5	4.00	4.10	−0.100	0.00036
6	3.30	3.20	0.100	0.00000
7	5.40	5.10	0.300	0.00044
8	5.40	5.70	−0.300	0.00152
9	5.10	4.60	0.500	0.00168
10	3.70	3.80	−0.100	0.00036

Average active return per period: 0.090%.

Sum of the squared deviations: $0.00829(\%)^2$.

Tracking risk: 0.30350%.

A portfolio's return and its benchmark's return are shown in Columns 2 and 3 of Exhibit 4. To calculate the standard deviation over the 10 periods, we calculate the active return for each period (in Column 4) and find the average active return (i.e., total return of 0.90 percent divided by 10 = 0.090 percent). We then subtract the average (or mean) active return from each period's active return and square each of the differences (Column 5). We add the values in Column 5 and divide the total by the number of sample periods minus one (i.e., 0.00829 percent/9), then take the square root of that value: $\sqrt{\dfrac{0.00829(\%)^2}{9}}$. The tracking risk is 0.30350 percent, or a little more than 30 bps.

Assume that the tracking risk for a portfolio is calculated to be 30 bps. Statistically, the area that is one standard deviation either side of the mean captures approximately 2/3 of all the observations if portfolio returns approximately follow a normal distribution. Therefore, a tracking risk of 30 bps would indicate that, in approximately two-thirds of the time periods, the portfolio return will be within a band of the benchmark index's return plus or minus 30 bps. The smaller the tracking risk, the more closely the portfolio's return matches, or tracks, the benchmark index's return.

---

[9] For Period 1, the calculation for the 5th column is $(0.200\% - 0.090\%)^2$ or $(0.000121\%)^2$.

Tracking risk arises primarily from mismatches between a portfolio's risk profile and the benchmark's risk profile.[10] The previous section listed seven primary risk factors that should be matched closely if the tracking risk is to be kept to a minimum. Any change to the portfolio that increases a mismatch for any of these seven items will potentially increase the tracking risk. Examples (using the first five of the seven) would include mismatches in the following:

1. *Portfolio duration.* If the benchmark's duration is 5.0 and the portfolio's duration is 5.5, then the portfolio has a greater exposure to parallel changes in interest rates, resulting in an increase in the portfolio's tracking risk.

2. *Key rate duration and present value distribution of cash flows.* Mismatches in key rate duration increase tracking risk. In addition, if the portfolio distribution does not match the benchmark, the portfolio will be either more sensitive or less sensitive to changes in interest rates at specific points along the yield curve, leading to an increase in the tracking risk.

3. *Sector and quality percent.* If the benchmark contains mortgage-backed securities and the portfolio does not, for example, the tracking risk will be increased. Similarly, if the portfolio overweights AAA securities compared with the benchmark, the tracking risk will be increased.

4. *Sector duration contribution.* Even though the sector percentages (e.g., 10 percent Treasuries, 4 percent agencies, 20 percent industrials) may be matched, a mismatch will occur if the portfolio's industrial bonds have an average duration of 6.2 and the benchmark's industrial bonds have an average duration of 5.1. Because the industrial sector's contribution to duration is larger for the portfolio than for the benchmark, a mismatch occurs and the tracking risk is increased.

5. *Quality spread duration contribution.* Exhibit 5 shows the spread duration for a 60-bond portfolio and a benchmark index based on sectors. The portfolio's

EXHIBIT 5	Contribution to Spread Duration					
	Portfolio			**Benchmark**		
Sector	**% of Portfolio**	**Spread Duration**	**Contribution to Spread Duration**	**% of Portfolio**	**Spread Duration**	**Contribution to Spread Duration**
Treasury	22.60%	0.00%	0.00%	23.20%	0.00%	0.00%
Agencies	6.80	6.45	0.44	6.65	4.43	0.29
Financial institutions	6.20	2.87	0.18	5.92	3.27	0.19
Industrials	20.06	11.04	2.21	14.20	10.65	1.51
Utilities	5.52	2.20	0.12	6.25	2.40	0.15
Non-U.S. credit	6.61	1.92	0.13	6.80	2.02	0.14
Mortgage	32.21	1.10	0.35	33.15	0.98	0.32
Asset backed	0.00	0.00	0.00	1.60	3.20	0.05
CMBS	0.00	0.00	0.00	2.23	4.81	0.11
Total	100.00%		3.43%	100.00%		2.77%

[10] Ignoring transaction costs and other expenses, the only way to completely eliminate tracking risk is to own all the securities in the benchmark. Even after all significant common risk factors are considered, it is possible to have some residual issue specific risk.

total contribution to spread duration (3.43) is greater than that for the benchmark (2.77). This difference is primarily because of the overweighting of industrials in the 60-bond portfolio. The portfolio has greater spread risk and is thus more sensitive to changes in the sector spread than the benchmark is, resulting in a larger tracking risk.

The remaining two factors are left for the reader to evaluate.

EXAMPLE 3

Interpreting and Reducing Tracking Risk

John Spencer is the portfolio manager of Star Bond Index Fund. This fund uses the indexing investment approach, seeking to match the investment returns of a specified market benchmark, or index. Specifically, it seeks investment results that closely match, before expenses, the Lehman Brothers Global Aggregate Bond Index. This index is a market-weighted index of the global investment-grade bond market with an intermediate-term weighted average maturity, including government, credit, and collateralized securities. Because of the large number of bonds included in the Lehman Brothers Global Aggregate Bond Index, John Spencer uses a representative sample of the bonds in the index to construct the fund. The bonds are chosen by John so that the fund's a) duration, b) country percentage weights, and c) sector- and quality-percentage weights closely match those of the benchmark bond index.

1. The target tracking risk of the fund is 1 percent. Interpret what is meant by this target.

2. Two of the large institutional investors in the fund have asked John Spencer if he could try to reduce the target tracking risk. Suggest some ways for achieving a lower tracking risk.

Solution to 1: The target tracking risk of 1 percent means that the objective is that in at least two-thirds of the time periods, the return on the Star Bond Index Fund is within plus or minus 1 percent of the return on the benchmark Lehman Brothers Global Aggregate Bond Index. The smaller the tracking risk, the more closely the fund's return matches the benchmark's index return.

Solution to 2: The target tracking risk could be reduced by choosing the bonds to be included in the fund so as to match the fund's duration, country percentage weights, sector weights, and quality weights to those of the benchmark, and to minimize the following mismatches with the benchmark:

　　a. key rate distribution and present value distribution of cash flows

　　b. sector duration contribution

　　c. quality spread duration contribution

　　d. sector, coupon, and maturity weights of the callable sectors

　　e. issuer exposure

3.2.4 Enhanced Indexing Strategies

Although there are expenses and transaction costs associated with constructing and rebalancing an indexed portfolio, there are no similar costs for the index itself (because it is, in effect, a paper portfolio). Therefore, it is reasonable to expect that a perfectly indexed portfolio will underperform the index by the amount of these costs. For this reason, the bond manager may choose to recover these costs by seeking to enhance the portfolio's return. Volpert (2000) has identified a number of ways (i.e., index enhancement strategies) in which this may be done:[11]

1. *Lower cost enhancements.* Managers can increase the portfolio's net return by simply maintaining tight controls on trading costs and management fees. Although relatively low, expenses do vary considerably among index funds. Where outside managers are hired, the plan sponsor can require that managers re-bid their management fees every two or three years to ensure that these fees are kept as low as possible.

2. *Issue selection enhancements.* The manager may identify and select securities that are undervalued in the marketplace, relative to a valuation model's theoretical value. Many managers conduct their own credit analysis rather than depending solely on the ratings provided by the bond rating houses. As a result, the manager may be able to select issues that will soon be upgraded and avoid those issues that are on the verge of being downgraded.

3. *Yield curve positioning.* Some maturities along the yield curve tend to remain consistently overvalued or undervalued. For example, the yield curve frequently has a negative slope between 25 and 30 years, even though the remainder of the curve may have a positive slope. These long-term bonds tend to be popular investments for many institutions, resulting in an overvalued price relative to bonds of shorter maturities. By overweighting the undervalued areas of the curve and underweighting the overvalued areas, the manager may be able to enhance the portfolio's return.

4. *Sector and quality positioning.* This return enhancement technique takes two forms:

   a. Maintaining a yield tilt toward short duration corporates. Experience has shown that the best yield spread per unit of duration risk is usually available in corporate securities with less than five years to maturity (i.e., short corporates). A manager can increase the return on the portfolio without a commensurate increase in risk by tilting the portfolio toward these securities. The strategy is not without its risks, although these are manageable. Default risk is higher for corporate securities, but this risk can be managed through proper diversification. (**Default risk** is the risk of loss if an issuer or counterparty does not fulfill contractual obligations.)

   b. Periodic over- or underweighting of sectors (e.g., Treasuries vs. corporates) or qualities. Conducted on a small scale, the manager may overweight Treasuries when spreads are expected to widen (e.g., before a recession) and underweight them when spreads are expected to narrow. Although this strategy has some similarities to active management, it is implemented on such a small scale that the objective is to earn enough extra return to offset some of the indexing expenses, not to outperform the index by a large margin as is the case in active management.

---

[11] See Volpert (2000, pp. 95–98).

5. *Call exposure positioning.* A drop in interest rates will inevitably lead to some callable bonds being retired early. As rates drop, the investor must determine the probability that the bond will be called. Should the bond be valued as trading to maturity or as trading to the call date? Obviously, there is a crossover point at which the average investor is uncertain as to whether the bond is likely to be called. Near this point, the actual performance of a bond may be significantly different than would be expected, given the bond's **effective duration**[12] (duration adjusted to account for embedded options). For example, for premium callable bonds (bonds trading to call), the actual price sensitivity tends to be less than that predicted by the bonds' effective duration. A decline in yields will lead to underperformance relative to the effective duration model's prediction. This underperformance creates an opportunity for the portfolio manager to underweight these issues under these conditions.

EXAMPLE 4

Enhanced Indexing Strategies

The Board of Directors of the Teachers Association of a Canadian province has asked its chairman, Jim Reynolds, to consider investing C$10 million of the fixed-income portion of the association's portfolio in the Reliable Canadian Bond Fund. This index fund seeks to match the performance of the Scotia Capital Universe Bond Index. The Scotia Capital Universe Bond Index represents the Canadian bond market and includes more than 900 marketable Canadian bonds with an average maturity of about nine years.

Jim Reynolds likes the passive investing approach of the Reliable Canadian Bond Fund. Although Reynolds is comfortable with the returns on the Scotia Capital Universe Bond Index, he is concerned that because of the expenses and transactions costs, the actual returns on the bond fund could be substantially lower than the returns on the index. However, he is familiar with the several index enhancement strategies identified by Volpert (2000) through which a bond index fund could minimize the underperformance relative to the index. To see if the fund follows any of these strategies, Reynolds carefully reads the fund's prospectus and notices the following.

> "Instead of replicating the index by investing in over the 900 securities in the Scotia Capital Universe Bond Index, we use stratified sampling. The fund consists of about 150 securities.
>
> . . . We constantly monitor the yield curve to identify segments of the yield curve with the highest expected return. We increase the holdings in maturities with the highest expected return in lieu of maturities with the lowest expected return if the increase in expected return outweighs the transactions cost. Further, the fund manager is in constant touch with traders and other market participants. Based on their information and our in-house analysis, we selectively overweight and underweight certain issues in the index."

1. Which of the index enhancement strategies listed by Volpert are being used by the Reliable Canadian Bond Fund?

---

[12] See Fabozzi (2004b, p. 235).

2. Which additional strategies could the fund use to further enhance fund return without active management?

Solution to 1: By investing in a small sample of 150 of over 900 bonds included in the index, the fund is trying to reduce transactions costs. Thus, the fund is following lower cost enhancements. The fund is also following yield curve positioning enhancement by overweighting the undervalued areas of the curve and underweighting the overvalued areas. Finally, the fund is following issuer selection enhancements by selectively over- and underweighting certain issues in the index.

Solution to 2: The fund could further attempt to lower costs by maintaining tight controls on trading costs and management fees. Additional strategies that the fund could use include sector and quality positioning and call exposure positioning.

3.3 Active Strategies

In contrast to indexers and enhanced indexers, an active manager is quite willing to accept a large tracking risk, with a large positive active return. By carefully applying his or her superior forecasting or analytical skills, the active manager hopes to be able to generate a portfolio return that is considerably higher than the benchmark return.

3.3.1 Extra Activities Required for the Active Manager

Active managers have a set of activities that they must implement that passive managers are not faced with. After selecting the type of active strategy to pursue, the active manager will:

1. *Identify which index mismatches are to be exploited.* The choice of mismatches is generally based on the expertise of the manager. If the manager's strength is interest rate forecasting, deliberate mismatches in duration will be created between the portfolio and the benchmark. If the manager possesses superior skill in identifying undervalued securities or undervalued sectors, sector mismatches will be pursued.

2. *Extrapolate the market's expectations (or inputs) from the market data.* As discussed previously, current market prices are the result of all investors applying their judgment to the individual bonds. By analyzing these prices and yields, additional data can be obtained. For example, forward rates can be calculated from the points along the spot rate yield curve. These forward rates can provide insight into the direction and level that investors believe rates will be headed in the future.

3. *Independently forecast the necessary inputs and compare these with the market's expectations.* For example, after calculating the forward rates, the active manager may fervently believe that these rates are too high and that future interest rates will not reach these levels. After comparing his or her forecast of forward rates with that of other investors, the manager may decide to create a duration mismatch. By increasing the portfolio's duration, the manager can profit (if he or she is correct) from the resulting drop in the yield curve as other investors eventually realize that their forecast was incorrect.

4. *Estimate the relative values of securities in order to identify areas of under- or overvaluation.* Again, the focus depends on the skill set of the manager.

Some managers will make duration mismatches while others will focus on undervalued securities. In all cases, however, the managers will apply their skills to try and exploit opportunities as they arise.

3.3.2 Total Return Analysis and Scenario Analysis

Before executing a trade, an active manager obviously needs to analyze the impact that the trade will have on the portfolio's return. What tools does the manager have in his or her tool bag to help assess the risk and return characteristics of a trade? The two primary tools are total return analysis and scenario analysis.

The **total return** on a bond is the rate of return that equates the future value of the bond's cash flows with the full price of the bond. As such, the total return takes into account all three sources of potential return: coupon income, reinvestment income, and change in price. **Total return analysis** involves assessing the expected effect of a trade on the portfolio's total return given an interest rate forecast.

To compute total return when purchasing a bond with semiannual coupons, for example, the manager needs to specify 1) an investment horizon, 2) an expected reinvestment rate for the coupon payments, and 3) the expected price of the bond at the end of the time horizon given a forecast change in interest rates. The manager may want to start with his prediction of the most likely change in interest rates.[13] The semiannual total return that the manager would expect to earn on the trade is:

$$\text{Semiannual total return} = \left(\frac{\text{Total future dollars}}{\text{Full price of the bond}} \right)^{\frac{1}{n}} - 1$$

where n is the number of periods in the investment horizon.

Even though this total return is the manager's most likely total return, this computation is for only *one* assumed change in rates. This total return number does very little to help the manager assess the risk that he faces if his forecast is wrong and rates change by some amount other than that forecast. A prudent manager will never want to rely on just one set of assumptions in analyzing the decision; instead, he or she will repeat the above calculation for different sets of assumptions or scenarios. In other words, the manager will want to conduct a **scenario analysis** to evaluate the impact of the trade on expected total return under all reasonable sets of assumptions.

Scenario analysis is useful in a variety of ways:

1. The obvious benefit is that the manager is able to assess the distribution of possible outcomes, in essence conducting a risk analysis on the portfolio's trades. The manager may find that, even though the expected total return is quite acceptable, the distribution of outcomes is so wide that it exceeds the risk tolerance of the client.

2. The analysis can be reversed, beginning with a range of acceptable outcomes, then calculating the range of interest rate movements (inputs) that would result in a desirable outcome. The manager can then place probabilities on interest rates falling within this acceptable range and make a more informed decision on whether to proceed with the trade.

3. The contribution of the individual components (inputs) to the total return may be evaluated. The manager's *a priori* assumption may be that a twisting of the yield curve will have a small effect relative to other factors. The

---

[13] We use the term "interest rates" rather generically here. For non-Treasury issues, the manager would likely provide a more detailed breakdown, such as the change in Treasury rates, the change in sector spreads, and so on.

results of the scenario analysis may show that the effect is much larger than the manager anticipated, alerting him to potential problems if this area is not analyzed closely.

4. The process can be broadened to evaluate the relative merits of entire trading strategies.

The purpose of conducting a scenario analysis is to gain a better understanding of the risk and return characteristics of the portfolio before trades are undertaken that may lead to undesirable consequences. In other words, scenario analysis is an excellent risk assessment and planning tool.

3.4 Monitoring/Adjusting the Portfolio and Performance Evaluation

Details of monitoring and adjusting a fixed-income portfolio (with its related performance evaluation) are essentially the same as other classes of investments. Because these topics are covered in detail in other readings, this reading will not duplicate that coverage.

MANAGING FUNDS AGAINST LIABILITIES   4

We have now walked our way through the major activities in managing fixed-income investment portfolios. However, in doing so, we took a bit of a shortcut. In order to see all the steps at once, we only looked at one branch of Exhibit 1—the branch having to do with managing funds against a bond market index benchmark. We now turn our attention to the equally important second branch of Exhibit 1—managing funds against a liability, or set of liabilities.

4.1 Dedication Strategies

Dedication strategies are specialized fixed-income strategies that are designed to accommodate specific funding needs of the investor. They generally are classified as passive in nature, although it is possible to add some active management elements to them. Exhibit 6 provides a classification of dedication strategies.

EXHIBIT 6	Dedication Strategies

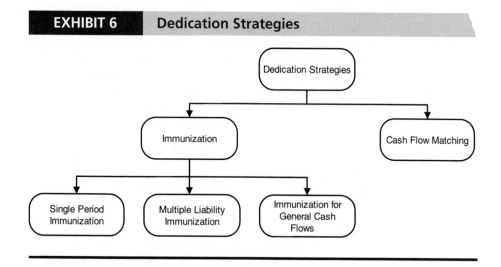

EXHIBIT 7	Classes of Liabilities	
Amount of Liability	**Timing of Liability**	**Example**
Known	Known	A principal repayment
Known	Unknown	A life insurance payout
Unknown	Known	A floating rate annuity payout
Unknown	Unknown	Post-retirement health care benefits

As seen in Exhibit 6, one important type of dedication strategy is immunization. **Immunization** aims to construct a portfolio that, over a specified horizon, will earn a predetermined return regardless of interest rate changes. Another widely used dedication strategy is **cash flow matching**, which provides the future funding of a liability stream from the coupon and matured principal payments of the portfolio. Each of these strategies will be more fully developed in the following sections followed by a discussion of some of the extensions based on them.

There are four typical types (or classes) of liabilities that can be identified. These are shown in Exhibit 7.

Obviously, the more uncertain the liabilities, the more difficult it becomes to use a passive dedication strategy to achieve the portfolio's goals. For this reason, as liabilities become more uncertain, managers often insert elements of active management. The goal of this action is to increase the upside potential of the portfolio while simultaneously ensuring a set of cash flows that are expected to be adequate for paying the anticipated liabilities. Examples of these more aggressive strategies, such as active/passive combinations, active/immunization combinations, and contingent immunization, are discussed later.

4.1.1 Immunization Strategies

Immunization is a popular strategy for "locking in" a guaranteed rate of return over a particular time horizon. As interest rates increase, the decrease in the price of a fixed-income security is usually at least partly offset by a higher amount of reinvestment income. As rates decline, a security's price increase is usually at least partly offset by a lower amount of reinvestment income. For an arbitrary time horizon, the price and reinvestment effects generally do not exactly offset each other: The change in price may be either greater than or less than the change in reinvestment income. The purpose of immunization is to identify the portfolio for which the change in price is exactly equal to the change in reinvestment income at the time horizon of interest. If the manager can construct such a portfolio, an assured rate of return over that horizon is locked in. The implementation of an immunization strategy depends on the type of liabilities that the manager is trying to meet: a single liability (e.g., a guaranteed investment contract), multiple liabilities (a defined-benefit plan's promised payouts), or general cash flows (where the cash flows are more arbitrary in their timing).

4.1.1.1 Classical Single-Period Immunization Classical immunization can be defined as the creation of a fixed-income portfolio that produces an assured return for a specific time horizon, irrespective of any parallel shifts in the yield curve.[14] In its most basic form, the important characteristics of immunization are:

---

[14] Any yield curve shift involves a change in the interest rate either up or down by the same amount at all maturities. The classical theory of immunization is set forth by Reddington (1952) and Fisher and Weil (1971).

1. Specified time horizon.
2. Assured rate of return during the holding period to a fixed horizon date.
3. Insulation from the effects of interest rate changes on the portfolio value at the horizon date.

The fundamental mechanism supporting immunization is a portfolio structure that balances the change in the value of the portfolio at the end of the investment horizon with the return from the reinvestment of portfolio cash flows (coupon payments and maturing securities). That is, immunization requires offsetting price risk and reinvestment risk. To accomplish this balancing requires the management of duration. Setting the duration of the portfolio equal to the specified portfolio time horizon assures the offsetting of positive and negative incremental return sources under certain assumptions, including the assumption that the immunizing portfolio has the same present value as the liability being immunized.[15] Duration-matching is a minimum condition for immunization.

EXAMPLE 5

Total Return for Various Yields

Consider the situation that a life insurance company faces when it sells a guaranteed investment contract (GIC). For a lump sum payment, the life insurance company guarantees that a specified payment will be made to the policyholder at a specified future date. Suppose that a life insurance company sells a five-year GIC that guarantees an interest rate of 7.5 percent per year on a bond-equivalent yield basis (3.75 percent every six months for the next 10 six-month periods). Also suppose that the payment the policyholder makes is $9,642,899. The value that the life insurance company has guaranteed the policyholder five years from now is thus $13,934,413. That is, the **target value** for the manager of the portfolio of supporting assets is $13,934,413 after five years, which is the same as a target yield of 7.5 percent on a bond-equivalent basis.

Assume that the manager buys $9,642,899 face value of a bond selling at par with a 7.5 percent yield to maturity that matures in five years. The portfolio manager will not be assured of realizing a total return at least equal to the target yield of 7.5 percent, because to realize 7.5 percent, the coupon interest payments must be reinvested at a minimum rate of 3.75 percent every six months. That is, the accumulated value will depend on the reinvestment rate.

EXHIBIT 8	Accumulated Value and Total Return after Five Years: Five-Year, 7.5% Bond Selling to Yield 7.5%
Investment horizon (years)	5
Coupon rate	7.50%
Maturity (years)	5
Yield to maturity	7.50%
Price	100.00000
Par value purchased	$9,642,899
Purchase price	$9,642,899
Target value	$13,934,413

(Exhibit continued on next page . . .)

---

[15] See Fabozzi (2004b) for further details.

EXHIBIT 8	(continued)

After Five Years

New Yield	Coupon	Interest on Interest	Bond Price	Accumulated Value	Total Return
11.00%	$3,616,087	$1,039,753	$9,642,899	$14,298,739	8.04%
10.50	3,616,087	985,615	9,642,899	14,244,601	7.96
10.00	3,616,087	932,188	9,642,899	14,191,175	7.88
9.50	3,616,087	879,465	9,642,899	14,138,451	7.80
9.00	3,616,087	827,436	9,642,899	14,086,423	7.73
8.50	3,616,087	776,093	9,642,899	14,035,079	7.65
8.00	3,616,087	725,426	9,642,899	13,984,412	7.57
7.50	3,616,087	675,427	9,642,899	13,934,413	7.50
7.00	3,616,087	626,087	9,642,899	13,885,073	7.43
6.50	3,616,087	577,398	9,642,899	13,836,384	7.35
6.00	3,616,087	529,352	9,642,899	13,788,338	7.28
5.50	3,616,087	481,939	9,642,899	13,740,925	7.21
5.00	3,616,087	435,153	9,642,899	13,694,139	7.14
4.50	3,616,087	388,985	9,642,899	13,647,971	7.07
4.00	3,616,087	343,427	9,642,899	13,602,414	7.00

Source: Fabozzi (2004b, p. 109).

To demonstrate this, suppose that immediately after investing in the bond above, yields in the market change, and then stay at the new level for the remainder of the five years. Exhibit 8 illustrates what happens at the end of five years.[16]

If yields do not change and the coupon payments can be reinvested at 7.5 percent (3.75 percent every six months), the portfolio manager will achieve the target value. If market yields rise, an accumulated value (total return) higher than the target value (target yield) will be achieved. This result follows because the coupon interest payments can be reinvested at a higher rate than the initial yield to maturity. This result contrasts with what happens when the yield declines. The accumulated value (total return) is then less than the target value (target yield). Therefore, investing in a coupon bond with a yield to maturity equal to the target yield and a maturity equal to the investment horizon does not assure that the target value will be achieved.

Keep in mind that to immunize a portfolio's target value or target yield against a change in the market yield, a manager must invest in a bond or a bond portfolio whose 1) duration is equal to the investment horizon and 2) initial present value of all cash flows equals the present value of the future liability.

---

[16] For purposes of illustration, we assume no expenses or profits to the insurance company.

4.1.1.2 Rebalancing an Immunized Portfolio   Textbooks often illustrate immunization by assuming a one-time instantaneous change in the market yield. In actuality, the market yield will fluctuate over the investment horizon. As a result, the duration of the portfolio will change as the market yield changes. The duration will also change simply because of the passage of time. In any interest rate environment that is different from a flat term structure, the duration of a portfolio will change at a different rate from time.

How often should a portfolio be rebalanced to adjust its duration? The answer involves balancing the costs and benefits of rebalancing. On the one hand, more frequent rebalancing increases transactions costs, thereby reducing the likelihood of achieving the target return. On the other hand, less frequent rebalancing causes the duration to wander from the target duration, which also reduces the likelihood of achieving the target return. Thus, the manager faces a trade-off: Some transactions costs must be accepted to prevent the duration from straying too far from its target, but some mismatch in the duration must be lived with, or transactions costs will become prohibitively high.

4.1.1.3 Determining the Target Return   Given the term structure of interest rates or the yield curve prevailing at the beginning of the horizon period, the assured rate of return of immunization can be determined. Theoretically, this immunization target rate of return is defined as the total return of the portfolio, assuming no change in the term structure. This target rate of return will always differ from the portfolio's present yield to maturity unless the term structure is flat (not increasing or decreasing), because by virtue of the passage of time, there is a return effect as the portfolio moves along the yield curve (matures). That is, for an upward-sloping yield curve, the yield to maturity of a portfolio can be quite different from its immunization target rate of return while, for a flat yield curve, the yield to maturity would roughly approximate the assured target return.

In general, for an upward-sloping yield curve, the immunization target rate of return will be less than the yield to maturity because of the lower reinvestment return. Conversely, a negative or downward-sloping yield curve will result in an immunization target rate of return greater than the yield to maturity because of the higher reinvestment return.

Alternative measures of the immunization target rate of return include the yield implied by a zero coupon bond of quality and duration comparable with that of the bond portfolio and an estimate based on results of a simulation that rebalances the initial portfolio, given scenarios of interest rate change.

The most conservative method for discounting liabilities—the method resulting in the largest present value of the liabilities—involves the use of the **Treasury spot curve** (the term structure of Treasury zero coupon bonds).

A more realistic approach utilizes the yield curve (converted to spot rates) implied by the securities held in the portfolio. This yield curve can be obtained using a curve-fitting methodology.[17] Because spreads may change as well as the term structure itself, the value of the liabilities will vary over time.

4.1.1.4 Time Horizon   The **immunized time horizon** is equal to the portfolio duration. Portfolio duration is equal to a weighted average of the individual security durations where the weights are the relative amounts or percentages invested in each.

A typical immunized time horizon is five years, which is a common planning period for GICs and allows flexibility in security selection because there is a fairly large population of securities to create the necessary portfolio duration. Securities in the portfolio should be limited to high-quality, very liquid instruments,

---

[17] See Vasicek and Fong (1982).

because portfolio rebalancing is required to keep the portfolio duration synchronized with the horizon date.

4.1.1.5 Dollar Duration and Controlling Positions   **Dollar duration** is a measure of the change in portfolio value for a 100 bps change in market yields.[18] It is defined[19] as

$$\text{Dollar duration} = \text{Duration} \times \text{Portfolio value} \times 0.01$$

A portfolio's dollar duration is equal to the sum of the dollar durations of the component securities.

EXAMPLE 6

Calculation of Dollar Duration

We have constructed a portfolio consisting of three bonds in equal par amounts of $1,000,000 each. The initial values and durations are shown in Exhibit 9. Note that the market value includes accrued interest.

EXHIBIT 9	Initial Durations of a Three-Bond Portfolio			
Security	**Price**	**Market Value**	**Duration**	**Dollar Duration**
Bond #1	$104.013	$1,065,613	5.025	$53,548
Bond #2	96.089	978,376	1.232	12,054
Bond #3	103.063	1,034,693	4.479	46,343
Dollar duration				$111,945

In a number of ALM applications, the investor's goal is to reestablish the dollar duration of a portfolio to a desired level. This rebalancing involves the following steps:

1. Move forward in time and include a shift in the yield curve. Using the new market values and durations, calculate the dollar duration of the portfolio at this point in time.

---

[18] Dollar duration is a traditional term in the bond literature; the concept applies to portfolios denominated in any currency. A related concept is the price value of a basis point (PVBP), also known as the dollar value of a basis point (DV01). The PVBP is equal to the dollar duration divided by 100.

[19] The use of the term "duration" in this reading (and in the equation) is consistent with Fabozzi (2004a, p. 228), who defines it as "the approximate percentage change in price for a 100 basis point change in rates." Taking a concept known as **Macaulay duration** (the percentage change in price for a *percentage change* in yield) as a baseline calculation measure, a tradition also exists for referring to "duration" as used in the equation as "modified duration" because it is equal to Macaulay duration modified to obtain a measure of price sensitivity for a change in the *level* of yields.

2. Calculate the **rebalancing ratio** by dividing the original dollar duration by the new dollar duration. If we subtract one from this ratio and convert the result to a percent, it tells us the percentage amount that each position needs to be changed in order to rebalance the portfolio.

3. Multiply the new market value of the portfolio by the desired percentage change in Step 2. This number is the amount of cash needed for rebalancing.

EXAMPLE 7

Rebalancing Based on the Dollar Duration

We now move forward one year and include a shift in the yield curve. The portfolio values at this point in time are given in Exhibit 10:

EXHIBIT 10	Durations of a Three-Bond Portfolio after One Year			
Security	**Price**	**Market Value**	**Duration**	**Dollar Duration**
Bond #1	$99.822	$1,023,704	4.246	$43,466
Bond #2	98.728	1,004,770	0.305	3,065
Bond #3	99.840	1,002,458	3.596	36,048
				$82,579

The portfolio dollar duration has changed from $111,945 to $82,579. Our requirement is to maintain the portfolio dollar duration at the initial level. To do so, we must rebalance our portfolio. We choose to rebalance using the existing security proportions of one-third each.

To calculate the rebalancing ratio, we divide the original dollar duration by the new dollar duration:

$$\frac{\$111,945}{\$82,579} = 1.356$$

Rebalancing requires each position to be increased by 35.6 percent. The cash required for this rebalancing is calculated as

$$\text{Cash required} = 0.356 \times (\$1,023,704 + 1,004,770 + 1,002,458)$$
$$= \$1,079,012$$

4.1.1.6 Spread Duration   Spread duration is a measure of how the market value of a risky bond (portfolio) will change with respect to a parallel 100 bps change in its spread above the comparable benchmark security (portfolio). Spread duration is an important measurement tool for the management of spread risk. Spreads do change and the portfolio manager needs to know the risks associated with such changes.

A characteristic of bonds with **credit risk** (risk of loss because of credit events such as default or downgrades in credit ratings)—sometimes called "spread product"—is that their yield will be higher than a comparable risk-free security. The large spectrum of bond products available in the marketplace leads to differing types of spread duration. The three major types are:

1. **Nominal spread**, the spread of a bond or portfolio above the yield of a certain maturity Treasury.
2. **Static spread** or zero-volatility spread, defined as the constant spread above the Treasury spot curve that equates the calculated price of the security to the market price.
3. **Option-adjusted spread (OAS)**, the current spread over the benchmark yield minus that component of the spread that is attributable to any embedded optionality in the instrument.

The spread duration of a portfolio is calculated as a market weighted average of the spread durations of the component securities. For a portfolio of non-Treasury securities, spread duration equals portfolio duration. However, because the spread duration of Treasury securities is zero, a portfolio that includes both Treasury and non-Treasury securities will have a spread duration that is different from the portfolio duration.

A bond index will have an overall spread duration as will each sector within the index. The manager can calculate the effect on the portfolio of a change in sector spreads. The effect due to a change in sector spreads is in addition to the effect that is implied by a general increase or decrease in interest rates.

EXAMPLE 8

Portfolio Immunization

The Managers of Reliable Life Insurance Company are considering hiring a consultant to advise them on portfolio immunization. Following are some of the statements that were made during these presentations:

1. A great thing about immunization is that it is a set-and-forget strategy. That is, once you have immunized your portfolio, there is no subsequent work to be done.
2. The immunization target rate of return is less than yield to maturity.
3. If a portfolio is immunized against a change in the market yield at a given horizon by matching portfolio duration to horizon, the portfolio faces no risk except for default risk.
4. The liquidity of securities used to construct an immunized portfolio is irrelevant.
5. In general, the entire portfolio does not have to be turned over to rebalance an immunized portfolio. Furthermore, rebalancing need not be done on a daily basis.

Critique the statements.

Solution to 1:   This statement is incorrect. One needs to rebalance the portfolio duration whenever interest rates change and as time elapses since the previous rebalancing.

Solution to 2:   This statement is only true if the yield curve is upward sloping. If the yield curve is downward-sloping, then this statement is not true as the immunization target rate of return would exceed the yield to maturity because of the higher reinvestment return.

Solution to 3:   The statement is incorrect. The portfolio described would be exposed to the risk of a change in interest rates that results in a change in the shape of the yield curve.

Solution to 4:   The statement is incorrect because immunized portfolios need to be rebalanced; the liquidity of securities used to construct an immunized portfolio is a relevant consideration. Illiquid securities involve high transaction costs and make portfolio rebalancing costly.

Solution to 5:   The statement is correct. The entire portfolio does not have to be turned over to rebalance it because shifting a small set of securities from one maturity range to another is generally enough. Also, to avoid excessive transactions costs, rebalancing is usually not done on a daily basis, which could involve excessive transaction costs.

4.1.2 *Extensions of Classical Immunization Theory*

Classical immunization theory is based on several assumptions:

1. Any changes in the yield curve are parallel changes, that is, interest rates move either up or down by the same amount for all maturities.
2. The portfolio is valued at a fixed horizon date, and there are no interim cash inflows or outflows before the horizon date.
3. The target value of the investment is defined as the portfolio value at the horizon date if the interest rate structure does not change (i.e., there is no change in forward rates).

Perhaps the most critical assumption of classical immunization techniques is the first one concerning the type of interest rate change anticipated. A property of a classically immunized portfolio is that the target value of the investment is the lower limit of the value of the portfolio at the horizon date if there are parallel interest rate changes.[20] According to the theory, if there is a change in interest rates that does not correspond to this shape-preserving shift, matching the duration to the investment horizon no longer assures immunization.[21] Non-shape-preserving shifts are the commonly observed case.

---

[20] See Fisher and Weil (1971) and Fabozzi (2004b).

[21] For a more complete discussion of these issues, see Cox, Ingersoll, and Ross (1979).

Exhibit 11 illustrates the nature of the portfolio value, given an immunized portfolio and parallel shifts in rates. The curve **aa′** represents the behavior of the portfolio value for various changes in rates, ranging from a decline to an increase as shown on the horizontal axis. Point V_0 on line **tt′** is the level of the portfolio value assuming no change in rates. As we note above, an immunized portfolio subjected to parallel shifts in the yield curve will provide at least as great a portfolio value at the horizon date as the assured target value, which thus becomes the minimum value. Therefore, if the assumptions of classical theory hold, immunization provides a minimum-risk strategy.

EXHIBIT 11	Changes in Portfolio Value Caused by Parallel Interest Rate Changes for an Immunized Portfolio

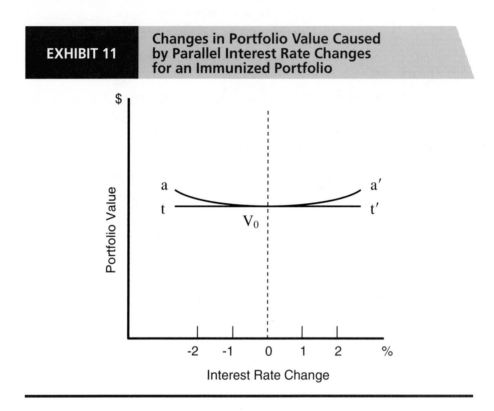

Exhibit 12 illustrates the relationship between the value of a classically immunized portfolio and interest rate changes when interest rates do not shift in a parallel fashion. Depending on the shape of the nonparallel shift, either the relationship shown in a) or that shown in b) will occur. This exhibit shows the possibility (in cases *d* and *e*) that the value of a classically immunized portfolio can be less than the target. The important point is that merely matching the duration of the portfolio to the investment horizon as the condition for immunization may not prevent significant deviations from the target value. As an example of the effect on accumulated value of a portfolio given nonparallel yield curve shifts, consider the return on a 6 year, 6.75 percent bond selling to yield 7.5 percent. Our horizon remains at 5 years.

The four yield curve changes shown in Exhibit 13 are applied to the existing yield curve. For example, Scenario 1 twists the existing yield curve by reducing the 3-month rate by 50 bps and increasing the 7-year rate by 100 bps. Intermediate points on the yield curve are linearly interpolated between the end points. The total return is then calculated and displayed in Exhibit 14.

A natural extension of classical immunization theory is to extend the theory to the case of nonparallel shifts in interest rates. Two approaches have been taken.

EXHIBIT 12	Two Patterns of Changes in Portfolio Value Caused by Nonparallel Interest Rate Shifts for an Immunized Portfolio

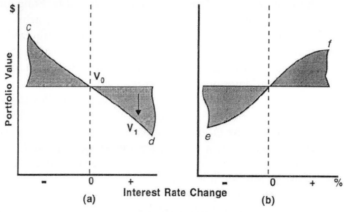

Source: Gifford Fong Associates.

EXHIBIT 13	Yield Curve Changes

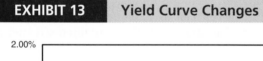

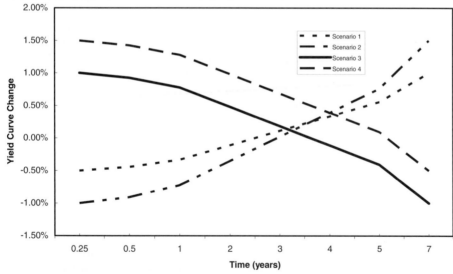

EXHIBIT 14	Total Return after Yield Curve Change

Scenario	Coupon	Interest on Interest	Price of the Bond	Accumulated Value	Total Return
Scenario 1	$3,375,000	$572,652	$9,999,376	$13,947,029	7.519%
Scenario 2	3,375,000	547,054	10,025,367	13,947,421	7.519
Scenario 3	3,375,000	679,368	9,894,491	13,948,860	7.522
Scenario 4	3,375,000	728,752	9,847,756	13,951,508	7.525

The first approach has been to modify the definition of duration so as to allow for nonparallel yield curve shifts, such as multifunctional duration (also known as **functional duration** or key rate duration). The second approach is a strategy that can handle any arbitrary interest rate change so that it is not necessary to specify an alternative duration measure. This approach, developed by Fong and Vasicek (1984), establishes a measure of immunization risk against any arbitrary interest rate change. The immunization risk measure can then be minimized subject to the constraint that the duration of the portfolio equals the investment horizon, resulting in a portfolio with minimum exposure to any interest rate movements. This approach is discussed later in the section.

A second extension of classical immunization theory applies to overcoming the limitations of a fixed horizon (the second assumption on which immunization depends). Marshall and Yawitz (1982) demonstrated that, under the assumption of parallel interest rate changes, a lower bound exists on the value of an investment portfolio at any particular time, although this lower bound may be below the value realized if interest rates do not change.

Fong and Vasicek (1984) and Bierwag, Kaufman, and Toevs (1979) extended immunization to the case of multiple liabilities. Multiple liability immunization involves an investment strategy that guarantees meeting a specified schedule of future liabilities, regardless of the type of shift in interest rate changes. Fong and Vasicek (1984) provided a generalization of the immunization risk measure for the multiple liability case. Moreover, it extends the theory to the general case of arbitrary cash flows (contributions as well as liabilities). Multiple liability immunization and the general case of arbitrary cash flows are discussed later in the reading.

In some situations, the objective of immunization as strict risk minimization may be too restrictive. The third extension of classical immunization theory is to analyze the risk and return trade-off for immunized portfolios. Fong and Vasicek (1983) demonstrated how this trade-off can be analyzed. Their approach, called "return maximization," is explained later in this reading.

The fourth extension of classical immunization theory is to integrate immunization strategies with elements of active bond portfolio management strategies. The traditional objective of immunization has been risk protection, with little consideration of possible returns. Leibowitz and Weinberger (1981) proposed a technique called **contingent immunization**, which provides a degree of flexibility in pursuing active strategies while ensuring a certain minimum return in the case of a parallel rate shift. In contingent immunization, immunization serves as a fall-back strategy if the actively managed portfolio does not grow at a certain rate.

Contingent immunization is possible when the prevailing available immunized rate of return is greater than the required rate of return. For example, if a firm has a three-year investment horizon over which it must earn 3 percent and it can immunize its asset portfolio at 4.75 percent, the manager can actively manage part or all of the portfolio until it reaches the safety net rate of return of 3 percent. If the portfolio return drops to this safety net level, the portfolio is immunized and the active management is dropped. The difference between the 4.75 percent and the 3 percent safety net rate of return is called the **cushion spread** (the difference between the minimum acceptable return and the higher possible immunized rate).

If the manager started with a $500 million portfolio, after three years the portfolio needs to grow to

$$P_I\left(1 + \frac{s}{2}\right)^{2T} = \$500\left(1 + \frac{0.03}{2}\right)^{2x3} = \$546.72$$

where dollar amounts are in millions and

P_I = initial portfolio value
s = safety net rate of return
T = years in the investment horizon

At time 0, the portfolio can be immunized at 4.75 percent, which implies that the required initial portfolio amount, where dollar amounts are in millions, is

$$\frac{\text{Required terminal value}}{\left(1 + \frac{i}{2}\right)^{2T}} = \frac{\$546.72}{\left(1 + \frac{0.0475}{2}\right)^{2 \times 3}} = \$474.90$$

The manager therefore has an initial dollar safety margin of $500 million − $474.90 million = $25.10 million.

If the manager invests the entire $500 million in 4.75 percent, 10-year notes at par and the YTM (yield to maturity) immediately changes, what will happen to the dollar safety margin?

If the YTM suddenly drops to 3.75 percent, the value of the portfolio will be $541.36 million. The initial asset value required to satisfy the terminal value of $546.72 million at 3.75 percent YTM is $489.06 million so the dollar safety margin has grown to $541.36 million − $489.06 million = $52.3 million. The manager may therefore commit a larger proportion of her assets to active management.

If rates rise so that the YTM is now 5.80 percent, the portfolio value will be $460.55 million and the initial asset value required will be $460.52 million. The dollar safety margin has gone to zero, and thus the portfolio must be immunized immediately.

Another example of the use of immunization as an adjunct to active return strategies is described by Fong and Tang (1988). Based on option valuation theory, a portfolio strategy can systematically shift the proportion between an active strategy and an immunized strategy in a portfolio to achieve a predetermined minimum return while retaining the potential upside of the active strategy.

4.1.2.1 Duration and Convexity of Assets and Liabilities   In order for a manager to have a clear picture of the **economic surplus** of the portfolio—defined as the market value of assets minus the present value of liabilities—the duration and convexity of both the assets and liabilities must be understood. Focusing only on the duration of a company's assets will not give a true indication of the total interest rate risk for a company.

As an example, assume that a company's assets and liabilities have the characteristics shown in Exhibit 15. We can consider two interest rate scenarios, up 100 bps and down 100 bps, with results shown in Exhibit 16 in Panels A and B, respectively. The economic surplus of the company has increased as rates rise. This increase is a result of the mismatch in duration between the assets and liabilities.

EXHIBIT 15	Balance Sheet Characteristics of a Company (Dollar Amounts in Millions)			
	Market Value	**Present Value**	**Economic Surplus**	**Duration**
Assets	$500	—	$100	4
Liabilities	—	$400	—	7

EXHIBIT 16	Interest Rate Scenarios (Dollar Amounts in Millions)		
	Approximate Market Value	Present Value	Economic Surplus
A. When Rates Increase by 100 bps			
Assets	$480	—	$108
Liabilities	—	$372	—
B. When Rates Decrease by 100 bps			
Assets	$520	—	$92
Liabilities	—	$428	—

Convexity also plays a part in changes in economic surplus. If liabilities and assets are duration matched but not convexity matched, economic surplus will be exposed to variation in value from interest rate changes reflecting the convexity mismatch.

The manager must continuously monitor the portfolio to ensure that asset and liability durations and convexities are well matched. If the duration/convexity mismatch is substantial, the portfolio should be rebalanced to achieve a closer match.

4.1.2.2 Types of Risk   As the market environment changes, the portfolio manager faces the risk of not being able to pay liabilities when they come due. Three sources of this risk are interest rate risk, contingent claim risk, and cap risk.

Interest rate risk.   Because the prices of most fixed-income securities move opposite to interest rates, a rising interest rate environment will adversely affect the value of a portfolio. If assets need to be sold to service liabilities, the manager may find a shortfall. Interest rate risk is the largest risk that a portfolio manager will face.

Contingent claims risk.   When a security has a contingent claim provision, explicit or implicit, there is an associated risk. In a falling rate environment, the manager may have lucrative coupon payments halted and receive principal (as is the case with mortgage-backed securities when the underlying mortgages prepay principal). The loss of the coupons is bad enough but now the principal must be reinvested at a lower rate. In addition, the market value of a callable security will level out at the call price, rather than continuing upwards as a noncallable security would.

Cap risk.   An asset that makes floating rate payments will typically have caps associated with the floating rate. The manager is at risk of the level of market rates rising while the asset returns are capped. This event may severely affect the value of the assets.

4.1.2.3 Risk Minimization for Immunized Portfolios   The Fong and Vasicek (1984) extension of classical immunization theory produced an immunized portfolio with a minimum exposure to any arbitrary interest rate change. One way of minimizing immunization risk is shown in Exhibit 17.

The spikes in the two panels of Exhibit 17 represent actual portfolio cash flows. The taller spikes depict the actual cash flows generated by securities at maturity, whereas the smaller spikes represent coupon payments. Both Portfolio A and

| EXHIBIT 17 | Illustration of Immunization Risk Measure |

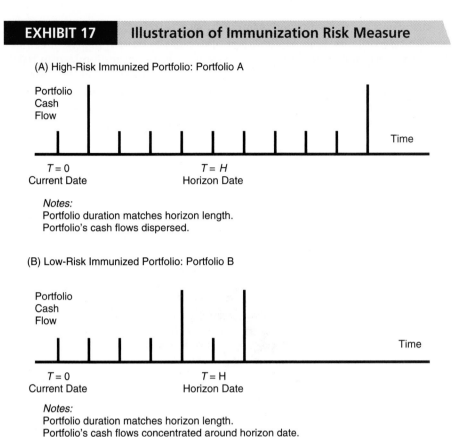

(A) High-Risk Immunized Portfolio: Portfolio A

Portfolio Cash Flow

Time

$T = 0$
Current Date

$T = H$
Horizon Date

Notes:
Portfolio duration matches horizon length.
Portfolio's cash flows dispersed.

(B) Low-Risk Immunized Portfolio: Portfolio B

Portfolio Cash Flow

Time

$T = 0$
Current Date

$T = H$
Horizon Date

Notes:
Portfolio duration matches horizon length.
Portfolio's cash flows concentrated around horizon date.

Source: Fabozzi (2004b, p. 123).

Portfolio B are composed of two bonds with durations equal to the investment horizon. Portfolio A is, in effect, a **barbell portfolio**—a portfolio made up of short and long maturities relative to the horizon date and interim coupon payments. Portfolio B, however is a **bullet portfolio**—the bond maturities are very close to the investment horizon.

If both portfolios have durations equal to the horizon length, both portfolios are immune to parallel rate changes. When interest rates change in an arbitrary nonparallel way, however, the effect on the value of the two portfolios differs— the barbell portfolio is riskier than the bullet portfolio.

Suppose, for instance, short rates decline while long rates go up. Both the barbell and bullet portfolios would realize a decline of the portfolio value at the end of the investment horizon below the target investment value, because they would experience a capital loss in addition to lower reinvestment rates.

The decline would be substantially higher for the barbell portfolio, however, for two reasons. First, the barbell portfolio experiences the lower reinvestment rates longer than the bullet portfolio does. Second, more of the barbell portfolio is still outstanding at the end of the investment horizon, which means that the same rate increase causes much more of a capital loss. In short, the bullet portfolio has less exposure to changes in the interest rate structure than the barbell portfolio.

It should be clear that reinvestment risk determines immunization risk. *The portfolio that has the least reinvestment risk will have the least immunization risk.* When there is a high dispersion of cash flows around the horizon date, as in the barbell portfolio, the portfolio is exposed to high reinvestment risk. When the cash flows are concentrated around the horizon date, as in the bullet portfolio, the portfolio is subject to minimal reinvestment risk. In the case of a pure discount instrument maturing at the investment horizon, immunization risk is zero because, with no interim cash flows, reinvestment risk is absent. Moving from pure discount instruments to coupon payment instruments, the portfolio manager is confronted with the task of selecting coupon-paying securities that provide the lowest immunization risk—if the manager can construct a portfolio that replicates a pure discount instrument that matures at the investment horizon, immunization risk will be zero.

Recall that the target value of an immunized portfolio is a lower bound on the terminal value of the portfolio at the investment horizon if yields on all maturities change by the same amount. If yields of different maturities change by different amounts, the target value is not necessarily the lower bound on the investment value.

Fong and Vasicek (1984) demonstrated that if forward rates change by any arbitrary function, the relative change in the portfolio value depends on the product of two terms.[22] The first term depends solely on the structure of the investment portfolio, while the second term, denoted M^2, is a function of interest rate movement only. The second term characterizes the nature of the interest rate shock. It is an uncertain quantity and, therefore, outside the control of the manager. The first term, however, is under the control of the manager, as it depends solely on the composition of the portfolio. The first term can be used as a measure of immunization risk because when it is small, the exposure of the portfolio to any interest rate change is small. The immunization risk measure M^2 is the variance of time to payment around the horizon date, where the weight for a particular time in the variance calculation is the proportion of the instrument's total present value that the payment received at that time represents.[23] The immunization risk measure may be called the **maturity variance**; in effect, it measures how much a given immunized portfolio differs from the ideal immunized portfolio consisting of a single pure discount instrument with maturity equal to the time horizon.

Given the measure of immunization risk that is to be minimized and the constraint that the duration of the portfolio equals the investment horizon, the optimal immunized portfolio can be found using **linear programming** (optimization in which the objective function and constraints are linear). Linear programming is appropriate because the risk measure is linear in the portfolio payments.

The immunization risk measure can be used to construct approximate confidence intervals for the target return over the horizon period and the target end-of-period portfolio value. A **confidence interval** represents an uncertainty band around the target return within which the realized return can be expected with a given probability. The expression for the confidence interval is:

Confidence interval = Target return ± (k)
× (Standard deviation of target return)

where k is the number of standard deviations around the expected target return. The desired confidence level determines k. The higher the desired confidence level, the larger k, and the wider the band around the expected target return.

---

[22] The Fong and Vasicek (1984) result is derived by expansion of the terminal portfolio value function into the first three terms of a Taylor series.

[23] The measure is $M^2 = \sum_{j=1}^{m}(s_j - H)^2 C_j P_0(s_j)/I_0$, where s_j is the time at which payment C_j is made, H is the horizon date, $P_0(s_j)$ is the present value of the payment(s) made at time s_j, and I_0 is initial portfolio value.

Fong and Vasicek (1983) demonstrated that the standard deviation of the expected target return can be approximated by the product of three terms:[24] 1) the immunization risk measure, 2) the standard deviation of the variance of the one-period change in the slope of the yield curve,[25] and 3) an expression that is a function of the horizon length only.[26]

4.1.3 Multiple Liability Immunization

Immunization with respect to a single investment horizon is appropriate where the objective of the investment is to preserve the value of the investment at the horizon date. This objective is appropriate given that a single liability is payable at, or a target investment value must be attained by, the horizon date. More often, however, there are a number of liabilities to be paid from the investment funds and no single horizon that corresponds to the schedule of liabilities. A portfolio is said to be immunized with respect to a given liability stream if there are enough funds to pay all the liabilities when due, even if interest rates change by a parallel shift.

Bierwag, Kaufman, and Toevs (1979) demonstrate that matching the duration of the portfolio to the average duration of the liabilities is not a sufficient condition for immunization in the presence of multiple liabilities. Instead, the portfolio payment stream must be decomposable in such a way that each liability is separately immunized by one of the component streams; there may be no actual securities providing payments that individually match those of the component payment streams.

Fong and Vasicek (1984) demonstrate the conditions that must be satisfied to assure multiple liability immunization in the case of parallel rate shifts. The necessary and sufficient conditions are:

1. The (composite) duration of the portfolio must equal the (composite) duration of the liabilities.[27]

2. The distribution of durations of individual portfolio assets must have a wider range than the distribution of the liabilities.[28]

An implication of the first condition is that to immunize a liability stream that extends 30 years, it is not necessary to have a portfolio with a duration of 30. The condition requires that the manager construct a portfolio so that the portfolio duration matches the weighted average of the liability durations. This fact is important because in any reasonable interest rate environment, it is unlikely that a portfolio of investment-grade coupon bonds could be constructed with a duration in excess of 15. Yet for corporate pension funds retired lives, the liability stream is typically a diminishing amount. That is, liabilities in the earlier years are the greatest, and liabilities toward the 30-year end are generally lower. Taking

---

[24] The derivation is based on the assumption that the immunization risk measure of an optimally immunized portfolio periodically rebalanced decreases in time in approximate proportion to the third power of the remaining horizon length.

[25] This term can be estimated empirically from historical yield changes.

[26] The expression for the third term for the standard deviation of the expected target return of a single-period liability immunized portfolio is $(7H)^{-1/2}$, where H is the length of the horizon.

[27] The duration of the liabilities is found as follows: $[(1)\ PVL_1 + (2)\ PVL_2 + \ldots + (m)\ PVL_m]/$ (Total present value of liabilities) where PVL_1 = present value of the liability at time t and m = time of the last liability payment.

[28] More specifically, the mean absolute deviation of the portfolio payments must be greater than or equal to the mean absolute deviation of the liabilities at each payment date.

a weighted average duration of the liabilities usually brings the portfolio duration to something manageable, say, 8 or 9.

The second condition requires portfolio payments to bracket (be more dispersed in time than) the liabilities. That is, the portfolio must have an asset with a duration equal to or less than the duration of the shortest-duration liability in order to have funds to pay the liability when it is due. And the portfolio must have an asset with a duration equal to or greater than the longest-duration liability in order to avoid the reinvestment rate risk that might jeopardize payment of the longest duration. This bracketing of shortest- and longest-duration liabilities with even shorter- and longer-duration assets balances changes in portfolio value with changes in reinvestment return.

To understand why the portfolio payments have to be more spread out in time than the liabilities to assure immunization, consider the case of a single investment horizon in which immunization is achieved by balancing changes in reinvestment return on coupon payments with changes in investment value at the investment horizon. The same bracketing of each liability by the portfolio payments is necessary in the multiple liability case, which implies that the payments have to be more dispersed in time than the liabilities. Thus, managers selecting securities to be included in the portfolio must not only keep track of the matching of duration between assets and liabilities but also maintain a specified distribution for assets in the portfolio.

The two conditions for multiple liability immunization assure immunization against parallel rate shifts only. Reitano (1991) has explored the limitations of the parallel shift assumption.[29] He has also developed models that generalize the immunization of multiple liabilities to arbitrary yield curve shifts. His research indicates that classical multiple period immunization can mask the risks associated with nonparallel yield curve shifts and that a model that protects against one type of yield curve shift may expose a portfolio to other types of shifts.

Fong and Vasicek (1984) also addressed the question of the exposure of an immunized portfolio to an arbitrary interest rate change and generalize the immunization risk measure to the multiple liability case. Just as in the single investment horizon case, they find that the relative change in the portfolio value if forward rates change by any arbitrary function depends on the product of two terms: a term solely dependent on the structure of the portfolio and a term solely dependent on the interest rate movement.

An optimal immunization strategy is to minimize the immunization risk measure subject to the constraints imposed by these two conditions (and any other applicable portfolio constraints). Constructing minimum-risk immunized portfolios can then be accomplished by the use of linear programming.

Approximate confidence intervals can also be constructed in the multiple liability case. The standard deviation of the expected target return is the product of the three terms indicated in the section on risk minimization.[30]

4.1.4 Immunization for General Cash Flows

In both the single investment horizon and multiple liability cases, we have assumed that the investment funds are initially available in full. What if, instead, a given schedule of liabilities to be covered by an immunized investment must

---

[29] See also Reitano (1992) for a detailed illustration of the relationship between the underlying yield curve shift and immunization.

[30] See Fong and Vasicek (1983). The expression for the third term in the multiple liability case is a function of the dates and relative sizes of the liabilities, as well as the horizon length.

be met by investment funds that are not available at the time the portfolio is constructed?

Suppose a manager has a given obligation to be paid at the end of a two-year horizon. Only one-half of the necessary funds, however, are now available; the rest are expected at the end of the first year, to be invested at the end of the first year at whatever rates are then in effect. Is there an investment strategy that would guarantee the end-of-horizon value of the investment regardless of the development of interest rates?

Under certain conditions, such a strategy is indeed possible. The expected cash contributions can be considered the payments on hypothetical securities that are part of the initial holdings. The actual initial investment can then be invested in such a way that the real and hypothetical holdings taken together represent an immunized portfolio.

We can illustrate this using the two-year investment horizon. The initial investment should be constructed with a duration of 3. Half of the funds are then in an actual portfolio with a duration of 3, and the other half in a hypothetical portfolio with a duration of 1. The total stream of cash inflow payments for the portfolio has a duration of 2, matching the horizon length. This match satisfies a sufficient condition for immunization with respect to a single horizon.

At the end of the first year, any decline in the interest rates at which the cash contribution is invested will be offset by a corresponding increase in the value of the initial holdings. The portfolio is at that time rebalanced by selling the actual holdings and investing the proceeds together with the new cash in a portfolio with a duration of 1 to match the horizon date. Note that the rate of return guaranteed on the future contributions is not the current spot rate but rather the forward rate for the date of contribution.

This strategy can be extended to apply to multiple contributions and liabilities, which produces a general immunization technique that is applicable to the case of arbitrary cash flows over a period. The construction of an optimal immunized portfolio involves quantifying and then minimizing the immunization risk measure. Linear programming methods can then be used to obtain the optimal portfolio.

4.1.5 Return Maximization for Immunized Portfolios

The objective of risk minimization for an immunized portfolio may be too restrictive in certain situations. If a substantial increase in the expected return can be accomplished with little effect on immunization risk, the higher-yielding portfolio may be preferred in spite of its higher risk.

Suppose that an optimally immunized portfolio has a target return of 8 percent over the horizon with a 95 percent confidence interval at ±20 bps. Thus, the minimum-risk portfolio would have a 1 in 40 chance of a realized return less than 7.8 percent. Suppose that another portfolio less well-immunized can produce a target return of 8.3 percent with a 95 percent confidence interval of ±30 bps. In all but one case out of 40, on average, this portfolio would realize a return above 8 percent compared with 7.8 percent on the minimum-risk portfolio. For many investors, the 8.3 percent target-return portfolio may be the preferred one.

The required terminal value, plus a safety margin in money terms, will determine the minimum acceptable return over the horizon period. As already mentioned, the difference between the minimum acceptable return and the higher possible immunized rate is known as the cushion spread. This spread offers the manager latitude in pursuing an active strategy. The greater the cushion spread, the more scope the manager has for an active management policy.

Fong and Vasicek's (1983) approach to the risk/return trade-off for immunized portfolios maintains the duration of the portfolio at all times equal to the horizon length. Thus, the portfolio stays fully immunized in the classical sense. Instead of minimizing the immunization risk against nonparallel rate changes, however, a trade-off between risk and return is considered. The immunization risk measure can be relaxed if the compensation in terms of expected return warrants it. Specifically, the strategy maximizes a lower bound on the portfolio return. The lower bound is defined as the lower confidence interval limit on the realized return at a given confidence level.

Linear programming can be used to solve for the optimal portfolio when return maximization is the objective. In fact, parametric linear programming can be employed to determine an efficient frontier for immunized portfolios analogous to those in the mean–variance framework.

4.2 Cash Flow Matching Strategies

Cash flow matching is an alternative to multiple liability immunization in asset/liability management. Cash flow matching is an appealing strategy because the portfolio manager need only select securities to match the timing and amount of liabilities. Conceptually, a bond is selected with a maturity that matches the last liability, and an amount of principal equal to the amount of the last liability is invested in this bond. The remaining elements of the liability stream are then reduced by the coupon payments on this bond, and another bond is chosen for the next-to-last liability, adjusted for any coupon payments received on the first bond selected. Going back in time, this sequence is continued until all liabilities have been matched by payments on the securities selected for the portfolio. Linear programming techniques can be employed to construct a least-cost cash flow matching portfolio from an acceptable universe of bonds.

Exhibit 18 provides a simple illustration of this process for a five-year liability stream. Exhibit 19 provides a cash flow analysis of sources and application of funds of a portfolio being used to cash flow match a series of remaining liabilities falling due on 31 December of 2004 to 2018. In the first row for 2004, the previous cash balance of €0 indicates that the previous liability was exactly met by maturing principal and coupon payments. Principal payments of €1,685, coupon payments of €2,340, and €13 from an account which accumulates interest on reinvested payments, suffice to meet the liability due year-end 2004 (€1,685 + €2,340 + €13 = €4,038). (The interest account reflects interest on payments expected to be received in advance of the liability that the payments will fund.) The last column in the exhibit shows the excess funds remaining at each period, which are reinvested at an assumed 1.2 percent reinvestment rate supplied by the portfolio manager. The more excess cash, the greater the risk of the strategy, because the reinvestment rate is subject to uncertainty.

4.2.1 Cash Flow Matching versus Multiple Liability Immunization

If all the liability flows were perfectly matched by the asset flows of the portfolio, the resulting portfolio would have no reinvestment risk and, therefore, no immunization or cash flow match risk. Given typical liability schedules and bonds available for cash flow matching, however, perfect matching is unlikely. Under such conditions, a minimum immunization risk approach should be as good as cash flow matching and likely will be better, because an immunization

EXHIBIT 18   **Illustration of Cash Flow Matching Process**

Assume: 5-year liability stream. Cash flow from bonds is annual.

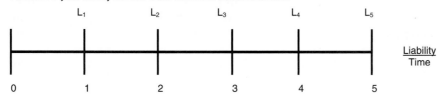

Step 1 – Cash flow from Bond A selected to satisfy L_5
Coupons = A_c ; Principal = A_p and $A_c + A_p = L_5$

Unfunded liabilities remaining:

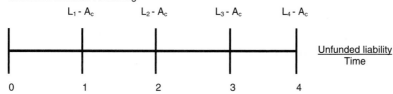

Step 2 – Cash flow from Bond B selected to satisfy $L_4 - A_c$
Coupons = B_c ; Principal = B_p and $B_c + B_p = L_4 - A_c$

Unfunded liabilities remaining:

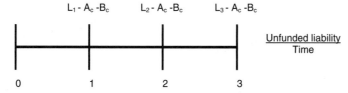

Step 3 – Cash flow from Bond C selected to satisfy $L_3 - A_c - B_c$
Coupons = C_c ; Principal = C_p and $C_c + C_p = L_3 - A_c - B_c$

Unfunded liabilities remaining:

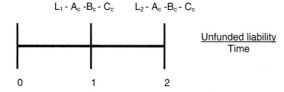

Step 4 – Cash flow from Bond D selected to satisfy $L_2 - A_c - B_c - C_c$
Coupons = D_c ; Principal = D_p and $D_c + D_p = L_2 - A_c - B_c - C_c$

Unfunded liabilities remaining:

$L_1 - A_c - B_c - C_c - D_c$

Unfunded liability
Time

0   1

Step 5 – Select Bond E with a cash flow of $L_1 - A_c - B_c - C_c - D_c$

Source: Fabozzi (2004b, p. 123).

EXHIBIT 19	Cash Flow Analysis of Sample Portfolio for Cash Flow Matching					
Year End (31 Dec)	Previous Cash Balance	Principal Payments	Coupon Payments	Interest on Reinvestment of Payments	Liability Due	New Cash Balance
2004	€0	€1,685	€2,340	€13	(€4,038)	€0
2005	0	1,723	2,165	13	(3,900)	0
2006	0	1,805	1,945	12	(3,762)	0
2007	0	1,832	1,769	23	(3,624)	0
2008	0	1,910	1,542	22	(3,474)	0
2009	0	1,877	1,443	10	(3,330)	0
2010	0	2,081	1,072	21	(3,174)	0
2011	0	2,048	950	14	(3,012)	0
2012	0	1,996	847	7	(2,850)	0
2013	0	3,683	768	9	(2,582)	1,878
2014	1,878	0	611	25	(2,514)	0
2015	0	1,730	611	5	(2,346)	0
2016	0	1,733	440	5	(2,178)	0
2017	0	1,756	233	15	(2,004)	0
2018	0	1,740	157	3	(1,900)	0

Reinvestment Rate: 1.2 percent; Evaluation Date: 31 December 2003

strategy would require less money to fund liabilities. Two factors contribute to this superiority.

First, cash flow matching requires a relatively conservative rate of return assumption for short-term cash and cash balances may be occasionally substantial. By contrast, an immunized portfolio is essentially fully invested at the remaining horizon duration. Second, funds from a cash flow–matched portfolio must be available when (and usually before) each liability is due, because of the difficulty in perfect matching. Because the reinvestment assumption for excess cash for cash flow matching extends many years into the future, a conservative interest rate assumption is appropriate. An immunized portfolio needs to meet the target value only on the date of each liability, because funding is achieved by a rebalancing of the portfolio.

Thus, even with the sophisticated linear programming techniques used, in most cases cash flow matching will be technically inferior to immunization. Cash flow matching is easier to understand than multiple liability immunization, however; this ease of use occasionally supports its selection in dedication portfolio strategies.

4.2.2 Extensions of Basic Cash Flow Matching

In basic cash flow matching, only asset cash flows occurring prior to a liability date can be used to satisfy the liability. The basic technique can be extended to allow cash flows occurring both before and after the liability date to be used to meet a liability.[31] This technique, called **symmetric cash flow matching**, allows for the short-term borrowing of funds to satisfy a liability prior to the liability due date. The opportunity to borrow short-term so that symmetric cash matching can be employed results in a reduction in the cost of funding a liability.

A popular variation of multiple liability immunization and cash flow matching to fund liabilities is one that combines the two strategies. This strategy, referred to as **combination matching** or horizon matching, creates a portfolio that is duration-matched with the added constraint that it be cash-flow matched in the first few years, usually the first five years. The advantage of combination matching over multiple liability immunization is that liquidity needs are provided for in the initial cash flow–matched period. Also, most of the curvature of yield curves is often at the short end (the first few years). Cash flow matching the initial portion of the liability stream reduces the risk associated with nonparallel shifts of the yield curve. The disadvantage of combination matching over multiple liability immunization is that the cost to fund liabilities is greater.

4.2.3 Application Considerations

In applying dedication strategies, the portfolio manager must be concerned with universe selection, optimization, monitoring, and transaction costs.

4.2.3.1 Universe Considerations Selection of the universe for construction of a single period immunized portfolio or a dedicated portfolio is extremely important. The lower the quality of the securities considered, the higher the potential risk and return. Dedication assumes that there will be no defaults, and immunization theory further assumes that securities are responsive only to overall changes in interest rates. The lower the quality of securities, the greater the probability that these assumptions will not be met. Further, securities with embedded options such as call options or prepayments options (e.g., mortgage-backed securities) complicate and may even prevent the accurate measurement of cash flow, and hence duration, frustrating the basic requirements of immunization and cash flow matching. Finally, liquidity is a consideration for immunized portfolios, because they must be rebalanced periodically.

4.2.3.2 Optimization Optimization procedures can be used for the construction of immunized and cash flow–matched portfolios. For an immunized portfolio, optimization typically takes the form of minimizing maturity variance subject to the constraints of matching weighted average duration and having the necessary duration dispersion (in multiple-liability immunization). For cash flow matching, optimization takes the form of minimizing the initial portfolio cost subject to the constraint of having sufficient cash at the time a liability arises. Further considerations such as average quality, minimum and maximum concentration constraints, and, perhaps, issuer constraints may be included. Throughout the process, it is critical to establish realistic guidelines and objectives. Accurate pricing is important because optimization is very sensitive to the prices of the securities under consideration. Because there are many inputs and variations available, the optimization process should be approached iteratively, with a final solution that is the result of a number of trials.

---

[31] See Fabozzi, Tong, and Zhu (1991).

4.2.3.3 Monitoring   Monitoring an immunized or cash flow–matched portfolio requires periodic performance measurement. For a bullet portfolio, performance monitoring may take the form of regular observations of the return to date linked with the current target return and annualized. This return should fluctuate only slightly about the original target return.

The performance of a multiple liability immunized plan can be monitored most easily by comparing the current market value of the assets with the present value of the remaining liabilities. The current internal rate of return on the immunized portfolio should be used to discount the remaining liabilities. (This rate is used because it is the expected rate of return that is necessary to provide sufficient cash flow to fund the liabilities.) These two quantities should track one another closely. It may also be useful to monitor the estimated standard deviation of the terminal value of the fund to make sure that it falls more or less uniformly to zero as the horizon date approaches.

4.2.3.4 Transactions Costs   Transactions costs are important in meeting the target rate for an immunized portfolio. They must be considered not only in the initial immunization (when the immunized portfolio is first created) but also in the periodic rebalancing necessary to avoid duration mismatch.

SUMMARY

The management of fixed-income portfolios is a highly competitive field requiring skill in financial and economic analysis, market knowledge, and control of costs. Among the points that have been made are the following:

▶ Because a benchmark is the standard with which the portfolio's performance will be compared, it should always reflect the portfolio's objective. If a portfolio has liabilities that must be met, that need is the paramount objective and thus is the most appropriate benchmark. If a portfolio has no liabilities, the most relevant standard is a bond market index that very closely matches the portfolio's characteristics.

▶ Bond indexing is attractive because indexed portfolios have lower fees than actively managed portfolios and broadly-based bond index portfolios provide excellent diversification.

▶ In selecting a benchmark index, the manager should choose an index with comparable market value risk, comparable income risk (comparable assured income stream), and minimal liability framework risk (minimal mismatch between the durations of assets and liabilities).

▶ For an indexed portfolio, the manager must carefully try to match the portfolio's characteristics to the benchmark's risk profile. The primary risk factors to match are the portfolio's duration, key rate duration and cash flow distribution, sector and quality percent, sector duration contribution, quality spread duration contribution, sector/coupon/maturity/cell weights, and issuer exposure.

▶ The indexing manager has a variety of strategies from which to choose ranging from a totally passive style to a very active style or points in between. The most popular of these strategies are pure bond indexing, enhanced indexing by matching primary risk factors, enhanced indexing by minor risk factor mismatches, active management by larger risk factor mismatches, and full-blown active management.

▶ Because a perfectly indexed portfolio will still underperform the benchmark by the amount of transactions costs, the manager may use a variety of techniques to enhance the return. These include lowering managerial and transactions costs, issue selection, yield curve positioning, sector and quality positioning, and call exposure positioning.

▶ Total return analysis and scenario analysis are methods of evaluating the impact of a trade given a change in interest rates and a range of changes in interest rates, respectively.

▶ The heart of a bond immunization strategy for a single liability is to match the average duration of the assets with the time horizon of the liability. However, this matching alone is not sufficient to immunize the portfolio, in general, because of the impact of twists and nonparallel changes in the yield curve. Care must be taken when designing the immunization strategy to ensure that the portfolio will remain immunized under a variety of different scenarios.

▶ In order to maintain the dollar duration of a portfolio, rebalancing may be necessary. Methods for achieving this include a) investing new funds (if necessary), b) changing the weight of a particular security to adjust the dollar duration, and c) using derivatives. If new funds are invested to rebalance, after an interest rate change, calculate the new dollar duration of the portfolio, calculate the rebalancing ratio, then multiply the new market value of the portfolio by the desired percentage change.

► Spread duration is a measure of how the market value of a risky bond (portfolio) will change with respect to a parallel 100 bps change in its spread above the comparable benchmark security (portfolio). Spread duration is an important factor influencing a portfolio's total return because spreads do change frequently.

► Because parallel shifts in the yield curve are rare, classical immunization will not immunize the portfolio adequately. Extensions to classical immunization provide better results. These extensions include modifying the definition of duration (to multifunctional duration), overcoming the limitations of a fixed horizon, analyzing the risk and return trade-off for immunized portfolios, and integrating immunization strategies with elements of active bond market strategies.

► Three categories that describe the risk of not being able to pay a portfolio's liabilities are interest rate risk, contingent claim, and cap risk. A rising interest rate environment (interest rate risk) comprises the largest risk that a portfolio manager will face. When a security has a contingent claim provision, the manager may have lucrative coupon payments halted (as is the case with mortgage-backed securities) or a leveling off in the market value of a callable security. An asset that makes floating rate payments will typically have caps associated with the floating rate. The manager is at risk of the level of market rates rising while the asset returns are capped.

► Multiple liabilities immunization requires the portfolio payment stream to be decomposed so that each liability is separately immunized by one of the component streams, the composite duration of the portfolio must equal the composite duration of the liabilities, and the distribution of individual portfolio assets must have a wider range than the distribution of the liabilities. For general cash flows, the expected cash contributions can be considered the payments on hypothetical securities that are part of the initial holdings. The actual initial investment can then be invested in such a way that the real and hypothetical holdings taken together represent an immunized portfolio.

► Risk minimization produces an immunized portfolio with a minimum exposure to any arbitrary interest rate change subject to the duration constraint. This objective may be too restrictive in certain situations however. If a substantial increase in the expected return can be accomplished with little effect on immunization risk, the higher-yielding portfolio may be preferred in spite of its higher risk.

Note: Part II of this reading is included in Study Session 10 under the title "Fixed-Income Portfolio Management—Part II."

PRACTICE PROBLEMS FOR READING 28

1. The table below shows the active return for six periods for a bond portfolio. Calculate the portfolio's tracking risk for the six-period time frame.

Period	Portfolio Return	Benchmark Return	Active Return
1	14.10%	13.70%	0.400%
2	8.20	8.00	0.200
3	7.80	8.00	−0.200
4	3.20	3.50	−0.300
5	2.60	2.40	0.200
6	3.30	3.00	0.300

2. The table below shows the spread duration for a 70-bond portfolio and a benchmark index based on sectors. Determine whether the portfolio or the benchmark is more sensitive to changes in the sector spread by determining the spread duration for each. Given your answer, what is the effect on the portfolio's tracking risk?

	Portfolio		Benchmark	
Sector	% of Portfolio	Spread Duration	% of Portfolio	Spread Duration
Treasury	22.70	0.00	23.10	0.00
Agencies	12.20	4.56	6.54	4.41
Financial institutions	6.23	3.23	5.89	3.35
Industrials	14.12	11.04	14.33	10.63
Utilities	6.49	2.10	6.28	2.58
Non-U.S. credit	6.56	2.05	6.80	1.98
Mortgage	31.70	1.78	33.20	1.11
Asset backed	—	2.40	1.57	3.34
CMBS	—	5.60	2.29	4.67
Total	100.00		100.00	

3. You are the manager of a portfolio consisting of three bonds in equal par amounts of $1,000,000 each. The first table below shows the market value of the bonds and their durations. (The price includes accrued interest.) The second table contains the market value of the bonds and their durations one year later.

Initial Values

Security	Price	Market Value	Duration	Dollar Duration
Bond #1	$106.110	$1,060,531	5.909	?
Bond #2	98.200	981,686	3.691	?
Bond #3	109.140	1,090,797	5.843	?
	Portfolio dollar duration =			?

After 1 year

Security	Price	Market Value	Duration	Dollar Duration
Bond #1	$104.240	$1,042,043	5.177	?
Bond #2	98.084	980,461	2.817	?
Bond #3	106.931	1,068,319	5.125	?
	Portfolio dollar duration =			?

As manager, you would like to maintain the portfolio's dollar duration at the initial level by rebalancing the portfolio. You choose to rebalance using the existing security proportions of one-third each. Calculate:

A. the dollar durations of each of the bonds.

B. the rebalancing ratio necessary for the rebalancing.

C. the cash required for the rebalancing.

Use the following information to answer Questions 4–9

The investment committee of Rojas University is unhappy with the recent performance of the fixed income portion of their endowment and has fired the current fixed-income manager. The current portfolio, benchmarked against the Lehman Brothers® U.S. Aggregate Index, is shown in Exhibit 1. The investment committee hires Alfredo Alonso, a consultant from MHC Consulting, to assess the portfolio's risks, submit ideas to the committee, and manage the portfolio on an interim basis.

EXHIBIT 1	Rojas University Endowment Fixed-Income Portfolio Information			
	Portfolio		**Index**	
Sector	**%**	**Duration***	**%**	**Duration***
Treasuries	47.74	5.50	49.67	5.96
Agencies	14.79	5.80	14.79	5.10
Corporates	12.35	4.50	16.54	5.61
Mortgage-backed securities	25.12	4.65	19.10	4.65

*Spread durations are the same as effective durations for all sectors with spread risk.

Alonso notices that the fired manager's portfolio did not own securities outside of the index universe. The committee asks Alonso to consider an indexing strategy, including related benefits and logistical problems. Alonso identifies three factors that limit a manager's ability to replicate a bond index:

1. a lack of availability of certain bond issues

2. a lack of available index data to position the portfolio

3. differences between the bond prices used by the manager and the index provider

Alonso has done further analysis of the current U.S. Treasury portion of the portfolio and has discovered a significant overweight in a 5-year Treasury bond ($10 million par value). He expects the yield curve to flatten and forecasts a six-month horizon price of the 5-year Treasury bond to be $99.50. Therefore, Alonso's strategy will be to sell all the 5-year Treasury bonds, and invest the proceeds in 10-year Treasury bonds and cash while maintaining the dollar duration of the portfolio. U.S. Treasury bond information is shown in Exhibit 2.

EXHIBIT 2	U.S. Treasury Bond Information		
Issue Description (Term to Maturity, Ticker, Coupon, Maturity Date)	**Duration**	**Price* ($)**	**Yield (%)**
5-year: T 4.125% 15May2011	4.53	100.40625	4.03
10-year: T 5.25% 15May2016	8.22	109.09375	4.14

*Prices are shown per $100 par value.

4. The duration of the Rojas University fixed-income portfolio in Exhibit 1 is *closest* to:

   A. 5.11.

   B. 5.21.

   C. 5.33.

5. The spread duration of the Rojas University fixed-income portfolio in Exhibit 1 is *closest* to:

   A. 2.58.

   B. 4.93.

   C. 5.21.

6. Based on the data in Exhibit 1, the bond portfolio strategy used by the fired manager can *best* be described as:

   A. pure bond index matching.

   B. enhanced indexing/matching risk factors.

   C. active management/larger risk factor mismatches.

7. Regarding the three factors identified by Alonso, the factor *least likely* to actually limit a manager's ability to replicate a bond index is:

   A. #1.

   B. #2.

   C. #3.

8. Using Alonso's forecasted price and the bond information in Exhibit 2, the expected 6-month total return of the Treasury 4.125% 15May2011 is *closest* to (assume zero accrued interest at purchase):

   A. −0.90%.

   B. 1.15%.

   C. 1.56%.

9. Using Exhibit 2, the par value of 10-year bonds to be purchased to execute Alonso's strategy is *closest* to:

   A. $5,072,000.

   B. $5,489,000.

   C. $5,511,000.

Use the following information to answer Questions 10–15

The State Retirement Board (SRB) provides a defined benefit pension plan to state employees. The governors of the SRB are concerned that their current fixed-income investments may not be appropriate because the average age of the state employee workforce has been increasing. In addition, a surge in retirements is projected to occur over the next 10 years.

Chow Wei Mei, the head of the SRB's investment committee, has suggested that some of the future pension payments can be covered by buying annuities from an insurance company. She proposes that the SRB invest a fixed sum to purchase annuities in seven years time, when the number of retirements is expected to peak. Chow argues that the SRB should fund the future purchase of the annuities by creating a dedicated fixed income portfolio consisting of corporate bonds, mortgage-backed securities, and risk-free government bonds. Chow states:

Statement #1: "To use a portfolio of bonds to immunize a single liability, and remove all risks, it is necessary only that 1) the market value of the assets be equal to the present value of the liability and 2) the duration of the portfolio be equal to the duration of the liability."

Chow lists three alternative portfolios that she believes will immunize a single, seven-year liability. All bonds in Exhibit 1 are option-free government bonds.

EXHIBIT 1	Alternative Portfolios for Funding an Annuity Purchase in Seven Years	
Portfolio	**Description**	**Portfolio Yield to Maturity (%)**
A	Zero-coupon bond with a maturity of 7 years	4.20
B	Bond with a maturity of 6 years	4.10
	Bond with a maturity of 8 years	
C	Bond with a maturity of 5 years	4.15
	Bond with a maturity of 9 years	

Chow then states:

Statement #2: "Because each of these alternative portfolios immunizes this single, seven-year liability, each has the same level of reinvestment risk."

The SRB governors would like to examine different investment horizons and alternative strategies to immunize the single liability. The governors ask

Chow to evaluate a contingent immunization strategy using the following assumptions:

► The SRB will commit a $100 million investment to this strategy.
► The horizon of the investment is 10 years.
► The SRB will accept a 4.50 percent return (semiannual compounding).
► An immunized rate of return of 5.25 percent (semiannual compounding) is possible.

Marshall Haley, an external consultant for the SRB, has been asked by the governors to advise them on the appropriateness of its investment strategies. Haley notes that, although state employee retirements are expected to surge over the next 10 years, the SRB will experience a continual stream of retirements over the next several decades. Hence, the SRB faces a schedule of liabilities, not a single liability. In explaining how the SRB can manage the risks of multiple liabilities, Haley makes the following statements:

Statement #1: "When managing the risks of a schedule of liabilities, multiple liability immunization and cash flow matching approaches do not have the same risks and costs. Whereas cash flow matching generally has less risk of not satisfying future liabilities, multiple liability immunization generally costs less."

Statement #2: "Assuming that there is a parallel shift in the yield curve, to immunize multiple liabilities, there are three necessary conditions: i) the present value of the assets be equal to the present value of the liabilities; ii) the composite portfolio duration be equal to the composite liabilities duration; and iii) I cannot remember the third condition."

Statement #3: "Horizon matching can be used to immunize a schedule of liabilities."

10. Is Chow's Statement #1 correct?
   A. Yes.
   B. No, because credit risk must also be considered.
   C. No, because the risk of parallel shifts in the yield curve must also be considered.

11. Is Chow's Statement #2 correct?
   A. No, Portfolio B is exposed to less reinvestment risk than Portfolio A.
   B. No, Portfolio B is exposed to more reinvestment risk than Portfolio C.
   C. No, Portfolio C is exposed to more reinvestment risk than Portfolio B.

12. Which of the following is *closest* to the required terminal value for the contingent immunization strategy?
   A. $100 million.
   B. $156 million.
   C. $168 million.

13. Is Haley's Statement #1 correct?

  A. Yes.

  B. No, because multiple liability immunization is generally less risky than cash flow matching.

  C. No, because cash flow matching is generally less costly than multiple liability immunization.

14. The condition that Haley cannot remember in his Statement #2 is that the:

  A. cash flows in the portfolio must be dispersed around the horizon date.

  B. cash flows in the portfolio must be concentrated around the horizon date.

  C. distribution of durations of individual assets in the portfolio must have a wider range than the distribution of the liabilities.

15. The *most* appropriate description of the strategy that Haley suggests in his Statement #3 is to create a portfolio that:

  A. has cash flows concentrated around the horizon date.

  B. is duration matched but uses cash flow matching in the later years of the liability schedule.

  C. is duration matched but uses cash flow matching in the initial years of the liability schedule.

SOLUTIONS FOR READING 28

1. The tracking risk is the standard deviation of the active returns. For the data shown in the problem, the tracking risk is 28.284 bps, as shown below:

Period	Portfolio Return	Benchmark Return	Active Return	$(AR - Avg. AR)^2$
1	14.10%	13.70%	0.400%	0.00090%
2	8.20	8.00	0.200	0.00010
3	7.80	8.00	−0.200	0.00090
4	3.20	3.50	−0.300	0.00160
5	2.60	2.40	0.200	0.00010
6	3.30	3.00	0.300	0.00040
Average active return per period =			0.100%	
Sum of the squared deviations =				0.00400%
Tracking risk (std. dev.) =				0.28284%

2. The portfolio is more sensitive to changes in the spread because its spread duration is 3.151 compared with the benchmark's 2.834. The portfolio's higher spread duration is primarily a result of the portfolio's greater weight on agency securities. The spread duration for each can be calculated by taking a weighted average of the individual sectors' durations. Because there is a difference between the portfolio's and the benchmark's spread duration, the tracking risk will be higher than if the two were more closely matched.

Sector	Portfolio % of Portfolio	Portfolio Spread Duration	Portfolio Contribution to Spread Duration	Benchmark % of Portfolio	Benchmark Spread Duration	Benchmark Contribution to Spread Duration
Treasury	22.70	0.00	0.000	23.10	0.00	0.000
Agencies	12.20	4.56	0.556	6.54	4.41	0.288
Financial institutions	6.23	3.23	0.201	5.89	3.35	0.197
Industrials	14.12	11.04	1.559	14.33	10.63	1.523
Utilities	6.49	2.10	0.136	6.28	2.58	0.162
Non-U.S. credit	6.56	2.05	0.134	6.80	1.98	0.135
Mortgage	31.70	1.78	0.564	33.20	1.11	0.369
Asset backed	–	2.40	0.000	1.57	3.34	0.052
CMBS	–	5.60	0.000	2.29	4.67	0.107
Total	100.00		3.151	100.00		2.834

3. Dollar duration is a measure of the change in portfolio value for a 100 bps change in market yields. It is defined as

$$\text{Dollar duration} = \text{Duration} \times \text{Dollar value} \times 0.01$$

A. A portfolio's dollar duration is the sum of the dollar durations of the component securities. The dollar duration of this portfolio at the beginning of the period is $162,636, which is calculated as

| Security | Initial Values | | | |
	Price	Market Value	Duration	Dollar Duration
Bond #1	$106.110	$1,060,531	5.909	$62,667
Bond #2	98.200	981,686	3.691	36,234
Bond #3	109.140	1,090,797	5.843	63,735
		Portfolio dollar duration =		$162,636

At the end of one year, the portfolio's dollar duration has changed to $136,318, as shown below.

| Security | After 1 Year | | | |
	Price	Market Value	Duration	Dollar Duration
Bond #1	$104.240	$1,042,043	5.177	$53,947
Bond #2	98.084	980,461	2.817	27,620
Bond #3	106.931	1,068,319	5.125	54,751
		Portfolio dollar duration =		$136,318

B. The rebalancing ratio is a ratio of the original dollar duration to the new dollar duration:

$$\text{Rebalancing ratio} = \$162,636/\$136,318 = 1.193$$

C. The portfolio requires each position to be increased by 19.3 percent. The cash required for this rebalancing is calculated as:

$$\begin{aligned} \text{Cash required} &= 0.193 \times (\$1,042,043 + 980,461 + 1,068,319) \\ &= \$596,529 \end{aligned}$$

4. B is correct. Portfolio duration is a weighted average of the component durations. In this problem, $(0.4774 \times 5.50) + (0.1479 \times 5.80) + (0.1235 \times 4.50) + (0.2512 \times 4.65) = 5.20735$. Round to 5.21.

5. A is correct. Spread duration is a measure of a non-Treasury security's price change as a result of a change in the spread between the security and a Treasury. The portfolio spread duration is the weighted average duration of those securities in the portfolio that have a yield above the default-free yield (i.e., non-Treasuries). In this problem, the agencies, corporates, and mortgage-backed securities have a spread. Using their original weights in the portfolio, the spread duration is $(0.1479 \times 5.80) + (0.1235 \times 4.50) + (0.2512 \times 4.65) = 2.58165$. Round to 2.58.

6. C is correct. Exhibit 1 makes clear that the portfolio weights differ and for some sectors quite dramatically from those of the index and that the durations of the portfolio components differ from their respective durations in the index. Thus the manager is using active management because he had both duration and sector mismatches and not on a small scale.

7. B is correct. Index data is readily available. Alonso is incorrect in identifying this as a limiting factor. Information (data) for the other two factors can be difficult or impossible to acquire.

8. B is correct. Calculate the holding period return for the Treasury 4.125% 15 May 2011 by using the current price of 100.40625 (Exhibit 2), Alonso's forecast of 99.50, and a semi-annual coupon of 2.0625. The problem informs that there is zero accrued interest. The 6-month total return is (99.50 + 2.0625 − 100.40625)/100.40625 = 1.15%.

9. A is correct. Alonso is not simply going to reinvest the entire proceeds of the sale into 10-year Treasuries because his stated desire is to maintain the dollar duration of the portfolio. The sale price of $10 million par value of the 5-year bond is found by multiplying $10,000,000 × 1.0040625 = $10,040,625. The dollar duration of the 5-year is 4.53 × $10,040,625 = $45,484,031.25. Now divide $45,484,031.25 by the duration of the 10-year to get the amount to invest in 10 years. This is divided by the quoted price to get the par value of the 10-years. The result is $45,484,031.25/(8.22 × 1.0909375) = $5,072,094.

10. B is correct. Chow's statement #1 is incorrect because what she describes does not remove all risks. Credit risk destroys the immunization match; therefore, the statement is incorrect. The risk to immunization comes from non-parallel shifts in the yield curve.

11. C is correct. Portfolio A is a zero-coupon bond and thus has no reinvestment rate risk. Portfolio B has lower dispersion in maturities than Portfolio C. Therefore, Portfolio C has more reinvestment rate risk than Portfolio B.

12. B is correct. The SRB will accept (i.e., require) a return of 4.50% (semiannual compounding). Find the time ten future value of $100 million at this rate. The answer is $100,000,000 × (1 + .045/2)^{20} = $156,050,920.

13. A is correct. Haley's statement #1 defines the risk-costs tradeoffs of cash flow matching versus multiple liabilities immunization.

14. C is correct. If the distribution of the durations of the assets is wider than that of the liabilities, the durations of the assets after a parallel yield curve shift (whether up or down) will envelope the durations of the liabilities after the shift. The immunization can be maintained, although rebalancing may be necessary.

15. C is correct. Horizon matching creates a duration-matched portfolio with the added constraint that it be cash-flow matched in the first few years. Cash flow matching the initial portion of the liability stream reduces the risk associated with nonparallel shifts of the yield curve.

RELATIVE-VALUE METHODOLOGIES FOR GLOBAL CREDIT BOND PORTFOLIO MANAGEMENT

by Jack Malvey, CFA

LEARNING OUTCOMES

The candidate should be able to:

Mastery

a. explain classic relative-value analysis, based on top-down and bottom-up approaches to credit bond portfolio management; ☐

b. discuss the implications of cyclical supply and demand changes in the primary corporate bond market and the impact of secular changes in the market's dominant product structures; ☐

c. summarize the influence of investors' short- and long-term liquidity needs on portfolio management decisions; ☐

d. discuss common rationales for secondary market trading, including yield-spread pickup trades, credit-upside trades, credit-defense trades, new issue swaps, sector-rotation trades, yield curve–adjustment trades, structure trades, and cash flow reinvestment; ☐

e. discuss and evaluate corporate bond portfolio strategies that are based on relative value, including total return analysis, primary market analysis, liquidity and trading analysis, secondary trading rationales and trading constraints, spread analysis, structure analysis, credit curve analysis, credit analysis, and asset allocation/sector analysis. ☐

INTRODUCTION   1

Corporate bonds are the second oldest and, for most asset managers, the most demanding and fascinating subset of the global debt capital markets. The label, "corporate," understates the scope of this burgeoning asset class. As commonly traded and administered within the context of an overall debt portfolio, the "corporate asset class" actually encompasses much more than pure corporate entities. Instead of the title "corporate asset class," this segment of the global bond market really should be classified as the "credit asset class," including any nonagency mortgage-backed securities (MBS), commercial mortgage-backed securities (CMBS), or asset-backed securities (ABS). Sovereigns and government-controlled entities with foreign currency debt issues thought to have more credit risk than the national government should also be included. In keeping with conventional practice in the fixed-income market, however, the application of the term "credit asset class" in this reading will pertain only to corporate bonds, sovereigns, and government-controlled entities.

From six continents, thousands of organizations (corporations, government agencies, projects and structured pools of debt securities) with different credit "stories" have sold debt to sustain their operations and to finance their expansion. These borrowers use dozens of different types of debt instruments (first mortgage bonds, debentures, equipment trust certificates, subordinated debentures, medium-term notes, floating rate notes, private placements, preferred stock) and in multiple currencies (dollars, yen, euros, Swiss francs, pounds) from maturities ranging from one year to even a thousand years. Sometimes these debt structures carry embedded options, which may allow for full or partial redemption prior to maturity at the option of either the borrower or the investor. Sometimes, the coupon payment floats with short-term interest rates or resets to a higher rate after a fixed interval or a credit rating change.

Investors buy credit assets because of the presumption of higher long-term returns despite the assumption of credit risk. Except near and during recessions, credit products usually outperform U.S. Treasury securities and other higher-quality "spread sectors" like U.S. agency securities, mortgage-backed securities, and asset-backed securities. In the 30-year period since the beginning of the Lehman indices (1973 through 2002), investment-grade credit outperformed U.S. Treasuries by 30 basis points (bps) per year on average (9.42% versus 9.12%).[1] As usual, an average masks the true daily, weekly, monthly, and annual volatility of credit assets' relative performance. Looking at the rolling 5-year excess returns of U.S. investment-grade credit from 1926 through early 2003 in Exhibit 1, one can observe extended periods of generous and disappointing returns for credit assets. Perhaps more meaningful, an examination of volatility-adjusted (Sharpe ratio) excess returns over Treasuries over a rolling 5-year period shown in Exhibit 2 further underscores the oscillations in relative credit performance.

Global credit portfolio management presents a complex challenge. Each day, hundreds of credit portfolio managers face thousands of choices in the primary (new issue) and secondary markets. In addition to tracking primary and secondary flows, investors have to keep tabs on ever-varying issuer fundamentals,

---

[1] Based on absolute returns of key Lehman indices from 1973.

EXHIBIT 1   Rolling 5-year U.S. Investment-Grade Credit Index Excess Returns[a] (bps) January 1926 through December 31, 2003

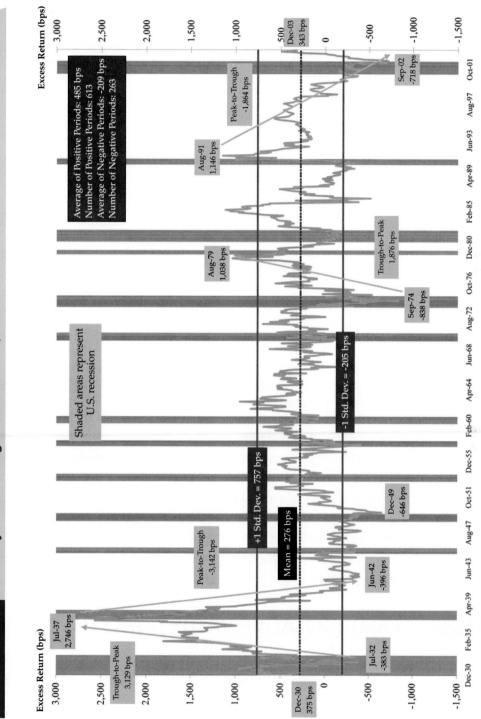

[a] Excess returns represent the difference, positive or negative, between the total return of all credit securities and Treasury securities along a set of key rate duration points across the term structure. This single statistic, excess return, therefore normalizes for the duration differential among debt asset classes, in this case between longer-duration credit and shorter-duration Treasuries.

Source: Data series from Ibbotson Associates prior to August 1988, Lehman Brothers data thereafter.

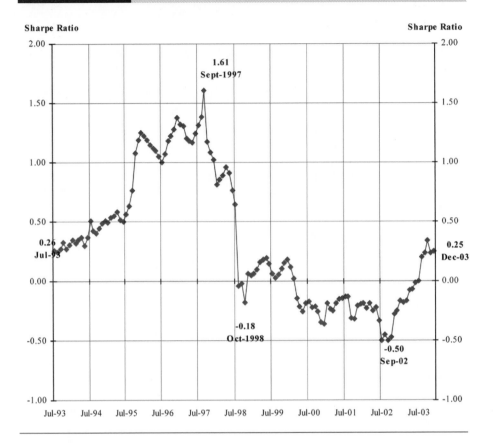

Source: Lehman Brothers U.S. Investment-Grade Credit Index.

credit-worthiness, acquisitions, earnings, ratings, etc. The task of global credit portfolio management is to process all of this rapidly changing information about the credit markets (issuers, issues, dealers, and competing managers) and to construct the portfolio with the best return for a given risk tolerance. This discipline combines the qualitative tools of equity analysis with the quantitative precision of fixed-income analysis. This reading provides a brief guide to methodologies that may help portfolio managers meet this formidable challenge.

2   CREDIT RELATIVE-VALUE ANALYSIS

Credit portfolio management represents a major subset of the multi-asset global portfolio management process illustrated in Exhibit 3. After setting the currency allocation (in this case, dollars were selected for illustration convenience) and distribution among fixed-income asset classes, bond managers are still left with a lengthy list of questions to construct an optimal credit portfolio. Some examples are:

► Should U.S. investors add U.S. dollar-denominated bonds of non-U.S. issuers?

EXHIBIT 3   Fixed-Income Portfolio Management Process

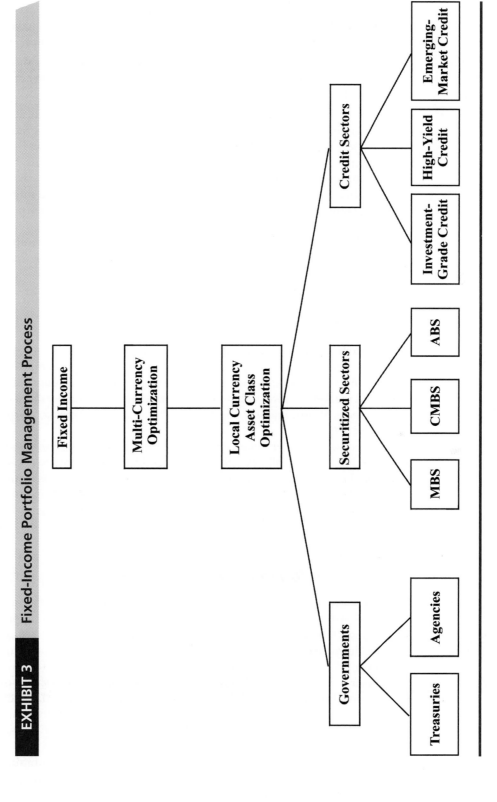

▶ Should central banks add high-quality euro-denominated corporate bonds to their reserve holdings?

▶ Should LIBOR-funded London-based portfolio managers buy fixed-rate U.S. industrial paper and swap into floating-rate notes?

▶ Should Japanese mutual funds own euro-denominated telecommunications debt, swapped back into dollars or yen using **currency swaps**?

▶ Should U.S. insurers buy perpetual floaters (i.e., floaters without a maturity date) issued by British banks and swap back into fixed-rate coupons in dollars using a currency/interest rate swap?

▶ When should investors reduce their allocation to the credit sector and increase allocation to governments, pursue a "strategic upgrade trade" (sell Baa/BBBs and buy higher-rated Aa/AA credit debt), rotate from industrials into utilities, switch from consumer cyclicals to non-cyclicals, overweight airlines and underweight telephones, or deploy a credit derivative (e.g., short the high-yield index or reduce a large exposure to a single issuer by selling an issuer-specific **credit default swap**) to hedge their portfolios?

To respond to such questions, managers need to begin with an analytical framework (relative-value analysis) and to develop a strategic outlook for the global credit markets.

A. Relative Value

Economists have long debated the concept and measurement of "value." But fixed-income practitioners, perhaps because of the daily pragmatism enforced by the markets, have developed a consensus about the definition of value. In the bond market, relative value refers *to the ranking of fixed-income investments by sectors, structures, issuers, and issues in terms of their expected performance during some future period of time.*

For a day trader, relative value may carry a maximum horizon of a few minutes. For a dealer, relative value may extend from a few days to a few months. For a total return investor, the relative value horizon typically runs from 1–3 months. For a large insurer, relative value usually spans a multi-year horizon. Accordingly, relative-value analysis refers to the methodologies used to generate such rankings of expected returns.

B. Classic Relative-Value Analysis

There are two basic approaches to global credit bond portfolio management—**top-down** approach and **bottom-up** approach. The top-down approach focuses on high-level allocations among broadly defined credit asset classes. The goal of top-down research is to form views on large-scale economic and industry developments. These views then drive asset allocation decisions (overweight certain sectors, underweight others). The bottom-up approach focuses on individual issuers and issues that will outperform their peer groups. Managers follow this approach hoping to outperform their benchmark due to superior security selection, while maintaining neutral weightings to the various sectors in the benchmark.

Classic relative-value analysis is a dialectical process combining the best of top-down and bottom-up approaches as shown in Exhibit 4. This process blends the macro input of chief investment officers, strategists, economists,

EXHIBIT 4   Credit Sector Portfolio Management Process: Classic, Dialectical Relative-Value Analysis

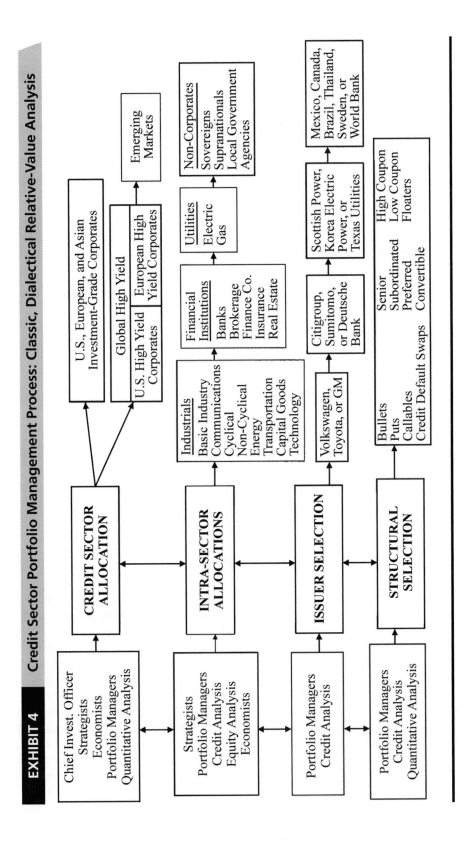

and portfolio managers with the micro input of credit analysts, quantitative analysts, and portfolio managers. The goal of this methodology is to pick the sectors with the most potential upside, populate these favored sectors with the best representative issuers, and select the structures of the designated issuers at the yield curve points that match the investor's for the benchmark yield curve.

For many credit investors, using classic relative-value analysis provides a measure of portfolio success. Although sector, issuer, and structural analyses remain the core of superior relative-value analysis, the increased availability of information and technology has transformed the analytical process into a complex discipline. Credit portfolio managers have far more data than ever on the total returns of sectors, issuers, and structures, quantity and composition of new-issue flows, investor product demand, aggregate credit-quality movements, multiple sources of fundamental and quantitative credit analyses on individual issuers, and yield spread data to assist them in their relative-value analysis.

C. Relative-Value Methodologies

The main methodologies for credit relative-value maximization are:

- ▶ total return analysis;
- ▶ primary market analysis;
- ▶ liquidity and trading analysis;
- ▶ secondary trading rationales and constraints analysis;
- ▶ spread analysis;
- ▶ structure analysis;
- ▶ credit curve analysis;
- ▶ credit analysis;
- ▶ asset allocation/sector analysis.

In the sections that follow, we discuss each of these methodologies.

3   TOTAL RETURN ANALYSIS

The goal of global credit portfolio management for most investors is to optimize the risk-adjusted total return of their credit portfolio. The best place to start is naturally total return analysis. Accordingly, credit relative-value analysis begins with a detailed dissection of past returns and a projection of expected returns. For the entire asset class and major contributing sub-sectors (such as banks, utilities, pipelines, Baa/BBB's, etc.), how have returns been formed? How much is attributed to credit spread movements, sharp changes in the fundamental fortunes of key issuers, and yield curve dynamics? If there are macro determinants of credit returns (the total return of the credit asset class), then credit markets may display regular patterns. For instance, the macroeconomic cycle is the major determinant of overall credit spreads. During recessions, the escalation of default risk widens spreads (which are risk premiums over underlying, presumably default-free, government securities [or swaps]) and reduces credit returns relative to Treasuries. Conversely, economic prosperity reduces bankruptcies and enhances overall credit fundamentals of most issuers. Economic prosperity usually leads to tighter credit spreads and boosts credit returns relative to Treasuries. For brief intervals, noncyclical technical factors can offset fundamentals. For example, the inversion of the U.S. Treasury yield curve in 2000 actually led to wider credit spreads and credit underperformance despite solid global economic growth and corporate profitability.

Thanks to the development of total return indices for credit debt (databases of prices, spreads, issuer, and structure composition), analyses of monthly, annual, and multi-year total returns have uncovered numerous patterns (i.e., large issue versus small issue performance variation, seasonality, election-cycle effects, and government benchmark auction effects) in the global credit market. Admittedly, these patterns do not always re-occur. But an awareness and understanding of these total-return patterns are essential to optimizing portfolio performance.

PRIMARY MARKET ANALYSIS   **4**

The analysis of primary markets centers on new issue supply and demand. Supply is often a misunderstood factor in tactical relative-value analysis. Prospective new supply induces many traders, analysts, and investors to advocate a defensive stance toward the overall corporate market as well as toward individual sectors and issuers. Yet the premise, "supply will hurt spreads," which may apply to an individual issuer, does not generally hold up for the entire credit market. Credit spreads are determined by many factors; supply, although important, represents one of many determinants. During most years, increases in issuance (most notably during the first quarter of each year) are associated with market-spread contraction and strong relative returns for credit debt. In contrast, sharp supply declines are accompanied frequently by spread expansion and a major fall in both relative and absolute returns for credit securities. For example, this counter-intuitive effect was most noticeable during the August–October 1998 interval when new issuance nearly disappeared in the face of the substantial increase in credit spreads. (This period is referred to as the "Great Spread-Sector Crash.")

In the investment-grade credit market, heavy supply often compresses spreads and boosts relative returns for credit assets as new primary valuations validate and enhance secondary valuations. When primary origination declines sharply, secondary traders lose reinforcement from the primary market and tend to reduce their bid spreads. Contrary to the normal supply-price relationship, relative credit returns often perform best during periods of heavy supply. For example, 2001 will be recalled for both the then all-time record for new credit origination as well as the best relative performance for U.S. credit securities in nearly two decades.

A. The Effect of Market-Structure Dynamics

Given their immediate focus on the deals of the day and week, portfolio managers often overlook short-term and long-term market-structure dynamics in making portfolio decisions. Because the pace of change in market structure is often gradual, market dynamics have less effect on short-term tactical investment decision-making than on long-term strategy.

The composition of the global credit bond market has shifted markedly since the early 1980s. Medium-term notes (MTN) dominate issuance in the front end of the credit yield curve. Structured notes and swap products have heralded the introduction of derivative instruments into the mainstream of the credit market. The high-yield corporate sector has become an accepted asset class. Global origination has become more popular for U.S. government agencies, supranationals (e.g., the World Bank), sovereigns, and large corporate borrowers.

Although the ascent of derivatives and high-yield instruments stands out during the 1990s, the true globalization of the credit market was the most important development. The rapid development of the Eurobond market since 1975, the introduction of many non-U.S. issuers into the dollar markets during the 1990s, and the birth of the euro on January 1, 1999, have led to the proliferation of truly transnational credit portfolios.

These long-term structural changes in the composition of the global credit asset class arise due to the desire of issuers to minimize funding costs under different yield curve and yield spread, as well as the needs of both active and asset/liability bond managers to satisfy their risk and return objectives. Portfolio managers will adapt their portfolios either in anticipation of or in reaction to these structural changes across the global credit markets.

B. The Effect of Product Structure

Partially offsetting this proliferation of issuers since the mid-1990s, the global credit market has become structurally more homogeneous. Specifically, bullet and intermediate-maturity structures have come to dominate the credit market. A bullet maturity means that the issue is not callable, putable, or sinkable prior to its scheduled final maturity. The trend toward bullet securities does not pertain to the high-yield market, where callables remain the structure of choice. With the hope of credit-quality improvement, many high-yield issuers expect to refinance prior to maturity at lower rates.

There are three strategic portfolio implications for this structural evolution. First, the dominance of bullet structures translates into scarcity value for structures with embedded call and put features. That is, credit securities with embedded options have become rare and therefore demand a premium price. Typically, this premium (price) is not captured by option-valuation models. Yet, this "scarcity value" should be considered by managers in relative-value analysis of credit bonds.

Second, bonds with maturities beyond 20 years are a small share of outstanding credit debt. This shift reduced the effective duration of the credit asset class and cut aggregate sensitivity to interest-rate risk. For asset/liability managers with long time horizons, this shift of the maturity distribution suggests a rise in the value of long credit debt and helps to explain the warm reception afforded, initially at least, to most new offerings of issues with 100-year maturities in the early and mid-1990s.

Third, the use of credit derivatives has skyrocketed since the early 1990s. The rapid maturation of the credit derivative market will lead investors and issuers to develop new strategies to match desired exposures to credit sectors, issuers, and structures.

5   LIQUIDITY AND TRADING ANALYSIS

Short-term and long-term liquidity needs influence portfolio management decisions. Citing lower expected liquidity, some investors are reluctant to purchase certain types of issues such as small-sized issues (less than $1.0 billion), private placements, MTNs, and non-local corporate issuers. Other investors gladly exchange a potential liquidity disadvantage for incremental yield. For investment-grade issuers, these liquidity concerns often are exaggerated.

The liquidity of credit debt changes over time. Specifically, liquidity varies with the economic cycle, credit cycle, shape of the yield curve, supply, and the season. As in all markets, unknown shocks, like a surprise wave of defaults, can reduce credit debt liquidity as investors become unwilling to purchase new issues at any spread and dealers become reluctant to position secondary issues except at very wide spreads. In reality, these transitory bouts of illiquidity mask an underlying trend toward heightened liquidity across the global credit asset class. With a gentle push from regulators, the global credit asset class is well along in converting from its historic "over-the-counter" domain to a fully transparent, equity/U.S. Treasury style marketplace. In the late 1990s, new technology led to creating ECNs (electronic communication networks), essentially electronic trading exchanges. In turn, credit bid/ask spreads generally have trended lower for very large, well-known corporate issues. This powerful twin combination of technological innovation and competition promises the rapid development of an even more liquid and efficient global credit market during the early 21st century.

SECONDARY TRADE RATIONALES   6

Capital market expectations constantly change. Recessions may arrive sooner rather than later. The yield curve may steepen rather than flatten. The auto and paper cycles may be moving down from their peaks. Higher oil and natural gas prices may benefit the credit quality of the energy sector. An industrial may have announced a large debt-financed acquisition, earning an immediate ratings rebuke from the rating agencies. A major bank may plan to repurchase 15% of its outstanding common stock (great for shareholders but leading to higher financial leverage for debtholders). In response to such daily information flows, portfolio managers amend their holdings. To understand trading flows and the real dynamics of the credit market, investors should consider the most common rationales of whether to trade and not to trade.

A. Popular Reasons for Trading

There are dozens of rationales to execute secondary trades when pursuing portfolio optimization. Several of the most popular are discussed below. The framework for assessing secondary trades is the total return framework.

1. Yield/Spread Pickup Trades

Yield/spread pickup trades represent the most common secondary transactions across all sectors of the global credit market. Historically, at least half of all secondary swaps reflect investor intentions to add additional yield within the duration and credit-quality constraints of a portfolio. If 5-year, Baa1/BBB General Motors paper trades at 150 bps, 10 bps more than 5-year, Baa1/BBB– Ford Motor, some investors will determine the rating differential irrelevant and purchase General Motors bond and sell the Ford Motor (an issue swap) for a spread gain of 10 bps per annum.

This "yield-first psychology" reflects the institutional yield need of long-term asset/liability managers. Despite the passage of more than three decades, this investor bias toward yield maximization also may be a methodological relic left over from the era prior to the introduction and market acceptance of total-return indices in the early 1970s. Yield measures have limitations as an indicator of potential performance. The total return framework is a superior framework for assessing potential performance for a trade.

2. Credit-Upside Trades

Credit-upside trades take place when the debt asset manager expects an upgrade in an issuer's credit quality that is not already reflected in the current market yield spread. In the illustration of the General Motors and Ford Motor trade described above, some investors may swap based on their view of potential credit-quality improvement for General Motors. Obviously, such trades rely on the credit analysis skills of the investment management team. Moreover, the manager must be able to identify a potential upgrade before the market, otherwise the spread for the upgrade candidate will already exhibit the benefits of a credit upgrade.

Credit-upside trades are particularly popular in the crossover sector—securities with ratings between Ba2/BB and Baa3/BBB—by two major rating agencies. In this case, the portfolio manager is expressing an expectation that an issue of the highest speculative grade rating (Ba1/BB+) has sufficiently positive credit fundamentals to be upgraded to investment grade (i.e., Baa3/BBB–). If this upgrade occurs, not only would the issue's spread narrow based on the credit improvement (with an accompanying increase in total return, all else equal), but the issue also would benefit from improved liquidity, as managers prohibited from buying high-yield bonds could then purchase that issue. Further, the manager would expect an improvement in the portfolio's overall risk profile.

3. Credit-Defense Trades

Credit-defense trades become more popular as geopolitical and economic uncertainty increase. Secular sector changes often generate uncertainties and induce defensive positioning by investors. In anticipating greater competition, in the mid-1990s some investors reduced their portfolio exposures to sectors like electric utilities and telecommunications. As some Asian currencies and equities swooned in mid-1997, many portfolio managers cut their allocation to the Asian debt market. Unfortunately because of yield-maximization needs and a general reluctance to realize losses by some institutions (i.e., insurers), many investors reacted more slowly to credit-defensive positioning. But after a record number of "fallen angels" in 2002, which included such major credit bellwether issuers as WorldCom, investors became more quick to jettison potential problem credits from their portfolios. Ironically once a credit is downgraded by the rating agencies, internal portfolio guidelines often dictate security liquidation immediately after the loss of single-A or investment-grade status. This is usually the worst possible time to sell a security and maximizes losses incurred by the portfolio.

4. New Issue Swaps

New issue swaps contribute to secondary turnover. Because of perceived superior liquidity, many portfolio managers prefer to rotate their portfolios gradually into more current and usually larger sized on-the-run issues. This disposition, reinforced by the usually superior market behavior of newer issues in the U.S. Treasury market (i.e., the on-the-run issues), has become a self-fulfilling prophecy for many credit issues. In addition, some managers use new issue swaps to add exposure to a new issuer or a new structure.

5. Sector-Rotation Trades

Sector-rotation trades, within credit and among fixed-income asset classes, have become more popular since the early 1990s. In this strategy, the manager shifts the portfolio from a sector or industry that is expected to underperform to a sector or industry which is believed will outperform on a total return basis. With the likely development of enhanced liquidity and lower trading transaction costs across the global bond market in the early 21st century, sector-rotation trades should become more prevalent in the credit asset class.

Such intra-asset class trading already has played a major role in differentiating performance among credit portfolio managers. For example, as soon as the Fed launched its preemptive strike against inflation in February 1994, some investors correctly exchanged fixed-rate corporates for floating-rate corporates. In 1995, the specter of U.S. economic weakness prompted some investors in high-yield corporates to rotate from consumer-cyclical sectors like autos and retailing into consumer non-cyclical sectors like food, beverage, and healthcare. Anticipating slower U.S. economic growth in 1998 induced a defensive tilt by some portfolio managers away from other cyclical groups like paper and energy. The resurrection of Asian and European economic growth in 1999 stimulated increased portfolio interest in cyclicals, financial institutions, and energy debt. Credit portfolio managers could have avoided a great deal of portfolio performance disappointment in 2002 by underweighting utilities and many industrial sectors.

6. Curve-Adjustment Trades

Yield curve-adjustment trades, or simply, curve-adjustment trades are taken to reposition a portfolio's duration. For most credit investors, their portfolio duration is typically within a range from 20% below to 20% above the duration of the benchmark index. If credit investors could have predicted U.S., euro, and yen yield curve movements perfectly in 2002, then they would have increased their credit portfolio duration at the beginning of 2002 in anticipation of a decrease in interest rates. Although most fixed-income investors prefer to alter the duration of their aggregate portfolios in the more-liquid Treasury market, strategic portfolio duration tilts also can be implemented in the credit market.

This is also done with respect to anticipated changes in the credit term structure or credit curve. For example, if a portfolio manager believes credit spreads will tighten (either overall or in a particular sector), with rates in general remaining relatively stable, they might shift the portfolio's exposure to longer spread duration issues in the sector.

7. Structure Trades

Structure trades involve swaps into structures (e.g., callable structures, bullet structures, and putable structures) that are expected to have better performance given expected movements in volatility and the shape of the yield curve. Here are some examples of how different structures performed in certain periods in the 1990s.

▶ During the second quarter of 1995, the rapid descent of the U.S. yield curve contributed to underperformance of high-coupon callable structures because of their negative convexity property.

▶ When the yield curve stabilized during the third quarter of 1995, investors were more willing to purchase high-quality callable bonds versus high-quality bullet structures to earn an extra 35 bps of spread.

▶ The sharp downward rotation of the U.S. yield curve during the second half of 1997 contributed to poor relative performance by putable structures. The yield investors had sacrificed for protection against higher interest rates instead constrained total return as rates fell.

▶ The plunge in U.S. interest rates and escalation of yield-curve volatility during the second half of 1998 again restrained the performance of callable structures compared to bullet structures.

▶ The upward rebound in U.S. interest rates and the fall in interest-rate volatility during 1999 contributed to the relative outperformance of callable structures versus bullet structures.

These results follow from the price/yield properties of the different structures. Structural analysis is also discussed in Section 8 of this reading.

8. Cash Flow Reinvestment

Cash flow reinvestment forces investors into the secondary market on a regular basis. During 2003, the sum of all coupon, maturity, and partial redemptions (via tenders, sinking funds, and other issuer prepayments) equaled approximately 100% of all new gross issuance across the dollar bond market. Before the allocation of any net new investment in the bond market, investors had sufficient cash flow reinvestment to absorb nearly all new bond supply. Some portfolio cash inflows occur during interludes in the primary market or the composition of recent primary supply may not be compatible with portfolio objectives. In these periods, credit portfolio managers must shop the secondary market for investment opportunities to remain fully invested or temporarily replicate the corporate index by using financial futures. Portfolio managers who incorporate analysis of cash flow reinvestment into their valuation of the credit market can position their portfolios to take advantage of this cash flow reinvestment effect on spreads.

B. Trading Constraints

Portfolio managers also should review their main rationales for not trading. Some of the best investment decisions are not to trade. Conversely, some of the worst investment decisions emanate from stale views based on dated and anachronistic constraints (e.g., avoid investing in bonds rated below Aa/AA). The best portfolio managers retain very open minds, constantly self-critiquing both their successful and unsuccessful methodologies.

1. Portfolio Constraints

Collectively, portfolio constraints are the single biggest contributor to the persistence of market inefficiency across the global credit market. Here are some examples:

▶ Because many asset managers are limited to holding securities with investment-grade ratings, they are forced to sell immediately the debt of issuers who are downgraded to speculative-gradings (Ba1/BB+ and below). In turn, this selling at the time of downgrade provides an opportunity for investors with more flexible constraints to buy such newly downgraded securities at a temporary discount (provided, of course, that the issuer's credit-worthiness stabilizes after downgrade).

▶ Some U.S. state employee pension funds cannot purchase credit securities with ratings below A3/A– due to administrative and legislative guidelines.

▶ Some U.S. pension funds also have limitations on their ownership of MTNs and non-U.S. corporate issues.

▶ Regulators have limited U.S. insurance companies' investment in high-yield corporates.

▶ Many European investors are restricted to issues rated at least single-A and sometimes Aa3/AA– and above, created originally in annual-pay Eurobond form.

▶ Many investors are confined to their local currency market—yen, sterling, euro, U.S. dollar. Often, the same issuer, like Ford, will trade at different spreads across different geographic markets.

▶ Globally, many commercial banks must operate exclusively in the floating-rate realm: all fixed-rate securities, unless converted into floating-rate cash flows via an interest rate swap, are prohibited.

2. "Story" Disagreement

"Story" disagreement can work to the advantage or disadvantage of a portfolio manager. Traders, salespersons, sell-side analysts and strategists, and buy-side credit researchers have dozens of potential trade rationales that supposedly will benefit portfolio performance. The proponents of a secondary trade may make a persuasive argument, but the portfolio manager may be unwilling to accept the "shortfall risk"[2] if the investment recommendation does not provide its expected return. For example in early 1998, analysts and investors alike were divided equally on short-term prospects for better valuations of Asian sovereign debt. After a very disappointing 1997 for Asian debt performance, Asia enthusiasts had little chance to persuade pessimists to buy Asian debt at the beginning of 1998. Technically, such lack of consensus in the credit market signals an investment with great outperformance potential. Indeed, most Asian debt issues recorded exceptional outperformance over the full course of 1998 and 1999. After a difficult 2002, the same "rebound effect" was observed in electric utilities during 2003. Of course, "story" disagreement can also work in the other direction. For example, Enron was long viewed as a very solid credit before its sudden bankruptcy in late 2001. An asset manager wedded to this long-term view might have been reluctant to act on the emergence of less favorable information about Enron in the summer of 2001.

3. Buy-and-Hold

Although many long-term asset/liability managers claim to have become more total return focused in the 1990s, accounting constraints (cannot sell positions at a loss compared with book cost or take too extravagant a gain compared with book cost) often limit the ability of these investors to trade. Effectively, these investors (mainly insurers) remain traditional "buy-and-hold" investors. Some active bond managers have converged to quasi-"buy-and-hold" investment programs at the behest of consultants to curb portfolio turnover. In the aftermath of the "Asian Contagion" in 1997–1998, this disposition toward lower trading turnover was reinforced by the temporary reduction in market liquidity provided

---

[2] Shortfall risk is the probability that the outcome will have a value less than the target return.

by more wary bond dealers. As shown in 2000–2002, however, a buy-and-hold strategy can gravely damage the performance of a credit portfolio. At the first signs of credit trouble for an issuer, many credit portfolios would have improved returns by reducing their exposure to a deteriorating credit.

4. Seasonality

Secondary trading slows at month ends, more so at quarter ends, and the most at the conclusion of calendar years. Dealers often prefer to reduce their balance sheets at fiscal year-end (November 30, December 31, or March 31 [Japan]). Also, portfolio managers take time to mark their portfolios, prepare reports for their clients, and chart strategy for the next investment period. During these intervals, even the most compelling secondary offerings can languish.

7   SPREAD ANALYSIS

By custom, some segments of the high-yield and emerging (EMG) debt markets still prefer to measure value by bond price or bond yield rather than spread. But for the rest of the global credit market, nominal spread (the yield difference between corporate and government bonds of similar maturities) has been the basic unit of both price and relative-value analysis for more than two centuries.

A. Alternative Spread Measures

Many U.S. practitioners prefer to value investment-grade credit securities in terms of option-adjusted spreads (OAS) so they can be more easily compared to the volatility ("vol") sectors (mortgage-backed securities and U.S. agencies).[3] But given the rapid reduction of credit structures with embedded options since 1990 (see structural discussion above), the use of OAS in primary and secondary pricing has diminished within the investment-grade credit asset class. Moreover, the standard one-factor binomial models[4] do not account for credit spread volatility. Given the exclusion of default risk in OAS option-valuation models, OAS valuation has seen only limited extension into the higher-risk markets of the quasi-equity, high-yield corporate, and EMG-debt asset classes.

Starting in Europe during the early 1990s and gaining momentum during the late 1990s, interest rate swap spreads have emerged as the common denominator to measure relative value across fixed- and floating-rate note credit structures. The U.S. investment-grade and high-yield markets eventually may switch to swap spreads to be consistent with Europe and Asia.

Other U.S. credit spread calculations have been proposed, most notably using the U.S. agency benchmark curve. These proposals emanate from the assumption of a persistent U.S. budgetary surplus and significant liquidation of outstanding U.S. Treasury securities during the first decade of the 21st century. As again demonstrated by 2002, history teaches that these budget assumptions

---

[3] These sectors are referred to as "vol" sectors because the value of the securities depends on expected interest rate volatility. These "vol" securities have embedded call options and the value of the options, and hence the value of the securities, depends on expected interest rate volatility.

[4] The model is referred to as a one-factor model because only the short-term rate is the factor used to construct the tree.

may unfortunately prove to be faulty. Although some practitioners may choose to derive credit-agency spreads for analytical purposes, this practice will be unlikely to become standard market convention.

Credit-default swap spreads have emerged as the latest valuation tool during the great stresses in the credit markets of 2000–2002. Most likely, credit-default swap spreads will be used as a companion valuation reference to nomial spreads, OAS, and swap spreads. The market, therefore, has an ability to price any credit instrument using multiple spread references. These include nominal spread, static or zero-volatility spread, OAS, credit-swap spreads (or simply swap spreads), and credit default spreads. The spread measures used the Treasury yield curve or Treasury spot rate curve as the benchmark. Given the potential that swap spreads will become the new benchmark, these same measures can be performed relative to swaps rather than relative to U.S. Treasuries. However, using swap rates as a benchmark has been delayed by the decoupling of traditional credit spreads (credit yield minus government yield) from swap spreads over 2000–2002. Effectively, credit risk during a global recession and its aftermath superseded the countervailing influence of strong technical factors like lower and steeper yield curves which affected the interest rate swap market differently.

B. Closer Look at Swap Spreads

Swap spreads became a popular valuation yardstick for credit debt in Europe during the 1990s. This practice was enhanced by the unique nature of the European credit asset class. Unlike its American counterpart, the European credit market has been consistently homogeneous. Most issuance was of high quality (rated Aa3/AA– and above) and intermediate maturity (10 years and less). Consequently, swap spreads are a good proxy for credit spreads in such a uniform market. Most issuers were financial institutions, natural swappers between fixed-rate and floating-rate obligations. And European credit investors, often residing in financial institutions like commercial banks, have been much more willing to use the swap methodology to capture value discrepancies between the fixed- and floating-rate markets.

Structurally, the Asian credit market more closely resembles the European than the U.S. credit market. As a result, the use of swap spreads as a valuation benchmark also became common in Asia.

The investment-grade segment of the U.S. credit market may well be headed toward an embrace of swap spreads. The U.S. MBS, CMBS, agency, and ABS sectors (accounting for about 55% of the U.S. fixed-income market) made the transition to swap spreads as a valuation benchmark during the second half of the 1990s. Classical nominal credit spreads derived directly from the U.S. Treasury yield curve were distorted by the special effects of U.S. fiscal surpluses and buybacks of U.S. Treasury securities in 2000 and 2001. Accordingly, many market practitioners envision a convergence to a single global spread standard derived from swap spreads.

Here is an illustration of how a bond manager can use the interest rate swap spread framework. Suppose that a hypothetical Ford Motor Credit 7 1/2's of 2008 traded at a bid price (i.e., the price at which a dealer is willing to buy the issue) of 113 bps over the 5-year U.S. Treasury yield of 6.43%. This equates to a yield-to-maturity of 7.56% (6.43% + 113 bps). On that date, 5-year swap spreads were 83 bps (to the 5-year U.S. Treasury). Recall that swaps are quoted where the fixed-rate payer pays the yield on a Treasury with a maturity equal to the initial term of the swap plus the swap spread. The fixed-rate payer receives

LIBOR flat—that is, no increment over LIBOR. So, if the bond manager invests in the Ford Motor Credit issue and simultaneously enters into this 5-year swap, the following would result:

Receive from Ford Motor Credit (6.43% + 113 bps)	7.56%
− Pay on swap (6.43% + 83 bps)	7.26%
+ Receive from swap	LIBOR
Net	LIBOR + 30 bps

Thus, a bond manager could exchange this Ford Motor Credit bond's fixed coupon flow for LIBOR + 30 bps. On the trade date, LIBOR was 6.24%, so that the asset swapper would earn 6.54% (= 6.24% + 30 bps) until the first reset date of the swap. A total return manager would want to take advantage of this swap by paying fixed and receiving floating if he expects interest rates to increase in the future.

The swaps framework allows managers (as well as issuers) to more easily compare securities across fixed-rate and floating-rate markets. The extension of the swap spread framework may be less relevant for speculative-grade securities, where default risk becomes more important. In contrast to professional money managers, individual investors are not comfortable using bond valuation couched in terms of swap spreads. The traditional nominal spread framework is well understood by individual investors, has the advantages of long-term market convention, and works well across the entire credit-quality spectrum from Aaa's to B's. However, this nominal spread framework does not work very well for investors and issuers when comparing the relative attractiveness between the fixed-rate and floating-rate markets.

C. Spread Tools

Investors should also understand how best to evaluate spread levels in their decision-making. Spread valuation includes mean-reversion analysis, quality-spread analysis, and percent yield spread analysis.

1. Mean-Reversion Analysis

The most common technique for analyzing spreads among individual securities and across industry sectors is mean-reversion analysis. The "mean" is the average value of some variable over a defined interval (usually one economic cycle for the credit market). The term "mean-reversion" refers to the tendency for some variable's value to revert (i.e., move towards) its average value. Mean-reversion analysis is a form of relative-value analysis based on the assumption that the spread between two sectors or two issuers will revert back to its historical average. This would lead investors to buy a sector or issuer identified as "cheap" because historically the spread has been tighter and will eventually revert back to that tighter spread. Also, this would lead investors to sell a sector or issuer identified as "rich" because the spread has been wider and is expected to widen in the future.

Mean-reversion analysis involves the use of statistical analysis to assess whether the current deviation from the mean spread is significant. For example, suppose the mean spread for an issuer is 80 basis points over the past six months and the standard deviation is 12 basis points. Suppose that the current spread of the issuer is 98 basis points. The spread is 18 basis points over the mean spread or equivalently 1.5 standard deviations above the mean spread. The manager can use that information to determine whether or not the spread deviation is sufficient to purchase the issue. The same type of analysis can be used to rank a group of issuers in a sector.

   Mean-reversion analysis can be instructive as well as misleading. The mean is highly dependent on the interval selected. There is no market consensus on the appropriate interval and "persistence" frequents the credit market, meaning cheap securities, mainly a function of credit uncertainty, often tend to become cheaper. Rich securities, usually high-quality issues, tend to remain rich.

2. Quality-Spread Analysis

Quality-spread analysis examines the spread differentials between low- and high-quality credits. For example, portfolio managers would be well advised to consider the "credit upside trade" discussed in Section 6 when quality-spreads collapse to cyclical troughs. The incremental yield advantage of lower-quality products may not compensate investors for lower-quality spread expansion under deteriorating economic conditions. Alternatively, credit portfolio managers have long profited from overweighting lower-quality debt at the outset of an upward turn in the economic cycle.

3. Percent Yield Spread Analysis

Dating from the early 20th century, percent yield spread analysis (the ratio of credit yields to government yields for similar duration securities) is another popular technical tool used by some investors. This methodology has serious drawbacks that undermine its usefulness. Percent yield spread is more a derivative than an explanatory or predictive variable. The usual expansion of credit percent yield spreads during low-rate periods like 1997, 1998, and 2002 overstates the risk as well as the comparative attractiveness of credit debt. And the typical contraction of credit percent yield spreads during upward shifts of the benchmark yield curve does not necessarily signal an imminent bout of underperformance for the credit asset class. Effectively, the absolute level of the underlying benchmark yield is merely a single factor among many factors (demand, supply, profitability, defaults, etc.) that determine the relative value of the credit asset class. These other factors can offset or reinforce any insights derived from percent yield spread analysis.

STRUCTURAL ANALYSIS   8

As explained earlier in this reading, there are bullet, callable, putable, and sinking fund structures. Structural analysis is simply analyzing the performance of the different structures discussed throughout this reading. While evaluating bond structures was extremely important in the 1980s, it became less influential in credit bond market since the mid-1990s for several reasons. First, the European credit bond market almost exclusively features intermediate bullets. Second, as can be seen in Exhibit 5, the U.S. credit and the global bond markets have moved to embrace this structurally homogeneous European bullet standard. Plenty of structural diversity still resides within the U.S. high yield and EMG debt markets, but portfolio decisions in these speculative-grade sectors understandably hinge more on pure credit differentiation than the structural diversity of the issue-choice set.

EXHIBIT 5	Changing Composition of the U.S. Investment-Grade Credit Markets	
	1990 (%)	**2003 (%)**
Bullets	24	94
Callables	72	3
Sinking Funds	32	1
Putables	5	2
Zeros	4	N/A

Note: Figures in table do not add to 100% given that some structures may have contained multiple options (e.g., a callable corporate bond may also have a sinking fund and put provision).

Source: Lehman Brothers U.S. Investment-Grade Credit Index.

Still, structural analysis can enhance risk-adjusted returns of credit portfolios. Leaving credit aside, issue structure analysis and structural allocation decisions usually hinge on yield curve and volatility forecasts as well as interpretation of option-valuation model outputs (see the discussion below). This is also a key input in making relative value decisions among structured credit issues, mortgage-backed securities, and asset-backed securities. In the short run and assuming no change in the perceived credit-worthiness of the issuer, yield curve and volatility movements will largely influence structural performance. Investors should also take into account long-run market dynamics that affect the composition of the market and, in turn, credit index benchmarks.

Specifically, callable structures have become rarer in the U.S. investment-grade credit bond market with the exception of the 2000 inversion. This is due to an almost continuously positively-sloped U.S. term structure since 1990 and the yield curve's intermittent declines to approximately multi-decade lows in 1993, 1997, 1998, and 2002. As a result, the composition of the public U.S. corporate bond market converged toward the intermediate-bullet Eurobond and euro-denominated bond market. To see this, we need only look at the structure composition of Lehman's U.S. Investment-Grade Credit Bond Index. Bullets increased from 24% of this index at the start of 1990 to 94% (principal value basis) by 2003. Over this interval, callables declined at a remarkable rate from 72% to just a 3% index share. Sinking-fund structures, once the structural mainstay of natural-gas pipelines and many industrial sectors, are on the "structural endangered species list" with a drop from 32% of the public bond market in 1990 to only 1% in 2003. Despite several brief flurries of origination in the mid-1990s and the late-1990s introduction of callable/putable structures, putable structure market share fell from 5% in 1990 to 2% by 2003. Pure corporate zeros are in danger of extinction with a fall from 4% market share in 1990 to negligible by 2003.

A. Bullets

Here is a review of how different types of investors are using bullet structures with different maturities.

Front-end bullets (i.e., bullet structures with 1- to 5-year maturities) have great appeal for investors who pursue a "barbell strategy" in which both the short and long end of the barbell are U.S. Treasury securities. There are "barbellers" who use credit securities at the front or short-end of the curve and Treasuries at the long-end of the yield curve. There are non-U.S. institutions who convert short bullets into floating-rate products by using interest rate swaps. The transactions are referred to as "asset swaps," and the investors who employ this transaction are referred to as "asset swappers."

Intermediate credit bullets (5- to 12-year maturities), especially the 10-year maturity sector, have become the most popular segment of the U.S. and European investment-grade and high-yield credit markets. Fifteen-year maturities, benchmarked off the 10-year bellwether Treasury, are comparatively rare and have been favored by banks that occasionally use them for certain types of swaps. Because new 15-year structures take five years to descend along a positively sloped yield curve to their underlying 10-year bellwether, 15-year maturities hold less appeal for many investors in search of return through price appreciation emanating from benchmark rolldown. In contrast, rare 20-year structures have been favored by many investors. Spreads for these structures are benched off the 30-year Treasury. With a positively sloped yield curve, the 20-year structure provides higher yield than a 10-year or 15-year security and less vulnerability (lower duration) than a 30-year security.

The 30-year maturity is the most popular form of long-dated security in the global credit market. In 1992, 1993, late 1995, and 1997, there was a minor rush to issue 50-year (half-centuries) and 100-year (centuries) securities in the U.S. credit bond market. These longer-dated securities provide investors with extra positive convexity for only a modest increase in effective (or modified-adjusted) duration.[5] In the wake of the "Asian Contagion" and especially the "Great Spread-Sector Crash" of August 1998, the cyclical increases in risk aversion and liquidity premiums greatly reduced both issuer and investor interest in these ultra-long maturities.

B. Callables

Typically after a 5-year or 10-year wait (longer for some rare issues), credit structures are callable at the option of the issuer at any time. Call prices usually are set at a premium above par (par + the initial coupon) and decline linearly on an annual basis to par by 5–10 years prior to final scheduled maturity. The ability to refinance debt in a potentially lower-interest rate environment is extremely valuable to issuers. Conversely, the risk of earlier-than-expected retirement of an above-current market coupon is bothersome to investors.

In issuing callables, issuers pay investors an annual spread premium (about 20 bps to 40 bps for high-quality issuers) for being long (from an issuer's perspective) the call option. Like all security valuations, this call premium varies through time with capital market conditions. Given the higher chance of exercise, this call option becomes much more expensive during low rate and high volatility periods. Since 1990, this call premium has ranged from approximately 15 bps to 50 bps for investment-grade issuers. Callables significantly underperform bullets when interest rates decline because of their negative convexity. When the bond market rallies, callable structures do not fully participate given the upper boundary imposed by call prices. Conversely, callable structures outperform bullets in bear bond markets as the probability of early call diminishes.

---

[5] The longer the maturity, the greater the convexity.

C. Sinking Funds

A sinking fund structure allows an issuer to execute a series of partial calls (annually or semiannually) prior to maturity. Issuers also usually have an option to retire an additional portion of the issue on the sinking fund date, typically ranging from 1 to 2 times the mandatory sinking fund obligation. Historically, especially during the early 1980s, total return investors favored the collection of sinking fund structures at sub-par prices. These discounted sinking funds retained price upside during interest rate rallies (provided the indicated bond price remained below par), and, given the issuers' requirement to retire at least annually some portion of the issue at par, the price of these sinking fund structures did not fall as much compared to callables and bullets when interest rates rose. It should be noted that astute issuers with strong liability management skills can sometimes satisfy such annual sinking fund obligations in whole or in part through prior open market purchases at prices below par. Nonetheless, this annual sinking fund purchase obligation by issuers does limit bond price depreciation during periods of rising rates.

D. Putables

Conventional put structures are simpler than callables. Yet in trading circles, put bond valuations often are the subject of debate. American-option callables grant issuers the right to call an issue at any time at the designated call price after expiration of the non-callable or non-redemption period. Put bonds typically provide investors with a one-time, one-date put option (European option) to demand full repayment at par. Less frequently, put bonds include a second or third put option date. A very limited number of put issues afford investors the privilege to put such structures back to the issuers at par in the case of rating downgrades (typically to below investment-grade status).

Thanks to falling interest rates, issuers shied away from new put structures as the 1990s progressed. Rather than incur the risk of refunding the put bond in 5 or 10 years at a higher cost, many issuers would prefer to pay an extra 10 bps to 20 bps in order to issue a longer-term liability.

Put structures provide investors with a partial defense against sharp increases in interest rates. Assuming that the issuer still has the capability to meet its sudden obligation, put structures triggered by a credit event enable investors to escape from a deteriorating credit. Perhaps because of its comparative scarcity, the performance and valuation of put structures have been a challenge for many portfolio managers. Unlike callable structures, put prices have not conformed to expectations formed in a general volatility-valuation framework. Specifically, the implied yield volatility of an option can be computed from the option's price and a valuation model. In the case of a putable bond, the implied volatility can be obtained using a valuation model such as the binomial model. The implied volatility should be the same for both puts and calls, all factors constant. Yet, for putable structures, implied volatility has ranged between 4%–9% since 1990, well below the 10%–20% volatility range associated with callable structures for the same time period. This divergence in implied volatility between callables (high) and putables (low) suggests that asset managers, often driven by a desire to boost portfolio yield, underpay issuers for the right to put a debt security back to the issuer under specified circumstances. In other words, the typical put bond should trade at a lower yield in the market than is commonly the case.

Unless put origination increases sharply, allowing for greater liquidity and the creation of more standardized trading conventions for this rarer structural issue, this assymetry in implied volatility between putable and corporate structures will persist. Meanwhile, this structure should be favored as an outperformance vehicle only by those investors with a decidedly bearish outlook for interest rates.

CREDIT CURVE ANALYSIS

The rapid growth of credit derivatives since the mid-1990s has inspired a groundswell of academic and practitioner interest in the development of more rigorous techniques to analyze the term structure (1–100 years) and credit structure (Aaa/AAA through B2/B's) of credit spread curves (higher risk higher-yield securities trade on a price rather than a spread basis).

Credit curves, both term structure and credit structure, are almost always positively sloped. In an effort to moderate portfolio risk, many portfolio managers take credit risk in short and intermediate maturities and to substitute less-risky government securities in long-duration portfolio buckets. This strategy is called a credit barbell strategy. Accordingly, the application of this strategy diminishes demand for longer-dated credit risk debt instruments by many total return, mutual fund, and bank portfolio bond managers. Fortunately for credit issuers who desire to issue long maturities, insurers and pension plan sponsors often meet long-term liability needs through the purchase of credit debt with maturities that range beyond 20 years.

Default risk increases non-linearly as credit-worthiness declines. The absolute risk of issuer default in any one year remains quite low through the investment-grade rating categories (Aaa/AAA to Baa3/BBB–). But investors constrained to high-quality investments often treat downgrades like quasi-defaults. In some cases like a downgrade from single-A to the Baa/BBB category, investors may be forced to sell securities under rigid portfolio guidelines. In turn, investors justifiably demand a spread premium for the increased likelihood of potential credit difficulty as rating quality descends through the investment-grade categories.

Credit spreads increase sharply in the high-yield rating categories (Ba1/BB+ through D). Default, especially for weak single-Bs and CCCs, becomes a major possibility. The credit market naturally assigns higher and higher risk premia (spreads) as credit and rating risk escalate. Exhibit 6 shows the credit curve for

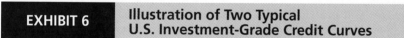

| EXHIBIT 6 | Illustration of Two Typical U.S. Investment-Grade Credit Curves |

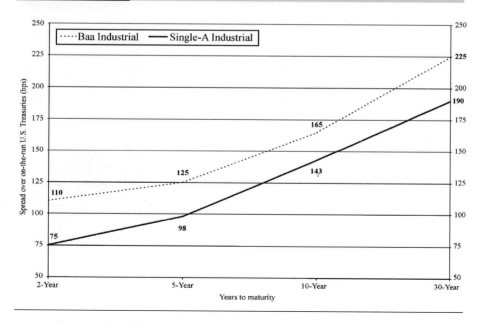

Source: Lehman Brothers U.S. Investment-Grade Credit Index, based on average corporate curves 1990–2003.

two credit sectors (Baa and single-A industrials) and also illustrates a higher spread is required as maturity lengthens.

In particular, the investment-grade credit market has a fascination with the slope of issuer credit curves between 10-year and 30-year maturities. Like the underlying Treasury benchmark curve, credit spread curves change shape over the course of economic cycles. Typically, spread curves steepen when the bond market becomes more wary of interest rate and general credit risk. Spread curves also have displayed a minor propensity to steepen when the underlying benchmark curve flattens or inverts. This loose spread curve/yield curve linkage reflects the diminished appetite for investors to assume both curve and credit risk at the long end of the yield curve when higher total yields may be available in short and intermediate credit products.

10 CREDIT ANALYSIS

In the continuous quest to seek credit upgrades and contraction in issuer/issue spread resulting from possible upgrades and, more importantly, to avoid credit downgrades resulting in an increase in issuer/issue spread, superior credit analysis has been and will remain the most important determinant of credit bond portfolio relative performance. Credit screening tools tied to equity valuations, relative spread movements, and the internet (information available tracking all related news on portfolio holdings) can provide helpful supplements to classic credit research and rating agency opinions. But self-characterized credit models, relying exclusively on variables like interest-rate volatility and binomial processes imported from option-valuation techniques, are not especially helpful in ranking the expected credit performance of individual credits like IBM, British Gas, Texas Utilities, Pohang Iron & Steel, Sumitomo, and Brazil.

Credit analysis is both non-glamorous and arduous for many top-down portfolio managers and strategists, who focus primarily on macro variables. Genuine credit analysis encompasses actually studying issuers' financial statements and accounting techniques, interviewing issuers' managements, evaluating industry issues, reading indentures and charters, and developing an awareness of (not necessarily concurrence with) the views of the rating agencies about various industries and issuers.

Unfortunately, the advantages of such analytical rigor may clash with the rapid expansion of the universe of issuers of credit bonds. There are approximately 5,000 different credit issuers scattered across the global bond market. With continued privatization of state enterprises, new entrants to the high-yield market, and expected long-term growth of the emerging-debt markets, the global roster of issuers could swell to 7,500 by 2010. The sorting of this expanding roster of global credit issues into outperformers, market performers, and underperformers demands establishing and maintaining a formidable credit-valuation function by asset managers.

11 ASSET ALLOCATION/SECTOR ROTATION

Sector rotation strategies have long played a key role in equity portfolio management. In the credit bond market, "macro" sector rotations among industrials, utilities, financial institutions, sovereigns, and supranationals also have a long history. During the last quarter of the 20th century, there were major variations in investor sentiment toward these major credit sectors. Utilities endured market wariness about heavy supply and nuclear exposure in the early-to-mid 1980s. U.S. and European financial institutions coped with investor concern about asset quality in the late 1980s and early 1990s. Similar investor skittishness affected demand for Asian financial institution debt in the late 1990s. Industrials embodied severe "event risk" in the mid-to-late 1980s, recession vulnerability during 1990–1992, a return of event risk in the late 1990s amid a general boom in corporate mergers and acquisitions, and a devastating series of accounting and corporate governance blows during 2001–2002. Sovereigns were exposed to periodic market reservations about the implications of independence for Quebec, political risk for various countries (i.e., Russia), the effects of the "Asian Contagion" during 1997–1998, and outright defaults like Argentina (2001).

In contrast, "micro" sector rotation strategies have a briefer history in the credit market. A detailed risk/return breakdown (i.e., average return and standard deviation) of the main credit sub-sectors (i.e., banks, brokerage, energy, electrics, media, railroads, sovereigns, supranationals, technology) was not available from credit index providers until 1993 in the United States and until 1999 in Europe. Beginning in the mid-1990s, these "micro" sector rotation strategies in the credit asset class have become much more influential as portfolio managers gain a greater understanding of the relationships among intra-credit sectors from these statistics.

Exhibit 7 illustrates the main factors bearing on sector rotation and issuer selection strategies. For example, an actual or perceived change in rating agency philosophy toward a sector and a revision in profitability expectations for a particular industry represent just two of many factors that can influence relative sectoral performance.

EXHIBIT 7   Some Outperformance Methodologies

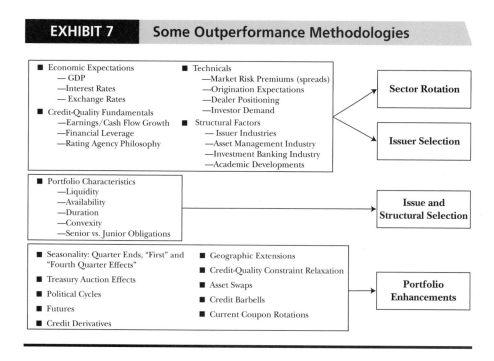

Common tactics to hopefully enhance credit portfolio performance are also highlighted in Exhibit 7. In particular, seasonality deserves comment. The annual rotation toward risk aversion in the bond market during the second half of most years contributes to a "fourth-quarter effect"—that is, there is underperformance of lower-rated credits, B's in high-yield and Baa's in investment-grade, compared to higher-rated credits. A fresh spurt of market optimism greets nearly every New Year. Lower-rated credit outperforms higher-quality credit—this is referred to as the "first-quarter effect." This pattern suggests a very simple and popular portfolio strategy: underweight low-quality credits and possibly even credit products altogether until the mid-third quarter of each year and then move to overweight lower-quality credits and all credit product in the fourth quarter of each year.

SUMMARY

- ▶ Superior credit analysis has been and will remain the most important determinant of the relative performance of credit bond portfolios, allowing managers to identify potential credit upgrades and to avoid potential downgrades.

- ▶ The "corporate asset class" includes more than pure corporate entities; this segment of the global bond market is more properly called the "credit asset class," including sovereigns, supranationals, agencies of local government authorities, nonagency mortgage-backed securities, commercial mortgage-backed securities, and asset-backed securities.

- ▶ Relative value refers to the ranking of fixed-income investments by sectors, structures, issuers, and issues in terms of their expected performance during some future interval.

- ▶ Relative-value analysis refers to the methodologies used to generate expected return rankings.

- ▶ Within the global credit market, classic relative-value analysis combines top-down and bottom-up approaches, blending the macro input of chief investment officers, strategists, economists, and portfolio managers with the micro input of credit analysts, quantitative analysts, and portfolio managers.

- ▶ The objective of relative value analysis is to identify the sectors with the most potential upside, populate these favored sectors with the best representative issuers, and select the structures of the designated issuers at the yield curve points that match the investor's outlook for the benchmark yield curve.

- ▶ The main methodologies for credit relative-value maximization are total return analysis, primary market analysis, liquidity and trading analysis, secondary trading rationales and constraints analysis, spread analysis, structure analysis, credit curve analysis, credit analysis, and asset allocation/sector analysis.

- ▶ Credit relative-value analysis starts with a detailed decomposition of past returns and a projection of expected returns.

- ▶ Primary market analysis refers to analyzing the supply and demand for new issues.

- ▶ The global credit market has become structurally more homogeneous, with intermediate maturity (5 to 10 years) bullet structure (noncallable issues) coming to dominate the investment-grade market.

- ▶ The trend toward bullet securities does not pertain to the high-yield market, where callable structures dominate the market.

- ▶ Short-term and long-term liquidity influence portfolio management decisions.

- ▶ Credit market liquidity changes over time, varying with the economic cycle, credit cycle, shape of the yield curve, supply, and the season.

- ▶ Despite the limitations of yield measures, yield/spread pickup trades account for the most common secondary market trades across all sectors of the global credit market.

- ▶ Credit-upside trades seek to capitalize on expectations of issues that will be upgraded in credit quality with such trades particularly popular in the crossover sector (securities with ratings between Ba2/BB and Baa3/BBB– by a major rating agency).

- ▶ Credit-defense trades involve trading up in credit quality as economic or geopolitical uncertainty increases.

▶ Sector-rotation trades involve altering allocations among sectors based on relative-value analysis; such strategies can be used within the credit bond market (intra-asset class sector rotation) and among fixed-income asset classes.

▶ Sector-rotation trades are not as popular in the bond market as in the equity market because of less liquidity and higher costs of trading; however, with the expected development of enhanced liquidity and lower trading transaction costs in the future, sector-rotation trades should become more prevalent in the credit asset class.

▶ Trades undertaken to reposition a portfolio's duration are called yield curve-adjustment trades, or simply, curve-adjustment trades.

▶ Structure trades involve swaps into structures (e.g., callable structures, bullet structures, and put structures) that are expected to have better performance given anticipated movements in volatility and the shape of the yield curve.

▶ Portfolio managers should review their main rationales for not trading.

▶ Portfolio constraints are the single biggest contributor to the persistence of market inefficiency across the global credit bond market.

▶ Many U.S. practitioners prefer to cast the valuations of investment-grade credit securities in terms of option-adjusted spreads (OAS), but given the rapid reduction of credit structures with embedded options since 1990, the use of OAS in primary and secondary pricing has diminished within the investment-grade credit asset class.

▶ Swap spreads have become a popular valuation yardstick for European credit, Asian credit, and U.S. MBS, CMBS, agency, and ABS sectors.

▶ In the global credit bond market, nominal spread (the yield difference between credit and government bonds of similar maturities) has been the basic unit of relative-value analysis.

▶ Mean-reversion analysis is the most common technique for analyzing spreads among individual securities and across industry sectors.

▶ Mean-reversion analysis can be misleading because the mean or average value is highly dependent on the time period analyzed.

▶ In quality-spread analysis, a manager examines the spread differentials between low- and high-quality credits.

▶ Structural analysis involves analyzing different structures' performance on a relative-value basis.

▶ Put structures provide investors with a partial defense against sharp increases in interest rates: this structure should be favored as an outperformance vehicle only by those investors with a decidedly bearish outlook for interest rates.

▶ Credit curves, both term structure and credit structure, are almost always positively sloped.

▶ In credit barbell strategies, many portfolio managers choose to take credit risk in short and intermediate maturities and to substitute less risky government securities in long-duration portfolio buckets.

▶ Like the underlying Treasury benchmark curve, credit spread curves change shape over the course of economic cycles; typically, spread curves steepen when the bond market becomes more wary of interest rate and general credit risk.

PRACTICE PROBLEMS FOR READING 29

1. What is meant by relative value in the credit market?

2. A. What is the dominant type of structure in the investment-grade credit market?

   B. What are the strategic portfolio implications of the dominant structure answer in Part (A)?

   C. What is the dominant structure in the high-yield corporate bond market and why is it not the same structure as discussed in Part (A)?

3. The following quote is from Lev Dynkin, Peter Ferket, Jay Hyman, Erik van Leeuwen, and Wei Wu, "Value of Security Selection versus Asset Allocation in Credit Markets," Fixed Income Research, Lehman Brothers, March 1999, p. 3:

> Most fixed income investors in the United States have historically remained in a single-currency world. Their efforts to outperform their benchmarks have focused on yield curve placement, sector and quality allocations, and security selection. The style of market participants is expressed in the amount of risk assumed along each of these dimensions (as measured by the deviation from their benchmarks), and their research efforts are directed accordingly.

   A. What is meant by "yield curve placement, sector and quality allocations, and security selection"?

   B. What is meant by the statement: "The style of market participants is expressed in the amount of risk assumed along each of these dimensions (as measured by the deviation from their benchmarks)"?

4. The following two passages are from Peter J. Carril, "Relative Value Concepts within the Eurobond Market," Chapter 29 in Frank J. Fabozzi (ed.), *The Handbook of Corporate Debt Instruments* (New Hope, PA: Frank J. Fabozzi Associates, 1998), p. 552.

   A. In discussing Eurobond issuers, Carril wrote: "Many first time issuers produce tighter spreads than one may anticipate because of their so called scarcity value." What is meant by scarcity value?

   B. In describing putable bonds Carril wrote: "Much analytical work has been devoted to the valuation of the put's option value, especially in the more mature U.S. investment-grade market." However, he states that in the high-yield market the overriding concern for a putable issue is one of credit concern. Specifically, he wrote: "traditional analysis used to quantify the option value which the issuer has granted the investor is overridden by the investor's specific view of the credit-worthiness of the issuer at the time of first put." Explain why.

5. In describing the approaches to investing in emerging markets credits, Christopher Taylor wrote the following in "Challenges in the Credit Analysis of Emerging Market Corporate Bonds," Chapter 16 in Frank J. Fabozzi (ed.), *The Handbook of Corporate Debt Instruments* (New Hope, PA: Frank J. Fabozzi Associates, 1998), p. 311:

> There traditionally have been two approaches to investing in emerging market corporate bonds: top-down and bottom-up. . . . The *top-down approach* essentially treats investing in corporates as "sovereign-plus." The *bottom-up approach* sometimes has a tendency to treat emerging market corporate as "U.S. credits-plus."

   What do you think Mr. Taylor means by "sovereign-plus" and "U.S. credits-plus"?

6. Chris Dialynas in "The Active Decisions in the Selection of Passive Management and Performance Bogeys" (in Frank J. Fabozzi (ed.), *Perspectives on Fixed Income Portfolio Management*, Volume 2) wrote:

> Active bond managers each employ their own methods for relative value analysis. Common elements among most managers are historical relations, liquidity considerations, and market segmentation. Market segmentation allegedly creates opportunities, and historical analysis provides the timing cure.

A. What is meant by "historical relations, liquidity considerations, and market segmentation" that Chris Dialynas refers to in this passage?

B. What is meant by: "Market segmentation allegedly creates opportunities, and historical analysis provides the timing cure?"

7. The following passages are from Leland Crabbe "Corporate Spread Curve Strategies," Chapter 28 in Frank J. Fabozzi (ed.), *The Handbook of Corporate Debt Instruments* (New Hope, PA: Frank J. Fabozzi Associates, 1998).

> In the corporate bond market, spread curves often differ considerably across issuers . . .

> Most fixed income investors understand the relation between the term structure of interest rates and implied forward rates. But some investors overlook the fact that a similar relation holds between the term structure of corporate spreads and forward corporate spreads. Specifically, when the spread curve is steep, the forward spreads imply that spreads will widen over time. By contrast, a flat spread curve gives rise to forwards that imply stability in corporate spreads. Essentially the forward spread can be viewed as a breakeven spread . . .

> Sometimes, investors may disagree with the expectations implied by forward rates, and consequently they may want to implement trading strategies to profit from reshapings of the spread curve.

A. What is meant by "spread curves" and in what ways do they differ across issuers?

B. Consider the relationship between the term structure of interest rates and implied forward rates (or simply forward rates). What is a "forward spread" that Mr. Crabbe refers to and why can it be viewed as a breakeven spread?

C. How can implied forward spreads be used in relative-value analysis?

8. What is the limitation of a yield-pickup trade?

9. Increases in investment-grade credit securities new issuance have been observed with contracting yield spreads and strong relative bond returns. In contrast, spread expansion and a major decline in both relative and absolute returns usually accompanies a sharp decline in the supply of new credit issues. These outcomes are in stark contrast to the conventional wisdom held by many portfolio managers that supply hurts credit spreads. What reason can be offered for the observed relationship between new supply and changes in credit spreads?

10. A. What is meant by the "crossover sector of the bond market"?

B. How do portfolio managers take advantage of potential credit upgrades in the crossover sector?

11. When would a portfolio manager consider implementing a credit-defense trade?

12. What is the motivation for portfolio managers to trade into more current and larger sized "on-the-run" issues?

13. A. Why has the swap spread framework become a popular valuation yardstick in Europe for credit securities?

   B. Why might U.S. managers embrace the swap spread framework for the credit asset class?

   C. Compare the advantages/disadvantage of the nominal spread framework to the swap spread framework.

14. An ABC Corporate issue trades at a bid price of 120 bps over the 5-year U.S. Treasury yield of 6.00% at a time when LIBOR is 5.70%. At the same time, 5-year LIBOR-based swap spreads equal 100 bps (to the 5-year U.S. Treasury).

   A. If a manager purchased the ABC Corporate issue and entered into a swap to pay fixed and receive floating, what spread over LIBOR is realized until the first swap reset date?

   B. Why would a total return manager buy the issue and then enter into a swap to pay fixed and receive floating?

15. The following was reported in the "Strategies" section of the January 3, 2000 issue of *BondWeek* ("Chicago Trust to Move Up in Credit Quality," p. 10):

> The Chicago Trust Co. plans to buy single-A corporate bonds with intermediate maturities starting this quarter, as the firm swaps out of lower-rated, triple B rated paper to take advantage of attractive spreads from an anticipated flood of single-A supply. . . .

The portfolio manager gave the following reasoning for the trade:

> . . . he says a lack of single-A corporate offerings during the fourth quarter has made the paper rich, and he expects it will result in a surge of issuance by single-A rated companies this quarter, blowing out spreads and creating buying opportunities. Once the issuance subsides by the end of the quarter, he expects spreads on the single-A paper will tighten.

   A. What type of relative value analysis is the portfolio manager relying on in making this swap decision and what are the underlying assumptions? (Note: When answering this question, keep the following in mind. The manager made the statement at either the last few days of December 1999 or the first two days in January 2000. So, reference to the fourth quarter means the last quarter in 1999. When the statement refers to the end of the quarter or to "this quarter" it is meant the first quarter of 2000.)

   B. Further in the article, it was stated that the portfolio manager felt that on an historical basis the corporate market as a whole was cheap. The portfolio manager used new cash to purchase healthcare credits, doubling the portfolio's allocation to the healthcare sector. The portfolio manager felt that the issuers in the healthcare sector he purchased for the portfolio had fallen out of favor with investors as a result of concerns with healthcare reform. He thought that the cash flows for the issuers purchased were strong and the concerns regarding reform were "overblown." Discuss the key elements to this strategy.

16. The following was reported in the "Strategies" section of the January 3, 2000 issue of *BondWeek* ("... Even as Wright Moves Down." p. 10):

> Wright Investors Services plans to buy triple B-rated corporate paper in the industrial sector and sell higher rated corporate paper on the view that stronger-than-anticipated economic growth will allay corporate bond investor fears.

In the article, the following was noted about the portfolio manager's view:

> spreads on higher rated investment grade paper already have come in some from last summer's wides, but he believes concerns over year-end and rising rates have kept investors from buying lower rated corporate paper, keeping spreads relatively wide.

Discuss the motivation for this strategy and the underlying assumptions.

17. The following appeared in the "Strategies" section of the September 27, 1999 issue of *BondWeek* ("Firm Sticks to Corps, Agencies," p. 6):

> The firm, which is already overweight in corporates, expects to invest cash in single A corporate paper in non-cyclical consumer non-durable sectors, which should outperform lower-quality, cyclicals as the economy begins to slow.

Discuss this strategy and its assumptions.

18. A. Suppose that a manager believes that credit spreads are mean reverting. Below are three issues along with the current spread, the mean (average) spread over the past six months, and the standard deviation of the spread. Assuming that the spreads are normally distributed, which issue is the most likely to be purchased based on mean-reversion analysis?

Issue	Current Spread	Mean Spread for Past 6 Months	Standard Deviation of Spread
A	110 bps	85 bps	25 bps
B	124	100	10
C	130	110	15

B. What are the underlying assumptions in using mean-reversion analysis?

19. Ms. Xu is the senior portfolio manager for the Solid Income Mutual Fund. The fund invests primarily in investment-grade credit and agency mortgage-backed securities. For each quarterly meeting of the board of directors of the mutual fund, Ms. Xu provides information on the characteristics of the portfolio and changes in the composition of the portfolio since the previous board meeting. One of the board members notices two changes in the composition of the portfolio. First, he notices that while the percentage of the portfolio invested in credit was unchanged, there was a sizeable reduction in callable credit relative to noncallable credit bonds. Second, while the portfolio had the same percentage of mortgage passthrough securities, there was a greater percentage of low-coupon securities relative to high-coupon securities.

When Ms. Xu was asked why she changed the structural characteristics of the securities in the portfolio, she responded that it was because the management team expects a significant drop in interest rates in the next quarter and the new structures would benefit more from declining interest rates than the structures held in the previous quarter. One of the directors asked why. How should Ms. Xu respond?

20. Ms. Smith is the portfolio manager of the Good Corporate Bond Fund, which invests primarily in investment-grade corporate bonds. The fund currently has an overweight within the retail industrial sector bonds of retailers. Ms. Smith is concerned that increased competition from internet retailers will negatively affect the earnings and cash flow of the traditional retailers. The fund is also currently underweighted in the U.S. dollar-denominated bonds of European issuers placed in the United States, which she believes should benefit from increased opportunities afforded by European Union. She believes that many of these companies may come to market with new U.S. dollar issues to fund some of their expansion throughout Europe.

Formulate and support a strategy for Ms. Smith that will capitalize on her views about the retail and European corporate sectors of her portfolio. What factors might negatively impact this strategy?

Use the following information to answer Questions 21–26. The questions are based on "Fixed-Income Portfolio Management—Part I" and this reading

Coughlin Fixed Income Funds is a family of mutual funds with assets totaling $4 billion, comprised primarily of U.S. corporate bonds. Hanover-Green Life Insurance Company has just under $1 billion in total assets primarily invested in U.S. corporate bonds. The two companies are considering combining their research and analysis units into one entity. They are also looking at possible synergies from consolidating their trading desks and/or back-office operations. Over a longer horizon, the companies also are open to the possibility of merger.

Gaven Warren is a senior portfolio manager with Hanover-Green. He has been asked to review the prospectuses for the various Coughlin funds and make recommendations regarding how the two companies might combine operations. Specifically, Warren is reviewing three of Coughlin's funds—The Select High-Performance Fund, the Yield Curve Plus Fund, and the Index

Match Fund. Highlights of the investment objectives of the three funds are shown below:

> The Select High-Performance Fund relies on the superior skills of its analyst team to discover hidden values among a wide range of corporate fixed-income securities. The fund will be approximately 95 percent invested in U.S. dollar denominated corporate bonds with medium-term to long-term maturities and Standard & Poors ratings of B or higher. The fund may use options, futures, and other derivative products to enhance returns. The primary goal of the fund is to maximize total return. The fund's annual total return target is to exceed the Lehman Brothers U.S. Corporate Bond Index total return by 200 basis points.

> The Yield Curve Plus Fund uses selected investments at key points along the yield curve to enhance portfolio returns. The fund will be approximately 95 percent invested in U.S. dollar denominated corporate bonds with medium-term to long-term maturities and Standard & Poors ratings of BBB or higher. The fund may use options, futures, and other derivative products to enhance returns. The primary goal of the fund is to outperform the Lehman Brothers U.S. Corporate Bond Index by analyzing the yield curve appropriate to pricing corporate bonds, identifying key rate durations for the bonds held in the portfolio, and positioning the portfolio to benefit from anticipated shifts in the slope and shape of the yield curve.

> The Index Match Fund seeks to match the return on the Lehman Brothers U.S. Corporate Bond Index. The fund will be approximately 98 percent invested in U.S. dollar denominated corporate bonds with medium-term to long-term maturities and Standard & Poors ratings of BBB or higher. The fund may use options, futures, and other derivative products to match the Lehman Brothers U.S. Corporate Bond Index returns.

As is typical of life insurance companies, Hanover-Green has estimated its liabilities using standard actuarial methods. The weighted-average duration of Hanover-Green's liabilities is about 12 years. The long-term focus of Hanover-Green means they can tolerate low liquidity in their portfolio. The primary management technique used by Hanover-Green has been contingent immunization. Because Warren anticipates a discussion with Coughlin regarding contingent immunization, he has prepared the following statements as part of a presentation.

Statement 1: "Contingent immunization requires the prevailing immunized rate of return to exceed the required rate of return."

Statement 2: "When interest rates fall, contingent immunization switches to more active management because the dollar safety margin is higher."

Although the Lehman Brothers U.S. Corporate Bond Index is the benchmark for the Coughlin funds, Warren is not certain that the index is appropriate for Hanover-Green. He compiled the data given in Exhibit 1 as a step toward deciding what index might be the best benchmark for Hanover-Green.

EXHIBIT 1	Selected Characteristics, Bond Indexes				
Index	Effective Duration	YTM (%)	Average Coupon (%)	Number of Securities	Weighting
Long-Term U.S. Corporate Bond Index	8.65	5.75	5.25	558	Value
Global Government Bond Index	5.15	6.30	5.85	520	Value
Selected Municipal Bonds Index	4.65	4.87	4.75	20	Value
Equal-Weighted Corporate Bond Index	4.70	5.19	5.75	96	Equal

Hanover-Green is considering a more active style for a small part of its portfolio. Warren is investigating several relative value methodologies. Two approaches are of particular interest—primary market analysis and spread analysis. Warren is worried that the primary market is about to enter a period where the supply of new issues will increase causing spreads to tighten, and furthermore, that most of the new issues will not be callable.

Regarding spread analysis, Hanover-Green is considering the addition of mortgage-backed securities (MBS) to its portfolio. Warren has investigated the MBS market and found that MBS analysis emphasizes the option-adjusted spread (OAS). Warren is considering using OAS to measure the risk of the corporate bonds in Hanover-Green's portfolio. Specifically, he wants to analyze the risks involved in holding several bonds whose credit ratings have deteriorated to speculative status.

21. The strategy used by the Yield Curve Plus Fund *most likely* attempts to enhance portfolio returns by taking advantage of:

    A. changes in credit spreads.

    B. changes in the level of interest rates.

    C. nonparallel changes in the yield curve.

22. The contingent immunization technique that Hanover-Green currently uses in managing their fixed-income portfolio is *best* described as:

    A. a passive management strategy similar to that of the Index Match Fund.

    B. an active management strategy similar to that of the Select High-Performance Fund.

    C. a mix of active and passive management strategies similar to that of the Yield Curve Plus Fund.

23. Are Warren's statements regarding contingent immunization *most likely* correct or incorrect?

	Statement 1	Statement 2
A.	Correct	Correct
B.	Correct	Incorrect
C.	Incorrect	Correct

24. Based solely on the information in Exhibit 1, which index is the *most* appropriate benchmark for Hanover-Green's portfolio?

 A. Global Government Bond Index.

 B. Long-Term U.S. Corporate Bond Index.

 C. Equal-Weighted Corporate Bond Index.

25. Consider Warren's expectations regarding the supply of new issues in the primary market. Given recent research into primary markets, is Warren *most likely* correct or incorrect regarding the effect on spreads and the probability of the bonds being callable?

	Effect on Spreads	Bonds Being Callable
A.	Correct	Correct
B.	Correct	Incorrect
C.	Incorrect	Correct

26. Which of the following statements *most* accurately evaluates the use of the option-adjusted spread (OAS) to analyze the bonds held in Hanover-Green's portfolio?

 A. OAS excludes default risk from its calculation; therefore OAS has limited applicability to the analysis of speculative grade bonds.

 B. OAS uses Monte Carlo simulation to factor out default risk from the spread; therefore OAS is not well suited to the analysis of speculative grade bonds.

 C. OAS is often used to evaluate bonds other than mortgage-backed securities. It is a very useful tool, especially appropriate for high-risk positions such as speculative grade bonds.

SOLUTIONS FOR READING 29

Note: Many of the questions are conceptual in nature. The solutions offered are one interpretation, and there may be other valid views.

1. Relative value refers to ranking credit sectors, bond structures, issuers, and issues in terms of their expected performance over some future time period.

2. **A.** The dominant structure in the investment-grade credit market is the bullet structure with an intermediate maturity.

   B. There are three strategic portfolio implications of the bullet structure with an intermediate maturity:

   i. The dominance of bullet structures creates a scarcity value for structures with embedded call and put features, resulting in premium price for bonds with embedded call options. This "scarcity value" should be considered by managers in relative-value analysis of credit bonds.

   ii. Because long-dated maturities have declined as a percentage of outstanding credit debt, there is a lower effective duration of all outstanding credit debt and, as a result, a reduction in the aggregate sensitivity to interest-rate risk.

   iii. There will be increased use of credit derivatives, whether on a stand-alone basis or embedded in structured notes, so that investors and issuers can gain exposure to the structures they desire.

   C. High-yield issuers will continue to issue callable bond structures in order to have the opportunity to refinance at a lower credit spread should credit quality improve.

3. **A.** Yield curve placement is simply the positioning of a portfolio with respect to duration and yield curve risk. Trades involving yield curve placement are referred to as curve adjustment trades in the reading. Sector and quality allocations refer to allocations based on relative value analysis of the different bond market sectors and quality sectors. Security selection involves the purchase or avoidance of individual issues based on some relative value basis.

   B. For a manager who is evaluated relative to some bond index, the deviation of the portfolio from the benchmark in terms of yield curve exposure, sector exposure, quality exposure, and exposure to individual issues is the appropriate way to measure risk.

4. **A.** Scarcity value means that an issue will trade at a premium price due to a lack of supply (relative to demand) for that issue. This is the same as saying that the issue will trade at a narrower spread. If investors want exposure to a first-time issuer, the spread can be narrower than otherwise comparable issuers.

   B. Analytical models for valuing bonds with embedded put options assume the issuer will fulfill the obligation to repurchase an issue if the bondholder exercises the put option. For high-yield issuers, there is the credit risk associated with the potential inability to satisfy the put obligation. Thus for high-yield issuers, the credit risk may override the value for a putable issue derived from a valuation model.

5. In general, the top-down approach involves beginning with a macro-economic outlook and making allocation decisions to sectors based on that outlook. With respect to credit in emerging markets, the top-down approach begins with the assessment of the economic outlook for emerging market countries and then basing the allocation of funds across emerging market credit issuers in different countries on that macroeconomic outlook. This is what Mr. Taylor means by "sovereign plus." The bottom-up approach focuses on the selection of corporate issuers in emerging market countries that are expected to outperform U.S. credit issuers. This is what Mr. Taylor means by "U.S. credits-plus."

6. A. Historical relations help a portfolio manager identify opportunities when current spreads are out of line and relative-value opportunities may be available. Liquidity considerations affect spreads and the ability to trade. Market segmentation means factors affecting supply and demand within sectors of the bond market due to impediments or restrictions on investors from reallocating funds across those bond sectors.

B. Market segmentation may create relative value opportunities when spreads get out of line due to obstructions that prevent or impede investors from allocating funds to certain sectors due to regulatory constraints and asset/liability constraints. Market segmentation may affect the supply of bonds in a sector for the same reasons. In pursuit of the optimal timing to move into or out of a sector (industry category, maturity neighborhood, or structure) or individual issuer, historical analysis of spreads, based on mean-reversion analysis can help identify when spreads might revert to some "normal" equilibrium.

7. A. Spread curves show the relationship between spreads and maturity. They differ by issuer or sector in terms of the amount of the spread and the slope of the spread curve.

B. Forward rates are derived from spot rates using arbitrage arguments. A forward spread, or an implied forward spread, can be derived in the same way. Also, forward rates were explained as basically hedgeable or breakeven rates—rates that will make an investor indifferent between two alternatives. For example, for default-free instruments a 2-year forward rate 3 years from now is a rate that will make an investor indifferent between investing in a 5-year zero-coupon default-free instrument or investing in a 3-year zero-coupon default-free instrument and reinvesting the proceeds for two more years after the 3-year instrument matures.

A forward spread can be interpreted in the same way. For example, a 2-year forward spread 3 years from now is the credit spread that will make an investor indifferent to investing in a 5-year zero-coupon instrument of an issuer or investing in a 3-year zero-coupon instrument of the same issuer and reinvesting the proceeds from the maturing instrument in a 2-year zero-coupon instrument of the same issuer.

The forward spread is a breakeven spread because it is the spread that would make the investor indifferent between two alternative investments with different maturities over a given investment horizon.

C. Because a forward spread is one that will make an investor indifferent between two alternatives, a manager must compare his or her expectations relative to the forward spread. Relative-value analysis involves making this comparison between expected spread and what is built into market prices (i.e., forward spread).

8. Yield measures are poor indicators of total return realized by holding a security to maturity or over some investment horizon. Thus, an asset manager does not know what a yield pickup of, say, 20 basis points means for subsequent total return. A bond manager can pick up yield on a trade (holding credit quality constant), but on a relative value basis underperform an alternative issue with a lower yield over the manager's investment horizon.

An example of this would be if at the beginning of the month, a portfolio manager sold the 5-year Ford issue at a spread of 140 basis points and purchased the 5-year General Motors issue at a spread of 150 basis points, for a yield pickup of 10 basis points. If the spread on the Ford issue continued to tighten throughout the month, while the General Motors issue's spread remained constant, the Ford issue would outperform the General Motors issue on a total return basis.

9. The reason suggested as to why heavy supply of new investment-grade credit issues will help spreads contract and enhance returns is that new primary bond valuations validate and enhance secondary valuations. In contrast, when new issuance declines sharply, secondary traders lose confirmation from the primary market and tend to require higher spreads on their bid offers.

10. **A.**   The crossover sector refers to the sector with issuers whose ratings are between Ba2/BB and Baa3/BBB− by a major rating agency. These issuers are on the border between investment grade and high yield.

   B.   A manager can purchase a below-investment grade issue which he believes will be upgraded to investment grade. If the manager is correct, then the issue will outperform due to spread narrowing resulting from the upgrade and also from increased liquidity as it becomes available to a broader class of investors.

11. A portfolio manager would consider implementing a credit-defense trade when the manager became increasingly concerned about geopolitical risk, the general economy, sector risk, or specific-issuer risk which could lead to widening credit spreads.

12. The motivation is to increase portfolio liquidity.

13. **A.**   The European credit market has been consistently homogeneous, having mostly high quality (rated Aa3/AA− and above) and intermediate maturity issues. So swap spreads were a good proxy for credit spreads. Because of the homogeneous character of the credit market in Europe, the swaps framework allows managers as well as issuers to more easily compare securities across fixed- and floating-rate markets. Moreover, in Europe, financial institutions such as commercial banks have been much more willing to use swap methodology to capture value discrepancies between the fixed- and floating-rate markets.

   B.   U.S. managers have embraced swap spreads for the MBS, CMBS, agency, and ABS sectors. This may gradually occur in the U.S. credit markets as well to help facilitate relative value comparisons across non-U.S. and non-credit sectors to U.S. credit securities.

   C.   Individual investors understand the traditional nominal spread framework as a market convention. Moreover despite its limitations, this framework can be used across the entire credit-quality spectrum from Aaa's to B's. The disadvantage is that the nominal spread framework does not work very well for investors and issuers in comparing the relative attractiveness between the fixed- and floating-rate markets. This is the advantage of using the swap framework.

14. A. By buying ABC Corporation issue and entering into a 5-year swap to pay fixed and receive floating, the spread over LIBOR until the first reset date for the swap is:

Receive from ABC Corp. (6.00% + 120 bps)	7.20%
− Pay on swap (6.00% + 100 bps)	7.00%
+ Receive from swap	LIBOR
Net	LIBOR + 20 bps

Since LIBOR is 5.70%, the manager is locking in a rate of 5.90% (= 5.70% + 20 basis points) until the first reset date.

B. If the manager expects that interest rates will increase, total return performance will be better using the swap.

15. A. The manager is relying on primary market analysis. The manager believes that one of the reasons why the spread on single-A rated issues may be out of line in the fourth quarter of 1999 is due to the lack of single-A rated issues coming to market in that quarter. The manager expects that in the first quarter of 2000, there will be a surge of single-A rated issues that will come to market, resulting in a widening of spreads and thereby providing an opportunity to purchase single-A rated issues relatively cheaply versus BBB issues.

The assumption is that the attractive level of the corporate spread for single-A rated issuers is driven principally by new issuance and not any structural issue or other factor that determines corporate spreads. Furthermore, it is assumed that once the market is cleared of the increase in supply of single-A rated issuers, the spread will narrow and provide better performance relative to BBB rated issuers.

B. The keys to this strategy are 1) that the cash flows will in fact remain strong, 2) that the spread for these health care issuers are not justified by the strong cash flow despite concerns with healthcare reform, and 3) that investors in the bond market will recognize this (by some time period), resulting in a decline in the credit spread for these issuers.

16. The motivation for this strategy is that while investment-grade issues may decline due to stronger-than-anticipated economic growth, a good amount of spread reduction has already occurred in above BBB rated sectors. Thus, on a relative basis, the decline in corporate spreads on investment grade bonds due to stronger-than-anticipated growth will be primarily in BBB rated sectors. The assumption is that spreads will contract more in the BBB rated sector.

17. This relative value strategy has two elements to it. First, there appears to be an allocation to single-A rated corporates versus lower-quality corporates. Hence, it appears to be a credit-defense trade because of a concern with the economy slowing down. Moreover, there is an allocation within the single-A rated corporates to a sector—non-cyclical consumer non-durables—that is expected to outperform an alternative sector—cyclicals—should the economy slow down.

18. A. One can use mean-reversion analysis in this question as follows. For each issue, the number of standard deviations that the current spread is above the historical average (the mean spread for the past six months) is computed as:

Issue	Number of Standard Deviations Above Mean
A	$(110 - 85)/25 = 1.0$
B	$(124 - 100)/10 = 2.4$
C	$(130 - 110)/15 = 1.3$

Issue B has the largest deviation above the mean and is therefore the one more likely to contract. Actually, based on a normal distribution, the probability associated with realizing a specified number of standard deviation above the mean can be determined.

B. The assumptions are that 1) the spreads will revert back to their historic means and 2) there have been no structural changes in the market that would render the historical mean and standard deviation useless for the analysis.

19. Ms. Xu should first explain that callable bonds exhibit negative convexity when interest rates decline, while noncallable bonds exhibit positive convexity. This means that when rates decline, the price appreciation for a callable bond will not be as great as an otherwise noncallable bond. Since the management team expects a significant drop in interest rates in the next quarter, to better participate in the rise in bond prices, there was a shift to noncallable credit securities.

All mortgage passthrough securities exhibit negative convexity. However, low-coupon issues exhibit less negative convexity than high-coupon issues. That is, there will be greater price appreciation for low-coupon issues when rates decline. Given the anticipated decline in interest rates, the low-coupon issues will appreciate more and hence the reason for the shift to such issues.

20. Ms. Smith could sell retail issues and use the proceeds to purchase U.S. dollar-denominated corporate bonds of European issuers. This would be consistent with her expectation of underperformance of the retail sector and outperformance of the European corporate sector. She could make her purchases in the new issue market, if she believes new issues will be attractively priced.

Ms. Smith should use credit analysis to select which issues to buy or sell within each sector. She must consider the possibility of a risk premium in the European corporate sector, as some managers cannot purchase bonds in that sector. Seasonality may also be a factor, depending on the timing of her purchases/sales.

21. C is correct. The Yield Curve Plus Fund is using key rate duration to enhance portfolio returns. Key rate duration attempts to profit from non-parallel shifts in the yield curve.

22. C is correct. Contingent immunization is a mix of the passive and active styles. Therefore, it is closest to the Yield Curve Plus Fund.

23. A is correct. Both statements regarding contingent immunization are correct.

24. B is correct. The Long-Term U.S. Corporate Bond Index's duration is closest to that of Hanover-Green's liabilities and reflects the corporate bonds that form the bulk of their assets.

25. A is correct. Warren is most likely correct regarding the effect on spreads and the probability of the bonds being callable. During most years, increases in issuance are associated with market-spread contraction. Bullet structures without call, put, or sinking fund options have come to dominate the credit market.

26. A is correct. OAS has limited use in the analysis of speculative grade bonds because default risk is excluded from the calculation.

STUDY SESSION 10
PORTFOLIO MANAGEMENT OF GLOBAL BONDS AND FIXED-INCOME DERIVATIVES

The previous study session builds on the basics of fixed-income portfolio management and introduces more targeted portfolio management strategies. This study session addresses international and emerging market strategies and the use of derivatives to manage interest rate and credit risks.

READING ASSIGNMENTS

Reading 30   Fixed-Income Portfolio Management—Part II
              Managing Investment Portfolios: A Dynamic Process,
              Third Edition, John L. Maginn, CFA, Donald L. Tuttle, CFA,
              Jerald E. Pinto, CFA, and Dennis W. McLeavey, CFA, editors

Reading 31   Hedging Mortgage Securities to Capture Relative Value
              Fixed Income Readings for the Chartered Financial Analyst®
              Program, Second Edition, Frank J. Fabozzi, CFA, editor

4% $4\tfrac{1}{16}$ $-\tfrac{3}{8}$

$5\tfrac{1}{2}$ $5\tfrac{1}{2}$ $-\tfrac{3}{8}$

$5\tfrac{1}{2}$ $21\tfrac{3}{16}$ $-\tfrac{1}{16}$

$20\tfrac{5}{8}$ $18\tfrac{1}{8}$ $+\tfrac{7}{8}$

$17\tfrac{3}{8}$ $6\tfrac{1}{2}$ $-\tfrac{1}{2}$

$6\tfrac{1}{2}$ $31\tfrac{1}{32}$ $-\tfrac{1}{8}$

$7\tfrac{1}{4}$ $15\tfrac{1}{16}$

$9\tfrac{1}{16}$ $\tfrac{9}{16}$

$7\tfrac{13}{16}$ $7\tfrac{15}{16}$

$7\tfrac{15}{16}$ $2\tfrac{1}{2}$ $+$

$2\tfrac{5}{8}$ $2\tfrac{11}{32}$ $2\tfrac{1}{4}$

$2\tfrac{3}{4}$ $2\tfrac{1}{4}$ $11\tfrac{3}{4}$ $+$

$61\tfrac{1}{2}$ $12\tfrac{1}{16}$ $11\tfrac{3}{8}$ $33\tfrac{1}{8}$ $-$

87 $33\tfrac{3}{4}$ 33 $25\tfrac{5}{8}$ $+$

602 $25\tfrac{5}{8}$ $24\tfrac{9}{16}$ $11\tfrac{7}{8}$ $+$

833 12 $11\tfrac{5}{8}$ $10\tfrac{1}{2}$ $-$

16 $10\tfrac{1}{2}$ $10\tfrac{1}{2}$ $15\tfrac{7}{8}$ $-$

78 $15\tfrac{7}{8}$ $15\tfrac{13}{16}$ $8\tfrac{1}{8}$ $+$

4508 $9\tfrac{1}{16}$ $8\tfrac{1}{4}$ $10\tfrac{1}{8}$

330 $11\tfrac{1}{4}$ $10\tfrac{1}{8}$

FIXED-INCOME PORTFOLIO MANAGEMENT—PART II

by H. Gifford Fong and Larry D. Guin, CFA

LEARNING OUTCOMES

The candidate should be able to:	Mastery
a. evaluate the effect of leverage on portfolio returns and duration;	☐
b. discuss the use of repurchase agreements (repos) to finance bond purchases and the factors that affect the repo rate;	☐
c. critique the use of standard deviation, target semivariance, shortfall risk, and value at risk as measures of fixed-income portfolio risk;	☐
d. demonstrate the advantages of using futures instead of cash market instruments to alter portfolio risk;	☐
e. construct and evaluate an immunization strategy based on interest rate futures;	☐
f. explain the use of interest rate swaps and options to alter portfolio cash flows and exposure to interest rate risk;	☐
g. compare and contrast default risk, credit spread risk, and downgrade risk and demonstrate the use of credit derivative instruments to address each risk in the context of a fixed-income portfolio;	☐
h. explain the sources of excess return for an international bond portfolio;	☐
i. evaluate 1) the change in value for a foreign bond when domestic interest rates change and 2) the bond's contribution to duration in a domestic portfolio given the duration of the foreign bond and the country beta;	☐
j. recommend and justify whether to hedge or not hedge currency risk in an international bond investment;	☐
k. illustrate how breakeven spread analysis can be used to evaluate the risk in seeking yield advantages across international bond markets;	☐
l. discuss the advantages and risks of investing in emerging market debt;	☐
m. discuss the criteria for selecting a fixed-income manager.	☐

Note: Part I of this reading is included in Study Session 9 under the title "Fixed-Income Portfolio Management—Part I."

Managing Investment Portfolios: A Dynamic Process, Third Edition, John L. Maginn, CFA, Donald L. Tuttle, CFA, Jerald E. Pinto, CFA, and Dennis W. McLeavey, CFA, editors. Copyright © 2007 by CFA Institute. Reprinted with permission.

105

5   OTHER FIXED-INCOME STRATEGIES

Whether managing against a bond market index or against a pool of liabilities, there are a range of combinations and alternatives that fixed-income managers might pursue in search of enhanced performance.

5.1 Combination Strategies

Although we have explained a number of basic portfolio strategies, the range of portfolio strategies really represents a continuum. At various phases during an interest rate cycle, a particular strategy may be most appropriate, but more often than not, a mix of alternatives is best for part or all of the cycle.

When decision makers have strong convictions, a one-strategy approach may be optimal; in the more likely case of uncertainty, strategy combinations may produce the best expected risk/return trade-off. A trade-off, for example, might be to tie a portion of the portfolio's risk and return to some baseline portfolio whose performance over the long term should provide satisfactory results, and actively manage the remaining portion. Retaining an active component preserves the opportunity for superior performance.

Two of the most popular combination strategies are active/passive and active/immunization. An **active/passive combination** allocates a core component of the portfolio to a passive strategy and the balance to an active component. The passive strategy would replicate an index or some sector of the market. In the active portion, the manager is free to pursue a return maximization strategy (at some given level of risk). A large pension fund might have a large allocation to a core strategy, consisting of an indexed portfolio, with additional active strategies chosen on the margin to enhance overall portfolio returns.

An **active/immunization combination** also consists of two component portfolios: The immunized portfolio provides an assured return over the planning horizon while the second portfolio uses an active high-return/high-risk strategy. The immunized portfolio is intended to provide an assured absolute return source. An example of an active immunization strategy is a surplus protection strategy for a fully funded pension plan in which the liabilities are immunized and the portion of assets equal to the surplus is actively managed.

5.2 Leverage

Frequently, a manager is permitted to use leverage as a tool to help increase the portfolio's return. In fact, the whole purpose of using leverage is to magnify the portfolio's rate of return. As long as the manager can earn a return on the investment of the borrowed funds that is greater than the interest cost, the portfolio's rate of return will be magnified. For example, if a manager can borrow €100 million at 4 percent (i.e., €4 million interest per year) and invest the funds to earn 5 percent (i.e., €5 million return per year), the difference of 1 percent (or €1 million) represents a profit that increases the rate of return on the entire portfolio. When a manager leverages a bond portfolio, however, the interest rate sensitivity of the equity in the portfolio usually increases, as will be discussed shortly.

5.2.1 Effects of Leverage

As we have just seen, the purpose of using leverage is to potentially magnify the portfolio's returns. Let us take a closer look at this magnification effect with the use of an example.

EXAMPLE 9

The Use of Leverage

Assume that a manager has $40 million of funds to invest. The manager then borrows an additional $100 million at 4 percent interest in the hopes of magnifying the rate of return on the portfolio. Further assume that the manager can invest all of the funds at a 4.5 percent rate of return. The return on the portfolio's components will be as follows:

	Borrowed Funds	Equity Funds
Amount Invested	$100,000,000	$40,000,000
Rate of Return @4.5%	4,500,000	1,800,000
Less Interest Expense @4.0%	4,000,000	0
Net Profitability	500,000	1,800,000
Rate of Return on Each Component	$\dfrac{\$500{,}000}{\$100{,}000{,}000} = 0.50\%$	$\dfrac{\$1{,}800{,}000}{\$40{,}000{,}000} = 4.50\%$

Because the profit on the borrowed funds accrues to the equity, the rate of return increases from 4.5 percent in the all-equity case to 5.75 percent when leverage is used:

$$\frac{\$1{,}800{,}000 + \$500{,}000}{\$40{,}000{,}000} = 5.75\%$$

Even though the net return on the borrowed funds is only 50 bps, the return on the portfolio's equity funds is increased by 125 bps (5.75 percent − 4.50 percent) because of the large amount of funds borrowed. The larger the amount of borrowed funds, the larger the magnification will be.

Leverage cuts both ways, however. If the manager cannot invest the borrowed money to earn at least the rate of interest, the leverage will serve as a drag on profitability. For example, in the illustration above, if the manager can only earn a 3.50 percent rate on the portfolio, the portfolio's net return will be 2.25 percent, which is 125 bps less than the unleveraged return. Exhibit 20 on the following page shows the portfolio return at various yields on the invested funds (and for varying levels of borrowed funds).

EXHIBIT 20	Portfolio Returns at Various Yields				
	Annual Rate of Return on Portfolio's Equity Funds				
Borrowed Funds	**2.50%**	**3.50%**	**4.50%**	**5.50%**	**6.50%**
$60,000,000	0.25%	2.75%	5.25%	7.75%	10.25%
80,000,000	−0.50	2.50	5.50	8.50	11.50
100,000,000	−1.25	2.25	5.75	9.25	12.75
120,000,000	−2.00	2.00	6.00	10.00	14.00
140,000,000	−2.75	1.75	6.25	10.75	15.25

Two relationships can be seen in the above exhibit:

1. The larger the amount of borrowed funds, the greater the variation in potential outcomes. In other words, the higher the leverage, the higher the risk.

2. The greater the variability in the annual return on the invested funds, the greater the variation in potential outcomes (i.e., the higher the risk).

Let us now examine the expressions for the returns on borrowed and equity components of a portfolio with leverage. Let us also develop the expression for the overall return on this portfolio. Suppose that

E = Amount of equity
B = Amount of borrowed funds
k = Cost of borrowing
r_F = Return on funds invested

R_B = Return on borrowed funds
= Profit on borrowed funds/Amount of borrowed funds
= $B \times (r_F - k)/B$
= $r_F - k$

As expected, R_B equals the return on funds invested less the cost of borrowing.

R_E = Return on equity
= Profit on equity/Amount of equity
= $E \times r_F/E$
= r_F

As expected, R_E equals the return on funds invested.

R_P = Portfolio rate of return
= (Profit on borrowed funds + Profit on equity)/Amount of equity
= $[B \times (r_F - k) + E \times r_F]/E$
= $r_F + (B/E) \times (r_F - k)$

For example, assume equity is €100 million and €50 million is borrowed at a rate of 6 percent per year. If the investment's return is 6.5 percent, portfolio return is 6.5 percent + (€50/€100)(6.5 percent − 6.0 percent) = 6.75 percent.

Besides magnification of returns, the second major effect of leveraging a bond portfolio is on the duration of the investor's equity in the portfolio. That duration is typically higher than the duration of an otherwise identical, but unleveraged, bond portfolio, given that the duration of liabilities is low relative to the duration of the assets they are financing. The expression for the duration of equity reflects the durations of assets and liabilities and their market values. With D_A denoting the duration of the assets (the bond portfolio) and D_L the duration of the liabilities (borrowings), the duration of equity, D_E, is given by[1]

$$D_E = \frac{D_A A - D_L L}{E}$$

In the above expression, A and L represent the market value of assets and liabilities, respectively.

To illustrate the calculation using the data from Example 9, suppose the $140 million bond portfolio (A = $140 million) has a duration of 4.00 (D_A = 4.00). However, $100 million of the value of the portfolio is borrowed (L = $100 million; $E = A - L$ = $40 million). Let us assume that the duration of the liabilities is 1.00 (D_L = 1.00). Then, stating quantities in millions of dollars,

$$D_E = \frac{4.00(\$140) - 1.00(\$100)}{\$40}$$
$$= \frac{\$460}{\$40}$$
$$= 11.50$$

Duration at 11.50 is almost three times larger than the duration of the unleveraged bond portfolio, 4.00.

As will be discussed later, derivatives such as interest rate futures are another means by which duration can be increased (or decreased, according to the investor's needs).

5.2.2 Repurchase Agreements

Managers may use a variety of financial instruments to increase the leverage of their portfolios. Among investment managers' favorite instruments is the repurchase agreement (also called a repo or RP). A **repurchase agreement** is a contract involving the sale of securities such as Treasury instruments coupled with an agreement to repurchase the same securities on a later date. The importance of the repo market is suggested by its colossal size, which is measured in trillions of dollars of transactions per year.

Although a repo is legally a sale and repurchase of securities, the repo transaction functions very much like a collateralized loan. In fact, the difference in selling price and purchase price is referred to as the "interest" on the transaction.[2] For example, a manager can borrow $10 million overnight at an annual

---

[1] See Saunders and Cornett (2003), Chapter 9, for related expressions.

[2] The repo "interest" should not be confused with the interest that is accruing on the security being used as loan collateral. The borrower is entitled to receive back the security that was put up as collateral as well as any interest paid or accrued on this instrument.

interest rate of 3 percent by selling Treasury securities valued at $10,000,000 and simultaneously agreeing to repurchase the same notes the following day for $10,000,833. The payment from the initial sale represents the principal amount of the loan; the excess of the repurchase price over the sale price ($833) is the interest on the loan.

In effect, the repo market presents a low-cost way for managers to borrow funds by providing Treasury securities as collateral. The market also enables investors (lenders) to earn a return above the risk-free rate on Treasury securities without sacrificing liquidity.

Term to maturity. RP agreements typically have short terms to maturity, usually overnight or a few days, although longer-term repos of several weeks or months may be negotiated. If a manager wants to permanently leverage the portfolio, he may simply "roll over" the overnight loans on a permanent basis by entering the RP market on a daily basis.

Transfer of securities (with related costs). Obviously, the buyer of the securities would like to take possession (or delivery) of the securities. Otherwise, complications may arise if the seller defaults on the repurchase of the securities. Also, if delivery is not insisted on, the potential exists for an unscrupulous seller to sell the same securities over and over again to a variety of buyers. Transfer agreements take a variety of forms:

▶ Physical delivery of the securities. Although this arrangement is possible, the high cost associated with physical delivery may make this method unworkable, particularly for short-term transactions.

▶ A common arrangement is for the securities to be processed by means of credits and debits to the accounts of banks acting as clearing agents for their customers (in the United States, these would be credit and debits to the banks' Federal Reserve Bank accounts). If desired, the banking system's wire transfer system may be used to transfer securities electronically in book-entry form from the seller (the borrower of funds) to the buyer (or lender of funds) and back later. This arrangement may be cheaper than physical delivery, but it still involves a variety of fees and transfer charges.

▶ Another common arrangement is to deliver the securities to a custodial account at the seller's bank. The bank takes possession of the securities and will see that both parties' interests are served; in essence, the bank acts as a trustee for both parties. This arrangement reduces the costs because delivery charges are minimized and only some accounting entries are involved.

▶ In some transactions, the buyer does not insist on delivery, particularly if the transaction is very short term (e.g., overnight), if the two parties have a long history of doing business together, and if the seller's financial standing and ethical reputation are both excellent.

Default risk and factors that affect the repo rate. Notice that, as long as delivery is insisted on, a repo is essentially a secured loan and its interest rate does not depend on the respective parties' credit qualities. If delivery is not taken (or is weakly secured), the financial stability and ethical characteristics of the parties become much more important.

A variety of factors will affect the repo rate. Among them are:

1. *Quality of the collateral.* The higher the quality of the securities, the lower the repo rate will be.

2. *Term of the repo.* Typically, the longer the maturity, the higher the rate will be. The very short end of the yield curve typically is upward sloping, leading to higher yields being required on longer-term repos.

3. *Delivery requirement.* If physical delivery of the securities is required, the rate will be lower because of the lower default risk; if the collateral is deposited with the bank of the borrower, the rate is higher; if delivery is not required, the rate will be still higher. As with all financial market transactions, there is a trade-off between risk and return: The greater control the repo investor (lender) has over the collateral, the lower the return will be.

4. *Availability of collateral.* Occasionally, some securities may be in short supply and difficult to obtain. In order to acquire these securities, the buyer of the securities (i.e., the lender of funds) may be willing to accept a lower rate. This situation typically occurs when the buyer needs securities for a short sale or to make delivery on a separate transaction. The more difficult it is to obtain the securities, the lower the repo rate.

5. *Prevailing interest rates in the economy.* The federal funds rate is often used to represent prevailing interest rates in the United States on overnight loans.[3] As interest rates in general increase, the rates on repo transactions will increase. In other words, the higher the federal funds rate, the higher the repo rate will be.

6. *Seasonal factors.* Although minor compared with the other factors, there is a seasonal effect on the repo rate because some institutions' supply of (and demand for) funds is influenced by seasonal factors.

The sections above demonstrate the motivation for managers to borrow money and discuss a major instrument used to raise this money—the repurchase agreement. Borrowed money often constitutes a single liability and, therefore, a single benchmark. Other managers are faced with multiple liabilities—managers of defined-benefit plans, for example. Regardless of whether the benchmark is single or multiple, a variety of investment strategies are available to the manager to satisfy the goal of generating cash flows to meet these liabilities. Let us now examine some of those strategies.

5.3 Derivatives-Enabled Strategies

Fixed-income securities and portfolios have sensitivities to various factors. These sensitivities are associated with return and risk characteristics that are key considerations in security selection and portfolio management. Factors include duration and convexity as well as additional factors for some securities such as liquidity and credit. We can call these sensitivities "factor exposures," and they provide a basis for understanding the return and risk characteristics of an investment.

The use of derivatives can be thought of as a means to create, reduce, or magnify the factor exposures of an investment. This modification can make use of basic derivatives such as futures and options in addition to combinations of factor exposures such as structured products.

In the following sections, we will review interest risk measurement and control and some of the most common derivatives used for such purposes, such as interest rate futures, interest rate swaps, credit options, credit swaps, and collateralized debt obligations.

5.3.1 Interest Rate Risk

The typical first-order source of risk for fixed-income portfolios is the duration or sensitivity to interest rate change. Conveniently, portfolio duration is

---

[3] The federal funds rate is the interest rate on an unsecured overnight loan (of excess reserves) from one bank to another bank.

a weighted average of durations of the individual securities making up the portfolio:

$$\text{Portfolio duration} = \frac{\sum_{i=1}^{n} D_i \times V_i}{V_p}$$

where

D_i = duration of security i
V_i = market value of security i
V_p = market value of the portfolio

In the course of managing a portfolio, the portfolio manager may want to replace one security in the portfolio with another security while keeping portfolio duration constant. To achieve this, the concept of dollar duration or the duration impact of a one dollar investment in a security can be used. Dollar duration is calculated using

$$\text{Dollar duration} = \frac{D_i \times V_i}{100}$$

where V_i = market value of the portfolio position if held; the price of one bond if not held.

To maintain the portfolio duration when one security is being exchanged for another, the dollar durations of the securities being exchanged must be matched. This matching can be accomplished by comparing the dollar durations of each side and thereby determining the necessary par value of the new bond. Specifically,

$$\text{New bond market value} = \frac{DD_O}{D_N} \times 100$$

where

DD_O = dollar duration of old bond
D_N = duration of new bond

EXAMPLE 10

Maintaining Portfolio Duration in Changing Portfolio Holdings

A portfolio manager wants to exchange one bond issue for another that he believes is undervalued. The existing position in the old bond has a market value of 5.5 million dollars. The bond has a price of $80 and a duration of 4. The bond's dollar duration is therefore 5.5 million × 4/100 or $220,000.

The new bond has a duration of 5 and a price of $90, resulting in a dollar duration of 4.5 ($90 × 5/100) per bond. What is the par value of the new bond needed to keep the duration of the portfolio constant?

Solution: The amount of the new bond required to keep the portfolio constant is $4.889 million ($220,000/4.5 × 100).

Although duration is an effective tool for measuring and controlling interest rate sensitivity, it is important to remember that there are limitations to this measure. For example, the accuracy of the measure decreases as the magnitude of the amount of interest rate change increases.

Duration is one measure of risk, related to sensitivity to interest rate changes. The following sections address statistical risk measures.

5.3.2 Other Risk Measures

The risk of a portfolio can be viewed as the uncertainty associated with the portfolio's future returns. Uncertainty implies dispersion of returns but raises the question, "What are the alternatives for measuring the dispersion of returns?"

If one assumes that portfolio returns have a normal (bell-shaped) distribution, then standard deviation is a useful measure. For a normal distribution, standard deviation has the property that plus and minus one standard deviation from the mean of the distribution covers 68 percent of the outcomes; plus and minus two standard deviations covers 95 percent of outcomes; and, plus and minus three standard deviations covers 99 percent of outcomes. The standard deviation squared (multiplied by itself) results in the variance of the distribution.

Realistically, the normality assumption may not be descriptive of the distribution, especially for portfolios having securities with embedded options such as puts, call features, prepayment risks, and so on.

Alternative measures have been used because of the restrictive conditions of a normal distribution. These have focused on the quantification of the undesirable left hand side of the distribution—the probability of returns less than the mean return. However, each of these alternatives has its own deficiency.

1. **Semivariance** measures the dispersion of the return outcomes that are below the target return.

   Deficiency: Although theoretically superior to the variance as a way of measuring risk, semivariance is not widely used in bond portfolio management for several reasons:[4]

   ▶ It is computationally challenging for large portfolios.

   ▶ To the extent that investment returns are symmetric, semivariance is proportional to variance and so contains no additional information. To the extent that returns may not be symmetric, return asymmetries are very difficult to forecast and may not be a good forecast of future risk anyway. Plus, because we estimate downside risk with only half the data, we lose statistical accuracy.

2. **Shortfall risk** (or risk of loss) refers to the probability of not achieving some specified return target. The focus is on that part of the distribution that represents the downside from the designated return level.

   Deficiency: Shortfall risk does not account for the magnitude of losses in money terms.

3. **Value at risk (VAR)** is an estimate of the loss (in money terms) that the portfolio manager expects to be exceeded with a given level of probability over a specified time period.

   Deficiency: VAR does not indicate the magnitude of the very worst possible outcomes.

---

[4] See Kahn (1997).

Unfortunately, a universal and comprehensive risk measure does not exist. Each alternative has its merits and limitations. It is important to keep in mind that the portfolio will have multiple risk exposures (factors) and the appropriate risk measures will vary with the particular requirements of the portfolio.

5.3.3 Bond Variance versus Bond Duration

The expected return of a portfolio is the weighted average of the expected returns of each individual security in the portfolio. The weight is calculated as the market value of each security as a percentage of the market value of the portfolio as a whole. The variance of a portfolio is determined by the weight of each security in the portfolio, the variance of each security, and the covariance between each pair of securities.

Two major problems are associated with using the variance or standard deviation to measure bond portfolio risk:

1. The number of the estimated parameters increases dramatically as the number of the bonds considered increases. The total number of variances and covariances that needs to be estimated can be found as follows:

    Number of bonds × (Number of bonds + 1)/2

    If a portfolio has 1,000 bonds, there would be 500,500 [i.e., 1,000 × (1,000 + 1) / 2] different terms to be estimated.

2. Accurately estimating the variances and covariances is difficult. Because the characteristics of a bond change as time passes, the estimation based on the historical bond data may not be useful. For instance, a bond with five years to maturity has a different volatility than a four-year or six-year bond. Besides the time to maturity factor, some securities may have embedded options, such as calls, puts, sinking fund provisions, and prepayments. These features change the security characteristics dramatically over time and further limit the use of historical estimates.

Because of the problems mentioned above, it is difficult to use standard deviation to measure portfolio risk.

We now turn our attention to a variety of strategies based on derivatives products. A number of these derivatives products are shown in Exhibit 21 and are explained in the following sections.

5.3.4 Interest Rate Futures

A **futures contract** is an enforceable contract between a buyer (seller) and an established exchange or its clearinghouse in which the buyer (seller) agrees to take (make) delivery of something at a specified price at the end of a designated period of time. The "something" that can be bought or sold is called the **underlying** (as in *underlying asset* or *underlying instrument*). The price at which the parties agree to exchange the underlying in the future is called the **futures price**. The designated date at which the parties must transact is called the **settlement date** or delivery date.

When an investor takes a new position in the market by buying a futures contract, the investor is said to be in a long position or to be long futures. If, instead, the investor's opening position is the sale of a futures contract, the investor is said to be in a short position or to be short futures.

EXHIBIT 21	Derivatives-Enabled Strategies

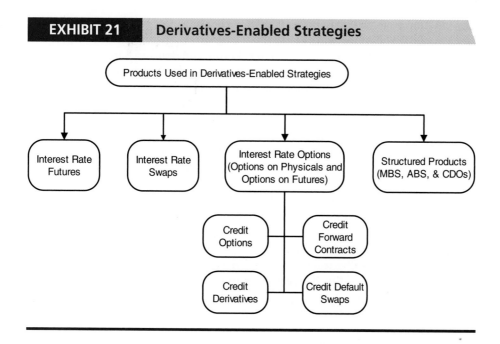

Interest rate futures contracts are traded on short-term instruments (for example, Treasury bills and the Eurodollars) and longer-term instruments (for example, Treasury notes and bonds). Because the Treasury futures contract plays an important role in the strategies we discuss below, it is worth reviewing the nuances of this contract. The government bond futures of a number of other countries, such as Japan and Germany, are similar to the U.S. Treasury futures contract.

The 30-year Treasury bond and 10-year U.S. Treasury note futures contracts are both important contracts. The 30-year contract is an important risk management tool in ALM; the 10-year U.S. Treasury note futures contract has become more important than the 30-year contract in terms of liquidity. The U.S. Treasury ceased issuing its 30-year bond in 2002 but reintroduced it in 2006. The following discussion focuses on the 30-year bond futures contract, which shares the same structure as the 10-year note futures contract.

The underlying instrument for the Treasury bond futures contract is $100,000 par value of a hypothetical 30-year, 6 percent coupon bond. Although price and yield of the Treasury bond futures contract are quoted in terms of this hypothetical Treasury bond, the seller of the futures contract has the choice of several actual Treasury bonds that are acceptable to deliver. The Chicago Board of Trade (CBOT) allows the seller to deliver any Treasury bond that has at least 15 years to maturity from the date of delivery if not callable; in the case of callable bonds, the issue must not be callable for at least 15 years from the first day of the delivery month. To settle the contract, an acceptable bond must be delivered.

The delivery process for the Treasury bond futures contract makes the contract interesting. In the settlement month, the seller of a futures contract (the short) is required to deliver to the buyer (the long) $100,000 par value of a 6 percent, 30-year Treasury bond. No such bond exists, however, so the seller must choose from other acceptable deliverable bonds that the exchange has specified.

To make delivery equitable to both parties, and to tie cash to futures prices, the CBOT has introduced **conversion factors** for determining the invoice price of each acceptable deliverable Treasury issue against the Treasury bond futures contract. The conversion factor is determined by the CBOT before a contract with a specific settlement date begins trading. The conversion factor is based on the price that a deliverable bond would sell for at the beginning of the delivery month if it were to yield 6 percent. The conversion factor is constant throughout the trading period of the futures contract. The short must notify the long of the actual bond that will be delivered one day before the delivery date.

In selecting the issue to be delivered, the short will select, from all the deliverable issues and bond issues auctioned during the contract life, the one that is least expensive. This issue is referred to as the **cheapest-to-deliver** (CTD). The CTD plays a key role in the pricing of this futures contract.

In addition to the option of which acceptable Treasury issue to deliver, sometimes referred to as the **quality option** or swap option, the short position has two additional options granted under CBOT delivery guidelines. The short position is permitted to decide when in the delivery month actual delivery will take place—a feature called the **timing option**. The other option is the right of the short position to give notice of intent to deliver up to 8:00 p.m. Chicago time after the closing of the exchange (3:15 p.m. Chicago time) on the date when the futures settlement price has been fixed. This option is referred to as the **wild card option**. The quality option, the timing option, and the wild card option (referred to in sum as the **delivery options**) mean that the long position can never be sure which Treasury bond will be delivered or when it will be delivered.

Modeled after the Treasury bond futures contract, the underlying for the Treasury note futures contract is $100,000 par value of a hypothetical 10-year, 6 percent Treasury note. Several acceptable Treasury issues may be delivered by the short. An issue is acceptable if the maturity is not less than 6.5 years and not greater than 10 years from the first day of the delivery month. The delivery options granted to the short position are the same as for the Treasury bond futures contract.

5.3.4.1 Strategies with Interest Rate Futures   The prices of an interest rate futures contract are negatively correlated with the change in interest rates. When interest rates rise, the prices of the deliverable bonds will drop and the futures price will decline; when interest rates drop, the price of the deliverable bonds will rise and the futures price will increase. Therefore, buying a futures contract will increase a portfolio's sensitivity to interest rates, and the portfolio's duration will increase. On the other hand, selling a futures contract will lower a portfolio's sensitivity to interest rates and the portfolio's duration will decrease.

There are a number of advantages to using futures contracts rather than the cash markets for purposes of portfolio duration control. Liquidity and cost-effectiveness are clear advantages to using futures contracts. Furthermore, for duration reduction, shorting the contract (i.e., selling the contract) is very effective. In general, because of the depth of the futures market and low transaction costs, futures contracts represent a very efficient tool for timely duration management.

Various strategies can use interest rate futures contracts and other derivative products, including the following.

Duration Management   A frequently used portfolio strategy targets a specific duration target such as the duration of the benchmark index. In these situations, futures are used to maintain the portfolio's duration at its target value when the weighted average duration of the portfolio's securities deviate from the target. The use of futures permits a timely and cost-effective modification of the portfolio duration.

More generally, whenever the current portfolio duration is different from the desired portfolio duration, interest rate futures can be an effective tool. For example, interest rate futures are commonly used in interest rate anticipation strategies, which involve reducing the portfolio's duration when the expectation is that interest rates will rise and increasing duration when the expectation is that interest rates will decline.

To change a portfolio's dollar duration so that it equals a specific target duration, the portfolio manager needs to estimate the number of future contracts that must be purchased or sold.

$$\text{Portfolio's target dollar duration} = \text{Current portfolio's dollar duration without futures} + \text{Dollar duration of the futures contracts}$$

$$\text{Dollar duration of futures} = \text{Dollar duration per futures contract} \times \text{Number of futures contracts}$$

The number of futures contracts that is needed to achieve the portfolio's target dollar duration then can be estimated by:

$$\text{Approximate number of contracts} = \frac{(D_T - D_I)\, P_I}{\text{Dollar duration per futures contract}}$$

$$= \frac{(D_T - D_I)\, P_I}{D_{CTD} P_{CTD}} \times \frac{D_{CTD} P_{CTD}}{\text{Dollar duration per futures contract}}$$

$$= \frac{(D_T - D_I)\, P_I}{D_{CTD} P_{CTD}} \times \text{Conversion factor for the CTD bond}$$

where

D_T = target duration for the portfolio
D_I = initial duration for the portfolio
P_I = initial market value of the portfolio
D_{CTD} = the duration of the cheapest-to-deliver bond
P_{CTD} = the price of the cheapest-to-deliver bond

Notice that if the manager wishes to increase the duration, then D_T will be greater than D_I and the equation will have a positive sign. Thus, futures contracts will be purchased. The opposite is true if the objective is to shorten the portfolio duration. It should be kept in mind that the expression given is only an approximation.

An expanded definition of D_{CTD} would be the duration of the cheapest-to-deliver bond to satisfy the futures contract. Whenever phrasing similar to the following is used, "a futures contract priced at y with a duration of x," what x actually represents is the duration of the cheapest-to-deliver bond to satisfy the futures contract.

EXAMPLE 11

Duration Management with Futures

A U.K.-based pension fund has a large portfolio of British corporate and government bonds. The market value of the bond portfolio is £50 million. The duration of the portfolio is 9.52. An economic consulting firm that provides economic forecasts to the pension fund has advised the fund that the chance of an upward shift in interest rates in the near term is greater than the market currently perceives. In view of this advice, the pension fund has decided to reduce the duration of its bond portfolio to 7.5 by using a futures contract priced at £100,000 that has a duration of 8.47. Assume that the conversion factor for the futures contract is 1.1.

1. Would the pension fund need to buy futures contracts or sell?

2. Approximately, how many futures contracts would be needed to change the duration of the bond portfolio?

Solution to 1: Because the pension fund desires to reduce the duration, it would need to sell futures contracts.

Solution to 2:

D_T = target duration for the portfolio = 7.5

D_I = initial duration for the portfolio = 9.52

P_I = initial market value of the portfolio = £50 million

D_{CTD} = the duration of the cheapest-to-deliver bond = 8.47

P_{CTD} = the price of the cheapest-to-deliver bond = £100,000

Conversion factor for the cheapest-to-deliver bond = 1.1

Approximate number of contracts

$$= \frac{(D_T - D_I)P_I}{D_{CTD}P_{CTD}} \times \text{Conversion factor for the CTD bond}$$

$$= \frac{(7.5 - 9.52) \times 50,000,000}{8.47 \times 100,000} \times 1.1 = -131.17.$$

Thus, the pension fund would need to sell 131 futures contracts to achieve the desired reduction in duration.

Duration Hedging   Fixed-income portfolios are commonly used for purposes of asset/liability management in which portfolio assets are managed to fund a specified set of liabilities. In the case of immunization, the use of duration is critical. The matching of the portfolio duration to the duration of liabilities to be funded by the portfolio is a form of hedging. Offsetting (reducing) the interest rate exposure of a cash position in a portfolio is also a form of hedging. Whenever an interest rate exposure must be reduced, futures can be used to accomplish the hedge. The following discussion reviews several important issues in hedging an existing bond position.

Hedging with futures contracts involves taking a futures position that offsets an existing interest rate exposure. If the hedge is properly constructed, as cash and futures prices move together any loss realized by the hedger from one position (whether cash or futures) will be offset by a profit on the other position.

In practice, hedging is not that simple. The outcome of a hedge will depend on the relationship between the cash price and the futures price both when a hedge is placed and when it is lifted. The difference between the cash price and the futures price is called the **basis**. The risk that the basis will change in an unpredictable way is called **basis risk**.

In some hedging applications, the bond to be hedged is not identical to the bond underlying the futures contract. This kind of hedging is referred to as **cross hedging**. There may be substantial basis risk in cross hedging, that is, the relationship between the two instruments may change and lead to a loss. An unhedged position is exposed to **price risk**, the risk that the cash market price will move adversely. A hedged position substitutes basis risk for price risk.

Conceptually, cross hedging requires dealing with two additional complications. The first complication is the relationship between the cheapest-to-deliver security and the futures contract. The second is the relationship between the security to be hedged and the cheapest-to-deliver security.

The key to minimizing risk in a cross hedge is to choose the right **hedge ratio**. The hedge ratio depends on exposure weighting, or weighting by relative changes in value. The purpose of a hedge is to use gains or losses from a futures position to offset any difference between the target sale price and the actual sale price of the asset. Accordingly, the hedge ratio is chosen with the intention of matching the volatility (specifically, the dollar change) of the futures contract to the volatility of the asset. In turn, the factor exposure drives volatility. Consequently, the hedge ratio is given by:

$$\text{Hedge ratio} = \frac{\text{Factor exposure of the bond (portfolio) to be hedged}}{\text{Factor exposure of hedging instrument}}$$

As the formula shows, if the bond to be hedged has greater factor exposure than the hedging instrument, more of the hedging instrument will be needed.

Although it might be fairly clear why factor exposure is important in determining the hedge ratio, "exposure" has many definitions. For hedging purposes, we are concerned with exposure in absolute money terms. To calculate the dollar factor exposure of a bond (portfolio), one must know the precise time at which exposure is to be calculated as well as the price or yield at which to calculate exposure (because higher yields generally reduce dollar exposure for a given yield change).

The relevant point in the life of the bond for calculating exposure is the point at which the hedge will be lifted. Exposure at any other point is essentially irrelevant, because the goal is to lock in a price or rate only on that particular day. Similarly, the relevant yield at which to calculate exposure initially is the target yield. Consequently, the "factor exposure of the bond to be hedged" referred to in the formula is the dollar duration of the bond on the hedge lift date, calculated at its current implied forward rate. The dollar duration is the product of the price of the bond and its duration.

The relative price exposures of the bonds to be hedged and the cheapest-to-deliver bond are easily obtained from the assumed sale date and target prices. In the formula for the hedge ratio, we need the exposure not of the cheapest-to-deliver bond, but of the hedging instrument, that is, of the futures contract. Fortunately, knowing the exposure of the bond to be hedged relative to the cheapest-to-deliver bond and the exposure of the cheapest-to-deliver bond relative to the futures contract, the relative exposures that define the hedge ratio can be easily obtained as follows:

$$\begin{aligned}\text{Hedge ratio} &= \frac{\text{Factor exposure of bond to be hedged}}{\text{Factor exposure of futures contract}}\\[2mm] &= \frac{\text{Factor exposure of bond to be hedged}}{\text{Factor exposure of CTD bond}}\\[2mm] &\quad\times \frac{\text{Factor exposure of CTD bond}}{\text{Factor exposure of futures contract}}\end{aligned}$$

Considering only interest rate exposure and assuming a fixed yield spread between the bond to be hedged and the cheapest-to-deliver bond, the hedge ratio is

$$\text{Hedge ratio} = \frac{D_H P_H}{D_{CTD} P_{CTD}} \times \text{Conversion factor for the CTD bond}$$

where D_H = the duration of the bond to be hedged and P_H = the price of the bond to be hedged. The product of the duration and the price is the dollar duration.

Another refinement in the hedging strategy is usually necessary for hedging nondeliverable securities. This refinement concerns the assumption about the relative yield spread between the cheapest-to-deliver bond and the bond to be hedged. In the discussion so far, we have assumed that the yield spread is constant over time. In practice, however, yield spreads are not constant over time. They vary with the maturity of the instruments in question and the level of rates, as well as with many unpredictable factors.

A hedger can use regression analysis to capture the relationship between yield levels and yield spreads. For hedging purposes, the variables are the yield on the bond to be hedged and the yield on the cheapest-to-deliver bond. The regression equation takes the form:

Yield on bond to be hedged = a + b(Yield on CTD bond) + Error term

The regression procedure provides an estimate of b, called the **yield beta**, which is the expected relative change in the two bonds. The error term accounts for the fact that the relationship between the yields is not perfect and contains a certain amount of noise. The regression will, however, give an estimate of a and b so that, over the sample period, the average error is zero. Our formula for the hedge ratio assumes a constant spread and implicitly assumes that the yield beta in the regression equals 1.0.

The formula for the hedge ratio can be revised to incorporate the impact of the yield beta by including the yield beta as a multiplier.

$$\text{Hedge ratio} = \frac{D_H P_H}{D_{CTD} P_{CTD}} \times \text{Conversion factor for the CTD bond} \times \text{Yield beta}$$

The effectiveness of a hedge may be evaluated after the hedge has been lifted. The analysis of hedging error can provide managers with meaningful insights that can be useful subsequently.

The three major sources of hedging error are incorrect duration calculations, inaccurate projected basis values, and inaccurate yield beta estimates. A good valuation model is critical to ensure the correct calculation of duration, especially for portfolios containing securities with embedded options.

5.3.5 Interest Rate Swaps

An **interest rate swap** is a contract between two parties (counterparties) to exchange periodic interest payments based on a specified dollar amount of principal (**notional principal amount**). The interest payments on the notional principal amount are calculated by multiplying the specified interest rate times the notional principal amount. These interest payments are the only amounts exchanged; the notional principal amount is only a reference value.

The traditional swap has one party (**fixed-rate payer**) obligated to make periodic payments at a fixed rate in return for the counter party (**floating-rate payer**) agreeing to make periodic payments based on a benchmark floating rate.

The benchmark interest rates used for the floating rate in an interest rate swap are those on various money market instruments: Treasury bills, the London Interbank Offered Rate (LIBOR), commercial paper, bankers' acceptances, certificates of deposit, the federal funds rate, and the prime rate.

5.3.5.1 Dollar Duration of an Interest Rate Swap   As with any fixed-income contract, the value of a swap will change as interest rates change and dollar duration is a measure of interest-rate sensitivity. From the perspective of the party who pays floating and receives fixed, the interest rate swap position can be viewed as

Long a fixed-rate bond + Short a floating-rate bond

This means that the dollar duration of an interest rate swap from the perspective of a floating-rate payer is just the difference between the dollar duration of the two bond positions that make up the swap:

Dollar duration of a swap	=	Dollar duration of a fixed-rate bond	−	Dollar duration of a floating-rate bond

The dollar duration of the fixed-rate bond chiefly determines the dollar duration of the swap because the dollar duration of a floating-rate bond is small.

5.3.5.2 Applications of a Swap to Asset/Liability Management   An interest rate swap can be used to alter the cash flow characteristics of an institution's assets or liabilities so as to provide a better match between assets and liabilities. More specifically, an institution can use interest rate swaps to alter the cash flow characteristics of its assets or liabilities: changing them from fixed to floating or from floating to fixed. In general, swaps can be used to change the duration of a portfolio or an entity's surplus (the difference between the market value of the assets and the present value of the liabilities).

Instead of using an interest rate swap, the same objectives can be accomplished by taking an appropriate position in a package of forward contracts or appropriate cash market positions. The advantage of an interest rate swap is that it is, from a transaction costs standpoint, a more efficient vehicle for accomplishing an asset/liability objective. In fact, this advantage is the primary reason for the growth of the interest rate swap market.

5.3.6 *Interest Rate Options*

Interest rate options can be written on cash instruments or futures. Several exchange-traded option contracts have underlying instruments that are debt instruments. These contracts are referred to as **options on physicals**. In general, however, **options on futures** have been far more popular than options on physicals. Market participants have made increasingly greater use of over-the-counter options on Treasury and mortgage-backed securities.

Besides options on fixed-income securities, there are OTC options on the shape of the yield curve or the yield spread between two securities (such as the spread between mortgage passthrough securities and Treasuries or between double-A rated corporates and Treasuries). A discussion of these option contracts, however, is beyond the scope of this section.

An option on a futures contract, commonly referred to as a futures option, gives the buyer the right to buy from or sell to the writer a designated futures contract at the strike price at any time during the life of the option. If the futures option is a call option, the buyer has the right to purchase one designated futures contract at the strike price. That is, the buyer has the right to acquire a long futures position in the designated futures contract. If the buyer exercises the call option, the writer of the call acquires a corresponding short position in the futures contract.

A put option on a futures contract grants the buyer the right to sell one designated futures contract to the writer at the strike price. That is, the option buyer has the right to acquire a short position in the designated futures contract. If the buyer exercises the put option, the writer acquires a corresponding long position in the designated futures contract.

5.3.6.1 Options and Duration   The price of an interest rate option will depend on the price of the underlying instrument, which depends in turn on the interest rate on the underlying instrument. Thus, the price of an interest rate option depends on the interest rate on the underlying instrument. Consequently, the interest-rate sensitivity or duration of an interest rate option can be determined.

The duration of an option can be calculated with the following formula:

$$\text{Duration for an option} = \text{Delta of option} \times \text{Duration of underlying instrument} \times (\text{Price of underlying})/(\text{Price of option instrument})$$

As expected, the duration of an option depends on the duration of the underlying instrument. It also depends on the price responsiveness of the option to a change in the underlying instrument, as measured by the option's **delta**. The leverage created by a position in an option comes from the last ratio in the formula. The higher the price of the underlying instrument relative to the price of the option, the greater the leverage (i.e., the more exposure to interest rates for a given level of investment).

The interaction of all three factors (the duration of the underlying, the option delta, leverage) affects the duration of an option. For example, all else equal, a deep out-of-the-money option has higher leverage than a deep in-the-money option, but the delta of the former is less than that of the latter.

Because the delta of a call option is positive, the duration of an interest rate call option will be positive. Thus, when interest rates decline, the value of an interest rate call option will rise. A put option, however, has a delta that is negative. Thus, duration is negative. Consequently, when interest rates rise, the value of a put option rises.

5.3.6.2 Hedging with Options   The most common application of options is to hedge a portfolio. There are two hedging strategies in which options are used to protect against a rise in interest rates: **protective put** buying and **covered call writing**. The protective put buying strategy establishes a minimum value for the portfolio but allows the manager to benefit from a decline in rates. The establishment of a floor for the portfolio is not without a cost. The performance of the portfolio will be reduced by the cost of the put option.

Unlike the protective put strategy, covered call writing is not entered into with the sole purpose of protecting a portfolio against rising rates. The covered call writer, believing that the market will not trade much higher or much lower than its present level, sells out-of-the-money calls against an existing bond portfolio. The sale of the calls brings in premium income that provides partial protection in case rates increase. The premium received does not, of course, provide the kind of protection that a long put position provides, but it does provide some additional income that can be used to offset declining prices. If, on the other hand, rates fall, portfolio appreciation is limited because the short call position constitutes a liability for the seller, and this liability increases as rates go down. Consequently, there is limited upside potential for the covered call writer. Covered call writing yields best results if prices are essentially going nowhere; the added income from the sale of options would then be obtained without sacrificing any gains.

Options can also be used by managers seeking to protect against a decline in reinvestment rates resulting from a drop in interest rates. The purchase of call options can be used in such situations. The sale of put options provides limited protection in much the same way that a covered call writing strategy does in protecting against a rise in interest rates.

Interest rate **caps**—call options or series of call options on an interest rate to create a cap (or ceiling) for funding cost—and interest rate **floors**—put options or series of put options on an interest rate—can create a minimum earning rate. The combination of a cap and a floor creates a **collar**.

Banks that borrow short term and lend long term are usually exposed to short-term rate fluctuation. Banks can use caps to effectively place a maximum interest rate on short-term borrowings; specifically, a bank will want the **cap rate** (the exercise interest rate for a cap) plus the cost of the cap to be less than its long-term lending rate. When short-term rates increase, a bank will be protected by the ceiling created by the cap rate. When short-term rates decline, the caps will expire worthless but the bank is better off because its cost of funds has decreased. If they so desire, banks can reduce the cost of purchasing caps by selling floors, thereby giving up part of the potential benefit from a decline in short-term rates.

On the opposite side, a life insurance company may offer a guaranteed investment contract that provides a guaranteed fixed rate and invest the proceeds in a floating-rate instrument. To protect itself from a rate decline while retaining the benefits from an interest rate increase, the insurance company may purchase a floor. If the insurance company wants to reduce the costs of purchasing a floor, it can sell a cap and give up some potential benefit from the rate increase.

5.3.7 Credit Risk Instruments

A given fixed-income security usually contains several risks. The interest rate may change and cause the value of the security to change (interest rate risk); the security may be prepaid or called (option risk); and the value of the issue may be affected by the risk of defaults, credit downgrades, and widening credit spreads (credit risk). In this section, we will focus on understanding and hedging credit risk.

Credit risk can be sold to another party. In return for a fee, another party will accept the credit risk of an underlying financial asset or institution. This party, called the **credit protection seller**, may be willing to take on this risk for several reasons. Perhaps the credit protection seller believes that the credit of an issuer will improve in a favorable economic environment because of a strong stock market and strong financial results. Also, some major corporate events, such as mergers and acquisitions, may improve corporate ratings. Finally, the corporate debt refinancing caused by a friendlier interest rate environment and more favorable lending rates would be a positive credit event.

There are three types of credit risk: default risk, credit spread risk, and downgrade risk. Default risk is the risk that the issuer may fail to meet its obligations. **Credit spread risk** is the risk that the spread between the rate for a risky bond and the rate for a default risk-free bond (like U.S. treasury securities) may vary after the purchase. **Downgrade risk** is the risk that one of the major rating agencies will lower its rating for an issuer, based on its specified rating criteria.

5.3.7.1 Products That Transfer Credit Risk   Credit risk may be represented by various types of credit events, including a credit spread change, a rating downgrade, or default. A variety of derivative products, known as **credit derivatives**, exist to package and transfer the credit risk of a financial instrument or institution to another party. The first type of credit derivative we examine is credit options.

Credit Options   Unlike ordinary debt options that protect investors against interest rate risk, credit options are structured to offer protection against credit risk. The triggering events of credit options can be based either on 1) the value decline of the underlying asset or 2) the spread change over a risk-free rate.

1. *Credit Options Written on an Underlying Asset*: **Binary credit options** provide payoffs contingent on the occurrence of a specified negative credit event.

   In the case of a binary credit option, the negative event triggering a specified payout to the option buyer is default of a designated reference entity. The term "binary" means that there are only two possible scenarios: default or no default. If the credit has not defaulted by the maturity of the option, the buyer receives nothing. The option buyer pays a premium to the option seller for the protection afforded by the option.

   The payoff of a binary credit option can also be based on the credit rating of the underlying asset. A credit put option pays for the difference between the strike price and the market price when a specified credit event occurs and pays nothing if the event does not occur. For example, a binary credit put option may pay the option buyer $X - V(t)$ if the rating of Bond A is below investment-grade and pay nothing otherwise, where X is the strike price and $V(t)$ is the market value of Bond A at time t. The strike price could be a fixed number, such as $200,000, or, more commonly, expressed as a spread (**strike spread**) that is used to determine the strike price for the payoff when the credit event occurs.

EXAMPLE 12

Binary Credit Option

The manager of an investment-grade fixed-income fund is concerned about the possibility of a rating downgrade of Alpha Motors, Inc. The fund's holding in this company consists of 5,000 bonds with a par value of $1,000 each. The fund manager doesn't want to liquidate the holdings in this bond, and instead decides to purchase a binary credit put option on the bond of Alpha Motors. This option expires in six months and pays the option buyer if the rating of Alpha Motors' bond on expiration date is below investment grade (Standard & Poor's/Moody's BB/Ba or lower). The payoff, if any, is the difference between the strike price and the value of the bond at expiration. The fund paid a premium of $130,000 to purchase the option on 5,000 bonds.

1. What would be the payoff and the profit if the rating of Alpha Motors' bond on expiration date is below investment grade and the value of the bond is $870?

2. What would be the payoff and the profit if the rating of Alpha Motors' bond on expiration date is investment grade and the value of the bond is $980?

> **Solution to 1:** The bond is in the money at expiration because its rating is below investment grade. The payoff on each bond is $1,000 − $870 = $130. Therefore, the payoff on 5,000 bonds is 5,000 × $130 = $650,000. The profit is $650,000 − $130,000 = $520,000.
>
> **Solution to 2:** The bond is out of the money at expiration because its rating is above investment grade. The payoff on each bond is zero. The premium paid of $130,000 is the loss.

2. *Credit Spread Options*: Another type of credit option is a call option in which the payoff is based on the spread over a benchmark rate. The payoff function of a credit spread call option is as follows:

$$\text{Payoff} = \text{Max} \left[(\text{Spread at the option maturity} - K) \times \text{Notional amount} \times \text{Risk factor, } 0 \right]$$

where K is the strike spread, and the risk factor is the value change of the security for a one basis point change in the credit spread. Max[A, B] means "A or B, whichever is greater."

Credit Forwards　Credit forwards are another form of credit derivatives. Their payoffs are based on bond values or credit spreads. There are a buyer and a seller for a credit forward contract. For the buyer of a credit forward contract, the payoff functions as follows:

$$\text{Payoff} = (\text{Credit spread at the forward contract maturity} - \text{Contracted credit spread}) \times \text{Notional amount} \times \text{Risk factor}$$

If a credit forward contract is symmetric, the buyer of a credit forward contract benefits from a widening credit spread and the seller benefits from a narrowing credit spread. The maximum the buyer can lose is limited to the payoff amount in the event that the credit spread becomes zero. In a credit spread option, by contrast, the maximum that the option buyer can lose is the option premium.

Example 13 illustrates the payoff of credit spread forward, and Example 14 contrasts binary credit options, credit spread options, and credit spread forwards.

EXAMPLE 13

Evaluating the Payoff of a Credit Spread Forward

The current credit spread on bonds issued by Hi-Fi Technologies relative to same maturity government debt is 200 bps. The manager of Stable Growth Funds believes that the credit situation of Hi-Fi Technologies will deteriorate over the next few months, resulting in a higher credit spread on its bonds. He decides to buy a six-month credit spread forward contract with the current spread as the contracted spread. The forward contract has a notional amount of $5 million and a risk factor of 4.3.

1. On the settlement date six months later, the credit spread on Hi-Fi Technologies' bonds is 150 bps. How much is the payoff to Stable Growth Funds?

2. How much would the payoff to Stable Growth Funds be if the credit spread on the settlement date is 300 bps?

3. How much is the maximum possible loss to Stable Growth Funds?

4. How much would the payoffs in Parts 1, 2, and 3 above be to the party that took the opposite side of the forward contract?

Solutions:

The payoff to Stable Growth Funds would be:

$$\text{Payoff} = (\text{Credit spread at the forward contract maturity} - 0.020) \times \$5 \text{ million} \times 4.3$$

1. Payoff = $(0.015 - 0.020) \times \$5$ million $\times 4.3 = -\$107,500$, a loss of $107,500.

2. Payoff = $(0.030 - 0.020) \times \$5$ million $\times 4.3 = \$215,000$.

3. Stable Growth Funds would have the maximum loss in the unlikely event of the credit spread at the forward contract maturity being zero. So, the worst possible payoff would be $(0.000 - 0.020) \times \$5$ million $\times 4.3 = -\$430,000$, a loss of $430,000.

4. The payoff to party that took the opposite side of the forward contract, that is, the party that took the position that credit spread would decrease, would be:

$$\text{Payoff} = (0.020 - \text{Credit spread at the forward contract maturity}) \times \$5 \text{ million} \times 4.3$$

The payoffs to this party would be the opposite of the payoffs to Stable Growth Fund. So, the payoffs would be a gain of $107,500 in Part 1, a loss of $215,000 in Part 2, and a maximum possible gain of $430,000 in Part 3. Because there is no limit to the increase in credit spread, the maximum possible loss for this party is limitless.

EXAMPLE 14

Binary Credit Option, Credit Spread Option, and Credit Spread Forward

The portfolio manager of a fixed-income fund is concerned about possible adverse developments in three of the bond holdings of the fund. The reason for his concern is different for the three bond holdings. In particular, he is concerned about the possibility of a credit rating downgrade for Company X, the possibility of a credit default by Company Y, and the possibility of a widening credit spread for Company Z. The portfolio manager contacts a credit derivative dealer. The dealer tells him that his firm offers several credit instruments, some of which are given on the next page.

For each of the following, indicate if it could be used to cover one or more of the three risks the portfolio manager is concerned about.

1. A binary credit put option with the credit event specified as a default by the company on its debt obligations.
2. A binary credit put option with the credit event specified as a credit rating downgrade.
3. A credit spread put option where the underlying is the level of the credit spread.
4. A credit spread call option where the underlying is the level of the credit spread.
5. A credit spread forward, with the credit derivative dealer firm taking a position that the credit spread will decrease.

Solution to 1: The fixed-income fund could purchase this put option to cover the risk of a credit default by Company Y.

Solution to 2: The fixed-income fund could purchase this put option to cover the risk of a credit rating downgrade for Company X.

Solution to 3: This option is not useful to cover any of the three risks. A credit spread put option where the underlying is the level of the credit spread is useful if one believes that credit spread will decline.

Solution to 4: The fixed-income fund could purchase this credit spread call option where the underlying is the level of the credit spread to cover the risk of an increased credit spread for Company Z.

Solution to 5: The fixed-income fund could enter into this forward contract to cover the risk of an increased credit spread for Company Z. The dealer firm would take a position that the credit spread will decrease, while the fixed-income fund would take the opposite position.

Credit Swaps   A number of different products can be classified as credit swaps, including credit default swaps, asset swaps, total return swaps, credit-linked notes, synthetic collateralized bond obligations, and basket default swaps. Among all credit derivative products, the **credit default swap** is the most popular and is commonly recognized as the basic building block of the credit derivative market. Therefore, we focus our discussion on credit default swaps.

A credit default swap is a contract that shifts credit exposure of an asset issued by a specified **reference entity** from one investor (protection buyer) to another investor (protection seller). The protection buyer usually makes regular payments, the swap premium payments (default swap spread), to the protection seller. For short-dated credit, investors may pay this fee up front. In the case of a **credit event**, the protection seller compensates the buyer for the loss on the investment, and the settlement can take the form of either physical delivery or a negotiated cash payment equivalent to the market value of the defaulted securities. The transaction can be schematically represented as in Exhibit 22.

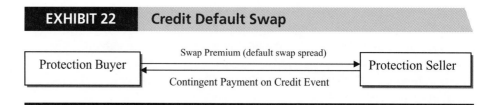

EXHIBIT 22   **Credit Default Swap**

Protection Buyer
— Swap Premium (default swap spread) →
← Contingent Payment on Credit Event —
Protection Seller

Credit default swaps can be used as a hedging instrument. Banks can use credit default swaps to reduce credit risk concentration. Instead of selling loans, banks can effectively transfer credit exposures by buying protections with default swaps. Default swaps also enable investors to hedge nonpublicly traded debts.

Credit default swaps provide great flexibility to investors. Default swaps can be used to express a view on the credit quality of a reference entity. The protection seller makes no upfront investment to take additional credit risk and is thus able to leverage credit risk exposure. In most cases, it is more efficient for investors to buy protection in the default swap market than selling or shorting assets. Because default swaps are negotiated over the counter, they can be tailored specifically toward investors' needs.

EXAMPLE 15

Credit Default Swap

We Deal, Inc., a dealer of credit derivatives, is quite bullish on the long-term debt issued by the governments of three countries in South America. We Deal decides to sell protection in the credit default swap market on the debt issued by these countries. The credit event in these transactions is defined as the failure by the borrower to make timely interest and/or principal payments. A few months later, the government of Country A defaults on its debt obligations, the rating of debt issued by Country B is lowered by Moody's from Baa to Ba because of adverse economic developments in that country, and the rating of debt issued by Country C is upgraded by Moody's from Baa to A in view of favorable economic developments in that country. For each of the countries, indicate whether We Deal suffers a loss.

Solution: In the protection sold by the dealer, the credit event was defined as the failure by the borrower to make timely interest and/or principal payments. This credit event occurred only in the case of Country A. Therefore, the dealer is likely to have suffered a loss only in the protection sold for Country A.

In the next section we broaden our view of fixed-income portfolio management by examining selected issues in international bond investing.

INTERNATIONAL BOND INVESTING

The motivation for international bond investing (i.e., investing in nondomestic bonds) includes portfolio risk reduction and return enhancement compared with portfolios limited to domestic fixed-income securities. In the standard Markowitz mean–variance framework, the risk reduction benefits from adding foreign-issued bonds to a domestic bond portfolio result from their less-than-perfect correlation with domestic fixed-income assets. Exhibit 23 illustrates historical correlations among a selection of developed fixed-income markets.

EXHIBIT 23	**Correlation Coefficients of Monthly Total Returns between International Government Bond Indices 1989–2003**

In US$

	Aus	Can	Fra	Ger	Jap	Net	Swi	U.K.	U.S.
Australia	1.00								
Canada	0.57	1.00							
France	0.27	0.26	1.00						
Germany	0.27	0.26	0.97	1.00					
Japan	0.16	0.12	0.43	0.46	1.00				
Netherlands	0.28	0.31	0.97	0.95	0.43	1.00			
Switzerland	0.20	0.14	0.88	0.90	0.49	0.86	1.00		
United Kingdom	0.24	0.33	0.67	0.66	0.35	0.69	0.58	1.00	
United States	0.27	0.49	0.43	0.42	0.19	0.41	0.37	0.48	1.00

In Local Currency

	Aus	Can	Fra	Ger	Jap	Net	Swi	U.K.	U.S.
Australia	1.00								
Canada	0.70	1.00							
France	0.45	0.46	1.00						
Germany	0.48	0.52	0.86	1.00					
Japan	0.25	0.27	0.20	0.29	1.00				
Netherlands	0.43	0.42	0.86	0.74	0.12	1.00			
Switzerland	0.34	0.35	0.61	0.68	0.27	0.55	1.00		
United Kingdom	0.51	0.59	0.67	0.71	0.24	0.58	0.53	1.00	
United States	0.63	0.71	0.56	0.62	0.26	0.46	0.47	0.57	1.00

The highest correlation was observed among the European markets because of the common monetary policy of the European Central Bank and introduction of the euro in 1999, which resulted in a larger, more liquid, and integrated European bond market. The correlation coefficients are the lowest among countries with the weakest economic ties to each other. When returns are converted to U.S. dollars, the correlation coefficients reflect the impact of currency exchange rates on international investment. For example, the correlation coefficient between U.S. and U.K. returns is 0.57 in local currency terms and only 0.48 in U.S. dollar terms.

Overall, local currency correlations tend to be higher than their U.S. dollar equivalent correlations. Such deviations are attributed to currency volatility, which tends to reduce the correlation among international bond indices when measured in U.S. dollars.

In summary, the low-to-moderate correlations presented in Exhibit 23 provide historical support for the use of international bonds for portfolio risk reduction. Expanding the set of fixed-income investment choices beyond domestic markets should reveal opportunities for return enhancement as well.

If the investor decides to invest in international fixed-income markets, what directions and choices may be taken? Clearly, certain issues in international bond investing, such as the choice of active or passive approaches, as well as many fixed-income tools (e.g., yield curve and credit analysis), are shared with domestic bond investing. However, international investing raises additional challenges and opportunities and, in contrast to domestic investing, involves exposure to **currency risk**—the risk associated with the uncertainty about the exchange rate at which proceeds in the foreign currency can be converted into the investor's home currency. Currency risk results in the need to formulate a strategy for currency management. The following sections offer an introduction to these topics.

6.1 Active versus Passive Management

As a first step, investors in international fixed-income markets need to select a position on the passive/active spectrum. The opportunities for active management are created by inefficiencies that may be attributed to differences in tax treatment, local regulations, coverage by fixed-income analysts, and even to differences in how market players respond to similar information. The active manager seeks to add value through one or more of the following means: bond market selection, currency selection, duration management/yield curve management, sector selection, credit analysis of issuers, and investing outside the benchmark index.

▶ *Bond market selection.* The selection of the national market(s) for investment. Analysis of global economic factors is an important element in this selection that is especially critical when investing in emerging market debt.

▶ *Currency selection.* This is the selection of the amount of currency risk retained for each currency, in effect, the currency hedging decision. If a currency exposure is not hedged, the return on a nondomestic bond holding will depend not only on the holding's return in local currency terms but also on the movement of the foreign/domestic exchange rate. If the investor has the ability to forecast certain exchange rates, the investor may tactically attempt to add value through currency selection. Distinct knowledge and skills are required in currency selection and active currency management more generally. As a result, currency management function is often managed separately from the other functions.

▶ *Duration management/yield curve management.* Once a market is chosen and decisions are made on currency exposures, the duration or interest rate exposure of the holding must be selected. Duration management strategies and positioning along the yield curve within a given market can enhance portfolio return. Duration management can be constrained by the relatively narrow selection of maturities available in many national markets; however, growing markets for fixed-income derivatives provide an increasingly effective means of duration and yield curve management.

▶ *Sector selection.* The international bond market now includes fixed-income instruments representing a full range of sectors, including government and corporate bonds issued in local currencies and in U.S. dollars. A wide assortment of coupons, ratings, and maturities opens opportunities for attempting to add value through credit analysis and other disciplines.

▶ *Credit analysis of issuers.* Portfolio managers may attempt to add value through superior credit analysis, for example, analysis that identifies credit improvement or deterioration of an issuer before other market participants have recognized it.

▶ *Investing in markets outside the benchmark.* For example, benchmarks for international bond investing often consist of government-issued bonds. In such cases, the portfolio manager may consider investing in nonsovereign bonds not included in the index to enhance portfolio returns. This tactic involves a risk mismatch created with respect to the benchmark index; therefore, the client should be aware of and amenable to its use.

Relative to duration management, the relationship between duration of a foreign bond and the duration of the investor's portfolio including domestic and foreign bonds deserves further comment. As defined earlier, portfolio duration is the percentage change in value of a bond portfolio resulting from a 100 bps change in rates. Portfolio duration defined this way is meaningful only in the case of a domestic bond portfolio. For this duration concept to be valid in the context of international bond investments, one would need to assume that the interest rates of every country represented in the portfolio simultaneously change by 100 bps. International interest rates are not perfectly correlated, however, and such an interpretation of international bond portfolio duration would not be meaningful.

The duration measure of a portfolio that includes domestic and foreign bonds must recognize the correlation between the movements in interest rates in the home country and each nondomestic market. Thomas and Willner (1997) suggest a methodology for computing the contribution of a foreign bond's duration to the duration of a portfolio.

The Thomas–Willner methodology begins by expressing the change in a bond's value in terms of a change in the foreign yields, as follows:

$$\text{Change in value of foreign bond} = -\text{Duration} \times \text{Change in foreign yield} \times 100$$

From the perspective of a Canadian manager, for example, the concern is the change in value of the foreign bond when domestic (Canadian) rates change. This change in value can be determined by incorporating the relationship between changes in domestic (Canadian) rates and changes in foreign rates as follows:

$$\text{Change in value of foreign bond} = -\text{Duration} \times \text{Change in foreign yield given a change in domestic yield} \times 100$$

The relationship between the change in foreign yield and the change in Canadian yield can be estimated empirically using monthly data for each country. The following relationship is estimated:

$$\Delta y_{\text{foreign}} = \alpha + \beta \, \Delta y_{\text{domestic}}$$

where

$\Delta y_{\text{foreign}}$ = change in a foreign bond's yield in month t
$\Delta y_{\text{domestic}}$ = change in domestic (Canadian) yield in month time t
β = correlation$(\Delta y_{\text{foreign},t}, \Delta y_{\text{domestic},t}) \times \sigma_{\text{foreign}}/\sigma_{\text{domestic}}$

The parameter β is called the **country beta**. The duration attributed to a foreign bond in the portfolio is found by multiplying the bond's country beta by the bond's duration in local terms, as illustrated in Example 16.

EXAMPLE 16

The Duration of a Foreign Bond

Suppose that a British bond portfolio manager wants to invest in German government 10-year bonds. The manager is interested in the foreign bond's contribution to the duration of the portfolio when domestic interest rates change.

The duration of the German bond is 6 and the country beta is estimated to be 0.42. The duration contribution to a British domestic portfolio is 2.52 = 6 × 0.42. For a 100 bps change in UK interest rates, the value of the German bond is expected to change by approximately 2.52 percent.

Because a portfolio's duration is a weighted average of the duration of the bonds in the portfolio, the contribution to the portfolio's duration is equal to the adjusted German bond duration of 2.52 multiplied by its weight in the portfolio.

6.2 Currency Risk

For the investor in international bonds, fluctuations in the exchange rate between domestic and foreign currencies may decrease or increase the value of foreign investments when converted into the investor's local currency. In particular, when a foreign currency depreciates against the investor's home currency (i.e., a given amount of the foreign currency buys less of the home currency) a currency loss occurs, but when it appreciates, a currency gain occurs. Currency risk is often substantial relative to interest rate risk in its effects on the returns earned on international bond portfolios.

In order to protect the value of international investments from adverse exchange rate movements, investors often diversify currency exposures by having exposure to several currencies. To the extent depreciation of one currency tends to be associated with appreciation of another—i.e., currency risks are less than perfectly correlated—a multi-currency portfolio has less currency risk than a portfolio denominated in a single currency.

The standard measure of the currency risk effect on foreign asset returns involves splitting the currency effect into 1) the expected effect captured by the **forward discount** or forward premium (the forward rate less the spot rate, divided by the spot rate; called the forward discount if negative) and 2) the unexpected effect, defined as the unexpected movement of the foreign currency relative to its forward rate. Every investor in the foreign markets can either remain exposed to this currency risk or hedge it. The investor may also have access to and may consider investing in **currency-hedged instruments**, which neutralize the currency exposure while maintaining the exposure to local bond price changes.

The bond investor should be aware of a basic result in economics concerning the forward discount/premium called covered interest rate parity as it suggests an approach to comparing (fully) hedged returns across international bond markets.

6.2.1 Interest Rate Parity

Interest rate parity (IRP) states that the forward foreign exchange rate discount or premium over a fixed period should equal the risk-free interest rate differential between the two countries over that period to prevent the opportunity for arbitrage profits using spot and forward currency markets plus borrowing or lending. Furthermore, as the interest rate differential between two countries changes, so should the forward discount or premium. To explain further, let the forward discount or premium, f, be given by

$$f = (F - S_0)/S_0$$

where

F = forward exchange rate (stated as domestic currency/foreign currency)

S_0 = spot exchange rate (stated as domestic currency/foreign currency)

The currency quotation convention used—domestic currency/foreign currency—called **direct quotation**, means that from the perspective of an investor in a foreign asset an increase in the spot exchange rate is associated with a currency gain from holding the foreign asset. According to IRP,[5]

$$f \approx i_d - i_f$$

where i_d and i_f are, respectively, the domestic and foreign risk-free interest rates over the time horizon associated with the forward exchange rate. For example, suppose the investor is based in the Eurozone and the available 1-year risk-free interest rate, at i_d = 3.0 percent, is lower than the 1-year U.S. risk-free interest rate, at i_f = 4.5 percent. Thus, the interest rate differential is $i_d - i_f$ = 3.0 percent − 4.5 percent = −1.5 percent. The spot exchange range is €0.8000 per dollar. According to IRP, the no-arbitrage forward exchange rate is €0.7880 per dollar because the resulting forward discount is (0.7880 − 0.8000)/0.8000 = −1.5 percent. If the Eurozone investor makes a U.S. dollar bank deposit, the higher interest earned is offset by a currency loss.

---

[5] For more details, including an explanation of the approximation, see Solnik and McLeavey (2004), Chapters 1 and 2.

6.2.2 Hedging Currency Risk

The decision on how much currency risk to hedge—from none to all—is important because currency movements can have a dramatic effect on the investor's return from international bond holdings. To illustrate the issue, Exhibit 24 shows the fluctuations in the U.S.–Australian dollar exchange rate over the period January 1993 to January 2004.

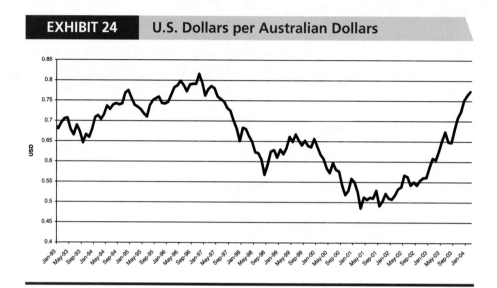

EXHIBIT 24	U.S. Dollars per Australian Dollars

During the period of a falling Australian dollar (1997 to mid-2001), hedged Australian investment positions generated higher returns in terms for U.S. investors than similar unhedged positions. From mid-2001 to the start of 2004, the trend reversed—the Australian currency appreciated—and hedged investments underperformed. Hedged and unhedged international investments with Australian dollar exposure generated drastically different returns in 2000 and 2003. Therefore, investors must carefully examine the decision to hedge and be familiar with hedging methods.

The three main methods of currency hedging are:

▶ forward hedging;

▶ proxy hedging; and

▶ cross hedging.

Forward hedging involves the use of a forward contract between the bond's currency and the home currency. **Proxy hedging** involves using a forward contract between the home currency and a currency that is highly correlated with the bond's currency. The investor may use proxy hedging because forward markets in the bond's currency are relatively undeveloped, or because it is otherwise cheaper to hedge using a proxy. In the context of currency hedging, **cross hedging** refers to hedging using two currencies other than the home currency and is a technique used to convert the currency risk of the bond into a different exposure that has less risk for the investor. The investment policy statement often provides guidance on permissible hedging methods.

The most popular hedging approach is forward hedging. For example, a German investor may be holding a position in Canadian bonds that is expected to pay C\$5 million at maturity in nine months. Forward contracts are used to lock in the current value of a currency for future delivery. To hedge this position, therefore, the investor enters a forward agreement to purchase euros nine months from today at a forward rate of €1.20 per Canadian dollar. By entering the forward agreement and arranging the receipt of €6 million = C\$5 million × 1.20€/C\$ nine months from now, the investor is hedging against fluctuations in the euro/Canadian dollar exchange rate over the next nine months.

Currency exposures associated with investments with variable cash flows, such as variable coupon bonds or collateralized debt obligations, cannot be hedged completely because forward contracts only cover the expected cash flows.[6] The actual investment payoff may differ from the expected, resulting in an over- or underhedged portfolio, in which case, the currency may have to be exchanged at the future spot rate.

This reading can only briefly introduce the subject of hedging currency risk, and the perspective taken will be tactical. A first, basic fact is that a foreign bond return stated in terms of the investor's home currency, the **unhedged return** (R), is approximately equal to the foreign bond return in local currency terms, r_l, plus the **currency return**, e, which is the percentage change in the spot exchange rate stated in terms of home currency per unit of foreign currency (direct quotation, as before):

$$R \approx r_l + e$$

If the investor can hedge fully with forward contracts, what return will the investor earn? The (fully) **hedged return**, HR, is equal to the sum of r_l plus the forward discount (premium) f, which is the price the investor pays (receives) to hedge the currency risk of the foreign bond. That is,

$$HR \approx r_l + f$$

If IRP holds, f is approximately equal to the interest rate differential, so that

$$HR \approx r_l + f \approx r_l + (i_d - i_f) = i_d + (r_l - i_f)$$

In other words, the hedged bond return can be viewed as the sum of the domestic risk-free interest rate (i_d) plus the bond's local risk premium (its excess return in relation to the local risk-free rate) of the foreign bond. If we compare the fully hedged return of international bond issues from different national markets, the expected difference in their fully hedged returns will reflect only the differences in their local risk premia. This idea provides an easy way to compare the hedged yields of bonds in different markets, as illustrated in Example 17.

---

[6] A **collateralized debt obligation** is a securitized pool of fixed-income assets.

EXAMPLE 17

Comparing Hedged Returns across Markets

Suppose a U.K. investor is making a choice between same maturity (and credit risk) Japanese and Canadian government bonds. Currently, 10-year yields on government bonds in Japan and in Canada are 2.16 percent and 3.40 percent, respectively. Short-term interest rates are 1.25 percent and 1.54 percent in Japan and Canada, respectively. Assume that IRP holds. Contrast the expected fully hedged returns on 10-year Japanese and Canadian government bonds.

Solution: The Japanese government bond's local risk premium is 0.91 percent = 2.16 percent − 1.25 percent, and the Canadian government bond's local risk premium is 1.86 percent = 3.40 percent − 1.54 percent. Because the local risk premium on the Canadian bond is higher, its expected fully hedged return will be higher as well.

Example 17 contrasted the hedged yields of two bonds. In Example 18, the investor chooses hedging with forwards over leaving an investment unhedged based on a comparison of the interest rate differential with the expected currency return.

EXAMPLE 18

To Hedge or Not with a Forward Contract (1)

A U.S. fixed-income fund has substantial holdings in euro-denominated German bonds. The portfolio manager of the fund is considering whether to leave the fund's exposure to the euro unhedged or fully hedge it using a dollar–euro forward contract. Assume that the short-term interest rates are 4 percent in the United States and 3.2 percent in Germany. The fund manager expects the euro to appreciate against the dollar by 0.6 percent. Assume that IRP holds. Explain which alternative has the higher expected return based on the short-term interest rates and the manager's expectations about exchange rates.

Solution: The interest rate differential between the dollar and the euro is 4 − 3.2 = 0.8 percent. Because this differential is greater than the expected return on euro of 0.6 percent, a forward hedged investment is expected to result in a higher return than an unhedged position.

Example 19 examines the tactical decision to hedge or not based on the expected **excess currency return**, which is defined as the expected currency return in excess of the forward premium or discount.

EXAMPLE 19

To Hedge or Not with a Forward Contract (2)

David Marlet is the portfolio manager of a French fund that has substantial holdings in the U.K. pound-denominated British government bonds. Simon Jones is the portfolio manager of a British fund that has large holdings in euro-denominated French government bonds. Both the portfolio managers are considering whether to hedge their portfolio exposure to the foreign currency using a forward contract or leave the exposure unhedged. Assume that the short-term interest rates are 3.2 percent in France and 4.7 percent in the United Kingdom and that the forward discount on the pound is $4.7 - 3.2 = 1.5$ percent. Marlet and Jones believe that the U.K. pound, the currency associated with the higher interest rate, will depreciate less relative to the euro than what the forward rate between the two currencies would indicate assuming interest rate parity.

1. Should Marlet use a forward contract to hedge the fund's exposure to the British pound?

2. Should Jones use a forward contract to hedge the fund's exposure to the euro?

Solutions:

Both portfolio managers expect that the pound will depreciate less than 1.5 percent.

1. If Marlet were to hedge using a forward contract, he would be locking in a currency return of -1.5 percent; that is, a 1.5 percent loss on currency. By remaining unhedged, however, he expects the loss on currency to be less than 1.5 percent. Based on expected returns alone, he should not hedge the currency risk using a forward contract.

2. The situation of Jones, the portfolio manager of the British fund, is exactly the opposite of the portfolio manager of the French fund. If Jones were to hedge using a forward contract, he would be locking in a currency return of 1.5 percent, that is, a 1.5 percent gain on currency. Jones expects the gain on currency to be less than 1.5 percent if he does not hedge. Therefore, Jones should hedge the currency risk. Because Jones's anticipated return on currency (less than 1.5 percent) is below the interest rate differential (1.5 percent), the currency risk should be hedged.

6.3 Breakeven Spread Analysis

One consideration in active international bond portfolio selection is bond and country yield advantages. Breakeven spread analysis can be used to quantify the amount of spread widening required to diminish a foreign yield advantage. Breakeven spread analysis does not account for exchange rate risk, but the information it provides can be helpful in assessing the risk in seeking higher yields. Yield relationships can change because of a variety of factors. Furthermore, even a constant yield spread across markets may produce different returns. One reason is that prices of securities that vary in coupon and maturity respond differently to changes in yield: Duration plays an important role in breakeven spread analysis. Also, the yield advantage of investing in a foreign country may disappear if domestic yields increase and foreign yields decline.

EXAMPLE 20

Breakeven Spread Analysis

Suppose the spread between Japanese and French bonds is 300 bps, providing Japanese investors who purchased the French bond with an additional yield income of 75 bps per quarter. The duration of the Japanese bond is 7. Let W denote the spread widening.

With a duration of 7, the price change for the Japanese bond will be seven times the change in yield. (For 100 bps change yield in yield, the price change for the Japanese bond will be 7 percent.)

$$\text{Change in price} = 7 \times \text{Change in yield}$$
$$\text{Change in price} = 7 \times W$$

Assuming that the increase in price caused by the spread widening will be 0.75 percent, the yield advantage of French bonds would be:

$$0.75 \text{ percent} = 7 \times W$$

Solving for the spread widening, W,

$$W = 0.1071 \text{ percent} = 10.71 \text{ bps}$$

Thus, a spread widening of 10.71 bps because of a decline in the yields in Japan would wipe out the additional yield gained from investing in the French bond for that quarter. A change in interest rates of only 10.71 bps in this case would wipe out the quarterly yield advantage of 75 bps.

Note that the breakeven spread widening analysis must be associated with an investment horizon (3 months in Example 20) and must be based on the higher of the two countries' durations. The analysis ignores the impact of currency movements.

The ability to choose individual sectors and/or securities varies considerably across the globe. For the developed countries, the same type of analysis for each of the respective fixed-income markets is appropriate. For the developing countries, such external influences as specific country or worldwide economic factors are relatively more important.

Emerging market security selection is especially limited. The resulting liquidity variation must be taken into account, which results in many countries limiting the choice to benchmark government bonds. In all cases, the details on settlements, taxation, and regulatory issues are important. Finally, as one builds a portfolio, the effects of currency positions add a critical dimension. Use of derivative products has enabled more flexibility but is usually available only at notional amounts in the tens of millions of dollars at a minimum.

6.4 Emerging Market Debt

Emerging markets comprise those nations whose economies are considered to be developing and are usually taken to include Latin America, Eastern Europe, Africa, Russia, the Middle East, and Asia excluding Japan. Emerging market debt (EMD) includes sovereign bonds (bonds issued by a national government) as well as debt securities issued by public and private companies in those countries.

Over the past 10 years, emerging market debt has matured as an asset class and now frequently appears in many strategic asset allocations. Because of its low correlation with domestic debt portfolios, EMD offers favorable diversification properties to a fixed-income portfolio. EMD has played an important role in **core-plus** fixed-income portfolios. Core-plus is a label for fixed-income mandates that permit the portfolio manager to add instruments with relatively high return potential, such as EMD and high-yield debt, to core holdings of investment-grade debt.[7]

6.4.1 Growth and Maturity of the Market

Although emerging market governments have always borrowed to meet their needs, the modern emerging markets debt sector originated in the 1980s when the Mexican financial crisis led to the creation of a secondary market in loans to that country. The Brady plan, which followed soon thereafter, allowed emerging country governments to securitize their outstanding external bank loans. A liquid market for these securities (called Brady bonds) soon followed. As a result of debt securitization, the majority of emerging market debt risk has now shifted from the banks to the private sector. The market has grown rapidly to its current substantial size—the International Monetary Fund (2005, p. 268) estimates the total size of the emerging external debt market in 2006 to be approximately $3.3 trillion.

The proportion of emerging market countries that are rated as investment grade has risen to about 40 percent of the countries represented in the emerging market indices. Mexico, for example, can now borrow almost as cheaply as the U.S. government. The quality of emerging market sovereign bonds has increased to the point that they now have frequencies of default, recovery rates, and ratings transition probabilities similar to corporate bonds as well as similar ratings. As a result, the spread of emerging market debt over risk-free rates has narrowed considerably.

The EMD market has also shown remarkable resiliency. During the Asian crisis of the late 1990s, the price of Asian debt fluctuated over wide ranges, but the market rebounded impressively, offering rates of return that exceeded those of many developed countries' equity markets in the post-crisis period. The market has dealt with crises in Latin America, Southeast Asia, and Russia with relatively little damage to investors, with the notable exception of the large Russian default in 1998.

Since 1992, the standard index in emerging markets has been the Emerging Markets Bond Index Plus (EMBI+). Although the index emphasizes the inclusion of highly liquid bonds, its main disadvantage is the lack of diversification in the securities that make up the index. An overwhelming percentage of the index (58 percent) is in Latin American securities, with Brazil and Mexico making up 37 percent of the total.

---

[7] For example, a core-plus manager might be officially benchmarked to the Lehman Aggregate Bond Index, but invest a fraction of the portfolio (perhaps up to 25 percent) outside the benchmark.

6.4.2 Risk and Return Characteristics

Emerging market debt frequently offers the potential for consistent, attractive rates of return. Sovereign emerging market governments possess several advantages over private corporations. They can react quickly to negative economic events by cutting spending and raising taxes and interest rates (actions that may make it more difficult for private corporations in these countries to service their own debt). They also have access to lenders on the world stage, such as the International Monetary Fund and the World Bank. Many emerging market nations also possess large foreign currency reserves, providing a shock absorber for bumps in their economic road. Using these resources, any adverse situation can be rapidly addressed and reversed.

Risks do exist in the sector however—volatility in the EMD market is high. EMD returns are also frequently characterized by significant negative skewness. Negative skewness is the potential for occasional very large negative returns without offsetting potential on the upside. An instance of an extreme negative event is the massive market sell-off that occurred from August 1997 to September 1998.

Other risks abound. Emerging market countries frequently do not offer the degree of transparency, court-tested laws, and clear regulations that developed market countries do. The legal system may be less developed and offer less protection from interference by the executive branch than in developed countries. Also, developing countries have tended to over borrow, which can damage the position of existing debt. If a default of sovereign debt occurs, recovery against sovereign states can be very difficult. Also, little standardization of covenants exists among various emerging market issuers. Sovereign debt also typically lacks an enforceable seniority structure, in contrast to private debt.

6.4.3 Analysis of Emerging Market Debt

Just as with any credit analysis, an investor in EMD securities must determine the willingness and ability of the issuers to pay their debt obligations. This analysis begins with a look at the country's fundamentals: the source of government revenues, fiscal and monetary policies, current debt levels, and willingness of the country's citizens to accept short-term sacrifices in order to strengthen the country's long-term economic situation. For example, consider the Russian default in 1998. A great deal of money was lent to Russia before its economic and financial collapse. Yet, even a cursory examination would have shown that the country had no experience in collecting taxes, had an extremely weak economic infrastructure, and was dependent on a single commodity (energy) for its revenues. Investors either forgot the fundamentals or chose to ignore them. Historically, the largest returns have come from countries with strong fundamentals, usually characterized by an export-oriented economy and a high savings rate.

In evaluating EMD, the risk of default remains a critical consideration, particularly when private debt is concerned. Investors should not simply accept a bond rating as the final measure of the issue's default risk. In some countries, the financial strength of a large company may be greater than that of the sovereign government. The underlying assets for the company can be quite valuable and may justify a high credit rating. However, the credit rating for the company debt will not be higher than that of sovereign debt. This restriction on private debt ratings creates opportunities for astute investors to purchase high-quality debt at prices below fair market value.

Whether investing in established or emerging markets, investment in foreign assets, while providing diversification benefits, carries the same types of risk of domestic investments plus some additional risks associated with converting the foreign investment cash flows into domestic currency. Political risk and currency risk are major sources of uncertainty for portfolios with international exposures. And, changes in liquidity and taxation may be additional sources of risk.

Political risk or geopolitical risk includes the risk of war, government collapse, political instability, expropriation, confiscation, and adverse changes in taxation. A common political risk is the uncertainty that investors will be able to convert the foreign currency holdings into their home currency as a result of constraints imposed by foreign government policies or political actions of any sort.

Sovereign governments may impose restrictions on capital flows, change rules, revise taxes, liberalize bankruptcy proceedings, modify exchange rate regimes, and create new market regulations, all of which add an element of uncertainty to financial markets by affecting the performance and liquidity of investments in those countries.

Political crises during the 1990s in Europe, Southeast Asia, Russia, Latin America, and the Middle East highlight the increasing global links among political risks. Today's political risks are often subtle, arising not only from legal and regulatory changes and government transitions but also from environmental issues, foreign policies, currency crises, and terrorism. Nevertheless, diversification among international securities is one means to controlling the effect of political risk on the investment performance. However, investments in countries with close economic and political links would afford less than investments in countries with looser links.

Investors in EMD face default risk as does any investor in debt. Sovereign EMD bears greater credit risk than developed market sovereign debt, reflecting less-developed banking and financial market infrastructure, lower transparency, and higher political risk in developing countries. Rating agencies issue sovereign ratings that indicate countries' ability to meet their debt obligations. Standard & Poor's investment-grade sovereign rating of BBB– and Moody's Baa3 are given to the most credit-worthy emerging markets countries. Increased transparency and availability of reliable foreign market data are valued in the marketplace and directly linked to foreign capital inflow. For example, some evidence indicates that U.S. investors in the early 2000s moved out of smaller markets and markets with low and declining credit ratings to countries with more transparent financial markets, open economies, and better inflation performance.[8]

In the next section, we turn our attention to the final topic of this reading, selecting a fixed-income portfolio manager.

SELECTING A FIXED-INCOME MANAGER   7

When funds are not managed entirely in-house, a search for outside managers must be conducted. Because the average institutional fixed-income portfolio has approximately 85 percent of the assets managed actively and 15 percent indexed, we focus our attention here on the selection of an active manager.

Active return and active risk (tracking risk) are intricately linked. The typical range for tracking risk in large fixed-income institutional portfolios is between 40 and 120 bps with the upper end of the range typically including a high-yield component and the lower end being more typical for core managers. Because

---

[8] See Burger and Warnock (2003).

active management fees typically range from 15 to 50 bps (plus custodial fees), it is clear that outperforming the benchmark on a net-of-fees basis is a challenging and difficult task.

The due diligence for selection of managers is satisfied primarily by investigating the managers' investment process, the types of trades the managers are making, and the manager's organizational strengths and weaknesses. The key to better performance is to find managers who can produce consistent positive style-adjusted alphas. Then, the portfolio can be constructed by optimizing the combination of managers in order to maximize the variety of styles and exposures contributed by each manager.

7.1 Historical Performance as a Predictor of Future Performance

Is a fixed-income manager's historical performance a good predictor of future performance? Studies indicate some evidence of persistence of outperformance by some managers relative to their peers over short periods of time. However, over long periods of time (15 years or more) and when fund fees and expenses are factored in, the realized alpha of fixed-income managers has averaged very close to zero and little evidence of persistence exits. So it is clear that selecting a manager purely on the basis of historical performance is not a good approach to manager selection.

7.2 Developing Criteria for the Selection

The value of due diligence is found in the details; a fundamental analysis of the manager's strategy must be conducted. Here are some of the factors that should be considered:

1. *Style analysis*: In large part, the active risk and return are determined by the extent to which the portfolio differs from the benchmark's construction—particularly with regard to overweighting of sectors and duration differences. An analysis of the manager's historical style may prove helpful in explaining how the types of biases and quality of the views reflected in the portfolio weighting have affected a portfolio's overall performance.

   For example, consider a style analysis of an individual core-plus manager. The analysis may demonstrate a significant style weight to MBS and high-yield bonds (consistent with the core-plus strategy), coupled with a persistent and large underweighting of investment-grade securities (relative to the Lehman Aggregate). Also, the manager may make consistent duration bets across the portfolio by investing in bonds with a longer duration than the benchmark. Under the right conditions, this approach could certainly lead to larger returns, but it will also likely lead to higher active risk. A close examination of the results should yield some insight into the manager's skill in using this approach.

2. *Selection bets*: If an active manager believes that she possesses superior credit or security analysis skills, she may frequently deviate from the weights in the normal portfolio. By forecasting changes in relative credit spreads and identifying undervalued securities, the manager may attempt to increase the active return of the portfolio. The manager's skill in this approach may be measured by decomposing the portfolio's returns.

3. *The organization's investment process*: The investor needs to be intimately familiar with the investment process of the manager's organization. What research methods are used by the organization? What are the main drivers of alpha? How are decisions regarding changes in the portfolio made? A manager is often only as good as the support staff. Before selection, the plan sponsor needs to spend quite a bit of time asking questions of several key people in the organization.

4. *Correlation of alphas*: The historical correlations of alpha across managers should also be examined. Many managers exhibit similarities in their management of a portfolio. If multiple managers are to be used, obviously the plan sponsor will prefer low to high correlation among managers' alphas to control portfolio risk.

7.3 Comparison with Selection of Equity Managers

Selecting a fixed-income manager has both similarities with and differences from the selection of an equity manager.

1. In both cases, a consultant is frequently used to identify a universe of suitable manager candidates (because of the consultants' large databases).

2. In both sectors, the available evidence indicates that past performance is not a reliable guide to future results.

3. The same qualitative factors are common to both analyses: philosophy of the manager and organization, market opportunity, competitive advantages, delegation of responsibility, experience of the professionals, and so on.

4. Management fees and expenses are vitally important in both areas, because they often reduce or eliminate the alpha that managers are able to earn gross of expenses. If anything, fees are more important in the fixed-income area, because fixed-income funds have a higher ratio of fees to expected outperformance. There is some evidence that fixed-income managers with the highest fees have the lowest information ratios (i.e., ratio of expected alpha to volatility of alpha), so the avoidance of high fees is clearly a defensible strategy.

Although limited space prevents discussion for all the relevant items here, Example 21 illustrates some of the key areas that should be investigated in a complete due diligence analysis.

EXAMPLE 21

Due Diligence Questionnaire for a U.S. Fixed-Income Portfolio

When conducting a search for managers, organizations will typically ask portfolio managers to submit answers to a wide variety of questions as part of the due diligence process. The following questionnaire illustrates the types of information typically asked of candidate managers:

1. Organization
   a. history (key events and date)
   b. structure

    c. ownership

    d. number of employees (last three years)

    e. awards/ratings

    f. flagship products and core competencies

    g. timeline of products/product development

    h. total assets, total fixed-income assets, and total core-plus assets

    i. significant client additions/withdrawals in last three years

    j. current lawsuits for investigations

    k. policy on market timing, excessive trading, and distribution fee arrangements

    l. Form ADV, Parts 1 and 2

2. Product (provide information based on a similar or composite portfolio)

    a. inception date

    b. investment philosophy

    c. nonbenchmark sectors and exposure to these sectors via commingled fund or direct investment

    d. return objective

    e. gross and net-of-fee performance versus the Lehman Brothers Aggregate Bond Index

        ▶ annualized returns for the quarter, year-to-date, 1 year, 3 years, 5 years, 10 years, and since inception

        ▶ annual returns for 1 through 10 years

        ▶ monthly returns for 1 through 5 years

    f. quantitative analysis—metrics such as:

        ▶ volatility, tracking risk, information ratio, Sharpe ratio, and so on

    g. sector allocation versus the Lehman Brothers Aggregate Bond Index, quarterly for the past three years

    h. portfolio characteristics versus the Lehman Brothers Aggregate Bond Index, quarterly for the past three years

        ▶ duration, average quality, average maturity, average yield, and so on

    i. permitted security types, including a statement on the use of short positions, derivative products, and leveraging

    j. description of any constraints/limits

        ▶ frequency of subscription/redemption

        ▶ cash limits

    k. average number of total holdings

    l. total management fees and additional fees, if any

    m. asset value data provider

    n. administrator, custodian, auditor, advisers for commingled funds, if any

    o. growth of assets under management of this product

    p. top clients by assets under management utilizing this product

    q. three current client references

3. Risk Management

    a. philosophy and process

    b. portfolio risk monitoring

    c. limits on single positions, regions/countries, industries/sectors, and so on

4. Investment Personnel

    a. structure of investment team

    b. responsibilities

    c. biographies of key personnel

    d. significant team departures in last five years

    e. additional products managed by same manager or management team

    f. compensation structure of investment team

    g. tenure of investment team

    h. a description of the client service resources that will be made available

5. Investment Process

    a. decisions by committee or by manager

    b. quantitative or fundamental analysis

    c. top-down or bottom-up approach

    d. use of internal and external research

    e. universal securities

    f. main alpha drivers/sources of value added

    g. significant changes in investment process over last 10 years or since inception

    h. process driven or people driven fund management

    i. sell discipline

    j. best execution trading policy

6. Reporting Capabilities

    a. sample monthly and quarterly reports

    b. online reporting/download capability

SUMMARY

The management of fixed-income portfolios is a highly competitive field requiring skill in financial and economic analysis, market knowledge, and control of costs. Among the points that have been made are the following:

▶ Standard deviation, target semivariance, shortfall risk, and value at risk have all been proposed as appropriate measures of risk for a portfolio. However, each has its own deficiency. For example, standard deviation (or variance) assumes that risk has a normal distribution (which may not be true). Semivariance often provides little extra information if returns are symmetric. Shortfall risk is expressed as a probability, not as a currency amount. Value at risk does not indicate the magnitude of the very worst possible outcomes.

▶ A repurchase agreement is subject to a variety of credit risks, including:

   a. *Quality of the collateral.* The higher the quality of the securities, the lower the repo rate will be.

   b. *Term of the repo.* Typically, the longer the maturity, the higher the rate will be.

   c. *Delivery requirement.* If physical delivery of the securities is required, the rate will be lower because of the lower credit risk.

   d. *Availability of collateral.* The buyer of the securities may be willing to accept a lower rate in order to obtain securities that are in short supply.

   e. *Prevailing interest rates in the economy.* As interest rates increase, the rates on repo transactions will generally increase.

   f. *Seasonal factors.* A seasonal effect may exist because some institutions' supply of funds varies by the season.

▶ The primary advantages to using futures to alter a portfolio's duration are increased liquidity and cost-effectiveness.

▶ Futures contracts can be used to shorten or lengthen a portfolio's duration. The contracts may also be used to hedge or reduce an existing interest rate exposure. As such, they may be combined with traditional immunization techniques to improve the results.

▶ Unlike ordinary bond options that protect against interest rate risk, credit options are structured to offer protection against credit risk. Binary credit option and binary credit option based on a credit rating are the two types of credit options written on an underlying asset. The former pays the option buyer in the event of default; otherwise nothing is paid. The latter pays the difference between the strike price and the market price when the specified credit rating event occurs and pays nothing if the event does not occur.

▶ Credit options are structured to offer protection against both default risk and credit spread risk, credit forwards offer protection against credit spread risk, and credit default swaps help in managing default risk.

▶ The sources of excess return for an international bond portfolio include bond market selection, currency selection, duration management/yield curve management, sector selection, credit analysis, and investing in markets outside the benchmark index.

▶ Emerging market debt has matured as an asset class. The spread of EMD over risk-free rates has narrowed considerably as the quality of sovereign bonds has increased to the point that they now have similar frequencies of default, recovery rates, and ratings transition probabilities compared with corporate bonds with similar ratings.

▶ Emerging market debt is still risky, however, and is characterized by high volatility and returns that exhibit significant negative skewness. Moreover, emerging market countries frequently do not offer the degree of transparency, court tested laws, and clear regulations found in established markets.

▶ For a change in domestic interest rates, the change in a foreign bond's value may be found by multiplying the duration of the foreign bond times the country beta. Because a portfolio's duration is a weighted average of the duration of the bonds in the portfolio, the contribution to the portfolio's duration is equal to the adjusted foreign bond duration multiplied by its weight in the portfolio.

▶ Breakeven spread analysis is used to estimate relative values between markets by quantifying the amount of spread widening required to reduce a foreign bond's yield advantage to zero. The breakeven spread can be found by dividing the yield advantage by the bond's duration.

▶ When funds are not managed entirely in-house, a search for outside managers must be conducted. The due diligence for selection of managers is satisfied primarily by investigating the managers' investment process, the types of trades the managers are making, and the organizational strengths.

1. Your client has asked you to construct a £2 million bond portfolio. Some of the bonds that you are considering for this portfolio have embedded options. Your client has specified that he may withdraw £25,000 from the portfolio in six months to fund some expected expenses. He would like to be able to make this withdrawal without reducing the initial capital of £2 million.

   A. Would shortfall risk be an appropriate measure of risk while evaluating the portfolios for your client?

   B. What are some of the shortcomings of the use of shortfall risk?

2. The market value of the bond portfolio of a French investment fund is €75 million. The duration of the portfolio is 8.17. Based on the analysis provided by the in-house economists, the portfolio manager believes that the interest rates are likely to have an unexpected decrease over the next month. Based on this belief, the manager has decided to increase the duration of its entire bond portfolio to 10. The futures contract it would use is priced at €130,000 and has a duration of 9.35. Assume that the conversion factor for the futures contract is 1.06.

   A. Would the fund need to buy futures contracts or sell?

   B. Approximately, how many futures contracts would be needed to change the duration of the bond portfolio?

3. The trustees of a pension fund would like to examine the issue of protecting the bonds in the fund's portfolio against an increase in interest rates using options and futures. Before discussing this with their external bond fund manager, they decide to ask four consultants about their recommendations as to what should be done at this time. It turns out that each of them has a different recommendation. Consultant A suggests selling covered calls, Consultant B suggests doing nothing at all, Consultant C suggests selling interest rate futures, and Consultant D suggests buying puts. The reason for their different recommendations is that although all consultants understand the pension fund's objective of minimizing risk, they differ with one another in regards to their outlook on future interest rates. One of the consultants believes interest rates are headed downward, one has no opinion, one believes that the interest rates would not change much in either direction, and one believes that the interest rates are headed upward. Based on the consultants' recommendations, could you identify the outlook of each consultant?

4. The current credit spread on bonds issued by Great Foods Inc. is 300 bps. The manager of More Money Funds believes that Great Foods' credit situation will improve over the next few months, resulting in a smaller credit spread on its bonds. She decides to enter into a six-month credit spread forward contract taking the position that the credit spread will decrease. The forward contract has the current spread as the contracted spread, a notional amount of $10 million, and a risk factor of 5.

   A. On the settlement date six months later, the credit spread on Great Foods bonds is 250 bps. How much is the payoff to More Money Funds?

   B. How much would the payoff to More Money Funds be if the credit spread on the settlement date is 350 bps?

   C. How much is the maximum possible gain for More Money Funds?

5. Consider a collateralized debt obligation (CDO) that has a $250 million structure. The collateral consists of bonds that mature in seven years, and the coupon rate for these bonds is the seven-year Treasury rate plus 500 bps. The senior tranche comprises 70 percent of the structure and has a floating coupon of LIBOR plus 50 bps. There is only one junior tranche that comprises 20 percent of the structure and has a fixed coupon of 7-year Treasury rate plus 300 bps. Compute the rate of return earned by the equity tranche in this CDO if the seven-year Treasury rate is 6 percent and the LIBOR is 7.5 percent. There are no defaults in the underlying collateral pool. Ignore the collateral manager's fees and any other expenses.

6. Assume that the rates shown in the table below accurately reflect current conditions in the financial markets.

Dollar/Euro Spot Rate	1.21
Dollar/Euro 1-Year Forward Rate	1.18
1-Year Deposit Rate:	
Euro	3%
U.S.	2%

In the table, the one-year forward dollar-euro exchange rate is mispriced, because it doesn't reflect the interest rate differentials between the U.S. and Europe.

A. Calculate the amount of the current forward exchange discount or premium.

B. Calculate the value that the forward rate would need to be in order to keep riskless arbitrage from occurring.

7. Assume that a U.S. bond investor has invested in Canadian government bonds. The duration of a 12-year Canadian government bond is 8.40, and the Canadian country beta is 0.63. Interest rates in the U.S. are expected to change by approximately 80 bps. How much can the U.S. investor expect the Canadian bond to change in value if U.S. rates change by 80 bps?

8. Assume that the spread between U.S. and German bonds is 300 bps, providing German investors who purchase a U.S. bond with an additional yield income of 75 bps per quarter. The duration of the German bond is 8.3. If German interest rates should decline, how much of a decline is required to completely wipe out the quarterly yield advantage for the German investor?

9. A portfolio manager of a Canadian fund that invests in the yen-denominated Japanese bonds is considering whether or not to hedge the portfolio's exposure to the Japanese yen using a forward contract. Assume that the short-term interest rates are 1.6 percent in Japan and 2.7 percent in Canada.

A. Based on the in-house analysis provided by the fund's currency specialists, the portfolio manager expects the Japanese yen to appreciate against the Canadian dollar by 1.5 percent. Should the portfolio manager hedge the currency risk using a forward contract?

B. What would be your answer if the portfolio manager expects the Japanese yen to appreciate against the Canadian dollar by only 0.5 percent?

10. A British fixed-income fund has substantial holdings in U.S. dollar-denominated bonds. The fund's portfolio manager is considering whether to leave the fund's exposure to the U.S. dollar unhedged or to hedge it using a U.K. pound–U.S. dollar forward contract. Assume that the short-term interest rates are 4.7 percent in the United Kingdom and 4 percent in the United States. The fund manager expects the U.S. dollar to appreciate against the pound by 0.4 percent. Assume IRP holds. Explain which alternative has the higher expected return based on the short-term interest rates and the manager's expectations about exchange rates.

Use the following information to answer Questions 11–16

Sheila Ibahn, a portfolio manager with TBW Incorporated, is reviewing the performance of L.P. Industries' $100 million fixed-income portfolio with Stewart Palme from L.P. Industries. TBW Incorporated employs an active management strategy for fixed-income portfolios. Ibahn explains to Palme that the portfolio return was greater than the benchmark return last year and states:

> "We outperformed our benchmark by using inter-sector allocation and individual security selection strategies rather than a duration management strategy. However, at this point in the interest rate cycle, we believe we can add relative return by taking on additional interest rate risk across the portfolio."

Ibahn recommends purchasing additional bonds to adjust the average duration of the portfolio. After reviewing the portfolio recommendations, Palme asks Ibahn:

> "How can we adjust the portfolio's duration without contributing significant funds to purchase additional bonds in the portfolio?"

Ibahn responds:

1. We could employ futures contracts to adjust the duration of the portfolio, thus eliminating the need to purchase more bonds.

2. We could lever the portfolio by entering into either an overnight or 2-year term repurchase agreement [repo] and use the repo funds to purchase additional bonds that have the same duration as the current portfolio. For example, if we use funds from a $25 million overnight repo agreement to purchase bonds in addition to the current $100 million portfolio, the levered portfolio's change in value for a 1% change in interest rates would equal $5,125,000 while giving you the portfolio duration you require. Unfortunately the current cost of the repo is high because the repo collateral is "special collateral" but the margin requirement is low because the collateral is illiquid.

After listening to Ibahn, Palme agrees to use a repo to lever the portfolio but leaves the repo term decision to Ibahn's discretion. Because the yield curve is inverted, the cost of both the overnight and the 2-year term repo is higher than the yield on the levered portfolio. As Ibahn and Palme discuss the repo term, Palme asks two final questions:

1. "What is the effect of leverage on a portfolio's range of returns if interest rates are expected to change?"
2. "If interest rates are unchanged over a six month period, what is the effect on the levered portfolio return compared to the unlevered portfolio return?"

11. Given Ibahn's recommendation, which of the following interest rate forecasts is TBW Incorporated *most likely* using?

   A.   A flattening of the yield curve.

   B.   An upward parallel shift in the yield curve.

   C.   A downward parallel shift in the yield curve.

12. Referring to Ibahn's first response to Palme, which of the following best describes TBW's *most likely* course of action?

   A.   Sell interest rate futures contracts to increase portfolio duration.

   B.   Buy interest rate futures contracts to increase portfolio duration.

   C.   Buy interest rate futures contracts to decrease portfolio duration.

13. Referring to Ibahn's second response to Palme, the levered portfolio would have:

   A.   the same duration if either the overnight repo or the 2-year term repo is used.

   B.   a longer duration if the overnight repo is used instead of the 2-year term repo.

   C.   a shorter duration if the overnight repo is used instead of the 2-year term repo.

14. In Ibahn's second response to Palme, the duration of the sample leveraged portfolio is *closest* to:

   A.   4.10.

   B.   5.13.

   C.   6.83.

15. Is Ibahn's second response to Palme regarding the cost and margin requirements for the repo *most likely* correct?

	High Repo Cost	Low Margin Requirement
A.	No	No
B.	Yes	Yes
C.	Yes	No

16. In response to Palme's two final questions, the levered portfolio's range of returns and six-month return when compared to the unlevered portfolio *most likely* would be:

	Levered Portfolio Range of Returns	Levered Portfolio Six-month Return
A.	narrower	lower
B.	narrower	higher
C.	wider	lower

Questions 17–22 relate to Autónoma Foundation and are based on Fixed-Income Portfolio Management—Parts I and II

The investment committee of the U.S.-based Autónoma Foundation has been dissatisfied with the performance of the fixed-income portion of their endowment and has recently fired the fixed-income manager.

The investment committee has hired a consultant, Julia Santillana, to oversee the portfolio on an interim basis until the search for a new manager is completed. She is also expected to assess the portfolio's risks and propose investment ideas to the committee.

Total Return Analysis and Scenario Analysis

During a meeting between Santillana and members of the committee, a member asks her to discuss the use of total return analysis and scenario analysis before executing bond trades. In her response, Santillana states:

▶ "To compute total return, the manager needs a set of assumptions about the investment horizon, the expected reinvestment rate, and the expected change in interest rates."

▶ "If the manager wants to evaluate how the individual assumptions affect the total return computation, she can use scenario analysis."

▶ "Scenario analysis can lead to rejection of a strategy that is acceptable from a total return perspective."

Use of Repurchase Agreements

During the meeting, Santillana reviews with the investment committee a hypothetical transaction in which leverage is used. A manager with $2 million of funds to invest purchases corporate bonds with a market value of $7 million. To partially finance the purchase, the manager enters into a 30-day repurchase agreement with the bond dealer for $5 million. The 30-day term repo rate is assumed to be 4.20 percent per year. At the end of the 30 days, when the transaction expires, the corporate bonds are assumed to have increased in value by 0.30 percent. Santillana uses this information to demonstrate the effects of leverage on portfolio returns.

Responding to a question asked by a committee member, Santillana explains: "The quality of collateral as well as short sellers' positions affect the repo rate."

International Bond Investing and Hedging

Santillana also mentions to the investment committee that the Foundation's current portfolio does not include international bonds. She describes the

EXHIBIT 1	Summary Information Relevant to International Bond Investing				
	U.K.	**Japan**	**Germany**	**Singapore**	**U.S.**
1-year interest rate (percent)	6.24	0.97	4.69	2.09	5.30
Yield on 10-year government bond/note (percent)	5.04	1.67	4.36	2.74	4.62
Expected one-year currency appreciation in percent (USD per local currency)	0.10	0.50	0.95	1.60	N/A
10-year bond duration	7.34	9.12	7.72	8.19	7.79

benefits of investing in international bonds and answers the committee's questions. Exhibit 1 displays information she uses during the meeting to clarify her answers. The 1-year interest rate is used as a proxy for the risk-free rate.

The committee is persuaded by Santillana's presentation and decides to invest in international bonds. As a result, Santillana considers whether she should recommend currency hedging using forward contracts, assuming that interest rate parity holds.

During the discussion on international bond investing, a member comments that investors in Japan and Singapore in particular should be investing in the United States because of the difference in bond yields. Santillana agrees but explains that investors should also perform a breakeven spread analysis when investing internationally.

17. Is Santillana correct in her statements about total return analysis *and* scenario analysis?

    A. Yes.

    B. No, because scenario analysis cannot evaluate how individual assumptions affect the total return computation.

    C. No, because scenario analysis cannot lead to a rejection of a strategy with an acceptable expected total return.

18. The 30-day rate of return on the hypothetical leveraged portfolio of corporate bonds is *closest* to:

    A. –0.05 percent.

    B. 0.05 percent.

    C. 0.18 percent.

19. Is Santillana correct in her explanation of factors affecting the repo rate?

    A. Yes.

    B. No, only the quality of collateral is correct.

    C. No, only the short sellers' position is correct.

20. Based on Exhibit 1 and assuming interest rates remain unchanged, which bond will have the *highest* hedged return?

    A. UK 10-year.

    B. Japan 10-year.

    C. Germany 10-year.

21. Based on Exhibit 1 and assuming interest rates remain unchanged, which bond will have the *highest* expected unhedged return?

  A. UK 10-year.

  B. Germany 10-year.

  C. Singapore 10-year.

22. Based on Exhibit 1, for investors that purchased 10-year U.S. notes, the spread widening in basis points that will wipe out the additional yield gained for a quarter is *closest* to:

  A. 6.03 in Singapore.

  B. 8.09 in Japan.

  C. 13.48 in the U.K.

Questions 23–28 relate to Salvatore Choo and are based on Fixed-Income Portfolio Management—Parts I and II

Salvatore Choo, the Chief Investment Officer at European Pension Fund (EPF), wishes to maintain the fixed-income portfolio's active management but recognizes that the portfolio must remain fully funded. The portfolio is run by World Asset Management, where Jimmy Ferragamo, a risk manager, is analyzing the portfolio (shown in Exhibit 1), whose benchmark has a duration of 5.6. None of the bonds in the portfolio have embedded options. However, EPF's liability has a duration of 10.2, creating an asset liability mismatch for the pension fund.

EXHIBIT 1	EPF Portfolio	
Maturity	**Market Value (000)**	**Duration**
2-year bond	€421,000	1.8
5-year bond	€1,101,000	4.8
10-year bond	€1,540,000	8.4
Total	€3,062,000	6.2

Choo is utilizing a contingent immunization (CI) approach to achieve better returns for the fund, so by his understanding of CI, he can use the entire fixed-income portfolio for active management until the portfolio drops below the safety net level or the terminal value.

Ferragamo runs the following risk statistics on the EPF portfolio to ensure that they are not outside the EPF trustee guidelines. He has the following comment:

> "The portfolio value at risk, as opposed to shortfall risk and standard deviation, determines the most the portfolio can lose in any month."

Ferragamo has collected the following data on the bund (German Bond) future, which has a conversion factor of 1.1, and the cheapest to deliver bond is priced at €100,000 and has a duration of 8.2.

In addition to his CIO responsibilities, Choo is also responsible for managing the funding liabilities for a new wing at the local hospital, which is currently fully funded utilizing a standard immunization approach with non-callable bonds. However, he is concerned about the various risks associated with the liabilities including interest rate risk, contingent claim risk, and cap risk.

Choo is interested in using cash flow matching rather than immunization to fund a liability for the new wing. The liability is denominated in euros and will be a lump sum payment in five years. The term structure of interest rates is currently a steep upward-sloping yield curve.

23. Given the term structure of interest rates and the duration mismatch between EPF's benchmark and its pension liability, the plan should be *most concerned* about a:

   A. flattening of the yield curve.

   B. steepening of the yield curve.

   C. large parallel shift up in the yield curve.

24. Choo's understanding of contingent immunization (CI) is:

   A. correct.

   B. incorrect, because CI does not use a terminal value.

   C. incorrect, because CI does not allow for active management.

25. Is Ferragamo's comment correct?

   A. Yes.

   B. No, because shortfall risk would provide this information.

   C. No, because value at risk does not indicate the magnitude of the very worst possible outcomes.

26. Based on the data Ferragamo collected on the bund and Exhibit 1, Choo can adjust the EPF portfolio duration to match the benchmark duration by selling:

   A. 2,240 contracts.

   B. 2,406 contracts.

   C. 2,465 contracts.

27. Are Choo's concerns regarding various risks of funding the hospital liability correct?

   A. Yes.

   B. No, because interest rate risk is not a factor.

   C. No, because contingent claim risk is not a factor.

28. Which of the following would best immunize the hospital liability?

   A. A five-year euro coupon bond.

   B. A five-year euro zero-coupon bond.

   C. Equal investment in three- and seven-year euro zero-coupon bonds.

The following problem is based on Fixed-Income Portfolio Management—Parts I and II

29. A portfolio manager decided to purchase corporate bonds with a market value of €5 million. To finance 60 percent of the purchase, the portfolio manager entered into a 30-day repurchase agreement with the bond dealer. The 30-day term repo rate was 4.6 percent per year. At the end of the 30 days, the bonds purchased by the portfolio manager have increased in value by 0.5 percent and the portfolio manager decided to sell the bonds. No coupons were received during the 30-day period.

    A. Compute the 30-day rate of return on the equity and borrowed components of the portfolio.

    B. Compute the 30-day portfolio rate of return.

    C. Compute the 30-day portfolio rate of return if the increase in value of the bonds was 0.3 percent instead of 0.5 percent.

    D. Use your answers to parts B and C above to comment on the effect of the use of leverage on the portfolio rate of return.

    E. Discuss why the bond dealer in the above example faces a credit risk even if the bond dealer holds the collateral.

SOLUTIONS FOR READING 30

1. **A.** Because you are considering bonds with embedded options, the returns of portfolios are unlikely to be normally distributed. Because shortfall risk is not based on normality assumption, however, it may be used as a risk measure. Furthermore, because the client has specified a minimum target return (£25,000/£2,000,000 or 1.25 percent over the next six months), shortfall risk could be a useful measure to look at.

   B. One of the shortcomings of shortfall risk is that it is not as commonly used as standard deviation, and there is relatively less familiarity with shortfall risk. Also, its statistical properties are not well known. Unlike VAR, it does not take the form of a dollar amount. Finally, the shortfall risk gives the probability of the returns from the portfolio falling below the specified minimum target return, but it does not provide any information about the extent to which the return may be below the specified minimum target.

2. **A.** Because the fund desires to increase the duration, it would need to buy futures contracts.

   B. D_T = target duration for the portfolio = 10

   D_I = initial duration for the portfolio = 8.17

   P_I = initial market value of the portfolio = €75 million

   D_{CTD} = the duration of the cheapest-to-deliver bond = 9.35

   P_{CTD} = the price of the cheapest-to-deliver bond = €130,000

   Conversion factor for the cheapest-to-deliver bond = 1.06

$$\text{Approximate number of contracts} = \frac{(D_T - D_I)\,P_I}{D_{CTD}P_{CTD}} \times \text{Conversion factor for the CTD bond}$$

$$= \frac{(10.0 - 8.17) \times 75,000,000}{9.35 \times 130,000} \times 1.06 = 119.69.$$

   Thus, the pension fund would need to buy 119 futures contracts to achieve the desired increase in duration.

3. Covered call writing is a good strategy if the rates are not going to change much from their present level. The sale of the calls brings in premium income that provides partial protection in case rates increase. The additional income from writing calls can be used to offset declining prices. If rates fall, portfolio appreciation is limited because the short call position is a liability for the seller, and this liability increases as rates go down. Consequently, there is limited upside potential for the covered call writer. Overall, this drawback does not have negative consequences if rates do not change because the added income from the sale of calls would be obtained without sacrificing any gains. Thus, Consultant A, who suggested selling covered calls, probably believes that the interest rates would not change much in either direction.

   Doing nothing would be a good strategy for a bondholder if he believes that rates are going down. The bondholder could simply gain from the increasing bond prices. Thus, Consultant B, who suggested doing nothing, likely believes that the interest rates would go down.

If one has no clear opinion about the interest rate outlook but would like to avoid risk, selling interest rate futures would be a good strategy. If interest rates were to increase, the loss in value of bonds would be offset by the gains from futures. Thus, Consultant C, who suggested selling interest rate futures, is likely the one who has no opinion.

Paying the premium for buying the puts would not be a bad idea if a bondholder believes that interest rates are going to increase. Thus, Consultant D is likely the one who believes that the interest rates are headed upward.

4. The payoff to More Money Funds would be:

Payoff = $(0.030 - \text{Credit spread at maturity}) \times \$10 \text{ million} \times 5$

A. Payoff = $(0.030 - 0.025) \times \$10 \text{ million} \times 5 = \$250,000$.

B. Payoff = $(0.030 - 0.035) \times \$10 \text{ million} \times 5 = \$250,000$, or a loss of $250,000.

C. The maximum gain would be in the unlikely event of credit spread at the forward contract maturity being zero. So, the best possible payoff is $(0.030 - 0.000) \times \$10 \text{ million} \times 5 = \$1,500,000$.

5. First, let us compute the amount in each of the three tranches in the CDO. The senior tranche is 70 percent of $250 million = $175 million. The junior tranche is 20 percent of $250 million = $50 million. The rest is the equity tranche = $250 million − $175 million − $50 million = $25 million.

Now let us compute the amount that would be received by the equity tranche. Annual interest generated by the collateral would be 6 + 5 = 11 percent of $250 million = $27.5 million. Annual interest received by the senior tranche would be 7.5 + 0.5 = 8 percent of $175 million = $14 million. Annual interest received by the junior tranche would be 6 + 3 = 9 percent of $50 million = $4.5 million. So, the amount to be received by the equity tranche is 27.5 − 14 − 4.5 = $9 million. This amount represents a return of 9/25 = 0.36 or 36 percent.

6. The mispricing occurs because the forward rate doesn't conform to the covered interest rate parity theorem.

A. The current discount rate is −2.48 percent [i.e., ($1.18 − $1.21)/$1.21]

B. The covered interest rate parity theorem states that the forward foreign exchange rate for a fixed period must be equal to the interest rate differentials between the two countries.

Forward rate = Spot rate × (1 + Domestic interest rate) / (1 + Foreign interest rate)

Substituting into the formula:

Forward rate = $1.21 (1 + 0.02)/(1 + 0.03)

Forward rate = $1.198

7. The investor can evaluate the change in value of the Canadian bond if U.S. rates change by 80 bps as follows:

Δ in value of Canadian bond = Canadian bond's duration × Canada country beta × Δ in U.S. rates

Δ in value of Canadian bond = 8.40 × 0.63 × 0.80 percent

Δ in value of Canadian bond = 4.23 percent

8. Let *W* denote the spread widening.

      Change in price = Duration × Change in yield

      Change in price = 8.3 × *W*

Assuming the increase in price caused by the spread widening will be 0.75 percent

      0.75 percent = 8.3 × *W*

Solving for the spread widening, *W*,

      W = 0.0904 percent = 9.04 bps

Thus, a spread widening of 9.04 bps would wipe out the additional yield gained from investing in the U.S. bond. The 0.0904 percent change in rates would wipe out the quarterly yield advantage of 75 bps.

9. The forward premium on the Japanese yen is 2.7 − 1.6 = 1.1 percent. So, the portfolio manager should hedge using a forward contract if the anticipated return on yen is less than 1.1 percent.

   A. Because the anticipated return on yen of 1.5 percent is greater than 1.1 percent, the portfolio manager should not hedge.

   B. Because the anticipated return on yen of 0.5 percent is less than 1.1 percent, the portfolio manager should hedge.

10. The interest rate differential between the U.K. pound and the U.S. dollar is 4.7 − 4.0 = 0.7 percent. Because this differential is greater than the 0.4 percent return on the U.S. dollar expected by the fund manager, the forward hedged position has a higher expected return than the unhedged position.

11. C is correct. TBW is most likely forecasting a decrease in interest rates based on the desire to take on additional interest rate risks. Based on the recommendation to adjust the average duration across the portfolio, rather than key rate duration adjustments, it conveys the expectation of a parallel yield curve shift.

12. B is correct. Because Ibahn wants to take on additional interest rate risk in the portfolio, she would extend duration. To extend duration, Ibahn would need to purchase interest rate futures contracts.

13. B is correct. The 2-year term leverage would shorten the total duration of the levered portfolio relative to overnight repo by the dollar duration of the 2-year liability. The levered portfolio duration would be longer using overnight repo because its proceeds are being invested in bonds to have the same duration as the unlevered portfolio—thus the net effect is a longer duration because the overnight repo duration is zero.

14. B is correct. The duration of the sample leveraged portfolio = (Total dollar duration/Investors' equity in the original portfolio) × 100 = ($5,125,000/100,000,000) × 100 = 5.13

15. A is correct. The cost of a repo on special collateral is actually lower than the standard cost of a repo because those needing that collateral are willing to lend funds at a lower cost to obtain that "special" collateral. The illiquidity of the collateral actually increases the margin requirement for the repo as those lending funds want more margin to offset the risk of them having to liquidate the collateral in the event of a borrower default (the entity using the repo to obtain the funds).

16. C is correct. The effect of leverage on a portfolio is that the distribution of returns widens, both to the upside and the downside. In this case, the cost of carry versus the yield on the portfolio causes the return on the levered portfolio to be lower than the return on the unlevered portfolio when interest rates are unchanged.

17. A is correct. Scenario analysis can help evaluate the contribution of individual assumptions (inputs, like the reinvestment rate assumption) to the total return computation. Also, the distribution of outcomes from a scenario analysis may be so wide that it exceeds a client's risk tolerance, even if the expected return is acceptable.

18. C is correct.

	Borrowed Funds	**Equity Funds**
Amount Invested	$5,000,000	$2,000,000
Rate of Return (0.30% increase in value)	$15,000	$6,000
Less Interest expense at 4.2% (4.2/12 = 0.35% per 30 day)	$17,500	
Net Profitability	−$2,500	$6,000
Rate of Return on Each Component	−0.05% (−2,500/5,000,000)	0.30%
Rate of Return	0.175% [(−2,500 + 6,000)/2,000,000]	

19. A is correct. The quality of the collateral affects the repo rate. Short sellers' needs can affect the demand/availability of the collateral, and hence the repo rate, when the lender of the funds needs the collateral for a short sale.

20. B is correct. The hedged return is equal to the sum of the domestic risk-free interest rate i_d plus the bond's local risk premium of the foreign bond $r_l - i_f$. The local risk premium of 0.70% on the Japanese bond (1.67 − 0.97) is higher than the local risk premium in any of the other countries.

21. B is correct. The unhedged return is approximately equal to the foreign bond return in local currency terms plus the currency return, which is the percentage change in the spot exchange rate stated in terms of home currency per unit of foreign currency. The expected unhedged return on the German bond is the bond yield of 4.36% plus the expected local currency appreciation of 0.95%, for a total of 5.31%.

22. B is correct. The spread widening equals the additional yield income per quarter (4.62 − 1.67)/4 = 0.7375% for Japan, divided by the higher of the two countries' durations, that is, 73.75/9.12 = 8.09.

23. A is correct. Given the mismatch in the liability and the benchmark they are running against, a flattening of the yield curve would cause the liability to increase faster than the asset.

24. A is correct. Contingent immunization does utilize the entire portfolio for active management.

25. C is correct. Value at risk does not indicate the magnitude of the very worst possible outcomes.

26. C is correct. (5.6 − 6.2) × 3,062,000,000/8.2/100,000 × 1.1 = 2,465

27. A is correct. Cap risk, interest rate risk, and contingent claim risk are all risks the portfolio manager faces.

28. B is correct. A five-year zero-coupon bond best matches the liability of five years.

29. A. Equity = E = 40 percent of €5 million = €2 million

Borrowed funds = B = 60 percent of €5 million = €3 million

k = Cost of borrowed funds = 4.6 percent per year
= 4.6/12 or 0.3833 percent per 30 days

r_F = Return on funds invested = 0.5 percent

Therefore,

R_E = Return on equity = r_F = 0.5 percent

R_B = Return on borrowed funds = $r_F - k$ = 0.5 − 0.3833
= 0.1167 percent

B. R_P = Portfolio rate of return = (Profit on borrowed funds + Profit on equity)/Amount of equity = $[B \times (r_F - k) + E \times r_F]/E$ =
[€3 million × (0.5 − 0.3833) + €2 million × 0.5]/€2 million =
0.6750 percent.

C. R_P = Portfolio rate of return = (Profit on borrowed funds + Profit on equity)/Amount of equity = $[B \times (r_F - k) + E \times r_F]/E$ =
[€3 million × (0.3 − 0.3833) + €2 million × 0.3]/€2 million =
0.1751 percent.

D. If the return on funds invested exceeds the cost of borrowing, then leverage magnifies the portfolio rate of return. This condition holds for the case in Part B, where the return on funds of 0.5 percent exceeds the cost of borrowing of 0.3833 percent, and therefore, the portfolio return (0.6750 percent) is greater than the return on funds.

If the return on funds invested is less than the cost of borrowing, then leverage is a drag on the portfolio rate of return. This condition holds for the case in Part C, where the return on funds of 0.3 percent is less than the cost of borrowing of 0.3833 percent, and therefore, the portfolio return (0.1751 percent) is less than the return on funds.

E. The bond dealer faces a credit risk even if he holds the collateral. The reason is that the value of the collateral may decline to such an extent that its market value falls below the amount lent. In such a situation, if the borrower defaults, the market value of the collateral will be insufficient to cover the amount lent.

$4\frac{5}{8}$ $4\frac{11}{16}$ $3\frac{3}{8}$

$5\frac{1}{2}$ $5\frac{1}{2}$ $- \frac{3}{8}$

$5\frac{1}{2}$ $21\frac{3}{16}$ $- \frac{1}{8}$

$20\frac{5}{8}$ $21\frac{3}{16}$

$17\frac{3}{8}$ $18\frac{1}{8}$ $+ \frac{7}{8}$

$9\frac{1}{2}$ $6\frac{1}{2}$ $6\frac{1}{2}$ $- \frac{1}{2}$

$7\frac{1}{4}$ $31\frac{1}{32}$ $- \frac{1}{8}$

$15\frac{7}{16}$ $9\frac{7}{8}$

$9\frac{9}{16}$

$1\frac{7}{32}$ $7\frac{15}{8}$

$7\frac{13}{16}$ $7\frac{15}{8}$

$7\frac{15}{16}$

$2\frac{5}{8}$ $2\frac{11}{32}$ $2\frac{1}{2}$ $+$

$2\frac{3}{4}$ $2\frac{1}{4}$ $2\frac{1}{4}$

$6\frac{1}{16}$ $12\frac{1}{16}$ $11\frac{3}{8}$ $11\frac{3}{4}$ $+$

87 $33\frac{3}{4}$ 33 $33\frac{1}{8}$ $-$

602 $25\frac{5}{8}$ $24\frac{9}{16}$ $25\frac{5}{8}$ $+$

833 12 $11\frac{5}{8}$ $11\frac{7}{8}$ $+$

16 $10\frac{1}{2}$ $10\frac{1}{2}$ $10\frac{1}{2}$ $-$

78 $15\frac{5}{8}$ $15\frac{13}{16}$ $15\frac{5}{8}$ $-$

$8\frac{1}{8}$ $+$

4508 $9\frac{1}{16}$ $8\frac{1}{4}$

430 $11\frac{1}{4}$ $10\frac{1}{8}$

HEDGING MORTGAGE SECURITIES TO CAPTURE RELATIVE VALUE

by Kenneth B. Dunn, Roberto M. Sella, and Frank J. Fabozzi, CFA

LEARNING OUTCOMES

The candidate should be able to:	Mastery
a. demonstrate how a mortgage security's negative convexity will affect the performance of a hedge;	☐
b. explain the risks associated with investing in mortgage securities and discuss whether these risks can be effectively hedged;	☐
c. contrast an individual mortgage security to a Treasury security with respect to the importance of yield-curve risk;	☐
d. compare and contrast duration-based approaches with interest rate sensitivity approaches to hedging mortgage securities.	☐

INTRODUCTION 1

Because of the spread offered on residential agency mortgage-backed securities, they often outperform government securities with the *same interest rate risk* and therefore they can be used to generate enhanced returns relative to a benchmark when the yield advantage of mortgage securities is attractive. However, to execute this strategy successfully, the prepayment risk of mortgage securities must be managed carefully. In this reading, we will see how this is done. Specifically, we will see how to "hedge" the interest rate risk associated with a

The authors thank Menglin Luo, CFA, for his assistance in providing the illustrations for this reading.

Fixed Income Readings for the Chartered Financial Analyst® Program, Second Edition, edited by Frank J. Fabozzi, CFA. Copyright © 2005 by CFA Institute. Reprinted with permission.

fixed rate mortgage security in order to capture the spread over Treasuries.[1] Note that we use the terms mortgage-backed securities and mortgage securities interchangeably in this reading. The most basic form of mortgage-backed security is the mortgage passthrough security. Securities that are created from mortgage passthrough securities include collateralized mortgage obligations and mortgage strips (interest-only and principal-only securities).

2 THE PROBLEM

To illustrate the problem faced by a portfolio manager who believes that the spread offered on a mortgage security is attractive and wants to hedge that spread, look at Exhibit 1. The exhibit shows the relationship between price and yield for a mortgage passthrough security. The yield for a mortgage security is the cash flow yield.[2] The price-yield relationship exhibits both positive and negative convexity. At yield levels above y^*, the mortgage security exhibits positive convexity; at yield levels below y^*, the mortgage security exhibits negative convexity.

EXHIBIT 1	Price-Yield Relationship for a Mortgage Passthrough Security

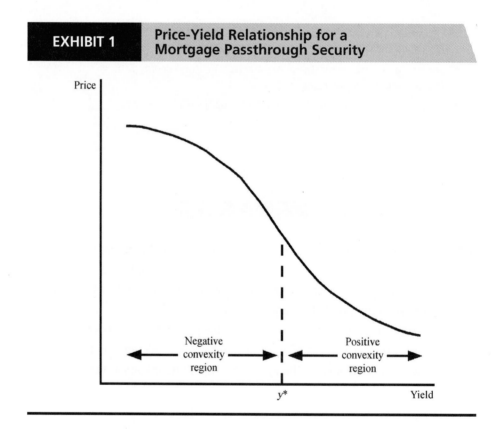

---

[1] In European countries where mortgage-backed securities are issued, the coupon rate is typically a floating rate.

[2] The cash flow yield is the interest rate (properly annualized) that makes the present value of the projected cash flows from a mortgage-backed security equal to its price.

EXHIBIT 2	**Price Changes Resulting from Positive and Negative Convexity**

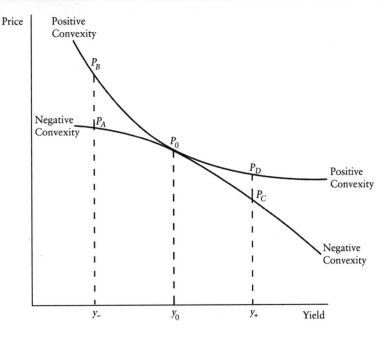

P_0 = initial price
P_A = price if yield decreases from y_0 to y_- for the negative convexity bond
P_B = price if yield decreases from y_0 to y_- for the positive convexity bond
P_C = price if yield increases from y_0 to y_+ for the negative convexity bond
P_D = price if yield increases from y_0 to y_+ for the positive convexity bond

Implications:
For a given change in yield, for a bond with positive convexity:
$\quad P_B - P_0 > |P_D - P_0|$ (i.e., gain is greater than the loss)
For a given change in yield, for a bond with negative convexity:
$\quad |P_C - P_0| > P_A - P_0$ (i.e., loss is greater than the gain)

It is important to understand this characteristic of a mortgage security. One way to understand it is to look at what happens to the change in price when interest rates move up and down by the same number of basis points. This can be seen in Exhibit 2, which shows the price-yield relationship for a security that exhibits positive convexity such as a Treasury security and a security that exhibits negative convexity. Let's look at what happens to the price change in absolute terms when interest rates change. From Exhibit 2 we observe the following property:

> For a security that exhibits positive convexity, the price increase when interest rates decline is greater than the price decrease when interest rates rise.

This is not the case for a security that exhibits negative convexity. Instead, we also observe from Exhibit 2 the following property:

> For a security that exhibits negative convexity, the price increase when interest rates decline is less than the price decrease when interest rates rise.

Why will a mortgage security exhibit negative convexity at some yield level? The explanation is the home-owner's prepayment option. The value of a mortgage security declines as the value of the prepayment option increases. As mortgage rates in the market decline, the value of the prepayment option increases. As a result, the appreciation due to a decline in interest rates that would result if there had not been a prepayment option will be reduced by the increase in the value of the option.

We can see this by thinking about an agency mortgage security as equivalent to a position in a comparable-duration Treasury security and a call option. We can express the value of the mortgage security as follows:

$$\text{Value of mortgage security} = \text{Value of a Treasury security} \\ - \text{Value of the prepayment option}$$

The reason for subtracting the value of the prepayment option is that the investor in a mortgage security has sold a prepayment option. Consider what happens as interest rates change. When interest rates decline, the value of the Treasury security component of the mortgage security's value increases. However, the appreciation is reduced by the increase in the value of the prepayment option which becomes more valuable as interest rates decline. The net effect is that while the value of a mortgage security increases, it does not increase by as much as a same-duration Treasury security because the increase in the value of the prepayment option offsets part of the appreciation.

When interest rates rise, we see the opposite effect of the prepayment option. A rise in interest rates results in a decline in the value of the Treasury security component of the mortgage security's value. At the same time, the value of the prepayment option declines. The net effect is that while the value of a mortgage security decreases, it does not decline in value as much as a same-duration Treasury security because the decline in the value of the prepayment option offsets part of the depreciation.

Another way of viewing positive and negative convexity is how the duration changes when interest rates change. Exhibit 3 shows tangent lines to the price/yield relationship for two securities, one exhibiting positive convexity and the other negative convexity. The tangent line is related to the duration. The steeper the tangent line, the higher the duration. Notice in Exhibit 3 the following:

	Effect on Duration When Interest Rates	
Convexity	Fall	Rise
Positive	Increases	Decreases
Negative	Decreases	Increases

That is, for a security that exhibits positive convexity, the duration changes in the desired direction; for a security that exhibits negative convexity, there is an adverse change in the duration.

While a mortgage security can exhibit both positive and negative convexity, a Treasury security exhibits only positive convexity. Look at the problem of hedging the interest rate risk associated with a mortgage security by either shorting Treasury securities or selling Treasury futures (i.e., hedging an instrument that has the potential for negative convexity with an instrument that only exhibits positive convexity). The hedging principle is that the change in the value of the mortgage security position for a given basis point change in interest rates will be offset by the change in the value of the Treasury position for the same basis point

EXHIBIT 3	Positive and Negative Convexity and Duration Changes

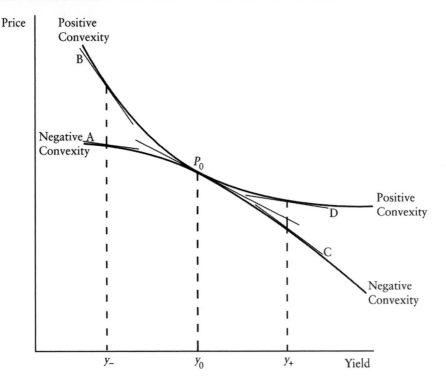

Duration at y_0 is the same for both the positive and negative convex securities.

When interest rates decrease, duration for the positively convex security (tangent line B) increases (i.e., becomes steeper) while the duration for negatively convex security (tangent line A) decreases (i.e., becomes flatter).

When interest rates increase, duration for the positively convex security (tangent line D) decreases (i.e., becomes flatter) while the duration for negatively convex security (tangent line C) increases (i.e., becomes steeper).

change in interest rates. When interest rates decline, prepayments cause the value of a mortgage security to increase less in value than that of a Treasury position with the same initial duration. Thus, when interest rates decline, simply matching the dollar duration of the Treasury position with the dollar duration of the mortgage security will not provide an appropriate hedge when the mortgage security exhibits negative convexity.

For this reason, many investors consider mortgages to be market-directional investments that should be avoided when one expects interest rates to decline.[3] Fortunately, when properly managed, mortgage securities are not market-directional investments. Proper management begins with separating mortgage valuation decisions from decisions concerning the appropriate interest-rate sensitivity of the portfolio. In turn, this separation of the value decision from the duration decision hinges critically on proper hedging. Without proper hedging

---

[3] This perception is exacerbated by the common practice of comparing the returns of the mortgage index with the returns of the government and corporate indices without adjusting for differences in duration. Because the mortgage index typically has less duration than either the corporate or government index, it generally has better relative performance when interest rates rise than when interest rates fall.

to offset the changes in the duration of mortgage securities caused by interest rate movements, the portfolio's duration would drift adversely from its target duration. In other words, the portfolio would be shorter than desired when interest rates decline and longer than desired when interest rates rise.

3   MORTGAGE SECURITY RISKS

Proper hedging requires understanding the principal risks associated with investing in mortgage securities. There are five principal risks: spread, interest-rate, prepayment, volatility, and model risk. The yield of a mortgage security—the cumulative reward for bearing all five of these risks—has two components: the yield on equal interest-rate risk Treasury securities plus a spread. This spread is itself the sum of the option cost, which is the expected cost of bearing prepayment risk, and the option-adjusted spread (OAS), which is the risk premium for bearing the remaining risks, including model risk.

A. Spread Risk

A portfolio manager would want to invest in mortgage securities when their spreads versus Treasuries are large enough to compensate for the risk surrounding the homeowner's prepayment option. Because the OAS can be thought of as the risk premium for holding mortgage securities, *a portfolio manager does not seek to hedge spread risk.* If a portfolio manager hedges against spread widening, she also gives up the benefit from spread narrowing. Instead, a portfolio manager seeks to capture the OAS over time by increasing the allocation to mortgage securities when yield spreads are wide and reducing exposure to mortgage securities when yield spreads are narrow.

To calculate the OAS for any mortgage security, a prepayment model is employed that assigns an expected prepayment rate every month—implying an expected cash flow—for a given interest rate path. These expected cash flows are discounted at U.S. Treasury spot rates to obtain their present value. This process is repeated for a large number of interest rate paths. Finally, the average present value of the cash flows across all paths is calculated. Typically, the average present value across all paths is not equal to the price of the security. However, we can search for a unique "spread" (in basis points) that, when added to the U.S. Treasury spot rates, equates the average present value to the price of the security. This spread is the OAS.

Historical comparisons are of only limited use for making judgments about current OAS levels relative to the past, because option-adjusted spreads depend on their underlying prepayment models. As a model changes, so does the OAS for a given mortgage security. There are periods where prepayment models change significantly, making comparisons to historical OASs tenuous. A portfolio manager should augment OAS analysis with other tools to help identify periods when spreads on mortgage securities are attractive, attempting to avoid periods when spread widening will erase the yield advantage over Treasuries with the same interest rate risk. The risk that the OAS may change, or **spread risk**, is managed by investing heavily in mortgage securities only when the initial OAS is large.

B. Interest Rate Risk

The interest rate risk of a mortgage security corresponds to the interest rate risk of comparable Treasury securities (i.e., a Treasury security with the same duration). This risk can be hedged directly by selling a package of Treasury notes or Treasury note futures. Once a portfolio manager has hedged the interest rate risk of a mortgage security, what can the manager earn? Recall that by hedging interest rate risk, a manager synthetically creates a Treasury bill and therefore earns the return on a Treasury bill. But what still remains after the interest rate risk is removed is the spread risk which, as just explained, is not hedged away. So, the portfolio manager after hedging interest rate risk can earn the Treasury bill return plus a spread over Treasuries. However, a portfolio manager cannot capture all of this spread because some of it is needed to cover the value of the homeowner's prepayment option. After netting the value of the option, the portfolio manager earns the Treasury bill rate plus the potential to capture the OAS.

Yield Curve Risk

Duration and convexity are measures of interest rate risk for "level" changes in interest rates. That is, if all Treasury rates shifted up or down by the same number of basis points, these measures do a good job of approximating the exposure of a security or a portfolio to a rate change. However, yield curves do not change in a parallel fashion. Consequently, portfolios with the same duration can perform quite differently when the yield curve shifts in a nonparallel fashion. **Yield curve risk** is the exposure of a portfolio or a security to a nonparallel change in the yield curve shape.

One approach to quantifying yield curve risk for a security or a portfolio is to compute how changes in a specific spot rate, holding all other spot rates constant, affect the value of a security or a portfolio. The sensitivity of the change in value of a security or a portfolio to a particular spot rate change is called rate duration. In theory, there is a rate duration for every point on the yield curve. Consequently, there is not one rate duration, but a profile of rate durations representing each maturity on the yield curve. The total change in value if all rates change by the same number of basis points is simply the duration of a security or portfolio to a change in the level of rates. That is, it is the duration measure for level risk (i.e., a parallel shift in the yield curve).

Vendors of analytical systems do not provide a rate duration for every point on the yield curve. Instead, they focus on key maturities of the spot rate curve. These rate durations are called key rate durations.

The impact of any type of yield curve shift can be quantified using key rate durations. A level shift can be quantified by changing all key rates by the same number of basis points and computing, based on the corresponding key rate durations, the effect on the value of a portfolio. The impact of a steepening of the yield curve can be found by 1) decreasing the key rates at the short end of the yield curve and determining the change in the portfolio value using the corresponding key rate durations, and 2) increasing the key rates at the long end of the yield curve and determining the change in the portfolio value using the corresponding key rate durations.

The value of an option-free bond with a bullet maturity payment (i.e., entire principal due at the maturity date) is sensitive to changes in the level of interest rates but not as sensitive to changes in the shape of the yield curve. This is because for an option-free bond whose cash flow consists of periodic coupon payments but only one principal payment (at maturity), the change of rates along the spot rate curve will not have a significant impact on its value. In contrast, while the value of a portfolio of option-free bonds is, of course, sensitive to changes in the level of interest rates, it is much more sensitive to changes in the shape of the yield curve than individual option-free bonds.

In the case of mortgage securities, the value of both an individual mortgage security and a portfolio of mortgage securities will be sensitive to changes in the shape of the yield curve, as well as changes in the level of interest rates. This is because a mortgage security is an amortizing security with a prepayment option. Consequently, the pattern of the expected cash flows for an individual mortgage security can be materially affected by the shape of the yield curve. To see this, look at Exhibit 4, which shows the key rate durations for a Ginnie Mae 30-year 10% passthrough, the current coupon passthrough at the time the graph was prepared. Exhibit 5 shows the key rate duration profile for a principal-only (PO) and an interest-only (IO) mortgage strip created from the Ginnie Mae passthrough whose key rate durations are shown in Exhibit 4.

From Exhibit 4 it can be seen that the passthrough exhibits a bell-shaped curve with the peak of the curve between 5 and 15 years. Adding up the key rate durations from 5 to 15 years (i.e., the 5-year, 7-year, 10-year, and 15-year key rate durations) indicates that of the total interest rate exposure, about 70% is within this maturity range. That is, the effective duration alone masks the fact that the interest rate exposure for this passthrough is concentrated in the 5-year to 15-year maturity range.

A PO will have a high positive duration. From the key rate duration profile for the PO shown in Exhibit 5 it can be seen that the key rate durations are negative up to year 7. Thereafter, the key rate durations are positive and have a high value. While the total risk exposure (i.e., effective duration) may be positive, there is exposure to yield curve risk. For example, the key rate durations suggest that if the long end of the yield curve is unchanged, but the short end of the yield curve (up to year 7) decreases, the PO's value will decline despite an effective duration that is positive.

EXHIBIT 4	Key Rate Duration Profile for a 30-Year Ginnie Mae Passthrough

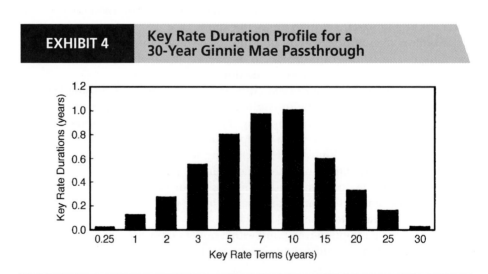

Source: Exhibit 12 in Thomas S.Y. Ho, "Key Rate Durations: Measures of Interest Rate Risks," *Journal of Fixed Income* (September 1992), p. 38. This copyrighted material is reprinted with permission from Institutional Investor, Inc. *Journal of Fixed Income,* 488 Madison Avenue, New York, NY 10022.

| EXHIBIT 5 | Key Rate Duration Profiles for a PO and an IO for Current Coupon Ginnie Mae |

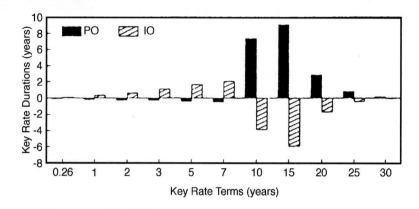

Source: Exhibit 13 in Thomas S.Y. Ho, "Key Rate Durations: Measures of Interest Rate Risks," *Journal of Fixed Income* (September 1992), p. 38. This copyrighted material is reprinted with permission from Institutional Investor, Inc. *Journal of Fixed Income,* 488 Madison Avenue, New York, NY 10022.

IOs have a high negative duration. However, from the key rate duration profile in Exhibit 5 it can be seen that the key rate durations are positive up to year 10 and then take on high negative values. As with the PO, this security is highly susceptible to how the yield curve changes.

While the key rate durations are helpful in understanding the exposure of a mortgage security or a portfolio to yield curve risk, we will present an alternative methodology for assessing the yield curve risk of a mortgage security when we discuss the hedging methodology in Section 5.

C. Prepayment Risk

When interest rates decline, homeowners have an economic incentive to prepay their existing mortgages by refinancing at a lower rate. As demonstrated earlier, because of the prepayment option the duration of mortgage securities varies in an undesirable way as interest rates change: extending as rates rise and shortening as rates fall. Therefore, the percentage increase in price of a mortgage security for successive 25 basis point declines in yield, for example, becomes smaller and smaller. Conversely, the percentage decline in price becomes greater as interest rates rise. Termed negative convexity, this effect can be significant—particularly for mortgage securities that concentrate prepayment risk such as interest-only strips.

When interest rates change we must offset the resultant change in mortgage durations in order to keep the overall interest rate risk of the portfolio at its desired target. Neglecting to do so would leave the portfolio with less interest rate risk than desired after interest rates decline and more risk than desired after rates increase. A portfolio manager should adjust for changes in durations of mortgage securities—or equivalently, manage negative convexity—either by buying options or by hedging dynamically.

Hedging dynamically requires lengthening duration—buying futures—after rates have declined, and shortening duration—selling futures—after rates have risen. Whether a portfolio manager employs this "buy high/sell low" dynamic strategy, or buys options, the portfolio's performance is bearing the cost associated with managing negative convexity by forgoing part of the spread over Treasuries.

D. Volatility Risk

An investment characteristic of an option is that its value increases with expected volatility. In the case of an interest rate option, the pertinent volatility is interest rate volatility. The prepayment option granted to a homeowner is an interest rate option and therefore the homeowner's prepayment option becomes more valuable when future interest rate volatility is expected to be high than when it is expected to be low. Because the OAS adjusts to compensate the investor for selling the prepayment option to the homeowner, OAS tends to widen when expected volatility increases and narrow when expected volatility declines.

A portfolio manager can manage volatility risk by buying options or by hedging dynamically. The selection depends on the following:

▶ When the volatility implied in option prices is high and the portfolio manager believes that future realized volatility will be lower than implied volatility, he should hedge dynamically.

▶ When implied volatility is low and the portfolio manager believes that actual future volatility will be higher than implied volatility, he should hedge by purchasing options.

Because it has been our experience that implied volatilities have tended to exceed subsequent realized volatility, we have generally hedged dynamically to a greater extent than we have hedged through the use of options.

E. Model Risk

Mortgage prepayment models generate cash flows for a given set of interest rate paths. But what happens when the models are wrong? In the rally of 1993, premium mortgages prepaid at much faster rates than predicted by most prepayment models in use at that time. Investors who had purchased interest-only strips (IOs) backed by premium mortgages, and had relied on the prepayment predictions of those models, sustained losses. It is important to note that prior to the rally, the OAS on IOs seemed attractive on a historical basis. However, the model OAS assumed a conditional prepayment rate (CPR) of 40% for premium mortgages; the actual CPR for premium mortgages was as high as 60%, causing the realized OAS to be negative.

Current models calibrate to historical experience. Although a portfolio manager does not know the magnitude of model error going forward, he can measure sensitivity to model error by increasing the prepayment rate assumed by the model for mortgage securities that are hurt by faster-than-expected prepayments and decreasing the prepayment rate assumed by the model for mortgage securities that are hurt by slower-than-expected prepayments.

Over time it has become cheaper to refinance mortgages as technological improvements have reduced the costs associated with refinancing. We expect this type of prepayment innovation to continue in the years ahead. Models calibrated to past behavior will understate the impact of innovation. Therefore, when evaluating mortgage securities that are vulnerable to this type of risk, a portfolio manager should carefully consider the likelihood and the effect of prepayment innovation in determining the size of a portfolio's mortgage securities.

Although a portfolio manager cannot hedge **model risk** explicitly, he can measure it and manage it by keeping a portfolio's exposure to this risk in line with that of the broad-based bond market indices.

HOW INTEREST RATES CHANGE OVER TIME
4

While key rate duration is a useful measure for identifying the exposure of a portfolio to different potential shifts in the yield curve, it is difficult to employ this approach to yield curve risk in hedging a portfolio. An alternative approach is to investigate how yield curves have changed historically and incorporate typical yield curve change scenarios into the hedging process. This approach has been used by several firms that specialize in the management of mortgage-backed securities.[4]

Empirically, studies have found that yield curve changes are not parallel. Rather, when the level of interest rates changes, studies have found that short-term rates move more than longer-term rates. Some firms develop their own proprietary models that decompose historical movements in the rate changes of Treasury strips with different maturities in order to analyze typical or likely rate movements. The statistical technique used to decompose rate movements is principal components analysis.

Most empirical studies, published and proprietary, find that more than 95% of historical movements in rate changes can be explained by changes in 1) the overall level of interest rates and 2) twists in the yield curve (i.e., steepening and flattening). For example, Morgan Stanley's proprietary model of the movement of monthly Treasury strip rates finds the following "typical" monthly rate change in basis points for three maturities:

Years	Level		Change From	
	Up	Down	Flattening	Steepening
2	23.0	−23.0	17.2	−17.2
5	25.8	−25.8	11.2	−11.2
10	24.3	−24.3	3.4	−3.4

"Typical" means one standard deviation in the change in the monthly rate. The last two columns in the above table indicate the change in the monthly rate found by principal components analysis that is due to a flattening or steepening of the yield curve. From the above table, the impact on the yield curve for a typical rise in the overall level of interest rates and a flattening of the yield curve is found as follows. To find the typical change in the slope of the 10-year–2-year yield-curve segment, the difference between the 17.2 basis points at 2-year, and 3.4 basis points at 10 years is computed. The difference of 13.8 basis points means that the typical monthly flattening is 13.8 basis points. The typical monthly steepening is 13.8 basis points.

---

[4] For example, the approach is used by Morgan Stanley as discussed in this reading and by Smith Breeden Associates. See Michael P. Schumacher, Daniel C. Dektar, and Frank J. Fabozzi, "Yield Curve Risk of CMO Bonds," Chapter 15 in Frank J. Fabozzi (ed.), *CMO Portfolio Management* (New Hope, PA: Frank J. Fabozzi Associates, 1994).

Because of the importance of yield curve risk for mortgage securities, a hedging methodology should incorporate this information about historical yield curve shifts. We will see how this is done in the next section.

5   HEDGING METHODOLOGY

Hedging is a special case of interest rate risk control where the portfolio manager seeks to completely offset the dollar price change in the instrument to be hedged by taking an opposite position in an appropriate hedging instrument that will produce the same dollar price change for the same change in interest rates.

To properly hedge the interest rate risk associated with a mortgage security, the portfolio manager needs to incorporate his knowledge of the following:

► how the yield curve changes over time, and
► the effect of changes in the yield curve on the homeowner's prepayment option.

Using this information, a portfolio manager can estimate how mortgage security prices will change as interest rates change.

A. Interest Rate Sensitivity Measure

Scott Richard and Benjamin Gord introduced the concept of interest rate sensitivity (IRS) and discussed why it is a better measure of interest rate risk than modified or effective duration.[5] IRS measures a security's or a portfolio's percentage price change in response to a shift in the yield curve.

Since two factors (the "level" and "twist" factors discussed in the previous section) have accounted for most of the changes in the yield curve, two Treasury notes (typically the 2-year and 10-year) can hedge virtually all of the interest rate risk in mortgage securities. Since two hedging instruments are used, the hedge is referred to as a two-bond hedge.

To create the two-bond hedge, we begin by expressing a particular mortgage security in terms of an "equivalent position" in U.S. Treasuries or "equivalent position" in Treasury futures contracts. We identify this equivalent position by picking a package of 2-year and 10-year Treasuries that—on average—has the same price performance as the mortgage security to be hedged under the assumed "level" and "twist" yield curve scenarios. For hedging purposes, the direction of the change—up or down in the case of the "level" factor, flattening or steepening in the case of the "twist" factor—is not known. (In calculating how the price will change in response to changes in the two factors, it is assumed that the OAS is constant.)

In this way, the portfolio manager can calculate the unique quantities of 2-year and 10-year Treasury notes or futures that will simultaneously hedge the mortgage security's price response to both "level" and "twist" scenarios. This combination is the appropriate two-bond hedge for typical yield curve shifts and therefore defines the interest rate sensitivity of the mortgage security in terms of 2-year and 10-year Treasury notes or futures.

---

[5] Scott F. Richard and Benjamin J. Gord, "Measuring and Managing Interest-Rate Risk," Chapter 7 in Frank J. Fabozzi (ed.), *Perspectives on Interest Rate Risk Management for Money Managers and Traders* (New Hope, PA: Frank J. Fabozzi Associates, 1998).

B. Computing the Two-Bond Hedge

The steps to compute the two-bond hedge are as follows:

Step 1: For an assumed shift in the level of the yield curve, compute the following:

▶ price of the mortgage security for an assumed increase in the level of interest rates;

▶ price for the mortgage security for an assumed decrease in the level of interest rates;

▶ price of the 2-year Treasury note (or futures) for an assumed increase in the level of interest rates;

▶ price of the 2-year Treasury note (or futures) for an assumed decrease in the level of interest rates;

▶ price of the 10-year Treasury note (or futures) for an assumed increase in the level of interest rates;

▶ price of the 10-year Treasury note (or futures) for an assumed decrease in the level of interest rates.

Step 2: From the prices found in Step 1, calculate the price change for the mortgage security, 2-year Treasury note (or futures), and 10-year Treasury note (or futures) for the assumed shift in the level of interest rates. There will be two price changes for each of the mortgage security, 2-year hedging instrument, and 10-year hedging instrument.

Step 3: Calculate the average price change for the mortgage security and the two hedging instruments for the assumed shift in the level of interest rates assuming that the two scenarios (i.e., increase and decrease) are equally likely to occur. The average price change will be denoted as follows:

MBS price$_L$ = average price change for the mortgage security for a level shift

2-*H* price$_L$ = average price change for the 2-year Treasury hedging instrument for a level shift

10-*H* price$_L$ = average price change for the 10-year Treasury hedging instrument for a level shift

Step 4: For an assumed twist (flattening and steepening) of the yield curve, compute the following:

▶ price of the mortgage security for an assumed flattening of the yield curve;

▶ price of the mortgage security for an assumed steepening of the yield curve;

▶ price of 2-year Treasury note (or futures) for an assumed flattening of the yield curve;

▶ price of 2-year Treasury note (or futures) for an assumed steepening of the yield curve;

▶ price of 10-year Treasury note (or futures) for an assumed flattening of the yield curve;

▶ price of 10-year Treasury note (or futures) for an assumed steepening of the yield curve.

Step 5: From the prices found in Step 4, calculate the price change for the mortgage security, 2-year Treasury note (or futures), and 10-year Treasury note (or futures) for the assumed twist in the yield curve. There will be two price changes for each of the mortgage security, 2-year hedging instrument, and 10-year hedging instrument.

Step 6: Calculate the average price change for the mortgage security and the two hedging instruments for the assumed twist in the yield curve assuming that the two scenarios (i.e., flattening and steepening) are equally likely to occur. The average price change will be denoted as follows:

> MBS price$_T$ = average price change for the mortgage security for a twist in the yield curve
>
> 2-H price$_T$ = average price change for the 2-year Treasury hedging instrument for a twist in the yield curve
>
> 10-H price$_T$ = average price change for the 10-year Treasury hedging instrument for a twist in the yield curve

Step 7: Compute the change in value of the two-bond hedge portfolio for a change in the level of the yield curve. This is done as follows. Let

> H_2 = amount of the 2-year hedging instrument per \$1 of market value of the mortgage security
>
> H_{10} = amount of the 10-year hedging instrument per \$1 of market value of the mortgage security

Our objective is to find the appropriate values for H_2 and H_{10} that will produce the same change in value for the two-bond hedge as the change in the price of the mortgage security that the portfolio manager seeks to hedge.

The change in value of the two-bond hedge for a change in the level of the yield curve is

$$H_2 \times (\text{2-}H\,\text{price}_L) + H_{10} \times (\text{10-}H\,\text{price}_L)$$

Step 8: Determine the change in value of the two-bond hedge portfolio for a twist in the yield curve. This value is

$$H_2 \times (\text{2-}H\,\text{price}_T) + H_{10} \times (\text{10-}H\,\text{price}_T)$$

Step 9: Determine the set of equations that equates the change in the value of the two-bond hedge to the change in the price of the mortgage security. To be more precise, we want the change in the value produced by the two-bond hedge to be in the opposite direction to the change in the price of the mortgage security. Using our notation, the two equations are:

> Level: $H_2 \times (\text{2-}H\,\text{price}_L) + H_{10} \times (\text{10-}H\,\text{price}_L) = -\text{MBS price}_L$
>
> Twist: $H_2 \times (\text{2-}H\,\text{price}_T) + H_{10} \times (\text{10-}H\,\text{price}_T) = -\text{MBS price}_T$

Step 10: Solve the simultaneous equations in Step 9 for the values of H_2 and H_{10}. Notice that for the two equations, all of the values are known except for H_2 and H_{10}. Thus, there are two equations and two unknowns.

In Step 9, a negative value for H_2 or H_{10} represents a short position and a positive value for H_2 or H_{10} represents a long position.

C. Illustrations of the Two-Bond Hedge

To illustrate the steps to compute the two-bond hedge, we will examine at two different dates: February 12, 2003, and March 4, 1997. Illustration 1 shows a combination of a long position and a short position in two hedging instruments to hedge the long position in a passthrough security. Illustration 2 involves a short position in two hedging instruments in order to hedge a long position in a passthrough security.

Illustration 1: Two-Bond Hedge with a Long and Short Position

In this illustration we will see how to hedge a position in the Fannie Mae 5% coupon passthrough on February 12, 2003. The price of this mortgage security was 99.126. In our illustrations we will use the 2-year and 10-year Treasury note futures as the hedging instruments for the two-bond hedge. The prevailing price for the 2-year Treasury note futures was 107.75. The prevailing price for the 10-year Treasury note futures was 114.813.

a. Finding the Two-Bond Hedge

Step 1: In computing the price resulting from a change in the level of interest rates, an increase and decrease of 24.3 basis points is used. (This is the typical monthly overall change in the level of rates.) The dollar price change per $100 of par value is shown below:

Instrument	Price For	
	Increase in Yield	Decrease in Yield
Fannie Mae 5%	97.787	100.334
2-year Treasury note futures	107.333	108.168
10-year Treasury note futures	113.137	116.510

For the Fannie Mae 5%, the Monte Carlo simulation model is used to calculate the price after the change in yield. The OAS is held constant at its initial value in the valuation model.

Step 2: From the prices found in Step 1, calculate the price changes:

Instrument	Price For	
	Increase in Yield	Decrease in Yield
Fannie Mae 5%	−1.339	1.208
2-year Treasury note futures	−0.417	0.418
10-year Treasury note futures	−1.676	1.697

Step 3: Calculate the average price change (using absolute values) for each instrument resulting from a level change:

$$\text{MBS price}_L = 1.274$$
$$\text{2-}H\text{ price}_L = 0.418$$
$$\text{10-}H\text{ price}_L = 1.687$$

Step 4: In computing the price resulting from a twist in the shape of the yield curve, the 2–10 slope is assumed to change by 13.8 bps. (Recall from Section 4 that this is the typical monthly twist in the shape of the yield curve.) The dollar price per $100 of par value is shown below:

Instrument	Price For	
	Flattening	Steepening
Fannie Mae 5%	98.89	99.363
2-year Treasury note futures	107.441	108.064
10-year Treasury note futures	114.342	115.285

Step 5: From the prices found in Step 4, calculate the price changes:

Instrument	Price For	
	Flattening	Steepening
Fannie Mae 5%	−0.236	0.237
2-year Treasury note futures	−0.309	0.314
10-year Treasury note futures	−0.471	0.472

Step 6: Calculate the average price change for each instrument resulting from a twist in the yield curve:

$$\text{MBS price}_T = 0.237$$
$$\text{2-}H\text{ price}_T = 0.312$$
$$\text{10-}H\text{ price}_T = 0.472$$

Step 7: The change in value of the two-bond hedge portfolio for a change in the level of the yield curve is:

$$H_2 \times (0.418) + H_{10} \times (1.687)$$

Step 8: The change in value of the two-bond hedge portfolio for a twist of the yield curve is:

$$H_2 \times (0.312) + H_{10} \times (0.472)$$

Step 9: The two equations that equate the change in the value of the two-bond hedge to the change in the price of the mortgage security are:

Level: $H_2 \times (0.418) + H_{10} \times (1.687) = -1.274$
Twist: $H_2 \times (0.312) + H_{10} \times (0.472) = -0.237$

Step 10: Solve the simultaneous equations in Step 9 for the values of H_2 and H_{10}. This is done as follows: Solve for H_2 in the "Level" equation:

$$H_2 = (-1.274 - 1.687 \, H_{10})/0.418 = -3.048 - 4.036 \, H_{10}$$

Substitute the above for H_2 in the "Twist" equation:

$$[-3.048 - 4.036 \, H_{10}] \, (0.312) + H_{10}(0.472) = -0.237$$
$$-0.950976 - 1.259232 \, H_{10} + 0.472 \, H_{10} = -0.237$$
$$-0.950976 - 0.787232 \, H_{10} = -0.237$$

Solve for H_{10}:

$$0.787232 \, H_{10} = -0.713976$$
$$H_{10} = -0.906945$$

To obtain H_2, we can substitute $H_{10} = -0.906945$ into the "Level" or the "Twist" equation and solve for H_2. Substituting into the "Level" equation we get:

$$H_2 \times (0.418) + (-0.906945) \times (1.687) = -1.274$$
$$H_2 \times (0.418) - 1.530016 = -1.274$$
$$H_2 = 0.612478$$

Thus, $H_2 = 0.612478$ and $H_{10} = -0.906945$.[6]

The value of 0.612478 for H_2 means that the par amount in the 2-year Treasury note futures will be 0.612478 per \$1 of par amount of the mortgage security to be hedged. So, if the par amount of the Fannie Mae 5% to be hedged against interest rate risk is \$1 million, then 2-year Treasury note futures with a notional value of \$612,478 (= 0.612478 × \$1 million) should be long (i.e., buying 2-year Treasury note futures). Notice that we have an example here of going long in a futures contract despite that we are seeking to hedge a long position!

The value of −0.906945 for H_{10} means that the par amount in the 10-year Treasury note futures will be 0.906945 per \$1 of par amount of the mortgage security to be hedged. Assuming again that the par amount of the Fannie Mae 5% to be hedged is \$1 million, then 10-year Treasury note futures with a notional value of \$906,945 (= 0.906945 × \$1 million) should be shorted.

b. Duration Hedge versus Two-Bond Hedge
It is interesting to note the difference between the potential performance of the bond hedge using duration only and the two-bond hedge that takes into consideration changes in both level and twist changes.

At the time of the hedge, the Fannie Mae 5% passthrough had an effective duration of 5.5. Using only duration to obtain the hedge position, it can be demonstrated that if the yield curve shift is a level one, the following price changes would result:

---

[6] The results can be verified by substituting these values into the "Level" or "Twist" equation.

	Fannie Mae 5%	Duration Hedge	Error
Increase in rates/Level up	−1.339	1.360	0.021
Decrease in rates/Level down	1.208	−1.379	−0.171

The above results indicate that if the duration hedge is used, when interest rates increase, the Fannie Mae 5% will decline by 1.339 points but the gain from the duration hedge will be 1.36 points. Hence, using a duration hedge the gain will be greater than the loss, resulting in a profit on the hedge. As can be seen from the results above, the opposite occurs if interest rates decline. This is the reason there is a market belief that mortgage securities are "market-directional" investments.

However, evidence using the two-bond hedge suggests otherwise: because the yield curve seldom moves in a parallel fashion, properly hedged mortgage securities are not market-directional. The two-bond hedge would produce the following results:

	Fannie Mae 5%	Two-Bond Hedge	Error
Increase in rates/Level up	−1.339	1.263	−0.076
Decrease in rates/Level down	1.208	−1.284	−0.076

As can be seen from the above table, when "likely level and twist" changes in the yield curve are accounted for, virtually all of the market-directionality is removed. The "error" in the two-bond hedge is a measure of the negative convexity of the Fannie Mae 5% passthrough. For a 24 basis point move (one stand deviation of monthly level shift) in the 10-year—assuming no rebalancing of the hedge—the Fannie Mae 5% passthrough would underperform its two-bond hedge using Treasury note futures by 8 basis points (or eight cents per $100 of par amount). This loss is more than offset by the carry advantage of a mortgage security over Treasuries (i.e., the higher interest earned on the mortgage security versus the cost of financing the Treasury positions). For example, the Fannie Mae 5% has a yield of 5.17% and a 200 basis point spread to Treasuries. This implies that every month this security has a carry advantage of 17 basis points (200 basis points/12), more than enough to offset the 8 basis point hedging loss.

Let's take a look at the Fannie Mae 5% duration and the duration implied for the two-bond hedging package. The duration for the Fannie Mae 5% is 5.5. We can obtain the implied duration of the two-bond hedge by computing the dollar value of a basis point (DV01) for the 2-year and 10-year Treasury note futures contracts.[7] The DV01 for the 2-year Treasury note futures is 0.0186. For the 10-year Treasury note futures the DV01 is 0.067. So the hedging package (i.e., the two-bond hedge) has a DV01 that is the weighted average of the two dollar durations as shown below:

$$0.612478 \times 0.0186 + (-0.906945) \times 0.067 = -0.049373$$

---

[7] The dollar value of a basis point, also called the price value of a basis point, is the change in the value of a position for a 1 basis point change in interest rates.

The sign is negative because of the inverse relationship between price change and interest rates. This implies that the two-bond hedge for the Fannie Mae 5% has a duration of $(0.049373/99.126) \times 10,000 = 4.98$. This is about 9% less than the duration of 5.5 for the Fannie Mae 5%.

Illustration 2: Two-Bond Hedge with Two Short Positions

The position to be hedged in Illustration 2 is the Freddie Mac 7.5% coupon passthrough on March 4, 1997. The price of this mortgage security was $99^{25/32}$. As with Illustration 1, we will use the 2-year and 10-year Treasury note futures as the hedging instruments for the two-bond hedge. While in Illustration 1 a long position was required in the 2-year Treasury note futures and a short position in the 10-year Treasury note futures, we will see that a short position is required in both hedging instruments in Illustration 2.

We will not go through all the steps but just provide the following basic information so that the positions in the hedging instruments can be computed:

$$\Delta \text{MBS price}_L = 1.22 \qquad \Delta 2\text{-}H\,\text{price}_L = 0.62 \qquad \Delta 10\text{-}H\,\text{price}_L = 1.69$$
$$\Delta \text{MBS price}_T = 0.25 \qquad \Delta 2\text{-}H\,\text{price}_T = 0.01 \qquad \Delta 10\text{-}H\,\text{price}_T = 0.55$$

Based on the above information, we can complete Steps 7 through 10 as shown below:

Step 7: The change in value of the two-bond hedge portfolio for a change in the level of the yield curve is found as follows:

$$H_2 \times (0.62) + H_{10} \times (1.69)$$

Step 8: The change in value of the two-bond hedge portfolio for a twist of the yield curve is found as follows:

$$H_2 \times (0.01) + H_{10} \times (0.55)$$

Step 9: The two equations that equate the change in the value of the two-bond hedge to the change in the price of the mortgage security are:

Level: $H_2 \times (0.62) + H_{10} \times (1.69) = -1.22$
Twist: $H_2 \times (0.01) + H_{10} \times (0.55) = -0.25$

Step 10: Solve the simultaneous equations in Step 9 for the values of H_2 and H_{10}. This is done as follows:

Solve for H_2 in the "Level" equation:

$$H_2 = \frac{-1.22 - 1.69\,H_{10}}{0.62} = -1.967742 - 2.725806\,H_{10}$$

Substitute the above for H_2 in the "Twist" equation:

$$[-1.967742 - 2.725806\,H_{10}]\,(0.01) + H_{10}(0.55) = -0.25$$
$$-0.019677 - 0.027258\,H_{10} + 0.55H_{10} = -0.25$$
$$-0.019677 + 0.522742\,H_{10} = -0.25$$

Solve for H_{10}:

$$0.522742\ H_{10} = -0.230323$$
$$H_{10} = -0.440605$$

To obtain H_2, we can substitute $H_{10} = -0.440605$ into the "Level" or the "Twist" equation and solve for H_2. Substituting into the "Level" equation we get:

$$H_2 \times (0.62) + (-0.440605) \times (1.69) = -1.22$$
$$H_2 \times (0.62) - 0.744622 = -1.22$$
$$H_2 = -0.766739$$

Thus, $H_2 = -0.766739$ and $H_{10} = -0.440605$.

These values indicate that a short position will be taken in both the 2-year and 10-year Treasury note futures. The value of 0.766739 for H_2 means that the par amount in the 2-year Treasury note futures will be 0.766739 per \$1 of par amount of the mortgage security to be hedged. So, if the par amount of the Freddie Mac 7.5% to be hedged against interest rate risk is \$1 million, then 2-year Treasury note futures with a par amount of \$766,739 (= 0.766739 × \$1 million) should be shorted. Similarly, the value of 0.440605 for H_{10} means that the par amount in the 10-year Treasury note futures will be 0.440605 per \$1 of par value of the mortgage security to be hedged.

Once again we see the value of using the two-bond hedge rather than using a duration hedge. At the time of the hedge, the Freddie Mac 7.5% passthrough had an effective duration of 4.4. Using only duration to obtain the hedge position, it can be demonstrated that if the yield curve shift is a parallel one, the following price changes would result:

	Freddie Mac 7.5%	Duration Hedge	Error
Increase in rates/Level up	−1.27	1.36	+0.09
Decrease in rates/Level down	1.18	−1.34	−0.16

As in Illustration 1, using a duration hedge the gain will be greater than the loss, resulting in a profit on the hedge and suggesting that mortgage securities are "market-directional" investments. However, for the two-bond hedge we would find the following:

	Freddie Mac 7.5%	Two-Bond Hedge	Error
Increase in rates/Level up	−1.27	1.25	−0.02
Decrease in rates/Level down	1.18	−1.20	−0.02

As can be seen from the above table, when typical changes in the yield curve are accounted for, virtually all of the market-directionality is removed.

D. Underlying Assumptions

Now that the underlying principles and mechanics for hedging the interest rate risk of a mortgage security have been covered, let's look at the underlying assumptions for the two-bond hedge. They are:

▶ The yield curve shifts used in constructing the two-bond hedge are reasonable.

▶ The prepayment model used does a good job of estimating how the cash flows will change when the yield curve changes.

▶ Assumptions underlying the Monte Carlo simulation model are realized (e.g., the interest rate volatility assumption).

▶ The average price change is a good approximation of how the mortgage security's price will change for a small movement in interest rates.

This last assumption may be unacceptable for certain types of mortgage securities as explained in the next section.

HEDGING CUSPY-COUPON MORTGAGE SECURITIES

6

In many cases, the "average" price change is a good approximation of how a mortgage security's price will change for a small movement in interest rates. This can be seen by the tangent line labeled "Current Coupon" in Exhibit 6. However, some mortgage securities are very sensitive to small movements in interest rates. For example, a mortgage security whose coupon is 100 basis points higher than the current coupon could be prepaid slowly if rates rise by 25 basis points but prepaid very quickly if rates fall by 25 basis points. Small changes in interest rates have large effects on prepayments for such securities and hence on their prices.

A mortgage security with this characteristic is referred to as a "cuspy-coupon" mortgage security. For such mortgage securities, averaging the price changes is not a good measure of how prices will change. In other words, the tangent line (labeled "Cuspy Coupon" in Exhibit 6) is not a good proxy for the price/yield

EXHIBIT 6	Mortgage Price/Yield Curve

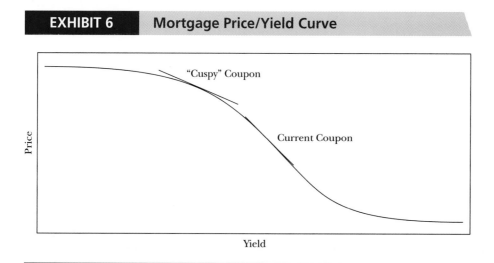

curve. At times, cuspy-coupon mortgage securities offer attractive risk-adjusted expected returns; however, they have more negative convexity than current-coupon mortgages.

Hedging cuspy-coupon mortgage securities only with Treasury notes or futures contracts may leave the investor exposed to more negative convexity than is desired. The negative convexity feature, as has been mentioned, is the result of the option that the mortgage security investor has granted to homeowners to prepay. That is, the investor has effectively sold an option to homeowners. To hedge the sale of an option (i.e., a short position in an option), an investor can buy an option. Thus, a portfolio manager can extend the two-bond hedge by buying interest rate options to offset some or all of a cuspy-coupon mortgage security's negative convexity.

We will use a Freddie Mac 8.5% passthrough, a cuspy-coupon mortgage security in February 1997, to illustrate how the two-bond hedging methodology is extended to include options. The price of the Freddie Mac 8.5% passthrough was 103.50.

Without going through the mechanics of how to construct the two-bond hedge, panel A in Exhibit 7 shows 1) the change in the price for the mortgage security and 2) the change in the value of the two-bond hedge for changes in the level and twist in the yield curve. The last column in panel A of the exhibit shows the error for the two-bond hedge. The error is due to the negative convexity characteristic of the Freddie Mac 8.5% passthrough (cuspy-coupon mortgage security).

Because the prepayment option of the Freddie Mac 8.5s is closer to the refinancing threshold than that of the Freddie Mac 7.5s at the time of the analysis, the two-bond hedge error is greater——0.05 for the 8.5s versus –0.02 for the 7.5s.

EXHIBIT 7   Alternatives for Hedging a Cuspy-Coupon Mortgage Security

A. Two-Bond Hedge

Yield Curve Change	Price Change for Freddie Mac 8.5%	Price Change for Two-Bond Hedge	Error for Two-Bond Hedge
"Level" up	–0.98	0.93	–0.05
"Level" down	0.85	–0.90	–0.05
"Twist" flattening	0.11	–0.12	–0.01
"Twist" steepening	–0.12	0.11	–0.01

B. Two-Bond Hedge plus Options

Yield Curve Change	Price Change for Freddie Mac 8.5%	Price Change for Two-Bond Hedge	Error Options Payoff	Two-Bond Hedge + Options
"Level" up	–0.98	0.93	0.05	0.00
"Level" down	0.85	–0.90	0.05	0.00
"Twist" flattening	0.11	–0.12	0.01	0.00
"Twist" steepening	–0.12	0.11	0.01	0.00

Buying calls and puts eliminates this drift. Specifically, we added the purchase of the following two option positions per $100 of the Freddie Mac 8.5s to be hedged:

▶ $18 6-month call option on a 10-year Treasury note with a strike price of 99.5;

▶ $17 6-month put option on a 10-year Treasury note with a strike price of 95.

(At the time, the 10-year Treasury was priced at $97^{15/32}$.) Determining how to obtain the positions in the options is beyond the scope of this reading.

Panel B of Exhibit 7 shows that adding the two option positions on the 10-year note offsets the two-bond hedge error, making the total package (mortgage security + two-bond hedge + options) insensitive to likely interest rate movements. Of course, buying these options requires paying a premium which amounted to about 7 basis points per month. Since the yield advantage of the 8.5s versus Treasuries was about 11 basis points, the expected excess return over Treasuries was about 4 basis points per month after we hedge out the negative convexity.

SUMMARY

▶ The price-yield relationship for a mortgage security exhibits both positive and negative convexity.

▶ For a security that exhibits negative convexity, the price increase when interest rates decline is less than the price decrease when interest rates rise.

▶ For a security that exhibits negative convexity, there is an adverse change in duration when interest rates change.

▶ Because of the negative convexity characteristics of a mortgage security, investors consider mortgages to be market-directional investments that should be avoided when one expects interest rates to decline.

▶ When properly managed, mortgage securities are not market-directional investments.

▶ At the portfolio level, without proper hedging to offset the changes in the duration of mortgage securities caused by interest rate movements, the portfolio's duration would drift adversely from its target duration.

▶ An agency mortgage security position is equivalent to a position in a comparable-duration Treasury security and selling a call option.

▶ The yield of a mortgage security is the sum of the yield on an equal interest rate risk Treasury security and a spread.

▶ For a mortgage security, the spread is the sum of the option cost (i.e., the expected cost of bearing prepayment risk) and the option-adjusted spread (i.e., the risk premium for bearing the remaining risks).

▶ There are five principal risks in mortgage securities: spread, interest rate, prepayment, volatility, and model risk.

▶ Because a portfolio manager wants to capture an attractive option-adjusted spread, the manager does not seek to hedge spread risk but only interest rate risk.

▶ After hedging the interest rate risk of a mortgage security, the portfolio manager has the potential to earn the Treasury bill rate plus the OAS.

▶ For a mortgage security, yield curve risk is considerably greater than for a Treasury security.

▶ A portfolio manager can manage volatility risk by buying options or hedging dynamically.

▶ A portfolio manager will hedge dynamically when the volatility implied in the option price is high and the portfolio manager believes that future realized volatility will be lower than implied volatility.

▶ A portfolio manager will hedge by purchasing options when the implied volatility in option prices is low and the portfolio manager believes that actual future volatility will be higher than implied.

▶ Implied volatility is computed using the Monte Carlo simulation valuation framework.

▶ In hedging a mortgage security, it is difficult to use key rate duration to manage yield curve risk.

▶ An alternative approach is to investigate how yield curves have changed historically and incorporate typical yield curve change scenarios into the hedging process.

► Studies have found that yield curve changes are not parallel and that when the level of interest rates changes, 2-year yields move about twice as much as long-term yields.

► Studies suggest that the two most important factors in explaining changes in the yield curve are changes in the level and twist (i.e., steepening and flattening).

► To properly hedge the interest rate risk associated with a mortgage security, the portfolio manager needs to estimate how mortgage security prices will change taking into account 1) how the yield curve can change over time and 2) the effect of changes in the yield curve on the prepayment option granted to homeowners.

► The interest rate sensitivity measure is superior to effective duration for assessing the impact of a change in the yield curve on the price of a mortgage security.

► The interest rate sensitivity measure quantifies a security's percentage price change in response to a shift in the yield curve.

► Since two factors (the "level" and "twist" factors) have accounted for most of the changes in the yield curve, in hedging a mortgage security two Treasury notes (typically the 2-year and 10-year) are used.

► A hedge in which two hedging instruments representing different maturity sectors of the yield curve are used is referred to as a two-bond hedge.

► The basic principle in constructing a two-bond hedge is to express a particular mortgage security's exposure to a change in the level and twist of the yield curve in terms of an equivalent position in U.S. Treasuries or an equivalent position in Treasury futures contracts.

► By mathematically expressing a mortgage security's exposure to a change in the level of interest rates and a twist in the yield curve, a portfolio manager can compute the unique quantities of the two hedging instruments that will simultaneously hedge the mortgage security's price response to both level and twist scenarios.

► Determining the amount of the two hedging instruments requires several steps that involve estimating the price changes of the mortgage security to be hedged and the two hedging instruments for an assumed change in the level of interest rates and an assumed change in the twist of the yield curve.

► One of the important assumptions in constructing the two-bond hedge is that the average price change is a good approximation of how a mortgage security's price will change for a small movement in interest rates.

► The average price change less accurately approximates price changes for a cuspy-coupon mortgage security than for a current-coupon mortgage security.

► A cuspy-coupon mortgage security is a mortgage security for which changes in interest rates have large effects on prepayments and hence on price. For such securities, using the average price change will not provide the correct information for hedging.

► Hedging cuspy-coupon mortgage securities only with Treasury notes or futures contracts exposes a portfolio manager to more negative convexity than is desired.

► The addition to a two-bond hedge of an appropriate number of interest rate options enables a portfolio manager to offset some or all of the negative convexity of a cuspy-coupon mortgage security.

1. Roger McFee is a fixed-income portfolio manager for Wells Asset Management Partners. In a meeting with his firm's client, Mr. McFee discussed his current strategy. He explained that it is his firm's view that there are a number of opportunities available in the mortgage sector of the fixed-income market for enhancing return. The strategy involved purchasing what were viewed to be undervalued mortgage products and hedging the interest rate risk. After Mr. McFee's presentation, the client questioned him as to the prudence of the strategy. The client stated: "If you are going to hedge the interest rate risk, then why bother buying mortgage products? After hedging, won't you be earning simply a short-term risk-free rate?"

    How should Mr. McFee respond to this question?

2. Laura Sze is the fixed-income strategist for a brokerage firm. She is responsible for setting the allocation of funds among the major sectors of the investment-grade fixed-income market. Her economic forecast is that interest rates will decline dramatically and that prepayments on mortgages will accelerate. Because of this she recommended in a report distributed to her firm's clients who manage funds versus a U.S. broad-based market index that they consider underweighting high-coupon mortgage passthroughs and overweighting Treasuries. After sending the report, she received the following e-mail message from the junior portfolio manager of an account customer: "Read your report. I am confused. If you expect interest rates to decline, why would I prefer Treasuries to mortgage passthroughs? Won't both Treasuries and passthroughs appreciate if interest rates decline? Please explain the rationale for your recommendation."

    How should Ms. Sze respond to this customer?

3. James Neutron is a trustee for a pension fund. In a recent report he received from one of the fund's asset managers, he noticed the overweighting of mortgage passthrough securities relative to the manager's benchmark. Mr. Neutron was concerned by the overweighting for the reason described in the following e-mail he sent to the asset manager, Ron Prain:

    Dear Mr. Prain:

    Just received your report on the portfolio composition. I am troubled by your overweighting of mortgage passthroughs. While I recognize that the investment guidelines grant you the authority to overweight as you have done, my concern is with the prudence of doing so. It is well known that mortgage passthrough securities are market-directional securities.

    Sincerely,

    James Neutron

    What should Mr. Prain's response be?

4. You are the portfolio manager of a mortgage portfolio. A new junior portfolio manager, Alexander Coffee, wants you to explain risk management strategies for the mortgage portfolio. Mr. Coffee understands that there are several risk exposures associated with the portfolio but is especially interested in knowing how volatility risk can be hedged. Explain to Mr. Coffee how this can be done.

5. What is the problem of using duration only to hedge a mortgage security?

6. Carol Ryan manages an MBS portfolio. She is considering the purchase of $10 million par value of a Freddie Mac passthrough selling at 99.895 because of its attractive option-adjusted spread. She would like to hedge against an adverse movement in interest rates in order to lock in the benefit from the attractive OAS and wants to do so using a two-bond hedge. The hedging instruments she will use are the 2-year and 10-year Treasury note futures. At the time of the purchase/hedge, the prices for the 2-year Treasury note futures and 10-year Treasury note futures are 106.650 and 111.190, respectively.

Using her firm's proprietary MBS valuation model, which computes the value of an MBS based on her firm's typical shift in the level and twist in the yield curve, the following prices are computed for the Freddie Mac passthrough to be hedged, per $100 of par value:

Price for increase in yield	97.955
Price for decrease in yield	101.100
Flattening of the yield curve	99.450
Steepening of the yield curve	100.350

Ms. Ryan's firm uses a standard model for pricing futures. Based on typical yield curve shifts used to obtain the price of the Freddie Mac passthrough above, the following prices for the futures are computed:

	Treasury Note Futures	
	2-Year	**10-Year**
Price for increase in yield	106.122	109.250
Price for decrease in yield	107.300	113.600
Flattening of the yield curve	106.104	110.850
Steepening of the yield curve	107.268	111.790

A. What type of convexity (positive or negative) does this passthrough exhibit based on the proprietary valuation model? Explain your answer.

B. Determine the appropriate hedge position in the two hedging instruments.

7. What are the critical assumptions underlying the hedging of a mortgage security?

SOLUTIONS FOR READING 31

1. Mr. McFee failed to communicate clearly what he intended to do. The client is correct that if Mr. McFee hedged all of the interest rate risk of the mortgage products in which he invested, then a return close to the short-term risk-free rate would be earned. However, that is not his strategy. The performance of the mortgage products in which he invests will depend on the movements of the level of interest rates and the mortgage spread (more specifically the option-adjusted spread). The purpose of the hedge is to eliminate the risk attributable to changes in interest rates so that the manager only has exposure to changes in the mortgage spread (i.e., OAS). That is, he does not seek to hedge spread risk. Mr. McFee is proposing to capture value from a change in the mortgage spread (not interest rates) that the market does not yet anticipate.

2. Ms. Sze should point out that while both mortgage passthroughs and Treasuries will appreciate when interest rates decline, the relative performance of the two sectors due to the expected decline in interest rates is what is important. Mortgage passthroughs exhibit negative convexity at levels of interest rates below the rate on the underlying mortgages while Treasuries, which are option-free securities, always exhibit positive convexity. Because of the negative convexity feature, while mortgage passthroughs will appreciate in value, Treasuries would appreciate more for a given initial duration. Hence the recommendation to underweight mortgages and overweight Treasuries.

3. There are investors who consider mortgages to be market-directional investments that should be avoided when one expects interest rates to decline. However, when properly managed by separating mortgage valuation decisions from decisions concerning the appropriate duration of the portfolio, mortgage securities are not market-directional investments. The ability to separate the value decision from the duration decision hinges critically on proper hedging. One must offset the interest rate-driven changes in the duration of mortgage securities to prevent the portfolio drifting adversely from its target. Hedged improperly, the portfolio's duration will be shorter than desired when interest rates decline and longer than desired when interest rates rise.

4. Volatility risk can be managed by buying options or by hedging dynamically. Hedging dynamically is selected when the volatility implied in option prices is high and it is believed that future realized volatility will be lower than implied volatility. When implied volatility is low and it is believed that actual future volatility will be higher than implied volatility, hedging by purchasing options would be the better alternative.

5. Mortgage securities are particularly sensitive to changes in the level and twist in the yield curve. Using just duration hedges a mortgage security to changes in the level of interest rates but not to twists in the yield curve.

6. A. One can assess the convexity characteristic of the passthrough by looking at the change in price when rates are changed. The answer then depends on how much rates are changed. In the illustration, the price increase when rates decline is 1.205 (101.100 − 99.895) while the price decrease when rates rise is 1.940 (99.895 − 97.955). This means that the loss (in absolute value) is greater than the gain. This is a property of an instrument that is expected to exhibit negative convexity.

Fixed Income Readings for the Chartered Financial Analyst® Program, Second Edition, edited by Frank J. Fabozzi, CFA.
Copyright © 2005 by CFA Institute. Reprinted with permission.

B. The position in the two hedging instruments is found by using the following ten steps described in the reading:

Step 1: Compute the prices for the passthrough and hedging instruments for typical level changes in the yield. The information for Step 1 is provided in the question. It is summarized below:

	Price For	
Instrument	**Increase in Yield**	**Decrease in Yield**
Freddie Mac passthrough	97.955	101.100
2-year Treasury note futures	106.122	107.300
10-year Treasury note futures	109.250	113.600

Step 2: From the prices found in Step 1, calculate the price changes:

	Price Change For	
Instrument	**Increase in Yield**	**Decrease in Yield**
Freddie Mac passthrough	−1.940	1.205
2-year Treasury note futures	−0.528	0.650
10-year Treasury note futures	−1.940	2.410

Step 3: Calculate the average value of the price change (using absolute values) for each instrument resulting from a level change:

$$\text{MBS price}_L = 1.573$$
$$2\text{-}H\,\text{price}_L = 0.589$$
$$10\text{-}H\,\text{price}_L = 2.175$$

Step 4: Compute the prices for the passthrough and hedging instruments for typical twists in the yield curve. The information for Step 4 is provided in the question. It is summarized below:

	Price For	
Instrument	**Flattening**	**Steepening**
Freddie Mac passthrough	99.450	100.350
2-year Treasury note futures	106.104	107.268
10-year Treasury note futures	110.850	111.790

Step 5: From the prices found in Step 4, calculate the price changes:

	Price Change For	
Instrument	**Flattening**	**Steepening**
Freddie Mac passthrough	−0.445	0.455
2-year Treasury note futures	−0.546	0.618
10-year Treasury note futures	−0.340	0.600

Step 6: Calculate the average value of the price change for each instrument resulting from a twist in the yield curve:

$$\text{MBS price}_T = 0.450$$
$$\text{2-}H\text{ price}_T = 0.582$$
$$\text{10-}H\text{ price}_T = 0.470$$

Step 7: The change in value of the two-bond hedge portfolio for a change in the level of the yield curve is found as follows:

$$H_2 \times (0.589) + H_{10} \times (2.175)$$

Step 8: The change in value of the two-bond hedge portfolio for a twist of the yield curve is found as follows:

$$H_2 \times (0.582) + H_{10} \times (0.470)$$

Step 9: The two equations that equate the change in the value of the two-bond hedge to the change in the price of the mortgage security are:

$$\text{Level: } H_2 \times (0.589) + H_{10} \times (2.175) = -1.573$$
$$\text{Twist: } H_2 \times (0.582) + H_{10} \times (0.470) = -0.450$$

Step 10: Solve the simultaneous equations in Step 9 for the values of H_2 and H_{10}. This is done as follows: Solve for H_2 in the "Level" equation:

$$H_2 = (-1.573 - 2.175\, H_{10})/0.589 = [-2.670628 - 3.692699\, H_{10}]$$

Substitute the above for H_2 in the "Twist" equation:

$$[-2.670628 - 3.692699\, H_{10}]\,(0.582) + H_{10}\,(0.470) = -0.450$$

Solving we would find that:

$$H_{10} = -0.657657$$

To obtain H_2, we can substitute $H_{10} = -0.657657$ into the "Level" or the "Twist" equation and solve for H_2. Substituting into the "Level" equation we get:

$$H_2 \times (0.589) + (-0.657657) \times (2.175) = -1.573$$
$$H_2 = -0.242099$$

Thus, $H_2 = -0.242099$ and $H_{10} = -0.657657$.

These values indicate that a short position will be taken in the two hedging instruments. The value of 0.242099 for H_2 means that the par amount in the 2-year Treasury note futures will be 0.242099 per \$1 of par amount of the mortgage security to be hedged. Since the par amount of the Freddie Mac passthrough to be hedged against interest rate risk is \$10 million, then 2-year Treasury note futures with a par amount of \$2,420,990 (0.242099 × \$10 million) should be shorted. Similarly, the value of 0.657657 for H_{10} means that the par amount in the 10-year Treasury note futures to be shorted will be 0.657657 per \$1 of par value of the mortgage security to be hedged.

7. The first assumption is that the yield curve shifts used in obtaining the prices that are used in computing the hedge are reasonable. In deriving the prices for a yield curve shift a prepayment model is used to obtain the mortgage price. Thus the second assumption is that the prepayment model does a good job of projecting changes in prepayments when the yield curve changes. The third assumption is that the other inputs into the Monte Carlo simulation model for obtaining the new prices when the yield curve shifts are reasonable and can be expected to be realized in the future. The last assumption deals with the use of average price changes used in deriving the position in each hedging instrument. It is assumed that the average price change is a good approximation of how the mortgage security's price will change for small yield curve shifts assumed in deriving the prices.

4⅛ 4⁷⁄₁₆ — ⅜

5½ 5½ —

5½ 213⁄₁₆ — ⅛

20⅝ 21³⁄₁₆ — ⅛

17⅜ 18⅛ + ⅞

6½ 6½ — ½

7¼ 31⁄₃₂ — ⅛

15⁄₁₆ 9⁄₁₆

9⁄₁₆

7¹⁵⁄₁₆ 7¹³⁄₁₆ 7¹⁵⁄₁₆

2⅝ 2¹¹⁄₃₂ 2½ +

2¾ 2¼ 2¼

12¹⁄₁₆ 11⅜ 11¾ +

87 33¾ 33 33⅛ —

602 25⅝ 24⁹⁄₁₆ 25⅜ +

833 12 11⅝ 11⅞ +

16 10½ 10½ 10½ —

78 15⅞ 15¹³⁄₁₆ 15⅞ —

4508 9¹⁄₁₆ 8¼ 8⅜ +

430 11¼ 10⅛

STUDY SESSION 11
EQUITY PORTFOLIO MANAGEMENT

Because equity securities represent a significant portion of many investment portfolios, equity management is often a critical component of overall investment success. This study session focuses on the role of equities in an investment portfolio, the three major approaches used to manage equity portfolios, and the evaluation of equity managers.

READING ASSIGNMENT

Reading 32   Equity Portfolio Management
              Managing Investment Portfolios: A Dynamic Process, Third
              Edition, John L. Maginn, CFA, Donald L. Tuttle, CFA,
              Jerald E. Pinto, CFA, and Dennis W. McLeavey, CFA, editors

$4\frac{5}{8}$ $4\frac{7}{8}$ $\frac{3}{8}$

$5\frac{1}{2}$ $5\frac{1}{2}$ $-$ $\frac{3}{8}$

$5\frac{1}{2}$ $21\frac{3}{16}$ $-$ $\frac{1}{16}$

$20\frac{5}{8}$ $21\frac{3}{16}$ $-$ $\frac{1}{16}$

$17\frac{3}{8}$ $18\frac{1}{8}$ $+$ $\frac{7}{8}$

$18\frac{1}{2}$ $6\frac{1}{2}$ $-$ $\frac{1}{2}$

$6\frac{1}{2}$ $6\frac{1}{2}$ $-$

$7\frac{1}{4}$ $31\frac{1}{32}$ $-$ $\frac{1}{8}$

$\frac{15}{16}$ $9\frac{5}{8}$

$9\frac{5}{8}$

$9\frac{1}{16}$

$\frac{1}{32}$ $7\frac{13}{16}$ $7\frac{15}{8}$

$7\frac{15}{16}$ $7\frac{13}{16}$

$2\frac{5}{8}$ $2\frac{11}{32}$ $2\frac{1}{2}$ $+$

$2\frac{3}{4}$ $2\frac{1}{4}$ $2\frac{1}{4}$

$6\frac{1}{2}$ $12\frac{1}{16}$ $11\frac{3}{8}$ $11\frac{3}{4}$ $+$

87 $33\frac{3}{4}$ 33 $33\frac{1}{8}$ $-$

$6\frac{1}{32}$ $25\frac{5}{8}$ $24\frac{9}{16}$ $25\frac{5}{8}$ $+$

833 12 $11\frac{5}{8}$ $11\frac{7}{8}$ $+$

16 $10\frac{1}{2}$ $10\frac{1}{2}$ $10\frac{1}{2}$ $-$

78 $15\frac{5}{8}$ $15\frac{13}{16}$ $15\frac{7}{8}$ $-$

608 $9\frac{1}{16}$ $8\frac{1}{4}$ $8\frac{1}{2}$ $+$

430 $11\frac{1}{4}$ $10\frac{1}{8}$

EQUITY PORTFOLIO MANAGEMENT

by Gary L. Gastineau, Andrew R. Olma, CFA, and Robert G. Zielinski, CFA

LEARNING OUTCOMES

The candidate should be able to:	Mastery
a. discuss the role of equities in the overall portfolio;	☐
b. discuss the rationales for passive, active, and semiactive (enhanced index) equity investment approaches and distinguish among those approaches with respect to expected active return and tracking risk;	☐
c. recommend an equity investment approach when given an investor's investment policy statement and beliefs concerning market efficiency;	☐
d. distinguish among the predominant weighting schemes used in the construction of major equity share indices and evaluate the biases of each;	☐
e. compare and contrast alternative methods for establishing passive exposure to an equity market, including indexed separate or pooled accounts, index mutual funds, exchange-traded funds, equity index futures, and equity total return swaps;	☐
f. compare and contrast full replication, stratified sampling, and optimization as approaches to constructing an indexed portfolio and recommend an approach when given a description of the investment vehicle and the index to be tracked;	☐
g. explain and justify the use of equity investment–style classifications and discuss the difficulties in applying style definitions consistently;	☐
h. explain the rationales and primary concerns of value investors and growth investors and discuss the key risks of each investment style;	☐
i. compare and contrast techniques for identifying investment styles and characterize the style of an investor when given a description of the investor's security selection method, details on the investor's security holdings, or the results of a returns-based style analysis;	☐
j. compare and contrast the methodologies used to construct equity style indices;	☐
k. interpret the results of an equity style box analysis and discuss the consequences of style drift;	☐

Managing Investment Portfolios: A Dynamic Process, Third Edition, John L. Maginn, CFA, Donald L. Tuttle, CFA, Jerald E. Pinto, CFA, and Dennis W. McLeavey, CFA, editors. Copyright © 2007 by CFA Institute. Reprinted with permission.

197

l.	explain the use of stock screens based on socially responsible investing criteria and discuss their potential effect on a portfolio's style characteristics;	☐
m.	compare and contrast long–short versus long-only investment strategies, including their risks and potential alphas, and explain why greater pricing inefficiency may exist on the short side of the market;	☐
n.	explain how a market-neutral portfolio can be "equitized" to gain equity market exposure and compare and contrast equitized market-neutral portfolios with short-extension portfolios;	☐
o.	compare and contrast the sell disciplines of active investors;	☐
p.	contrast derivatives-based versus stock-based enhanced indexing strategies and justify enhanced indexing on the basis of risk control and the information ratio;	☐
q.	discuss and justify, in a risk–return framework, the optimal portfolio allocations to a group of investment managers;	☐
r.	explain the core-satellite approach to portfolio construction and discuss the advantages and disadvantages of adding a completeness fund to control overall risk exposures;	☐
s.	distinguish among the components of total active return ("true" active return and "misfit" active return) and their associated risk measures and explain their relevance for evaluating a portfolio of managers;	☐
t.	explain alpha and beta separation as an approach to active management and demonstrate the use of portable alpha;	☐
u.	review the process of identifying, selecting, and contracting with equity managers, including the development of a universe of suitable candidates based on both qualitative and quantitative factors, the composition of equity manager questionnaires, and the analysis of fee structures;	☐
v.	contrast the top-down and bottom-up approaches to equity research.	☐

1 INTRODUCTION

E quities constitute a significant part of many investment portfolios' value. For numerous investors, the decision of how to invest the equity allocation among competing investment approaches ranks second in importance only to the decision of how much of the portfolio to allocate to equities in the first place.

This reading presents a broad overview of equity portfolio management organized as follows: Section 2 summarizes the role of equities in investors' portfolios. Sections 3 through 6 introduce and discuss three broad approaches to equity investing and their subdisciplines. Section 7 discusses managing a portfolio of managers so that the overall equity allocation achieves the investor's purposes. Section 8 presents the important subject of identifying, selecting, and contracting with equity portfolio managers. Section 9 discusses structuring equity research and security selection, and the final section summarizes the reading.

THE ROLE OF THE EQUITY PORTFOLIO

2

Equities represent a significant source of wealth in the world today. As of 30 September 2004, the aggregate market value of the equities in the Morgan Stanley Capital International All Country World Index (MSCI ACWI) was more than $19 trillion, of which almost half represented markets outside the United States.[1] Furthermore, nearly 5 percent of the $19 trillion total, equal to a market value of nearly $950 billion, represented emerging markets.

This vast pool of equity assets is held in both individual and institutional portfolios. Exhibit 1 shows the equity allocation weighting for institutional clients in various markets.[2] Both domestic and international equities play a large role in these portfolios—domestic equities are in the investor's home markets; international equities are outside those markets. Exhibit 1 makes clear that international equities constitute differing proportions of the average equity portfolio in different countries. These differences probably reflect, at least in part, differences in the market capitalizations (values) of investors' home equity markets in relation to a global portfolio of equities: The larger the domestic market's global weight, the more we might expect investors to emphasize that market. Different attitudes and investment constraints may also affect these international differences.

EXHIBIT 1	Equity Allocations for Institutional Investors

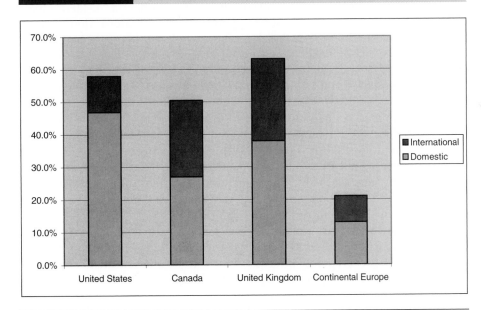

Source: Greenwich Associates, 2003.

---

[1] This index covers 49 developed and emerging markets and is intended to represent approximately 85 percent of each country's equity market value.

[2] According to a 2003 survey by the Pension Fund Association in Japan, covering 1,316 Japanese pension plans, the average allocations to domestic and international equities were 28.2 percent and 15.1 percent, respectively (43.3 percent in total). Although focusing on corporate pension plans rather than all institutional investors as in Exhibit 1, this survey suggests that Japanese equity allocations tend to be smaller than those in North American and U.K. markets, but larger than those in continental Europe. The survey is available at www.pfa.or.jp.

Investing across multiple markets also offers diversification benefits, because no one market fully captures all global economic factors. Furthermore, many companies located outside of an investor's home market have no exact home-market equivalent, regardless of whether the domestic market is small or as large and diverse as in the United States.

Most investors worry about inflation, and inflation hedging ability is a sought-after characteristic. Informally, an asset is an **inflation hedge** if its returns are sufficient on average to preserve purchasing power during periods of inflation. More formally stated, an inflation hedge's nominal returns tend to be highly correlated with inflation rates. As residual real claims on businesses, common equities should offer superior protection against unanticipated inflation compared with conventional bonds. This phenomenon is so because companies' earnings tend to increase with inflation, whereas payments on conventional bonds are fixed in nominal terms. Nevertheless, companies do face challenges in coping with inflation. Reported earnings often overstate their real economic value to varying degrees. Corporate income taxes and capital gains tax rates are typically not inflation indexed, so inflation can cut into investors' after-tax real returns unless share prices fully reflect (through lower prices) the interaction of inflation and taxation. Furthermore, individual equities differ in their sensitivities to inflation because of industry, competitive, and other types of factors. Companies' abilities to raise output prices and revenues to keep pace with increases in input prices vary inversely with the amount of price competition in their markets. Yet the historical record indicates that the very long-run real return on stocks in the United States has been relatively insensitive to realized inflation rates, in contrast to bonds, whose returns have been negatively related to inflation.[3] Evidence from many markets indicates that using long measurement periods (longer than annual), equities on average do have value as an inflation hedge.[4] That fact has been an argument for equity investment not only for investors with general inflation concerns but also for defined-benefit plan sponsors, which may be exposed through the terms of the pension benefit formula to increasing nominal wage and salary costs.

Finally, equities' comparatively high historical long-term real rates of return have been important in establishing the widely held perspective that they play a growth role in a portfolio. Exhibit 2, showing historical real rates of return on equity, is taken from a Dimson, Marsh, and Staunton (2006) survey of capital market returns internationally. Their analysis shows that during the 106 years from 1900 to 2005, the long-term real rates of return to equities have exceeded that of bonds in all 17 countries listed in Exhibit 2.[5]

For all the reasons discussed, many successful long-term investors have had an equity bias in their asset allocation, diversifying with instruments such as bonds to obtain an acceptable level of risk and/or income. In the next sections we discuss how investors approach equity investment.

---

[3] See Siegel (2002), p. 195. Siegel examined 30-year holding periods from 1871 to 2001. Equities have not been effective inflation hedges, however, for the short-term (Siegel 2002) or in periods of high (4.00 percent to 7.99 percent) or extraordinary inflation (8.00 percent and above). See Ibbotson and Brinson (1987).

[4] See Boudoukh and Richardson (1993), focusing on U.S. data; Ely and Robinson (1997) for an international focus; and Luintel and Paudyal (2006), focusing on U.K. data.

[5] See Dimson, Marsh, and Staunton (2006) for data on historical bond returns.

EXHIBIT 2	Equity Real Rates of Return, 1900–2005		
	Mean		Standard
Country	Geometric	Arithmetic	Deviation
Australia	7.7%	9.2%	17.6%
Belgium	2.4	4.6	22.1
Canada	6.2	7.6	16.8
Denmark	5.2	6.9	20.3
France	3.6	6.1	23.2
Germany (excludes 1922–23)	3.1	8.2	32.5
Ireland	4.8	7.0	22.1
Italy	2.5	6.5	29.1
Japan	4.5	9.3	30.0
The Netherlands	5.3	7.2	21.3
Norway	4.3	7.1	27.0
South Africa	7.3	9.5	22.6
Spain	3.7	5.9	21.9
Sweden	7.8	10.1	22.6
Switzerland	4.5	6.3	19.7
United Kingdom	5.5	7.4	20.0
United States	6.5	8.5	20.2
World	5.7	7.2	17.2

Source: Dimson, Marsh, and Staunton (2006).

APPROACHES TO EQUITY INVESTMENT

3

There are a number of different approaches to managing equity portfolios, each of which we will discuss in more detail later in this reading.

In **passive management**, the investor does not attempt to reflect his investment expectations through changes in security holdings. The dominant passive approach is **indexing**, which involves investing in a portfolio that attempts to match the performance of some specified benchmark. Although passive in the sense of not incorporating the investor's expectations concerning securities, indexed portfolios are anything but passive in implementation. When a stock is added to or dropped from an index, or when the weight of a given stock changes because of a corporate action (such as a share buyback, or a **secondary offering**—an offering after the initial public offering of securities), the portfolio must be adjusted. Pioneered in the 1970s, indexing has quickly grown to the point that the United States alone has more than $1 trillion in institutional indexed equities. Today, indexed portfolios often function as the core holding in an investor's overall equity allocation.

Another approach is **active management**, which historically is the principal way that investors have managed equity portfolios. An active manager seeks to outperform a given benchmark portfolio (the portfolio against which the manager's performance will be evaluated). The manager does this by identifying which stocks she thinks will perform comparatively well versus the benchmark portfolio, buying or holding those, and avoiding stocks she believes will underperform the benchmark. Despite indexing's growing popularity during the last few decades, active equity management still accounts for the overwhelming majority of equity assets managed.

The final approach is **semiactive management** (also called enhanced indexing or risk-controlled active management) and is in reality a variant of active management. In a semiactive portfolio, the manager seeks to outperform a given benchmark, as do active managers in general. A semiactive portfolio manager, however, worries more about tracking risk than an active manager does and will tend to build a portfolio whose performance will have very limited volatility around the benchmark's returns.

Exhibit 3 below compares the typical expected active return, tracking risk, and information ratio for successful (first-quartile) practitioners of these three different approaches. **Active return** is the portfolio's return in excess of the return on the portfolio's benchmark. **Tracking risk**, the annualized standard deviation of active returns, measures **active risk** (risk relative to the portfolio's benchmark).[6]

The **information ratio** equals a portfolio's mean active return divided by tracking risk and represents the efficiency with which a portfolio's tracking risk delivers active return. What can we infer from Exhibit 3 about how an investor in each of these categories views equity market informational efficiency? Investors who believe that an equity market is efficient will usually favor indexing because they think that equity research will not provide a sufficient increment in return to overcome their research and transaction costs. Active investors believe that the equity market is often inefficient and that good research will allow them to outperform the market net of all costs. Enhanced indexers fall somewhere between the two, believing that they can extract information about companies that has not been embedded in stock prices, but attempting to do so in a way that limits tracking risk.

EXHIBIT 3	Indexing, Enhanced Indexing, and Active Approaches: A Comparison		
	Indexing	**Enhanced Indexing**	**Active**
Expected active return	0%	1%–2%	2%+
Tracking risk	<1%	1%–2%	4% + r
Information ratio[a]	0	0.75	0.50

[a] Estimated values expected of first-quartile portfolio managers.

Source: Authors' estimates.[7]

_____

[6] Tracking risk has also been called tracking error and tracking error volatility.

[7] An information ratio (IR) of 0.50 is frequently viewed as distinguishing top-quartile active equity managers. For a summary of empirical results, see Grinold and Kahn (2000), p. 131. Jorion (2002), Table 4, finds that the first quartile of enhanced index funds is close to 0.75. The IR that distinguishes a top-quartile manager may change over time, however, and more research is needed on the distribution of IRs.

Within any of these three broad investment approaches, the investor needs to define the investment universe from which to select common stock. Considerations such as fund size and investment horizon affect the desired minimal level of holdings' liquidity. Tax concerns particularly concern individual and taxable corporate investors. Social concerns (e.g., corporate performance in matters such as governance and ethics, environment, workplace conditions, product safety and impact, and human rights) may matter to any type of investor. The mandates that clients give their investment managers will reflect these constraints.

PASSIVE EQUITY INVESTING 4

Passive investment philosophy has its roots in the history of equity indexing. The first indexed portfolio, launched in 1971 by Wells Fargo, was created for a single pension fund client. In 1973, Wells Fargo organized a commingled index fund for trust accounts. In 1976, Wells Fargo combined the funds, using capitalization-weighted S&P 500 Index as the template for the combined portfolios. By 1981, Wells Fargo had established a fund designed to track the broader market of companies outside the S&P 500. By holding these two funds in market cap weights, an investor could effectively capture the return of the U.S. equity market. Indexed investments became available for individual investors too. John Bogle at The Vanguard Group, Inc., launched the first broad-market index fund for retail investors in 1975.

Several early advocates of indexing were influential in establishing indexing as a major investment approach. Burton Malkiel called for "A New Investment Instrument" in the first edition of his best seller, *A Random Walk Down Wall Street* (1973). He wrote, "What we need is a no-load, minimum-management-fee mutual fund that simply buys the hundreds of stocks making up the broad stock-market averages and does no trading from security to security in an attempt to catch the winners." Other early advocates included Paul Samuelson (1974) and Charles D. Ellis in "The Loser's Game" (1975), one of the most widely cited papers in the literature of both finance and tennis. Ellis marshaled some simple facts illustrating that the institutionalization of the equity markets in the 1960s and early 1970s had made it probable that the *average* institutional investment manager would typically underperform the market as measured by a representative index. According to Ellis, the increased institutional share of the market left too little stock in the hands of nonprofessional investors for amateurs to fill the ranks of underperformers by themselves. Given the costs of trading, administrative expenses, and management fees as well, average active institutional investors inevitably would underperform the unmanaged market indices over time. In his classic article "The Arithmetic of Active Management," William F. Sharpe (1991) explains why the average investor cannot hope to beat a comprehensive equity index. His argument is unassailably clear and simple: "If 'active' and 'passive' management styles are defined in sensible ways, it *must* be the case that:

► before costs, the return on the average actively managed dollar will equal the return on the average passively managed dollar; and

► after costs, the return on the average actively managed dollar will be less than the return on the average passively managed dollar."

History has generally proven Ellis and Sharpe right. Appropriately designed performance studies have generally found that the *average* active institutional portfolio fails to beat the relevant comparison index after expenses.[8] Frequently, the difference in performance has been found to be close to the average expense disadvantage of active management.[9] Therefore, compared with the average actively managed fund that has similar objectives, a well-run indexed fund's major advantage is expected superior long-term net-of-expenses performance because of relatively low portfolio turnover and management fees (often 0.10 percent of assets or less). For tax-sensitive investors, indexing's often relatively high tax efficiency (i.e., post-tax returns that are close to pre-tax returns) is appealing. That tax efficiency comes from turnover that is usually low compared with active investing.

Indexing has advantages in a broad range of equity market segments. The relatively high informational efficiency of prices in large-cap equity markets favors indexing. In typically less efficient market segments, such as small cap, the supply of active investment opportunities may be larger but transaction costs are higher. Indexing is also a logical choice to gain exposure to markets with which an investor may be unfamiliar (e.g., an overseas market), because active investing when one may be at an informational disadvantage is usually ill-advised.

To thoroughly understand the implementation of indexing, we need to discuss the construction and maintenance of equity indices. The way indices are created, selected, and used may be passive investing's weakest link.

4.1 Equity Indices

Investment performance is undeniably important to an equity portfolio manager, whether he takes an active or passive investment approach. It makes little difference how well a manager can identify great companies, make long-term earnings estimates, or forecast the economy if his investment performance is consistently inferior. Equity portfolio managers frequently evaluate their performance against equity benchmark indices designed to show how the overall stock market or some subsector of the market has performed.[10]

The benchmark is not just about measuring asset-class performance. A well-chosen benchmark index for a portfolio manager also represents that manager's investment "neighborhood." If a manager's benchmark is the S&P 500, he is unlikely to be investing in Russian stocks. Investors find it easier to manage their aggregate portfolios if an index well captures the investment universe of their investment managers, and to compartmentalize managers for the purposes of comparison with peers.

In addition to their role as portfolio management benchmarks, stock indices are also used to measure the returns of a market or market segment, as the basis for creating an index fund, to study factors that influence share price movements, to perform technical analysis, and to calculate a stock's systematic risk (or beta).

Four choices determine a stock index's characteristics: the boundaries of the index's universe, the criteria for inclusion in the index, how the stocks are weighted, and how returns are calculated. The first choice, the boundaries of the stock index's universe, is important in determining how well the index repre-

---

[8] Equity mutual funds have been perhaps the most intensively and rigorously researched institutional equity segment. See Daniel, Grinblatt, Titman, and Wermers (1997) and the references therein for equity mutual funds for empirical findings, as well as Ennis (2005).

[9] See Daniel et al.

[10] See the reading on performance evaluation for details and alternative approaches to evaluation.

sents a specific population of stocks. The greater its number of stocks and the more diversified by industry and size, the better the index will measure broad market performance. A narrower universe will measure performance of a specific group of stocks. The second choice, the criteria for inclusion, establishes any specific characteristics desired for stocks within the selected universe. The third, the weighting of the stocks, is usually a choice among price weighting, value (or float) weighting, or equal weighting. The fourth choice, computational method, includes variations such as price only and total return series that include the reinvestment of dividends. Only total return series capture the two sources of equity returns, capital appreciation and dividends.

4.1.1 Index Weighting Choices

Probably the greatest differences among indices covering similar universes lie in how the index components are weighted. The three basic index weighting methods are price weighting, value (or float) weighting, and equal weighting.

- ▶ **Price weighted**. In a price-weighted index, each stock in the index is weighted according to its absolute share price. In other words, the index is simply the sum of the share prices divided by the adjusted number of shares in the index (adjustments are for the purpose of ensuring that the index value does not change merely because of stock splits or changes in index components since the base or launch date of the index). *The performance of a price-weighted index represents the performance of a portfolio that simply bought and held one share of each index component.*

- ▶ **Value weighted** (or market-capitalization weighted). In a value-weighted index (also called a market-capitalization weighted index or a market capitalization index), each stock in the index is weighted according to its market cap (share price multiplied by the number of shares outstanding). *The performance of a value-weighted index would represent the performance of a portfolio that owns all the outstanding shares of each index component.* A given percentage change in a value-weighted index is equal to the change in the total value of all included companies. A value-weighted index self-corrects for stock splits, reverse stock splits, and dividends because such actions are directly reflected in the number of shares outstanding and price per share for the company affected.

  A subcategory of the value-weighted method involves adjustment of market cap weights for each issue's **floating supply of shares** or free float— the number of shares outstanding that are actually available to investors. The resulting index is called a free float–adjusted market capitalization index, or float-weighted index for short. Float adjustments usually exclude corporate cross-holdings, large holdings by founding shareholders, and government holdings of shares in partly privatized companies.[11] The weight of a stock in a float-weighted index equals its market-cap weight multiplied by a free-float adjustment factor (a number between 0 and 1 representing the fraction of shares that float freely). A float-weighted index is concerned with the *investable* market values of equity issues—the market values actually available to be held by the public. *The performance of a float-weighted index represents the performance of a portfolio that buys and holds all the shares of each*

---

[11] For instance, in Example 1 given later, two stocks (Wal-Mart and Microsoft) have substantial free-float adjustments. In both cases, substantial shareholdings of founding executives, their heirs, or foundations that they established are expected never to be liquidated.

index component that are available for trading. Thus, the (total) return of a float-weighted index will represent the return to the average dollar invested passively in the index's securities (ignoring costs). If the index securities are the manager's investment universe, such a float-weighted index represents a plausible performance benchmark for him. With the changeover of Standard & Poor's principal U.S. indices (the S&P 500, the S&P MidCap 400 Index, and the S&P SmallCap 600 Index) and the principal Japanese index (TOPIX) to float weighting, all major value-weighted indices are now free-float adjusted.

For brevity, in the reading we will use "value-weighted/float-weighted indices" to refer to value-weighted indices without float adjustment (sometimes called for emphasis *full* market-cap indices) and value-weighted indices with float adjustment as a group.

▶ **Equal weighted**. In an equal-weighted index, each stock in the index is weighted equally. *The performance of an equal-weighted index represents the performance of a portfolio in which the same amount of money is invested in the shares of each index component.* Equal-weighted indices must be rebalanced periodically (e.g., monthly, quarterly, or annually) to reestablish the equal weighting, because varying individual stock returns will cause stock weights to drift from equal weights.

These different weighting schemes can lead to a number of biases. A price-weighted index is biased toward the highest-priced share. For example, a stock with a price of €50 will have twice the weight in a price-weighted index as a stock with a price of €25. Therefore, a 10 percent increase in the higher-priced stock will have the same effect on the index as a 20 percent increase in the lower-priced stock. The absolute level of a share price is an arbitrary figure, however, because a company can change its share price through a stock split, a stock dividend, or a reverse split. It makes no sense to invest money merely in proportion to an absolute share price, which is what such an index would dictate. Some price-weighted averages, such as the Nikkei 225 for Japanese equities, systematically reduce the weighting of very high-priced stocks to minimize such arbitrary distortion of the index by very high-priced shares.

A price-weighted index's main advantage lies in the simplicity of its construction. Straightforwardly, the share prices are added up and then divided by the number of shares in the index adjusted to maintain continuity in the series, taking account of stock splits and additions/deletions of components. Stock price data series are also easier to obtain historically than market value series. Consequently, price-weighted index series can go back far into the past. Price-weighted indices can be created with a rich, if sometimes hypothetical, history. The oldest and most widely followed equity index, the Dow Jones Industrial Average, is calculated this way. When that index was first published in 1896, the weighting choices most index users prefer today were impractical.

A value-weighted index is biased toward the shares of companies with the largest market capitalizations. In other words, a 10 percent share price increase for a large-cap company would affect the index more than would a 10 percent share price increase for a smaller company. Such an index excels at conveying the effect of a change in companies' total value, or aggregate investor wealth. Float adjustments to capitalization weights exclude shares that are unavailable to investors, making float-weighted indices most representative of the range of securities and weights that public investors as a group can buy and hold. The bias toward large market cap issues in value-weighted/float-weighted indices, however, means that such indices will tend to be biased toward:

► large and probably mature companies, and

► overvalued companies, whose share prices have already risen the most.

Arnott (2005) argues that even if pricing errors are random, the largest-cap stocks are more likely to incorporate positive pricing errors than negative pricing errors. Arnott, Hsu, and Moore (2005) have suggested the weighting of component securities by fundamentals (adjusting the market cap of components downward or upward when price-to-fundamentals metrics such as P/Es are high or low, respectively) as a means of addressing such biases.[12] Another criticism of value-weighted/float-weighted indices is that a portfolio based on such an index may be concentrated in relatively few issues and, hence, less diversified than most actively managed portfolios.[13] Furthermore, because of regulatory or other restrictions on maximum holdings, indexing to some concentrated indices may be infeasible. Although controversy exists (as on many investment issues), float-weighting is generally regarded as today's gold standard for indexing portfolios because it facilitates the minimization of tracking risk and portfolio turnover, and because it results in indices that well represent asset-class performance.

In an equal-weighted index, all stocks are treated the same. Small companies have the same weight in the index as very large companies. An equal-weighting methodology introduces a small-company bias because such indices include many more small companies than large ones. Moreover, to maintain equal weighting, this type of index must be rebalanced periodically. Frequent rebalancing can lead to high transaction costs in a portfolio tracking such an index. Another limitation of equal-weighted indices as indexing benchmarks is that not all components in such an index may have sufficiently liquid markets to absorb the demand of indexers.

Example 1 contrasts the various types of indices.

EXAMPLE 1

A Problem of Benchmark Index Selection

Stephen Alcorn is a portfolio manager at Amanda Asset Management, Inc. (AAM). At the end of 2002, a wealthy client engaged Alcorn to manage $10,000,000 for one year in an active focused (concentrated) equity style. The investment management contract specified a symmetric incentive fee of $10,000 per 100 basis points (bps) of capital appreciation relative to that of an index of the stocks selected for investment.[14] (*Symmetric* means that the incentive fee will reduce the investment management fee if benchmark-relative performance is negative.) In an oversight, the contract leaves open the method by which the benchmark index will be calculated. Alcorn invests in shares of Eastman Kodak Company, McDonald's Corporation, Intel Corporation, Merck & Co., Wal-Mart Stores, and Microsoft Corporation, achieving a 15.9 percent price return for the year. Exhibit 4 gives information on the six stocks.

---

[12] See Arnott, Robert D., Jason Hsu, and Philip Moore, "Fundamental Indexation." *Financial Analysts Journal,* Vol. 61, No. 2 (March/April 2005) 83–99.

[13] See Bernstein (2003).

[14] To simplify the calculations, the problem is stated in terms of capital appreciation. In practice, the incentive fee would usually be stated in terms of total return.

| EXHIBIT 4 | Equity Market Data for the Shares of Six Companies | | | | | |

	Share Price 31-Dec-02	Share Price 31-Dec-03	Price Change	Market Value of Shares 31-Dec-02 (Millions)	Market Value of Shares 31-Dec-03 (Millions)	Free Float Factor
Kodak	$35.04	$24.85	−29.1%	$ 10,056	$ 7,132	1
McDonald's	16.08	24.09	49.8	20,406	30,570	1
Intel	15.57	31.36	101.4	101,703	204,844	1
Merck	53.58	45.10	−15.8	119,216	100,348	1
Wal-Mart	50.51	53.05	5.0	221,992	233,154	0.6
Microsoft	25.85	27.37	5.9	277,060	293,352	0.85
Total				$750,433	$869,400	

Using only the information given, address the following:

1. For each of the six shares, explain the price-only return calculation on the following indices for the period 31 December 2002 to 31 December 2003:

    i. price-weighted index

    ii. value-weighted index

    iii. float-weighted index

    iv. equal-weighted index

2. Recommend the appropriate benchmark index for calculating the performance incentive fee on the account and determine the amount of that fee.

Solution to 1:

　i. As Exhibit 5 illustrates, the value of the price-weighted index on 31 December 2002 is found by adding the six share prices as of that date and dividing by 6: 196.63/6 = 32.77. As of 31 December 2003, the value of the index is 205.82/6 = 34.30. Thus the one-year return is (34.30 − 32.77)/32.77 = 0.047, or 4.7 percent. At 31 December 2002, the index gives a 53.58/196.63 = 27.2 percent weight to Merck and a 50.51/196.63 = 25.7 percent weight to Wal-Mart, the highest-priced shares.

EXHIBIT 5	Price-Weighted Index				
	Share Price 31-Dec-02	**Share Price 31-Dec-03**	**Price Change**	**Percentage of Index 31-Dec-02**	**Contribution to Return**
Kodak	$ 35.04	$ 24.85	−29.1%	17.82%	−5.19%
McDonald's	16.08	24.09	49.8	8.18	4.07
Intel	15.57	31.36	101.4	7.92	8.03
Merck	53.58	45.10	−15.8	27.25	−4.31
Wal-Mart	50.51	53.05	5.0	25.69	1.28
Microsoft	25.85	27.37	5.9	13.15	0.78
Total	$196.63	$205.82	4.7%	100%	4.7%
Index	32.77	34.30			

ii. A value-weighted index is calculated by multiplying the share price by the number of shares outstanding to arrive at each company's market value, then summing these values to create an index. As Exhibit 6 shows, such an index would have risen by 15.9 percent in 2003, because it would have had almost 14 percent of assets in Intel, which doubled, and only 1 percent in Kodak, which fell by the largest amount. Note that for real world value-weighted indices, if X is the total market values of the index components, the index vendor will normalize X by dividing it by the total market value as of some baseline date, and multiply that result by some value such as 100 to represent the starting index value. In the case of Exhibit 6 data, for example, if 31 December 2002 were chosen as the starting date and 100 as the beginning value, then an index vendor would give the index value as of 31 December 2002 as 100, and its value as of 31 December 2003 as (869,400/750,433) × 100 = 115.85.

EXHIBIT 6	Value-Weighted Index				
	Market Value of Shares 31-Dec-02 (Millions)	**Market Value of Shares 31-Dec-03 (Millions)**	**Value Change**	**Percentage of Index 31-Dec-02**	**Contribution to Return**
Kodak	$ 10,056	$ 7,132	−29.1%	1.34%	−0.39%
McDonald's	20,406	30,570	49.8	2.72	1.36
Intel	101,703	204,844	101.4	13.55	13.74
Merck	119,216	100,348	−15.8	15.89	−2.51
Wal-Mart	221,992	233,154	5.0	29.58	1.48
Microsoft	277,060	293,352	5.9	36.92	2.18
Index	$750,433	$869,400	15.9%	100%	15.9%

iii. A float-weighted index is calculated the same way as a value-weighted index, except that the market value is adjusted by a float factor that represents the fraction of shares outstanding actually available to investors. As shown in Exhibit 7, the market values are identical to those given in Exhibit 6 for the value-weighted index except for Wal-Mart and Microsoft, which have free-float factors below 1.0. A free-float index would have risen by 18.1 percent in 2003, or a bit over 2 percentage points more than a simple value-weighted index. The pickup results from the fact that the effect of Wal-Mart and Microsoft's relatively poor performance in 2003 decreases because of their smaller weights after adjusting for free float.

EXHIBIT 7   Float-Weighted Index

	Market Value 31-Dec-02 (Millions)	Market Value 31-Dec-03 (Millions)	Value Change	Percentage of Index 31-Dec-02	Contribution to Return
Kodak	$ 10,056	$ 7,132	−29.1%	1.62%	−0.47%
McDonald's	20,406	30,570	49.8	3.29	1.64
Intel	101,703	204,844	101.4	16.40	16.63
Merck	119,216	100,348	−15.8	19.23	−3.04
Wal-Mart	133,195	139,892	5.0	21.48	1.07
Microsoft	235,501	249,349	5.9	37.98	2.24
Index	$620,077	$732,135	18.1%	100.00%	18.1%

iv. An equal-weighted index assumes an equal investment in each of the six stocks. Its performance would be the average performance of the six stocks over the year, or 19.5 percent. In Exhibit 8, the base value of each of the six components on 31 December 2002 is 100/6 = 16.67. The value of a component shown for 31 December 2003 is found by multiplying its 31 December 2002 value by 1 plus the return over the year. For Kodak, for example, 16.67(1 − 0.291) = 11.82 on 31 December 2003. The weights of the components would then be rebalanced to 16.67 to reestablish equal weighting.

EXHIBIT 8   Equal-Weighted Index

	Index 31-Dec-02	Index 31-Dec-03	Price Change	Percentage of Index 31-Dec-02	Contribution to Return
Kodak	16.67	11.82	−29.1%	16.67%	−4.85%
McDonald's	16.67	24.97	49.8	16.67	8.3
Intel	16.67	33.57	101.4	16.67	16.90
Merck	16.67	14.04	−15.8	16.67	−2.63
Wal-Mart	16.67	17.50	5.0	16.67	0.83
Microsoft	16.67	17.65	5.9	16.67	0.98
Index	100	119.55	19.5%	100%	19.5%

Solution to 2: A float-weighted index of the six shares is the recommended benchmark index because it represents the return to the average dollar invested passively in the six stocks, reflecting the supply of shares actually available to the public. Because the portfolio underperformed that index by 220 basis points, AAM management fees should be reduced by (220/100) × $10,000 = $22,000. Exhibit 9 below summarizes the dispersion of active returns for the various ways in which the benchmark index might be calculated. The manager greatly outperformed a price-weighted index of the six shares, matched a value-weighted index, and underperformed float-weighted and equal-weighted indices.

EXHIBIT 9	Summary of Weighting Method Results	
Weighting Method	**Index Return**	**Active Return to Benchmark**
Price-weighted	4.7%	11.2%
Value-weighted	15.9	0.0
Float-weighted	18.1	−2.2
Equal-weighted	19.5	−3.6

4.1.2 Equity Indices: Composition and Characteristics of Major Indices

A large number of stock price indices exist for measuring share performance on a global, regional, country, and sector basis. The sector category includes indices designed to reflect results for large stocks, small stocks, growth stocks, value stocks, and specific industries.

Exhibit 10 compares some of the major stock market indices. The exhibit first gives facts on indices within the currently very small group of major price-weighted and equal-weighted equity indices. The list of important value-weighted/float-weighted indices is very long: even giving summary facts on them would run to many pages. Exhibit 10 thus covers indices that are discussed in text examples, examples from each of the world's six largest equity markets (which are, in alphabetical order: Canada, France, Germany, Japan, the United Kingdom, and the United States), and an example of a global index family.[15]

---

[15] The country weights in the MSCI World Index as of 30 September 2005 were used to select the six largest equity markets worldwide.

EXHIBIT 10　　Some Representative Equity Indices Worldwide

	Representing	Number of Stocks	Weighting of Index	Special Characteristics	Drawbacks/Comments
Dow Jones Industrial Average	U.S. blue chip companies	30	Price-weighted	The oldest and most widely followed U.S. equity index	30 stocks chosen by *Wall Street Journal* editors; large, mature blue chip companies
Nikkei Stock Average	Japanese blue chip companies	225	Modified price-weighted	Originally formulated by Dow Jones & Company, using essentially the same method as the DJIA	Also known as the Nikkei 225. There is a huge variation in share price levels of the component companies, and some high-priced shares are weighted at a fraction of their share price. Some component stocks are illiquid.
Value Line Arithmetic Composite Index	Equities traded in U.S. markets	Approximately 1,700	Equal-weighted	Represents the performance of the stocks covered in the *Value Line Investment Survey*	A well-known equal-weighted index. The Value Line Geometric Composite Index is based on the same stocks but calculates index changes using a geometric rather than arithmetic mean.
S&P TSX Composite	Broad market cap stocks listed on the Toronto Stock Exchange	Varies	Float-weighted	Very comprehensive index	Widely used Canadian equities benchmark
CAC 40	French blue chip companies	40	Float-weighted	Chosen from the 100 largest market cap stocks on the Paris Bourse (Euronext Paris)	
DAX 30	German blue chip companies	30	Float-weighted	Published by the Frankfurt Stock Exchange	Widely used German equities benchmark
TOPIX	All listed companies on the Tokyo Stock Exchange 1st Section	Varies	Value-weighted[16]	Includes all stocks listed on the TSE 1st Section, which represents about 93% of the market value of all equities in Japan	The index contains a large number of very small, illiquid stocks, making it difficult to replicate exactly.
FTSE 100	The 100 largest publicly traded stocks on the London Stock Exchange	100	Float-weighted	A large-cap index, pronounced "Footsie 100"	There are also a FTSE Mid 250 for mid-cap stocks and a small-cap index.

(Exhibit continued on next page . . .)

[16] The TOPIX became float weighted in three stages: October 2005, February 2006, and June 2006.

EXHIBIT 10   (continued)

	Representing	Number of Stocks	Weighting of Index	Special Characteristics	Drawbacks/Comments
Russell 3000	The 3,000 largest stocks in the United States by market cap	3,000 selected on the last trading day of May. The new composition becomes effective on the last Friday in June.	Float-weighted and value-weighted available	Very comprehensive index	The Russell indices are reconstituted annually based on market cap data as of the last day of May. Widely used institutional benchmark.
Russell 1000	The 1,000 largest stocks in the Russell 3000	1,000 on the day the new composition is determined	Float-weighted	A large-cap index	Competes with the S&P 500 as a large-cap benchmark.
Russell 2000	The smallest 2,000 stocks in the Russell 3000	2,000 on the day the new composition is determined	Float-weighted	A small-cap index	The many U.S. small-cap index funds tracking this index and the consequent annual reconstitution costs and possible tax consequences make this a relatively high-cost benchmark for a U.S. small-cap index fund.
S&P 500	Predominantly large-cap companies representative of the U.S. stock market	500	Float-weighted	Membership determined by a committee of S&P employees	Its popularity with indexers causes new components to earn average positive abnormal returns on the announcement that they are joining the index.[17]
MSCI Index Family	Separate series for individual developed and emerging markets; regions; world developed markets—MSCI World; and All Country World (developed and emerging markets)—MSCI ACWI	Varies	Float-weighted	Most widely used global index family. The MSCI World ex U.S., ex Japan (MSCI Kokusai), ex U.K., and ex EMU, are some indices used as benchmarks for nondomestic equities in various markets.	Other major families of global benchmark indices are published by FTSE, Dow Jones, and S&P/Citigroup.

[17] See Lynch and Mendenhall (1997) and Malkiel and Radisich (2001) for more information and a discussion of competing explanations for this phenomenon.

The first entry is the oldest equity index, the Dow Jones Industrial Average. Interestingly, the DJIA consists of only 30 companies, but since its creation in 1896 it has had a total of more than 100 different constituents. As leading companies of their time go into decline, they are routinely taken out of the index. Many disappeared long ago. General Electric is the only one of the original 12 constituents in the DJIA currently in the index, and it has been in and out of the DJIA a few times over the years. One moral of DJIA's story for equity investors is that if an investor holds a single stock long enough, he is about as likely to lose most or all of his money as to accumulate great wealth. The history of changes in the Dow's composition is one of the best arguments for diversification.

An indexer's choice of index to track has important consequences. Committee-determined indices tend to have lower turnover than those reconstituted regularly according to an algorithm. Thus indexing on the former type of index may have transaction cost and tax advantages. On the other hand, indices (and index funds based on them) that are not reconstituted regularly may drift away from the market segment they are intended to cover. The indexer should also be aware of liquidity differences among the component securities of the various indices that cover the same market segment. For example, liquidity and relatively adequate float are criteria for selection to the S&P SmallCap 600 Index but not the Russell 2000 Index. On the other hand, investing in less liquid shares may allow the indexer to capture an illiquidity premium. In choosing the index to replicate, a fund must evaluate the trade-off between differences in transaction costs and differences in return premiums among the indices.

4.2 Passive Investment Vehicles

Having described the array of equity indices, in the following sections we describe specific passive investment vehicles. The major choices are:

▶ investment in an indexed portfolio;

▶ a long position in cash plus a long position in futures contracts on the underlying index, when such markets are available and adequately liquid; and

▶ a long position in cash plus a long position in a swap on the index. (That is, in the swap the investor pays a fixed rate of interest on the swap's notional principal and in return receives the return on the index.)

4.2.1 Indexed Portfolios

The three most important categories of indexed portfolios are:

▶ conventional index mutual funds;

▶ exchange-traded funds (ETFs), which are based on benchmark index portfolios; and

▶ separate accounts or pooled accounts, mostly for institutional investors, designed to track a benchmark index.

The most obvious difference between conventional index mutual funds and ETFs is that shareholders in mutual funds usually buy shares from the fund and sell them back to the fund at a net asset value determined once a day at the market close.[18] ETF shareholders buy and sell shares in public markets anytime during the trading day. Dealers can create and redeem ETF shares with in-kind deposits and withdrawals at each day's market close.

The principal difference between index mutual funds and exchange-traded funds on the one hand, and indexed institutional portfolios, on the other hand, is cost. Indexed institutional portfolios managed as separate accounts with a single shareholder or, increasingly, as pooled accounts, are extremely low-cost products. Depending on the nature of the securities used in the portfolio, total annual expenses may be as low as a few basis points. Occasionally, where securities with an active lending market are involved, the revenue from securities lending can equal or exceed total portfolio management and custody expenses.[19]

Conventional index mutual funds vary greatly in their cost structure. Elton, Gruber, and Busse (2004) examined and compared the expenses and performance of all conventional S&P 500 mutual funds continuously available in the United States from 1996 to 2001. A large part of the difference in performance among these funds came from differences in the funds' expense ratios, but other significant differences affected performance as well. For example, funds use securities lending as a source of income to varying degrees. The difference between the best-performing S&P 500 fund and the worst-performing fund for that six-year period was an average of 209 bps (2.09 percent) a year. Clearly, S&P 500 index funds and index portfolio managers are sometimes not the "commodities" they are often thought to be. Other differences among index funds become apparent when exchange-traded funds are added to the range of choices.

At least four economically significant differences separate conventional index mutual funds from exchange-traded funds (which in the United States are currently all index funds):[20]

1. Shareholder accounting at the fund level can be a significant expense for conventional mutual funds in some markets, but ETFs do not have fund level shareholder accounting.

2. Exchange-traded funds generally pay much higher index license fees than conventional funds.

3. Exchange-traded funds are often much more tax-efficient than conventional funds in many markets, including the United States.

4. Users of exchange-traded funds pay transaction costs including commissions to trade them, but for their ongoing shareholders, ETFs provide inherently better protection from the cost of providing liquidity to shareholders who are selling fund shares.

To the extent that a fund has a large number of small shareholders, shareholder record-keeping will be a significant cost reflected in the fund's expense ratio. Some funds attempt to cope with this cost and to allocate it to the shareholders who are responsible for it by charging a maintenance fee for accounts

[18] A few funds in the United States and all funds in some countries make more-frequent net asset value calculations: once an hour in some cases, and almost continuously in others.

[19] Securities lending is a common practice in most equity and fixed-income markets around the world. The securities lender typically receives cash equal or slightly greater in value than the securities lent. The lender invests this cash and typically shares the interest with the securities borrower. In some cases, when a security has great value in the lending market because it is popular with short sellers, the securities lender may keep all the interest and even receive an additional premium for lending the securities.

[20] As of mid-2005, U.S. ETFs were all index funds, although a few actively managed ETFs exist outside of the United States. In mid-2005, some actively managed U.S. ETFs were in the planning stages.

below a certain size and/or by offering funds with a lower expense ratio to very large investors. For example, Vanguard imposes a periodic fee on certain small accounts; the Vanguard Admiral share class (offered to investors who buy more than $250,000 worth of shares in a fund) typically has a 6 bps (0.06 percent) lower expense ratio than Vanguard's Investor share class.[21] Exchange-traded funds have no shareholder accounting at the fund level, so their expense ratios are typically lower than conventional mutual fund expense ratios for funds linked to comparable indices. Brokers who carry these shares for investors may levy inactivity fees on ETF shareholders if they trade rarely, and of course there are transaction costs associated with buying and selling ETF shares in the marketplace.

Another important difference between index mutual funds and exchange-traded funds is that, at least in the United States, exchange-traded funds are usually more tax efficient in the sense that they are less likely than mutual funds to make taxable capital gains distributions. At the investor level, mutual fund buyers are affected by a fund's cost basis for its positions, which may differ quite a bit from the positions' current values. As a result, at the time of purchase an investor may buy into a potential tax liability if the positions show a gain.

At the fund level, the most significant tax difference between conventional funds and ETFs is in the process by which fund shares are redeemed. A traditional mutual fund will usually experience a tax event from selling portfolio securities when holders of a significant number of shares redeem their positions for cash. Unlike a traditional mutual fund that will ordinarily sell stocks inside the fund and pay cash to a fund shareholder who is redeeming shares, the redemption mechanism for an exchange-traded fund is usually "in kind" in the sense of being an exchange of shares. The fund typically delivers a basket of the fund's portfolio stocks to a redeeming dealer who has turned in shares of the fund for this exchange. In the United States, this transaction is not taxable from the fund's perspective, and there is no distributable gain on the redemption. Occasionally, a conventional fund—particularly a non-index fund—will deliver stock in kind to a large redeeming shareholder; but most conventional funds offer limited opportunities to redeem fund shares by delivering portfolio stock in kind. The in-kind creation and redemption process of ETFs also insulates long-term ETF shareholders from the costs of supplying liquidity to traders, a persistent problem with mutual funds in a number of markets.[22]

Turning to indexed institutional portfolios, a relatively small number of quantitatively oriented investment management organizations manage the majority of the money in such indexed accounts. The same organization may manage institutional portfolios, conventional funds, and ETFs. Management of these different portfolios may be assigned to separate groups of managers or integrated, with the portfolio management and trading functions consolidated in a single indexing group. Investment management firms' aggressiveness in implementing index composition changes varies, and in fact may vary from one type of account to another within the same firm. Indeed, index fund managers have sometimes come under scrutiny for failing to implement anticipated index composition changes aggressively because of their concern for minimizing tracking risk. The issue arises because changes to indexes are often predictable or announced in advance of the effective date, but index funds may not effect the

---

[21] Vanguard and other managers also offer even lower expense ratio share classes to "institutional" investors.

[22] In the United States, the inconsistent application of deadlines for accepting mutual fund buy and sell orders has been a related problem for long-term mutual fund shareholders.

forthcoming changes as soon as they are foreseeable because of a concern with minimizing tracking risk relative to the current index components. In the interim, arbitrageurs may trade on the basis of the anticipated changes, affecting prices and causing an implicit loss to index fund investors.[23]

If an index contains less than, say, 1,000 stocks, and the stocks are liquid, the index fund manager will usually attempt to manage the portfolio with **full replication** of the index—that is, every issue in the index will be represented in the portfolio, and each portfolio position will have approximately the same weight in the fund as in the index. As the number of issues in the index passes 1,000, it is increasingly likely that the manager will construct the portfolio using either **stratified sampling** (also called representative sampling) or **optimization**. In some cases, the preferred method depends on portfolio size and the availability of active trading in an index basket by means of portfolio trades. For example, an indexer may use full replication for a large fund (e.g., an ETF) tracking the Russell 2000, making use of standard Russell 2000 basket trades, but may choose optimization for smaller, separately managed accounts indexed to the same index.

Full replication, where the number and liquidity of the issues permit using it, should result in minimal tracking risk. Apart from minimizing tracking risk, a full replication portfolio based on a value-weighted (or float-weighted) index has the advantage of being self-rebalancing because the stock weights in the portfolio will mirror changes in the index weights resulting from constantly changing stock prices. Self-rebalancing is a desirable characteristic because it implies that trading is needed only for the reinvestment of dividends and to reflect changes in index composition. Full replication is the most common procedure for indices such as the S&P 500 that are composed of highly liquid securities. Typically, the return on a full replication index fund may be less than the index return by an amount equal to the sum of:

▶ the cost of managing and administering the fund;

▶ the transaction costs of portfolio adjustments to reflect changes in index composition;

▶ the transaction costs of investing and disinvesting cash flows; and

▶ in upward-trending equity markets, the drag on performance from any cash positions.[24]

Attempting to fully replicate an index containing a large proportion of illiquid stocks will usually result in an index portfolio that underperforms the index.[25] This phenomenon occurs because indices do not have to bear transaction costs but a real portfolio does. These transaction costs include brokerage commissions, bid–offer spreads, taxes, and the market impact of trades (the effect of large trades on the market price).[26] There are two ways to build an index-tracking portfolio using a subset of stocks in the index: stratified sampling and optimization. Skillful use of these techniques should permit a portfolio manager to index successfully to even a very broad index containing illiquid securities.

---

[23] See Chen, Noronha, and Singal (2006).

[24] In the long run, we expect equity returns to exceed the returns on cash, justifying the inclusion of this factor.

[25] Nevertheless, superior tax reclaims (of withheld taxes) on large international index funds can deliver a significant boost to performance relative to most international indices, which use conservative assumptions on tax reclaims.

[26] Taxes are levied on transactions in some countries. For example, a stamp duty of 0.50% is paid on the value of each stock purchase in the United Kingdom.

Using stratified sampling, a portfolio manager divides the index along a number of dimensions (e.g., market capitalization, industry, value, and growth), creating multidimensional cells. Each index stock is placed into the cell that best describes it. For instance, a simple cell structure could focus on market cap and industry. A manager trying to build a portfolio mimicking the TOPIX index would then place a stock such as Toyota into a cell that is defined by automobile stocks with a market cap greater than ¥5 trillion. Next, she would characterize all stocks in the index in this way and determine the weight of each cell in the index by totaling the market cap for all stocks in that cell. The manager would then build a portfolio by selecting a random sample of stocks from each cell and ensuring that the sum of the weights of the stocks purchased from each cell corresponds to the cell's weight in the index.

For example, suppose that a cell contains 2 percent of the weight of the index and that two stocks chosen to represent the cell have index weights of 0.3 percent and 0.5 percent, leaving a balance of $2.0\% - 0.8\% = 1.2\%$. By overweighting each security by $1.2\%/2 = 0.6$ percentage points (i.e., holding them in weights of $0.3\% + 0.6\% = 0.9\%$ and $0.5\% + 0.6\% = 1.1\%$), the index fund can achieve the same exposure to the cell factors as the index.[27] Stratified sampling allows the manager to build a portfolio that retains the basic characteristics of the index without having to buy all of the stocks in the index. Generally speaking, the greater the number of dimensions and the finer the divisions, the more closely the portfolio will resemble the index.

Sometimes an index with relatively few components or with a few heavily weighted components is not naturally compliant with regulatory requirements for fund diversification (which often place maximums on how much of the portfolio may be invested in any one issuer). In such cases, stratified sampling techniques may be used to create an index fund variation loosely based on the non-diversification-compliant index. In the United States, the relevant diversification requirements are the rules for Regulated Investment Company (RIC) diversification in Sub-Chapter M of the Internal Revenue Code. In the European Union, the appropriate rules cover Undertakings for Collective Investment in Transferable Securities (UCITS). As of early 2006, the EU member states were considering adoption of modifications to the UCITS requirements that would allow index funds with an EU passport (approved for offering in all EU jurisdictions) to hold up to 20 percent of assets in one security if the index called for such.[28] Increasingly, ETF issuers and index publishers who develop indices specifically for the ETF market are designing indices to be inherently RIC-compliant in the United States and UCITS-compliant in Europe. If the fund can replicate the index and comply with local diversification requirements simultaneously, a fund analyst can better evaluate the fund's portfolio manager and the fund management process.

Another technique commonly used to build portfolios containing only a subset of an index's stocks is optimization. Optimization is a mathematical approach to index fund construction involving the use of:

▶ a multifactor risk model, against which the risk exposures of the index and individual securities are measured, and

---

[27] This simple approach to weight adjustment has been used in practice. A more precise approach would be to increase the securities weights so as to maintain their relative proportion of $0.3/0.5 = 0.6$: weights of 0.75 percent and 1.25 percent for the first and second securities, respectively $(0.75\%/1.25\% = 0.60$ and $0.75\% + 1.25\% = 2\%)$.

[28] EU member states could increase the limit to 35 percent under exceptional market circumstances.

▶ an objective function that specifies that securities be held in proportions that minimize expected tracking risk relative to the index subject to appropriate constraints.

The multifactor model might include factors such as market capitalization, beta, and industry membership, as well as macroeconomic factors such as interest rate levels. The objective function seeks to match the portfolio's risk exposures to those of the index being tracked. An advantage of optimization compared with stratified sampling is that optimization takes into account the covariances among the factors used to explain the return on stocks. The stratified sampling approach implicitly assumes the factors are mutually uncorrelated.

Optimization has several drawbacks as an approach to indexation. First, even the best risk models are likely to be imperfectly specified. That is, it is virtually impossible to create a risk model that exactly captures the risk associated with a given stock, if only because risks change over time and risk models are based on historical data. Furthermore, the optimization procedure seeks to maximally exploit any risk differences among securities, even if they just reflect sampling error (this is the problem known as overfitting the data). Even in the absence of index changes and dividend flows, optimization requires periodic trading to keep the risk characteristics of the portfolio lined up with those of the index being tracked. As a result of these limitations, the predicted tracking risk of an optimization-based portfolio will typically understate the actual tracking risk. That said, indexers have found that the results of an optimization approach frequently compare well with those of a stratified sampling approach, particularly when replication is attempted using relatively few securities. With either stratified sampling or optimization, the indexer may fully replicate (purchase in index-weight proportions) the largest stocks and create an optimized/sampled portfolio for the rest.

EXAMPLE 2

Passive Portfolio Construction Methods

An investment manager has been given a mandate for managing a Russell 2000 index fund for a moderate-size foundation. The manager must choose either full replication or optimization for managing the portfolio. Recommend the most appropriate method for constructing this index portfolio.

Solution: Optimization is the most appropriate method. Each of the techniques for building an index portfolio has strengths and weaknesses. Generally, when the index contains highly liquid stocks, full replication is usually the preferred index construction method. Apart from minimizing tracking risk, a full replication portfolio has the advantage of being self-rebalancing (given that it is based on a value- or float-weighted index). That said, the Russell 2000 is dominated by smaller-cap companies, and replication may not be the most cost-effective choice given the costs of transacting in small-cap issues.

Stratified sampling and optimization are preferred when a portfolio manager wishes to track an index containing a large number of stocks, particularly stocks that are more difficult and costly to trade. In this case, however, stratified sampling is not under consideration. Therefore, the pension plan should use optimization to construct the index portfolio.

4.2.2 Equity Index Futures

Institutional indexed portfolios and conventional indexed mutual funds, which date back to the 1970s, are the earliest index products and are probably the most familiar to investors. In the 1980s, two additional indexing products, **portfolio trades** (also known as basket trades or program trades) and **stock index futures**, arrived. These products grew in tandem because they were closely related; the success of each was closely linked to the success of the other. A portfolio trade is simply a basket of securities traded as a basket or unit, whereas a traditional security trade is done one share issue at a time. A portfolio trade is made when all of the stocks in the basket—most commonly, the components of an index—are traded together under relatively standardized terms.

In the United States, the most popular trading basket by far is the S&P 500 basket. In the early 1980s, trading in such baskets increased dramatically in conjunction with the introduction of S&P 500 index futures contracts on the Chicago Mercantile Exchange (CME). By the end of that decade, trading in S&P 500 portfolios accounted for a growing share of trading in U.S. securities, and the notional value of trading in the S&P 500 futures contract regularly surpassed the notional value of trading in the underlying securities. The e-mini S&P 500 futures contract, with a notional value of 50 times the value of the S&P 500 (compared with 250 times for the standard S&P 500 contract), became a very liquid vehicle favored by traders in the early 2000s.[29] Trading in these index instruments interacted and found a variety of applications. Trading index securities as a basket and exchanging the stock basket for the futures contract on the index—a transaction called an Exchange of Futures for Physicals—permits sharp reductions in transaction costs.[30] Using an EFP, a futures position can be translated into a portfolio position. The product interchangeability through the EFP process facilitates risk-management transactions for many participants in the securities markets.

Although the S&P 500 portfolios are still the largest such standardized portfolios, trading in a variety of other index baskets and futures contracts has grown significantly throughout the world. Among the most liquid stock index futures contracts are those on the FTSE 100, the Nikkei 225, the CAC 40, and DAX 30.[31]

The limited life of a futures contract and the fact that the most active trading in the futures market is in the nearest expiration contract means that a futures position must be rolled over periodically to maintain appropriate market exposure. Trading a basket of stocks can be relatively cumbersome at times, particularly on the short side where any uptick rule historically impeded basket transactions in U.S. markets. (**Uptick rules** require that a short sale must not be on a downtick relative to the last trade at a different price.)[32] Exchange-traded funds historically have been exempt from the uptick rule for short sales. This fact, and their lack of an expiration date, has made ETFs instruments of choice for many indefinite-term portfolio hedging and risk management applications.

---

[29] The e-mini futures contracts trade on CME's Globex electronic trading system.

[30] In an EFP, one party buys cash market assets and sells futures contracts, and the opposite party sells the cash market assets and buys futures contracts. For example, a long position in equity futures can be exchanged for a long position in a portfolio of securities representative of the index composition. The counterparties privately set the prices, quantities, and other terms of the transaction.

[31] The CME launched futures on equity style indices in 1995, but they did not develop a useful amount of liquidity. See Hill (2003).

[32] A **tick** is the smallest possible price movement of a security. Uptick and downtick in this context refer to any up- or down-price change, whatever the size. In 2007, the U.S. uptick rule was repealed.

4.2.3 Equity Total Return Swaps

Conceptually, equity swaps resemble the more widely known fixed-income and currency swaps. The distinct feature of an equity swap is that at least one side of the transaction receives the total return of either an equity instrument or, more commonly, an equity index portfolio. The other side can be either another equity instrument or index or an interest payment. The most common non-equity swap counter payments are U.S. dollar LIBOR for equity swaps based on U.S. securities, or LIBOR in the appropriate currency for equity swaps based on non-U.S. stocks.

Equity swaps enjoyed a brief and intense popularity in the United States as a way for high-tax bracket investors to achieve diversification, by exchanging the return on a single stock or an undiversified stock basket for the return on a broad stock market index. Changes in U.S. tax law, however, sharply curtailed this application. Today, most equity swap applications are motivated by differences in the tax treatment of shareholders domiciled in different countries or by the desire to gain exposure to an asset class in asset allocation. The tax-oriented applications focus primarily on differences in tax treatment accorded domestic and international recipients of corporate dividends in many countries. Dividend withholding taxes, and an often cumbersome process for obtaining appropriate relief from part of the withholding tax, give many cross-border investors an incentive to use an equity total return swap. They receive the total return of a nondomestic equity index in return for an interest payment to a counterparty that holds the underlying equities more tax-efficiently. Although many cross-border tax differences have been reduced, as long as tax differences persist, equity swaps can provide significant tax-saving opportunities to many large cross-border investors.

Equity swaps have another important application: asset allocation transactions. A manager can use equity swaps to rebalance portfolios to the strategic asset allocation. Total costs to rebalance by trading the underlying securities may exceed the cost of an equity swap. Consequently, effecting the asset allocation change with a swap is often more efficient. Equity swaps are used in tactical asset allocation for similar reasons.

ACTIVE EQUITY INVESTING   5

The active equity portfolio manager's primary job is to deliver the best possible performance relative to the benchmark's performance working within the risk and other constraints specified in the client's mandate. To add value, the active manager must sharpen information, investment insights, and investment tools to the point at which he has a distinct competitive advantage over his peers. Investment tools include the area of equity valuation models, a subject of study in itself.[33] The following sections on active investing focus on macro choices of orientation and strategy that distinguish the different approaches to active equity investing.

Indexing, discussed earlier, sprang from the efficient markets theory initiated in academia during the 1960s. In the subsequent three decades, however, academic and practitioner research identified a variety of possible opportunities for active management. These developments have reinvigorated active management,

---

[33] See Stowe, Robinson, Pinto, and McLeavey (2002).

allowing portfolio managers to justify the higher expenses of active management compared with passive management. Furthermore, demand for performance in excess of broad market averages has been and probably will continue to be a regular feature of both the individual and institutional investor landscape. That said, many investment managers offer a range of equity investment products from active to passive to suit the differing interests of a broad spectrum of investors.

5.1 Equity Styles

To understand the landscape of active equity portfolio management today, we must discuss the concept of equity styles. Most broadly, an **investment style** is a natural grouping of investment disciplines that has some predictive power in explaining the future dispersion of returns across portfolios.[34] As we will discuss in detail later, a traditional equity style contrast is between **value** (focused on paying a relatively low share price in relation to earnings or assets per share) and growth (focused on investing in high-earnings-growth companies) disciplines. **Market oriented** is often specified as an intermediate grouping for investment disciplines that cannot be clearly categorized as value or growth. Furthermore, the market-capitalization segment(s) in which an equity investor operates is frequently specified in describing an investor's style.

Style plays roles in both risk management and performance evaluation. If an equity portfolio manager adopts a specific style and is evaluated relative to a benchmark that reflects that style, then investors who hire the manager can readily determine whether she is talented or is just earning the generic returns to a style, which might be more inexpensively obtained by indexing on an appropriate equity **style index** (an index intended to reflect the average returns to a given style). Certain categories of stocks (e.g., value stocks) can outperform the overall market for years. A mediocre value stock investor might be beating a broad market benchmark consistently while actually underperforming his chosen style as represented by a benchmark for a value style.

Identifying true talent became an important issue with the emergence of the pension fund consultant in the 1980s. Pension fund consultants are hired to identify good portfolio managers, track their performance, and recommend their replacement if necessary. To accomplish this, the consultants partition managers according to the style that each follows. In this environment, an active equity portfolio manager who claims he follows no definable style automatically excludes himself from consideration by many pension funds and other institutional accounts.

The groundbreaking work in style and performance measurement was done by Nobel Laureate William F. Sharpe (1988, 1992). Sharpe set out to explain U.S. equity mutual funds' returns in terms of their exposures to the four asset classes into which he divided the U.S. institutional equity universe: large-cap value, large-cap growth, medium cap, and small cap. Exhibit 11 reproduces Sharpe's original diagram. The horizontal lines divide total market cap into the fraction accounted for by large-cap, mid-cap, and small-cap equities; the vertical line divides large-cap equities into equal halves of large-cap value and large-cap growth.

---

[34] See Brown and Goetzmann (1997).

| EXHIBIT 11 | Composition of Four Domestic Equity Classes |

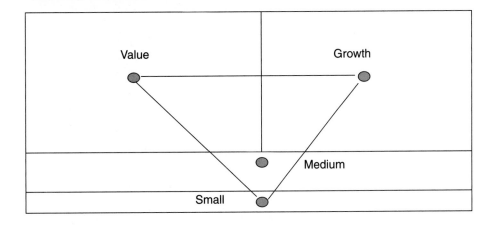

Source: Sharpe (1992).

Sharpe's purpose was to define style to facilitate performance measurement and to reflect the distinct and useful differences in the way active portfolio managers structured their portfolios. As he observed in 1992,

> Much has been written about both the small-stock and the value/growth phenomena. While the terms "value" and "growth" reflect common usage in the investment profession, they serve only as convenient names for stocks that tend to be similar in several respects. As is well known, across securities there is significant positive correlation among: book/price, earnings/price, low earnings growth, dividend yield and low return on equity. Moreover, the industry compositions of the value and growth groups differ (e.g., companies with high research budgets tend to have low book values relative to their stock prices).

Thus style distinctions recognize the similarities and differences among active equity managers. The contrast between value and growth stocks is fuzzy, however, particularly when we categorize stocks in a forward-looking sense rather than using historical data. Almost any stock can be categorized as cheap or expensive depending on one's expectations for the future. Fuzziness in the growth–value contrast coincides with a movement in some quarters to give portfolio managers greater flexibility to use a wide range of techniques and instruments to add value wherever they perceive it lies.[35]

EXAMPLE 3

Same Stock, Different Opinions

Value and growth investors have opposite views on the best way to invest, and they thus tend to reach different conclusions about a stock. In 2004, one example was the Eastman Kodak Company ("Kodak"), the world's largest photography company and one of the oldest members of the DJIA.

---

[35] Bernstein (2003).

For most of its history, Kodak was a growth company. It had a dominant market share in photographic films, photographic paper, and cameras. Its only real rival has been Fuji Photo of Japan. Kodak's earnings, dividends, and cash flow were strong throughout its history. The company was unsuccessful in its attempts to diversify out of photography, however, and in recent years has suffered from the rapid growth of digital cameras. In 2003, its share price fell approximately 28 percent, primarily because digital cameras caused its sales of film and paper to collapse. The company announced sweeping job cuts, slashed its dividend, and came out with a plan to focus on digital imaging.

A growth investor would simply dismiss Kodak's stock as a potential investment. The company has not increased its sales in a decade, and those sales are expected to fall further as demand for film and photo paper continues to decline. Its earnings will be under pressure from restructuring charges and its new strategic investments. Although Kodak is trying to find a niche in the digital imaging market, its strategic repositioning may be too late. In contrast to the film business, the digital imaging market has many competitors.

A value investor, however, would point to the fact that Kodak was trading on a P/E of 12.4x versus 20x for the DJIA, that its shares fell 28 percent in 2003 versus an approximate 25 percent gain for the DJIA, and that it still had one of the strongest brand names in the world, similar in public recognition to those of Coca-Cola and Sony. Although Kodak is struggling to make the transition to digital photography, it is a technologically advanced company with an excellent distribution network. For a value investor, Kodak might be a buy.

In the following sections, we examine the major types of investment styles.

5.1.1 Value Investment Styles

All else being equal, value investors are more concerned about buying a stock that is deemed relatively cheap in terms of the purchase price of earnings or assets than about a company's future growth prospects. They may make several possible arguments to justify buying such stocks. One is that companies' earnings may have a tendency to revert to a mean value; if valuation multiples for a set of stocks are depressed because of recent earnings problems, an investor in those stocks may benefit from reversion to the mean in earnings accompanied by expansion in P/Es. The flip side of the argument is that investments in stocks that are relatively expensive expose the investor to the risk of contractions in multiples and in earnings. Value investors often believe that investors inherently overpay for "glamour" stocks—those seen as having particularly good growth prospects—while neglecting those with less favorable prospects.

All of these arguments presume that investors as a whole do not accurately judge forward-looking risk and return prospects, and so this line of thinking relates closely to the behavioral argument that investors overreact to bad news and thus provide opportunities for value investors. In contrast, Fama and French (1996) suggest that stocks that are cheap in terms of assets—in particular, stocks having a relatively high ratio of book value of equity to market value of equity (equivalent to a *low* price-to-book ratio, or P/B)—have a higher risk of financial distress and thus offer higher expected returns as fair compensation for that risk.[36] Empirically, most studies have found that in the long run a value style may earn a positive return premium relative to the market.[37] Evidence on this phenomenon is still evolving, however. For example, using U.S. data from 1980 through 2001, Phalippou (2004) found that the extra return to value is concentrated in the smallest 7 percent of equities by market value. That segment is relatively illiquid. Various commentators have suggested that, in general, value investors may earn a return premium for supplying liquidity to the market, buying when short-term excess supply causes shares to decline.

The main risk for a value investor is that he has misinterpreted a stock's cheapness. The stock may be cheap for a very good economic reason that the investor does not fully appreciate. Value investors also face the risk that the perceived undervaluation will not be corrected within the investor's investment time horizon. Questions that the value investor should ask include the following:

▶ How long is it expected to take for price to rise to reflect the shares' perceived higher intrinsic value?

▶ What catalyst (triggering event or change) will make the price rise?

▶ Is the expected timeframe for the price to correct acceptable?

The value investing style has at least three substyles: **low P/E**, **contrarian**, and **high yield**.[38] A low P/E investor will look for stocks that sell at low prices to current or normal earnings. Such stocks are generally found in industries categorized as defensive, cyclical, or simply out-of-favor. The investor buys on the expectation that the P/E will at least rise as the stock or industry recovers. A contrarian investor will look for stocks that have been beset by problems and are generally selling at low P/Bs, frequently below 1. Such stocks are found in very depressed industries that may have virtually no current earnings. The investor buys on the expectation of a cyclical rebound that drives up product prices and demand. A yield investor focuses on stocks that offer high dividend yield with prospects of maintaining or increasing the dividend, knowing that in the long run, dividend yield has generally constituted a major portion of the total return on equities.[39]

5.1.2 Growth Investment Styles

In contrast to value investors, who are more concerned with price, growth investors are more concerned with earnings. Their underlying assumption is that if a company can deliver future growth in earnings per share and its P/E does not decline, then its share price will appreciate at least at the rate of EPS growth. Growth investors generally will pay above-market earnings multiples for companies that have superior growth rates. They also tend to invest in companies in growth industries, such as (during the decade ending in 2005) technology, health care, and consumer products. Growth stocks have high sales growth relative to the overall market and tend to trade at high P/Es, P/Bs, and price-to-sales ratios (P/Ss). The major risk facing growth investors is that the forecasted EPS

---

[36] They postulate that distress risk is highly correlated across firms so that it is nondiversifiable and commands a premium.

[37] See Bodie, Kane, and Marcus (2005).

[38] See Christopherson and Williams (1997) for this classification.

[39] See Siegel (2002) for a popular account and details of these substyles focused on the U.S. experience.

growth does not materialize as expected. In that event, P/E multiples may contract at the same time as EPS, amplifying the investor's losses.

The growth style has at least two substyles: **consistent growth** and **earnings momentum**. Companies with consistent growth have a long history of unit-sales growth, superior profitability, and predictable earnings. They tend to trade at high P/Es and be the leaders in consumer-oriented businesses. An example of such a growth stock as of 2005 is Dell, Inc. Companies with earnings momentum have high quarterly year-over-year earnings growth (e.g., EPS for the first quarter of 2006 represents a large increase over EPS for the first quarter of 2005). Such companies may have higher potential earnings growth rates than consistent growth companies, but such growth is likely to be less sustainable. Some growth investors also include price momentum indicators such as relative strength indicators in their investment disciplines, relying on possible patterns of price persistence for certain (usually relatively short) time horizons.[40] (**Relative strength indicators** compare a stock's performance during a specific period either to its own past performance or to the performance of some group of stocks.)

The growth investor who buys a stock at a premium to the overall market is counting on the market to continue paying a premium for the earnings growth that a company has been providing and may continue to deliver. During an economic expansion, earnings growth is abundant—even in the depressed stocks preferred by a value investor—which *may* cause this premium to above-average growth to shrink or vanish. By contrast, when companies with positive earnings momentum become scarce, as in a slowing economy, earnings growth becomes a scarce resource commanding a higher price, and growth investors may do relatively well.[41]

5.1.3 Other Active Management Styles

Market-oriented investors do not restrict themselves to either the value or growth philosophies. The term "market-oriented style" (also sometimes called a blend or core style) gathers an eclectic group of approaches, with the common element that the valuation metrics of market-oriented portfolios resemble those of a broad market index more than those of a value or growth index, averaged over a full market cycle.[42] Market-oriented investors may be willing to buy stocks no matter where they fall on the growth/value spectrum, provided they can buy a stock below its perceived intrinsic value. They might use a discounted cash flow model or other discipline to estimate intrinsic value. Market-oriented style investors might buy a stock with a high P/E provided the price can be justified through future growth expected in EPS. They might also buy a depressed cyclical issue provided that they foresee some recovery in product pricing in the future. The potential drawback of a market-oriented active style is that if the portfolio achieves only marketlike returns, indexing or enhanced indexing based on a broad equity market index will likely be the lower-cost and thus more effective alternative.

---

[40] See Chan, Jegadeesh, and Lakonishok (1999) for a discussion of price persistence and reversal.

[41] See Bernstein (1995), pp. 61–62.

[42] Morningstar replaced "blend" with "core" in 2002. Many investors, however, use "core" in the sense of *playing a central role in the portfolio*, as in the *core-satellite* approach to managing a portfolio of managers discussed later. A "market-oriented" portfolio may be appropriate for a central role but is not absolutely required for it. Because *core* adds a connotation of role unnecessarily, rather than focusing on characteristics, we prefer the more descriptive term "market oriented."

Among the recognized subcategories of market-oriented investors are market-oriented with a value bias, market-oriented with a growth bias, growth-at-a-reasonable-price, and style rotators. As the names imply, value bias and growth bias investors tilt their portfolios toward value and growth respectively, but not so distinctively as to clearly identify them as value or growth investors. They typically hold well-diversified portfolios. Growth-at-a-reasonable-price investors favor companies with above-average growth prospects that are selling at relatively conservative valuation levels compared with other growth companies. Their portfolios are typically somewhat less well diversified than those of other growth investors. Style rotators invest according to the style that they believe will be favored in the marketplace in the relatively near term.

Another characteristic often used in describing the style of equity investors is the typical market capitalization of the issues they hold. Small-capitalization equity investors (also called small-cap or small-stock investors) focus on the lowest market-capitalization stocks in the countries in which they invest. (Micro-cap is sometimes used to characterize investors in the lowest capitalization range within the small-cap segment.) The underlying premise of this style is that more opportunity exists to find mispriced stocks through research in the small-cap universe than in the less numerous and more intensely researched universe of large-cap blue chip firms.[43] Another rationale is that smaller companies tend to have better growth prospects (if their business model is sound) because their business is starting from a smaller base and their product line tends to be more focused. Also, the chance of earning a very high rate of return on one's money is much better if the starting market capitalization is small. Small-cap investors can also focus on value, growth, or market-orientation within the small-cap universe.

In some equity markets, mid-cap equity investors have defined an investment segment focusing on middle-capitalization equities; in the United States, such investors typically focus on stocks that are between the 200th and 1,000th largest by market cap.[44] Mid-cap investors argue that the companies in this segment may be less well researched than the largest-cap companies but financially stronger and less volatile than small-cap companies.

Large-cap equity investors focus on large-cap equities. Such investors favor the relative financial stability of large-cap issues and believe that they can add value through superior analysis and insight.

Small-cap, mid-cap, and large-cap investors are frequently also classified as value, growth, or market-oriented investors within their capitalization domain.

EXAMPLE 4

One Style or Two?

Jeff Fujimori is responsible for the investment of a new ¥10 billion contribution to the Honshu Bank's pension fund. The mandate is to invest with active managers. The equity portion of the pension plan has a broad equity market benchmark. Discuss the advantages and disadvantages of hiring a single manager in either a growth or value style, one manager in each style, or one manager in a market-oriented style.

---

[43] Kritzman and Page (2003).

[44] See Christopherson and Greenwood (2004).

Solution:

Value *or* growth manager (but not both). *Advantage*: If the investor has a position on the desirability of these equity investment styles, this choice would lead to a portfolio expressing the clear conviction of the investor. Such a portfolio has the potential for strong gains if the investor's style is favored by the market. *Disadvantages*: The choice creates tracking risk relative to the equity benchmark. Substantial underperformance may occur if the manager's style is not in favor. Furthermore, Fujimori must confirm that Honshu Bank finds it acceptable to deviate from an overall broad market orientation of the benchmark before undertaking this alternative.

Value *and* growth manager. *Advantage*: We would expect this choice to have lower tracking risk relative to the benchmark than investing in a single growth or value-oriented portfolio, because it does not make an overall style bet. It is a kind of barbell approach to achieving an overall market orientation, which may have the advantage of combining the expertise of two managers. *Disadvantage*: This choice may have higher overall management fees than investing in a single portfolio. The investor must rely on security selection alone to overcome the transaction costs and higher fees associated with active management.

One manager with a market-oriented style. *Advantage*: This is the simplest way to invest consistently with the equity benchmark. *Disadvantage*: Fujimori needs to confirm that the market-oriented style reflects an appropriate and consistent process that promises to add value, as opposed to an unfocused process that has averaged to a market orientation. With that qualification, no obvious disadvantages to this approach exist.

5.1.4 Techniques for Identifying Investment Styles

Two major approaches to identifying style are returns-based style analysis, which relies on portfolio returns, and holdings-based style analysis (also called composition-based style analysis), which relies on an analysis of the characteristics of individual security holdings. The analyst can use the information from either technique to identify a manager's style for performance attribution purposes and/or to formulate expectations about the manager's future performance.

The first technique of style identification was Sharpe's (1988, 1992) **returns-based style analysis** (RBSA). This technique focuses on characteristics of the overall portfolio as revealed by a portfolio's realized returns. It involves regressing portfolio returns (generally monthly returns) on return series of a set of securities indices. In principle, these indices are:

► mutually exclusive;

► exhaustive with respect to the manager's investment universe; and

► distinct sources of risk (ideally they should not be highly correlated).[45]

---

[45] Sharpe (1992), examining U.S. mutual funds, used 12 indices representing U.S. Treasury bills, intermediate-term government bonds, long-term government bonds, corporate bonds, mortgage-related securities, large-cap value stocks, large-cap growth stocks, mid-cap stocks, small-cap stocks, non-U.S. bonds, European stocks, and Japanese stocks.

Returns-based style analysis involves a constraint that the coefficients or betas on the indices are nonnegative and sum to 1.[46] That constraint permits us to interpret a beta as the portfolio's proportional exposure to the particular style (or asset class) represented by the index.[47] For example, if a portfolio had a beta of 0.75 on a large-cap value index, a beta of 0 on a large-cap growth index, a beta of 0.25 on a small-stock value index, and a beta of 0 on a small-stock growth index, we would infer that the portfolio was run as a value portfolio with some exposure to small stocks. The factor weights on large-cap value, large-cap growth, small-cap value, and small-cap growth indices are 75 percent, 0, 25 percent, and 0, respectively. (The factor weights are also known as style weights or Sharpe style weights.) We expect the portfolio to move 0.75 times whatever happens to large-cap value stocks (holding everything else constant) and 0.25 times whatever happens to small-cap value stocks (holding everything else constant).

The large-cap value index and the small-cap value index held in weights of 0.75 and 0.25, respectively, would constitute a natural benchmark for this portfolio, given that the overall fit of the model was excellent. Such a benchmark is sometimes referred to as the **normal portfolio** or normal benchmark for a manager.[48] As defined in the reading on performance evaluation, a normal portfolio is a portfolio with exposures to sources of systematic risk that are typical for a manager, using the manager's past portfolios as a guide. A manager's normal portfolio or normal benchmark in effect represents the universe of securities from which a manager normally might select securities for his portfolio.

EXAMPLE 5

The Choice of Indices in Returns-Based Style Analysis

In the example just given in the text, the style analysis used four indices. Suppose that instead we used the following three indices:

► a large-cap value index

► a large-cap growth index

► a small stock index

We find a large weight on large-cap value, no weight on large-cap growth, and a small weight on small stocks and we conclude that the portfolio was run as a value portfolio with some exposure to small stocks. Critique the conclusion.

---

[46] With this constraint, the model must be solved using quadratic programming (e.g., Solver in Microsoft Excel). It is possible to do a returns-based style analysis constraining the coefficients to sum to 1 but not constraining the coefficients to be nonnegative; that approach could capture elements such as the use of leverage (a negative coefficient on T-bills, included as an index).

[47] Furthermore, Lobosco and DiBartolomeo (1997) have shown how to calculate approximate confidence intervals for the weights.

[48] As defined in the reading on performance evaluation, a normal portfolio is a portfolio with exposures to sources of systematic risk that are typical for a manager, using the manager's past portfolios as a guide.

Solution: The evidence does not contradict the conclusion, but does not completely validate the value characterization. In particular, the portfolio's weight on small stocks might be explained (at least in part) by a positive weight on small-cap growth. By breaking down small stocks into small-cap value and small-cap growth and running the style analysis with four indices (including large-cap value and large-cap growth), we can remove all ambiguity.

We can use a returns-based style analysis to calculate a coefficient of determination measuring style fit. The quantity 1 minus the style fit equals selection, the fraction of return variation unexplained by style. The error term in the style analysis equation—the difference between the portfolio's return and a passive asset mix with the same style as the portfolio—represents selection return (the return from active security selection ability).

Example 6 shows the use of returns-based style analysis to independently evaluate a portfolio manager's style. In this example, Exhibit 13 is a rolling style chart showing the evolution of a portfolio's style exposures through time.

EXAMPLE 6

Returns-Based Style Analysis (1)

Giles Hébert is chief pension officer of Compagnie Minière de l'Ouest SA (CMO). One of Hébert's outside managers for the U.S. equity portion of his portfolio is Arizona Capital Partners (ACP). Hébert is conducting a review of ACP's performance as of mid-2003. CMO decided to pursue a large-cap growth strategy for its U.S. equity investments and selected ACP's U.S. large-cap growth strategy for the investment of part of its allocation to U.S. large-cap growth stocks. When the relationship was established, Hébert and ACP agreed that the Russell 1000 Growth Index fairly represents the investment universe of this strategy. CMO uses returns-based style analysis in evaluating its investment managers.

Hébert knows from the portfolio's custodian that, following its mandate, the portfolio has remained fully invested in U.S. equities. He thus selects the following four benchmarks as the independent variables for a returns-based style analysis:

▶ Russell 1000 Growth Index (R1000G)
▶ Russell 1000 Value Index (R1000V)
▶ Russell 2000 Growth Index (R2000G)
▶ Russell 2000 Value Index (R2000V)

Hébert includes the R1000G because it is the account's benchmark. He adds the R1000V to capture the degree to which the manager may not be adhering to a growth orientation. Finally, Hébert includes the

R2000G and R2000V to capture the degree to which ACP may be failing to adhere to a large-cap orientation. Exhibit 12 gives the results of the returns-based style analysis. Hébert also notes the following facts:

▶ Exhibit 12 is based on the most recent three years of monthly data as of 31 March 2003.

▶ Exhibit 13 is based on rolling three-year monthly data ending 31 March 2003.

▶ For the data period shown in Exhibit 12, selection is 8.1 percent and the style fit is 91.9 percent.

▶ For the data period shown in Exhibit 12, the annualized active return is −0.38 percent and the annualized tracking risk is 6.58 percent.

EXHIBIT 12 | **Returns-Based Style Analysis: Effective Style as of 31 March 2003**

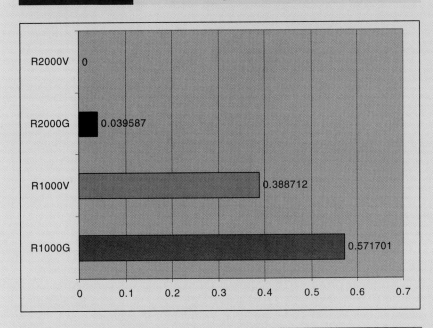

Note: Based on 36 months of data ending 31 March 2003.

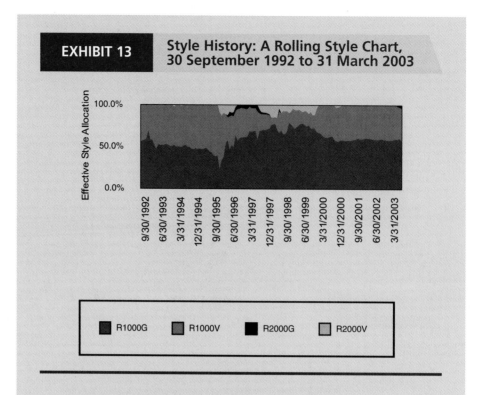

EXHIBIT 13   Style History: A Rolling Style Chart, 30 September 1992 to 31 March 2003

Legend: R1000G, R1000V, R2000G, R2000V

Using the information given, address the following:

1. State and justify whether the ACP product in which CMO is invested is accurately described as a U.S. large-cap growth active equity product.
2. Characterize the historical style of the ACP product and evaluate whether the historical analysis supports the answer to the previous question.
3. Calculate and interpret the information ratio of the ACP product.
4. Recommend a course of action to CMO.

Solution to 1: The ACP product cannot accurately be described as a U.S. large-cap growth active equity product. The product does indeed appear to be actively managed, because the fraction of return variation unexplained by style (selection) is 8.1 percent; the product is not merely replicating the returns on more-passive benchmarks. The very low weights on the R2000G and R2000V small-cap indices, at 4 percent and 0 respectively, also confirm that the product is essentially large-cap. Furthermore, the largest factor weight at 57.2 percent is on the manager's large-cap benchmark, the R1000G. However, the product has a substantial factor weight of 38.9 percent on large-cap value as represented by the R1000V. Considering all these facts, the portfolio appears to be an actively managed large-cap market-oriented portfolio with a growth bias.

Solution to 2: As Exhibit 13 shows, the ACP product has generally had substantial exposure to both large-cap growth and large-cap value; the factor weight on large-cap value was greatest in the first third of the overall period, peaking in 30 September 1995 when it exceeded the weight on large-cap growth. In the middle period, the factor weight on large-cap growth increased at the expense of large-cap value; however, the weight on small-cap stocks, particularly small-cap value, increased to noticeable levels. Since the end of 2000, the style weights have been fairly close to the values shown in Exhibit 12. The ACP product appears to always have had a meaningful weight on value. For the most part, the ACP product has adhered to its specified large-cap orientation. Thus the historical analysis supports the conclusions reached in the previous question.

Solution to 3: The information ratio is the mean historical active return divided by the tracking risk, or $-0.38\%/6.58\% = -0.0578$. For each percentage point of tracking risk, the ACP product earned approximately -0.06 percentage points of active return. Thus the portfolio's active risk has been unrewarded.

Solution to 4: CMO wants to pursue a large-cap growth strategy for its U.S. equity investments. The ACP U.S. large-cap growth active equity product does not meet its needs because it is essentially a large-cap market-oriented fund with a growth bias. The product was not correctly represented by ACP, which indicated that the Russell 1000 Growth Index fairly represented the product's investment universe. An appropriate recommendation would be to move the funds invested in the ACP growth strategy to another investment manager.

Example 7 shows an error that can occur in returns-based style analysis.

EXAMPLE 7

Returns-Based Style Analysis (2)

Frank Harvey is analyzing a U.S. equity mutual fund that states the investment objective of investing for growth and income, with an orientation to mid-cap stocks within the universe of U.S.-domiciled companies. Harvey may select from the following indices for use in a returns-based style analysis:

► the S&P/Citigroup 500 Growth and Value indices, which have a large-cap orientation;

► the Russell 2000 Growth and Value indices, which have a small-cap orientation;

► the Russell 1000 Growth and Value indices, which include large-cap and mid-cap shares;

▶ the Russell Top 200 Growth and Value indices, which together represent the 200 largest market-cap securities in the Russell 1000 Index; and

▶ the Russell Midcap Growth and Value indices, which together represent the 800 smallest market-cap issues in the Russell 1000 Index (the Russell Top 200 Index and the Russell Midcap Index together constitute the Russell 1000 Index).

Harvey selects the S&P/Citigroup 500 Growth and Value indices and the Russell 2000 Growth and Value indices for the style analysis.

1. Critique Harvey's selection.

2. Recommend a more appropriate selection of indices.

Solution to 1: Harvey's choice omits from coverage a substantial number of stocks: those with market caps too small for the S&P 500 but too large for the Russell 2000. Many of the excluded stocks could be characterized as mid-cap. This omission is significant because Harvey should seek to confirm whether the fund being analyzed is actually oriented to mid-cap stocks as it claims to be. The selection of indices should be mutually exclusive and at least approximately exhaustive with respect to the investment manager's universe. The results of an RBSA using a faulty set of indices can be misleading.

Solution to 2: The following selection of indices would be best:

▶ Russell Top 200 Growth

▶ Russell Top 200 Value

▶ Russell Midcap Growth

▶ Russell Midcap Value

▶ Russell 2000 Growth

▶ Russell 2000 Value

This selection of indices is not only exhaustive, in contrast to the one critiqued in Part 1, but also adequate for determining a distinct style weight for mid-cap issues (because it breaks out mid-cap issues via the Russell Midcap indices).

A less satisfactory selection, but an improvement over Harvey's selection, is the Russell 1000 Growth and Value indices and the Russell 2000 Growth and Value indices. This selection is exhaustive, in contrast to Harvey's selection, but would be inferior to the one recommended: It does not suffice to give a specific weight for mid-cap because the Russell 1000–based indices include both large- and mid-cap stocks.

The second major broad approach to style identification is **holdings-based style analysis**, which categorizes individual securities by their characteristics and aggregates results to reach a conclusion about the overall style of the portfolio at a given point in time. For example, the analyst may examine the following variables:

▶ *Valuation levels.* A value-oriented portfolio has a very clear bias toward low P/Es, low P/Bs, and high dividend yields. A growth-oriented portfolio exhibits the opposite characteristics. A market-oriented portfolio has valuations close to the market average.

▶ *Forecast EPS growth rate.* A growth-oriented portfolio will tend to hold companies experiencing above-average and/or increasing earnings growth rates (positive earnings momentum). Typically, trailing and forecast EPS growth rates are higher for a growth-oriented portfolio than for a value-oriented portfolio. The companies in a growth portfolio typically have lower dividend payout ratios than those in a value portfolio, because growth companies typically want to retain most of their earnings to finance future growth and expansion.

▶ *Earnings variability.* A value-oriented portfolio will hold companies with greater earnings variability because of the willingness to hold companies with cyclical earnings.

▶ *Industry sector weightings.* Industry sector weightings can provide some information on the portfolio manager's favored types of businesses and security characteristics, thus furnishing some information on style. In many markets, value-oriented portfolios tend to have larger weights in the finance and utilities sectors than growth portfolios, because of these sectors' relatively high dividend yields and often moderate valuation levels. Growth portfolios often have relatively high weights in the information technology and health care sectors, because historically these sectors have often included numerous high-growth enterprises. Industry sector weightings must be interpreted with caution, however. Exceptions to the typical characteristics exist in most if not all sectors, and some sectors (e.g., consumer discretionary) are quite sensitive to the business cycle, possibly attracting different types of investors at different points in the cycle.

Example 8 illustrates the use of a holdings-based style analysis.

EXAMPLE 8

Do Portfolio Characteristics Match the Stated Investment Style?

Charles Simpson is a consultant analyzing a portfolio for consistency with the portfolio manager's stated value investment style. Exhibit 14 summarizes the characteristics of the portfolio and those of a representative market benchmark portfolio.

EXHIBIT 14	Simpson's Portfolio Analysis (1)	
	Portfolio	Market Benchmark
Number of stocks	30	750
Weighted-average market cap	$37 billion	$45 billion
Dividend yield	3%	2.1%
P/E	15	20
P/B	1.2	2
EPS growth (5-year projected)	10%	12%
Sector		
Consumer Discretionary	18%	13%
Consumer Staples	5	10
Energy	11	9
Finance	25	20
Health Care	2	7
Industrials	10	9
Information Technology	2	7
Materials	10	8
Telecommunications	5	10
Utilities	12	7

What can Simpson infer about the firm's investment style?

Solution: Simpson can be fairly confident that the manager is following a value style. The portfolio's P/E and P/B are below those of the benchmark, but the dividend yield is above that of the benchmark, consistent with a value bias. EPS growth expectations that are slightly below average support the inference that the portfolio is not growth oriented. The sector breakdown suggests value as well. Finance and utilities tend to have relatively high dividend yield and moderate P/Es. On the other hand, sectors with a greater growth orientation, in particular health care and information technology, are underweighted. Thus the portfolio appears to follow a value discipline.

In Example 8, Simpson included some of the types of variables previously mentioned in the text (market capitalization and valuation ratios, such as dividend yield, P/E, P/B, and industry sector weightings) but not others (e.g., earnings variability). Such variation is typical of holdings-based style analysis. Holdings-based analysis involves a number of modeling decisions. One decision is the set of characteristics that discriminate among different styles: Analysts use a variety of sets of discriminating characteristics. The number of discriminating characteristics may run from one (such as the value of the P/B) to a large set, as in the Barra fundamental multifactor risk models, commercial models that have been used in holdings-based analysis. Besides modeling characteristics, a decision must be made on aggregating security-level information. A security may be assigned:

► to value exclusively or to growth exclusively in all instances;

► to value exclusively or to growth exclusively but only if the value of some characteristic exceeds or is less than a specified threshold value; or

► in part to growth and in part to value.

Threshold values must be specified in order to make exclusive (also known as "0-1") assignments. For example, in the first-given assignment method, the market value–weighted average value of an attribute (or set of attributes) may determine the cutoff point for assigning a stock to growth or to value. To illustrate the second approach, assuming that the classification focuses on the P/E, if the P/E is below a specified value (e.g., 16.50) it would be assigned to value; if it is above a higher value (e.g., 24.50) it would be assigned to growth, and if it is in between (i.e., between 16.50 and 24.50), it would be viewed as neither value nor growth. In the description of the final assignment approach, "in part" means up to 100 percent so that the assignments to value and growth sum to 100 percent. To use the terminology of Lazzara (2004), in the first two approaches, style is viewed as a *category*; in the third approach, in which a stock can be "spread over" growth and value, style is viewed as a *quantity*.

Exhibit 15 contrasts the advantages and disadvantages of returns-based and holdings-based style analysis. Because of its less intense data needs, returns-based style analysis might often be performed first and suffice by itself; however, an analysis of holdings obviously can reveal important details of a manager's investment discipline. Both approaches have uses in practice.

The next section discusses the increasing variety of style indices available.

EXHIBIT 15	Two Approaches to Style Analysis: Advantages and Disadvantages	
	Advantages	**Disadvantages**
Returns-based style analysis	► Characterizes entire portfolio ► Facilitates comparisons of portfolios ► Aggregates the effect of the investment process ► Different models usually give broadly similar results and portfolio characterizations ► Clear theoretical basis for portfolio categorization ► Requires minimal information ► Can be executed quickly ► Cost effective	► May be ineffective in characterizing current style ► Error in specifying indices in the model may lead to inaccurate conclusions
Holdings-based style analysis	► Characterizes each position ► Facilitates comparisons of individual positions ► In looking at present, may capture changes in style more quickly than returns-based analysis	► Does not reflect the way many portfolio managers approach security selection ► Requires specification of classification attributes for style; different specifications may give different results ► More data intensive than returns-based analysis

5.1.5 Equity Style Indices

Significant debate exists—and probably should—about how to divide the stock universe into growth and value components. Allocating stocks between growth and value indices can be as simple as ranking them by a single variable such as P/B, or it can involve multiple variables. The clear trend has been to construct style indices based on multiple variables.[49] Typical elements in many classification approaches include price, earnings, book value, dividends, and past and projected growth rates in these or other elements. Each element can be part of more than one factor in a multifactor growth/value stock allocation system, creating some (probably) benign redundancy. Attention to the details of style index construction has increased as index publishers compete to serve and capture licensing fees from ETFs and other investment products.

Exhibit 16 summarizes information on some major style indices. Characteristically, all the indices in this exhibit essentially feature holding-based style analysis, focusing on individual stock or company attributes. In the exhibit, "overlap" means that some securities may be assigned in part to both value and growth. **Buffering** refers to rules for maintaining the style assignment of a stock consistent with a previous assignment when the stock has not clearly moved to a new style. Buffering reduces turnover in style classification and serves to reduce the transaction expenses of funds that track the style index.

EXHIBIT 16	Select Style Index Families: Principal Growth/Value Allocation Criteria and Rebalancing Rules		
Index Family	**Criteria**	**Rebalancing**	**Comments**
Dow Jones Wilshire	Projected P/E Projected earnings growth P/B Dividend yield Trailing P/E Trailing earnings growth	March, September (with buffering)	Two categories (value, growth), no overlap.
FTSE	*Value* P/B P/S Dividend yield Price/Cash flow *Growth* 3-year historical sales growth rate 3-year historical EPS growth rate 2-year forward sales growth estimate 2-year forward EPS growth estimate	June and December	Two categories (value, growth). Constituents are members of the FTSE All-World Index, and Value and Growth indices are calculated for the FTSE World Index, derivatives of the FTSE World Index, plus regional and country indices in the FTSE World index.

(Exhibit continued on next page . . .)

[49] With the replacement of the S&P/BARRA style indices (which were based only on P/B) by the S&P/Citigroup style indices in December 2005, all major commercial style indices employ multiple factors.

EXHIBIT 16	(continued)			

Index Family	Criteria		Rebalancing	Comments
FTSE (continued)	Internal growth rate (ROE × [1 − Payout ratio]) Long-term Past book value growth			Constituents showing high growth (value) characteristics are assigned to growth (value); an intermediate group is apportioned to both growth and value.
Morningstar	*Value* Price/Projected earnings P/B P/S Price/Cash flow Dividend yield	*Weight* 50.0% 12.5 12.5 12.5 12.5	June, December (with buffering)	Three categories (value, core, growth), no overlap.
	Growth Long-term projected earnings growth Past earnings growth Past sales growth Past cash flow growth Past book value growth	*Weight* 50.0% 12.5 12.5 12.5 12.5		
MSCI	*Value* P/B 12-month forward earnings/Price Dividend yield *Growth* Long-term forward EPS growth rate Short-term forward EPS growth rate Long-term historical EPS growth trend Long-term historical sales per share		May, November (with buffering)	Two categories (value, growth), no overlap.
Russell	P/B IBES growth estimates		Approximately June 30	Two categories (value, growth), with overlap.
S&P/ Citigroup World	*Value* Book/Price Sales/Price Cash flow/Price Dividend yield *Growth* 5-year average internal growth rate[50] 5-year historical EPS growth rate 5-year historical sales per share growth rate		July 1	Style Index series: two categories (value, growth), with overlap. Pure Style Index series: two categories (value, growth), no overlap.

Source: www.djindexes.com, www.ftse.com, indexes.morningstar.com, www.msci.com, www.russell.com/US/Indexes, www.globalindices.standardandpoors.com.

---

[50] The internal growth rate is defined as Return on equity × Earnings retention rate.

As Exhibit 16 illustrates (and consistent with our earlier discussion of holdings-based style analysis), style index publishers use growth and value either as categories (no overlap) or as quantities (with overlap).[51] If MSCI, a categorizer, assigns a stock to the growth or value category, the company will be labeled as either growth or value and is never divided between the two. In contrast, index providers that treat growth and value as quantities will often assign a stock partly to growth and partly to value. This split allocation recognizes that some stocks do not fit neatly into either growth or value. Among the style index families in Exhibit 16, Morningstar confronts this issue most directly by explicitly distinguishing three mutually exclusive categories (value, core, and growth). The two-category value/growth split of other index families reflects the consideration that most active equity mandates specifying style are an order for the portfolio manager to manage according to one of these two styles (value or growth).

EXAMPLE 9

Returns-Based and Holdings-Based Style Analyses

John Whitney is a consultant being asked to evaluate a portfolio managed by California Investment Management. He uses proprietary software to do both returns-based and holdings-based style analyses.

Returns-Based Style Analysis

- ► Effective Style for 36 monthly periods ending 30 June 2004
- ► 44.9 percent S&P/Citigroup Growth
- ► 55.1 percent S&P/Citigroup Value
- ► Style Fit: 99.5 percent; Selection: 0.5 percent

Holdings-Based Style Analysis (Based on 30 June 2004 Holdings)

EXHIBIT 17	Holdings-Based Analysis, 30 June 2004		
	Portfolio	S&P 500 Index	Difference
P/E	18.34	19.54	−1.20
P/B	2.87	2.96	−0.09
Dividend yield	1.53%	1.70%	−0.17%
Size (Market-Cap) Analysis			
Largest quintile	25.40%	24.87%	0.53%
Quintile 2	22.34	26.00	−3.66
Quintile 3	23.75	24.37	−0.62
Quintile 4	22.03	21.74	0.29
Smallest quintile	6.48	3.02	3.46

[51] See Lazzara (2004) for more information.

How should Whitney interpret the style analysis results from the two approaches?

Solution: The two methods offer complementary and essentially confirming views of the portfolio. The holdings-based analysis suggests a market-oriented portfolio with a very slight tilt to value (the portfolio's P/E and P/B both are slightly lower than those of S&P 500, suggesting a tilt toward value, although dividend yield is also lower, suggesting a tilt toward growth). The portfolio also seems to have a slight bias toward smaller-cap stocks relative to the S&P 500.

The returns-based analysis produces similar conclusions. The results also suggest a market orientation, with perhaps a slight leaning toward value. The style fit (R^2) is very high at 99.5 percent. Any performance difference between this portfolio and the S&P 500 can likely be attributed to the slight tilts toward value and smaller stocks.

5.1.6 The Style Box

Today, the style box is probably the most popular way of, literally, looking at style. Although an early version of the style box with four component boxes appeared in Sharpe's 1992 paper (see Exhibit 11), his original style divisions were only between growth and value among large-cap funds and among large-cap, mid-cap, and small-cap funds on the market capitalization dimension. The most widely recognized version of the style box is probably Morningstar's because of that firm's high-profile use of the 3×3-style box to categorize mutual funds and, more recently, individual common stocks. The Morningstar style box, shown in Exhibit 18, divides a fund portfolio or stock universe by market capitalization (large-cap through mid-cap to small-cap, from top to bottom), and style (value through core to growth, from left to right), creating a total of nine boxes.[52] Morningstar uses holdings-based style analysis and classifies roughly one-third of its stock universe as growth, one-third as value, and another third as core. We see from Exhibit 18 that most of the value of Vanguard Mid-Cap Growth Fund is indeed centered in mid-cap growth holdings as defined by Morningstar.

EXHIBIT 18	Morningstar Style Box for Vanguard Mid-Cap Growth Fund		
	Value	Core	Growth
Large-cap	2	1	13
Mid-cap	3	17	60
Small-cap	0	1	3

Source: www.morningstar.com.

[52] Core was formerly called blend by Morningstar.

Different criteria may lead to noticeably different style box characterizations for the same portfolio. The techniques used to categorize a stock or the components of a portfolio by size are relatively standard, if the size division is based on market capitalization.[53] The specifics of the techniques used to distinguish among value, growth, and (sometimes) market-oriented stocks, however, are almost as diverse as the firms selling style-based indices and financial products/services can make them. Price relative to earnings or book value or some other measure(s) typically forms the basis of value categorization and measurement, whereas historical, forecast, or implied (by market valuation) growth in earnings, sales, or dividends typically forms the basis for growth categorization. The market-oriented category is characterized by a mix of growth and value characteristics in a portfolio. The market-oriented designation usually reflects an inability to clearly categorize a stock or a portfolio as definitively growth or value in nature. In rare cases (e.g., Morningstar's style box and the Morningstar equity style indices), a technique makes a deliberate attempt to define a group of stocks as being *neither* growth *nor* value. An alternative interpretation is that the group constitutes a *blend* of growth and value characteristics.

The numbers in each box represent the percentage of this fund's portfolio value consisting of stocks that fall in that style box (using Morningstar's own index classification). For example, in the Vanguard Mid-Cap Growth Fund, 60 percent of the portfolio by market value falls in the mid-cap growth box and 17 percent falls in the mid-cap core box. All boxes except small-cap value are represented by at least one position in this Vanguard Mid-Cap Growth Fund portfolio.

5.1.7 Style Drift

Professional investors view inconsistency in style, or **style drift**, as an obstacle to investment planning and risk control. Ordinarily a value manager holding what is perceived by the market to be a growth stock would have some trouble explaining that holding to his or her clients. One stock in isolation may not be much of an issue; but if a manager is hired as a value manager and over time begins to hold stocks that would be primarily characterized as growth stocks, that manager can be said to be experiencing style drift. Investors should be concerned about style drift because they hired the investment manager (bought the mutual fund or unit trust) to achieve a particular exposure to an equity market segment—be it large-cap, mid-cap, small-cap, value, growth or market-oriented. Managers are also hired for their expertise in a given style. Consequently, when a manager begins to stray from her stated style to the style currently in favor, the investor understandably should worry—the investor may no longer be getting exposure to the particular style desired, and the manager may now be operating outside her area of expertise.

---

[53] Most float-weighted indices rank companies by total capitalization before adjusting their index weightings for float.

EXAMPLE 10

Style Drift or Not?

Six months later, Charles Simpson is reexamining the portfolio that he analyzed in Example 8. In that example, we determined that the portfolio was managed according to a value style. Exhibit 19 provides the portfolio's current characteristics. What can Simpson infer about consistency of the firm's investment style?

EXHIBIT 19	Simpson's Portfolio Analysis (2)	
	Portfolio	**Market Benchmark**
Number of stocks	45	750
Weighted-average market cap	$46 billion	$45 billion
Dividend yield	2.0%	2.1%
P/E	19	20
P/B	1.9	2
EPS growth (5-year projected)	13%	12%
Sector		
Consumer Discretionary	15%	13%
Consumer Staples	8%	10%
Energy	11%	9%
Finance	22%	20%
Health Care	5%	7%
Industrials	10%	9%
Information Technology	5%	7%
Materials	10%	8%
Telecommunications	5%	10%
Utilities	9%	7%

Solution: The portfolio's style has definitely drifted from value (in Example 8) to become market oriented. Looking at the valuation measures, the portfolio does not deviate much from the market benchmark. Although the sector weights still lean very slightly toward value (see the weights on finance, utilities, and information technology, and health care), the magnitudes of these biases relative to the market benchmark have decreased significantly compared with the prior period.

5.2 Socially Responsible Investing

Socially responsible investing, also called ethical investing, integrates ethical values and societal concerns with investment decisions. With increasing demand for SRI coming from individual investors, public pension fund sponsors, religious-affiliated groups, and others in many of the world's major markets, an increasing number of equity portfolio managers are responsible for, or have contact with, SRI mandates.

SRI commonly involves the use of stock screens involving SRI-related criteria. SRI stock screens include negative screens and positive screens. Negative SRI screens apply a set of SRI criteria to reduce an investment universe to a smaller set of securities satisfying SRI criteria. SRI criteria may include:

▶ industry classification, reflecting concern for sources of revenue judged to be ethically questionable (tobacco, gaming, alcohol, and armaments are common focuses); and

▶ corporate practices (for example, practices relating to environmental pollution, human rights, labor standards, animal welfare, and integrity in corporate governance).

Positive SRI screens include criteria used to identify companies that have ethically desirable characteristics. Internationally, SRI portfolios most commonly employ negative screens only, a smaller number employ both negative and positive screens, and even fewer employ positive screens only.[54] The particulars of the SRI screening process should reflect the concerns and values communicated by the client.

Portfolio managers should be alert to an SRI discipline's effects on a portfolio's financial characteristics. In particular, managers should track any style biases induced by the SRI portfolio selection process. For example, applying a negative screen, the portfolio manager may exclude (because of environmental concerns) companies from basic industries and energy, which sometimes present a concentration of value stocks; as a result the portfolio could have a growth bias.[55] SRI mutual funds have been documented to have an average market-cap bias toward small-cap shares.[56] At least two benefits for the client can result from measuring and managing these style biases. First, the portfolio manager may be able to address the SRI mandate fully while neutralizing any style biases inconsistent with the client's financial objectives or risk tolerance. Second, the manager can choose an appropriate performance benchmark given an accurate picture of the SRI portfolio's style. Among the methods used to identify and measure progress toward addressing issues of style bias is returns-based style analysis.

5.3 Long–Short Investing

Whereas style investing is concerned with portfolio characteristics (low P/E, high earnings growth, etc.), long–short investing focuses on a constraint. Essentially, many investors face an investment policy and/or regulatory constraint against selling short stocks. Indeed, the constraint is so common and pervasive that many investors do not even recognize it as a constraint.

---

[54] See Ali and Gold (2002) and the references therein.

[55] For example, see Guerard (1997), who found a growth bias in the Domini Social Index relative to the S&P 500, and Bauer, Koedijk, and Otten (2005), who found a growth bias tendency among German, U.S., and U.K. mutual funds.

[56] See Bauer, Koedijk, and Otten and references therein.

In a traditional long-only strategy, the value added by the portfolio manager is called **alpha**—the portfolio's return in excess of its required rate of return, given its risk. Equivalently, alpha is the portfolio's return in excess of that on a risk-matched benchmark. In a market-neutral long–short strategy, however, the value added can be equal to two alphas. This is because the portfolio manager can use a given amount of capital to purchase a long position and to support a short position. One alpha can come from the long position and another from the short position. In addition, a market-neutral strategy is constructed to have an overall zero beta and thus show a pattern of returns expected to be uncorrelated with equity market returns. As discussed later, the alpha from such a strategy is **portable**—that is, it can be added to a variety of different systematic (beta) risk exposures.

In the basic long–short trade, known as a **pairs trade** or pairs arbitrage, an investor is long and short equal currency amounts of two common stocks in a single industry (long a perceived undervalued stock and short a perceived overvalued stock), and the risks are limited almost entirely to the specific company risks. Even such a simple convergence trade can go terribly wrong, however, if the value of the short position surges and the value of the long position collapses.

Probably the greatest risk associated with a long–short strategy involves leveraging. In order to magnify the difference in alphas between two stocks, long–short managers (in particular hedge fund managers) sometimes leverage their capital as much as two to three times using borrowed money. Although leverage magnifies the opportunity to earn alpha, it also magnifies the possibility that a negative short-term price move may force the manager to liquidate the positions prematurely in order to meet margin calls (requests for additional capital) or return borrowed securities.

5.3.1 Price Inefficiency on the Short Side

Some investors believe that more price inefficiency can be found on the short side of the market than the long side for several reasons.

First, many investors look only for undervalued stocks, but because of impediments to short selling, relatively few search for overvalued stocks. These impediments prevent investor pessimism from being fully expressed. For example, in order to short a stock, a short seller must borrow the shares from someone who already owns them.[57] When the original investor wants to sell, the securities loan is called and the short seller must return the stock. When many investors are willing to lend the stock, a replacement loan of stock is quickly arranged. When a stock is a popular short (e.g., many internet stocks during the late 1990s) and few shares are available to borrow, the short seller may have to cover the loan by buying back the stock at an inopportune time.

Second, opportunities to short a stock may arise because of management fraud, "window-dressing" of accounts, or negligence. Few parallel opportunities exist on the long side because of the underlying assumption that management is honest and that the accounts are accurate. Rarely do corporate managers deliberately understate profits.

Third, sell-side analysts issue many more reports with buy recommendations than with sell recommendations.[58] One explanation for this phenomenon is related to commissions that a recommendation may generate: Although most

---

[57] Borrowing can be done in a number of ways. Institutional investors typically borrow/lend shares through securities lending programs run by custodian banks or prime brokers.

[58] See Womack (1996) and Dhiensiri, Mandelker, and Sayrak (2005) for more-recent evidence on the distribution of buy and sell recommendations.

customers may be potential buyers of a stock, only those who already own shares or who are short sellers—usually a smaller group—can sell it. Moreover, those customers who already own a stock may become angry when an analyst issues a sell recommendation because it can cause them to lose money.[59]

Fourth, sell-side analysts may be reluctant to issue negative opinions on companies' stocks for reasons other than generic ones such as that a stock has become relatively expensive. Most companies' managements have a vested interest in seeing their share price rise because of personal shareholdings and stock options. After an analyst issues a sell recommendation, therefore, he can find himself suddenly cut off from communicating with management and threatened with libel suits.[60] His employer may also face the prospect of losing highly lucrative corporate finance business.[61] Although such retaliations have occurred, they are not consistent with the Best Practice Guidelines Governing Analyst/ Corporate Issue Relations sponsored by the CFA Centre for Financial Market Integrity and the National Investor Relations Institute. Furthermore, despite any such pressures, CFA Institute members and candidates are bound by the Code of Ethics and Standards of Professional Conduct, including Standard I(B) requiring independence and objectivity.[62]

Long–short strategies can make better use of a portfolio manager's information because both rising and falling stocks offer profit potential. Rather than simply avoiding a stock with a bad outlook, a long–short manager can short it, thereby earning the full performance spread.

5.3.2 *Equitizing a Market-Neutral Long–Short Portfolio*

A market-neutral long–short portfolio can be **equitized** (given equity market systematic risk exposure) by holding a permanent stock index futures position (rolling over contracts), giving the total portfolio full stock market exposure at all times. In carrying out this strategy, the manager may establish a long futures position with a notional value approximately equal to the value of the cash position resulting from shorting securities. Equitizing a market-neutral long–short portfolio is appropriate when the investor wants to add an equity-beta to the skill-based active return the investor hopes to receive from the long–short investment manager. The rate of return on the total portfolio equals the sum of the gains or losses on the long and short securities positions, the gain or loss on the long futures position, and any interest earned by the investor on the cash position that results from shorting securities, all divided by the portfolio equity.

Depending on carrying costs and the ability to borrow ETF shares for short selling, ETFs may be a more attractive way than futures to equitize or de-equitize a long–short alpha over a longer period than the life of a single futures contract. The general ease of borrowing ETF shares for institutional-sized short-sale transactions, as well as the fact that the fund's expense ratio lowers the expected cost of shorting, can making shorting ETFs an attractive alternative to rolling short futures contracts.[63]

---

[59] Irvine (2000) provides evidence that sell-side analysts' choice to cover a security is positively related to the security's potential to generate commission revenue for their firm.

[60] Lim (2001) finds evidence consistent with this hypothesis.

[61] See Michaely and Womack (1999) and references therein.

[62] See the *Standards of Practice Handbook* (2005). Furthermore, a variety of self-regulatory organizations (e.g., the New York Stock Exchange in the United States) have issued rules for their members concerning analyst conflicts of interest.

[63] Individual investors often find it difficult to borrow a small number of ETF shares or other securities to sell short. Small stock loan transactions are often uneconomic for a brokerage firm to arrange.

A long–short spread can be transported to various asset classes. An investment with no systematic risk should earn the risk-free rate. Therefore, a market-neutral portfolio's performance should be measured against a nominally risk-free rate such as a Treasury bill return, provided the portfolio is truly market neutral rather than simply leveraged equity. If the long–short portfolio has been equitized, then it should be treated as equity, with returns benchmarked against the index underlying the equitizing instrument.

5.3.3 The Long-Only Constraint

Long–short strategies have an inherent efficiency advantage over long-only portfolios. That inherent advantage is the ability to act on negative insights that the investor may have, which can never be fully exploited in a long-only context. First, consider the example of the long-only investor whose benchmark is the FTSE 100 and whose portfolio holds 45 stocks. One way of thinking about that portfolio is to characterize each stock held relative to that stock's weight in the FTSE 100. A stock that is 4 percent of the portfolio but whose index weight is 3 percent can be said to have an active weight of 1 percent. A stock not included in the portfolio but whose index weight is 5 percent is said to have an active weight of −5 percent, and so on.

Looking at the portfolio this way, the investor can think of the portfolio as being long–short (positive active weights/negative active weights) around the FTSE 100 index. The problem with this portfolio, however, is that its maximum short position (negative active weight) in any given stock is limited by that stock's index weight. If the investor has a strong negative view on a company with a 5 percent index weight, the best she could do is not to hold it at all. On the other hand, if the investor has a very favorable view on a company with a 1 percent index weight, she can (at least theoretically) invest the entire portfolio in that company. The bottom line is that the investor's opportunity set is not symmetric.

A true long–short portfolio, built around a cash benchmark, solves this problem of symmetry. Subject to borrowing constraints and other risks outlined above, a long–short portfolio allows an investor to fully exploit both positive and negative views on a stock. One significant caveat exists, however. The investor needs to have both positive and negative insights about stocks in the investment universe. Stocks excluded from further research because they fail to pass some preliminary screen are not necessarily good candidates for shorting.

5.3.4   Short Extension Strategies

Short extension strategies (also known as partial long–short strategies) modify equity long-only strategies by specifying the use of a stated level of short selling. These strategies attempt to benefit from a partial relaxation of the long-only constraint while controlling risk by not relaxing it completely. In contrast to market-neutral long–short strategies which specify long and short positions of equal value and an overall market beta of zero, short extension strategies are generally designed to have a market beta of one with long positions of 100 percent + x percent and short positions of x percent of capital invested. For example, a common implementation of the short extension strategy is a 130/30 portfolio. In this type of portfolio, for every €100 received from the client, the portfolio manager shorts $0.30(€100) = €30$ worth of securities and invests $€100 + €30 = €130$ long—the initial €100 plus €30 provided by short sales proceeds. The costs of a short extension strategy include trade execution costs and stock loan fees paid to brokers lending securities for short sale.

The idea behind short extension strategies is that the partial relaxation of the long-only constraint allows the portfolio manager to make more efficient use of his or her information. In a long-only portfolio, the manager's maximum response to negative information is to avoid holding the stock (selling an existing position or not adding it to the portfolio). With a short extension strategy, the manager can also go short the stock. This shorting activity has the follow-on effect of releasing money with which to take on larger long positions than would otherwise be possible (apart from using borrowed money). That is to say, every €1 of shorts allows a portfolio manager to invest €1 in long positions that he would not otherwise have been able to establish. That €1 in longs could be an addition to an equity already held or an entirely new equity. This is an important point because the long-only constraint not only limits the portfolio manager's ability to take advantage of negative information, but also limits his or her ability to exploit positive information.

A 130/30 short extension strategy is inherently different from a 100/0 long-only strategy plus a 30/30 strategy. The key difference is that in the 130/30 strategy, portfolio decisions on long and short positions are coordinated, whereas with a combination of 100/0 and 30/30 strategies they are generally not. In managing a 130/30 portfolio, the portfolio manager thinks in terms of a single portfolio rather than two separate portfolios. Separate 30/30 and 100/0 strategies, by contrast, may be uncoordinated to the extent of having offsetting positions in the two portfolios, particularly if the 100/0 strategy is an indexed portfolio. For example, the 100/0 strategy could have a 0.5 percent long position in an issue, matching the issue's benchmark weight, at the same time that the 30/30 strategy has a short position (e.g., −2 percent) in the issue.

A short extension strategy has several potential advantages. In contrast to a long–short market neutral portfolio that is equitized using futures or swaps, a short extension strategy can be established even in the absence of a liquid swap or futures market. Another advantage is that relaxing the long-only constraint even to the extent of 20 percent to 30 percent can result in an appreciable increase in the proportion of a manager's investment insight that is incorporated in the portfolio. The long-only constraint's effects on the portfolio manager's opportunity set are more serious in the case of negative information about small and mid-sized companies than they are in the case of such information about large-sized companies, given that the manager's benchmark is market capitalization weighted. Therefore, relaxing the long-only constraint helps the portfolio manager first in the place where the long-only constraint is most limiting, namely, stocks with small market capitalizations.

A disadvantage of short extension strategies is that they gain their market return and earn their alpha from the same source. By contrast, with an equitized long–short market neutral portfolio, it is possible to earn the market return from one source and the alpha from another. This is an appealing feature to investors because it gives them flexibility to pursue alpha wherever it may be found without having to adjust their strategic asset allocation.

Short extension strategies also differ from long–short market neutral strategies in how investors tend to perceive them. Because they are beta zero, long–short market neutral strategies are typically seen by investors as an alternative investment (even if the underlying investments are equities). Short extension strategies, however, are often seen as a substitute for long-only strategies in an investor's portfolio largely because of their inherent market exposure.

EXAMPLE 11

Long–Short and Market Structure

Jim Summers is being asked to investigate two alternatives for his company's pension plan. The first is a market-oriented active long-only portfolio benchmarked to the FTSE 100 index. Only moderate tracking risk with respect to the FTSE 100 is acceptable. The second alternative involves building a long–short portfolio using British stocks and then overlaying that portfolio with FTSE 100 futures. Summers is familiar with the FTSE 100 index and knows that the nine largest stocks account for slightly more than 50 percent of the index's weight. Explain a rationale for choosing a long–short strategy.

Solution: Summers recognizes that a market-oriented active manager will have some difficulty outperforming the FTSE 100 index because relatively few stocks make up such a large portion of the index's weight. He reasons that if the portfolio is to be market oriented, the investment manager will have to produce a portfolio with an average market capitalization somewhat in line with the index. The fact that only nine stocks make up half the index weight means that roughly half of the portfolio value will also need to be concentrated in these largest companies. The availability of insights concerning these nine stocks (a relatively small number) would have an important effect on the portfolio's benchmark-relative results. Summers concludes that this concentration of market value in a small number of issues will hinder the market-oriented active manager's ability to outperform the benchmark.

Summers then examines the long–short approach and quickly concludes that not only can the investment manager take equivalent long or short positions in all 100 stocks in the index, to increase the opportunity set the manager may also be able to use stocks not included in the index.

5.4 Sell Disciplines/Trading

Equity portfolios are not unchanging. Besides sales associated with rebalancing or a change in asset allocation, investors may sell stocks from their portfolios to raise needed cash or replace existing holdings with other stocks. Turnover may be related to the investment discipline. Several recognized categories of selling disciplines exist.

First, an investor can follow a strategy of substitution. In this situation, the investor is constantly looking at potential stocks to include in the portfolio and will replace an existing holding whenever a better opportunity presents itself. This strategy revolves around whether the new stock being added will have a higher risk-adjusted return than the stock it is replacing net of transaction costs and taking into account any tax consequences of the replacement. Such an approach may be called an opportunity cost sell discipline. Based on the portfolio manager's ongoing review of portfolio holdings, the manager may conclude that a company's business prospects will deteriorate, initiating a reduction or elimination of the position. This approach may be called a deteriorating fundamentals sell discipline.

Another group of sell disciplines is more rule driven. A value investor purchasing a stock based on its low P/E multiple may choose to sell if the multiple reaches its historical average. This approach may be called a valuation-level sell discipline. Also rule based are down-from-cost, up-from-cost, and target price sell disciplines. As an example of a down-from-cost sell discipline, the manager may decide at the time of purchase to sell any stock in the portfolio once it has declined 15 percent from its purchase price; this strategy is a kind of stop-loss measure. An up-from-cost may specify at purchase a percent or absolute gain that will trigger a sale. At the time of purchase, the manager may specify a target price, representing an estimate of intrinsic value, and the stock reaching that price triggers a sale.

The manager may use a combination of sell disciplines. Sales typically generate realized capital gains or losses. Thus, the implications of a sell discipline need to be evaluated on an after-tax basis for tax-sensitive investors such as private wealth investors and certain institutional investors such as insurance companies.

So how much trading in a portfolio is normal? To answer that question, we need to understand what drives the manager's stock selection. Ultimately, the nature of the ideas motivating the purchase should determine what level of turnover is reasonable. Value investors frequently have relatively low turnover; they buy cheap stocks hoping to reap a longer-term reward. Annual turnover levels for a value manager typically range from 20 percent to 80 percent.[64] Growth managers are trying to capitalize on earnings growth and stability. Company earnings are reported quarterly, semiannually, or annually, depending on the stock's country of domicile. In any case, it is easy to understand that a growth portfolio would generally tend to have higher turnover than value—a range of 60 percent to several hundred percent for more short-term oriented investors.

6　SEMIACTIVE EQUITY INVESTING

Semiactive strategies (also known as "enhanced index" or "risk-controlled active" strategies) are designed for investors who want to outperform their benchmark while carefully managing their portfolio's risk exposures. An enhanced index portfolio is designed to perform better than its benchmark index without incurring much additional risk. The portfolio manager creates such a portfolio by making use of his investment insights while neutralizing the portfolio's risk characteristics inconsistent with those insights. Although tracking risk (also called active risk) will increase, the enhanced indexer believes that the incremental returns more than compensate for the small increase in risk. Such a portfolio is expected to perform better than the benchmark on a risk-adjusted basis. As Exhibit 3 showed, enhanced indexing strategies with their strict control of tracking risk have tended to have the highest information ratios.

Semiactive equity strategies come in two basic forms: derivatives based (also called synthetic) and stock based. Derivatives-based semiactive equity strategies intend to provide exposure to the desired equity market through a derivative and the enhanced return through something other than equity investments. A common and straightforward derivatives-based semiactive equity strategy is to equitize a cash portfolio and then attempt to add value by altering the duration

---

[64] This level of turnover translates to a holding period of between 1.25 and 5 years.

of the underlying cash.[65] For example, one simple approach could be to vary the duration between 90-day bills (cash) and 3-year notes based on yield curve slope. When this segment of the yield curve slopes steeply, the manager should invest in longer-duration fixed income, because the higher yield compensates the investor for the increased risk. When the slope is flat, the manager should stay short because no increased yield exists for investing in longer maturities. In this way, a portfolio manager can attempt to achieve some incremental return over cash from the short-term fixed-income portfolio while obtaining equity exposure through the futures market, thereby creating an enhanced index fund.

Enhanced indexing strategies based on stock selection attempt to generate alpha by identifying stocks that will either outperform or underperform the index. Risk control is imposed in order to limit the degree of individual stock underweighting or overweighting and the portfolio's exposure to factor risks and industry concentrations. The resulting portfolio is intended to look like the benchmark in all respects except in those areas on which the manager explicitly wishes to bet.

One way of thinking about an enhanced index stock-selection strategy versus traditional active management involves considering the investment manager's frame of reference. A traditional active manager begins with a pool of investment capital, tries to identify stocks that will appreciate the most, and includes those in the portfolio. Whatever that manager's benchmark, if the manager is uninformed about a particular stock, she will not hold it in the portfolio. In an enhanced index stock selection strategy, the neutral portfolio is the benchmark. If the manager has no opinion about a given stock, that manager holds the stock at its benchmark weight. Every portfolio position is evaluated relative to the benchmark weight.

How do semiactive equity managers try to generate alpha using stock selection? Mostly, they do it the same way traditional active managers do. They may look at broad themes relating to a company's valuation or growth. They may also build complex models to process vast quantities of information in their quest for alpha. But the bottom line is that these portfolio managers are essentially active managers who build portfolios with a high degree of risk control.

In addition to a high degree of risk control, another reason for the popularity of enhanced index portfolios can be explained in terms of Grinold and Kahn's **Fundamental Law of Active Management**.[66] The law states that

$$\text{IR} \approx \text{IC}\sqrt{\text{Breadth}} \qquad\qquad \textbf{(1)}$$

Translated, this means that the information ratio (IR) is approximately equal to what you know about a given investment (the **information coefficient** or IC)[67] multiplied by the square root of the investment discipline's breadth, which is defined as the number of independent, active investment decisions made each year. Therefore, a lower-breadth strategy necessarily requires more accurate insight about a given investment to produce the same IR as a strategy with higher breadth. Well-executed enhanced indexed strategies may have a relatively high

[65] To equitize is to go long on sufficient futures contracts to provide equity exposure to the underlying cash investment. For example, to equitize cash using a $10 million cash portfolio with S&P 500 futures, divide $10 million by the notional value of each S&P 500 contract to determine how many long position contracts are required. (In practice, a small adjustment called "tailing" is made to this calculation to account for the time value of money on the daily futures marks received or paid. A discussion of tailing is outside the scope of this reading.)

[66] See Grinold and Kahn (2000) for a complete development.

[67] The information coefficient is more formally defined as the correlation between forecast return and actual return. In essence, it measures the effectiveness of investment insight.

combination of insight and breadth, resulting from the disciplined use of information across a wide range of securities that differ in some important respects. (Note, however, that the number of *independent* decisions available per period does not *necessarily* increase with the size of the research universe.)

EXAMPLE 12

Illustration of the Fundamental Law of Active Management

Gerhardt Holz is evaluating two investment managers:

▶ Manager A follows 500 stocks with annual forecasts, and the IC for each of the forecasts is 0.03.

▶ Manager B follows 100 stocks with annual forecasts, and the IC for each of the forecasts is twice that of Manager A's security forecasts.

Based only on the above information, which manager should Holz select?

Solution: Manager A's breadth of 500 and IC of 0.03 translates into an information ratio of approximately $0.03\sqrt{500} = 0.67$ (on an annual basis). Manager B's breadth of 100 and IC of 0.06 translates into an information ratio of approximately $0.06\sqrt{100} = 0.60$ (on an annual basis). Based only on the information given, Holz would select Manager A.

A semiactive stock-selection approach has several possible limitations. The first is that any technique that generates positive alpha may become obsolete as other investors try to exploit it. A successful enhanced indexer is always innovating. Also, quantitative and mathematical models derived from analysis of historical returns and prices may be invalid in the future. Markets undergo secular changes, lessening the effectiveness of the past as a guide to the future. Markets also occasionally undergo shocks that, at least temporarily, render forecasting or risk models ineffective. Example 13 illustrates a comparison made in terms of alpha and tracking risk.[68]

EXAMPLE 13

Derivatives-Based versus Stock-Based Semiactive Strategies

Heidi Erikson is an investment officer with a large Swedish pension plan. Her supervisor is thinking about investing in an enhanced index product focused on Japanese equities benchmarked against the Index. He asks Erikson to investigate the various alternative approaches. Exhibit 20 presents her findings.

---

[68] In the example, the use of alpha rather than active return in calculating the information ratio means only that the portfolio's benchmark has been matched in terms of systematic risk.

EXHIBIT 20	Semiactive Alternatives	
	Expected Alpha	Tracking Risk
Stock-based semiactive	1.2%	2.7%
Derivative-based semiactive	1.0	2.1

Using the information given, address the following:

1. Contrast stock-based and derivative-based semiactive investment strategies.

2. State an appropriate quantitative criterion for evaluating alternative semiactive approaches.

3. Recommend and justify a semiactive approach for the pension plan.

Solution to 1: A stock-based semiactive approach involves controlled under- and overweighting of securities relative to their index weights. This approach attempts to pick up active return through equity insights. By contrast, a derivative-based semiactive approach involves using derivatives to equitize cash and attempting to pick up active return by adjusting the duration of the fixed-income position.

Solution to 2: The information ratio (IR), defined as mean active return divided by tracking risk, is the appropriate quantitative criterion for evaluating alternative active strategies because it permits comparison based on the mean active return gained for bearing a unit of active risk in each strategy.

Solution to 3: The stock-based semiactive strategy has an IR of $1.2/2.7 = 0.44$ versus $1/2.1 = 0.48$ for the derivative-based strategy. Because it has the higher information ratio, based only on the information given, Erikson should recommend using a derivative-based strategy.

MANAGING A PORTFOLIO OF MANAGERS   7

When investing a pool of assets, every investor must decide first on the overall asset allocation of the investments—which asset classes to use and how much to invest in each. The investor then needs to decide how to invest the assets within each class. Should the investor use index funds or have the money managed actively? What is the correct level of active risk? How many managers should be used?

When developing an asset allocation policy, the investor seeks an allocation to asset classes that maximizes expected total return subject to a given level of *total* risk. The framework of optimizing allocations to a group of managers (in this context, equity managers within the equity allocation) takes a parallel form, but with the investor now maximizing active return for a given level of active risk determined by his level of aversion to active risk:[69]

$$\underset{\substack{\text{Maximize} \\ \text{by choice of managers}}}{} \quad U_A = r_A - \lambda_A \sigma_A^2 \qquad\qquad (2)$$

where

U_A = expected utility of the active return of the manager mix

r_A = expected active return of the manager mix

λ_A = the investor's trade-off between active risk and active return; measures risk aversion in active risk terms

σ_A^2 = variance of the active return

The efficient frontier specified by this objective function is drawn in active risk and active return space, because once active or semiactive managers are potentially in the mix, the investor's trade-off becomes one of active return versus active risk (the asset allocation decision determines the trade-off between total risk and return). How much active risk an investor wishes to assume determines the mix of specific managers. For example, an investor wishing to assume no active risk at all would hold an index fund. On the other hand, investors desiring a high level of active risk and active return may find their mix skewed toward some combination of higher active risk managers with little or no exposure to index funds.

Take the hypothetical case of Yasu Nakasone, an investment officer with the pension fund of RBG Electronics. Nakasone wants to invest ¥60 billion in Japanese equities benchmarked to TOPIX. He is considering the managers shown in Exhibit 21. The active managers and semiactive managers follow distinct investment styles.[70]

EXHIBIT 21	Portfolio Statistics	
	Expected Active Return	**Expected Tracking Risk**
Index	0.0%	0%
Semiactive	1.5	2
Active A	2.0	3
Active B	3.0	5
Active C	4.0	8

For his analysis, Nakasone assumes that all five managers' active returns are uncorrelated; he generates the efficient frontier in Exhibit 22 using a mean–variance optimizer. The question Nakasone must ask himself is how much active risk he wishes to take in the aggregate equity portfolio. The answer will help him determine the required manager mix.

---

[69] See Waring, Whitney, Pirone, and Castille (2000), on which this discussion is based. The objective function shown does not consider fees and other costs associated with the mix of managers. Investment management fees and custody costs also must be considered, and these will be higher for active and semiactive managers than for index funds. One way of incorporating costs into the optimization is simply to subtract them from each manager's expected returns.

[70] Because these investment managers have different investment styles, the assumption of uncorrelated alphas made subsequently is reasonable. The model also applies if alphas are correlated, although the details will be more complex.

EXHIBIT 22	Efficient Frontier of Managers

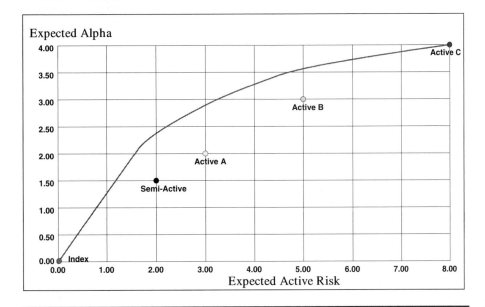

In addition to generating the efficient frontier, Nakasone has also put together a "waterfall" chart (Exhibit 23) that breaks down manager mix for each level of active risk.

EXHIBIT 23	Manager Allocation by Active Risk Level

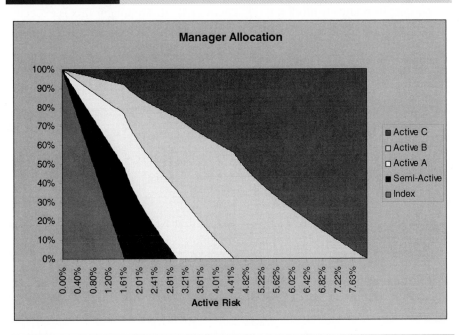

Nakasone must now select the appropriate level of active risk. Generally, investors are far more risk averse in active risk terms than in total risk terms, for several reasons. For example, an investor can achieve the benchmark return by purchasing an index portfolio. To achieve an active return in his portfolio, however, Nakasone must believe both that successful active management is possible and that he has the necessary skill to select active managers who will outperform. Second, Nakasone is responsible for the whole equity portfolio, and his superiors will judge him based on how well the overall portfolio performs relative to the benchmark. Successful active management is difficult, and many who attempt it underperform.[71] This fact produces a sort of institutional conservatism on the part of many investors. Finally, Nakasone realizes that as one moves up on the efficient frontier assuming more active risk, less manager diversification exists. For institutional investors, an overall active risk budget (target) in the range of 1.5 percent to 2.5 percent is fairly typical.[72]

Nakasone decides that he is willing to assume only 1.51 percent active risk, leading him to select the portfolio shown in Exhibit 24:

EXHIBIT 24	RBG Pension Fund Manager Mix
	Allocation
Index	8%
Semiactive	44
Active A	26
Active B	14
Active C	8

Despite its relatively modest level of active risk, this manager mix is expected to produce an active return of 1.92 percent, leading to a very strong IR of 1.27. The active return for the overall portfolio is a weighted average of the active returns for the individual managers.

$$\text{Portfolio active return} = \sum_{i=1}^{n} h_{Ai} r_{Ai}$$

where

h_{Ai} = weight assigned to the ith manager
r_{Ai} = active return of the ith manager

The active risk is a bit more complex. Recall that Nakasone assumes the active returns are uncorrelated. Therefore,

$$\text{Portfolio active risk} = \sqrt{\sum_{i=1}^{n} h_{Ai}^2 \sigma_{Ai}^2}$$

---

[71] The average actively managed dollar, yen, euro, etc. must necessarily underperform, per Sharpe (1991).

[72] See Waring et al. (2000).

where

h_{Ai} = the weight assigned to the ith manager

σ_{Ai} = the active risk of the ith manager

The portfolio active risk in this case is the square root of the weighted sum of the individual managers' variances.[73]

7.1 Core-Satellite

The type of portfolio that Nakasone constructed in the previous section is referred to as a **core-satellite portfolio**.[74] Specifically, 52 percent of the overall portfolio—the index and semiactive managers—constitutes the core holding, and the three active managers represent a ring of satellites around this core. When we apply the optimization shown in Equation 2 to a group of equity managers that includes effective indexers and/or enhanced indexers and successful active managers (as judged by information ratios), a core-satellite portfolio is a likely result.

Core-satellite portfolios can be constructed using Nakasone's rigorous approach or much more simply, as demonstrated in Example 14 below. In either case, the objective is to anchor a strategy with either an index portfolio or an enhanced index portfolio and to use active managers opportunistically around that anchor to achieve an acceptable level of active return while mitigating some of the active risk associated with a portfolio consisting entirely of active managers. The index or enhanced index portfolios used in the core generally should resemble as closely as possible the investor's benchmark for the asset class. The satellite portfolios may also be benchmarked to the overall asset class benchmark, but there is greater latitude for them to have different benchmarks as well (e.g., having a growth or value focus rather than the more likely core benchmark for the asset class).

EXAMPLE 14

A Pension Fund's Performance Objectives

Jim Smith manages the international equity portion of the pension portfolio of ACME Minerals, a large Australian mining company. Smith is responsible for a portfolio of A\$700 million of non-Australian equities. Smith's annual compensation is related to the performance of this portfolio versus the MSCI World ex-Australia Index, the benchmark for the pension portfolio's international equity portion. He has hired the following managers with expected alphas and active risk shown.

---

[73] Had the active returns been correlated, the portfolio active risk equation would also have included covariance terms under the square root sign.

[74] Core-satellite is sometimes discussed as an approach to overall asset allocation in which certain asset classes are held in a passively managed core while others (believed to be inefficiently priced) are held in actively managed satellites. See Singleton (2005). The text discusses the concept in terms of allocating assets within a single asset class, another frequent usage of the term.

EXHIBIT 25	Portfolio Managers' Characteristics		
	AUM (Millions)	Expected Alpha	Expected Tracking Risk
Manager A	A$400	0%	0%
Manager B	100	2	4
Manager C	100	4	6
Manager D	100	4	6

All four managers' alphas are uncorrelated and are measured against the MSCI World ex-Australia benchmark.

The pension fund's trustees have stated objectives of achieving a ratio of alpha to tracking risk of 0.6 or greater, with tracking risk of no more than 2 percent a year. An optimization based on Equation 2 results in weights on Managers A, B, C, and D of 4/7, 1/7, 1/7, and 1/7, respectively. Based only on the information given, address the following:

1. Identify the investment approach of Manager A.
2. Characterize the structure of the optimal portfolio of managers.
3. Evaluate whether the optimal portfolio of managers is expected to meet the trustees' investment objectives.

Solution to 1: Because Manager A has expected tracking risk of 0 percent, we can infer that this manager is an indexer.

Solution to 2: The portfolio of managers represents a core-satellite portfolio. An indexed investment (Manager A) represents more than half the portfolio's value and functions as the core. Actively managed portfolios (Managers B, C, and D) represent the satellite portfolios surrounding the core.

Solution to 3: We need to calculate the expected alpha and active tracking risk for the portfolio of managers to evaluate whether this portfolio meets the trustees' performance objectives. The portfolio's expected alpha is

$$(4/7)(0\%) + (1/7)(2\%) + (1/7)(4\%) + (1/7)(4\%) = 1.43\%$$

The portfolio's tracking risk is

$$[(4/7)^2 0^2 + (1/7)^2 (4\%)^2 + (1/7)^2 (6\%)^2 + (1/7)^2 (6\%)^2]^{1/2} = 1.34\%$$

Tracking risk of 1.34 percent satisfies the trustees' objective of tracking risk of no more than 2 percent annually. The ratio of $1.43\%/1.34\% = 1.07$ exceeds the target of 0.6. Thus the portfolio of managers meets the performance requirements of the trustees. Note that the tracking risk calculation used the assumption that the managers' alphas are uncorrelated.

Example 14 assumed that the managers under consideration were all benchmarked to the benchmark for the overall international equity allocation—that is, all of the managers are essentially broad capitalization market-oriented managers. In reality, investors often wish to consider managers that are either value or growth and perhaps specialize within a given range of market capitalization. To evaluate such managers, it is useful to divide their total active return into two components:

1. Manager's return − Manager's normal benchmark = Manager's "true" active return
2. Manager's normal benchmark − Investor's benchmark = Manager's "misfit" active return

To review, the manager's normal benchmark (normal portfolio) represents the universe of securities from which a manager normally might select securities for her portfolio. The term **investor's benchmark** refers to the benchmark the investor uses to evaluate performance of a given portfolio or asset class.

The standard deviation of "true" active return is called manager's "true" active risk (or "true" active risk); the standard deviation of "misfit" active return is manager's "misfit" risk (or "misfit" risk). The manager's total active risk, reflecting both "true" and "misfit" risk, is

$$\text{Manager's total active risk} = [(\text{Manager's "true" active risk})^2 + (\text{Manager's "misfit" active risk})^2]^{1/2}$$

The most accurate measure of the manager's risk-adjusted performance is the IR computed as (Manager's "true" active return)/(Manager's "true" active risk).

The "true"/"misfit" distinction has two chief uses: One relates to performance appraisal, and the other relates to optimizing a portfolio of managers. We can illustrate the technically less complex of these two uses, that related to performance appraisal, using the numbers given in Exhibit 25 in Example 14, and the following additional facts:

▶ Manager C is a value-oriented manager;
▶ the MSCI World ex-Australia Value Index well represents Manager C's investment universe;
▶ Manager C, the MSCI World ex-Australia Index, and the MSCI World ex-Australia Value Index respectively return 12 percent, 10 percent, and 15 percent per year, for a given time period; and
▶ Manager C's total active risk computed with respect to MSCI World ex-Australia Index is 5.5 percent annually. The manager's "misfit" risk is 4 percent annually.

Based on the second fact above, the MSCI World ex-Australia Value Index is appropriate as Manager C's normal benchmark. By contrast, the MSCI World ex-Australia Index is the investor's benchmark. Although Manager C appears to outperform the asset class benchmark (12 percent versus 10 percent), in reality the manager has not done such a great job:

▶ The manager's "true" active return is $12\% - 15\% = -3\%$.
▶ The manager's "misfit" active return is $15\% - 10\% = 5\%$.

Measuring the manager's results against the normal benchmark rather than the investor's benchmark far more accurately evaluates performance. The positive "misfit" active return indicates that the manager would be expected to outperform the asset class benchmark for the simple reason that value stocks outperformed the investor's benchmark. The manager's negative "true" active return, however, indicates that the manager actually underperformed a passive investment in the normal benchmark. The manager's performance relative to the investor's benchmark reflects the sum of "true" active return and "misfit" active return and misleadingly nets to a positive value: $-3\% + 5\% = 2\%$. To complete the picture, we need to calculate the manager's IR based on "true" active risk and "true" active return. Using the expression for manager's total active risk and letting X represent "true" active risk, $5.5\% = [X^2 + (4\%)^2]^{1/2}$, $X = 3.775\%$ is "true" active risk. The manager's "true" IR was thus quite poor: $-3\%/3.775\% = -0.7947$.

The second use of the "true"/"misfit" distinction is in optimization. By disaggregating the active risk and return into two components, it is possible to create optimal solutions that maximize total active return at every level of total active risk and that also allow for the optimal level of "misfit" risk. Although it may seem that no "misfit" risk is desired, a nonzero amount may actually be optimal, because a high level of "true" active return may more than compensate for a given level of "misfit" risk.

7.2 Completeness Fund

The Nakasone and Smith examples illustrated a rigorous approach to constructing a portfolio of managers. Some investors will construct a portfolio of active managers using an equal-weighting approach or other heuristic. Whether the active manager's normal portfolio is the overall equity benchmark or some other benchmark (especially in this latter case), the aggregate portfolio of active managers may have any number of risk exposures or biases, such as sector underweighting or overweighting, relative to the investor's overall equity benchmark. The portfolios of bottom-up stock pickers often evidence industry concentrations as an outcome of their stock selection processes rather than intentional macro bets.

In such cases, the fund sponsor should consider establishing a completeness fund for the equity portfolio. A **completeness fund**, when added to active managers' positions, establishes an overall portfolio with approximately the same risk exposures as the investor's overall equity benchmark.[75] For example, the completeness fund may be constructed with the objective of making the overall portfolio sector and/or style neutral with respect to the benchmark while attempting to retain the value added from the active managers' stock-selection ability. The completeness portfolio may be managed passively or semiactively. This portfolio needs to be re-estimated periodically to reflect changes in the active portfolios.

One drawback of completeness portfolios is that they essentially seek to eliminate misfit risk. As stated above, a nonzero amount of misfit risk may be optimal. In seeking to eliminate misfit risk through a completeness fund, a fund sponsor may be giving up some of the value added from the stock selection of the active managers.

---

[75] Completeness funds are sometimes referred to as dynamic completion funds or as bias control funds. Tierney and Winston (1990) offer an early presentation of the rationale for this technique.

7.3 Other Approaches: Alpha and Beta Separation

Another method which may be used to build a portfolio of multiple managers involves what has become known as **alpha and beta separation**. A typical long active equity portfolio provides an investor with exposure to the market (beta) as well as to the active manager's stock selection ability (alpha). As previously discussed, a market-neutral long–short strategy is a pure alpha strategy with no beta exposure.

For example, an investor might choose to hire a comparatively inexpensive index fund manager to provide beta exposure and pay explicitly for alpha by hiring a market-neutral long–short manager. The second approach adds the advantage of allowing the investor to mix and match beta and alpha in a way that long-only active management cannot accomplish. For example, an investor may need beta exposure to a relatively efficient part of the equity market (e.g., the Russell Top 200, representing the 200 largest securities in the Russell 3000) but will also want to outperform that part of the market. This may be difficult to do with long-only active management. The investor, however, may choose to hire a Russell Top 200 index fund manager and a manager that seeks to add 4 percent annual alpha by managing a long–short portfolio of Japanese equities. Assuming that the long–short portfolio is also market neutral (i.e., beta of zero with respect to the Japanese equity market) and that the long–short manager delivers on the alpha target, the strategy becomes a Russell Top 200 + 4% strategy. This is an example of **portable alpha**—that is, alpha available to be added to a variety of systematic risk exposures.

One of this approach's big advantages is that an investor can obtain the beta exposure desired while broadening the opportunity set for alpha to cover styles and even asset classes outside the beta asset class. In the example above, the long–short manager could also have been a bond manager. Alpha and beta separation allows the investor to manage the market and active risks more effectively than if dealing solely with long-only managers. In doing so, the investor can also very clearly understand the fees being paid to capture market (inexpensive) and active (costly) returns. That said, certain markets may constrain the ability to manage long–short alpha-generating strategies. Short positions may be very costly to establish in smaller or emerging markets. Also, investors need to realize that not all long–short strategies that appear to be market neutral really are. Some may have a degree of market risk.

Some investors may be explicitly precluded from investing on a long–short basis. These investors may still be able to use portable alpha, although in a less efficient way than described above. For example, assume that an investor desires S&P 500 market exposure but has identified a capable active manager of Japanese equities benchmarked to the TOPIX index. The investor can port the manager's alpha by taking a short futures position in TOPIX and a corresponding long position in S&P 500 futures.[76] The resulting portfolio is S&P 500 plus an alpha associated with the Japanese equity portfolio.

---

[76] The short exposure to TOPIX can be seen as a hedge of sorts and might not violate specific pension plan restrictions in the way that an explicit net short position in an equity issue would.

8   IDENTIFYING, SELECTING, AND CONTRACTING WITH EQUITY PORTFOLIO MANAGERS

Institutional and private wealth investors face critical decisions when deciding what funds (if any) to manage themselves and, second, what investment managers to engage for the funds they delegate to outside management. Frequently, investors will work with a consultant in an investment manager search. The following sections address some of the issues that investors will face in identifying, selecting, and contracting with equity managers.

8.1 Developing a Universe of Suitable Manager Candidates

The process of developing a universe of suitable manager candidates starts with a general evaluation of the large number of investment managers, and then researching and monitoring those that are worthy of further consideration. Investment consultants typically have a research staff whose job is to collect information on investment managers and to meet with them to understand the managers' investment approach and organization. Consultants employ various tools to determine which managers have talented individuals and truly add value in their investment style.

Consultants use both qualitative and quantitative factors in evaluating investment managers. The qualitative factors include the people and organizational structure, the firm's investment philosophy, the decision-making process, and the strength of its equity research. The quantitative factors include performance comparisons with benchmarks and peer groups, as well as the measured style orientation and valuation characteristics of the firm's portfolios. At all times, the investment consultant seeks consistency between a firm's *stated* philosophy and process and its *actual* practices.

8.2 The Predictive Power of Past Performance

Anyone who invests in the stock market is well aware that the best performing stock or sector in any given year is rarely the best performer in the next. In fact, one reasonable approach to investing could be simply to sell the winners and buy the losers (although many investors tend to do the opposite). The same holds true of investment performance, which is one reason why fund managers are legally required to state in their advertisements that "past performance is no guarantee of future results."

The evidence generally supports this caution. For example, the Frank Russell Company, a multimanager investment strategies firm, found that of the 81 managers who were in the top quartile of their 293 U.S. equity manager database in 1997, only 16 remained in the top quartile in 1998, and only 7 remained in 1999. None of these original top performers in 1997 was still in the top quartile in 2000, 2001, or 2002. This result does not mean that past performance goes unexamined, however. A portfolio manager who has consistently underperformed his benchmark is unlikely to be considered for an active manager role, because an active manager is expected to generate positive alpha.

Investors and their consultants place considerable weight on an equity manager's investment process and the strength of the manager's organization. A good investment record achieved by the same set of managers over a long period, following consistent investment disciplines, is more likely to indicate future satisfactory results for the client than a record with comparable statistics but an underlying history of manager turnover and shifts in investment orientation.

8.3 Fee Structures

Investors must pay attention to the management fees of the investment managers that they hire. Absent such fees, the investor would realize exactly the same alpha that the manager achieves (after transactions costs). With management fees, the investor earns a net-of-fee alpha that is smaller and possibly negative even when the manager's alpha (gross of fees) is positive. In short, the investment management fee represents a wedge between managerial skill and investor results.[77]

Fees are typically set in one of two basic ways: ad valorem and performance based. **Ad valorem fees** are calculated by multiplying a percentage by the value of assets managed (e.g., 0.60 percent on the first £50 million, and 0.45 percent on assets above £50 million). Ad valorem fees are also called assets under management (AUM) fees.

A simple **performance-based fee** is usually specified by a combination of a base fee plus sharing percentage (e.g., 0.20 percent on all assets managed plus 20 percent of any performance in excess of the benchmark return). Performance-based fees can also include other features such as fee caps and "high water marks." A **fee cap** limits the total fee paid regardless of performance and is frequently put in place to limit the portfolio manager's incentive to aim for very high returns by taking a high level of risk. A **high water mark** is a provision requiring the portfolio manager to have cumulatively generated outperformance since the last performance-based fee was paid. As an example, ABC Investments charged a performance-based fee based on its performance in 2001. In 2002, however, the firm underperformed its benchmark and could collect only the base fee. If ABC is subject to a high water mark provision, in 2003 it will need to outperform its benchmark by an amount greater than the 2002 underperformance in order to collect a performance-based fee.

Ad valorem fees have the advantage of simplicity and predictability. If a plan sponsor must budget fees in advance, an ad valorem approach makes estimation much simpler. In contrast, performance-based fees are typically quite involved, as every term of the performance-based fee must be precisely defined. But performance-based fees—particularly symmetric incentive fees that reduce as well as increase compensation—may align the plan sponsor's interests with those of the portfolio manager by spurring the manager to greater effort. The better the manager's performance, the greater the reward for both sides. For the client, the impact of poor performance is reduced by the smaller fees paid to the investment manager. On the other hand, reliance on such arrangements can create revenue volatility for the investment manager, which might present practical issues (e.g., staff retention) when the manager performs relatively poorly in a year in which its competitors have done better.[78] A one-sided performance-based fee, by contrast, conveys a call option to the investment manager whose value can be determined by option pricing methodology and whose expected net cost to the fund sponsor may be judged relative to expected fee if a strictly ad valorem compensation contract were in place.

---

[77] Ennis (2005) quantifies the extent of this wedge for various fee levels and levels of managerial skill.

[78] See Arnott (2005) for a further discussion.

8.4 The Equity Manager Questionnaire

A typical equity manager questionnaire examines five key areas: organization/people, philosophy/process, resources, performance, and fees. The questionnaire creates a formal basis for directly comparing different investment firms.

In the questionnaire's first section, Organization/People, the investment firm must describe the firm's organization and who will be managing the portfolio. Equity portfolio management is a people business; nothing is more important than having the right people in place. Typical questions cover such areas as the vision of the firm, its competitive advantages, and how it defines success; the organization of the group and the role of portfolio managers, traders, and analysts; the delegation of responsibility for decisions on asset allocation, portfolio construction, research, and security selection; the structure of the compensation program, with an emphasis on the manner in which talented individuals are rewarded; the background of the professionals directly involved in managing the assets, such as prior experience, education, and professional qualifications such as the CFA designation; and finally, the length of time the team has been together and the reasons for any turnover.

The second section, Philosophy/Process, asks questions about how the equity portfolio will be managed. Typical questions concern:

▶ the firm's investment philosophy and the market inefficiency that it is trying to capture, along with any supporting evidence for this inefficiency;

▶ the research process, including whether or not a top-down analysis is applied (**top-down** analysis is analysis that proceeds from the macroeconomy to the economic sector level to the industry level to the firm level);

▶ the risk management function, including management and monitoring of risk and risk models;

▶ how the firm monitors the portfolio's adherence to its stated investment style, philosophy, and process;

▶ the stock selection process, including unique sources of information, and how the buy or sell decision is made; and

▶ the portfolio construction process.

The third section, Resources, looks at the allocation of resources within the organization. In particular, the focus is on the research process: how and by whom research is conducted, the outputs of this research, how the research outputs are communicated, and how the research is incorporated into the portfolio construction process. In addition, there are questions addressing any quantitative models used in research and portfolio construction, and the investments that have been made in technology. Finally, the trading function is examined in terms of turnover, traders, trading strategies, and the measurement of costs.

The fourth section, Performance, asks questions about what the equity manager considers to be an appropriate benchmark (and why) and what level of excess return is appropriate. There are also questions about how performance is evaluated within the firm, including causes of dispersion in the returns of similarly managed portfolios. The firm must then normally submit monthly or quarterly returns as well as holdings, so that the evaluator can calculate performance for all candidates in the same way.

The final section deals with fees. Questions are typically about what is included in the fee, the type of fee (ad valorem or performance based), and any specific terms and conditions relating to the fees quoted.

The equity manager questionnaire is used to identify a short list of the fund managers most suitable for the sponsor's needs. This process is followed up with face-to-face interviews (and sometimes on-site visits) to better understand the fund manager and to ask additional questions raised by any responses to the questionnaire before the final selection decision.

EXAMPLE 15

Equity Manager Questionnaire (Excerpt)

A. Organization, Structure, and Personnel

1. Provide a brief history of the firm, including:

   a. the month and year of SEC 1940 Act registration;

   b. the month and year the subject product was introduced; and

   c. ownership structure.

2. Form of ownership (if an affiliate, designate percent of parent firm's total revenue generated by your organization).

3. If the firm is a joint venture partner, identify the percentage of ownership and revenues recognized by each partner to the combined association.

4. Provide an organizational chart diagramming the relationships between the professional staff as well as the parent–subsidiary, affiliate, or joint venture entities.

5. Describe the levels (U.S. dollar amounts) of coverage for SEC-required (17g-1) fidelity bonds, errors and omissions coverage, and any other fiduciary coverage which your firm carries. List the insurance carriers supplying the coverage.

6. During the past five years, has your organization or any of its affiliates or parent, or any officer or principal been involved in any business litigation, regulatory, or legal proceedings? If so, provide a detailed explanation and indicate the current status. Also provide complete Form ADV (Parts I and II) or explain the nature of the exemption.

7. Has your firm been the subject of an audit, censure (fine), inquiry, or administrative action by the SEC, IRS, State Attorney General, or Department of Labor in the past seven years? If so, explain findings and provide a copy, as well as evidence of any changes in procedures implemented as a result of such audit.

8. Describe in detail the material developments in your organization (changes in ownership, restructuring, personnel, business, etc.) during the past three years.

9. Provide the location and function of each of your firm's offices.

10. Provide details on the financial condition of the firm (i.e., most recent annual report filed with the SEC).

11. Investment Professionals

    a. List all senior investment professionals and portfolio managers involved with the subject product. Please also separately provide appropriate biographical information. Highlight the person(s) who would be responsible for this account.

b. Indicate when and why any investment professionals left or joined the firm in the last three years. In which products were they involved? For personnel who have left, indicate job titles and years with the firm. Please include all additions and departures, regardless of seniority.

c. Discuss your organization's compensation and incentive program. How are professionals evaluated and rewarded? What incentives are provided to attract and retain superior individuals? If equity ownership is possible, on what basis is it determined and distributed? How is the departure of a shareholder treated?

d. Describe your firm's backup procedures in the event the key investment professional assigned to this account should leave the firm.

For Items 12 through 14, please provide the following information for the years ending on 30 June from 1999 through 2004 (all in $ millions and number of accounts, counting funds as one account):

12. Total assets under management—all products.

13. Total discretionary U.S. equity assets—all products.

14. Total assets in subject product—distinguish between retail and institutional.

15. Provide the names and the size of the mandate for your top five clients.

16. Provide the names and the size of your top five clients in the strategy under review.

17. List all clients (or the number and type) and asset amounts gained in the subject product during the past five years as of June 30, 2004.

18. List all clients (or the number and type) and asset amounts lost in the subject product during the past five years as of June 30, 2004.

19. Identify three clients that have terminated accounts in the subject product during the past three years that can be contacted as references. Provide the firm name, contact person and title, phone number, product name, and reason for termination.

20. Provide the client name, address, phone number, contact name, title, and account type (e.g., defined benefit, defined contribution, endowment) of three accounts, who are invested in the subject product that can be contacted as references. Also indicate the length of your relationship and AUM for each reference.

B. Investment Philosophy, Policy, and Process

1. Describe your investment philosophy for the product.

a. What market anomaly or inefficiency are you trying to capture?

b. Why do you believe this philosophy will be successful in the future?

c. Provide any evidence or research that supports this belief.

d. How has this philosophy changed over time?

e. What are the product's shortcomings or limitations?

    f. In what market environment(s) will your product have difficulty outperforming?

2. Describe your investment decision process and valuation approaches used in regard to the following:

    a. security selection;

    b. sector selection; and

    c. portfolio construction.

3. Indicate what fundamental/quantitative factors are used to analyze a stock and indicate their relative importance in the decision-making process. If applicable, who developed and maintains your quantitative models?

4. Describe the techniques used to identify and control overall portfolio risk. What limits/constraints do you establish, if any?

    a. What is the market liquidity criteria applied by your firm for the companies in which it invests?

    b. Provide the typical number of securities in a portfolio of $50 million, $100 million, $1 billion, and $2 billion.

    c. Describe the use of futures, options, or other derivatives (when and how much?).

5. Describe the decision process used to make sell decisions. When would your firm deviate from its sell disciplines?

6. Over what time horizon could your strategy be expected to meet performance objectives?

7. Provide the average annual portfolio turnover for the past three years and the source of this turnover.

8. Describe your firm's policy regarding cash and cash equivalents. Would your firm accept a "fully invested" mandate?

9. Describe your firm's process for executing trades. Include answers to the following:

    a. Does your firm use electronic trading systems?

    b. What guidelines do you have pertaining to dealing/trading execution parameters/costs?

    c. How are trading costs monitored? How are these costs minimized?

    d. Describe how your firm evaluates trading execution.

    e. What is the firm's average commission (cents/share) for the product in question?

    f. Does your firm trade with an affiliate broker/dealer?

10. Submit a sample portfolio (an actual portfolio) as of June 30, 2004, that reflects the investments of the product proposed for this account.

11. Provide the following characteristics as of June 30, 2004 and for the years ending 1999 through 2003:

    ▶ typical number of holdings

    ▶ typical turnover rate

    ▶ average market capitalization

- ▶ median market capitalization
- ▶ P/E
- ▶ P/B
- ▶ beta
- ▶ sector limitations
- ▶ highest sector weightings
- ▶ tracking error
- ▶ since-inception information ratio

C. Research Capabilities and Resources

1. Explain your firm's research process as it pertains to the product.

2. Rate your firm's reliance on the following sources of research; average rating should approximate 3 (*1=very important, 5=unimportant*).

   a. Internal

   b. Broker/dealer

   c. Third-party fundamental research

   d. External economists

   e. Company visits

   f. Other (explain)

3. Describe the software packages used to manage portfolios. If owned, were they internally developed and by whom? Are they internally maintained? How long have the current systems been in place?

D. Historical Performance/Risk Factors

1. Provide your monthly gross and net-of-fees composite performance in the subject product, since the inception of the product, in an attached Microsoft Excel spreadsheet file in the following format:

	A	B	C
1	Date	Gross Returns	Net Returns
2	12/1990	1.01	0.81
3	1/1991	−3.04	−3.24
4	2/1991	5.02	4.82
5	3/1991	12.10	11.90

2. Provide a description of composite:

   a. Number of accounts and market value of assets represented in composite as of each annual period shown.

   b. Include low/high and median return for each annual period.

   c. Is composite in compliance with AIMR Performance Presentation Standards?

   d. Has composite been verified for compliance? If not, why not?

   e. Is there a period for which composite is not in compliance?

3. What benchmark is most appropriate for evaluating the performance results of your process?

E.   Fee Structure

1. Provide a proposed fee schedule for the proposed strategy, including any breakpoints. In addition, please provide a proposed fee schedule for the various portfolio sizes of: $50 million, $100 million, and $500 million.

2. Will you certify that the fee schedule provided above is the most favorable fee schedule that the firm offers for accounts of similar size? If not, please explain why.

3. Do you offer clients performance-based fees?

Note: Exhibits and other sections omitted.

Example 16 shows a highly simplified fee proposal. In practice, fees stated as annual rate are usually paid at regular intervals during the year, and asset valuations within a given payment interval are important. For instance, in practice an ad valorem fee of 0.50 percent a year of assets under management might be billed at the end of each quarter at a rate of $0.50\%/4 = 0.125\%$, based on the average AUM during the quarter. Nevertheless, the principles involved would be the same as those illustrated.

EXAMPLE 16

A Fee Proposal

Helen Warburton is evaluating a fee proposal from Buckingham Equity Investors. She has been quoted both ad valorem and performance-based fees.

Ad Valorem
First £25 million @ 0.80%
Next £25 million @ 0.60%
Balance @ 0.40%
The above fees are payable in advance.

Performance Based
Base fee of 0.20% of beginning AUM plus 20% of outperformance versus the FTSE All-Share Index, to be paid annually at the end of each 12-month period.

Warburton expects to invest a £100 million lump sum, and based on Buckingham's questionnaire response, she expects the firm to outperform the FTSE All-Share by 2.50 percent gross of fees. If Warburton assumes that the FTSE All-Share returns 0 percent, what fee approach should she choose? What other considerations might she make in deciding which fee structure makes more sense?

Solution: The fees for a £100 million account given Buckingham's expected performance are:

Ad Valorem
£550,000 = (£25 million)(0.80%) + (£25 million)(0.60%) + (£50 million)(0.40%)
Performance Based
£700,000 = (£100 million)(0.20%) + (£100 million)(20%)(2.50%)

The ad valorem fee is lower assuming that Buckingham delivers its expected outperformance. Investors should consider a firm's performance history when determining which approach to choose. If Buckingham's FTSE All-Share strategy has a very high information ratio, implying a high degree of consistency in annual outperformance, Warburton might prefer using an ad valorem fee because Warburton might expect to pay higher fees over time under a performance-based fee arrangement. The reverse is true if Buckingham's history of outperformance was less consistent. (Note that in setting its fee structure, Buckingham could factor in the volatility of its outperformance. This element would make both Buckingham and Warburton indifferent to the fee structure.)

9   STRUCTURING EQUITY RESEARCH AND SECURITY SELECTION

Equity research is a necessary component of both active and semiactive investing. The security selection process varies from firm to firm, but some generalities apply.

9.1 Top-Down versus Bottom-Up Approaches

Investors focusing their research primarily on macroeconomic factors or investment themes are said to use a top-down approach. For example, an investor focused on a single country might favor certain defensive industries like consumer staples and utilities if she believes the economy may be heading into a recession. Although top-down investors build portfolios from individual stocks, they want those stocks to reflect their macro insights.

A more complex top-down example might involve a global portfolio. The investor might wish to identify:

1. themes affecting the global economy;
2. the effect of those themes on various economic sectors and industries;
3. any special country or currency considerations; and
4. individual stocks within the industries or economic sectors that are likely to benefit most from the global themes.

On the other hand, an investor focusing on company-specific fundamentals or factors such as revenues, earnings, cash flow, or new product development is said to follow a **bottom-up** approach. This investor pays attention to company specifics when doing research and building a portfolio. For example, a value investor might screen stocks based on P/E or dividend yield. His focus is on the individual company. Bottom-up investors have little interest in the state of the economy or other macro factors but rather try to put together the best portfolio of stocks based on company-specific information.

A more complex bottom-up example might also involve a global portfolio. The investor might approach the problem by:

1. identifying factors with which to screen the investment universe (e.g., stocks in the lowest P/E quartile that also have expected above-median earnings growth);

2. collecting further financial information on companies passing the screen; and

3. identifying companies from this subset that may be potential investments based on other company-specific criteria.

That said, many investors use some combination of the two approaches. An investor managing a global portfolio can, for example, decide which countries to favor based on a top-down analysis but build the portfolio of stocks within each country based on a bottom-up analysis. Furthermore, some analysts use technical analysis, which attempts to predict future stock prices from the time series of their past values.

9.2 Buy-Side versus Sell-Side Research

The terms "buy side" and "sell side" refer to the source of the equity research. **Buy side** refers to those who do research with the intent of assembling a portfolio, such as investment management firms. **Sell side** refers either to independent researchers who sell their work, or to investment banks/brokerage firms that use research as a means to generate business for themselves. Sell-side research is also what most people hear on TV or read about in the newspaper. Buy-side research by its very nature is generally inaccessible to those outside of the investment firm generating the research.

Sell-side and buy-side research frequently are developed in a different manner. Sell-side research is generally organized by sector/industry with a regional delineation (e.g., U.S. autos, European telecommunications, Japanese banks, etc.). Analysts work either in teams or by themselves and produce reports on individual companies and also on the industries they cover. In addition to providing information such as earnings forecasts, sell-side analysts also rate companies as buy, hold, or sell (the nomenclature varies from firm to firm).

Because buy-side research is concerned with assembling a portfolio rather than just rating a company, decisions on buy-side research are usually made through a committee structure. An analyst may investigate a particular theme or individual company, but usually an investment committee makes the decisions. The analyst prepares a report to substantiate the idea and why it should be included in the portfolio or sold; she then uses the research to persuade the investment committee.

EXAMPLE 17

Top Down or Bottom Up?

Maria Ramirez is watching a financial program on television in which a unit trust portfolio manager is explaining the investment approach he uses in managing the global equity unit trust. He says, "Right now, I really like Japan. The economic growth we see there looks to us like it is solid and driven as much by consumer demand as it is by capital investment. One market that we really don't like very much is the U.K., which we are avoiding because we fear further interest rate hikes by the Bank of England." From this brief statement what can Maria conclude about the portfolio manager's research approach?

Solution: The portfolio manager is employing a top-down approach, because his comments are focused exclusively on macro factors driving the British and Japanese markets. A bottom-up investor might also have favored Japan over the United Kingdom but would have emphasized that he finds more stocks that are attractive investments in one market rather than another.

9.3 Industry Classification

Many equity research departments are organized along industry or sector lines. Given the need to do sector/industry research across many countries, it is important to have a system for like companies to be classified in the same categories. Developed by Standard & Poor's and MSCI, the Global Industry Classification Standard is one representative industry classification method that does exactly this. GICS divides stocks into:

▶ 10 Sectors (Consumer Discretionary, Consumer Staples, Energy, Financials, Health Care, Industrials, Information Technology, Materials, Telecommunication, and Utilities);

▶ 24 Industry Groups;

▶ 62 Industries;

▶ 132 Sub-Industries.

GICS assigns a company to a particular category based on the percentage of revenue derived from each of that company's businesses. The company is then categorized into one and only one sector, industry group, industry, and sub-industry. For example, Michelin is included in the Consumer Discretionary Sector, the Automobiles & Components Industry Group, the Auto Components Industry, and the Tires & Rubber Sub-Industry. Other classification systems include:

▶ the Industry Classification Benchmark, proprietary to FTSE International Ltd and Dow Jones & Co., consisting of 10 industries (Oil & Gas, Basic Materials, Industrials, Consumer Goods, Health Care, Consumer Services, Telecommunications, Utilities, Financials, and Technology), 18 supersectors, 39 sectors and 104 subsectors; and

▶ the highly detailed North American Industry Classification System (NAICS—pronounced "nakes"), sponsored by the U.S., Canadian, and Mexican governments.

SUMMARY

Equity portfolio management is not only challenging; for many investors, the skill applied to it can determine their long-term investment success. This reading has provided a detailed introduction to the major concepts and tools that professional equity investors use.

► Equities play a growth role in investment portfolios.

► The major investment approaches are passive, active, and semiactive. The major passive approach is indexing, which is based on the rationale that after costs, the return on the average actively managed dollar should be less than the return on the average passively managed dollar. Active management is historically the dominant approach to investment and is based on the rationale that markets offer opportunities to beat a given equity benchmark. Semiactive or enhanced indexing is a growing discipline based on the rationale that markets offer opportunities to achieve a positive information ratio with limited risk relative to a benchmark.

► A successful active equity manager will have an expected active return of 2 percent or higher, but his tracking error is likely to be more than 4 percent. Hence, his information ratio will be 0.5 or lower. At the opposite end of the spectrum, an index fund will have minimal tracking risk and an expected active return of 0 percent, implying an information ratio of zero. Enhanced indexing strategies tend to have the highest information ratios, often in the range of 0.5 to 2.0.

► An indexer must choose the index that the portfolio will track and understand the details of the index's construction. The major types of index are:

   ► *Price weighted.* In a price-weighted index, each stock in the index is weighted according to its absolute share price.

   ► *Value weighted* (or *market-capitalization weighted*). In a value-weighted index, each stock in the index is weighted according to its market capitalization (share price multiplied by the number of shares outstanding). A subset of the value-weighted method is the float-weighted method, which adjusts value weights for the floating supply of shares (the fraction of shares outstanding that is actually available to investors).

   ► *Equal weighted.* In an equal-weighted index, each stock in the index is weighted equally.

   A price-weighted index is biased toward shares with the highest price, and a value- or float-weighted index is biased toward the largest market cap companies, which may reflect positive valuation errors. An equal-weighted index is biased toward smaller-cap companies.

► Indexed separate or pooled accounts, index mutual funds, exchange traded funds, equity index futures, and equity total return swaps are the major methods for implementing an indexing strategy. Indexed separate or pooled accounts are typically very low cost. Index mutual funds are a widely accessible alternative with a considerable range of cost structures. Exchange traded funds may have structural advantages compared with mutual funds and also permit short positions. Equity index futures are relatively low-cost vehicles for obtaining equity market exposure that require a rollover to maintain longer term. Equity total return swaps are a relatively low-cost way to obtain long-term exposure to an equity market that may offer tax advantages.

▶ Three methods of indexation include full replication (in which every index security is held in approximately the same weight in the fund as in the index), stratified sampling (which samples from the index's securities organized into representative cells), and optimization (which chooses a portfolio of securities that minimizes expected tracking risk relative to the index based on a multifactor model of index risk exposures). Full replication is the most common procedure for indices composed of highly liquid securities. Stratified sampling and optimization are applicable when full replication is not feasible or cost-effective.

▶ All else being equal, value investors are more concerned about buying a stock that is deemed relatively cheap in terms of the purchase price of earnings or assets than about the company's future growth prospects. In contrast to value investors' focus on price, growth investors are more concerned with earnings growth. Value has substyles of low P/E, contrarian, and high yield. Growth has substyles of consistent growth and earnings momentum.

▶ The main risk for a value investor is the potential for misinterpreting a stock's cheapness; it may be cheap for a very good economic reason that the investor does not fully appreciate. The major risk for growth investors is that the forecasted EPS growth fails to materialize as expected. In that event, P/E multiples may contract at the same time as EPS, amplifying the investor's losses.

▶ Two major approaches to identifying style are returns-based style analysis, based on portfolio returns, and holdings-based style analysis based on analysis of security holdings. Returns-based style analysis is quickly executed, cost-effective, and requires minimal information. Holdings-based style analysis requires detailed information on security holdings and can give an up-to-date and detailed picture of a manager's style. Most current style indices are constructed using a holdings-based approach.

▶ The style box is a means of visualizing a manager's style exposures, which is typically based on a holdings-based analysis. It may contain as many as nine cells representing a portfolio on value–market-oriented–growth and small–mid–large spectrums.

▶ Inconsistency in style, or style drift, is of concern to investors because 1) the investor may no longer have exposure to the particular style desired and 2) the manager may be operating outside her area of expertise.

▶ A long-only strategy can capture one overall alpha. With a long–short strategy, however, the value added can be equal to two alphas, one from the long position and one from the short position. A market-neutral strategy is constructed to have an overall zero beta. Long–short strategies may benefit from pricing inefficiencies on the short side (a greater supply of overvalued than undervalued securities).

▶ The Fundamental Law of Active Management states that $IR \approx IC\sqrt{Breadth}$, which implies that the information ratio approximately equals what the investor knows about the company multiplied by the square root of the number of independent active investment decisions made each year.

▶ The framework for optimizing allocations to a group of managers (in this context, equity managers within the equity allocation) involves maximizing active return for a given level of active risk determined by the investor's aversion to active risk.

▶ A core-satellite portfolio involves an indexed and/or enhanced indexed core portfolio and actively managed satellite portfolios.

▶ A completion fund may be used to neutralize unintended bets against the overall equity benchmark.

▶ Investment management contracts may involve an ad valorem fee schedule and/or an incentive fee schedule.

▶ Selecting and monitoring good managers is as complex a process as selecting and managing good investments.

1. Katrina Lowry works for the pension department of National Software. Her supervisor has asked her to evaluate the different style alternatives for a large-cap mandate and to highlight their differences.

   A. State the three main large-cap styles.

   B. Describe the basic premise and risks of each style identified in Part A.

2. Juan Varga is concerned about the performance and investment positions of an investment firm he hired five years ago. The firm, Galicia Investment Management, has been tasked with managing an active portfolio with a developed market mandate (MSCI World countries). Galicia is a well-known value manager. Varga performs some returns-based style analysis and finds the following results for the last two years (each quarterly snapshot is the result of a regression using the prior 36 months return data).

	MSCI World Value (%)	MSCI World Growth (%)	Other (%)
1Q 2002	83	16	1
2Q 2002	77	20	3
3Q 2002	79	19	2
4Q 2002	68	29	3
1Q 2003	55	40	5
2Q 2003	48	45	7
3Q 2003	52	45	3
4Q 2003	55	43	2

   What reasonable conclusions can Varga reach regarding the Galicia investment process?

3. David Burke is considering investing in a mutual fund that is classified generically under the term "growth and income." In preparation for his CFA exams, Burke studied style investing. Using publicly available data sources, he gathered the following information about the mutual fund in question. How should he characterize the fund based on what he has learned in his CFA exam preparation?

	Fund	Market Benchmark
Number of stocks	80	600
Weighted-average market cap	$37 billion	$40 billion
Dividend yield	2.5%	2.1%
P/E	16	19
P/B	1.6	1.9
EPS growth (5-year projected)	11%	12%
Sector		
Consumer Discretionary	16%	10%
Consumer Staples	9	12
Energy	9	9
Finance	15	20
Health Care	9	7
Industrials	12	9
Information Technology	8	7
Materials	5	8
Telecommunications	7	10
Utilities	10	7

4. Phillipa Jenkins has been asked to manage internally a FTSE 100 index fund. Because the index's 10 largest stocks make up more than 50 percent of its weight, Jenkins is considering using optimization to build the portfolio using many fewer than 100 stocks. All 100 stocks in the index are considered liquid. Is optimizing the best approach?

5. Shawn Miller plans to use returns-based style analysis to analyze his global portfolio. He will use style indices as a proxy for style in the analysis and is debating whether to use indices like Dow Jones (which categorizes stocks as value, growth, or neutral) or like MSCI (which categorize stocks only as value or growth).

    A. What are the benefits and drawbacks of each method?

    B. Does it matter which type Miller chooses for a returns-based style analysis?

6. Explain the principal benefit of a market-neutral long–short portfolio. What risks are inherent in such a portfolio that a long-only equity portfolio lacks?

7. Simon Hayes is a long–short portfolio manager with Victoria Investment Management in London. His expertise lies in building market-neutral long–short strategies using U.K. equities. After meeting with his most important client, Hayes learns that the client is planning to hire an investment firm to manage a Japanese equity portfolio. How can Hayes satisfy this mandate using U.K. equities and no Japanese equities?

8. Yoko Suzuki manages an enhanced index portfolio benchmarked to the index for Kyushu Motors' pension fund. The strategy has a target alpha of 1.5 percent annually with an annualized active risk of 2 percent. Her client is quite pleased that the portfolio has met its stated objective for the last five years. Kyushu's other investment managers have not done so well against their objectives, however, and the pension fund now suffers from a large shortfall between its assets and liabilities. To make up this shortfall, Kyushu asks her to double the portfolio's active risk with the intention of doubling the alpha as well. How should Suzuki respond to this suggestion?

9. Mike Smith is a consultant evaluating a market neutral long–short strategy for his client. Based on the holdings data he receives from the client, Smith notices a small but persistent difference between the alphas generated on the long side and those generated on the short side. State which of the two alphas is more likely the larger one, and provide three reasons why that might be the case.

10. Karen Johnson is responsible for the U.S. equity portion of her company's pension plan. She is thinking about trying to boost the overall alpha in U.S. equities by using an enhanced index fund to replace her core index fund holding.

    A. The U.S. equity portion of the pension plan currently consists of three managers (one index, one value, and one growth) and is expected to produce a target annual alpha of 2.4 percent with a tracking risk of 2.75 percent. By replacing the index manager with an enhanced indexer the target alpha changes to 2.8 percent with a tracking risk of 2.9 percent. Does this change represent an improvement? Why?

    B. Johnson also needs to decide whether she prefers a stock-based or a synthetic enhanced index manager. What are the advantages and disadvantages of each?

11. Stephanie Whitmore is evaluating several alternatives for the U.S. equity portfolio of her company's pension plan, involving the following managers:

	Active Return	Active Risk (with Respect to Normal Benchmark)	Normal Benchmark
Index	0%	0%	Russell 3000
Semiactive	1	1.5	Russell 3000
Active A (Value)	3	5	Russell 1000 Value
Active B (Growth)	4	6	Russell 1000 Growth
Long–Short	6	6	Cash with Russell 1000 overlay

Active A's misfit risk is 7.13 percent. In all of the questions below, assume that the active returns are uncorrelated. The overall equity portfolio benchmark is the Russell 3000.

A. Whitmore has taken the information in the table above and used a mean variance optimizer to create an implementation efficient frontier. The highest risk point on the efficient frontier is a 100 percent allocation to the long–short manager with a 100 percent Russell 1000 overlay. The active risk of this portfolio is 6.1 percent. Why is the risk greater than 6 percent?

B. Calculate the total active risk for Active A.

C. Whitmore's current equity manager allocation is 30 percent Index and 70 percent Semiactive. Calculate this portfolio's current expected active return, active risk, and information ratio.

D. After determining the desired level of active risk, Whitmore selected the appropriate portfolio from the efficient frontier. The portfolio allocates 39 percent to the Index manager, 34 percent to the Semiactive manager, 7 percent to Active Manager A, 8 percent to Active Manager B, and 12 percent to the Long–Short manager. This portfolio has an expected active return of 1.59 percent and an expected active risk of 1.10 percent. Does this portfolio represent an improvement over the current allocation? If so, by how much?

E. Upon further investigation of the long–short manager, Whitmore learns that approximately 20 percent of the active return generated comes from equity positions in non-U.S. companies. Is this a concern? Why or why not?

Use the following information to answer Questions 12–17

Carl Tyner is a portfolio manager for the Gibson State University (GSU) Endowment Fund. The GSU Endowment's Investment Policy Statement mandates a core-satellite portfolio for the equity portion of the Endowment's assets. The portfolio assets are managed with institutional commingled (or pooled) investment funds. The details for the managers of each of the commingled funds are presented in Exhibit 1.

EXHIBIT 1	Investment Manager Data		
	Manager A	**Manager B**	**Manager C**
Assets under management ($ millions)	$678	$4,200	$1,600
Weighted-average market cap (billions)	$50.60	$52.30	$54.10
P/E	12.20	15.55	19.61
EPS growth (long-term projected)	8.50%	11.00%	14.00%
Dividend yield	2.90%	1.65%	1.00%
Portfolio active return	2.50%	0.00%	2.50%
Portfolio active risk	4.00%	0.00%	4.00%
Management fees & expenses (% of portfolio)	0.40%	0.18%	0.41%
Allocation to GSU Endowment Equity Portfolio	20%	45%	35%

The investment committee would like Tyner to invest a small portion, $2.0 million, in international equities. The committee suggests that the MSCI ACWI Index would be an appropriate benchmark for the international equity exposure. Tyner responded that there are several index strategies that GSU could use to gain exposure to the MSCI ACWI index. The committee wants Tyner to use a strategy that will minimize tracking error.

12. Which of the managers *most likely* is following a passive investment strategy?

   A. Manager A.

   B. Manager B.

   C. Manager C.

13. Which of the managers is *most likely* following a growth investment style?

   A. Manager A.

   B. Manager B.

   C. Manager C.

14. Which of the following substyles is *least consistent* with Manager A's investment style?

   A. Contrarian.

   B. High Yield.

   C. Momentum.

15. The portfolio active return and portfolio active risk for GSU Endowment's equity portfolio are *closest to*:

	Portfolio Active Return	Portfolio Active Risk
A.	1.38%	1.61%
B.	1.38%	3.27%
C.	1.67%	3.27%

16. Which of the following index strategies for the international equity exposure is *most* appropriate given the investment committee's goal related to tracking error?

　　A. Optimization.

　　B. Style Indexing.

　　C. Full replication.

17. Which of the following is *most likely* to have the highest investment cost associated with meeting the investment committee's tracking error goal?

　　A. MSCI ACWI ETF.

　　B. MSCI ACWI mutual fund.

　　C. Full replication of the index.

Questions 18–23 relate to Roy Bernard

Roy Bernard is a portfolio manager with an institutional investment management firm. He has several U.S.-based clients seeking domestic and international equity exposure. Three of these clients are discussed below.

Satellite Fund

Satellite Fund is a new client seeking international equity management services. Simon Day, President of Satellite Fund, tells Bernard that the fund's objectives are to exploit information not reflected in current stock prices, maximize the information ratio, and maintain a low tracking error. The portfolio's constraints include substantial unpredictable cash inflows and outflows.

Day asks Bernard for assistance in selecting a suitable international benchmark. Bernard advises him of the various trade-offs to consider when choosing an international index benchmark.

Eastern Reserve College

A second client, Eastern Reserve College, has chosen to index a portion of its large endowment fund to the S&P 500 Index. The college's finance director wants to minimize ongoing rebalancing costs and tracking error. Bernard recommends stratified sampling as the indexing strategy that best meets the college's objectives and constraints.

The college wants another portion of its endowment fund managed to maximize alpha by fully exploiting available investment opportunities in international equity markets. Bernard suggests a market-neutral, long–short portfolio using U.K. equities. He makes the following statements comparing the market-neutral, long–short portfolio strategy to a long-only portfolio strategy:

　　Statement 1:　A market-neutral, long–short portfolio can generate two alphas, one from the long position and one from the short position.

　　Statement 2:　In a long-only portfolio, alpha can be doubled by doubling the active risk.

　　Statement 3:　The opportunity set for a long-only portfolio strategy is asymmetrical.

Gardelli

Bernard has another client, Gardelli Fund, that has inquired about semiactive portfolio management. Paolo Caruso, the manager of the fund, says he wants to avoid benchmarks biased toward small-capitalization stocks.

Bernard evaluates two forms of semiactive equity styles for Gardelli's fund, stock based and derivatives based.

Bernard prepares Exhibit 1 comparing the two:

EXHIBIT 1	Semiactive Equity Styles	
	Expected Alpha	Tracking Risk
Stock–based semiactive	1.5%	2.9%
Derivatives–based semiactive	1.2%	2.1%

18. The investment approach *most* consistent with Satellite Fund's objectives is:
    A. enhanced indexing.
    B. active management.
    C. indexing using optimization.

19. Given Satellite Fund's constraints, the *most* appropriate international benchmark will favor:
    A. investability over breadth.
    B. float bands over judgment-based construction.
    C. fewer reconstitution effects over fewer crossing opportunities.

20. Is stratified sampling the *most* appropriate construction method for the indexed portion of the Eastern Reserve endowment fund?
    A. Yes.
    B. No, optimization is more appropriate.
    C. No, full replication is more appropriate.

21. Which of Bernard's statements comparing the market-neutral, long–short strategy to the long-only strategy is incorrect?
    A. Statement 1.
    B. Statement 2.
    C. Statement 3.

22. The type of index that would *least likely* address Caruso's concern about bias is:
    A. a price-weighted index.
    B. a value-weighted index.
    C. an equal-weighted index.

23. Which is the *most* appropriate strategy for Bernard to recommend for Gardelli's fund?
    A. The derivatives-based strategy, because it has lower tracking risk.
    B. The stock-based strategy, because it has a higher information ratio.
    C. The derivatives-based strategy, because it has a higher information ratio.

SOLUTIONS FOR READING 32

1. **A.** The three main large-cap styles are value, growth, and market oriented.

   B. Value managers seek to buy stocks below their intrinsic value. That said, the stocks may be cheap for good reason. Also, it may take a long time for stocks to reach their intrinsic value. Growth managers buy stocks of companies with either steadily growing earnings or companies whose earnings they expect to sharply appreciate. On the other hand, they may overpay for these earnings or the expected earnings may not materialize. Managers following the third style, market oriented, may forecast stock returns using a combination of growth or value considerations but endeavor to build portfolios that more closely resemble the market than either value or growth managers. If their fees are relatively high for achieving market-like returns, indexing or enhanced indexing may be a more cost-effective alternative.

2. The portfolio managed by Galicia is experiencing style drift. The threefold increase in the weighting of growth stocks suggests that Galicia has decided to shift to more of a market orientation, although some or all of the drift may have occurred because the stocks in the portfolio have become less value-like during the two year period. The relatively low percentages given to "Other" suggest that Galicia's style bets explain the overwhelming majority of the portfolio's performance.

3. The fund has a modest value orientation. Dividend yield, P/E, P/B, and EPS growth are all slightly lower than the market benchmark. The sector weights are a bit more mixed. Some sectors that typically contain stocks with value characteristics (consumer discretionary and utilities) are overweight, while others (finance and energy) are underweight or equal weight to the benchmark. Also, traditionally growth oriented sectors like health care and information technology are modestly overweight—unlikely in a deep value portfolio.

4. A better approach would be full replication. The main justification for using full replication is that all the components of the FTSE 100 are very liquid, so full replication can be accomplished readily and inexpensively. Because full replication minimizes tracking risk, it is the preferred method when the index consists of liquid securities. Another point is that full replication allows for the creation of a self-rebalancing portfolio in the case of a value-weighted (or float-weighted index): Trading is required only to reinvest dividends and to reflect changes in index composition. A self-rebalancing portfolio is one in which the portfolio moves in line with the index without any need for trading activity. An optimized portfolio may indeed hold fewer than 100 stocks. Because it does not contain every stock in the index in the proper capitalization weight, however, periodic trading will be required (even in the absence of index changes and dividend flows) simply to realign the portfolio's characteristics with those of the index. Over time, the trading-related costs will drag down performance. In general, optimization should be used only in situations in which full replication would result in substantial transaction costs.

5. **A.** The principal benefit of all stocks being categorized as either growth or value (MSCI approach) is that it is collectively exhaustive. That said, many stocks are "border" stocks (i.e., have characteristics that place

Solutions to 1–10 taken from *Managing Investment Portfolios: A Dynamic Process*, Third Edition, John L. Maginn, CFA, Donald L. Tuttle, CFA, Jerald E. Pinto, CFA, and Dennis W. McLeavey, CFA, editors. Copyright © 2007 by CFA Institute. Reprinted with permission. All other solutions copyright © CFA Institute.

them near the value/growth border) that don't really exhibit significant value or growth characteristics but are categorized in one of these styles anyway. The Dow Jones method's neutral/core category eliminates this problem, but the value and growth indices by definition do not contain all of the stocks in the broad index.

B. Either set of indices can be used for returns-based style analysis. That said, Miller is likely to obtain a higher R^2 in a regression of the portfolio returns on the style index returns if he uses the more "granular" set of style indices—those by Dow Jones. For example, if the portfolio is a deep value portfolio or a strong growth portfolio, the Dow Jones indices are more likely to better explain the portfolio's style than a set of style indices in which every stock is forced into either value or growth. Specifically, the deep value portfolio will be better represented by the Dow Jones Value Index because that index focuses more on deep value stocks. That same portfolio's returns regressed versus the MSCI Value Index is likely to show a lower R^2.

6. The principal benefit of a market-neutral long–short portfolio is absence of a long-only constraint. A long-only constraint penalizes portfolios in two ways. First, it prevents the portfolio manager from fully exploiting a negative forecast on a given stock. Second, in a long-only portfolio, being unable to fully exploit a negative forecast also limits the ability of the portfolio manager to maximize positive forecasts. The main risk with long–short portfolios is the unlimited liability on the short trades. If a stock in which an investor has a long position loses all of its value, the most that could happen is that the investor loses his entire investment. With a short position, however, the investor's upside is limited (stock goes to zero) but the liability is unlimited (theoretically, a stock can appreciate infinitely).

7. Hayes can produce such a portfolio through the use of a portable alpha. He submits a proposal to manage a market-neutral long–short portfolio of U.K. stocks. This strategy generates alpha (α). To produce beta (β), the Japanese equity exposure, Hayes takes a long position in a notional value of futures equal to the size of the portfolio.

8. Suzuki tells her client that although she can certainly double the portfolio's tracking risk to 4 percent, the portfolio's alpha will increase but not double. The problem is that as an investor increases a portfolio's tracking risk, the long-only constraint increasingly limits the portfolio manager from taking full advantage of her investment insights. Remember, $IR \approx IC \sqrt{Breadth}$. If the breadth is constant but the IC falls because a smaller portion of the manager's insight is translated into the portfolio, then the IR must also fall.

9. The short side alpha is likely the larger of the two. Many investors look for cheap stocks in which to take long positions, but comparatively few look for expensive stocks to short. Shorting is operationally more cumbersome than taking a long position, which contributes to the limited use of shorting by most investors. Also, sell recommendations from the analyst community are relatively uncommon. Analysts are more likely to simply not cover a stock on which they have an unfavorable opinion. Also, analysts working for investment banking firms have a strong incentive not to issue negative reports on companies with which the bank may wish to do business.

10. **A.** The change is in fact positive (assuming that Johnson is willing to accept a slightly higher level of tracking risk) because the information ratio improves. Her current portfolio has an information ratio of 0.87 (2.4%/2.75%). The portfolio with the enhanced indexer has an information ratio of 0.97 (2.8%/2.9%).

B. Stock-based enhanced indexing begins with an index portfolio and then over- or underweights individual stocks based on the portfolio manager's return expectations for those stocks. The portfolio is built to look like its target benchmark but to add some level of outperformance on a fairly consistent basis. The advantage of this approach is greater breadth than the synthetic approach. That said, as with all active strategies, obtaining a satisfactory IC or level of investment insight is the challenge. Synthetic enhanced index strategies involve gaining exposure to the benchmark with futures (or a swap) while generating an alpha, typically using fixed income. This strategy has the advantage of being straightforward. It generally has narrower breadth (usually a duration or credit bet) and so requires a high IC to produce the same level of IR as the stock-based approach.

11. A. The total active risk is greater than 6 percent because in the calculation, the long-short manager would be benchmarked to the Russell 1000 rather than the manager's normal benchmark, which most closely captures the manager's orientation. We can see this by noting the positive level of misfit risk. The misfit risk is calculated with the equation $\sqrt{6.0\%^2 + (\text{Misfit risk})^2} = 6.1\%$, which equals 1.1 percent.

B. The total active risk is $\sqrt{5\%^2 + 7.13\%^2} = 8.71\%$.

C. The expected total active return is $(0.3 \times 0\%) + (0.7 \times 1\%) = 0.7\%$.

The expected total active risk for the portfolio is
$$\sqrt{(0.3^2 \times 0\%^2) + (0.7^2 \times 1.5\%^2)} = 1.05\%.$$

The expected IR is $0.7\%/1.05\% = 0.67$.

D. The efficient combination of managers leads to a portfolio with an IR of $1.59\%/1.10\% = 1.45$. Hence, despite the slightly greater active risk exposure, the overall portfolio IR increases by a factor of 2.17 versus the current mix.

E. In general, the exposures to non-U.S. equities in the long–short portfolio should not concern Whitmore as long as she believes that the manager has skill in managing non-U.S. equities. As shown in Part A of this problem, the misfit risk for the strategy is relatively small because the manager overlays the long–short portfolio with Russell 1000 futures and thus has a high correlation with the Russell 3000 benchmark. The large majority of the strategy's total active risk is driven by the manager's active return volatility.

12. B is correct. Both the active return and active risk are expected to be 0.00%, which would indicate a passive or index investment style.

13. C is correct. Relative to the other managers' portfolio characteristics, Portfolio C has characteristics most like a growth portfolio, such as a higher average P/E, higher average earnings growth rate, and lower average dividend-yield.

14. C is correct. Manager A most likely is pursuing a value investment style, not a growth investment style. This is evidenced by the relatively low long-term projected EPS growth. Contrarian and high yield, along with low P/E, are examples of value investment substyles. Momentum is an investment substyle consistent with a growth investment style.

Reading 32 • Equity Portfolio Management

15. A is correct. Portfolio active return and portfolio active risk are calculated as follows:

Portfolio active return = (0.20 × 0.025) + (0.45 × 0.0) + (0.35 × 0.025)
= 0.01375 = 1.38%

Portfolio active risk = $[(0.20^2 \times 0.04^2) + (0.45^2 \times 0.0^2) + (0.35^2 \times 0.04^2)]^{0.5} = (0.000260)^{0.5} = 0.0161 = 1.61\%$

16. C is correct. Full replication of an index is the indexing methodology that is most likely to have the least tracking error because every issue in the index is represented in the portfolio in approximately the same weight as in the index.

17. C is correct. Full replication is likely to have the highest investment cost. The other choices are low-cost index options of large pooled investments. While full replication of an index will generally have the least tracking error, a portfolio of just $2.0 million on an index as large as the MSCI ACWI would be very inefficient and cost-ineffective due to the inherent costs of managing and administering the portfolio, transaction costs of portfolio adjustments, transaction costs of investing and disinvesting cash flows, and a drag on performance from cash positions in an upward-trending equity market.

18. A is correct. Enhanced indexing seeks to outperform a given index (exploit information not yet reflected in stock prices) and limit tracking risk: ". . . enhanced indexing strategies with their strict control of tracking risk have tended to have the highest information ratios."

19. A is correct. A client with unpredictable cash inflows and outflows needs greater liquidity and furthermore would not want an index with a large number of stocks.

20. C is correct. Full replication has self-rebalancing properties when used for a float-weighted index, which would translate into lower costs from lower transaction fees and also should result in minimal tracking risk. In addition, full replication is generally the preferred index construction method for indices such as the S&P 500 that are composed of highly liquid securities. It is usually used for indexes with fewer than 1,000 stocks.

21. B is correct. You cannot double a long-only portfolio's alpha by doubling its risk. As tracking risk increases, the long-only constraint limits the investor's investment opportunity set. Because IR (active return/active risk) = IC (effectiveness of investment insight, or correlation between forecast return and actual return) * √breadth (number of independent active decisions made), if the breadth is constant but the IC falls because a smaller portion of the manager's insight is translated into the portfolio, then the IR must also fall.

22. C is correct. An equal-weighted index is biased toward small-cap companies.

23. C is correct. An enhanced indexed portfolio is designed to perform better than its benchmark index without incurring much additional risk. The derivatives-based strategy has the higher information ratio of the two, meaning it generates a higher mean active return for each unit of active risk:

Stock based   1.5/2.9 = .52
Derivatives based   1.2/2.1 = .57

www.cfainstitute.org/toolkit—Your online preparation resource

STUDY SESSION 12
EQUITY PORTFOLIO MANAGEMENT

" **C**orporate Governance" addresses the alignment of interests between a corporation's managers and its equity shareholders. Although other investor classes are also concerned with corporate governance, the issue is particularly relevant for equity portfolio managers. Agency problems and conflicts of interest reduce a company's appeal to investors and thus directly affect its valuation. The reading concludes with an examination of the relationship between a corporation and its stakeholders and the arguments for and against a stakeholder-based governance structure.

Management techniques, such as benchmark selection and style analysis, are presented as tools for effectively measuring and controlling equity portfolio attributes in an international environment in "International Equity Benchmarks."

"Emerging Market Finance" presents a summary of financial and economic research relevant to investors in emerging markets.

READING ASSIGNMENTS

4⅝ 4¹¹/₁₆

4⅝ 4¹¹/₁₆ — ⅜

5½ 5½ — ⅜

5½ 21³/₁₆ — ⅛

20⅝ 21³/₁₆ — ⅛

17⅜ 18⅛ + ⅞

6½ 6½ — ½

7¼ 6½ — ⅛

31/32 —

15/16

9/16 9/16

5/32

7¹⁵/₁₆ 7¹³/₁₆ 7¹⁵/₁₆

2⅝ 2¹¹/₃₂ 2½ +

2¾ 2¼ 2¼

6½ 12¹/₁₆ 11⅜ 11¾ +

87 33¾ 33 33¼

502 25⅝ 24⁹/₁₆ 25⅜ +

833 12 11⅝ 11⅝ +

16 10½ 10½ 10½ —

78 15⅞ 15¹³/₁₆ 15⅞ —

508 9⁹/₁₆ 8¼ 8⅛ +

430 11¼ 10⅝

CORPORATE GOVERNANCE
by Jean Tirole

LEARNING OUTCOMES

The candidate should be able to:	Mastery
a. explain the ways in which management may act that are not in the best interest of the firm's owners (moral hazard) and illustrate how dysfunctional corporate governance can lead to moral hazard;	☐
b. evaluate explicit and implicit incentives that can align management's interests with those of the firm's shareholders;	☐
c. explain the shortcomings of boards of directors as monitors of management and state and discuss prescriptions for improving board oversight;	☐
d. discuss why active monitoring by investors requires control, the various mechanisms by which control is exercised, and the limitations of active monitoring;	☐
e. critique the effectiveness of debt as a corporate governance mechanism;	☐
f. explain the social responsibilities of the corporation in a "stakeholder society" and evaluate the advantages and disadvantages of a corporate governance structure based on stakeholder rather than shareholder interests;	☐
g. discuss the Cadbury Report recommendations for best practice in maintaining an effective board of directors whose interests are aligned with those of shareholders.	☐

In 1932, Berle and Means wrote a pathbreaking book documenting the separation of ownership and control in the United States. They showed that shareholder dispersion creates substantial managerial discretion, which can be abused. This was the starting point for the subsequent academic thinking on corporate governance and corporate finance. Subsequently, a number of corporate problems around the world have reinforced the perception that managers are unwatched. Most observers are now seriously concerned that the best managers may not be selected, and that managers, once selected, are not accountable.

The Theory of Corporate Finance, by Jean Tirole. Copyright © 2006. Reprinted with permission of Princeton University Press.

289

Thus, the premise behind modern corporate finance in general and this reading in particular is that corporate insiders need not act in the best interests of the providers of the funds. This reading's first task is therefore to document the divergence of interests through both empirical regularities and anecdotes. As we will see, moral hazard comes in many guises, from low effort to private benefits, from inefficient investments to accounting and market value manipulations.

Two broad routes can be taken to alleviate insider moral hazard. First, insiders' incentives may be partly aligned with the investors' interests through the use of performance-based incentive schemes. Second, insiders may be monitored by the current shareholders (or on their behalf by the board or a large shareholder), by potential shareholders (acquirers, raiders), or by debtholders. Such monitoring induces interventions in management ranging from mere interference in decision making to the threat of employment termination as part of a shareholder- or board-initiated move or of a bankruptcy process. We document the nature of these two routes.

This reading is organized as follows. Section 1 sets the stage by emphasizing the importance of managerial accountability. Section 2 reviews various instruments and factors that help align managerial incentives with those of the firm: monetary compensation, implicit incentives, monitoring, and product-market competition. Sections 3–6 analyze monitoring by boards of directors, large shareholders, raiders, and banks, respectively. Section 7 discusses differences in corporate governance systems. Section 8 and the supplementary section conclude the reading by a discussion of the objective of the firm, namely, whom managers should be accountable to, and tries to shed light on the long-standing debate between the proponents of the stakeholder society and those of shareholder-value maximization.

1   INTRODUCTION: THE SEPARATION OF OWNERSHIP AND CONTROL

The governance of corporations has attracted much attention in the past decade. Increased media coverage has turned "transparency," "managerial accountability," "corporate governance failures," "weak boards of directors," "hostile takeovers," "protection of minority shareholders," and "investor activism" into household phrases. As severe agency problems continued to impair corporate performance both in companies with strong managers and dispersed shareholders (as is frequent in Anglo-Saxon countries) and those with a controlling shareholder and minority shareholders (typical of the European corporate landscape), repeated calls have been issued on both sides of the Atlantic for corporate governance reforms. In the 1990s, study groups (such as the Cadbury and Greenbury committees in the United Kingdom and the Viénot committee in France) and institutional investors (such as CalPERS in the United States) started enunciating codes of best practice for boards of directors. More recently, various laws and reports[1] came in reaction to the many corporate scandals of the late 1990s and early 2000s (e.g., Seat, Banesto, Metallgesellschaft, Suez, ABB, Swissair, Vivendi in Europe, Dynergy, Qwest, Enron, WorldCom, Global Crossing, and Tyco in the United States).

But what is corporate governance?[2] The dominant view in economics, articulated, for example, in Shleifer and Vishny's (1997) and Becht et al.'s (2002) surveys on the topic, is that corporate governance relates to the "ways in which the suppliers of finance to corporations assure themselves of getting a return on their investment." Relatedly, it is preoccupied with the ways in which a corporation's insiders can credibly commit to return funds to outside investors and can thereby attract external financing. This definition is, of course, narrow. Many politicians, managers, consultants, and academics object to the economists' narrow view of corporate governance as being preoccupied solely with investor returns; they argue that other "stakeholders," such as employees, communities, suppliers, or customers, also have a vested interest in how the firm is run, and that these stakeholders' concerns should somehow be internalized as well.[3] Section 8 will return to the debate about the stakeholder society, but we should indicate right away that the content of this reading reflects the agenda of the narrow and orthodox view described in the above citation. The rest of Section 1 is therefore written from the perspective of shareholder value.

1.1 Moral Hazard Comes in Many Guises

There are various ways in which management may not act in the firm's (understand: its owners') best interest. For convenience, we divide these into four categories, but the reader should keep in mind that all are fundamentally part of the same problem, generically labeled by economists as "moral hazard."

Insufficient effort. By "insufficient effort," we refer not so much to the number of hours spent in the office (indeed, most top executives work very long hours), but rather to the allocation of work time to various tasks. Managers may find it unpleasant or inconvenient to cut costs by switching to a less costly supplier, by reallocating the workforce, or by taking a tougher stance in wage negotiations (Bertrand and Mullainathan 1999).[4] They may devote insufficient effort to the oversight of their subordinates; scandals in the 1990s involving large losses inflicted by traders or derivative specialists subject to insufficient internal control (Metallgesellschaft, Procter & Gamble, Barings) are good cases in point. Lastly, managers may allocate too little time to the task they have been hired for because they overcommit themselves with competing activities (boards of directors, political involvement, investments in other ventures, and more generally activities not or little related to managing the firm).

---

[1] In the United States, for example, the 2002 Sarbanes-Oxley Act, and the U.S. Securities and Exchange Commission's and the Financial Accounting Standards Board's reports.

[2] We focus here on corporations. Separate governance issues arise in associations (see Hansmann 1996; Glaeser and Shleifer 2001; Hart and Moore 1989, 1996; Kremer 1997; Levin and Tadelis 2005) and government agencies (see Wilson 1989; Tirole 1994; Dewatripont et al. 1999a,b).

[3] A prominent exponent of this view in France is Albert (1991). To some extent, the German legislation mandating codetermination (in particular, the Codetermination Act of 1976, which requires that supervisory boards of firms with over 2,000 employees be made up of an equal number of representatives of employees and shareholders, with the chairperson—a representative of the shareholders—deciding in the case of a stalemate) reflects this desire that firms internalize the welfare of their employees.

[4] Using antitakeover laws passed in a number of states in the United States in the 1980s and firm-level data, Bertrand and Mullainathan find evidence that the enactment of such a law raises wages by 1–2%.

Extravagant investments. There is ample evidence, both direct and indirect, that some managers engage in pet projects and build empires to the detriment of shareholders. A standard illustration, provided by Jensen (1988), is the heavy exploration spending of oil industry managers in the late 1970s during a period of high real rates of interest, increased exploration costs, and reduction in expected future oil price increases, and in which buying oil on Wall Street was much cheaper than obtaining it by drilling holes in the ground. Oil industry managers also invested some of their large amount of cash into noncore industries. Relatedly, economists have long conducted event studies to analyze the reaction of stock prices to the announcement of acquisitions and have often unveiled substantial shareholder concerns with such moves (see Shleifer and Vishny 1997; see also Andrade et al. (2001) for a more recent assessment of the long-term acquisition performance of the acquirer-target pair). And Blanchard et al. (1994) show how firms that earn windfall cash awards in court do not return the cash to investors and spend it inefficiently.

Entrenchment strategies. Top executives often take actions that hurt shareholders in order to keep or secure their position. There are many entrenchment strategies. First, managers sometimes invest in lines of activities that make them indispensable (Shleifer and Vishny 1989); for example, they invest in a declining industry or old-fashioned technology that they are good at running. Second, they manipulate performance measures so as to "look good" when their position might be threatened. For example, they may use "creative" accounting techniques to mask their company's deteriorating condition. Relatedly, they may engage in excessive or insufficient risk taking. They may be excessively conservative when their performance is satisfactory, as they do not want to run the risk of their performance falling below the level that would trigger a board reaction, a takeover, or a proxy fight. Conversely, it is a common attitude of managers "in trouble," that is, managers whose current performance is unsatisfactory and are desperate to offer good news to the firm's owners, to take excessive risk and thus "gamble for resurrection." Third, managers routinely resist hostile takeovers, as these threaten their long-term positions. In some cases, they succeed in defeating tender offers that would have been very attractive to shareholders, or they go out of their way to find a "white knight" or conclude a sweet nonaggression pact with the raider. Managers also lobby for a legal environment that limits shareholder activism and, in Europe as well as in some Asian countries such as Japan, design complex cross-ownership and holding structures with double voting rights for a few privileged shares that make it hard for outsiders to gain control.

Self-dealing. Lastly, managers may increase their private benefits from running the firm by engaging in a wide variety of self-dealing behaviors, ranging from benign to outright illegal activities. Managers may consume perks[5] (costly private jets,[6] plush offices, private boxes at sports events, country club memberships, celebrities on payroll, hunting and fishing lodges, extravagant entertainment expenses, expensive art); pick their successor among their friends or at least like-minded individuals who will not criticize or cast a shadow on their past management; select a costly supplier on friendship or kinship grounds; or finance political parties of their liking. Self-dealing can also reach illegality as in the case of thievery (Robert Maxwell stealing from the employees' pension fund,

---

[5] Perks figure prominently among sources of agency costs in Jensen and Meckling's (1976) early contribution.

[6] Personal aircraft use is one of the most often described perks in the business literature. A famous example is RJR Nabisco's fleet of 10 aircraft with 36 company pilots, to which the chief executive officer (CEO) Ross Johnson's friends and dog had access (Burrough and Helyar 1990).

managers engaging in transactions such as below-market-price asset sales with affiliated firms owned by themselves, their families, or their friends),[7] or of insider trading or information leakages to Wall Street analysts or other investors.

Needless to say, recent corporate scandals have focused more on self-dealing, which is somewhat easier to discover and especially demonstrate than insufficient effort, extravagant investments, or entrenchment strategies.

1.2 Dysfunctional Corporate Governance

The overall significance of moral hazard is largely understated by the mere observation of managerial misbehavior, which forms the "tip of the iceberg." The submerged part of the iceberg is the institutional response in terms of corporate governance, finance, and managerial incentive contracts. Yet, it is worth reviewing some of the recent controversies regarding dysfunctional governance; we take the United States as our primary illustration, but the universality of the issues bears emphasizing. Several forms of dysfunctional governance have been pointed out:

Lack of transparency. Investors and other stakeholders are sometimes imperfectly informed about the levels of compensation granted to top management. A case in point is the retirement package of Jack Welch, chief executive officer (CEO) of General Electric.[8] Unbeknownst to outsiders, this retirement package included continued access to private jets, a luxurious apartment in Manhattan, memberships of exclusive clubs, access to restaurants, and so forth.[9]

The limited transparency of managerial stock options (in the United States their cost for the company can legally be assessed at zero) is also a topic of intense controversy.[10] To build investor trust, some companies (starting with, for example, Boeing, Amazon.com, and Coca-Cola) but not all have recently chosen to voluntarily report stock options as expenses.

Perks[11] are also often outside the reach of investor control. Interestingly, Yermack (2004a) finds that a firm's stock price falls by an abnormal 2% when firms first disclose that their CEO has been awarded the aircraft perk.[12] Furthermore, firms that allow personal aircraft use by the CEO underperform the market by about 4%. Another common form of perks comes from recruiting practices; in many European countries, CEOs hire family and friends for important positions; this practice is also common in the United States.[13]

---

[7] Another case in point is the Tyco scandal (2002). The CEO and close collaborators are assessed to have stolen over $100 million.

[8] Jack Welch was CEO of General Electric from 1981 to 2001. The package was discovered only during divorce proceedings in 2002.

[9] Similarly, Bernie Ebbers, WorldCom's CEO, borrowed over $1 billion from banks such as Citigroup and Bank of America against his shares of WorldCom (which went bankrupt in 2001) and used it to buy a ranch in British Columbia, 460,000 acres of U.S. forest, two luxury yachts, and so forth.

[10] In the United States grants of stock options are disclosed in footnotes to the financial statements. By the mid 1990s, the U.S. Congress had already prevented the Financial Accounting Standards Board from forcing firms to expense managerial stock options.

[11] Such as Steve Jobs's purchase of a $90 million private jet.

[12] As Yermack stresses, this may be due to learning either that corporate governance is weak or that management has undesirable characteristics (lack of integrity, taste for not working hard, etc.). See Rajan and Wulf (2005) for a somewhat different view of perks as enhancing managerial productivity.

[13] Retail store Dillard's CEO succeeded in getting four of his children onto the board of directors; Gap's CEO hired his brother to redesign shops and his wife as consultant. Contrast this with Apria Healthcare: in 2002, less than 24 hours after learning that the CEO had hired his wife, the board of directors fired both.

Level. The total compensation packages (salary plus bonus plus long-term compensation) of top executives has risen substantially over the years and reached levels that are hardly fathomable to the public.[14] The trend toward higher managerial compensation in Europe, which started with lower levels of compensation, has been even more dramatic.

Evidence for this "runaway compensation" is provided by Hall and Liebman (1998), who report a tripling (in real terms) of average CEO compensation between 1980 and 1994 for large U.S. corporations,[15] and by Hall and Murphy (2002), who point at a further doubling between 1994 and 2001. In 2000, the annual income of the average CEO of a large U.S. firm was 531 times the average wage of workers in the company (as opposed to 42 times in 1982).[16]

The proponents of high levels of compensation point out that some of this increase comes in the form of performance-related pay: top managers receive more and more bonuses and especially stock options,[17] which, with some caveats that we discuss later, have incentive benefits.

Tenuous link between performance and compensation. High levels of compensation are particularly distressing when they are not related to performance, that is, when top managers receive large amounts of money for a lackluster or even disastrous outcome (Bebchuk and Fried 2003, 2004). While executive compensation will be studied in more detail in Section 2, let us here list the reasons why the link between performance and compensation may be tenuous.

First, the compensation package may be poorly structured. For example, the performance of an oil company is substantially affected by the world price of oil, a variable over which it has little control. Suppose that managerial bonuses and stock options are not indexed to the price of oil. Then the managers can make enormous amounts of money when the price of oil increases. By contrast, they lose little from the lack of indexation when the price of oil plummets, since their options and bonuses are then "out-of-the money" (such compensation starts when performance—stock price or yearly profit—exceeds some threshold), not to mention the fact that the options may be repriced so as to reincentivize executives. Thus, managers often benefit from poor design in their compensation schemes.

Second, managers often seem to manage to maintain their compensation stable or even have it increased despite poor performance. In 2002, for example, the CEOs of AOL Time Warner, Intel, and Safeway made a lot of money despite a bad year. Similarly, Qwest's board of directors awarded $88 million to its CEO despite an abysmal performance in 2001.

Third, managers may succeed in "getting out on time" (either unbeknownst to the board, which did not see, or did not want to see, the accounting manipulations or the impending bad news, or with the cooperation of the board). Global Crossing's managers sold shares for $735 million. Tenet Health Care's CEO in January 2002 announced sensational earnings prospects and sold shares for an amount of $111 million; a year later, the share price had fallen by 60%. Similarly, Oracle's CEO (Larry Ellison) made $706 million by selling his stock options in January 2001 just before announcing a fall in income forecasts. Unsurprisingly, many reform proposals have argued in favor of a higher degree of vesting of managerial shares, forcing top management to keep shares for a long time

---

[14] For example, in 1997, twenty U.S. CEOs had yearly compensation packages over $25 million. The CEO of Traveler's group received $230 million and that of Coca-Cola $111 million. James Crowe, who was not even CEO of WorldCom, received $69 million (*Business Week*, April 20, 1998).

[15] Equity-based compensation rose from 20 to 50% of total compensation during that period.

[16] *A New Era in Governance*, McKinsey Quarterly, 2004.

[17] For example, in 1979, only 8% of British firms gave bonuses to managers; more than three-quarters did in 1994. The share of performance-based rewards for British senior managers jumped from 10 to 40% from 1989 to 1994 (*The Economist*, January 29, 1994, p. 69).

(perhaps until well after the end of their employment),[18] and of an independent compensation committee at the board of directors.

Finally, managers receive large golden parachutes[19] for leaving the firm. These golden parachutes are often granted in the wake of poor performance (a major cause of CEO firing!). These high golden parachutes have been common for a long time in the United States, and have recently made their way to Europe (witness the $89 million golden parachute granted to ABB's CEO).

The Sarbanes-Oxley Act (2002) in the United States, a regulatory reaction to the previously mentioned abuses, requires the CEO and chief financial officer (CFO) to reimburse any profit from bonuses or stock sales during the year following a financial report that is subsequently restated because of "misconduct." This piece of legislation also makes the shares held by executives less liquid by bringing down the lag in the report of sales of executive shares from ten days to two days.[20]

Accounting manipulations. We have already alluded to the manipulations that inflate company performance. Some of those manipulations are actually legal while others are not. Also, they may require cooperation from investors, trading partners, analysts, or accountants. Among the many facets of the Enron scandal[21] lie off-balance-sheet deals. For example, Citigroup and JPMorgan lent Enron billions of dollars disguised as energy trades. The accounting firm Arthur Andersen let this happen. Similarly, profits of WorldCom (which, like Enron, went bankrupt) were assessed to have been overestimated by $7.1 billion starting in 2000.[22]

Accounting manipulations serve multiple purposes. First, they increase the apparent earnings and/or stock price, and thereby the value of managerial compensation. Managers with options packages may therefore find it attractive to inflate earnings. Going beyond scandals such as those of Enron, Tyco, Xerox,[23] and WorldCom in the United States and Parmalat in Europe, Bergstresser and Philippon (2005) find more generally that highly incentivized CEOs exercise a large number of stock options during years in which discretionary accruals form a large fraction of reported earnings, and that their companies engage in higher levels of earnings management.

Second, by hiding poor performance, they protect managers against dismissals or takeovers or, more generally, reduce investor interference in the managerial process. Third, accounting manipulations enable firms not to violate bank covenants, which are often couched in terms of accounting performance. Lastly, they enable continued financing.[24]

When pointing to these misbehaviors, economists do not necessarily suggest that managers' actual behavior exhibits widespread incompetency and moral

---

[18] The timing of exercise of executives' stock options is documented in, for example, Bettis et al. (2003). They find median values for the exercise date at about two years after vesting and five years prior to expiration.

[19] Golden parachutes refer to benefits received by an executive in the event that the company is acquired and the executive's employment is terminated. Golden parachutes are in principle specified in the employment contract.

[20] See Holmström and Kaplan (2003) for more details and an analysis of the Sarbanes-Oxley Act, as well as of the NYSE, NASDAQ, and Conference Board corporate governance proposals.

[21] For an account of the Enron saga and, in particular, of the many off-balance-sheet transactions, see, for example, Fox (2003). See also the special issue of the *Journal of Economic Perspectives* devoted to the Enron scandal (Volume 12, Spring 2003).

[22] Interestingly, one WorldCom director chaired Moody's investment services, and it took a long time for the rating agency to downgrade WorldCom.

[23] A restatement by the Securities and Exchange Commission reduced Xerox's reported net income by $1.4 billion over the period 1997–2001. Over that period, the company's CEO exercised options worth over $20 million.

[24] For example, WorldCom, just before bankruptcy, was the second-largest U.S. telecommunications company, with 70 acquisitions under its belt.

hazard. Rather, they stress both the potential extent of the problem and the endogeneity of managerial accountability. They argue that corporate governance failures are as old as the corporation, and that control mechanisms, however imperfect, have long been in place, implying that actual misbehaviors are the tip of an iceberg whose main element represents the averted ones.

2   MANAGERIAL INCENTIVES: AN OVERVIEW

2.1 A Sophisticated Mix of Incentives

However large the scope for misbehavior, explicit and implicit incentives, in practice, partly align managerial incentives with the firm's interest. Bonuses and stock options make managers sensitive to losses in profit and in shareholder value. Besides these explicit incentives, less formal, but quite powerful implicit incentives stem from the managers' concern about their future. The threat of being fired by the board of directors or removed by the market for corporate control through a takeover or a proxy fight, the possibility of being replaced by a receiver (in the United Kingdom, say) or of being put on a tight leash (as is the case of a Chapter 11 bankruptcy in the United States) during financial distress, and the prospect of being appointed to new boards of directors or of receiving offers for executive directorships in more prestigious companies, all contribute to keeping managers on their toes.

Capital market monitoring and product-market competition further keep a tight rein on managerial behavior. Monitoring by a large institutional investor (pension fund, mutual fund, bank, etc.), by a venture capitalist, or by a large private owner restricts managerial control, and is generally deemed to alleviate the agency problem. And, as we will discuss, product-market competition often aligns explicit and implicit managerial incentives with those of the firm, although it may create perverse incentives in specific situations.

Psychologists, consultants, and personnel officers no doubt would find the economists' description of managerial incentives too narrow. When discussing incentives in general, they also point to the role of intrinsic motivation, fairness, horizontal equity, morale, trust, corporate culture, social responsibility and altruism, feelings of self-esteem (coming from recognition or from fellow employees' gratitude), interest in the job, and so on. Here, we will not enter the debate as to whether the economists' view of incentives is inappropriately restrictive.[25] Some of these apparently noneconomic incentives are, at a deeper level, already incorporated in the economic paradigm.[26] As for the view that economists do not

---

[25] For references to the psychology literature and for views on how such considerations affect incentives, see, for example, Bénabou and Tirole (2003, 2004, 2005), Camerer and Malmendier (2004), Fehr and Schmidt (2003), and Frey (1997).

[26] For example, explicit or implicit rules mandating "fairness" and "horizontal equity" can be seen as a response to the threat of favoritism, that is, of collusion between a superior and a subordinate (as in Laffont 1990). The impact of morale can be partly apprehended through the effects of incentives on the firm's or its management's reputation (see, for example, Tirole 1996). And the role of trust has in the past twenty years been one of the leitmotivs of economic theory since the pioneering work of Kreps et al. (1982) (see, for example, Kreps 1990). Economists have also devoted some attention to corporate culture phenomena (see Carrillo and Gromb 1999; Crémer 1993; Kreps 1990). Economists may not yet have a fully satisfactory description of fairness, horizontal equity, morale, trust, or corporate culture, but an *a priori* critique of the economic paradigm of employee incentives as being too narrow is unwarranted, and more attention should be devoted to exactly what can and cannot be explained by the standard economic paradigm.

account for the possibility of benevolence, it should be clear that economists are concerned with the study of the residual incentives to act in the firm's interests over and beyond what they would contribute in the absence of rewards and monitoring. While we would all prefer not to need this sophisticated set of explicit and implicit incentives, history has taught us that even the existing control mechanisms do not suffice to prevent misbehavior.

2.2 Monetary Incentives

Let us first return to the managerial compensation problem and exposit it in more detail than was done in the introduction to the reading.

The compensation package.[27] A typical top executive receives compensation in three ways: salary, bonus, and stock-based incentives (stock, stock options). The salary is a fixed amount (although revised over time partly on the basis of past performance). The risky bonus and stock-based compensations are the two incentive components of the package.[28] They are meant to induce managers to internalize the owners' interests. Stock-based incentives, the bulk of the incentive component, have long been used to incentivize U.S. managers. The compensation of executives in Germany or in Japan has traditionally been less tied to stock prices (which does not mean that the latter are irrelevant for the provision of managerial incentives, as we later observe). Everywhere, though, there has been a dramatic increase in equity-based pay, especially stock options. For example, in the United States, the *sensitivity* of top executives pay to shareholder returns has increased tenfold between the early 1980s and late 1990s (see, for example, Hall and Liebman 1998; Hall 2000).

Needless to say, these compensation packages create an incentive to pursue profit-maximization only if the managers are not able to undo their incentives by selling the corresponding stakes to a third party. Indeed, third parties would in general love to offer, at a premium, insurance to the managers at the expense of the owners, who can no longer count on the incentives provided by the compensation package they designed. As a matter of fact, compensation package agreements make it difficult for managers to undo their position in the firm through open or secret trading. Open sales are limited for example by minimum-holding requirements while secret trading is considered insider trading.[29] There are, however, some loopholes that allow managers to undo some of their exposure to

---

[27] See, for example, Smith and Watts (1982) and Baker et al. (1988) for more detailed discussions of compensation packages.

[28] More precisely, *earnings-related compensation* includes bonus and performance plans. Bonus plans yield short-term rewards tied to the firm's yearly performance. Rewards associated with performance plans (which are less frequent and less substantial than bonus plans) are contingent on earnings targets over three to five years. Many managerial contracts specify that part or all of the bonus payments can be transformed into stock options (or sometimes into phantom shares), either at the executive's discretion or by the compensation committee. (Phantom shares are units of value that correspond to an equivalent number of shares of stock. Phantom stock plans credit the executive with shares and pay her the cash value of these shares at the end of a prespecified time period.) This operation amounts to transforming a safe income (the earned bonus) into a risky one tied to future performance. *Stock-related compensation* includes stock options or stock appreciation rights, and restricted or phantom stock plans. Stock options and stock appreciation rights are more popular than restricted or phantom stock plans, which put restrictions on sale: in 1980, only 14 of the largest 100 U.S. corporations had a restricted stock plan as opposed to 83 for option plans. Few had phantom stock plans, and in about half the cases these plans were part of a bonus plan, and were therefore conditional on the executive's voluntarily deferring his bonus. Stock appreciation rights are similar to stock options and are meant to reduce the transaction costs associated with exercising options and selling shares.

[29] Securities and Exchange Commission (SEC) rules in the United States constrain insider trading and short selling.

the firm's profitability through less strictly regulated financial instruments, such as equity swaps and collars.[30]

While there is widespread consensus in favor of some linkage between pay and performance, it is also widely recognized that performance measurement is quite imperfect. Bonus plans are based on accounting data, which creates the incentive to manipulate such data, making performance measurement systematically biased. Profits can be shifted backward and forward in time with relative ease. Equity-based compensation is less affected by this problem provided that the manager cannot sell rapidly, since stock prices in principle reflect the present discounted value of future profits. But stock prices are subject to exogenous factors creating volatility.

Nevertheless, compensation committees must use existing performance measures, however imperfect, when designing compensation packages for the firm's executives.

Bonuses and shareholdings: substitutes or complements? As we saw, it is customary to distinguish between two types of monetary compensation: bonuses are defined by current profit, that is, accounting data, while stocks and stock options are based on the value of shares, that is, on market data.

The articulation between these two types of rewards matters. One could easily believe that, because they are both incentive schemes, bonuses and stock options are substitutes. An increase in a manager's bonus could then be compensated by a reduction in managerial shareholdings. This, however, misses the point that bonuses and stock options serve two different and complementary purposes.[31]

A bonus-based compensation package creates a strong incentive for a manager to privilege the short term over the long term. A manager trades off short- and long-term profits when confronting subcontracting, marketing, maintenance, and investment decisions. An increase in her bonus increases her preference for current profit and can create an imbalance in incentives. This imbalance would be aggravated by a reduction in stock-based incentives, which are meant to encourage management to take a long-term perspective. Bonuses and stock options therefore tend to be complements. An increase in short-term incentives must go hand in hand with an increase in long-term incentives, in order to keep a proper balance between short- and long-term objectives.

---

[30] An interesting article by Bettis et al. (1999) documents the extent of these side deals.

Equity swaps and collars (among other similar instruments) are private contracts between a corporate insider (officer or director) and a counterparty (usually a bank). In an equity swap, the insider exchanges the future returns on her stock for the cash attached to another financial instrument, such as the stock market index. A collar involves the simultaneous purchase of a put option and sale of a call option on the firm's shares. The put provides the insider with insurance against the firm's stock price decreases, and the call option reduces the insider's revenue from a price increase.

In the United States, the SEC, in two rulings in 1994 and 1996, mandated reporting of swaps and collars. Bettis et al. argue that the reporting requirements have remained ambiguous and that they have not much constrained their use by insiders (despite the general rules on insider trading that prohibit insiders from shorting their firm's stock or from trading without disclosing their private information).

Swaps and collars raise two issues. First, they may enable insiders to benefit from private information. Indeed, Bettis et al. show that insiders strategically time the purchase of these instruments. Swap and collar transactions occur after firms substantially outperform their benchmarks (by a margin of 40% in 250 trading days), and are followed by no abnormal returns in the 120 trading days after the transaction. Second, they provide insurance to the insiders and undo some of their exposure to the firm's profitability and thereby undo some of their incentives that stocks and stock options were supported to create. Bettis et al. estimate that 30% of shares held by top executives and board members in their sample are covered by equity swaps and collars.

[31] This discussion is drawn from Holmström and Tirole (1993).

The compensation base. It is well-known that managerial compensation should not be based on factors that are outside the control of the manager.[32] One implication of this idea is that managerial compensation should be immunized against shocks such as fluctuations in exchange rate, interest rate, or price of raw materials that the manager has no control over. This can be achieved, for example, by indexing managerial compensation to the relevant variables; in practice, though, this is often achieved more indirectly and only partially through corporate risk management, a practice that tends to insulate the firm from some types of aggregate risks through insurance-like contracts such as exchange rate or interest rate swaps.

Another implication of the point that managerial compensation should be unaffected by the realization of exogenous shocks is relative performance evaluation (also called "yardstick competition"). The idea is that one can use the performance of firms facing similar shocks, e.g., firms in the same industry facing the same cost and demand shocks, in order to obtain information about the uncontrollable shocks faced by the managers. For example, the compensation of the CEO of General Motors can be made dependent on the performance of Ford and Chrysler, with a better performance of the competitors being associated with a lower compensation for the executive. Managers are then rewarded as a function of their *relative* performance in their peer group rather than on the basis of their absolute performance (see Holmström 1982a).[33] There is some controversy about the extent of *implicit* relative performance evaluation (see, for example, Baker et al. 1988; Gibbons and Murphy 1990), but it is fairly clear that relative performance evaluation is not widely used in *explicit* incentive schemes (in particular, managerial stock ownership).

Bertrand and Mullainathan (2001) provide evidence that there is often too little filtering in CEO compensation packages, and that CEOs are consequently rewarded for "luck." For example, in the oil industry, pay changes and changes in the price of crude oil correlate quite well, even though the world oil price is largely beyond the control of any given firm; interestingly, CEOs are not always punished for bad luck, that is, there is an asymmetry in the exposure to shocks beyond the CEO's control. Bertrand and Mullainathan also demonstrate a similar pattern for the sensitivity of CEO compensation to industry-specific exchange rates for firms in the traded goods sector and to mean industry performance. They conclude that, roughly, "CEO pay is as sensitive to a lucky dollar as to a general dollar," suggesting that compensation contracts are poorly designed.

As Bertrand and Mullainathan note, it might be that, even though oil prices, exchange rates, and industry conditions are beyond the control of managers, investors would like them to forecast these properly so as to better tailor production and investment to their anticipated evolution, in which case it might be efficient to create an exposure of CEO compensation to "luck." Bertrand and Mullainathan, however, show that better-governed firms pay their CEOs less for luck; for example, an additional large shareholder on the board reduces CEO pay for luck by between 23 and 33%.

---

[32] The formal version of this point is Holmström's (1979) sufficient statistic result according to which optimal compensation packages are contingent on a sufficient statistic about the manager's unobserved actions.

[33] A cost of relative-performance-evaluation schemes is that they can generate distorted incentives, such as the tendency to herding; for example, herding has been observed for bank managers (perhaps more due to implicit rather than explicit incentives), as it is sometimes better to be wrong with the rest of the pack than to be right alone.

As Keynes (1936, Chapter 12) said, "Wordly wisdom teaches that it is better for reputation to fail conventionally than to succeed unconventionally."

This evidence suggests that the boards in general and the compensation committees in particular often comprise too many friends of the CEOs (see also Bertrand and Mullainathan 2000), who then de facto get to set their executive pay. We now turn to why they often gain when exposed to "luck": their compensation package tends to be convex, with large exposure in the upper tail and little in the lower tail.

Straight shares or stock options? Another aspect of the design of incentive compensation is the (non)linearity of the reward as a function of performance. Managers may be offered stock options, i.e., the right to purchase at specified dates stocks at some "exercise price" or "strike price."[34] These are call options. The options are valueless if the realized market price ends up being below the exercise price, and are worth the difference between the market price and the exercise price otherwise. In contrast, managerial holdings of straight shares let the manager internalize shareholder value over the whole range of market prices, and not only in the upper range above the exercise price.

Should managers be rewarded through straight shares or through stock options?[35] Given that managers rarely have a personal wealth to start with and are protected by limited liability or, due to risk aversion,[36] insist on a base income, stock options seem a more appropriate instrument. Straight shares provide management with a rent even when their performance is poor, while stock options do not. In Figure 1(a), the managerial reward when the exercise or strike price is P^S and the stock price is P at the exercise date is $\max(0, P - P^S)$ for the option; it would be P for a straight share. Put another way, for a given expected cost of the managerial incentive package for the owners, the latter can provide managers with stronger incentives by using stock options. This feature explains the popularity of stock options.

Stock options, on the other hand, have some drawbacks. Suppose that a manager is given stock options to be (possibly) exercised after two years on the job; and that this manager learns after one year that the firm faces an adverse shock (on which the exercise price of the options is not indexed), so that "under normal management" it becomes unlikely that the market price will exceed the strike price at the exercise date. The manager's option is then "under water" or "out of the money" and has little value unless the firm performs remarkably well during the remaining year. This may encourage management to take substantial risks in order to increase the value of her stock options. Such "gambling for resurrection" is also likely to occur under implicit/career-concern incentives, namely, when a poorly performing manager is afraid of losing her job. This situation is represented in Figure 1(b) by stock option 2 with high strike price P_2^S. That figure depicts two possible distributions (densities) for the realized price P depending on whether a safe or a risky strategy is selected. The value of this out-of-the money option is then much higher under a risky strategy than under a safe one.[37] The manager's benefit from gambling is much lower when the option is in the money (say, at strike price P_1^S in the figure).[38]

---

[34] In the United States, stock option plans, when granted, are most often at-the-money options.

[35] We ignore tax considerations. Needless to say, these may play a role. For example, in the United States (and at the time of writing, accounting rules are likely to change in the near future), stock options grants, unlike stock grants, create no accounting expense for the firm.

[36] There is a large literature on hedging by risk-averse agents (see, for example, Anderson and Danthine 1980, 1981).

[37] Whether the manager is better off under the risky strategy depends on her risk aversion. However, if a) the manager is risk neutral or mildly risk averse and b) the risky strategy is a mean-preserving spread or more generally increases risk without reducing the mean too much relative to the safe strategy, then the manager will prefer the risky strategy.

[38] In the figure, option 1 is almost a straight stock in that it is very unlikely that the option turns out to be valueless.

FIGURE 1   Straight Shares and Stock Options

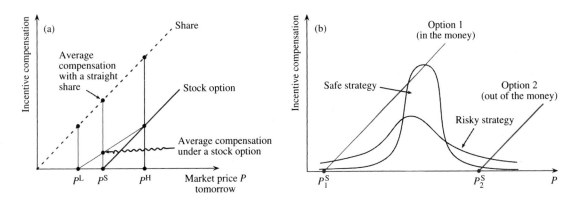

(a) Expected rents (P^L: low price (option "out of the money"); P^S: strike price; P^H: high price (option "in the money")).
(b) Risk preferences under a stock option.

Another issue with "underwater options" relates to their credibility. Once the options are out of the money, they either induce top management to leave or create low or perverse incentives, as we just saw. They may be repriced (the exercise price is adjusted downward) or new options may be granted.[39] To some extent, such *ex post* adjustments undermine *ex ante* incentives by refraining from punishing management for poor performance.[40]

In contrast, when the option is largely "in the money," that is, when it looks quite likely that the market price will exceed the exercise price, a stock option has a similar incentive impact as a straight share but provides management with a lower rent, namely, the difference between market and exercise price rather than the full market price.

The question of the efficient mix of options and stocks is still unsettled. Unsurprisingly, while stock options remain very popular, some companies, such as DaimlerChrysler, Deutsche Telekom, and Microsoft, have abandoned them, usually to replace them by stocks (as in the case of Microsoft).

The executive compensation controversy. There has been a trend in executive compensation towards higher compensation as well as stronger performance linkages. This trend has resulted in a public outcry. Yet some have argued that the performance linkage is insufficient. In a paper whose inferences created controversy, Jensen and Murphy (1990) found a low sensitivity of CEO compensation to firm performance (see also Murphy 1985, 1999). Looking at a sample of the CEOs of the 250 largest publicly traded American firms, they found that a) the median public corporation CEO holds 0.25% of his/her firm's equity and b) a $1,000 increase in shareholder wealth corresponds on average to a $3.25 increase in total CEO compensation (stock and stock options, increase in this

---

[39] Consider, for example, Ascend Communications (*New York Times*, July 15, 1998, D1). In 1998, its stock price fell from $80 to $23 within four months. The managerial stock options had strike prices ranging up to $114 per share. The strike price was reduced twice during that period for different kinds of options (to $35 a share and to $24.50, respectively).

[40] At least, if the initial options were structured properly. If repricing only reflects general market trends (after all, more than half of the stock options were out of the money in 2002), repricing may be less objectionable (although the initial package is still objectionable, to the extent that it would have rewarded management for luck).

For theories of renegotiation of managerial compensation and its impact on moral hazard, see Fudenberg and Tirole (1990) and Hermalin and Katz (1991).

and next year's salary, change in expected dismissal penalties). This sounds tiny. Suppose that your grocer kept 0.3 cents out of any extra $1 in net profit, and gave 99.7 cents to other people. One might imagine that the grocer would start eating the apples on the fruit stand. Jensen and Murphy argue that CEO incentives not to waste shareholder value are too small.

Jensen and Murphy's conclusion sparked some controversy, though. First, managerial risk aversion and the concomitant diminishing marginal utility of income implies that strong management incentives are costly to the firm's owners. Indeed, Haubrich (1994) shows that the low pay-performance sensitivity pointed out by Jensen and Murphy is consistent with relatively low levels of managerial risk aversion, such as an index of relative risk aversion of about 5. Intuitively, changes in the value of large companies can have a very large impact on CEO performance-based compensation even for low sensitivity levels. Second, the CEO is only one of many employees in the firm. And so, despite the key executive responsibilities of the CEO, other parties have an important impact on firm performance. Put another way, overall performance results from the combined effort and talent of the CEO, other top executives, engineers, marketers, and blue-collar workers, not to mention the board of directors, suppliers, distributors, and other "external" parties. In the economic jargon, the joint performance creates a "moral hazard in teams," in which many parties concur to a common final outcome. Ignoring risk aversion, the only way to properly incentivize all these parties is to promise each $1,000 any time the firm's value increases by $1,000. This is unrealistic, if anything because the payoff must be shared with the financiers.[41] Third, the work of Hall and Liebman (1998) cited earlier, using a more recent dataset (1980 to 1994), points to a substantial increase in performance-based compensation, which made Jensen and Murphy's estimates somewhat obsolete. They find that the mean (median) change in CEO wealth is $25 ($5.30) per $1,000 increase in firm value.

2.3 Implicit Incentives

Managers are naturally concerned about keeping their job. Poor performance may induce the board to remove the CEO and the group of top executives. The board either voluntarily fires the manager, or, often, does so under the implicit or explicit pressure of shareholders observing a low stock price or a low profit. Poor performance may also generate a takeover or a proxy fight, or else may drive a fragile firm into bankruptcy and reorganization. Finally, there is evidence that the fraction of independent directors rises after poor performance, so that top management is on a tighter leash if it keeps its position (Hermalin and Weisbach 1988). There is substantial normative appeal for these observations: efficient contracting indeed usually requires that poor performance makes it less likely that managers keep their position, more likely that they be starved of liquidity, and more likely that they surrender control rights or that control rights be reshuffled among investors towards ones who are less congruent with management, i.e., debtholders.

There is a fair amount of evidence that executive turnover in the United States is correlated with poor performance, using either stock or accounting data

---

[41] Suppose a "source" (i.e., an outside financier) brings $(n-1)$ thousand dollars to the firm for any $1,000 increase in firm value, so that the n parties responsible for the firm's overall performance receive $1,000 each. First, this financing source would be likely not to be able to break even, since the n insiders would be unable to pay out money in the case of poor performance. Second, the n insiders could collude against the source (e.g., borrow one dollar to receive n dollars from the source).

FIGURE 2   Top Executive Turnover and Stock Returns

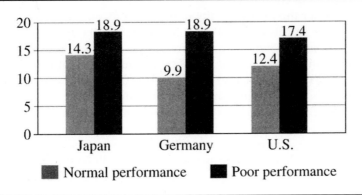

Source: Built from data in Kaplan (1994a,b).

(see Kojima (1997, p. 63) and Subramanian et al. (2002) for a list of relevant articles). The sensitivity of CEO removal to performance is higher for firms with more outside directors (Weisbach 1988) and smaller in firms run by founders (Morck et al. 1989). Thus, a tight external monitoring and a less complacent board are conducive to managerial turnover after a poor performance.

Perhaps more surprisingly in view of the substantial institutional differences, the relationship between poor performance and top executive turnover is similar in the United States, Germany, and Japan: see Figure 2, drawn from the work of Kaplan. More recent research (see, for example, Goyal and Park 2002) has confirmed the dual pattern of an increase in forced executive turnover in the wake of poor performance and of an increased sensitivity of this relationship when there are few insiders on the board.

The threat of bankruptcy also keeps managers on their toes. Even in the United States, a country with limited creditor protection and advantageous treatment of managers during restructurings,[42] 52% of financially distressed firms experience a senior management turnover as opposed to 19% for firms with comparably poor stock performance but not in financial distress (Gilson 1989).

Are explicit and implicit incentives complements or substitutes? The threat of dismissal or other interferences resulting from poor performance provides incentives for managers over and beyond those provided by explicit incentives. Explicit and implicit incentives are therefore substitutes: with stronger implicit incentives, fewer stocks and stock options are needed to curb managerial moral hazard. While this substitution effect is real,[43] the strengths of implicit and explicit incentives are codetermined by sources of heterogeneity in the sample and so other factors impact the observed relationship between implicit and explicit incentives (the survey by Chiappori and Salanié (2003) provides an

---

[42] Under U.S. law's Chapter 11, which puts a hold on creditor claims, the firm is run as a going concern and no receiver is designated.

[43] Gibbons and Murphy (1992) analyze the impact of implicit incentives on optimal explicit incentive contracts in a different context. They posit career concerns *à la* Holmström (1982b): successful employees receive with a lag external offers, forcing their firm to raise their wage to keep them. Their model has a fixed horizon (and so does not apply as it stands to the executive turnover issue); it shows that implicit and explicit incentives are indeed substitutes: as the employee gets closer to retirement, career concerns decrease and the employer must raise the power of the explicit incentive scheme. Gibbons and Murphy further provide empirical support for this theoretical prediction.

extensive discussion of the need to take account of unobserved heterogeneity in the econometrics of contracts).

First, consider the heterogeneity in the intensity of financial constraints. A recurrent theme of this book will be that the tighter the financing constraint, the more concessions the borrower must make in order to raise funds. And concessions tend to apply across the board. Concessions of interest here are reductions in performance-based pay and in the ability to retain one's job after poor performance, two contracting attributes valued by the executive. Thus, a tightly financially constrained manager will accept both a lower level of performance-based rewards and a smaller probability of keeping her job after a poor performance, where the probability of turnover is determined by the composition of the board, the presence of takeover defenses, the specification of termination rights (in the case of venture capital or alliance financing) and other contractual arrangements. The heterogeneity in the intensity of financial constraints then predicts a positive comovement of turnover under poor performance and low-powered incentives. Implicit and explicit incentives then appear to be complements in the sample.

Second, consider adverse selection, that is, the existence of an asymmetry of information between the firm and its investors. Investors are uncertain about the likely performance of the executive. An executive who is confident about the firm's future prospects knows that she is relatively unlikely to achieve a poor performance, and so accepting a high turnover in the case of poor performance is less costly than it would be if she were less confident in her talent or had unfavorable information about the firm's prospects. Thus, the confident executive is willing to trade off a high performance-based reward against an increased turnover probability in the case of poor performance. By contrast, less confident managers put more weight on their tenure and less on monetary compensation. The prediction is then one of a negative covariation between turnover in the case of poor performance[44] and low-powered incentives. Put differently, implicit and explicit incentives come out as being substitutes in the sample.[45]

Interestingly, Subramanian et al. (2002) find that, in their sample, CEOs with greater explicit incentives also face less secure jobs.

2.4 Monitoring

Monitoring of corporations is performed by a variety of external (nonexecutive) parties such as boards of directors, auditors, large shareholders, large creditors, investment banks, and rating agencies. To understand the actual design of monitoring structures, it is useful to distinguish between two forms of monitoring, active and speculative, on the basis of two types of monitoring information, prospective and retrospective.

Active monitoring consists in interfering with management in order to increase the value of the investors' claims. An active monitor collects information that some policy proposed or followed by management (e.g., the refusal to sell the firm to a high bidder or to divest some noncore assets) is value-decreasing and intervenes to prevent or correct this policy. In extreme cases, the intervention may be the removal of current management and its replacement by a new man-

---

[44] Note that this is indeed a *conditional* probability: confident managers are less likely to reach a poor performance.

[45] The theoretical model in Subramanian et al. (2002) emphasizes a third consideration by making learning from performance about talent sensitive to managerial effort. Then a high-powered incentive scheme, by increasing effort, also increases the informativeness of performance. This increased informativeness, if turnover is otherwise unlikely due to switching costs, in turn may raise turnover. Put differently, the manager is more likely to be found untalented if she exerts a high effort and fails.

agement more able to handle the firm's future environment. Active monitoring is *forward looking* and analyzes the firm's past actions only to the extent that they can still be altered to raise firm value or that they convey information (say, about the ability of current management) on which one can act to improve the firm's prospects.

The mechanism by which the change is implemented depends on the identity of the active monitor. A large shareholder may sit on the board and intervene in that capacity. An institutional investor in the United States or a bank holding a sizeable number of the firm's shares as custodian in Germany may intervene in the general assembly by introducing resolutions on particular corporate policy issues; or perhaps they may be able to convince management to alter its policy under the threat of intervention at the general meeting. A raider launches a takeover and thereby attempts to gain control over the firm. Lastly, creditors in a situation of financial distress or a receiver in bankruptcy force concessions on management.

While active monitoring is intimately linked to the exercise of control rights, *speculative monitoring* is not. Furthermore, speculative monitoring is partly *backward looking* in that it does not attempt to increase firm value, but rather to measure this value, which reflects not only exogenous prospects but also past managerial investments. The object of speculative monitoring is thus to "take a picture" of the firm's position at a given moment in time, that is, to take stock of the previous and current management's accomplishments to date. This information is used by the speculative monitor in order to adjust his position in the firm (invest further, stay put, or disengage), or else to recommend or discourage investment in the firm to investors. The typical speculative monitor is the stock market analyst, say, working for a passive institutional investor, who studies firms in order to maximize portfolio return without any intent to intervene in the firms' management.

But, as the examples above suggest, it would be incorrect to believe that speculative monitoring occurs only in stock markets. A short-term creditor's strategy is to disengage from the firm, namely, to refuse to roll over the debt, whenever he receives bad news about the firm's capacity to reimburse its debt. Or, to take other examples, an investment bank that recommends purchasing shares in a company or a rating agency that grades a firm's public debt both look at the firm's expected value and do not attempt to interfere in the firm's management in order to raise this value. They simply take a picture of the firms' resources and prospects in order to formulate their advice.

Another seemingly unusual category of speculative monitoring concerns legal suits by shareholders (or by attorneys on behalf of shareholders) against directors. Like other instances of speculative monitoring, legal suits are based on backward-looking information, namely, the information that the directors have not acted in the interest of the corporation in the past; per se they are not meant to enhance future value, but rather to sanction past underperformance. Two kinds of legal suits are prominent in the United States: class-action suits on behalf of shareholders, and derivative suits on behalf of the corporation (that is, mainly shareholders, but also creditors and other stakeholders to the extent that their claim is performance-sensitive), which receives any ensuing benefits.

It is worth mentioning here that speculative monitoring does discipline management in several ways. Speculative monitoring in the stock market makes the firm's stock value informative about past performance; this value is used directly to reward management through stock options and, indirectly, to force reluctant boards to admit poor performance and put pressure on or remove management. Speculative monitoring by short-term creditors, investment banks, or rating agencies drains liquidity from (or restricts funding to) poorly performing firms. Either way, speculative monitoring helps keep managers on their toes.

A second and important point is that monitoring is performed by a large number of other "eyeballs": besides stock analysts, rating agencies assess the strength of new issues. Auditors certify the accounts, which in part requires discretionary assessments such as when they evaluate illiquid assets or contingent liabilities. A long-standing issue has resurfaced with the recent scandals. These eyeballs may face substantial *conflicts of interest* that may alter their assessment (indeed, many reform proposals suggest reducing these conflicts of interest). For example, a bank's analysts may overhype a firm's stocks to investors in order to please the firm from which the investment banking branch tries to win business in mergers and acquisitions and in security underwriting.[46]

Accountants may face similar conflicts of interest if they also, directly or indirectly, act as directors, brokers, underwriters, suppliers of management or tax consulting services, and so forth.[47] Unsurprisingly, a number of countries (e.g., United States, United Kingdom, Italy) have moved from self-regulation of the accounting profession to some form of government regulation. In the United States, the Sarbanes-Oxley Act of 2002 created a regulatory body[48] to set rules for, inspect, and impose penalties on public accounting firms.[49]

2.5 Product-Market Competition

It is widely agreed that the quality of a firm's management is not solely determined by its design of corporate governance, but also depends on the firm's competitive environment. Product-market competition matters for several reasons. First, as already mentioned, close competitors offer a yardstick against which the firm's quality of management can be measured. It is easier for management to attribute poor performance to bad luck when the firm faces very idiosyncratic circumstances, say, because it is a monopoly in its market, than when competitors presumably facing similar cost and demand conditions are doing well. There is no arguing that this benchmarking is used, at least implicitly, in the assessment of managerial performance.

Actually, product-market competition improves performance measurement even if the competitors' actual performance is not observed.[50] The very existence of product-market competition tends to filter out or attenuate the exogenous shocks faced by the firm. Suppose the demand in the market is high or the cost of supplies low. The management of a firm in a monopoly position then benefits substantially from the favorable conditions. It can either transform these favor-

[46] For example, Merrill Lynch was imposed a $100 million penalty by the New York Attorney General (2002) when internal emails by analysts described as "junk" stocks they were pushing at the time. Merrill Lynch promised, among other things, to delink analyst compensation and investment banking (*Business Week*, October 7, 2002). In the same year, Citigroup, or rather its affiliate, Salomon Smith Barney, was under investigation for conflicts between stock research and investment banking activities.

[47] In 2001, nonaudit fees made up for over 50% of the fees paid to accounting firms by 28 of the 30 companies constituting the Dow Jones Industrial Average. The California Public Employees' Retirement System (CalPERS) announced that it would vote against the reappointment of auditors who also provide consulting services to the firm.

[48] The Public Company Accounting Oversight Board, overseen by the SEC.

[49] DeMarzo et al. (2005) argue that self-regulation leads to lenient supervision. Pagano and Immordino (2004), building on Dye (1993), explicitly model management advisory services as bribes to auditors and study the optimal regulatory environment under potential collusion between firms and their auditors. They show that good corporate governance reduces the incentive to collude and calls for more demanding auditing standards.

[50] This argument is drawn from Rey and Tirole (1986), who, in the context of the choice between exclusive territories and competition between retailers, argue that competition acts as an insurance device and thus boosts incentives. Hermalin (1992) and Scharfstein (1988) study the impact of product-market competition on the agency cost in a Holmström (1979) principal-agent framework.

able circumstances into substantial monetary rents if its compensation is very sensitive to profits, or it can enjoy an easy life while still reaching a decent performance, or both. This is not so for a competitive firm. Suppose, for instance, that production costs are low. While they are low for the firm, they are also low for the other firms in the industry, which are then fierce competitors; and so the management is less able to derive rents from the favorable environment.

Another related well-known mechanism through which product-market competition affects managerial incentives is the bankruptcy process. Management is concerned about the prospect of bankruptcy, which often implies the loss of the job and in any case a reduction in managerial prerogatives. To the extent that competition removes the cosy cash cushion enjoyed by a monopolist, competition keeps managers alert.[51]

While competition may have very beneficial effects on managerial incentives, it may also create perverse effects. For example, firms may gamble in order to "beat the market." A case in point is the intensely competitive market for fund management. Fund managers tend to be obsessed with their ranking in the industry, since this ranking determines the inflow of new investments into the funds and, to a lesser extent due to investor inertia, the flow of money out of the fund. This may induce fund managers to adopt strategies that focus on the ranking of the fund relative to competing funds rather than on the absolute return to investors.

It should also be realized that competition will never substitute for a proper governance structure. Investors bring money to a firm in exchange for an expected return whether the firm faces a competitive or protected environment. This future return can be squandered by management regardless of the competitiveness of the product market. And indeed, a number of recent corporate governance scandals (e.g., Barings, Credit Lyonnais, Gan, Banesto, Metallgesellschaft, Enron, WorldCom) have occurred in industries with relatively strong competition. Similarly, the reaction of the big three American automobile manufacturers to the potential and then actual competition from foreign producers was painfully slow.

THE BOARD OF DIRECTORS　　3

The board of directors[52] in principle monitors management on behalf of shareholders. It is meant to define or, more often, to approve major business decisions and corporate strategy: disposal of assets, investments or acquisitions, and tender

---

[51] Aghion et al. (1999) develop a Schumpeterian model in which management may be unduly reluctant to adopt new technologies, and show that a procompetition policy may improve incentives in those firms with poor governance structures.

[52] We will here be discussing the standard board structure. There are, of course, many variants. One variant that has received much attention is the German two-tier board. For instance, AGs (*Aktien-gesellschaften*) with more than 2,000 employees have a) a management board (*Vorstand*) with a leader (*Sprecher*) playing somewhat the role of a CEO and meeting weekly, say, and b) a supervisory board (*Aufsichtsrat*) meeting three or four times a year, appointing members of the Vorstand, and approving or disapproving accounts, dividends, and major asset acquisitions or disposals proposed by the Vorstand. The Vorstand is composed of full-time salaried executives with fixed-term contracts, who cannot be removed except in extreme circumstances, a feature that makes it difficult for an outsider to gain control over the firm.

Firm managers cannot be members of the Aufsichtsrat. Half of the members of the Aufsichtsrat are nonexecutive representatives of the shareholders, and half represents employees (both employee delegates and external members designated by trade unions). The shareholders' representatives are nonexecutives but they are not independent in the Anglo-Saxon sense since they often represent firms or banks with an important business relationship with the firm. The chairman is drawn from the shareholders' representatives, and breaks ties in case of a deadlock. For more detail about the German two-tier system, see, for example, Charkham (1994, Chapter 2), Edwards and Fischer (1994), Kojima (1997, Section 4.1.2), and Roe (2003).

offers made by acquirers. It is also in charge of executive compensation, oversight of risk management, and audits. Lastly, it can offer advice and connections to management. To accomplish these tasks, boards operate more and more often through committees such as the compensation, nominating, and audit committees. Boards have traditionally been described as ineffective rubber-stampers controlled by, rather than controlling, management. Accordingly, there have recently been many calls for more accountable boards.[53]

3.1 Boards of Directors: Watchdogs or Lapdogs?

The typical complaints about the indolent behavior of boards of directors can be found in Mace's (1971) classic book. Directors rarely cause trouble in board meetings for several reasons.

Lack of independence. A director is labeled "independent" if she is not employed by the firm, does not supply services to the firm, or more generally does not have a conflict of interest in the accomplishment of her oversight mission. In practice, though, directors often have such conflicts of interest. This is most obvious for insiders sitting on the board (executive directors), who clearly are simultaneously judge and party.[54] But nonexecutive directors are often not independent either. They may be hand-picked by management among friends outside the firm. They may be engaged in a business relationship with the firm, which they worry could be severed if they expressed opposition to management. They may belong to the same social network as the CEO.[55] Finally, they may receive "bribes" from the firm; for example, auditors may be asked to provide lucrative consultancy and tax services that induce them to stand with management.

In the United States, as in France, the chairman of the board (who, due to his powers, exercises a disproportionate influence on board meetings) is most often the firm's CEO, although the fraction of large corporations with a split-leadership structure has risen from an historical average of about one-fifth to

---

[53] In France, the corporate governance movement is scoring points, partly due to the increase in foreign shareholdings (70% of stock market value, but only 13% of the seats on the boards in 1997) and to privatizations. Firms publicize their compliance with the 1995 Viénot report setting up a code of behavior for boards. Yet, the corporate governance movement is still in its infancy. There are very few independent directors. A Vuchot-Ward-Howell study (cited by *La Tribune,* March 10, 1997) estimated that only 93 directors among the 541 directors of the largest publicly traded French corporations (CAC40) are independent (although French firms widely advertise "outside directors" as "independent directors"). Many are part of a club (and often went to the same schools and issued from the same corps of civil servants) sitting on each other's boards. The composition of board committees is not always disclosed. And general assemblies are still largely perfunctory, although minority shareholder movements are developing and recent votes demonstrate (minority) opposition to managerial proposals in a number of large companies.

[54] The argument that is sometimes heard that insiders should be board members (implying: with full voting rights) in order to bring relevant information when needed is not convincing, since insiders without voting rights could participate in part or all of the board meetings.

[55] Kramarz and Thesmar (2004) study social networks in French boardrooms. They identify three types of civil-service related social networks in business (more than half of the assets traded on the French stock market are managed by CEOs issued from the civil service). They find that CEOs appoint directors who belong to the same social network. Former civil servants are less likely to lose their job following a poor performance, and they are also more likely than other CEOs to become director of another firm when their own firm is doing badly.

Bertrand et al. (2004) investigates the consequences of French CEOs' political connections. There is a tight overlap between the CEOs and cabinet ministers, who often come from the same corps of civil servants or more generally belong to the same social networks associated with the Ecole Polytechnique or the Ecole Nationale d'Administration. Bertrand et al. find that firms managed by connected CEOs create more (destroy fewer) jobs in politically contested areas, and that the quid pro quo comes in the form of a privileged access to government subsidy programs.

one-third in 2004.[56] Nonexecutive chairmen are much more frequent in the United Kingdom (95% of all FTSE 350 companies in 2004) and in Germany and in the Netherlands (100% in both countries), which have a two-tier board.

An executive chairmanship obviously strengthens the insiders' hold on the board of directors. Another factor of executive control over the board is the possibility of mutual interdependence of CEOs. This factor may be particularly relevant for continental Europe and Japan, where cross-shareholdings within broadly defined "industrial groups" or keiretsus in Japan creates this interdependence. But, even in the United States, where cross-shareholdings are much rarer, CEOs may sit on each others' boards (even perhaps on each others' compensation committees!).

Insufficient attention. Outside directors are also often carefully chosen so as to be overcommitted. Many outside directors in the largest U.S. corporations are CEOs of other firms. Besides having a full workload in their own company, they may sit on a large number of boards. In such circumstances, they may come to board meetings (other than their own corporation's) unprepared and they may rely entirely on the (selective) information disclosed by the firm's management.

Insufficient incentives. Directors' compensation has traditionally consisted for the most part of fees and perks. There has often been a weak link between firm performance and directors' compensation, although there is a trend in the United States towards increasing compensation in the form of stock options for directors.[57]

Explicit compensation is, of course, only part of the directors' monetary incentives. They may be sued by shareholders (say, through a class-action suit in the United States). But, four factors mitigate the effectiveness of liability suits. First, while courts penalize extreme forms of moral hazard such as fraud, they are much more reluctant to engage in business judgments about, say, whether an investment or an acquisition *ex ante* made good economic sense. Judges are not professional managers and they have limited knowledge of past industry conditions. They therefore do not want to be drawn into telling managers and directors how they should run their companies. Since corporate charters almost always eliminate director liability for breaches of duty of care, it is difficult for shareholders and other stakeholders to bring a suit against board members. Second, firms routinely buy liability insurance for their directors.[58] Third, liabilities, if any, are often paid by the firms, which indemnify directors who have acted in good faith. Fourth, plaintiff's lawyers may be inclined to buy off directors (unless they are extremely wealthy) in order to settle. Overall, for Black et al. (2004), as long as outside directors refrain from enriching themselves at the expense of the company, the risk of having to pay damages or legal fees out of their own pocket

---

[56] According to a September 2004 study by Governance Metrics International, a corporate governance rating agency based in New York (cited in Felton and Wong 2004). Among the firms that have recently separated the roles of chairman and CEO are Dell, Boeing, Walt Disney, MCI, and Oracle.

[57] Yermack (2004b), looking at 766 outside directors in Fortune 500 firms between 1994 and 1996, estimates incentives from compensation, replacement, and opportunity to obtain other directorships. He finds that these incentives together yield 11 cents per $1,000 increase in firm value (shareholder wealth) to an outside director. Thus, performance-based incentives are not negligible for outside directors even though they remain much lower than those for CEOs (e.g., $5.29 per $1,000 increase in firm value for the median CEO in 1994, as reported by Hall and Liebman (1998)).

[58] As well as officers (these insurance policies are labeled directors and officers (D&O) insurance policies).

is very small in the United States,[59] as well as in other countries such as France, Germany, or Japan, where lawsuits are much rarer.

This undoing of the impact of liability suits has two perverse effects: it makes directors less accountable, and, in the case of indemnification by the firm, it deters shareholders from suing the directors since the fine paid in the case of a successful suit comes partly out of their pocket.

Avoidance of conflict. Except when it comes to firing management, it is hard even for independent directors to confront management; for, they are engaged in an ongoing relationship with top executives. A conflictual relationship is certainly unpleasant. And, perhaps more fundamentally, such a relationship is conducive neither to the management's listening to the board's advice nor to the disclosure to the board of key information.

In view of these considerations, it may come as a surprise that boards have any effectiveness. Boards actually do interfere in some decisions. They do remove underperforming managers, as we discussed in Section 2. They may also refuse to side with management during takeover contests. A well-known case in point is the 1989 RJR Nabisco leveraged buy-out (LBO) in which a group headed by the CEO made an initial bid and the outside directors insisted on auctioning off the company, resulting in a much more attractive purchase by an outsider.

It should be realized, though, that the cozy relationship between directors and management is likely to break down mainly during crises. Directors are then more worried about liability and more exposed to the spotlight. Furthermore, their relationship with management has shorter prospects than during good times. And, indeed, directors have historically been less effective in preventing management from engaging in wasteful diversification or in forcing it to disgorge excess cash than in removing underperforming managers. Relatedly, there is evidence that decreases in the share price lead to an increase in board activity, as measured by the annual number of board meetings (Vafeas 1999).

Bebchuk and Fried (2004) offer a scathing view of board behavior. They argue that most directors choose to collude with CEOs rather than accomplish their role of guardian of shareholders' interests. Directors dislike haggling with or being "disloyal" to the CEO, have little time to intervene, and further receive a number of favors from the CEO: the CEO can place them on the company's slate, increasing seriously their chance of reelection, give them perks, business deals (perhaps after they have been nominated on the board, so that they are formally "independent"), extra compensation on top of the director fee, and charitable contributions to nonprofit organizations headed by directors, or reciprocate the lenient oversight in case of interlocking directorates. A key argument of Bebchuk and Fried's book is that the rents secured by directors for the CEO involve substantial "camouflage"; that is, these rents should be as discrete or complex as possible so as to limit "outrage costs" and backlash. This camouflage yields inefficient compensation for officers. For example, compensation committees[60] fail to filter out stock price rises or general market trends and use conventional stock-option plans (as discussed in Section 2); and they grant substantial ability to managers to

---

[59] It was a shock to directors when ten former executive directors of WorldCom agreed to pay a total of $18 million from their own savings and ten former Enron directors paid $13 million (still, the insurance companies are expected to pay out the bulk of the money: $36 million for WorldCom and $155 million for Enron (*The Economist*, January 15, 2005, p. 65). It is hard to predict whether this indicates a new trend, as these cases involved extreme misbehaviors.

D&O insurance policies are less prevalent in Europe because of the lower probability of lawsuits, but they are likely to become very widespread as lawsuits become more common.

[60] Despite their independence (in the United States, and unlike for some other committees, such as the nomination committee, directors sitting on the compensation committee are mostly independent directors).

unload their options and shares. They also grant large cash payments in the case of an acquisition, generous retirement programs, and follow-on consulting contracts. Directors also happily acquiesce to takeover defenses.[61]

3.2 Reforming the Board

The previous description of indolent boards almost smacks of conspiracy theory. Managers carefully recommend for board nomination individuals who either have conflicts of interest or are overcommitted enough that they will be forced to rubberstamp the management's proposals at the board meetings. And managers try to remove incentives to monitor by giving directors performance-insensitive compensation and by insuring them against liability suits, and "bribe" them in the various ways described in Bebchuk and Fried's book. Most of these managerial moves must, of course, be approved by the board itself, but board members may find their own benefit to colluding with management at the expense of shareholders.

While there is obviously some truth in this description, things are actually more complex for a couple of reasons.

Teammates or referees? As we observed, board members may actually be in an uncomfortable situation in which they attempt to cooperate with top executives while interfering with their decisions. Such relationships are necessarily strenuous. These different functions may sometimes conflict. The advisory role requires the directors be supplied with information that the top management may be unwilling to disclose if this information is also used to monitor and interfere with management.[62]

Knowledge versus independence? Parties close to the firm, and therefore susceptible to conflict of interest, are also likely to be the best informed about the firm and its environment. Similarly, professional managers are likely to be good monitors of their peers, even though they have an undue tendency to identify with the monitored.

What link from performance to board compensation? Providing directors with stock options rather than fixed fees goes in the right direction, but, for the same reasons as for managers, stock options have their own limitations. In particular, if managers go for a risky strategy that reduces investor value but raises the value of their stock options, directors may have little incentive to oppose the move if they themselves are endowed with stock options. Similarly, directors' exposure to liability suits has costs. While the current system of liability insurance clearly impairs incentives, exposing directors fully to liability suits could easily induce them to behave in a very conservative fashion or (for the most talented ones) to turn down directorial jobs.

With these caveats in mind, there is still ample scope for board reform. Save a few legal and regulatory rules (such as the 1978 New York Stock Exchange rule that listed firms must have audit committees made up of nonexecutives), directors and managers faced few constraints in the composition and governance of boards. New regulations and laws may help in this respect, but, as usual, one must ask whether government intervention is warranted; in particular, one should wonder why the corporate charter designers do not themselves draw better rules for their boards, and, relatedly, why more decentralized solutions

---

[61] Another example of "camouflaged rent" is the granting of executive loans, now prohibited by the 2002 Sarbanes-Oxley Act.

[62] Adams and Ferreira (2003) build a model of board composition based on this premise and show that, in some circumstances, a management-friendly board may be optimal.

cannot be found, in which shareholders force (provided they have the means to) boards to behave better. That is, with better information of and coordination among shareholders, capital market pressure may be sufficient to move boards in the right direction.

In this spirit, several study groups produced codes of good conduct or of best practice for boards (e.g., the 1992 Cadbury report in the United Kingdom and the 1995 Viénot report in France). Abstracts from the Cadbury report are reproduced at the end of this reading. Among other proposals, the Cadbury report calls for a) the nomination of a recognized senior outside member where the chairman of the board is the CEO,[63] b) a procedure for directors to take independent professional advice at the company's expense, c) a majority of independent directors (namely, nonexecutive directors free from business relationship with the firm), and d) a compensation committee dominated by nonexecutive directors and an audit committee conferred to nonexecutive directors, most of whom should be independent. In contrast, the Cadbury report recommends against performance-based compensation of directors.

In the United States, the largest public pension fund, CalPERS, with $165.3 billion in assets in August 2004, drew in the mid 1990s a more ambitious list of 37 principles of good practice for a corporate board, 23 "fundamental" and 14 "ideal." CalPERS would like the companies to consider the ideal principles, such as a limit on the number of directors older than 70, but has stated it would be more open-minded on these principles than on the fundamental ones. CalPERS monitors the companies' compliance (in spirit, if not the letter) with these principles and publicizes the results, so as to generate proxy votes for companies that comply least. As of 1997, most firms failed to comply with a substantial number of CalPERS criteria, although some of these criteria were usually satisfied by most corporations (see Table 1).

While the CalPERS list is stringent and some of its criteria controversial, it illustrates well the investors' current pressure for more accountable boards.

More recently, in the wake of the many corporate scandals at the turn of the century, expert recommendations regarding the board of directors have been bolder. For example, they suggest regular meetings of the board or specific committees in the absence of executives, a policy already adopted by a number of corporations.[64] Such meetings promote truth telling and reduce individual directors' concern about the avoidance of conflict with management. A number of experts have also recommended self-evaluation of boards; for example, at regular intervals the director with the worst "grade" would be fired.[65] There have also been calls for strict limits (e.g., three) on the number of board mandates that a director can accept, for limited director tenures, and for a mandatory retirement age.

Monetary incentives have also been put forward. The directors' compensation would be more systematically related to the firm's stock value. Here the recommendation is for directors to hold a minimum number of shares in the firm.[66]

---

[63] The U.K. Combined Code (the successor to the Cadbury Code) states that chairman should be independent at the time of appointment.

[64] Korn/Ferry International (2003) estimated that in 2003 87% of U.S. Fortune 1000 boards held Executive Sessions without their CEO present. By contrast, only 4% of Japanese boards gather without the CEO present.

[65] In 2003, 29% of U.S. boards (41% in Asia Pacific) conducted individual director evaluation reviews (Korn/Ferry International 2003).

[66] An example often cited by the proponents of this view is that of G. Wilson, who was for twelve years director of the Disney Corporation and held no share of Disney despite a personal wealth exceeding $500 million!

TABLE 1	Compliance of U.S. Companies with a Few CalPERS Criteria in 1997	
Has outside chairman		5%
Only one insider on the board		18%
Some form of mandatory retirement for directors		18%
Independent nominating committee		38%
Fewer than 10% of directors over 70		68%
Independent governance committee		68%
No retired chief executive on the board		82%
Independent ethics committee		85%
Independent audit committee		86%
A majority of outside directors on the board		90%
Independent compensation committee		91%

Source: Analysis by the *New York Times* (August 3, 1997) of data compiled by Directorship from the 861 public companies on the Fortune 1000 list. "Independent" here means "composed of outside directors."

Some experts[67] have proposed a direct or intermediated (through an ombudsman) access of whistle-blowers to independent directors. This is probably a good suggestion, although it has one flaw and its impact is likely to be limited for two reasons. The drawback of whistleblowing is that companies react to its threat by a) intensively screening employees in order to pick those who are likely to prove "loyal," and b) reducing information flows within the firm, which reduces the benefit of whistleblowing in terms of transparency and accountability.[68] Second, employees have relatively low incentives to blow the whistle. If discovered by the company (even formal anonymity does not guarantee that there will not be suspicion about the source of information), they will probably be fired. And whistleblowers notoriously have a hard time finding a new job in other firms who fear that they will blow the whistle again.[69] In particular, employers

---

[67] See, for example, *Getting Governance Right*, McKinsey Quarterly, 2002.

[68] More generally, a cost of using informers is that it destroys trust in social groups, as has been observed in totalitarian regimes (e.g., in Eastern Germany, where people were concerned that family members or friends would report them to the Stasi).

[69] Consider the example of Christine Casey, who blew the whistle on Mattel, the toy manufacturer, which reported very inflated sales forecasts to its shareholders (see, for example, *The Economist*, January 18, 2003, p. 60). Some managers kept two sets of figures, and consistently misled investors. In February 1999, Ms. Casey approached a Mattel director. After being screamed at by executives and basically demoted, in September 1999, she telephoned the SEC. She ended up resigning, filed an unsuccessful lawsuit against Mattel, and in 2003 was still without a job.

Zingales (2004) reviews the (rather bleak) evidence on what happens to whistleblowers after they have denounced management and after they quit their firm. To counteract the strong incentives not to blow the whistle, he proposes that whistleblowers receive a fraction (say, 10%) of all fees and legal awards imposed on the company (with, of course, some punishments for frivolous whistleblowing and a requirement to denounce to the SEC rather than in public). Such rewards already exist for people who help the U.S. government to recover fraudulent gains by private agents at its expense (whistleblowers are entitled to between 15% and 30%).

Friebel and Guriev (2004) argue that internal incentives are designed so as to limit whistleblowing. In their theoretical model, division managers may have evidence that top managers are inflating earnings. Top management, however, provides lower level managers with a pay structure similar to theirs so as to make them allies. Friebel and Guriev thus provide an explanation for the propagation of short-term incentives in corporate hierarchies.

routinely check prospective employees' litigation record. The proposal of letting whistleblowers have a direct or indirect access to independent directors is therefore likely to be most effective when a) the sensitive information is held by a number of employees, so that whistleblower anonymity can really be preserved, and b) the directors can check the veracity of the information independently, that is, without resorting to the whistleblower. Lastly, it must be the case that directors pay attention to the information that they receive from the whistleblower (the Enron board failed to follow up on allegations by a whistleblower). For this, they must not be swamped by tons of frivolous whistleblowing messages; and, of course, they must have incentives to exercise their corporate governance rights.

Lastly, the Sarbanes-Oxley Act (2002) in the United States requires the audit committee to hire the outside auditor and to be composed only of directors who have no financial dealing with the firm. It also makes the board more accountable for misreporting.

3.3 A Few Final Comments

Scope of codes. First, codes are not solely preoccupied with boards of directors. They also include, for example, recommendations regarding reporting (auditor governance, financial reporting), executive compensation, shareholders voting, or antitakeover defenses. Second, they are now commonplace. As of 2004, fifty countries had their own code of governance, emanating from regulators, investor associations, the industry itself, or supranational organizations. They differ across countries as shown by Table 2, which reports some key features of a few recently drawn codes.

Do codes matter? Codes are only recommendations and have no binding character. Probably the main reason why they seem to have an impact is that they educate the general public, including investors. To the extent that they are drawn by expert and independent bodies they carry (real) authority in indicating the conditions that are conducive to efficient governance. They further focus the debate on pointing at some "reasonable" or "normal" practices, a deviation from which ought to be explained. For example, it is often asserted that the 1992 Cadbury Code of Best Practice, by pointing at the cost of conflating the positions of chairman of the board and CEO, was instrumental in moving the fraction of the top U.K. companies that operated a separation from 50 to 95% in 2004. In performing this educative role, the codes finally may help the corresponding practices enjoy the "network externalities" inherent in familiar institutions: investors, judges, and regulators in charge of enforcing the laws gain expertise in the understanding of the meaning and implications of most often used charters; contractual deviations by individual firms therefore run the risk of facing a lack of familiarity by these parties.

Do codes suffice? Unlike codes, corporate laws do have a binding impact on the design of corporate charters, even though the exact nature of the regulatory constraint is subject to debate as courts are sometimes willing to accept contractual innovations in corporate charters in which the parties opt out of the legal rules and set different terms.[70] In the long-standing normative debate on contractual freedom in corporate law, there is relative agreement on the usefulness of corporate law as creating a default point that lowers the cost of contracting for all parties who do not want to spend considerable resources into drafting

---

[70] On the role of courts, see, for example, Coffee (1989).

TABLE 2	Some Recent Codes of Good Governance					
	Independent Directors?	Separation of Chairman-CEO Roles?	Rotation of External Auditor?	Frequency of Financial Reporting?	"Comply or Explain" Requirement?	Selected Country-Specific Governance Issues
Brazil						
CVM Code (2002)	As many as possible	Clear preference for split	Not covered	Quarterly	No	Adoption of IAS/U.S. GAAP[a] Fiscal boards[b] Tag-along rights[c]
France						
Bouton Report (2002)	At least one-half of board	No recommendation	Regularly, for lead auditors	No recommendation given	No	Dual statutory auditors
Russia						
CG Code (2002)	At least one-quarter of board	Split required by law	Not covered	Quarterly	No	Managerial boards
Singapore						
CG Committee (2001)	At least one-third of board	Recommended	Not covered	Quarterly	Yes	Disclosure of pay for family members of directors/CEOs
United Kingdom						
Cadbury Code (1992)	Majority of nonexecutive directors	Recommended	Periodically, for lead auditors	Semiannually	Yes	
Combined Code (2003)	At least one-half of board	Clear preference for split	Not covered[b]	Semiannually, per listing rules	Yes	
United States						
Conference Board (2003)	Substantial majority of board	Separation is one of three acceptable options	Recommended for audit firm[c]	Quarterly, as required by law	No	

[a] IAS. International Accounting Standards; GAAP, generally accepted accounting principles; fiscal boards are akin to audit committees, but members are appointed by shareholders; tag-along rights protect minority shareholders by giving them the right to participate in transactions between large shareholders and third parties.

[b] In the United Kingdom, the accounting profession's self-regulatory body requires rotation of lead audit partner every seven years. Combined Code recommends that companies annually determine auditor's policy on partner rotation.

[c] Sarbanes-Oxley Act requires rotation of lead audit *partner* every five years. Circumstances that warrant changing auditor *firm* include audit relationship in excess of ten years, former partner of audit firm employed by company, and provision of significant nonaudit services.

Source: Coombes and Wong (2004).

agreements.[71] Legal experts in contrast disagree on the desirability of the compulsory nature of the law. Advocates of deregulation, such as Easterbrook and Fischel (1989), argue that one size does not fit all and that a mandatory law at the very least prevents contractual innovations that would benefit all parties; they may further argue that existing rules need not be optimal even in the set of rigid rules. Others are opposed to permitting shareholders to opt out from the mandatory core of corporate law. Arguments in favor of keeping corporate law mandatory include: the absence of some concerned parties at the initial bargaining table; the possibility that inefficient governance allows managers to change the rules of the game along the way thanks to investors' apathy,[72] and the possibility that asymmetric information at the initial contracting stage engenders dissipative costs.

Even if it is not mandatory, corporate law matters for roughly the same reasons that codes are relevant. First, the transaction costs of contracting around the default point may be substantial. Second, there are the "network externalities" alluded to above in the context of codes. In particular, abiding by the statutes provides for a more competent enforcement by the legal infrastructure. These network externalities could, of course, suggest an equilibrium focus on contractual provisions that differ from existing rules; but the existence of transaction costs (the first argument) tends to make the rule a focal point.

Finally, note that a state or a country's codes and legal rules matter most when firms cannot choose where to incorporate and/or be listed. Competition among codes and legal rules[73] encourages international convergence towards standards that facilitate the corporations' access to financing (although firms' interests with respect to the regulatory environment may not be aligned).

4   INVESTOR ACTIVISM

Active monitors intervene in such matters as the firm's strategic decisions, investments, and asset sales, managerial compensation, design of takeover defenses, and board size and composition. We first describe various forms of investor activism, leaving aside takeovers and bank monitoring, which will be discussed in latter sections. We then point to a number of limitations of investor activism.

4.1 Investor Activism Comes in Many Guises

Active monitoring requires control. Monitoring per se does not alter corporate policy. In order to implement new ideas, or to oppose bad policies of managers, the active monitor must have *control*. Control can come in two forms:[74] formal and

---

[71] On this, see, for example, Ayres and Germer (1989, 1992). Easterbrook and Fischel (1989), among others, point out that the story that corporate law is there to provide off-the-shelf terms for parties who want to economize on contracting costs is incomplete in that the default rules could be designed alternatively by law firms, corporate service bureaus, or investment banks. They argue nonetheless that the supply of default rules has the nature of a public good, if only because the court system can develop a set of precedents on how to deal with contract incompleteness.

[72] Bebchuk (1989) emphasizes that the questions of contractual freedom in the initial charter and in midstream (after the charter has been drawn) are different. The amendment process is imperfect, as the shareholders' insufficient incentive to become informed may not preclude value-decreasing amendments.

[73] There is a large literature on competition between legal environments. See, for example, Bar-Gill et al. (2003) and Pagano and Volpin (2005c) and the references therein.

[74] This dichotomy is an expositional oversimplification. Actual control moves more continuously than suggested by the dichotomy.

real. Formal control is enjoyed by a family owner with a majority of voting shares, by headquarters over divisions in a conglomerate, or by a venture capitalist with explicit control rights over a start-up company. Formal control thus enables a large owner to, directly and unencumbered (except perhaps by fiduciary duties), implement the changes he deems necessary. In contrast, real control is enjoyed by a minority owner who persuades other owners, or at least a fraction of them sufficient to create a dissenting majority, of the need for intervention. The extent to which a minority owner is able to convince other owners to move against management depends on two factors: ease of communication and of coalition-building with other investors, and congruence of interest among owners. The degree of congruence is determined by the active monitor's reputation (is he competent and honest?), by the absence of conflict of interest (will the monitor benefit from control in other ways than his fellow shareholders?), and by his stake in the firm (how much money will the monitor lose in case of a misguided intervention?). The latter factor explains why minority block shareholders are often described (a bit abusively) as having a "control block" even though they do not formally control the firm, and why dissidents in proxy contests are less trusted if their offer is not combined with a cash tender offer.

Proxy fights. In a proxy contest, a stockholder or a group of stockholders unhappy with managerial policies seeks either election to the board of directors with the ultimate goal of removing management, or support by a majority of shareholders for a resolution on a specific corporate policy. Sometimes, the *threat* of a proxy contest suffices to achieve the active monitor's aims, and so the contest need not even occur. For example, active monitors may use a political campaign to embarrass directors and force them to remove the CEO: or they may meet with directors or management and "convince" them of the necessity to alter their policies.

Proxy fights are an important element of corporate discipline in the United States. For example, in 1992–1993, financial institutions claimed the scalps of the CEOs of American Express, Borden, General Motors, IBM, Kodak, and Westinghouse. They also pressed for smaller boards and a larger fraction of outside directors, and forced large pay cuts on the bosses of ITT, General Dynamics, and U.S. Air (*The Economist,* August 19, 1996, p. 5). Proxy fights are associated with low accounting earnings, but, perhaps surprisingly, seem to have little relationship with the firm's stock returns (see DeAngelo 1988; DeAngelo and DeAngelo 1989; Pound 1988).

As we discussed, the existence and success of proxy fights depend not only on whether the initiator is trusted by other shareholders,[75] but also on their cost and feasibility. The competition between management (who can use corporate resources) and dissidents must be fair. And shareholders must be able to communicate among themselves. Until 1992, U.S. regulations made it very difficult for institutional investors (many of whom typically own a small piece of the firm, as we will see) to communicate. A 1992 SEC rule change has allowed freer communication. Furthermore, the 1992 new SEC rules have lowered the cost of a proxy fight from over $1 million to less than $5,000 (*The Economist,* January 29, 1994, p. 24 of a survey on corporate governance).

Proxy fights are rare in many other countries, and almost unheard of in Japan, where general assemblies tend to be perfunctory.

---

[75] Proxy votes may be ineffective if the dissenters do not succeed in building a majority. For example, in 2003, Disney was able to ignore in large part a proxy vote in which about 40% of the votes were cast against management.

4.2 Pattern of Ownership

Investor activism is intimately linked to the structure of ownership. A brief review of this structure (in the context of publicly held companies) is therefore in order.

Table 3 looks at the ownership of common stock for listed and unlisted companies. It shows that, as of 2002, countries differ substantially as to who owns equity. In the United States, households and institutional investors other than banks hold most of the shares.[76] Households (other than owners of family firms) have much lower stockholdings in France, Germany,[77] and Japan.

Table 3(b), for the same year, specializes to *listed companies*. Note that foreign ownership is substantially higher, indicating that foreign equity portfolios tend to specialize in listed companies.

Figures 3 and 4 describe the intertemporal evolution of listed-equity ownership in France and the United Kingdom, respectively.

Institutional investors do not all have the same incentives to monitor, as we will later discuss. It is therefore interesting to have a closer look at the decomposition of shareholdings among these investors. Table 4 describes this decomposition for the United States in 2004.

Pension funds play a much more minor role in other countries such as France, Germany, Italy, or Japan; in these countries, they are quasi nonexistent,

| TABLE 3 | Ownership of Common Stock (as a Percentage of Total Outstanding Common Shares in 2002) for (a) All Equity and (b) Listed Equity | | | | | | | |

	(a)				(b)			
	U.S.	Japan	France	Germany	U.K.	Japan	France	Germany
Banks and other financial institutions	2.3	9.0	12.1	10.5	12.6	7.42	12.6	33.5
Insurance companies	7.3	4.3 ⎫	4.5	9.9	19.9	7.32 ⎫	7.0	7.4
Pension funds	16.9	5.4 ⎭			15.6	5.62 ⎭		
Mutual funds	19.5	1.9	5.9	11.3	4.5	6.58	19	4.6
Households	42.5	14.0	19.5	14.7	14.3	16.84	6.5	22.9
Nonfinancial business	n.a.	43.7	34.3	34.2	0.8	38.12	20.2	11.7
Government	0.7	14.0	4.5	2.7	0.1	4.12	3.6	1.9
Foreign	10.6	7.7	19.2	16.6	32.1	13.98	31.2	18.1

Note: This table was assembled by David Sraer. The details of its construction can be found in Appendix 33B.

---

[76] We here focus on the ownership of common stock. Needless to say, the ownership pattern for assets in general may be quite different. For example, U.S. banks held almost no equity due in part to the prohibition contained in the 1933 Glass-Steagall Act, an act passed by Congress prohibiting commercial banks from participating in investment banking or to collaborating with full-service brokerage firms (this act was repealed in 1999). In contrast, their market share of total assets among U.S. financial institutions in 1994 was 28.7% (as opposed to 15.3% for insurance companies, 14.6% for private pension funds, 7.1% for public pension funds, 9.5% for mutual funds, 3.5% for money market funds, and 21.3% for other institutions). Source: Board of Governors of the Federal Reserve System. Flow of Funds Accounts 1995, cited by Sametz (1995).

[77] For further information about the ownership of German corporations, see Franks and Mayer (2001).

**FIGURE 3   Evolution of Listed-Equity Ownership by Sectors
in France (1977–2003)**

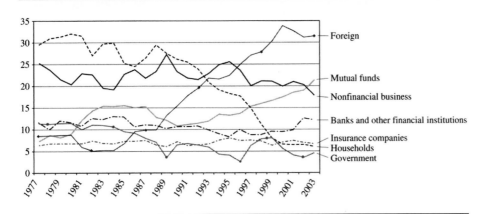

Note: Assembled by David Sraer.

because retirement benefits are publicly funded on a pay-as-you-go basis (as in France), or because pension funds are just a liability item on the firms' balance sheet and do not stand as independent investors (as in Germany).

The absence or weakness of pension funds is not the only characteristic of non-Anglo-Saxon countries. As we will see, *ownership concentration* is substantial. Also, *cross-shareholdings* among firms is widespread, as shown by the ownership share of nonfinancial business. There is a complex web of cross-participations within loosely defined or more structured industrial groups. For example, Table 5 reproduces findings of a study of the Japanese Fair Trade Commission summarizing cross-share holdings in the major Japanese industrial groups.

Another interesting international difference relates to the *size of the stock market*. Anglo-Saxon countries have well-developed stock markets; the capitalizations of the U.S. and U.K. stock markets in June 1996 made up about 90% and 120% of their respective GDPs (gross domestic products). With some exceptions (e.g., Japan and Switzerland), other stock markets are smaller (under 40% of GDP in France; Germany and Italy around the same date); for example, many relatively large German firms choose to remain private.

**FIGURE 4   Evolution of Listed-Equity Ownership by Sectors
in the United Kingdom (1963–2002)**

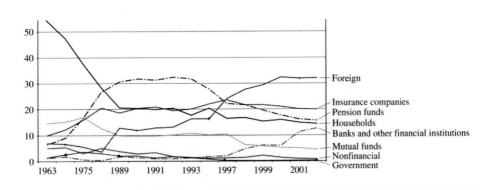

Note: Assembled by David Sraer.

TABLE 4   Institutional Investors' Equity Holdings as a Percentage of the Total U.S. Equity Market by Category

Type of Institution	IEH[a]	TEM (%)[b]
Banks	213.7	1.8
Commercial banking	3.5	0.0
Savings institutions	29.1	0.2
Banks, personal trusts and estates	181.1	1.5
Insurance companies	861.2	7.3
Life insurance companies	708.9	6.0
Other insurance companies	152.3	1.3
Pension funds	2015.0	17.0
Private pension funds	1096.7	9.2
State and local government retirement funds	869.8	7.3
Federal government retirement funds	48.5	0.4
Investment companies	2394.8	20.2
Mutual funds	2188.0	18.4
Closed-end funds	33.7	0.3
Exchange-traded funds	98.2	0.8
Brokers and dealers	74.9	0.6
All institutions	5484.7	46.2

[a] Institutional Equity Holdings ($ Billion)
[b] Total Equity Market
Note: Assembled by David Sraer. The details of its construction can be found in Appendix 33B.

Ownership concentration. There are also wide variations in the concentration of shares across countries.

In the majority of publicly listed Italian firms, for example, one shareholder holds above 50% of the shares (Franks et al. 1996). Family-owned firms there play an important role, as they do in France, Germany, and Sweden (see Table 6). Using a sample of 5,232 listed firms in 13 countries, Faccio and Lang (2002) provide a systematic analysis of ownership in Western Europe, pointing out the wide diversity of institutions (dual-class shares, cross-holdings, pyramidal structures[78]) and concentration. They find that 54% of European firms have only one controlling owner and that more than two-thirds of the family-controlled firms have top managers from the controlling family. Widely held firms account for 37% of the sample and family-controlled ones for 44%.

Similarly, Claessens et al. (2000) investigate the ownership structure of 2,980 publicly traded firms in nine East Asian countries (see, in particular, Table 7). In all countries, control vastly exceeds what would be predicted by cash-flow rights and is enhanced through pyramid structures and cross-holdings between firms.

---

[78] Pyramids refer to the indirect control of one corporation by another that does not totally own it.

TABLE 5   Average Percentage of Shares Owned by Firms in the Keiretsu Divided by Total Outstanding Shares in 1992

Mitsui	19.3%
Mitsubishi	38.2%
Sumitomo	28%
Fuyo	16.9%
Sanwa	16.7%
Dai-ichi Kangin	14.2%

Source: Kojima (1997, p. 57).

In their sample, more than two-thirds of the firms are controlled by a single shareholder, and about 60% of the firms that are not widely held are managed by someone related to the family of the controlling shareholder. There are significant variations across countries, though: for example, corporations in Japan are often widely held while those in Indonesia and Thailand are mainly family owned.

In contrast, ownership concentration is much smaller in Anglo-Saxon countries. For example, the mean and the median of the "three-shareholder concentration ratio," namely, the fraction of ownership by the three largest shareholders, for the largest listed firms, are 0.19 and 0.15 for the United Kingdom, 0.34 and 0.68 for France, and 0.48 and 0.50 for Germany (La Porta et al. 1998).

TABLE 6   The Identity of Controlling Owners in Europe (%) (1996–2000)

Country	France	Germany	Italy	Sweden	U.K.
Widely held	14	10	13	39	63
Family	65	64	60	47	24
Identified families	26	27	39	23	12
Unlisted firms	39	38	20	24	11
State	5	6	10	5	0
Widely held corporation	4	4	3	0	0
Widely held financial	11	9	12	3	9
Miscellaneous	1	3	1	6	3
Cross-holdings	0	2	1	0	0
Number of firms	607	704	208	245	1953

Source: Faccio and Lang (2002). Reprinted from *Journal of Financial Economics*. Volume 65, M. Faccio and L. Lang, the ultimate ownership of Western European corporations, pp. 365–395. Copyright (2002), with permission from Elsevier. A detailed description can be found in Appendix 33B.

TABLE 7	The Identity of Controlling Owners in Asia (%) (1996)						
Country	Hong Kong	Japan	Korea	Malaysia	Singapore	Taiwan	Thailand
Widely held	7	79.8	43.2	10.3	5.4	26.2	6.6
Family	66.7	9.7	48.4	67.2	55.4	48.2	61.6
State	1.4	0.8	1.6	13.4	23.5	2.8	8
Widely held corporation	19.8	3.2	6.1	6.7	11.5	17.4	15.3
Widely held financial	5.2	6.5	0.7	2.3	4.1	5.3	8.6
Number of firms	330	1240	345	238	221	141	167

Source: Claessens et al. (2000). Reprinted from *Journal of Financial Economics,* Volume 58. S. Claessens, S. Djankov, and L. Lang. The separation of ownership and control in East Asian corporations, pp. 81–112, Copyright (2000), with permission from Elsevier. A detailed description can be found in Appendix 33B.

Ownership is extremely dispersed in the United States. While Shleifer and Vishny (1986) report that above 50% of the Fortune 500 firms have at least one shareholder holding a block exceeding 5%, large blocks are relatively rare (except, of course, in the case of leveraged buyouts or family-held firms). The median largest shareholder has only 9% of the firm's equity, and a number of moderate size block shareholders typically coexist; 20% (respectively, 15%) of firms traded on the New York Stock Exchange, the Amex, and the over-the-counter market have a nonofficer (respectively, officer) holding more than 10% of shares (Barclay and Holderness 1989). Institutional investors often hold (individually) a very small amount of the firm's stock; for example, in 1990, the most visible "active investor," CalPERS, reportedly held less than 1% of the firms it invested in (Kojima 1997, p. 22).

Stable holdings versus active portfolio management. Another point of departure among countries is the degree of stability of stock holdings.

Simplifying somewhat, Japanese and German investors have traditionally been in for the long haul, while Anglo-Saxon investors reshuffle their portfolios frequently. Institutional investors dominate liquidity trading in the United States. Mutual funds and actively managed pension funds hold their shares, on average, for 1.9 years (Kojima 1997, p. 84). In contrast, shareholdings are very stable in Japan. Kojima (1997, p. 31) assesses that, for a typical Japanese firm, about 60% of shareholdings are stable. In Japan, business corporations (which hold substantial amounts of stocks through cross-shareholdings) and financial institutions view themselves as engaged in a long-term relationship with the firms they invest in.[79] Table 8 confirms the low turnover rate for corporate and institutional investors.

4.3 The Limits of Active Monitoring

For all its benefits, investor activism encounters a number of limits, grouped below in four categories.

Who monitors the monitor? Active monitors are in charge of mitigating the agency problem within the firms they invest in. The same agency problem, however, often applies, with a vengeance, to the monitors themselves. In particular,

---

[79] See Aoki (1984, 1990), Aoki and Patrick (1995), Tsuru (1995), and Kojima (1994, 1997) for discussions of long-term financial relationships in Japan.

TABLE 8	Stock Trading by Type of Investor in Terms of Average Percentage Turnover Rates (for the Years 1990–92)		
Life and casualty insurance companies		sales	4.9
		purchases	5.0
Business corporations		sales	8.5
		purchases	8.4
Banks		sales	12.3
		purchases	12.8
Individuals		sales	24.9
		purchases	24.7
Foreigners		sales	61.4
		purchases	65.1
Investment trusts		sales	65.3
		purchases	64.9

Source: Tsuru (1995, p. 15) and Economic Planning Agency White Papers (1992).

pension and mutual funds have a very dispersed set of beneficiaries and no large shareholder! Coffee (1991) argues that there are very few mechanisms holding U.S. institutional money managers accountable: most face no threat of hostile takeover or proxy fights; pension funds have no debt and therefore face less pressure to generate profits than ordinary corporations; and executive compensation is hard to design, as well as constrained by the regulatory framework (compensation is a function of assets under management rather than an incentive compensation based on the fund's capital appreciation, which is contrary to federal securities laws).

Thus, monitoring may be impaired by the fact that monitors may not act in the interest of the beneficiaries. Corporate managers usually argue, in this respect, that institutional investors are too preoccupied by short-term profit, presumably because the managers of pension and mutual funds are keen to keep their positions and to manage larger funds. Some corporate managers also complain that the institutions' managers monitoring them have limited managerial competency.

Congruence with other investors. Even if the agency problem between the active monitor and its beneficiaries is resolved (say, because the two coincide, as in the case of a large private owner), the active monitor does not internalize the welfare of other investors and therefore may not monitor efficiently. This may give rise to:

Undermonitoring. A pension fund owning 1 or 2% of a corporation has vastly suboptimal incentives to acquire strategic information and launch a proxy fight, as it receives only 1 or 2 cents per dollar it creates for the shareholders. Substantial free riding may thus be expected, for example, when institutional ownership is very dispersed.

Collusion with management. Relatedly, a monitor may enter into a quid pro quo with management or be afraid of retaliation in case it dissents (for example, noncooperative fund managers in a proxy fight may not be selected to manage the firm's pension plan).

Self-dealing. Large blockholders monitoring a firm may use their private information to extract rents from the firm through transactions with affiliated firms and the like. How much they can extract depends on the strength of legal enforcement of shareholders rights as well as on the (non)existence of other large shareholders who are not made part of the sweet deals and can denounce the abuse.

Cost of providing proper incentives to the monitor. Again, leaving aside agency problems within the monitor, several authors, most notably Coffee (1991), Porter (1992), and Bhide (1993a), have argued that only "long-term players" are good monitors. Their basic idea is that investors have little incentive to create long-run value improvement (exert voice) if they can easily exit by reselling their shares at a fair price. They further argue that illiquidity, promoted, say, by privately placed equity, large blocks with limited marketability, taxes on realized capital gains, or equity with limited resale rights (letter stocks), would enhance the quality of monitoring, and they point at the long-term, stable relationships in Japan and Germany between the investors and the corporations they invest in.[80] These authors recognize that illiquidity is costly to the institutional investors but they argue that this cost is limited for some institutional investors such as pension funds. The point that properly structuring the active monitor's incentives may entail some illiquidity costs is valid.

Perverse effects on the monitorees. While monitoring is generally beneficial, it does not come without side effects for the monitoree. There may be overmonitoring and a reduction in initiative, and the firm's managers may become overly preoccupied by short-run news that will determine their tenure in the firm. They may then devote much time to manipulating short-term earnings and trying to secure the cooperation of the largest institutional investors.

Legal, fiscal, and regulatory obstacles. A number of authors, most notably Roe (1990), Coffee (1991), and Bhide (1993a), have emphasized the legal, fiscal, and regulatory impediments to investor activism in the United States, and argued that U.S. regulators have discouraged efficient governance.

First, stockholders who sit on a firm's board are exposed to SEC and class-action suits.[81] Furthermore, an individual or a group that possesses "control" of a company is deemed an "affiliate" and faces volume and holding-period restrictions on reselling shares.[82] Section 16(b) of the Securities Exchange Act of 1934 stipulates that any gain that an officer, director, or 10% holder of a security receives on purchases or sales of the security within six months of an earlier purchase or sale must be paid back to the corporation. These rules create illiquidity, which add to the natural illiquidity of big blocks. These are therefore particularly costly for mutual funds, which face redemptions and therefore must be able to sell.

Another rule affecting institutional control is the diversification rule. In order to receive favorable tax treatment as a diversified fund, a pension fund or mutual fund cannot hold more than 10% of the stock of any firm (even though a holding above 10% may be small relative to the fund's total managed assets, so that the rule has no virtue in terms of diversification and prudential regulation!). It is therefore not surprising that U.S. institutional investors hold small fractions of shares of individual firms so as to avoid restrictions on short-term (insider) trading and receive favorable tax treatment, and that they avoid sitting on boards.

While the details of regulation are country- and time-specific, it should be borne in mind that they can have a nonnegligible impact on corporate governance.

---

[80] With respect to this last point, it should be noted that these contributions were written in the late 1980s to early 1990s when the "GJ" model (for "Germany–Japan") was fashionable. The economic evolution of the 1990s made observers much less keen on endorsing this model, and more keen (probably too keen) on embracing the Anglo-Saxon paradigm.

[81] Section 20 of 1934 Securities Exchange Act.

[82] Securities Act of 1933.

TAKEOVERS AND LEVERAGED BUYOUTS   5

One of the most controversial aspects of corporate governance, and certainly one that varies most across countries, is the market for corporate control. The explosion of hostile takeovers and of leveraged buyouts (LBOs) in the United States in the 1980s[83] has been perceived with awe, horror, and admiration. In Japan and continental Europe, where acquisitions are usually negotiated with management, they represent the worst of an American capitalism based on greed and myopia. In Anglo-Saxon countries, in contrast, many view them as an original mode of corporate governance that substitutes efficient teams for entrenched, money-wasting managers (Manne 1965).[84]

Although they are divided on the topic, economists are in agreement on many of the costs and benefits of takeovers, and hold much more dispassionate views on the topic than practitioners and laymen. On the managerial side, takeovers may be needed to keep managers on their toes, if the board and general assembly are ineffective monitors and thus traditional corporate governance fails. But, as for other forms of incentive based on the termination of employment, they may induce managers to act "myopically" and boost their short-term performance at the expense of the long-term one. On the corporate policy front, takeovers may put in place a new managerial team with fresh ideas on how to run the firm and less keen on sticking to former strategy mistakes. But they may also let a value-reducing raider gain control from uncoordinated shareholders. Finally, takeovers may shatter implicit contracts with other stakeholders.

Let us begin with three salient features of the U.S. corporate environment of the 1980s. First, while definitely smaller than that of the subsequent merger wave (see below), the volume of mergers and acquisitions was very high by historical standards during the decade. Indeed, 143 of the 1980 Fortune 500 firms had become acquired by 1989. About $1.3 trillion changed hands in the 1980s. Of course, most acquisitions were or looked "friendly" (it is hard to measure the extent to which negotiated acquisitions are influenced or driven by the threat of a takeover); out of 3,336 transactions that occurred in 1986, only 40 were hostile[85] and 110 corresponded to tender offers unopposed by management. Yet the size of some hostile takeovers, their wide media coverage, the personality characteristics of the participants,[86] and the anxiety of managers (few keep their job after a successful raid, so that one of a manager's worst nightmares is to become the target of a takeover bid) all concurred to draw substantial attention to the phenomenon.

---

[83] There are several excellent reviews of the takeover and LBO boom of the 1980s, including Bhagat et al. (1990), Holmström and Kaplan (2001, 2003), Kaplan (1993), Milgrom and Roberts (1992, Chapter 15), and the papers by Shleifer and Vishny, Jensen, Jarrell et al., and Scherer in the 1988 symposium of the *Journal of Economic Perspectives*.

[84] This view is, of course, far from being uniform, for example, Peter Drucker, a leading management guru, argued in 1986 that "there can be absolutely no doubt that hostile takeovers are exceedingly bad for the economy." He characterized the high leverage of acquired companies as "severely impairing the company's potential for economic performance." And he condemned the sell-off of the most valuable parts of the acquired businesses (see Bhide 1993b).

[85] "Hostile" refers to the fact that the raider invites shareholders to accept the offer whether the board recommends it or not.

[86] Bosses under siege and raiders such as Boone Pickens, Goldsmith, Perelman, Campeau, and Icahn became almost household names. Books about hostile acquisitions, such as *Barbarians at the Gate* by B. Burrough and J. Helyar (New York: Harper & Row, 1990) relating the $25 billion takeover of RJR Nabisco by KKR (a spectacular takeover which started as a management buyout (MBO), but in which management ultimately lost to KKR, who paid more than twice the price prevailing before the bidding war began), turned into bestsellers.

FIGURE 5   Going Private Volume as Percentage of Average Total Stock Market Value 1979–2003

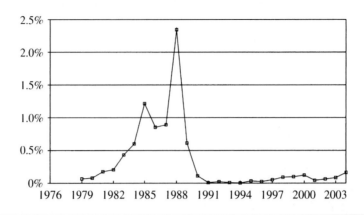

Source: Holmström and Kaplan (2001) and S. Kaplan (personal communication, 2005).

Second, many publicly traded firms were turned back private through leveraged buyouts, especially management buyouts (see Figure 5).

Third, corporate leverage increased substantially during the decade. Firms bought back their own shares, and sometimes put them into Employee Stock Ownership Plans. Furthermore, and associated with the takeover and LBO wave, a new form of public debt, namely, risky or junk bonds, appeared and grew remarkably fast: $32.4 billion of junk bonds were issued in 1986, and the stock of junk bonds had swollen to $175 billion by the fall of 1988 (Stigum 1990, p. 100).

The trend stopped around 1989–1990. The junk bonds used for LBOs and takeovers, especially those issued in the second half of the decade, started defaulting. A number of Savings and Loans, who had been big buyers of junk bonds, went bankrupt.[87] The creator of junk bonds (Michael Milken) and his employer (the investment bank Drexel-Burnham-Lambert, which subsequently went bankrupt) were sued and found guilty of a number of misdemeanors and criminal offenses (insider trading, stock manipulation, fraud, falsified records). Hostile takeovers declined (see Figure 6).

While the risky bond market recovered around 1992–1993 (see Figure 7), it was then much less related to mergers and acquisitions.

Simultaneously, the popularity of LBOs had waned. Buyouts of public corporations fell from $60 billion in 1988 to $4 billion in 1990 (W. T. Grimm's Mergerstat Review 1991). Takeovers in general collapsed in 1990. Most states had by then put in place restrictive antitakeover laws, partly under the pressure of the Business Roundtable (composed of the CEOs of the 200 largest U.S. corporations).

It should be noted, though, that the volume of mergers and acquisitions was substantially higher in the 1990s than in the 1980s. The recent merger wave,[88] culminating in the 1998–2001 period, was the largest in American history and associated with high stock valuations and the use of equity as a form of payment;

---

[87] The difficulties faced by the S&Ls did not stem from junk bonds, but with the interest rate shock of the late 1970s, and several mistakes of prudential regulators in the 1980s. However, the S&L disaster added to the general negative feelings about junk bonds.

[88] Documented, for example, in Moeller et al. (2003).

FIGURE 6 Contested Tender Offers as a Percentage of Total 1974–2004

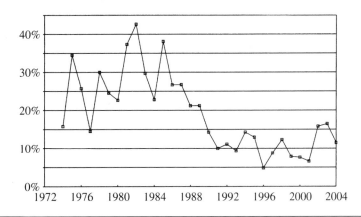

Source: Holmström and Kaplan (2001) and S. Kaplan (personal communication, 2005).

but more takeover defenses were in place than in the 1980s. What died out in the 1990s were hostile takeovers.[89]

Lastly, firms tried to accomplish internally very much what takeovers and LBOs were about. Cost-cutting and leanness became fashionable through concepts such as reengineering, downsizing, focus, and EVA.[90] Share repurchases allowed firms to increase their leverage. And proxy fights such as those led by institutional investors and facilitated by the 1992 new SEC rules provided a substitute mechanism for interfering with management when takeover defenses and

FIGURE 7 Noninvestment Grade Bond Volume (as a Percentage of Average Total Stock Market Capitalization) 1977–1999

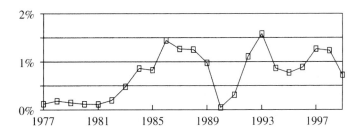

Source: Holmström and Kaplan (2001).

[89] Meanwhile, hostile takeovers have gained a bit more prominence in Europe, where they have traditionally been very rare. British-based Vodafone's 2000 takeover of the German company Mannesmann for $183 billion, for example, attracted much attention, caused several law suits, and created a public debate about the large golden parachutes for Mannesmann executives (including 31 million euros for its chairman).

[90] EVA refers to "economic value added," a technique promoted by management consulting companies such as Stern Stewart, and which consists of imputing a cost of capital to guide internal investment decisions. See Rogerson (1997) for more detail.

antitakeover laws made it difficult to acquire control by purchasing a large number of shares. Before discussing these phenomena, we first review some of the institutional innovations of the decade.

5.1 Takeover Bids and Defenses

Although it is generally preceded by a purchase of a "toehold" by the potential acquirer, a takeover process really starts with a tender offer, that is, with an invitation to buy the firm's shares at an announced price. The offer may concern part or all of the stock. And it may be conditional on a certain number of shares being effectively tendered, the idea being that the bidder is often interested in the shares only if he obtains a controlling stake. The bid may also be multitiered, that is, specify a different price for shares beyond some threshold level, or may offer a uniform price for all shares (multitier offers are allowed in the United States, but British raiders cannot pay less to minority shareholders once 30% of the shares have been acquired).

While hostile takeovers have long been part of the American corporate scene, there has been a phenomenal volume of such takeovers in the 1980s, with a peak in 1988–1989. They have been particularly prominent in such industries as oil and gas, mining and minerals, banking and finance, and insurance. Jensen (1988) has argued that takeovers facilitate exit and cash disgorgement in slow-growth industries, where management refuses to unwind its empire and uses the available cash, where there is any, to engage in wasteful diversifications. Relatedly, Morck et al. (1990) find that firms in industries with low ratios of market value of securities over the accounting value of assets (that is, with low "Tobin's Qs") are more likely to be the target of takeover bids.

Management reacted not only by lobbying for restrictive antitakeover laws,[91] but also by adopting (or by convincing shareholders or the board to adopt) takeover defenses. Takeover defenses come in many guises and are sometimes quite ingenious. (See Jarrell et al. (1988) and Malatesta (1992) for more detailed discussions.)

Some defenses, called corporate charter defenses, just *make it technically difficult for the raider to acquire control.* With a *staggered board,* only a fraction of members rather than all directors are up for reelection in a given year, so that a successful raider has to wait for some time after the acquisition to acquire full control. Under a *supermajority rule,* a raider needs x% of the votes in order to effect a merger or another significant corporate reorganization, such as large asset sales, where x may be 80 or 90 rather than 50 (as it would be under a simple majority rule). *Fair price clauses* attempt to force an acquirer to offer a premium for all shares by imposing a very stringent supermajority clause (nearing shareholder unanimity) unless a high and uniform price is offered for all shares (where "high," for example, means that the bid must exceed the highest share price during the preceding year). Another variation on the supermajority rule consists in placing a number of shares in an Employee Stock Ownership Plan (ESOP). To the extent that employees will vote with management in the event of a takeover (which is likely), ESOPs make it more difficult for a raider to gain

---

[91] For a description of the main antitakeover laws (control share laws, fair price laws, and freeze-out laws), see, for example, Malatesta (1992).

Comment and Schwert (1995) express skepticism about the deterrence effect of antitakeover laws and argue that the collapse of the market for corporate control at the end of the 1980s is due to other factors, such as the recession and the resulting credit crunch. They find, however, that takeover premia paid by raiders are higher when target firms are protected by state laws or by poison pills.

control.[92] In the same spirit, *differential voting rights* provide privileged voting rights to shares that are held for an extended period (and so the raider cannot benefit from the corresponding privileges); and *dual-class recapitalizations* provide management or family owners with more votes than would be warranted by their shares. Still another way for a firm to deter takeovers is to change its state of incorporation and *move to a state with tougher antitakeover statutes*.

A second group of takeover defenses amount to diluting the raider's equity, often at the expense of the corporation. The idea is to make the firm less attractive to the raider, perhaps at the cost of making the firm less attractive to anybody else as well. *Scorched-earth policies* consist in selling, possibly at a low price, assets which the raider is particularly keen on acquiring, either because they would create synergies with his own operations or because they would generate a steady flow of cash that would help finance the often highly leveraged acquisition (relatedly, management may try to increase leverage or reduce the amount of corporate cash that can be enjoyed by a potential raider). Entering *litigation* against the raider may also prove an effective deterrent. For, even if the raider is reasonably confident of winning the case, the very cost of litigation may make the prey much less desirable.

Lastly, a wide variety of *poison pills* have been conceived. Poison pills generally refer to special rights of the target's shareholders to purchase additional shares at a low price or sell shares to the firm at a high price conditionally, say, on a raider acquiring a certain fraction of the target's shares. That is, poison pills are call or put options for the target shareholders that have value only in case of a hostile takeover. Poison pills thus reduce the value of equity in the event of a takeover. Popular poison pills include flip-over plans, which, inter alia, allow the shareholder to buy shares in the surviving or merged firm at a substantial discount, say 50%.[93]

To complete this brief description, let us also mention two common practices used by managers, once the takeover process has started, to repel raiders at the expense of shareholder value. Managers sometimes look for a *white knight*, namely, an alternative acquirer with a friendlier attitude vis-à-vis current management and willing to bid up the price; the presence of the white knight may discourage the raider (who, remember, has to find the funds for the takeover attempt) and the firm may end up being sold at a relatively low price to the white knight. Perhaps the most controversial defense of all is the practice of *greenmail* (or targeted block stock repurchases), through which management, using company money, purchases at a premium the raider's block of the target's stock. Greenmail can be viewed as a form of collusion between management and the raider at the expense of other shareholders.

---

[92] See, for example, Pagano and Volpin (2005a) for the deterrent effect of ESOPs in hostile takeover attempts. Dhillon and Ramirez (1994) point out that ESOPs, like many other antitakeover devices, have two effects: a reduction in the occurrence of takeovers and an increase in the relative bargaining power of the firm vis-à-vis the raider; using the 1989 Delaware court decision on Polaroid's ESOP, establishing the legality of ESOPs as a takeover defense, Dhillon and Ramirez find that the overall stock price reaction upon the announcement of an ESOP tended to be positive over their sample period, consistent with the relative bargaining power effect, but that, after the Delaware court decision, it was strongly negative for those firms that were already subject to takeover speculation, consistent with the managerial entrenchment hypothesis.

[93] The term "flip-over" refers to the fact that formally the plans are call options given as dividends to the target shareholders. The shareholder can exercise these options at a high price in the case of a takeover and the firm can redeem these options at a nominal fee before a bid or acquisition. The impediment resides mainly in the flip-over provision, which gives old shareholders the right to dilute the firm after a takeover.

Let us conclude this discussion of takeover institutions and strategies with a puzzle. Leaving aside statutory defenses, which lie outside the firm's control, one may question the process through which corporate charter (supermajority amendments, fair price clauses, staggered boards, changes in the state of incorporation) and other defenses (greenmail, litigation against the raider, poison pills) come about. The former require ratification by the shareholders, while the latter are subject to board approval without shareholder ratification. In view of the substantial conflict of interest faced by management in such matters and of the fact that greenmail and the adoption of poison pills are usually greeted by a negative stock price reaction,[94] it is not *a priori* clear why boards exert so little control and why corporate charter defenses are so often approved by shareholders. This rubber-stamping of managerial proposals in the matter of takeover defenses raises the question of whether they increase incumbent shareholders' wealth (for one thing, they may force the raider to bid a higher price) or whether this is just another illustration of managerial entrenchment and poor corporate governance.

5.2 Leveraged Buyouts

Roughly speaking, a leveraged buyout (LBO) consists in taking a firm private by purchasing its shares and allocating them to a concentrated ownership composed of management, a general partner, and other investors (the limited partners or LBO fund). Due to the dearth of equity of the owners, the new entity is highly leveraged. Typically, top-level managers (either incumbent managers, often under the threat of a takeover, or a dissenting team) ally with an LBO specialist who brings equity of his own and also finds investors to cofinance the LBO. An LBO involving current management is called a management buyout (MBO).[95] Either way, the coalition acquires the outstanding shares and divides equity in roughly the following fashion: management receives 10–30%,[96] and the buyout partnership, namely, the LBO specialist (who sits on the board) and the investors, pick up the remainder. An LBO specialist such as KKR (Kohlberg-Kravis-Roberts) as a general partner typically has 20% of the nonexecutive shares while the limited partners purchase the remaining 80%.[97]

The flip side of concentrated ownership is that the coalition must also issue a substantial amount of debt. Leverage ratios in LBOs were as high as 20:1 in the 1980s (and fell below 5:1 in the 1990s; typical debt-to-equity LBO ratios have only been 40–60% in recent years). In Kaplan's (1990) sample, the average ratio of long-term debt over debt plus equity for firms subject to a buyout was about 20% before the buyout and 85% after completion of the buyout.

Substantial managerial stock ownership is all the more important as the LBO sponsor usually has a very lean structure. The sponsor intervenes actively in key strategic decisions, but must operate arm's-length vis-à-vis everyday operating choices. Jensen's (1989a) survey of LBO partnerships finds an average staff of 13 professionals and 19 nonprofessionals in an LBO partnership. The world's largest LBO partnership, KKR, had 16 professionals and 44 additional employees.[98]

---

[94] See, for example, Jarrell et al. (1998) and Malatesta (1992) for reviews of the evidence.

[95] The ownership pattern much resembles the financing of start-ups by venture capitalists. There are a couple of differences, though. In particular, start-ups generate lower income, and are therefore not much leveraged, while LBOs often concern firms with steady cash flows and are highly leveraged.

[96] The median management equity ownership of the post-buyout companies in the Kaplan and Stein (1993) sample of MBOs was 22.3% (as opposed to 5% in the pre-buyout entities).

[97] All shares are owned by the private equity group. The sharing rule just alluded to governs the split of the capital gains once the investment is exited.

[98] Interestingly, it took over companies with large headquarters, sometimes exceeding 5,000 employees.

Typically, banks provide two types of loan: long-term senior loans with maturity of, say, seven years, and short-term loans that are used as bridges until junk bonds are issued. Junk bonds are public debt which is junior to bank debt in several respects: they are unsecured and include few covenants; their principal is not amortized before maturity; and their maturity, ten years, say, exceeds that of bank loans. Junk bonds are evidently risky and are often renegotiated (towards reduced interest payments, stretched-out maturities, and equity-for-debt swaps). In 1986, they were held mainly by mutual funds (32%), insurance companies (32%), pension funds (12%), individuals (12%), and thrifts (8%).[99]

The proclaimed virtues of the buyout partnership arrangement are a) stronger monetary incentives for the firm's managers relative to those of a publicly traded corporation,[100] b) active monitoring taken seriously, in which the general partner has both the incentives and the means of intervention, and c) high leverage, which forces management and the partnership to work out cost reductions and improvements in efficiency, and to sell divisions (possibly in the form of MBOs with the managers of these divisions!).

It is worth emphasizing that buyout partnerships do not function as conglomerates. For example, KKR, a well-known general partner in LBOs,[101] keeps its companies[102] separate. The companies thus operate as stand-alone entities and do not cross-subsidize each other. As a matter of fact, cross-subsidization is prohibited by the statutes of the partnership. The LBO sponsor must ask its institutional investors for permission to transfer any cash from one LBO division to another. And LBO funds must return capital from exited investments to the limited and general partners and are not allowed to reinvest the funds.

Another point worth noting is that KKR sticks to the companies for five to ten years before exiting. This gives it nonnegligible incentives to invest for the long run. When successful, it resells its share to another large investor or takes the company public again. As is the case for a venture capitalist, these exit options allow KKR to free equity to invest in new ventures.[103]

Concerning leverage, LBO targets have to generate large and steady cash flows in order to service the high debt payments. Thus LBOs can be successful only for mature industries with these cash-flow characteristics. Examples of such industries that have been mentioned in the literature are oil and gas, mining and chemicals, forest products, broadcasting, tobacco, food processing, and tyres.[104] Still, there have been a number of defaults, mainly for the deals that took place

---

[99] S. Rasky, "Tracking junk bond owners." *The New York Times,* December 7, 1986, cited in Perry and Taggart (1993).

[100] Jensen (1989a,b) estimates that in the 1980s the average CEO in an LBO firm receives $64 per $1,000 increase in shareholder value, as opposed to $3 for the average Fortune 1000 firm.

[101] KKR is not only known for spectacular takeovers such as the RJR Nabisco one. It has also rewarded its investors (wealthy individuals, commercial banks, pension funds) over a span of 20 years with a 23.5% annual return, compared with around 15% for the stock market index (S&P 500) (*The Economist,* August 2, 1997, p. 77).

KKR itself has been very profitable. Its profits do not come solely from the capital gains on its equity investments (merchant banker activity). As an agent for the investors, it receives a 1.5% management fee, a retainer fee for monitoring performance, and a fee for servicing on boards of directors (agency activity). Lastly, it receives a 1% fee after the deals are completed (investment banking activity). See Kauffman et al. (1995, Chapter 10).

[102] That is, 15 in April 1991, with combined revenues $40 billion.

[103] The exit may be fully planned in the original deal; for example, the limited partnership may be limited to last ten years.

[104] One-third of the LBOs in the manufacturing sector between 1978 and 1988 took place in the food and tobacco industries. Seventy percent of LBOs in the nonmanufacturing sector concerned retail trade and services (Rappaport 1990).

in the second half of the decade. Kaplan and Stein (1993) analyze a sample of 124 large MBOs completed during the 1980s. Of the 41 deals completed between 1980 and 1984, only one defaulted on its debt; in contrast, 22 of the 83 deals put together between 1985 and 1989 defaulted. Kaplan and Stein find that the MBOs put together in the second half of the decade were characterized by a) high purchase prices (relative to cash flows), b) riskier industries, c) smaller and more secured positions held by banks, and substantial junk bond financing, and d) more up-front payments to management and deal makers. In a nutshell, the MBOs became riskier during the decade. As Kaplan and Stein note, this evidence is consistent with loose statements about an "overheated buyout market" and "too much financing chasing too few good deals" in the second half of the decade, but it does not quite explain why financial markets made such mistakes.

LBOs are, most likely, a circumscribed phenomenon. Most observers (including Jensen) agree that they can apply only to firms with specific characteristics, namely, strong and predictable cash flows. It would be a mistake, for example, to burden firms in growth industries (in which investment needs exceed the cash flows) with high levels of debt; similarly, debt may be a dangerous form of finance for firms with risky cash flows. Rappaport (1990) further argues that the "reliquification objective" implies that LBOs are a transitory form of organization. LBO sponsors and limited partners want to be able to cash out, in the form of a return to public corporation status or negotiated sales, in order to be able to invest in new firms (sponsors) or to face their liquidity needs (institutions). Not only do most LBO limited-partnership agreements have a limited duration (often ten years), but the exit option is often exercised before the end of the partnership. Rappaport cites a Kidder Peabody study on 90 initial public offerings (IPOs) for buyout corporations between 1983 and 1988, in which 70% of the companies were taken public within three years of their LBO date.

5.3 The Rise of Takeovers and the Backlash: What Happened?

There are several competing hypotheses for what happened in the 1980s in the United States. None of these hypotheses is a satisfactory explanation by itself, but all offer some insights about the events.[105]

Hypothesis 1: Decline of corporate governance. The first possibility, stressed by Jensen (1984, 1988, 1989a,b) and Jensen and Ruback (1983) among others, is that the previous system of corporate governance was basically broken. The lack of monitoring by the board and large shareholders was, of course, nothing new in 1980, but it may have been particularly costly in a period of excess liquidities, i.e., in a period in which managers had substantial amounts of cash to spend. According to Jensen, entrenched managers refused (and were not forced by boards) to disgorge their excess cash flow and rather invested it in unattractive projects. Furthermore, international competition, deregulation and technological change implied that a number of firms had to exit or downsize. The proponents of this hypothesis thus argue that the capital market substituted for a deficient corporate governance, and helped fire inefficient managers, allocate corporate cash to its most efficient uses, and create an efficient exit.

---

[105] A more complete and very useful discussion of the hypotheses can be found in Holmström and Kaplan (2001, 2003).

Hypothesis 2: Financial innovation. Another and complementary hypothesis, also often associated with Jensen, holds that LBOs created a new and superior form of corporate governance for mature industries. High-powered executive compensation, "external management" by active monitors such as KKR, and high leverage all created, according to Jensen, better incentives for efficiency.[106] The financing of these LBOs was facilitated by the development of a junk bond market during the decade. The fact that few industries are good candidates for LBOs and the decline of LBOs in the 1990s imply that this explanation has only limited scope.

Hypothesis 3: Break-up of conglomerates. According to this hypothesis, takeovers targeted the conglomerate empires built in the 1960s and 1970s. These conglomerates had proved unmanageable, but managers did not want to reduce the size of their empires through "bust-ups" (sales of divisions to other companies) and "spin-offs" (transformations of divisions into independent companies). An external intervention was called for that had to downsize these conglomerates and make them focus on their core business.[107]

A variant of this hypothesis demonstrates the lenient enforcement of antitrust statutes under the Republican administrations of the 1980s. This relaxation of competition policy resulted in new opportunities for horizontal and vertical mergers. In this variant, the driver for the bust-ups is not the lack of focus of the existing conglomerates, but rather the nonrealization of "synergies" (understand: exploitation of market power) under the existing structures.

There are a number of other hypotheses for the takeover wave of the 1980s, including speculative excesses and transfers from employees, the bondholders, and the Treasury (to which we come back shortly).

What is the verdict for the 1980s?

Large gain for target shareholders. The winners were without doubt the target shareholders. While estimates differ and also vary with the type of takeover,[108] a 30% premium is definitely in the ballpark.

Neutral outcome for the acquirer. Most estimates show that the bidders neither gained nor lost, or else that they lost slightly in value (see Kaplan (1997) for a review). There are several possible explanations for this fact. The first is consistent with the notion that takeovers create value and is based on Grossman and Hart's (1980) free-riding argument. According to this argument, a raider cannot offer less than the post-acquisition value of the firm and have the target shareholders tender their shares: for, it would then be optimal for an individual shareholder to refuse to tender his shares and to enjoy the higher value of the post-acquisition firm. But if all shareholders behave this way, the raider cannot acquire control and the value-increasing changes are never implemented. While the free-rider problem is important and certainly contributes to explaining low returns for the acquirers, it depicts only an extreme case and there is every reason to believe that a raider should be able to make some profit. So, another argument seems needed if we want to explain the neutral or negative effect of takeovers on the acquirers' value. One possibility, less consistent with the view that takeovers are value enhancing, is that acquirers themselves are agents and misuse the resources entrusted to them. And, indeed, acquisitions are a quick

---

[106] Kaplan (1989) provides evidence of improvements in operating profits in a sample of leveraged buyouts pulled together in the 1980s.

[107] See, for example, Bhagat et al. (1990) and Kaplan and Weisbach (1992), Kaplan (1997), reviewing the evidence, argues that there was no deconglomeration in the 1980s in the United States. But there was, perhaps, unwinding of bad diversification.

[108] For example, Kaplan and Stein find a 43% premium for their sample of MBOs.

and easy way for managers to expand the scope of their control and build empires.[109]

Where does the overall gain come from? Takeovers are associated with an increase in total value (target plus acquirer). Somehow, investors must believe that gains will result from the change in control. Where do these gains come from? Again, there are two possible views on this. The antitakeover view asserts that they primarily result from transfers from stakeholders (laid-off employees, expropriated bondholders and Treasury, consumers hurt by the merged firms' market power) to shareholders. There is little evidence that takeovers reduce wages and generate unemployment,[110] although they may do so in particular instances: the takeover of TWA by Icahn implied wage losses for unionized workers (Shleifer and Summers 1988). More likely, white-collar employees may be laid off when a merger leads to a cut in redundant headquarters personnel. In any case, the transfers from employees to shareholders do not seem commensurate with the overall gain to shareholders.[111] Several papers have similarly studied the possibility the increased leverage could have hurt the bondholders, or the Treasury due to tax shields (see Jarrell et al. 1988). These studies too conclude that these effects are small on average (although they can be significant in specific transactions). All these studies combined suggest that the pro-takeover view, according to which takeovers are efficiency enhancing, must have at least some validity for the 1980s (see below for a contrast with the 1990s). It is quite possible that takeovers indeed prevented some managers from wasting free cash flow and forced some exit or curtailments in excess capacity. And it seems that takeovers did not have a large negative impact on long-term investments such as R&D expenditures (see, for example, Hall 1990).

Contrast with subsequent mergers and acquisitions. As discussed above the merger wave that peaked in the 1998–2001 period was the largest in American history. It differs from that of 1980s not only through its reduced emphasis on hostile takeovers: it also seems to have led to wealth destruction. Moeller et al. (2003) estimate that, from 1998 through 2001, shareholders of acquiring firms lost $240 billion and that this loss was not offset by a larger gain by shareholders of the target firms. Indeed, the combined loss when adding the targets' gains was still $134 billion.

How meaningful is the overall-gain test? Suppose that it is established empirically that a sizeable fraction of the net gains from takeovers to shareholders does not come from transfers from other stakeholders. This still does not quite settle the takeover debate for two reasons. First, there are hidden benefits and costs of takeovers that may not be properly accounted for. On the benefit side, those managers whose firm ends up not being taken over may still operate value enhancements through fear that inaction would trigger a takeover. Such benefits from the "contestability" of the managerial position may be hard to measure. On the cost side, the possibility of takeovers creates incentives to underinvest in unobservable long-term investments. Takeovers may also induce managers to engage in costly defenses or to focus most of their attention on producing good

---

[109] Shleifer and Vishny (1988). Morck et al. (1990) point out that half of the announcements of takeovers are greeted with a negative stock price reaction from the bidder's shareholders. Behavioral hypotheses (in terms of managerial hubrist) have also been offered to explain the lack of profits of acquirers: see the introduction to the book for references to the behavioral literature.

[110] Bhagat et al. (1990) and Lichtenberg and Siegel (1990) find a limited impact of hostile takeovers on employment (except, perhaps, for redundant white-collar employees).

[111] For a review of the evidence, see Kaplan (1997), who further points out that many firms that did not undergo a takeover laid off workers over the 1980s and early 1990s: for example, General Motors and General Electric reduced the workforce by over 200,000 and 100,000, respectively.

earnings reports or looking for white knights. Such costs are also hard to measure. A second issue is that of the reference point. In particular, one must ask whether the benefits of takeovers cannot be achieved in other ways, for example, through improved corporate governance and whether these alternative ways would not generate the same costs as takeovers. More theoretical and empirical work is needed in order to have a better assessment of the benefits and costs of takeovers.[112]

DEBT AS A GOVERNANCE MECHANISM   6

Our discussion so far has largely focused on the impact of shareholders in corporate governance. We now turn to that of debt claims.

6.1 Debt as an Incentive Mechanism

Leaving aside the possible tax advantages of debt, which are sometimes an important consideration in the design of financial structures but are country- and time-specific, debt is often viewed as a disciplining device, especially if its maturity is relatively short. By definition, debt forces the firm to disgorge cash flow. In so doing, it puts pressure on managers in several related ways.

▶ By taking cash out of the firm, it prevents managers from "consuming" it. That is, it reduces their ability to turn their "free cash flow" into lavish perks or futile negative net present value investments.

▶ Debt incentivizes the company's executives. Managers must contemplate their future obligation to repay creditors on time, and therefore must pay attention to generate cash flows beyond the future debt repayments or else enhance their firm's prospect so as to facilitate future issues of claims. Absent such efforts, they may become cash-strapped and be unable to sink even desirable reinvestments. This threat of illiquidity has a positive disciplining effect on management.

At the extreme, the firm may be liquidated in the context of a bankruptcy process, leading to an increase in the probability of termination of employment, frustration, and stigma for the managers who led the firm to its end.[113]

▶ Under financial distress, but in the absence of liquidation, the nonrepayment of debt puts the creditors in the driver's seat. Roughly speaking, creditors acquire control rights over the firm. They need not formally acquire such rights. But they hold another crucial right: that of forcing the firm into bankruptcy. This threat indirectly gives them some control over the firm's policies.

---

[112] Despite obvious selection biases, clinical analyses may also shed some light about value creation and destruction in mergers and acquisitions. For example, the analysis of two acquisitions in Kaplan et al. (1997) sheds some light on the potential pitfalls: lack of understanding of the target by the managers of the acquiring firm, failure to realize synergies, diversion of the acquiring firm's management's attention, complexity of compensation design, and so forth.

[113] In Zwiebel (1996), managers choose debt as a commitment to produce high profits in the short run. The bankruptcy process is viewed as facilitating managerial turnover in the case of poor performance, relative to equity-based channels of managerial turnover (takeovers, or dismissal via the board, or a proxy fight). Issuing debt or distributing dividends (or, more generally, any policy that makes a liquidity crisis in the case of poor performance more likely) therefore increases sensitivity of turnover to poor performance and makes shareholders more comfortable with current management.

As we will later discuss, management is not indifferent as to who exercises control over their firms: different claimholders, through the cash-flow rights attached to their claims, have different incentives when interfering with the firm's management. In particular, debtholders tend to be more "conservative" than equityholders, as they get none of the upside benefits and in contrast suffer from downside evolutions. They are therefore more inclined to limit risk, especially by cutting investment and new projects.[114]

▶ Finally, when the managers hold a substantial amount of claims over the firm's cash flow, debtholding by investors has the benefit of making managers by and large residual claimants for their performance. An (extreme) illustration of this point arises when an entrepreneur's borrowing needs are relatively small and there is enough guaranteed future income (collateral, or certain cash flow) to repay the corresponding debt. Then, issuing debt to investors implies that any increase in the firm's profit goes to the entrepreneur. Put differently, the entrepreneur fully internalizes the increase in profit brought about by her actions, and so faces the "right incentives" to minimize cost and maximize profit.

6.2 Limits to Debt as a Governance Mechanism

We emphasize that debt is by no means a panacea. There are several reasons why this is so; this section emphasizes two such reasons.

Cost of illiquidity. The flip side of threatening management with a shortage of future cash flow is that cash disgorgements may actually end up depriving the firm from the liquidities it needs to finance ongoing projects and start on new ones, since the firm's cash flow and reinvestment needs are affected by uncertainty that lies beyond the reach of managerial control: input prices may rise, competitors may enter the market, projects may face hardships over which managers have no control, and so forth. Furthermore, risk management opportunities may be limited; that is, the firm may not be able to insure at a reasonable cost against these exogenous shocks.

The firm, when facing an adverse shock to its cash flow or its reinvestment needs, could, of course, return to the capital market and raise funds by issuing new securities (bonds, bank debt, equity), as stressed, in particular, by Myers (1977). For several reasons, though, returning to the capital markets is unlikely to provide enough liquidity. First, issuing new securities in good conditions may take time, and liquidity needs, for example, for paying employees and suppliers, may be pressing. Second, and more fundamentally,[115] the capital market may be reluctant to refinance the firm. They will not be able to recoup fully the benefits attached to refinancing as some of these benefits will necessarily go to insiders. Furthermore, they may be uncertain about the firm's prospects and the value of existing assets, and therefore worry about adverse selection—the possibility that securities have low value. Consequently, debt claims, especially of short maturity,

---

[114] At the extreme, debtholders are more keen on liquidating a firm than shareholders: for the former, a bird in the hand—the value of liquidated assets—is worth two in the bush—the uncertain prospect of full repayment.

[115] Note that the two reasons are related. Suppose, for example, that information about the firm's state is widely available. Then it should not take long to raise cash by issuing new securities. It is in part because investors are uncertain about the firm's prospects and the value of existing assets that they need time to analyze the firm's condition and that it takes time to issue securities.

expose the firm to the risk of liquidity associated with credit rationing in the refinancing market.

Bankruptcy costs. At the extreme, the firm's inability to repay the debt coupons may push it into bankruptcy. Bankruptcy processes vary substantially across the world, but to fix our ideas, it may be useful to take the U.S. case as an illustration (with the caveat that the U.S. bankruptcy institutions are particularly lenient on managers as compared with other countries). There are two main forms of bankruptcy. Under Chapter 7, the firm's assets are liquidated by a court-appointed trustee; the priority of claims (who is paid first?) is respected.[116] Firms rarely file bankruptcy under Chapter 7 directly, however. Rather, they use Chapter 11, which allows for a workout in which a reorganization plan is designed and thus liquidation is at least temporarily avoided.[117] Indeed, it may be the case that the firm is unable to pay its debt, but has a positive ongoing value for investors as a whole. To let the firm continue, it is then necessary for creditors to make concessions, for example, by forgiving some of their debt and taking equity in exchange.[118] Management is then given six months (or more if the bankruptcy judge extends the period) to formulate a reorganization plan. Creditors can propose their own plan afterwards. A reorganization plan must be approved by a qualified majority (e.g., one-half in number, two-thirds in amount).[119] In the absence of approval, creditors can finally force the firm into entering Chapter 7.

Chapter 11 is often heralded by its proponents as enabling firms to design plans that let them continue if they have valuable assets or prospects; its critics, in contrast, argue that management, equityholders, and junior, unsecured creditors have the ability to delay the resolution, at great cost to senior creditors. They further argue that the bankruptcy process is not as strong a disciplining device as it should be. Gilson (1990), based on a study of 111 U.S. firms, reports that 44% of CEOs (and 46% of directors) are still in place four years after the start of the bankruptcy process. Even if managers must cope with stricter covenants and often more powerful monitoring (by a large block shareholder) after bankruptcy, the process still proves relatively lenient towards them.

Workouts are desirable if they serve to protect stakeholders (including employees) who would suffer from a liquidation, and are undesirable if their main function is to hold up senior creditors and delay a liquidation that is socially efficient.

The workout *process* may fail for several reasons.

Transaction costs. It is difficult to bring to the bargaining table many groups of stakeholders. Even leaving aside employees and fiscal authorities, who have claims over the firm, a number of claimholders with very dissonant objectives must be induced to engage in serious bargaining: holders of debt claims with various covenants, maturities, degree of collateralization, and trade creditors (just think of the number of trade creditors involved in the bankruptcy of a large

[116] The "Absolute Priority Rule" (APR) distributes the firm's pay-offs according to priority. In particular, junior claimholders receive nothing until senior claimholders are fully paid.

[117] Under Chapter 11, all payments to creditors are suspended (automatic stay), and the firm can obtain additional financing by granting new claims seniority over existing ones. A number of proposals have been made in the literature to replace Chapter 11, deemed too slow in removing inefficient management, by a new bankruptcy procedure that would still facilitate the renegotiation of existing claims (see, in particular, Bebchuk 1988; Aghion et al. 1992).

[118] Exchange offers are only one of the actions that can be taken to reorganize the company. Others include asset sales, reduced capital expenditures, and private debt restructuring.

[119] See Asquith et al. (1994) and Gertner and Scharfstein (1991) for empirical evidence and theoretical considerations relative to workouts.

retailer!). Other stakeholders may have a stake in the firm without having formal claims over its cash flow. For example, if a supplier of Boeing or Airbus is about to go bankrupt, then the airplane manufacturer may bend over backwards and enter into a long-term supply agreement in order to keep the supplier afloat. This example illustrates the fact that even parties without an existing claim in the firm may need to be brought to the bargaining table.

Bargaining inefficiencies. Bargaining between the various parties may be inefficient—the Coase Theorem may not apply—for a variety of reasons. Prominent among them is asymmetric information, between insiders and outsiders and among outsiders.[120] Each party may be reluctant to enter a deal in which it suspects that other parties are willing to sign because it is favorable to them. Relatedly, some bargaining parties may attempt to hold up other parties by delaying the resolution.[121] Their ability to do so depends on the specifics of the bankruptcy process. A unanimity rule, applied either within a class of claimholders or across classes of claimholders, aims at protecting all claimholders; but it gives each individual claimholder or each class of claimholders the ability to hold up the entire reorganization process: they can threaten not to sign up and wait until they are bought out at a handsome price. This is why bankruptcy processes often specify only qualified majorities.[122]

Costs of the bankruptcy process can be decomposed into two categories:

Direct costs include the legal and other expenses directly attached to the process. Most studies have found that direct costs are relatively small, a few percent of market value of equity plus book value of debt (see, for example, Warner 1977; Altman 1984; Weiss 1990).

Indirect costs, associated with managerial decisions in anticipation of or during bankruptcy, are much harder to define and to measure; but they seem to be much more substantial than direct costs. In principle, bankruptcy costs may include the actions, such as gambling, taken by incumbent management in order to avoid entering the bankruptcy process, and the costs of cautious management during the process.[123]

INTERNATIONAL COMPARISONS OF THE POLICY ENVIRONMENT

We emphasize the many contractual concessions firms make to investors in order to boost pledgeable income and raise funds: covenants, monitoring structures, control rights, board composition, takeover defenses, financial structure, and so forth. Bilateral and multilateral agreements between firms and their investors do

---

[120] Asymmetric information between insiders and outsiders is stressed, for example, in Giammarino (1989).

[121] Free riding was first emphasized in Grossman and Hart (1980).

[122] The debate between unanimity and qualified majority rules has a long-standing counterpart in international finance. In particular, many sovereign bonds are issued under New York law, which requires unanimity for renegotiation (i.e., agreement to forgive some of the debt). In contrast, sovereign bonds issued under U.K. law specify only a qualified majority for approval of a deal renegotiated with the issuing country. Proponents of the New York law approach argue that it is precisely because renegotiations are difficult that discipline is imposed on the government. Critics, in contrast, point at the holdups and inefficiencies brought about by the unanimity rule. Much more detailed descriptions and analyses of the debate can be found in, for example, Eichengreen and Portes (1997, 2000) and Bolton and Jeanne (2004).

[123] We refer to Senbet and Seward (1995) for a discussion of these as well as for a broader survey of the bankruptcy literature.

not occur in an institutional vacuum, though. Rather, the firms' ability to commit to return funds to their investors depends on a policy environment that is exogenous to individual firms. "Contracting institutions" refer to the laws and regulations that govern contracts and contract enforcement, as well as, more broadly, to the other policy variables such as taxes, labor laws, and macroeconomic policies that affect pledgeable income and value. Contracting institutions vary substantially across countries, and so, as a result, do financial development and corporate governance.[124]

An active line of research, initiated by La Porta, Lopez-de-Silanes, Shleifer, and Vishny (1997, 1998, 1999, 2000),[125] studies the relationship between countries' legal structures and corporate finance. La Porta et al. consider two broad legal traditions. *Common law,* which prevails in most English-speaking countries, emphasizes judiciary independence, reactivity to precedents, and limited codification. *Civil law,* in contrast, stresses codification (e.g., the Napoleonic and Bismarckian codes) and is historically more associated with politically determined careers for judges (judges have only recently gained their independence in France, for example); furthermore, its more centralized determination makes it easier for interest groups to capture it than under common law. There are three broad subcategories of civil law: French, German, and Scandinavian. Both common law and civil law have spread through conquest, colonization, import, or imitation.[126]

La Porta et al. derive some interesting correlations between legal systems and investor protection. They measure investor protection through a list of qualitative variables: e.g., one-share-one-vote, proxy by mail allowed, judicial venue for minority shareholders to challenge managerial decisions, preemptive rights for new issues of stocks, ability to call extraordinary shareholders' meetings, in the case of *shareholder protection*: and creditors' consent to file for reorganization, inability for the debtor to retain administration of property during a reorganization, ability for secured creditors to gain possession of that security, respect of priority rules in bankruptcy, in the case of *creditor protection*. Shareholder rights are then aggregated in an "antidirector rights index," and creditor rights in a "creditor rights index."

A key finding is that the protection of shareholders is strongest in common law countries, weakest in French-style civil law countries, with German- and Scandinavian-style law countries somewhere in between.[127]

As one would expect, the extent of investor protection impacts the development of financial markets. Indeed, the work of La Porta et al. was partly motivated by country-specific observation. La Porta et al. (1997) documented a positive covariation between shareholder protection and the breadth of the equity market.[128] For example, in Italy (French-origin civil law system) (see Pagano et al.

---

[124] This section briefly reviews some of the empirical work on comparative corporate governance. As we discussed in this reading, there is also a large institutional literature comparing the main financial systems (see, for example, Allen and Gale 2000, Part 1; Berglöf 1988; Charkham 1994; Kindelberger 1993).

[125] See also La Porta, Lopez-de-Silanes, and Shleifer (1999).

[126] Glaeser and Shleifer (2002) argue that the foundations for English and French common and civil laws in the twelfth and thirteenth centuries were reactions to the local environments.

[127] The exception to this rule is that *secured* creditors are best protected in German- and Scandinavian-origin legal systems.

[128] Pagano and Volpin (2005b) also find a positive covariation, although a weaker one, for their panel data. They show, in particular, that the dispersion in shareholder protection has declined since the La Porta et al. study, in that the La Porta et al. measures of shareholder protection have substantially converged towards the best practice in the 1993–2002 interval.

1998), companies rarely go public, and the voting premium (the price difference between two shares with the same cashflow rights but different voting rights) is much larger than in the United States (a common law country).[129] Similarly, Germany's stock market capitalization is rather small relative to GDP.

More generally, common law countries have the highest ratio of external capital (especially equity) to GDP. (But, as Rajan and Zingales (2003) note, legal origins alone cannot explain why, in 1913, the ratio of stock market capitalization over GDP was twice as high in France as in the United States.) Common law countries also have the largest numbers of firms undergoing IPOs. The reader will find in Rajan and Zingales (2003) both a series of measures of countries' financial development[130] as well as a discussion of the relevance of such measures.

Relatedly, we would also expect systems with poor investor protection to resort to substitute mechanisms. La Porta et al. (1998) consider two such mechanisms. One is the use of bright-line rules, such as the possibility of mandatory dividends in countries with poor shareholder protection. More importantly, one would expect such countries to have a more concentrated ownership structure, since such a structure creates incentives for high-intensity monitoring and curbs managerial misbehavior. La Porta et al. (1998, Table 8) indeed find a sharply higher concentration of ownership in countries with French-style civil law.[131]

La Porta, Lopez-de-Silanes, and Shleifer (1999) more generally document that large firms in non-Anglo-Saxon countries are typically controlled by large resident shareholders or a group of shareholders. Looking at the top 20 firms in each country as ranked by market capitalization of common equity at the end of 1995, they show that, on average, 36% are "widely held," 31% "family controlled," 18% "state-controlled," and 15% in "residual categories" (defining categories is no straightforward task; see their paper for details). Quite crucially, widely held firms are much more common in countries with a good investor protection: for example, all top 20 firms in the United Kingdom and 16 out of the top 20 firms in the United States are widely held.[132] A similar picture emerges for medium-size firms. Specific evidence on the control of European firms can be found in the book edited by Barca and Becht (2002), whose findings (summarized by Becht and Mayer) confirm the sharp contrast between continental Europe and Anglo-Saxon countries. Control is concentrated in Europe not only because of the presence of large investors, but also by the absence of significant holdings by others. In the United States and the United Kingdom, in contrast, the second and third shareholders are often not noticeably smaller than the first.

Davydenko and Franks (2004) make similar observations on the debt side using a sample of small firms defaulting in their bank debt in France, Germany,

---

[129] Premia commanded by voting shares are 5.4% for the United States, 13.3% in the United Kingdom, 29% in Germany, 51.3% in France, and 81.5% in Italy (compilation by Faccio and Lang (2002) of various studies).

[130] For example, equity issues over gross fixed capital formation for the corporate sector, deposits over GDP for the banking sector, stock market capitalization, or number of companies listed related to GDP.

[131] They also find that large economies and more equal societies have a lower ownership concentration.

[132] While La Porta et al. attribute dispersed ownership in the United States to good investor protection Roe (1994) in contrast emphasizes populist regulatory impediments to concentrated ownership in that country.

and the United Kingdom. Of the three countries, France clearly exhibits the weakest protection of creditor rights: court-administered procedures are mandated by law to pursue the preservation of the firm as a going concern and the maintenance of employment; and, in the case of liquidation, even secured lenders rank behind the state and the employees in terms of priority. By contrast, U.K. secured creditors can impose the privately contracted procedure specified by the debt contract and they receive absolute priority in recovering their claims. Davydenko and Franks indeed find that medium recovery rates for creditors are 92% in the United Kingdom, 67% in Germany, and 56% in France.[133] The theory developed in Section 4.3 predicts that French firms will want to offer more collateral in order to make up for the shortage in pledgeable income. Davydenko and Franks show that collateralization (in particular of receivables) is high in France.

This analysis raises a number of interesting questions. First, the relative convergence between common and civil law systems makes it unlikely that legal origins by themselves can explain the current differences in corporate governance and financial institutions, between, say, the United States and the United Kingdom on the one hand, and continental Europe on the other. Some source of hysteresis must be involved that preserves systems with strong (weak) investor protection. This brings us to a second point: legal institutions, and more broadly contracting institutions, are endogenous; they are fashioned by political coalitions, which themselves depend, among other things, on financial outcomes. A case in point is the emergence of stricter antitakeover legislation in the United States in the wake of the hostile takeover wave of the 1980s. The broader theme of a political determination of corporate finance institutions is developed at length by, for example, Roe (2003).[134,135]

Remark (determinants of institutions). La Porta et al.'s correlation between legal system and investor protection is revisited in Acemoglu et al. (2001), who look at European colonization and argue that the mode of settlement, more than the legal system, had a bigger impact on contracting institutions. They divide colonies into two broad categories: those (Africa, Central America, Caribbean, South Asia) where the Europeans had little interest in settling—perhaps due to high mortality rates—and developed "extractive institutions," which allowed little protection for private property and few checks and balances against government expropriation; and those in which Europeans settled in larger numbers (United States, Canada, Australia, New Zealand) and therefore developed institutions that were far more protective of private property. There is, of course, a correlation between the British Empire and the latter category.[136]

---

[133] Their sample covers the 1996–2003 period, except for France (1993–2003 period).

[134] See also Krosner and Strahan (1999) on bank branching regulation, Hellwig (2000) on corporate governance regulation, and Rajan and Zingales (2003), who argue that incumbent firms may be leading opponents to reforms facilitating financial development.

The endogeneity of political institutions is, of course, a broader theme in economics: see Laffont (2000) (other theoretical books emphasizing the political determination of policy include Dixit (1996), Laffont and Tirole (1993), and Persson and Tabellini (2000).

[135] Corporate governance systems may also be forced to converge if companies can cross-list in jurisdictions (countries) with better shareholder protection or engage in cross-border merger and acquisition activity. The literature on convergence towards best practice corporate governance includes Coffee (1999), Gilson (2001), and Pagano and Volpin (2005c).

[136] The impact of extractive institutions as upsetting existing ones is further explored in Acemoglu et al. (2002), who attempt to account for a reversal of prosperity after the sixteenth century between the then poor (United States, Canada, Australia, etc.) and rich (India, China, Incas, Aztecs, etc.) colonies.

8

SHAREHOLDER VALUE OR STAKEHOLDER SOCIETY?

The corporate governance debates reviewed in this reading are framed in terms of shareholder value; as we noted in the introduction to this reading, economists, and for that matter much of the legal framework, have always asserted, on the grounds that prices reflect the scarcity of resources, that management should aim at maximizing shareholder wealth. To many noneconomists, economists in this respect appear "oblivious to redistributional issues," "narrow-minded," or "out of touch with social realities." A widespread view in politics and public opinion is that corporations should serve a larger social purpose and be "responsible," that is, they should reach out to other stakeholders and not only to shareholders.

8.1 The Corporate Social Responsibility View

An economist would rephrase the position of the proponents of the stakeholder society as the recommendation that management and directors internalize the externalities that their decisions impose on various groups. Examples of such externalities and concomitant duties toward stakeholders, according to the proponents of the stakeholder society, can be found in the following list.

Duties toward employees. Firms should refrain from laying off workers when they make sizeable profits (the "downsizing" move of the 1990s and events such as the January 1996 laying off of 40,000 employees by a record-profit-making AT&T and the $14 million annual compensation of its chairman created uproars on the left and the right of the American political spectrum): firms should also protect minorities, provide generous training and recreational facilities, and carefully monitor safety on the job.

Duties toward communities. Firms should refrain from closing plants in distressed economic areas except when strictly necessary; in normal times they should contribute to the public life of its communities.

Duties toward creditors. Firms should not maximize shareholder value at the expense of creditor value.

Ethical considerations. Firms ought to protect the environment even if this reduces profit. They should refrain from investing in countries with oppressive governments, or with weak protection of or respect for the minorities (child labor, apartheid, etc.). Firms should not evade taxes, or bribe officials in less developed countries, even when such behavior raises profit on average.

Many managers view their role within society in an even broader sense (satisfaction of consumer wants, support of the arts, political contributions, etc.) than suggested by this list.

According to Blair (1995, p. 214), even in the United States, which traditionally has been much less receptive to the stakeholder society idea than most other developed countries (especially outside the Anglo-Saxon world), "by the late 1960s and early 1970s corporate responsiveness to a broad group of stakeholders had become accepted business practice." Charitable contributions, divestitures from (apartheid-practicing) South Africa, and paid leave for employees engaging in public service activities, for example, became commonplace and were upheld by the courts. The consensus for some internalization of stakeholder welfare partly broke down in the 1980s. Proponents of shareholder value gained influence. Yet, the hostile takeover wave of that decade sparked an intense debate as to whether the increase in shareholder wealth associated with the takeover did not partly come to the detriment of employees and communities (see, for example, Shleifer and Summers 1988).

The popularity of the stakeholder society view in the public is to be contrasted with the strong consensus among financial economists that maximizing shareholder value has major advantages over the pursuit of alternative goals. A particularly influential advocate of the shareholder-value approach has been Milton Friedman (1970).[137]

Economists have long argued in favor of a proper internalization of externalities. And certainly the vast majority of them have no objections to the goals advanced by the proponents of the stakeholder society. A scientific debate therefore focuses on how to achieve these goals, rather than on the goals themselves.

8.2 What the Stakeholder Society Is and What It Is Not

Some management gurus have surfed the stakeholder society wave and have argued that "stakeholding" makes commercial sense. In a nutshell, the recommendation is to treat employees fairly through job security, training facilities, etc. The reasoning is that, by building a reputation for fairness, the firm will be able to attract the most talented employees and to induce them to invest in the firm, as the employees will know that they are engaged in a long-term relationship with the firm and that their firm-specific investments will be rewarded. This argument can, of course, be extended to, say, suppliers and communities, who are inclined to offer lower prices or larger subsidies, respectively, to a more trustworthy firm.

Such recommendations smack of social responsiveness: but in fact they are about shareholder value: intertemporal value maximization often trades off short-run sacrifices (investments) for the prospect of higher long-term

---

[137] "In a free-enterprise, private-property system, a corporate executive is an employee of the owners of the business. He has direct responsibility to his employers. That responsibility is to conduct the business in accordance with their desires, which generally will be to make as much money as possible while conforming to the basic rules of the society, both those embodied in law and those embodied in ethical custom. Of course, in some cases his employers may, of course, have a different objective. A group of persons might establish a corporation for an eleemosynary purpose for example, a hospital or a school. The manager of such a corporation will not have money profit as his objective but the rendering of certain services.

"Of course, the corporate executive is also a person in his own right. As a person, he may have many other responsibilities that he recognizes or assumes voluntarily—to his family, his conscience, his feelings of charity, his church, his clubs, his city, his country. He may feel impelled by these responsibilities to devote part of his income to causes he regards as worthy, to refuse to work for particular corporations, even to leave his job, for example, to join his country's armed forces. If we wish, we may refer to some of these responsibilities as 'social responsibilities.' But in these respects he is acting as a principal, not an agent; he is spending his own money or time or energy, not the money of his employers or the time or energy he has contracted to devote to their purposes. If these are 'social responsibilities,' they are the social responsibilities of individuals, not of business.

"The stockholders or the customers or the employees could separately spend their own money on the particular action if they wished to do so. The executive is exercising a distinct 'social responsibility,' rather than serving as an agent of the stockholders or the customers or the employees, only if he spends the money in a different way than they would have spent it.

"But if he does this, he is in effect imposing taxes, on the one hand, and deciding how the tax proceeds shall be spent, on the other.

"Here the businessman—self-selected or appointed directly or indirectly by stockholders—is to be simultaneously legislator, executive and jurist. He is to decide whom to tax by how much and for what purpose, and he is to spend the proceeds—all this guided only by general exhortations from on high to restrain inflation, improve the environment, fight poverty and so on and on."

profits.[138] Treating stakeholders fairly in order to raise intertemporal profit is not what the stakeholder society is about. Rather, *the "socially responsible corporation" is one that consciously makes decisions that reduce overall profits.*[139]

Similarly, we do not classify actions whose primary interest is to restore the firm's public image under the corporate social responsibility heading. It is perhaps no coincidence that multinationals, and in particular ones that, for good or bad reasons, have a poor public image (tobacco, oil, pharmaceutical companies), have eagerly embraced the concepts of corporate social responsibility and sustainable development and created senior executive positions in charge of the firm's social responsibility.

Before discussing the implementation of the stakeholder society, let me address the issue of what the concept exactly refers to. On the one hand, the stakeholder society may refer to a *broad mission of management.* According to this view, management should aim at maximizing the sum of the various stakeholders' surpluses (adopting an utilitarian approach); and, if management is not naturally inclined to do so, incentives should be designed that induce management to account for the externalities imposed on all stakeholders. On the other hand, the stakeholder society may refer to the *sharing of control by stakeholders,* as is, for example, the case for codetermination in Germany.[140] Presumably, the two notions are related; for instance, it would be hard for a manager to sacrifice profit to benefit some stakeholder if a profit-maximizing raider can take over the firm and replace her, unless that very stakeholder can help the manager deter the takeover (see Pagano and Volpin 2005a).[141] In what follows, we will take the view that the stakeholder society means both a broad managerial mission and divided control.

We focus on optimal contracting among stakeholders (including investors) and wonder whether managerial incentives and a control structure can be put in

---

[138] To again quote from Friedman (1970), who is highly critical of the stakeholder society concept: "Of course, in practice the doctrine of social responsibility is frequently a cloak for actions that are justified on other grounds rather than a reason for those actions.

"To illustrate, it may well be in the long run interest of a corporation that is a major employer in a small community to devote resources to providing amenities in that community or to improving its government. That may make it easier to attract desirable employees, it may reduce the wage bill or lessen losses from pilferage and sabotage or have other worthwhile effects. Or it may be that, given the laws about the deductibility of corporate charitable contributions, the stockholders can contribute more to charities they favor by having the corporation make the gift than by doing it themselves, since they can in that way contribute an amount that would otherwise have been paid as corporate taxes.

"In each of these and many similar cases, there is a strong temptation to rationalize these actions as an exercise of 'social responsibility.' In the present climate of opinion, with its wide spread aversion to 'capitalism,' 'profits,' the 'soulless corporation' and so on, this is one way for a corporation to generate goodwill as a by-product of expenditures that are entirely justified in its own self-interest.

"It would be inconsistent of me to call on corporate executives to refrain from this hypocritical window dressing because it harms the foundations of a free society. That would be to call on them to exercise a 'social responsibility'! If our institutions, and the attitudes of the public make it in their self-interest to cloak their actions in this way, I cannot summon much indignation to denounce them. At the same time, I can express admiration for those individual proprietors or owners of closely held corporations or stockholders of more broadly held corporations who disdain such tactics as approaching fraud."

[139] Interestingly, in the 1960s and 1970s, U.S. courts accommodated socially responsible activities such as donations to charities by arguing that short-run diversion of shareholder wealth may be good for the shareholders "in the long run." Courts thereby avoided conceding that directors did not have a primary duty to maximize shareholder wealth (see Blair 1996, p. 215).

[140] Porter (1992) argues in favor of board representation of customers, suppliers, financial advisors, employees, and community representatives.

[141] In this sense, there may be some consistency in the German corporate governance system between shared control, the absence or small level of managerial stock options, and the inactivity of the takeover market.

place that efficiently implement the concept of stakeholder society. Another layer of difficulty is added by the existence of a regulatory environment that restricts the set of contracts that can be signed among stakeholders. Interestingly, countries such as France, Germany, and Japan, which traditionally are more sympathetic to the stakeholder society than the United States and the United Kingdom, also have legal, regulatory, and fiscal environments that are assessed by most economists as creating weaker governance systems (see Section 7).

As in other areas of contract law, a hard question is, why does one need a law in the first place? Couldn't the parties reach efficient agreements by themselves, in which case the role of courts and of the government is to enforce private contracts and not to reduce welfare by constraining feasible agreements? For example, why can't a mutually agreeable contract between investors and employees allow employee representation on the board, stipulate reasonable severance pay for laid-off workers, and create incentives that will induce management to internalize the welfare of employees, thus substituting for an enlarged fiduciary duty by the management toward employees, legal restrictions on layoffs, or mandated collective bargaining?

Besides the standard foundations for the existence of laws (transaction-costs benefits of standard form contracts well understood by all parties, *ex post* completion of a (perhaps rationally) incomplete contract by judges in the spirit of the original contract, contract writing under asymmetric information or under duress, etc.), a key argument for regulatory intervention in the eyes of the proponents of the stakeholder society has to do with tilting the balance of bargaining power away from investors and toward stakeholders. This position raises the questions of whether redistribution is best achieved through constraining feasible contractual arrangements (as opposed to through taxation, say), and whether regulation even serves its redistributive goals in the long run, to the extent that it may discourage investment and job creation and thereby end up hurting employees' interests.

Whatever its rationale, regulatory intervention in favor of stakeholder rights plays an important role in many countries. Thus, besides the normative question of whether laws protecting stakeholders can be justified on efficiency grounds, the positive question of how such laws actually emerge is also worthy of study. Clearly, political economy considerations loom large in the enacting of pro-stakeholder regulations. In this respect, one may also be suspicious of the motives behind the endorsement of the stakeholder society concept by some managers, to the extent that they do not propose to replace shareholder control by a different, but strong, governance structure. That is, the stakeholder society is sometimes viewed as synonymous with the absence of effective control over management. (That the shareholder-stakeholder debate neglects the role of management as a party with specific interests has been strongly emphasized by Hellwig (2000), who discusses extensively the "political economy" of corporate governance.)

8.3 Objections to the Stakeholder Society

Four different arguments can be raised against a stakeholder-society governance structure. The first is that giving control rights to noninvestors may discourage financing in the first place. For example, suppose the community of "natural stakeholders" is composed of management and employees, who do not have the funds to pay for investment themselves, and that the investors are concerned that they will not be able to recoup their investment in the firm if they share control with the stakeholders; that is, there may not be enough "pledgeable income" that the stakeholders can credibly promise to pay back when they have a say in the governance structure. The stakeholders probably will then want to hand control over to the investors, even in situations in which control by investors reduce total surplus. "Shareholder value" may be the only way to obtain the required money.

The second and third objections are developed in a bit more detail in the supplementary section. The second objection is also relative to the governance structure. The issue with the sharing of control between investors and natural stakeholders is not only that it generates less pledgeable income and therefore less financing than investor control, but also that it may create inefficiencies in decision making. On many decisions, investors and natural stakeholders have conflicting objectives. They may not converge to mutually agreeable policies. In particular, deadlocks may result from the sharing of control.

The third issue with the concept of stakeholder society is managerial accountability. A manager who is instructed to maximize shareholder value has a relatively well-defined mission; her performance in this mission—stock value or profit—is relatively objective and well-defined (even though we repeatedly emphasize the substantial imperfections in performance measurement). In contrast, the socially responsible manager faces a wide variety of missions, most of which are by nature unmeasurable. Managerial performance in the provision of positive externalities to stakeholders is notoriously ill-defined and unverifiable. In such situations managerial incentives are known to be poor (see Dewatripont et al. 1999b).

Concretely, the concern is that the management's invocation of multiple and hard-to-measure missions may become an excuse for self-serving behavior, making managers less accountable. For example, an empire builder may justify the costly acquisition of another firm on the grounds that this acquisition will save a few jobs. Or a manager may select a costly supplier officially on the grounds that this supplier has a better environmental policy, while actually entering in a sweet deal with a friend or reciprocating a favor. As a last example, an inefficient manager may install antitakeover defenses on the grounds that employees must be protected against potential layoffs implemented by a profit-maximizing raider.

The fourth argument is that a successful popular push for corporate social responsibility de facto imposes a tax on business, whose proceeds escape control by political process. While there are sometimes good reasons to subtract public policy from political pressures by handing it over to less politically accountable bodies such as independent agencies and nongovernmental organizations, it is not obvious that social goals are best achieved by directors and officers eager to pander to their own constituencies (in particular, their customers and policy makers who affect their firm's stake).

8.4 The Shareholder-Value Position

Proponents of the maximization of shareholder value (hopefully) do not object to the goals of the stakeholder society. Rather, they disagree on how these goals are to be reached. Implicit in their position is the view that externalities are best handled through the contractual and legal apparatus, rather than through some discretionary action by the firm's officers and directors. Shareholders can substantially expropriate creditors by picking risky moves, or by disgorging cash and assets, leaving the creditors with an empty shell. Then, creditors should (and actually do on a routine basis) insist on a set of covenants that will protect them against expropriation. Maximization of value can come at the expense of the firm's workforce. Then, employees and unions should enter collective agreements with the firm specifying rules for on-the-job safety, severance pay, and unemployment benefits.[142] And so forth.

We just saw that it is important to use the contractual apparatus in order to reduce the externalities imposed by the choices of the controlling shareholders. There are *two ways of creating contractual protections* for the noncontrolling stakeholders. The first is to circumscribe the action set available to the controlling stakeholder by ruling out those actions that are more likely to involve strong negative externalities on other stakeholders; this reduction in the size of the action set involves transaction and flexibility costs, but it may still create value. The second is to make the claims of noncontrolling stakeholders as insensitive to biased decision making as possible. This idea is illustrated in Figure 8 for the case of creditors and employees.

Debt contracts impose a large number of positive and negative covenants, which can be summarized as defining the action set for shareholders. Making the creditors' claim less sensitive to shareholders' actions has two aspects: *flat claims* and *exit options*. First, the creditors' final claim is often a fixed nominal claim; and collateral further helps limit the creditors' potential losses in the case of nonreimbursement of the debt. Second, debt contracts often provide creditors with exit options that can be exercised before the value of the claim's payout is realized. This is most evident in the case of short-term debt, which gives debtholders the choice between rolling over the debt and getting out if bad news accrues; debt that is convertible into equity protects debtholders against excessive risk taking by shareholders. Debt contracts thus often limit the creditors' exposure to biased decision making by shareholders.

The same logic can be applied to the protection of employees. Let us here focus on the exit options. Exit options are, of course, facilitated by the firm's policies with respect to general training, vesting of retirement plans, and so forth. But quite importantly, exit options for employees as well as their welfare when they are laid off depend heavily on a variable over which the employment contract between the firm and its employees has no control, namely, the firm's economic environment and the flexibility of the labor market. While being laid off is always quite costly to a worker, this cost is currently much higher in a country like France, which has high unemployment (in particular, long-term unemployment)

FIGURE 8   Protecting Noncontrolling Stakeholders

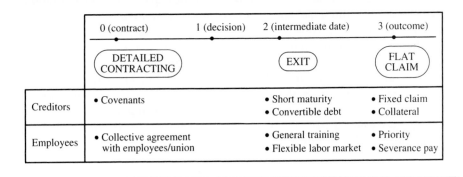

	0 (contract) DETAILED CONTRACTING	2 (intermediate date) EXIT	3 (outcome) FLAT CLAIM
Creditors	• Covenants	• Short maturity • Convertible debt	• Fixed claim • Collateral
Employees	• Collective agreement with employees/union	• General training • Flexible labor market	• Priority • Severance pay

---

[142] This position underlies the use of layoff taxes and experience rating (see Blanchard and Tirole (2004, 2005) for a policy discussion and an optimal mechanism approach, respectively).

and low mobility for a variety of reasons (such as close family ties and the fiscal environment[143]), than in Anglo-Saxon economies, where it is currently easier for laid-off workers to find a job of comparable quality. One could therefore conjecture that one of the reasons why shareholder value is currently less controversial in Anglo-Saxon countries than in continental Europe is that the externalities exerted by shareholder control on employees are smaller in the former.

Of course, proponents of shareholder value recognize that contracts are imperfect. They then point at the role of the legal environment. Courts can fill in the details of imprecise or incomplete contracts as long as they abide by the spirit of the original contracts. And, in the case of externalities not covered by any private contract (as is the case, for instance, with diffuse pollution externalities), courts (in reaction to lawsuits), or regulators (say, through environmental taxation), can substitute for the missing contracts.

The counterargument to this last point is that the legal and regulatory framework is itself imperfect. It sometimes lags the collective will (if such a thing exists). And it is often influenced by intense interest group lobbying (see, for example, Pagano and Volpin 2005b). So, when laws are "suboptimal," managers may need to substitute for the required reforms (but, as noted above, nothing guarantees that they will better represent the "collective will" than the courts or legislators).

While incentive and control considerations plead in favor of shareholder value and against social responsibility[144] shareholder-value maximization is, of course, very much a second-best mandate. In view of some imperfections in contracts and the laws, extremist views on shareholder value are distasteful. It implies, for instance, that management should bribe dictators or government officials in less developed countries when this practice is not sanctioned in the firm's home country; or that firms should have little concern for the environment when environmental taxes are thwarted by intense lobbying or measurement problems. New forms of intervention should then be designed in order to reconcile shareholder value and social responsibility in such instances of contract failure, although it should be recognized that proper incentives are then hard to design.

Green funds (investing in businesses that exert efforts to protect the environment) or more broadly ethical funds and consumer boycotts have attempted to do just that. They are interesting and well-meaning attempts at substituting for an imperfect regulation of externalities, but have their own limitations. a) One limitation is that both investors and consumers have poor information: incentives provided by individual investors and consumers require these actors to be well-informed about the actual facts as well as to be capable of interpreting these facts (for example, the social and economic impacts of a policy are often misunderstood). Presumably, trustworthy informational intermediaries are needed to guide their choice. b) Another limitation is free riding in the (costly) production of sanctions against socially irresponsible firms: as the evidence shows, a nonnegligible fraction of investors are willing to accept a slightly lower rate of return in order to avoid funding firms that behave in an unethical way. Most are, however, unlikely to be willing to take a low rate of return, in the same way that households are indignant when a park or an old neighborhood is converted into luxury condominium buildings but rush to acquire the resulting units.

---

[143] For example, high real estate transaction taxes have traditionally reduced owners' mobility. Similarly, for nonowners, laws related to rentals have made the rental market rather illiquid.

[144] An early exponent of this view was Berle himself. He argued that "you cannot abandon emphasis on the view that business corporations exist for the sole purpose of making profits for their stockholders until such time as you are prepared to offer a clear and reasonably enforceable scheme of responsibilities to someone else" (1932, cited by Blair 1995).

SUPPLEMENTARY SECTION— THE STAKEHOLDER SOCIETY: INCENTIVES AND CONTROL ISSUES

This supplementary section, which draws in part on Tirole (2001), develops the analysis of Section 8.3 on the implementation of the stakeholder society in a little more detail.

9.1 Monetary Incentives

To implement the stakeholder society, managerial incentives should be designed so as to align the managers' incentives with the sum of the stakeholders' surpluses rather than just the equityholders' surplus. We thus consider sequentially the provision of explicit and implicit incentives.

As discussed in this reading, managerial incentives that explicitly emphasize shareholder value are provided through bonuses and stock options that encourage management to devote most of its effort to enhancing profitability and favor this objective when trading off the costs and benefits of alternative decisions. Similarly, managerial incentives that would explicitly emphasize stakeholder value would be provided by rewarding management on the basis of some measure of the aggregate welfare of the stakeholders (including investors). The key issue here is whether such a measure of aggregate welfare is readily available. I would argue that it is harder to measure the firm's contribution to the welfare of employees, of suppliers, or of customers than to measure its profitability. For one thing, there is no *accounting* measure of this welfare, although in some examples one can find imperfect proxies, such as the number of layoffs.[145] For another thing, there is no *market* value of the impact of past and current managerial decisions on the future welfare of stakeholders; that is, there is no counterpart to the stock market measurement of the value of assets in place, since the employment, supply, or other relationships with the firm are not traded in liquid markets, unlike the shareholder relationship. (Besides, if a measure of the impact of managerial decisions upon stakeholders' welfare were available (which I do not believe to be the case), then there would be no objection to shareholder value since the firm could be forced to internalize the externalities through contracts specifying that the firm will compensate the stakeholders for the externalities!)

Relatedly, to avoid giving management a blank check to pursue whatever policy pleases it, management could be made subject to an enlarged fiduciary duty: stakeholders could take management to court and try to demonstrate that managerial actions do not follow the mandate of the stakeholder society. An enlarged fiduciary duty would therefore be an attempt to make management accountable for the welfare of stakeholders.

Those familiar with the difficulty of implementing the restricted concept of fiduciary duty toward shareholders will easily imagine the limitations of an enlarged fiduciary duty. In a nutshell, management can almost always rationalize any action by invoking its impact on the welfare of *some* stakeholder. An empire builder can justify a costly acquisition by a claim that the purchase will save a couple of jobs in the acquired firm; a manager can choose his brother-in-law as

---

[145] And their duration. A clever aspect of the experience rating system for layoff taxes is that the amount paid by the company depends on the level of benefits received by the employee it laid off, and so firing someone who remains unemployed for two years is much more costly than firing someone who will find a job the next day.

supplier on the grounds that the latter's production process is environmentally friendly.

In the absence of a reliable measure of stakeholders' welfare that could be incorporated into a formal compensation contract, managers could still receive profit-based compensation as under the paradigm of shareholder value. Unfortunately, multitask explicit incentives theory (e.g., Holmström and Milgrom 1991) has taught us that designing pay that is sensitive to the performance of a single task leads to a neglect of the other tasks.[146] We therefore infer that the stakeholder society is likely to be best promoted through *flat* managerial compensation, that is, through a fixed wage rather than performance-based incentives. There is in this respect some consistency between the lenient views in the French, German, and Japanese populations toward the stakeholder society and the historically low power of the managerial incentive schemes in these countries.[147]

9.2 Implicit Incentives and Managerial Missions

The previous discussion raises the issue of what management will maximize under flat explicit incentive schemes. The optimistic view is that management will choose what is best for society, that is, will maximize the sum of the stakeholders' surpluses. This view is sometimes vindicated: consider caritative organizations. Such organizations by definition aim at raising the welfare of the poor, of the hungry, or at providing access to cultural services to a broad audience, to give a few examples. Profit-maximizing behaviors would obviously defeat the purpose of such organizations. The key to success for caritative organizations is to empower idealistic employees who will derive private benefits from promoting social welfare.

While this paradigm works relatively well in some contexts, it would, however, be naive to trust it can be transposed to general environments. Most economic agents indeed place their own welfare above that of society. Thus, we cannot assume that managers facing flat compensation schemes will maximize the total surplus. Their incentives are then generally governed by their career concerns. The existence of multiple missions associated with the welfare of each stakeholding group suggests an investigation of the economics of multitask career concerns (which are actually the incentives faced by politicians, bureaucrats, and most employees, who have little performance-related pay).

Implicit incentives stem from an economic agent's desire to signal characteristics, such as ability, to what is broadly called the agent's "labor market," namely, whoever will in the future take actions that reflect beliefs about these characteristics and will impact the agent's welfare: board of directors, potential employers, voters, and so forth (Holmström 1999). Implicit incentives substitute (imperfectly) for explicit ones in environments in which performance cannot be well-described *ex ante*, but can be better assessed after the fact due to the accrual of new information.[148]

---

[146] Unlike Sinclair-Desgagne (1999), we assume that the nonmonetary dimension cannot be subjected to an audit. Otherwise, in some circumstances, it may be possible to provide high-powered multitask incentives (as Sinclair Desgagne shows) through a combination of compensation based on the monetary dimension together with an audit of the other tasks when monetary performance is high.

[147] As discussed in the text of the reading, entrepreneurial incentive schemes have become more high-powered in the last decade in non-Anglo-Saxon countries as well.

[148] More technically, a missing "deciphering key" does not allow the contracting parties to describe at the contracting stage the meaning of a "good performance"; it is only later when the uncertainty unfolds that it becomes clearer what a good performance means.

Implicit incentives are less proficient than explicit ones simply because the link from performance to reward cannot be fully controlled by a contract. This is particularly the case in a multitask environment. Indeed, multitasking impairs informal incentives just as it impairs formal ones (Dewatripont et al. 1999a,b). One reason is that managerial performance becomes noisier when the manager pursues multiple missions; the absence of "focus" on a specific task is therefore costly. Another reason is that multitasking may give rise to "fuzzy missions," that is, to situations in which the agent's labor market no longer knows which missions the agent is trying to pursue (although it tries to infer them by looking at what the agent has done best). The manager then does not know along which lines he will be evaluated. This uncertainty can be shown to further reduce the agent's incentives.

We are thus led to the view that the design of (explicit and implicit) managerial incentives for the stakeholder society is a particularly complex issue. This conclusion should not come as a surprise. After all, governments may be the ultimate stakeholder-society organizations, since they are instructed to balance the welfares of many different interest groups. It is well-known that proper incentives for bureaucrats and politicians are hard to design.

9.3 The Costs and Benefits of Shared Control: Lessons from Input Joint Ventures for the Stakeholder Society

We now come to the second aspect of the stakeholder society: the control structure. The stakeholder society is unlikely to be promoted by the undivided control structure that prevails under the shareholder-value paradigm. Nor is it likely to be sustainable if control goes entirely to nonfinanciers: for, consider undivided control by other stakeholders such as employees or customers. Such control structures are not mirror images of shareholder control. Employee or customer control makes it difficult to protect investors by contractual means. While covenants can restrict the payment of dividends to shareholders (so as to prevent shareholders from leaving creditors and other stakeholders with an empty shell), it is much harder to prevent employees or customers from paying themselves large "dividends" when they have control. For this point, the distinction between "natural stakeholder" (management, employees, customers, etc.) and "stakeholder by design" (the investors) is crucial. Dividends paid to shareholders are highly visible and verifiable; dividends paid to natural stakeholders may not be: employees may enjoy large perks and customers may select gold-plated designs. The partial lack of control over dividends in kind severely impairs the effectiveness of governance structures in which investors are not represented.

Let us therefore discuss the sharing of control among stakeholders in the form of a generalized codetermination.[149] To help us think through alternative control structures, let us use the analogy of the organization of a production process with multiple users needing a common input. This input can be manufactured by a

---

[149] We focus here on the sharing of all major control rights among stakeholders. Alternatively, multiple control rights could be shared among stakeholders, but some could be allocated fully to specific shareholders. In some circumstances, the two can be closely related: different stakeholders may threaten to hurt each other substantially through the exercise of their proprietary control rights; the parties must then cooperate on a global deal as if they shared all control rights. A case in point is the failed attempt in the mid 1990s by Mr. Schrempp, the chairman of Daimler-Benz, to take advantage of a newly passed law in Germany offering firms the possibility of limiting the payments to sick employees. The board of directors took back the decision a few days later because the envisioned restructuring of Daimler-Benz required the cooperation of employees. The chairman, up to that time a strong proponent of shareholder value, declared that he would never mention the phrase shareholder value again.

third party, either a not-for-profit or a for-profit corporation, controlled by players that are independent from the users (structural separation); or by one of the users, who then sells it to the other users (vertical integration); or else by a specific-purpose entity controlled jointly by the users (joint venture or association). For example, an electricity transmission network may be controlled by a distribution company or a generator (vertical integration), a group of users (joint venture), or an independent organization (not-for-profit as in the case of an independent system operator, or for-profit as in the case of a transmission company).

We can gain some insights into the costs and benefits of shared control from looking at the familiar case of a production of a joint input and apply them to the corporate governance debate. Indeed, input joint ventures are quite common: credit card associations such as Visa and MasterCard,[150] some stock exchanges, Airbus, research and farm cooperatives, telecommunications, biotechnology, and automobile alliances are all examples of joint ventures. Joint ventures, partnerships, and associations can be viewed as instances of stakeholder societies to the extent that players with conflicting interests share the control. But it should also be noted that the first argument in favor of shareholder value, the dearth of pledgeable income (see Section 8.3), may not apply to them: partners in joint ventures can more easily bring capital than employees in a corporation; the need for borrowing from independent parties is therefore much reduced. In other words, self-financing by the users of the input of a joint venture implies that the dearth of pledgeable income is not a key factor here.

An interesting lesson drawn from the work of Hansmann (1996) and from much related evidence is that the heterogeneity of interests among the partners of a joint venture seriously impedes the joint venture's efficacy. As one might expect, conflicts of interest among the partners create mistrust and lead to deadlocks in decision making.[151]

---

[150] MasterCard became for-profit in 2003.

[151] These deadlocks can be attributed primarily to asymmetries of information, but sometimes may stem from limited compensation abilities of some of the parties. This is where the Coase Theorem fails.

APPENDIX 33A

CADBURY REPORT

Report of the Committee on the Financial Aspects of Corporate Governance

Introduction

1. The Committee was set up in May 1991 by the Financial Reporting Council, the London Stock Exchange, and the Accountancy profession to address the financial aspects of corporate governance.

2. The Committee issued a draft report for public comment on 27 May 1992. Its final report, taking account of submissions made during the consultation period and incorporating a Code of Best Practice, was published on 1 December 1992. This extract from the report sets out the text of the Code. It also sets out, as Notes, a number of further recommendations on good practice drawn from the body of the report.

3. The Committee's central recommendation is that the boards of all listed companies registered in the United Kingdom should comply with the Code. The Committee encourages as many other companies as possible to aim at meeting its requirements.

4. The Committee also recommends:
   a. that listed companies reporting in respect of years ending after 30 June 1993 should make a statement in their report and accounts about their compliance with the Code and identify and give reasons for any areas of non-compliance;
   b. that companies' statements of compliance should be reviewed by the auditors before publication. The review by the auditors should cover only those parts of the compliance statement which relate to provisions of the Code where compliance can be objectively verified (see note 14).

5. The publication of a statement of compliance, reviewed by the auditors, is to be made a continuing obligation of listing by the London Stock Exchange.

6. The Committee recommends that its sponsors, convened by the Financial Reporting Council, should appoint a new Committee by the end of June 1995 to examine how far compliance with the Code has progressed, how far its other recommendations have been implemented, and whether the Code needs updating. In the meantime the present Committee will remain responsible for reviewing the implementation of its proposals.

7. The Committee has made clear that the Code is to be followed by individuals and boards in the light of their own particular circumstances. They are responsible for ensuring that their actions meet the spirit of the Code and in interpreting it they should give precedence to substance over form.

8. The Committee recognises that smaller listed companies may initially have difficulty in complying with some aspects of the Code. The boards of smaller listed companies who cannot, for the time being, comply with parts of the Code should note that they may instead give their reasons for

non-compliance. The Committee believes, however, that full compliance will bring benefits to the boards of such companies and that it should be their objective to ensure that the benefits are achieved. In particular, the appointment of appropriate non-executive directors should make a positive contribution to the development of their businesses.

The Code of Best Practice

1. The Board of Directors

1.1. The board should meet regularly, retain full and effective control over the company and monitor the executive management.

1.2. There should be a clearly accepted division of responsibilities at the head of a company, which will ensure a balance of power and authority, such that no one individual has unfettered powers of decision. Where the chairman is also the chief executive, it is essential that there should be a strong and independent element on the board, with a recognised senior member.

1.3. The board should include non-executive directors of sufficient calibre and number for their views to carry significant weight in the board's decisions. (Note 1.)

1.4. The board should have a formal schedule of matters specifically reserved to it for decision to ensure that the direction and control of the company is firmly in its hands. (Note 2.)

1.5. There should be an agreed procedure for directors in the furtherance of their duties to take independent professional advice if necessary, at the company's expense. (Note 3.)

1.6. All directors should have access to the advice and services of the company secretary, who is responsible to the board for ensuring that board procedures are followed and that applicable rules and regulations are complied with. Any question of the removal of the company secretary should be a matter for the board as a whole.

2. Non-Executive Directors

2.1. Non-executive directors should bring an independent judgement to bear on issues of strategy, performance, resources, including key appointments, and standards of conduct.

2.2. The majority should be independent of management and free from any business or other relationship which could materially interfere with the exercise of their independent judgement, apart from their fees and shareholding. Their fees should reflect the time which they commit to the company. (Notes 4 and 5.)

2.3. Non-executive directors should be appointed for specified terms and reappointment should not be automatic. (Note 6.)

2.4. Non-executive directors should be selected through a formal process and both this process and their appointment should be a matter for the board as a whole. (Note 7.)

3. Executive Directors

3.1. Directors' service contracts should not exceed three years without shareholders' approval. (Note 8.)

3.2. There should be full and clear disclosure of directors' total emoluments and those of the chairman and the highest-paid UK director, including pension, contributions and stock options. Separate figures should be given for salary and performance-related elements and the basis on which performance is measured should be explained.

3.3. Executive directors' pay should be subject to the recommendations of a remuneration committee made up wholly or mainly of non-executive directors. (Note 9.)

4. Reporting and Controls

4.1. It is the board's duty to present a balanced and understandable assessment of the company's position. (Note 10.)

4.2. The board should ensure that an objective and professional relationship is maintained with the auditors.

4.3. The board should establish an audit committee of at least three non-executive directors with written terms of reference which deal clearly with its authority and duties. (Note 11.)

4.4. The directors should explain their responsibility for preparing the accounts next to a statement by the auditors about their reporting responsibilities. (Note 12.)

4.5. The directors should report on the effectiveness of the company's system of internal control. (Note 13.)

4.6. The directors should report that the business is a going concern, with supporting assumptions or qualifications. (Note 13.)

Notes

These notes include further recommendations on good practice. They do not form part of the Code.

1. To meet the Committee's recommendations on the composition of sub-committees of the board, boards will require a minimum of three non-executive directors, one of whom may be the chairman of the company provided he or she is not also its executive head. Additionally, two of the three non-executive directors should be independent in the terms set out in paragraph 2.2 of the Code.

2. A schedule of matters specifically reserved for decision by the full board should be given to directors on appointment and should be kept up to date. The Committee envisages that the schedule would at least include:

   a. acquisition and disposal of assets of the company or its subsidiaries that are material to the company;

   b. investments, capital projects, authority levels, treasury policies and risk management policies.

   The board should lay down rules to determine materiality for any transaction, and should establish clearly which transactions require multiple board signatures. The board should also agree to the procedures to be followed when, exceptionally, decisions are required between board meetings.

3. The agreed procedure should be laid down formally, for example in a Board Resolution, in the Articles, or in the Letter of Appointment.

4. It is for the board to decide in particular cases whether this definition of independence is met. Information about the relevant interests of directors should be disclosed in the Directors' Report.

5. The Committee regards it as good practice for non-executive directors not to participate in share option schemes and for their service as non-executive directors not to be pensionable by the company, in order to safeguard their independent position.

6. The Letter of Appointment for non-executive directors should set out their duties, term of office, remuneration, and its review.

7. The Committee regards it as good practice for a nomination committee to carry out the selection process and to make proposals to the board. A nomination committee should have a majority of non-executive directors on it and be chaired either by the chairman or a non-executive director.

8. The Committee does not intend that this provision should apply to existing contracts before they become due for renewal.

9. Membership of the remuneration committee should be set out in the Directors' Report and its chairman should be available to answer questions on remuneration principles and practice at the Annual General Meeting. Best practice is set out in PRO NED's Remuneration Committee Guidelines published in 1992.

10. The report and accounts should contain a coherent narrative, supported by the figures of the company's performance and prospects. Balance requires that setbacks should be dealt with as well as successes. The need for the report to be readily understood emphasises that words are as important as figures.

11. The Committee's recommendations on audit committees are as follows:

    a. They should be formally constituted as subcommittees of the main board to whom they are answerable and to whom they should report regularly; they should be given written terms of reference which deal adequately with their membership, authority and duties; and they should normally meet at least twice a year.

    b. There should be a minimum of three members. Membership should be confined to the nonexecutive directors of the company and a majority of the non-executives serving on the committee should be independent of the company, as defined in paragraph 2.2 of the Code.

    c. The external auditor and, where an internal audit function exists, the head of internal audit should normally attend committee meetings, as should the finance director. Other board members should also have the right to attend.

    d. The audit committee should have a discussion with the auditors at least once a year, without executive board members present, to ensure that there are no unresolved issues of concern.

    e. The audit committee should have explicit authority to investigate any matters within its terms of reference, the resources which it needs to do so, and full access to information. The committee should be able to obtain outside professional advice and if necessary to invite outsiders with relevant experience to attend meetings.

    f. Membership of the committee should be disclosed in the annual report and the chairman of the committee should be available to answer questions about its work at the Annual General Meeting.

    Specimen terms of reference for an audit committee, including a list of the most commonly performed duties, are set out in the Committee's full report.

12. The statement of directors' responsibilities should cover the following points:

    ▶ the legal requirements for directors to prepare financial statements for each financial year which give a true and fair view of the state of affairs of the company (or group) as at the end of the financial year and of the profit and loss for that period;

▶ the responsibility of the directors for maintaining adequate accounting records, for safeguarding the assets of the company (or group), and for preventing and detecting fraud and other irregularities;

▶ confirmation that suitable accounting policies, consistently applied and supported by reasonable and prudent judgements and estimates, have been used in the preparation of the financial statement;

▶ confirmation that applicable accounting standards have been followed, subject to any material departures disclosed and explained in the notes to the accounts. (This does not obviate the need for a formal statement in the notes to the accounts disclosing whether the accounts have been prepared in accordance with applicable accounting standards.)

The statement should be placed immediately before the auditors' report which in future will include a separate statement (currently being developed by the Auditing Practices Board) on the responsibility of the auditors for expressing an opinion on the accounts.

13. The Committee notes that companies will not be able to comply with paragraphs 4.5 and 4.6 of the Code until the necessary guidance for companies has been developed as recommended in the Committee's report.

14. The company's statement of compliance should be reviewed by the auditors in so far as it relates to paragraphs 1.4, 1.5, 2.3, 2.4, 3.1 to 3.3 and 4.3 to 4.6 of the Code.

APPENDIX 33B

NOTES TO TABLES

1. Notes to Table 3

Sources: a) Federal Reserve, Banque de France, Bank of Japan, and Eurostat; b) Bank of England, Banque de France, Bank of Japan, and Eurostat. Data are not available for a) the United Kingdom or b) the United States.

Construction for both parts is as follows.

a) *United States*. 1. *Sources*: Federal Reserve of the United States, Flow of Funds Accounts of the United States (Release of December 9, 2004). Level Tables. Table 1.213 (www.federalreserve.gov/releases/zl/Current/zlr-4.pdf).

2. *Details*: Corporate equities are shares of ownership in financial and nonfinancial corporate businesses. The category comprises common and preferred shares issued by domestic corporations and U.S. purchases of shares issued by foreign corporations, including shares held in the form of American depositary receipts (ADRs); it does not include mutual fund shares. Data on issuance and holdings of corporate equities are obtained from private data-reporting services, trade associations, and regulatory and other federal agencies. Purchases of equities by the households and nonprofit organizations sector are found as the residual after the purchases of all other sectors have been subtracted from total issuance. *Construction*: "insurance companies" = "life insurance companies" + "other insurance companies"; "banks and other financial institutions" = "commercial banking" + "saving institutions" + "bank and personal trusts and estate" + "brokers and dealers"; "mutual funds" = "mutual funds" + "closed-end funds" + "exchange-traded funds"; "pension funds" = "private pension funds" + "state and local government retirement funds" + "federal government retirement funds."

France. 1. *Sources*: Banque de France, Comptes Nationaux Financiers, Séries Longues, Accès par Opération, Encours, Actif: F51 Actions et Autres Participations hors titre d'OPCVM, 2002 (www.banque-france.fr/fr/stat_conjoncture/series/eptsnatfinann/html/tof_ope_fr_encours_actif.htm).

2. *Construction*: "insurance companies" + "pension funds" = "sociétés d'assurance et fonds de pension"; "mutual funds" = "autres intermédiaires financiers"; "banks and other financial institutions" = "sociétés financieres" − "autres intermédiaires financiers" − "sociétés d'assurance et fonds de pension."

Germany. 1. *Sources*: Eurostat, Comptes des patrimoines, Actifs financiers, Actions et autres participations, à l'exclusion des parts d'organismes de placement collectif, 2002 (europa.eu.int/comm/eurostat/).

2. *Construction*: see France.

Japan. 1. *Sources*: Bank of Japan, Flow of Funds (Annual Data (2002)/Financial assets and liabilities), Column AP (shares and other equity) (www2.boj.or.jp/en/diong/flow/flow12.htm#01).

2. *Construction*: "banks and other financial institutions" = "financial institutions" − "insurance" − "pension total" − "securities investment trust."

b) 1. *Sources*: National Statistics Bureau of the U.K., 2002 Share Ownership Report, Table A: Beneficial Ownership of U.K. Shares, 1963–2002 (www.statistics .gov.uk/downloads/theme_economy/ShareOwnership2002.pdf).

2. *Description*: contains details on the beneficial ownership of U.K. listed companies as at December 31, 2002. The survey uses data downloaded from the CREST settlement system to assign shareholdings to National Accounts sectors.

3. *Construction*: "mutual funds" = "unit trust" + "investment trust" + "charities"; "banks and other financial institutions" = "banks" + "other financial institutions"; "pension funds" = "insurance companies"; "insurance companies" = "insurance"; "mutual funds" = "securities investment trust."

2. Notes to Table 4

Sources: Federal Reserve of the United States. Flow of Funds Accounts of the United States (Release of December 9, 2004). Level Tables. Table 1.213 (www.federalreserve.gov/releases/zl/Current/zlr-4.pdf). *Other financial institutions*: includes securities held by brokers and security dealers investing on their own account rather than for clients; venture capital companies; unauthorized investment trusts; unauthorized unit trusts; and other financial institutions not elsewhere specified.

3. Notes to Tables 6 and 7

Description of Table 6: ultimate control of publicly traded firms. Data relating to 5,232 publicly traded corporations are used to construct this table. The table presents the percentage of firms controlled by different controlling owners at the 20% threshold. Data are collected at various points in time between 1996 and 2000, depending on countries. Controlling shareholders are classified into six types:

Family A family (including an individual or a firm) that is unlisted on any stock exchange.

Widely Held Financial Institution A financial firm (SIC 6000-6999) that is widely held at the control threshold.

State A national government (domestic or foreign), local authority (county, municipality, etc.), or government agency.

Widely Held Corporation A nonfinancial firm, widely held at the control threshold.

Cross-holdings The firm Y is controlled by another firm, which is controlled by Y, or directly controls at least 20% of its own stocks.

Miscellaneous Charities, voting trusts, employees, cooperatives, or minority foreign investors.

Companies that do not have a shareholder controlling at least 20% of votes are classified as widely held.

Description of Table 7: Assembled data for 2,980 publicly traded corporations (including both financial and nonfinancial world) and supplemented with information from country-specific sources. In all cases, the ownership structure was collected as of the end of fiscal year 1996 or the closest possible date. This table presents result defining control on a 20% threshold of ownership.

4⅝ 4... ⅜
5½ 5½ — ⅜
5½ 21³⁄₁₆ — ⅛
20⅝ 21³⁄₁₆ — ⅞
17⅜ 18⅛ + ½
6½ 6½ — ½
7¼ 6½ — ⅛
15⁄₁₆ 3¹⁄₃₂ —
9⁄₁₆ 9⁄₁₆
19⁄₃₂ 7¹⁵⁄₁₆
7¹³⁄₁₆ 7¹⁵⁄₁₆
7⁵⁄₁₆ 7¹³⁄₁₆
2⅝ 2¹¹⁄₃₂ 2½ +
2¾ 2¼ 2¼
6½ 12¹⁄₁₆ 11⅜ 11⅜ +
87 33¾ 33 33¹⁄₁₆ —
602 25⅝ 24⁹⁄₁₆ 25⅝ +
833 12 11⅝ 11⅝ +
16 10½ 10½ 10½ —
78 15⅝ 15¹³⁄₁₆ 15⅝ —
808 9¹⁄₁₆ 8¼ 8⅝ +
430 11¼ 10⅝ 10⅝

INTERNATIONAL EQUITY BENCHMARKS

by Laurence B. Siegel

LEARNING OUTCOMES

The candidate should be able to:	Mastery
a. discuss the need for float adjustment in the construction of international equity benchmarks;	☐
b. discuss the trade-offs involved in constructing international indices, including 1) breadth versus investability, 2) liquidity and crossing opportunities versus index reconstitution effects, 3) precise float adjustment versus transactions costs from rebalancing, and 4) objectivity and transparency versus judgment;	☐
c. discuss the effect that a country's classification as either a developed or an emerging market can have on market indices and on investment in the country's capital markets.	☐

INTRODUCTION

International (that is, non-U.S.) equity benchmarks differ from U.S. equity benchmarks in some distinct ways:[1]

► Float adjustment is much more important for international stocks.

► The convention is to divide international equity markets into developed and emerging categories, and the decision as to which countries belong in which category has consequences for both the benchmarks and the countries' markets.

► An investor/manager must keep track of currencies and construct both local-currency and investor-currency versions of the benchmark.

---

[1] I thank Mark Sladkus of Morgan Stanley Capital International for providing an interview used in this reading, and I thank Steven Schoenfeld of Active Index Advisors for sharing many of the ideas and much of the data in Schoenfeld and Ginis (2002). Schoenfeld was at Barclays Global Investors when he did the work referred to in this reading.

Benchmarks and Investment Management, by Laurence B. Siegel. Copyright © 2003 by AIMR, Research Foundation. Reprinted with permission.

361

Expressing benchmark returns in more than one currency is straightforward. Float adjustment and the division of the world into developed and emerging markets, however, are sources of controversy.

The discussion in this reading will focus on international equity benchmarks from the viewpoint of U.S. investors. I will also review the trade-offs involved in international equity index construction and touch on the impact of benchmarking in international markets.

1   EARLY DEVELOPMENT OF INDEXES

Stock indexes around the world, including the United States, were first typically compiled by newspapers. Examples include the Dow Jones in the United States, the Nikkei in Japan, the DAX in Germany, and the *Financial Times* indexes in the United Kingdom. Such indexes were price-only (not total-return) indexes and were generally not capitalization weighted. Academic or brokerage-affiliated researchers also created stock indexes in some countries.[2] But although stock indexes already existed in a number of countries long before the mid-1960s, the first usable benchmarks were initiated by Nilly Sikorsky of the Capital Group in November 1968.[3] Unlike most investors who struggle to capitalize on their inventions, the Capital Group's successor company in index construction, Morgan Stanley Capital International (MSCI), became and has remained the dominant provider of international equity indexes.[4]

The Capital Group constructed the MSCI benchmarks to help investors measure active management performance. (Index funds had not been invented yet.) Unlike earlier efforts, the MSCI indexes followed the basic principles of good index construction—market-cap weighting, publication of constituent lists, and historical reconstruction of data so that they would be useful for analyzing asset allocation. These indexes did, however, have one quirk: They sought to capture only 60 percent of the market cap of the countries and sectors they covered. This percentage was small even by the modest standards of the time. MSCI justified this limited capitalization coverage on liquidity grounds and decided that it would be more consistent to have one capitalization coverage standard for all countries rather than cover a larger percentage of capitalization in the more liquid countries, such as the United States and the United Kingdom.

The emergence of international equity indexes of reasonable quality (that is, indexes that were good enough to double as practical benchmarks) meshed nicely with a trend toward internationalization of portfolios that had been developing in the 1970s and that came to the forefront in the 1980s. International portfolios had been available to U.S. investors for a long time, mostly from European managers, such as Robeco. In the late 1970s and early 1980s, however, U.S. investors began to perceive their home country as having inferior economic performance and began more aggressively to seek higher rates of return in booming Japanese, German, and other non-U.S. markets.

---

[2] For an excellent general discussion of global equity returns and indexes and a 101-year historical reconstruction in 16 countries based on returns from various carefully documented sources, see Dimson, Marsh, and Staunton (2002).

[3] See Sikorsky (1982). The November 1968 date represents a test launch, and the indexes were backdated to 1959. The eventual MSCI indexes had an initiation and base date of 1 January 1970.

[4] Sikorsky is president of Capital International S.A., an operating unit of the Capital Group; MSCI is a joint venture of Morgan Stanley and Capital International and is now controlled by Morgan Stanley.

U.S. investors in the late 1970s and the 1980s were also influenced by a number of academic studies showing that international investing had delivered a risk premium (Solnik 1974; Bergstrom 1975). Although international stocks had outperformed U.S. stocks in the historical period for which data were available, some investors (and academics) naively interpreted the results of these studies as meaning that international stocks would permanently offer a risk premium in the future. I have always been puzzled by this train of thought: Investors in any country might see investing in countries other than their own as risky. In other words, they might have a "home country bias," so they would require a higher return to entice them to invest in a different country. But that logic works both ways: U.S. investors would require a risk premium to invest in non-U.S. markets and non-U.S. investors would require a premium to invest in the United States. If the markets are roughly the same size (and they are), the two premiums should cancel each other out.[5] Investors should invest internationally for many reasons—for diversification and because the industrial mix of every country is different—but capturing a risk premium is not one of them.

Where there are portfolios, there need to be benchmarks. During this same period, the MSCI EAFE Index was pretty much the only international equity index available, so it became the almost universal standard for international equity benchmarks.[6] It remains so even though EAFE omits Canada and another index using the same methodology (the MSCI World ex-U.S. Index) that includes Canada has been available for quite some time.

NEED FOR FLOAT ADJUSTMENT   2

In the late 1980s, the Japanese equity market entered a super-boom phase that caused the weight of Japan in EAFE to soar to almost 60 percent by the end of 1989. The implications of this development for portfolio management were peculiar. As Japanese stocks took on higher and higher multiples, they became less and less attractive to most fundamentals-oriented active managers. To minimize tracking error to the benchmark, however—and to stay even with the benchmark's performance, which was boosted by its large weight in Japan—portfolio managers had to hold larger and larger Japanese equity positions.

Part of Japan's large weight in EAFE was a result of growth of the country's real economy and was, therefore, justified on fundamental grounds. And part of the large weight was caused by the high multiples that prevailed in the Japanese market. But part of the weight was the result of a large volume of cross-holdings in Japan. In cross-holding, one company owns shares of another, so including the full capitalization of both companies in an index is double counting. In addition, many shares were closely held, so they were unavailable to the public even if they did not represent cross-holdings.

To correct these problems, some managers tried to persuade clients to use either an "EAFE light" benchmark with an artificially reduced weight in Japan or a benchmark weighted by gross domestic product. Free-float adjustment, however, seemed to be a more natural solution.[7]

---

[5] For the two premiums to cancel each other out, U.S. and non-U.S. investors would also need roughly the same amount of aversion to the risk represented by investing in each other's markets.

[6] Originally, "EAFE" stood for Europe/Australia/Far East Index. Later, the name was changed to the Europe/Australasia/Far East Index.

[7] Free-float weighting does not eliminate distortions caused by high market prices (valuations), as it should not if a cap-weighted benchmark is the goal.

Salomon-Russell was the first organization (that I know of) to introduce float-adjusted benchmarks. Although the Salomon-Russell (now Citigroup) indexes did not attract a large market share because of the reluctance of sponsors and managers to change benchmarks, the superiority of its methodology was widely recognized. As a result, all the indexes introduced by new providers were float adjusted. Finally, after years of preparation, MSCI converted its indexes to a float-adjusted basis on 31 May 2002. Some details of this conversion and its effect on market prices are discussed later in this reading. In the meantime, note the differences in capitalizations and weights between MSCI's full-capitalization and free-float indexes shown in Table 1.

TABLE 1	Composition of MSCI Float-Adjusted and Full-Cap World Indexes, 30 November 2001					
	MSCI World Provisional Index (Float Adjusted, 85% Cap Coverage)			MSCI World Index (Full Cap, 60% Cap Coverage)		
Country	No. of Companies	Market Cap (Millions)	Index Weight	No. of Companies	Market Cap (Millions)	Index Weight
Australia	71	$ 243,658	1.54%	53	$ 236,243	1.50%
Austria	12	6,580	0.04	15	12,545	0.08
Belgium	17	50,496	0.32	16	70,735	0.45
Canada	86	336,853	2.13	68	340,053	2.16
Denmark	25	45,338	0.29	19	67,676	0.43
Finland	21	143,153	0.91	27	143,997	0.92
France	54	577,055	3.66	50	773,886	4.92
Germany	50	426,671	2.70	45	567,913	3.61
Greece	23	24,711	0.16	23	24,711	0.16
Hong Kong	28	99,401	0.63	28	143,944	0.91
Ireland	14	54,775	0.35	13	48,108	0.31
Italy	42	218,979	1.39	40	312,164	1.98
Japan	322	1,295,698	8.21	274	1,526,191	9.70
Netherlands	25	350,249	2.22	23	386,266	2.46
New Zealand	15	8,047	0.05	11	9,187	0.06
Norway	25	27,141	0.17	21	34,682	0.22
Portugal	10	23,418	0.15	10	37,240	0.24
Singapore	35	45,494	0.29	28	58,947	0.37
Spain	27	206,809	1.31	31	226,677	1.44
Sweden	38	137,015	0.87	34	167,619	1.07
Switzerland	38	467,962	2.97	35	491,214	3.12
United Kingdom	137	1,718,828	10.89	111	1,591,282	10.11
United States	413	9,270,878	58.75	322	8,462,332	53.79
Total	1,528	$15,779,217	100.00%	1,297	$15,733,613	100.00%

Source: MSCI.

When Japanese stocks were rising in the 1980s, managers struggled to stay even with full-cap benchmarks, and as Japanese stocks plunged in the 1990s, they found the full-cap indexes easy to beat. (With all benchmarks now float adjusted and with Japan constituting only 21 percent of EAFE as of March 2003, managers may not find that benchmark as easy to beat in the future.) When a benchmark is either very easy or very difficult for a large proportion of managers to beat, something is probably wrong with the benchmark—not with the theory that says active management is a zero-sum game!

The question of full-capitalization versus float-adjusted benchmarks is still a source of controversy for the U.S. equity market. For international equity benchmarks, however, the question has been resolved. Although the precise nature of the float adjustment varies from provider to provider (see Schoenfeld and Ginis 2002), no international equity benchmark uses full capitalization anymore.

INTERNATIONAL EQUITY INDEXES COMPARED   3

Today, major providers of international equity indexes include MSCI, Citigroup, FTSE, Standard & Poor's, and Dow Jones and Company. Exhibit 1 presents the basic characteristics of each index and provides a brief description of how each suite of indexes is constructed. Schoenfeld and Ginis described in detail how each of these indexes is constructed, enumerated the key criteria by which a good international index can be identified, and rated each index according to each of the criteria.

EXHIBIT 1	Basic Characteristics of Major International Equity Benchmarks, 30 June 2002					
Provider	Index	Country Coverage	No. of Securities	No. of Countries	Target Market Cap by Country (%)	Historical Inception Date
MSCI	All Country World Index ex-U.S.	Integrated	1,799	48	85	Jan 1988
MSCI	World ex-U.S.	Developed markets	1,101	22	85	Jan 1970
MSCI	EAFE	Developed markets	1,021	21	85	Jan 1970
FTSE	All-World ex-U.S.	Integrated	1,815	48	85–90	Jan 1994
FTSE	World Developed ex-North America	Developed markets	1,294	21	85–90	Jan 1994
Citigroup	Broad Market Index Global ex-U.S.	Integrated	4,875	49	95	Jul 1989
Citigroup	Primary Markets Index—Europe Pacific	Developed markets	663	21	95	Jul 1989
Citigroup	Global 1200 ex-U.S.	Modified integrated[a]	700	30	70 (by region)	Oct 1989
Dow Jones	Global ex-U.S.	Modified integrated[a]	2,200	33	70 (by region)	Jan 1992

[a] Includes advanced emerging markets.

Note: "Integrated" indexes include developed and emerging markets.

Sources: Schoenfeld and Ginis and data collected by the author.

Trade-Offs in Constructing International Indexes

As discussed for the domestic equity indexes, constructing any benchmark involves trade-offs, but the trade-offs differ somewhat from one asset class to another. Trade-offs discussed in this section are specific to international equity benchmarks or have special resonance when a U.S. investor is deciding which international equity benchmark to use (for more, see Schoenfeld and Ginis).

▶ *Breadth versus investability.* International indexes face a direct trade-off between breadth (the number of different stocks in an index) and investability. (An index is investable to the extent that you can readily buy and sell the stocks in it with a minimum of price-pressure effects and other transaction costs.) With international indexes—not only emerging market but also developed country indexes—the illiquidity of the smallest-cap and most closely held stocks is a greater problem than in the United States. Although most indexes exclude the smallest, least liquid securities, when selecting a benchmark you might want to take the extra measure of choosing an index that errs on the side of less breadth and greater liquidity (see Exhibit 1 for the number of stocks in each index). For example, the manager of an index fund with substantial cash flows in and out might not want the job of holding all 2,200 stocks in the Dow Jones Global ex-U.S. Index.

▶ *Liquidity and crossing opportunities versus index reconstitution effects.* Indexes that are most popular and most widely used as benchmarks or as the basis for index funds have greater index-level liquidity—that is, liquidity for investors seeking to buy or sell an index fund position or an actively managed position whose contents resemble, at least to some degree, those of the index. Of particular interest to institutional investors are crossing opportunities in such indexes. Crossing is the process by which an investment manager matches its own clients' buy and sell orders without using a broker and without incurring the transaction costs associated with brokerage. Crossing avoids transaction costs except for a small fee paid to the investment management firm doing the crossing.

Program trades, sometimes called portfolio trades, are another way that investors can buy or sell indexed or "benchmarked" positions. Program trades involve a broker bidding on the right to buy or sell a whole portfolio at an agreed-on price. A popular and liquid benchmark results in a lower bid from the broker because the broker's own costs are lower for such a benchmark.

Popular indexes—domestic and international—suffer, however, from index reconstitution (inclusion and deletion) effects. These effects consist of upward price pressure on stocks chosen for inclusion in an index and downward price pressure on stocks taken out of the index. The size of the effect on a portfolio manager is, logically, proportional to the amount of assets indexed or benchmarked to the particular index. Reconstitution effects are detrimental to performance, although the underperformance does not show up in conventional performance evaluation as a negative alpha because the reconstitution effect affects the benchmark as well as the investor's actual portfolio.

Indexes with more index-level liquidity and crossing opportunities may have poorer performance because of reconstitution effects. Of the developed country equity indexes, MSCI EAFE provides by far the most opportunity to investors seeking to cross trades or otherwise take advantage of index-level liquidity, and it is also the most likely to suffer from reconstitution effects because it is the most popular index.[8]

---

[8] Although not specifically discussed in previous readings, this trade-off also applies to the U.S. equity market and should be taken into consideration when selecting a U.S. equity benchmark.

▶ *Precise float adjustment versus transaction costs from rebalancing.* As noted, float adjustment for international equity indexes is no longer a matter of controversy. All the indexes are float adjusted in one way or another. In international markets, however, where float adjustment has a large effect on the constituent weights, the exact method of adjustment makes a difference. Indexes that make precise float adjustments and that revise these adjustments frequently impose higher transaction costs on those benchmarking against them than indexes that use float bands or broad categories. Float bands are categories of, say, 15–25 percent, 25–50 percent, 50–75 percent, and 75–100 percent, in which the percentage represents the portion of a company's full capitalization that the index constructors regard as freely floating. Citigroup makes precise float adjustments, whereas MSCI and FTSE use bands. Float bands make sense because transaction costs are a real loss to the investor; what is to be gained by replicating the float of the market exactly is not as clear.

▶ *Objectivity and transparency versus judgment.* Objective and clearly stated rules for index construction convey as large an advantage to international equity indexes as to U.S. indexes. They enable both index funds and active managers to predict what will be in the benchmark and, as a result, to trade more effectively in anticipation of changes in benchmark contents. They also make benchmarks easier to understand and to use as proxies for asset classes in asset allocation.

From this perspective, MSCI's judgment-based method for constructing EAFE and its other indexes is difficult to defend (as is S&P's use of an index committee to construct the S&P 500). When MSCI's indexes contained (by design) only 60 percent of the capitalization of each country and sector, however, it had little choice but to use judgment to select the companies. An odd result of this situation was that the MSCI U.S. index did not contain Ford Motor Company because General Motors Corporation accounted for more than 60 percent of the U.S. automotive sector and "crowded out" the other U.S. auto companies, even mega-cap Ford. Thus, a manager using the MSCI U.S. index as a benchmark would have incurred tracking error simply by holding Ford at its market-cap weight. Now that MSCI's indexes capture 85 percent of capitalization, MSCI's use of judgment to pick the stocks has less impact on index contents.

The advantages of benchmarking to a widely accepted index, such as EAFE or the S&P 500, include ease of communication and a high degree of index-level liquidity, which may overcome the disadvantages associated with using a judgment-based index.

Style/Size Indexes

The size and value-growth distinctions are as important for international equities as they are in the U.S. market.[9] Of the index constructors shown in Exhibit 1, MSCI and Citigroup calculate style and size subindexes. The MSCI indexes, in particular, also have a substantial back history, which is helpful for understanding and comparing style effects in various countries. These effects are at least as dramatic outside the U.S. market as within it.

An understanding of the specific construction methods of the subindexes is important before attempting to use them as benchmarks or buying index funds

---

[9] For a full discussion of the size effect internationally, see Clothier, Waring, and Siegel (1998).

based on them. Describing them is beyond the scope of this reading, but you can find information on international style indexes in Schoenfeld and Ginis.

4   CLASSIFICATION OF COUNTRIES AS DEVELOPED OR EMERGING

The division of non-U.S. markets into developed and emerging categories dates back to 1981 when Antoine van Agtmael, an investment manager at the World Bank, referred (in a flash of marketing brilliance) to what were then called third-world or developing countries as emerging markets (Thomas 1999). Mark Mobius of the Franklin Templeton (then, simply Templeton) organization was among the other managers who quickly capitalized on the trend to invest in countries, such as the Asian tigers, Mexico, Brazil, and (later) the formerly communist countries of Central and Eastern Europe, that were not in any established equity benchmark.[10] The emergence of China as a capitalist society in the 1990s reinforced the level of interest in (although not the performance of) emerging markets, and Russia and India are now having an impact. With the rising interest of institutional investors in the emerging markets came the need for benchmarks, so a number of index providers stepped up to the plate to provide them.

The first emerging market benchmarks were provided by the International Finance Corporation (IFC) and Baring Securities (now ING Barings). Soon afterward, MSCI and Citigroup constructed emerging market indexes. MSCI's Emerging Markets Free Index (EMF) gained an early popular lead, just as MSCI's EAFE had for developed markets. (The "free" in EMF refers not to free float but to the ability of investors from outside a given country to transact freely in that country's market. Such freedom includes the unrestricted exchange of currencies and movement of capital across borders.)

Today, the leading providers of emerging market benchmarks are the same as the leading providers of developed market benchmarks identified in Exhibit 1. The Barings indexes have been folded into the FTSE, and the IFC indexes have been folded into the Standard & Poor's series of indexes. All of the providers shown in Exhibit 1 also constructed integrated (that is, developed + emerging markets) indexes.

Boundary between Developed and Emerging Markets

When an index constructor decides that a country is going to be in the developed category or the emerging category, that decision has consequences for the characteristics of the benchmark and, potentially, for the country itself. First, the index constructor may be undecided about where to put the country because the country's market capitalization is large relative to an emerging market index. For example, South Korea's equity market is in the MSCI EMF and other emerging market indexes, but its market is quite well developed and has a capitalization of $100.7 billion, equal to 19.9 percent of the EMF. Thus, the decision to include or exclude Korea in the EMF had a real impact on the average company size and

---

[10] The traditional "Asian tigers" were Hong Kong, South Korea, Singapore, and Taiwan; later, the term was sometimes expanded to include Malaysia, Thailand, and other countries. Mexico was in the original MSCI suite of indexes discussed in Sikorsky (1982). The former communist countries were typically not strangers to equity investing; Hungary, for example, had the world's fourth largest stock exchange in 1900.

average level of country development in that index. As a constituent of EAFE (which it is scheduled to become), Korea will be a small rather than a huge player.

For the country, being in a developed index is highly desirable because far more assets are committed to developed than to emerging markets. For example, Korean companies would rather have a small weight in EAFE than a large weight in the EMF. This preference reflects the fact that when a country graduates from MSCI's emerging markets indexes to EAFE, as Portugal, Greece, Ireland, and many other countries have done and as Korea may do soon, a new source of capital becomes available to that country's companies. Inclusion in a broadly followed index of developed countries, in itself, makes a country more developed.

Acceptance of Integrated Indexes

There is no compelling reason why international managers should segregate themselves into developed and emerging markets specialists or why clients should establish separate allocations to these categories of markets. A historical reason is the desire of clients (investors) to reassure themselves that they are not taking undue risk. They pursued this goal by investing only in developed markets believed to have transparent accounting rules, liquid exchanges, and stable currencies. Investors also sought to avoid capital-control risk by holding only developed market securities. Today, however, the largest companies in the emerging markets are traded on the New York Stock Exchange and are thus free of capital-control risk (as well as subject to the exchange's transparency and liquidity standards). And some of these companies are globally dominant in their industries. Therefore, the developed–emerging distinction seems less important than it once was and investment managers increasingly find that the skills used to identify attractive stocks play equally well in developed and emerging economies.

As a result, integrated mandates (mandates for a single manager to invest in all non-U.S. markets, whether developed or emerging) are growing rapidly. Schoenfeld and Ginis reported that 48 percent of all new international mandates in the first half of 2002 were for integrated portfolios, up from 20 percent in 2000 and 13.6 percent in 1999.[11] The benchmark for such mandates is typically the MSCI All Country World Index ex-U.S.

IMPACT OF BENCHMARKING ON INTERNATIONAL MARKETS

5

The impact of inclusion of a stock in a benchmark on that stock's price has been less thoroughly studied in international markets than in the United States. Two recent events, however, offer evidence on the consequences of benchmarking for international markets.

The Odd Case of Malaysia

Up to 1998, Malaysia was a constituent of both the EAFE and EMF indexes because of an odd historical situation. The countries of Singapore and Malaysia were united until 1965, and their stock exchanges developed as a unit in the early 1970s (even after the countries separated politically), when MSCI was contemplating adding a number of countries to the developed market EAFE index. Singapore

---

[11] Schoenfeld and Ginis were citing data from InterSec Research Corporation.

was clearly a developed country, but no separate MSCI Singapore index existed, only a Singapore/Malaysia index. In a press release, Capital International, which at the time was the constructor of the MSCI indexes, later explained:

> Although the two markets became increasingly independent, the joint MSCI Singapore/Malaysia Index remained a constituent of the EAFE index for the next 20 years (to avoid disruption to the index, and to the markets). In May 1993, the MSCI Singapore/Malaysia index was finally split into two separate indexes. At that time, in view of Malaysia's long history of inclusion in the MSCI EAFE index, it was decided that it would remain, temporarily, in both the [EAFE and EMF] series.[12]

The result was a double-counting situation in which an investor who held one portfolio benchmarked to EAFE and another benchmarked to the EMF would receive a double weight in Malaysia (the only country in the world in this position). As of 2 September 1998, Malaysia represented 0.37 percent of EAFE and 4.40 percent of the EMF.

Then, in the wake of the Asian financial crisis of 1998, Malaysia imposed capital controls, motivating MSCI to remove that country from EAFE as of 30 September 1998. Capital International stated, "In light of the recent developments in Malaysia, it is time to put an end to this transition period."

If Malaysia had been removed from EAFE to avoid double counting at a time when no externally caused turmoil was occurring in the markets, researchers would have had a noteworthy experimental condition. They could have observed how the change in demand from indexing and benchmarking affected the Malaysian stock index relative to the stock indexes of other, roughly comparable countries, such as Thailand and Indonesia. The imposition of capital controls that spurred MSCI to make the index change, however, also ruined the experiment: Investors wanted to flee Malaysian stocks for reasons having nothing to do with their exclusion from EAFE.

Nevertheless, if only to satisfy curiosity, I've compared the returns on Malaysian stocks with stocks and indexes for the relevant period, 1998–2000, as shown in Figure 1. Because the decision to remove Malaysia from EAFE was announced on 4 September 1998 and was to take effect on 30 September of the same year, you can see the effects of the decision by looking at returns in September and October 1998. For September 1998, Malaysia did not have the lowest return in Southeast Asia; in October 1998, it had the lowest return in the region but the return was positive. Thus, without conducting any statistical tests but simply by inspecting the results visually, you can see that the returns for Malaysia appear to have been not much different from those for other countries in the region. Malaysia's returns are also not much different from those for the broad EMF in the period surrounding Malaysia's removal from EAFE.[13]

On 30 November 1998, MSCI also removed Malaysia from the EMF because of the capital controls. When Malaysia was restored to the EMF on 23 May 2000, it had already experienced huge gains (to more than four times the 1998 low in U.S. dollar terms) and was, in fact, at a high that it still has not surpassed.[14]

---

[12] This quotation and the next one are from "Malaysia to Be Removed from MSCI EAFE," Capital International press release, 4 September 1998: www.msci.com/pressreleases/archive/pr199809a.html.

[13] On a daily basis, the results are quite confusing. The volatile MSCI Malaysia Index actually rose, in U.S. dollars, by 75.0 percent between 1 September and 7 September 1998. By 30 September, it had fallen back to its old low. Currency depreciation was responsible for part of the decline after 7 September but had almost no impact on the 1–7 September advance. The reasons for these dramatic price moves might be a fruitful research topic for those interested in index-inclusion effects (or the effects of capital controls).

[14] As of 30 June 2003.

**FIGURE 1   Cumulative Returns on Malaysian
and Other Equity Markets, 1998–2000**

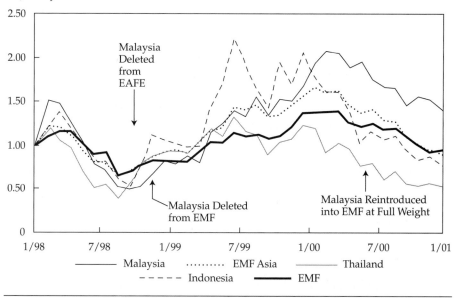

Growth of US$1.00 Invested
31 January 1998

Source: MSCI.

Either investors had been buying Malaysian stocks in anticipation of its reintroduction to the EMF or investors were ignoring Malaysia's absence from it. There was no measurable Malaysian EAFE deletion effect and there was no measurable Malaysian EMF inclusion effect.

The Biggest Index Change Ever

Recognizing that international investors had long held a strong preference for float-adjusted benchmarks and that they had sustained their loyalty to MSCI largely because of the difficulties that sponsors and managers have in switching benchmarks, MSCI converted its indexes to a float-adjusted format in a stepwise process. The process began on 31 May 2001, when the Provisional indexes were introduced. These float-adjusted indexes captured 85 percent of the capitalization of each country and of each country's industrial sectors, and they were designed to run in parallel with the Standard or original indexes for a year. (Recall that the original indexes, which were not float adjusted, captured 60 percent of capitalization by country and sector.) After a year—that is, on 31 May 2002—the Standard indexes were to be discontinued and the Provisional indexes would become the permanent MSCI indexes.

This procedure was designed to allow investors to adjust to the new index construction methods. Both the demand side—index funds and benchmark-sensitive active funds—and the supply side—brokers, hedge funds, and active managers seeking to profit from providing liquidity to the demand side—had plenty of opportunity to observe how the new indexes were constructed and what their constituents would be and to trade in anticipation of the full changeover on 31 May 2002.

Note that the conversion from full capitalization to free float and from 60 percent to 85 percent capitalization coverage affected the MSCI index weight of most of the large- and mid-cap stocks in the world. It was, to borrow the title of a Barclays Global Investors report, "the world's biggest index change ever."[15] Although little of the U.S. equity market is indexed or benchmarked to the MSCI U.S. Index, a large portion of non-U.S. equities are indexed or benchmarked to EAFE or to other MSCI indexes.

One way to measure the success of this effort is by the return differential, or spread, between the Provisional and Standard indexes (both overall and country by country). As liquidity suppliers bought stocks in the Provisional index in the hope of later selling them to indexed or benchmarked investors whose Standard index was about to be abandoned, the Provisional index should have earned an incremental return over the Standard one. In other words, the Provisional-to-Standard spread would be a measure of the transaction costs being paid by investors in the Standard index.

The original forecast was that investors could lose well over 1 percent in performance through transaction costs and/or by not switching benchmarks, Barclays noted.[16] The overall Provisional–Standard spread for the year ended 31 May 2002, however, was only 0.32 percent for the flagship EAFE index. "The World spread finished in negative territory," according to Barclays. Thus, much of the transaction cost that might have been paid was instead avoided through careful planning and a high degree of index transparency.

Results differed, of course, from country to country, and the spreads did not line up cleanly with the amount by which a country gained or lost share in EAFE and other broad indexes. For example, the United Kingdom, the country whose weight in EAFE increased the most as a result of the transition, had a generally strong market (it beat EAFE) and might have also been expected to have a high Provisional–Standard spread (because of a perceived "shortage" of UK stocks), but the spread actually turned out to be negative. Japan, the country that lost the most from the transition, had weak markets and might also have been expected to have a negative spread (because of a "glut" of Japanese stocks), but the spread turned out to be close to zero.[17]

Interestingly, in the first half of the transition year, the Provisional–Standard spread dove into negative territory because liquidity providers, reacting to the information in the Provisional with enthusiasm (also known as greed), grossly overestimated the demand for the stocks they were buying whereas investors on the demand side seemed confused or indifferent. Later in the transition, however, liquidity providers appeared to lose enthusiasm while demand-side investors were coming under increasing pressure to move to the weights in the Provisional indexes. So, the spread turned positive.

The lessons of this episode are not only that investors, managers, and index constructors can cooperate to avoid unnecessary transaction costs but also that markets appear to "work" quite well at the micro level (if the word micro can be used to describe this vast and complex change in an industry-dominant benchmark). They work, that is, to provide liquidity with a reasonable degree of efficiency when it is needed and to make transaction costs, which could have been huge and unpredictable, quite small.

---

[15] Unpublished report, Barclays Global Investors, San Francisco (14 December 2001).

[16] This and the following quotation are from "The MSCI Reconstitution: What Happened?" Unpublished report, Barclays Global Investors, San Francisco (2002).

[17] I use quote marks to describe "shortages" and "gluts" in this context because in open markets, supply–demand imbalances (shortages and gluts) exist only at the current price; the imbalance is resolved by a change in price that calls forth additional supply or that removes some of the excess supply.

EMERGING MARKETS FINANCE[1]

by Geert Bekaert and Campbell R. Harvey

LEARNING OUTCOMES

The candidate should be able to:	Mastery
a. discuss the process of financial liberalization and explain the expected impact on pricing and expected returns as a segmented market evolves into an integrated market;	☐
b. explain the benefits that may accrue to an emerging market economy as a result of financial liberalization;	☐
c. discuss the major issues confronting emerging market investors, including excess correlations during times of crisis (contagion), corporate governance, price discovery, and liquidity.	☐

Note:
Candidates should focus on the issues and concepts examined in this reading rather than the specific results of studies cited by the authors.

INTRODUCTION 1

Emerging markets have long posed a challenge for finance. Standard models are often ill suited to deal with the specific circumstances arising in these markets. However, the interest in emerging markets has provided impetus for both the adaptation of current models to new circumstances in these markets and the development of new models. The model of market integration and segmentation is our starting point. Next, we emphasize the distinction between market liberalization and integration. We explore the financial effects of market integration as well as the impact on the real economy. We also consider a host of other issues such as contagion, corporate finance, market microstructure and

---

[1] We have benefited from discussions with Karl Lins and Chris Lundblad. We appreciate the comments of Stijn Claessens, Vihang Errunza, Kristin Forbes, Andrew Frankel, Eric Ghysels, Angela Ng, Enrico Perotti, Roberto Rigobon, Frank Warnock. We thank Frank Warnock for providing us with an early release of his U.S. holdings estimates.

373

stock selection in emerging markets. Apart from surveying the literature, this reading contains new results regarding political risk and liberalization, the volatility of capital flows and the performance of emerging market investments.

In the early 1990s, developing countries regained access to foreign capital after a decade lost in the aftermath of the debt crisis of the mid-1980's. Not only did capital flows to emerging markets increase dramatically, but their composition changed substantially as well. Portfolio flows (fixed income and equity) and foreign direct investment replaced commercial bank debt as the dominant sources of foreign capital. This could not have happened without these countries embarking on a financial liberalization process, relaxing restrictions on foreign ownership of assets, and taking other measures to develop their capital markets, often in tandem with macroeconomic and trade reforms. New capital markets emerged as a result, and the consequences were dramatic. For example, in 1985, Mexico's equity market capitalization was 0.7% of gross domestic product (GDP) and the market was only accessible by foreigners through the Mexico Fund that traded on the New York Stock Exchange. In 2000, equity market capitalization had risen to 21.8% of GDP and U.S. investors alone were holding through a variety of channels about 25% of the market.[2]

These developments raise a number of intriguing questions. From the perspective of investors in developed markets, what are the diversification benefits of investing in these newly available emerging markets? And from the perspective of the developing countries themselves, what are the effects of increased foreign capital on domestic financial markets and ultimately on economic growth?

Market integration is central to both questions. In finance, markets are considered integrated when assets of identical risk command the same expected return irrespective of their domicile. In theory, liberalization should bring about emerging market integration with the global capital market, and its effects on emerging equity markets are then clear. Foreign investors will bid up the prices of local stocks with diversification potential while all investors will shun inefficient sectors. Overall, the cost of equity capital should go down, which in turn may increase investment and ultimately increase economic welfare.

Foreign investment can also have adverse effects, as the 1994 Mexican and 1997 South Asian crises illustrated. For example, foreign capital flows may complicate monetary policy, drive up real exchange rates and increase the volatility of local equity markets. Moreover, in diversifying their portfolios toward emerging markets, rational international investors should consider that the integration process might lower expected returns and increase correlations between emerging market and world market returns. To the extent that the benefits of diversification are

---

[2] See Thomas and Warnock (2002) for the estimates of U.S. holdings.

severely reduced by the liberalization process, there may be less of an increase in the original equity price. Ultimately, all of these questions require empirical answers, which a growing body of research on emerging markets has attempted to provide.

Of course, it is unlikely that liberalization will lead to the full integration of any emerging market into the global capital market. After all, the phenomenon of home asset preference leads many international economists to believe that even developed markets are not well integrated. In fact, much of the literature has proceeded to compute the benefits of full market integration in the context of theoretical models of market integration and international risk sharing. The results of these counterfactual exercises depend very much on the model assumptions (see Lewis, 1996; Van Wincoop, 1999). The liberalization process in emerging markets offers an ideal laboratory to test directly some of the predictions of the market integration and risk sharing theoretical literature.

In this reading, we start in Section 2 by focusing on market integration and how it is related to the liberalization process in emerging markets. We discuss the theoretical effects of financial market liberalization and the problems in measuring when market integration has effectively taken place. Section 3 surveys the financial effects of market integration, from the cost of capital and equity return volatility to diversification benefits.

We also present some new results that examine the volatility of capital flows, the impact of financial liberalizations on country risk, and the performance of emerging market investments. Some of these results challenge conventional wisdom. For example, we find that capital flows to emerging markets as a group are less volatile than capital flows to developed countries as a group. We also find that despite growing reports on the irrational behavior of foreign investors in emerging markets, the emerging market portfolios of U.S. investors outperform a number of natural benchmarks.

Section 4 shifts attention to the real sector. We examine the effects of the liberalization process on economic growth, real exchange rates and income inequality. We present empirical evidence that suggests that for equity market liberalizations, there is a positive average effect. Nevertheless, a large literature stresses the disastrous effects freewheeling capital has had through severe currency, equity and banking crises in Mexico in 1995, Asia in 1997 and Russia in 1998. A comprehensive review of this evidence is beyond the scope of this reading; however, in Section 5, we do offer a brief survey and suggest a somewhat different perspective on the rapidly growing contagion literature. In Section 6, we briefly review the important aspects of emerging market finance we do not discuss elsewhere in detail, including corporate finance and governance issues, the microstructure of emerging equity markets, the emerging fixed income markets and individual security analysis in emerging markets. Some concluding remarks are offered in Section 7.

2 MARKET INTEGRATION AND LIBERALIZATION

2.1 The Theory of Market Integration

It is important to be clear by what we mean by financial liberalization. In the development literature, it often refers to domestic financial liberalization (see Gelos and Werner, 2001; Beim and Calomiris, 2001 for example), which may include banking sector reforms or even privatizations. By financial liberalization, we mean allowing inward and outward foreign equity investment. In a liberalized equity market, foreign investors can, without restriction, purchase or sell domestic securities. In addition, domestic investors can purchase or sell foreign securities.

There are other forms of financial openness regarding bond market, banking sector and foreign exchange reforms. The popular International Monetary Fund (IMF) capital account openness measure lumps all of these together in a 0/1 variable (see below).

Even with our limited focus, the liberalization process is extremely complex and there is no established economic model that adequately describes the dynamics of the process. That is, while there are general equilibrium models of economies in integrated states and segmented states, there is no model that specifies the economic mechanism that moves a country from segmented to integrated status.[3]

To gain some intuition, we consider a simple model that traces the impact of market integration on security prices from the perspective of an emerging market. The model is a straightforward extension of the standard static integration/ segmentation model; (see Errunza and Losq (1985), Eun and Janakiramanan (1986), Alexander, Eun and Janakiramanan and Errunza, Senbet and Hogan (1998), and Martin and Rey (2000)). Within the context of a simple quadratic utility specification, we examine a three-period problem for the world market and an emerging market. We assume that there is one share outstanding of each asset. In period three, dividends are paid out and, hence, there are only two trading periods. In period two, the government in the developing/emerging country may integrate the market with the world market or it may not. Each market has a price-taking agent, who only consumes in the third period. In period one, agents attach a probability, λ, to the government integrating the market with the world market in the second period.

For simplicity, the risk-free rate is set equal to zero and currency considerations are ignored. Risky assets in the world market (emerging market) yield a random per capita payoff of $D_i^W (D_i^E)$ with $i = 1, \ldots, N_W$, ($i = 1, \ldots, N_E$) in the third period. Denote the aggregate, market payoff as $D_M^W = \Sigma_{i=1}^{N_W} D_i^W$ and $D_M^E = \Sigma_{i=1}^{N_E} D_i^E$.

We focus on equity prices in the emerging markets. The second-period prices under perfect integration or perfect segmentation are well known:

$$P_2^S = E[D_M^E] - \rho \text{Var}[D_M^E]$$
$$P_2^I = E[D_M^E] - \rho \text{Cov}[D_M^E, D_M^W]$$

where ρ is the risk aversion coefficient and where we assumed the weight of the emerging market in the global world market to be negligible.

---

[3] One possibility is to model investments in international markets as being taxed by the host country (Stulz, 1981). A segmented (integrated) country is a country that imposes taxes (no taxes) on incoming and outgoing investments. A change in regime is a change in the tax rate. For a simple version of this idea, see Bacchetta and Wincoop (2000). The Errunza and Losq (1985) model, a limiting case of Stulz (1981), also lends itself to an analysis of a continuum of market structures.

In period 1, agents know that prices in period 2 will either be P_2^S or P_2^I. The attraction of the quadratic utility framework is that in period 1, the price will be:

$$P_1 = \lambda P_2^I + (1 - \lambda) P_2^S$$

where λ is the probability (in period 1) that the government will integrate the market in period 2. It is important to realize that $P_2^S < P_2^I$, since the variability of local cash flows will be high whereas the covariance between local and world cash flows may be quite low.

Suppose the government announces a liberalization in period 1 to occur in period 2. The model predicts that prices will jump up and that the size of the jump is related both to the credibility of the government's announcement (and policies in general) as captured by the λ parameter, and the diversification benefits to be gained from integrating the market, as reflected in P_1^I. Foreign capital flows in when the market finally liberalizes (in period 2) and the price rises again since all uncertainty is resolved. This last price rise may be small if the announcement was credible.

Figure 1 presents the implications of this simple model for equity prices and capital flows. Of course, this model is very stylized and ignores many dynamic effects. This simple model suggests that variables such as dividend yields and market capitalization to GDP may change significantly during liberalization as they embed permanent price changes. This simple story already reveals complex timing issues. Market prices can change upon announcement of a liberalization or as soon as investors anticipate liberalization may occur in the future. However, foreign ownership can only be established when allowed by the authorities. That is, capital flows may only occur after the "return to integration" has already taken place, so that foreign investors may not enjoy this return. (Note that we assume that capital inflows exceed capital outflows upon liberalization).

The model suggests that expected returns (cost of capital) should decrease. The reason is that the volatility of emerging market returns is much higher than their covariances with world market returns. Holding the variances and covariances constant, this implies that prices should rise (expected returns decrease) when a market moves from a segmented to an integrated state. However, when a market is opened to international investors, it may become more sensitive to world events (covariances with the world may increase). Even with this effect, it is likely that these covariances are still much smaller than the local variance, which would imply rising prices.

It also makes sense that the liberalization process may be reflected in activity in the local market. As foreigners are allowed to access the local market, liquidity may increase along with trading volume.

There could also be some structural changes in the market. For example, if the cost of capital decreases, new firms may present initial public offerings. Market concentration may decrease as a result of these new entrants. In addition, individual stocks may become less sensitive to local information and more sensitive to world events. This may cause the cross-correlation of individual stocks within a market to change. Morck et al. (2000) find that stock prices in poor economies move together more (that is, the cross-correlation is higher) than in rich countries, but they link this phenomenon to the absence of strong public investor property rights in emerging markets.

The liberalization process is intricately linked with the macro-economy. Liberalization of markets could coincide with other economic policies directed at inflation, exchange rates, or the trade sector (see Henry, 2000a for details) and it may be correlated with other financial reforms aimed at developing the domestic financial system. Liberalization may also be viewed as a positive step by

FIGURE 1   Asset Prices and Market Integration

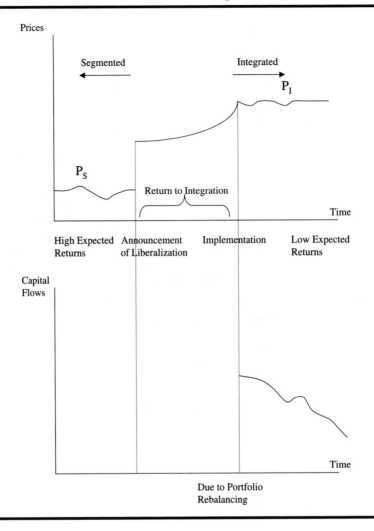

international bankers that may lead to better country risk ratings. Hence, these ratings may contain valuable information regarding the integration process as well as the credibility of reforms.

2.2 Measuring Market Integration

Once we leave the pristine world of theory, it soon becomes clear that the degree of market integration is very difficult to measure. Investment restrictions may not be binding, or there may be indirect ways to access local equity markets for example, through country funds or American Depository Receipts (ADRs). For example, the Korea Fund was launched in 1986, well before the liberalization of the Korean equity market. Also, there are many kinds of investment barriers, and the liberalization process is typically a complex and gradual one.

Bekaert (1995) distinguishes between three different kinds of barriers. First are legal barriers arising from the different legal status of foreign and domestic investors with regard to, for example, foreign ownership restrictions and taxes on foreign investment. Second are indirect barriers arising from differences in available information, accounting standards, and investor protection. Third are barriers arising from emerging market specific risks (EMSRs) that discourage foreign investment and lead to de facto segmentation. EMSRs include liquidity risk, political risk, economic policy risk, and perhaps currency risk. Nishiotis (2002) uses country fund data to examine the differential pricing effects of these types of barriers and finds indirect barriers and EMSRs to have often more important pricing effects than direct barriers.

Some might argue that these risks, are in fact, diversifiable and not priced; however, World Bank surveys of institutional investors in developed markets found that liquidity problems were seen as major impediments to investing in emerging markets. Moreover, Bekaert, Erb, Harvey and Viskanta (1997) find political risk to be priced in emerging market securities. When Bekaert (1995) measures the three types of broadly defined investment barriers for nine emerging markets, he finds that direct barriers to investment are not significantly related to a return-based quantitative measure of market integration. However, indirect barriers, such as poor credit ratings and the lack of a high-quality regulatory and accounting framework, are strongly related cross-sectionally with the integration measure. These results reveal the danger in measuring market integration purely by investigating the market's regulatory framework. Nevertheless, many researchers have tried this, including Kim and Singal (2000), Henry (2000a) and Bekaert and Harvey (2000a). Bekaert and Harvey provide an Internet site with detailed time lines for 45 emerging markets that provided the basis for the dates in Bekaert and Harvey (2000a).[4] Bekaert (1995) and more recently, Edison and Warnock (2001) have proposed to use the ratio of market capitalization represented by the International Finance Corporation (IFC) Investable Indices, which correct for foreign ownership, to the market capitalization represented by the IFC Global Indices. This ratio has the advantage that it captures gradual liberalizations as in South Korea where foreign ownership restrictions were relaxed gradually over time.[5]

There are a number of potential solutions to the problems posed in trying to date regulatory reforms.

First, Bekaert and Harvey (1995) measure the degree of integration directly from equity return data using a parameterized model of integration versus segmentation (a regime-switching model). The model yields a time-varying measure of the extent of integration between 0 and 1. Importantly, the model allows for the possibility of gradual integration, as in Korea where foreign ownership restrictions were gradually relaxed. In many countries, with Thailand as a stark example, variation in the integration measure coincides with capital market reforms. In contrast to general perceptions at the time of this article was written, its results suggest that some countries became less integrated over time.[6]

Carrieri et al. (2002) study eight emerging markets over the period 1976–2000. Their results suggest that although local risk is the most relevant factor in explaining time-variation in emerging market expected returns, global risk is also conditionally priced for three countries, while for two countries it exhibits marginal significance. Further, there are substantial cross-market differences in

---

[4] See www.duke.edu:80/charvey/Country_risk/chronology/chronology_index.htm. Also see Bekaert and Harvey (2000b) and Bekaert, Harvey and Lundbland (2003a).

[5] De Jong and De Roon (2002) apply this measure to a model of emerging market expected returns. Bae et al. (2002a) use the measure to model time-varying volatility.

[6] The Bekaert and Harvey (1995) model has been extended in Bhattacharya and Daouk (2002), Hardouvelis et al. (2000), Carrieri et al. (2002) and Adler and Qi (2002). A related model in Bekaert and Harvey (1997) is extended by Rockinger and Urga (2001).

the degree of integration. More interestingly, they observe evolution towards more integrated financial markets. This conforms to our a priori expectations based on the reduction in barriers to portfolio flows, the general liberalization of capital markets, the increased availability of ADRs and country funds, better information and investor awareness. Finally, their results strongly suggest the impropriety of using correlations of market-wide index returns as a measure of market integration.

Laeven and Perotti (2001) argue that credibility of liberalizations evolves over time. Their evidence suggests that the positive impact of privatizations occurs during the actual privatization rather than the announcement period. This is consistent with the importance of allowing for gradual integration.

Second, Bekaert and Harvey (2000a,b) use bilateral capital flow data in conjunction with IFC index returns to construct measures of U.S. holdings of the emerging market equities as a percentage of local market capitalization. The use of more liquid securities represented in the IFC indices to compute the returns of foreign investors is consistent with Kang and Stulz (1997) who show that foreign investors in Japan mostly buy large and liquid stocks. Bekaert and Harvey then determine the time at which capital flows experienced a structural break as a proxy for when foreign investors may have become marginal investors in these markets. Although this measure avoids the necessity of having to specify an asset-pricing model and avoids noisy return data, the capital flow data that they use are complicated by the existence of financial intermediary centers (e.g., large flows to the U.K. are channeled to other countries), and by the fact that the United States is the only country for which we have detailed data on bilateral monthly flows with emerging markets.[7]

In Table 1, we show the U.S. holdings measure for various periods for 16 emerging markets. We contrast its value in the 1980s versus the 1990s and pre- and post-liberalization, where the liberalization date is the Official Liberalization date from Bekaert and Harvey (2000a). The message here is simple: on average, liberalizations are associated with increased capital flows. In dollar terms, U.S. holdings increase 10-fold in the 5-years post-liberalization versus the 5-years pre-liberalization, but in percent of market capitalization, the increase is much more modest, but still quite substantial (from 6.2% to 9.4%). This modest percentage increase is influenced by the steep drop in holdings in the Philippines, where American capital was substantially present before the official liberalization. Also the dating of the liberalization may be incorrect. Finally the results are influenced by the fact that, comparing the 1980s to the 1990s, the U.S. share of the IFC market capitalization increased from 6.6% to 12.9%.

Third, Bekaert, Harvey, and Lumsdaine (2002b) exploit the idea that market integration is an all-encompassing event that should change the return-generating process, and with it the stochastic process governing other economic variables. They use a novel methodology both to detect breaks and to "date" them, looking at a wide set of financial and economic variables. The resulting break dates are mostly within 2 years of one of four alternative measures of a liberalization event: a major regulatory reform liberalizing foreign equity investments; the announcement of the first ADR issue; the first country fund launching; and a large increase in capital flows.[8]

---

[7] Also see Warnock and Cleaver (2002), and Tesar and Werner (1995) for an earlier study.

[8] Garcia and Ghysels (1998) also find strong evidence of structural change when applying different asset pricing models to emerging markets but they do not "date" the changes.

TABLE 1   Estimates of U.S. Share of MSCI Market Capitalization around Liberalizations

Country	U.S. Holdings in Millions		U.S. Share of Market Capitalization		U.S. Share of Market Capitalization	
	5-Year Pre-Liberalization ($)	5-Year Post-Liberalization ($)	5-Year Pre-Liberalization (%)	5-Year Post-Liberalization (%)	1980s (%)	1990s (%)
Argentina	193.5	3031.7	20.7	22.5	19.4	28.4
Brazil	243.9	6856.7	1.8	10.3	0.8	14.3
Chile	491.0	3261.8	7.6	10.3	7.1	10.6
Colombia	10.7	191.6	1.2	3.0	1.1	4.1
Greece	4.2	119.3	0.2	2.4	0.5	6.2
India	138.2	2779.1	0.7	5.4	0.6	5.4
Indonesia	46.7	776.0	NA	9.3	14.2	14.5
Jordan	NA	NA	NA	NA	NA	NA
Korea	754.0	6200.6	2.1	6.5	2.0	9.5
Malaysia	225.7	2128.8	1.5	4.7	1.7	8.1
Mexico	1184.5	16,197.8	18.0	26.0	17.0	29.9
Nigeria	NA	NA	NA	NA	NA	NA
Pakistan	NA	NA	NA	NA	NA	NA
Philippines	457.0	2219.1	16.8	12.7	18.8	16.3
Portugal	29.6	219.0	6.3	5.9	5.8	14.2
Taiwan	145.4	746.1	0.2	0.8	0.2	1.8
Thailand	107.3	1000.1	5.5	8.6	6.3	12.9
Turkey	44.4	425.5	3.8	6.3	3.8	13.7
Venezuela	47.5	444.9	6.9	15.2	6.9	16.6
Zimbabwe	NA	NA	NA	NA	NA	NA
Total/average	4123.4	46,597.8	6.2	9.4	6.6	12.9

Finally, the macroeconomic and development literature has mostly focused on a broader concept of financial or capital market openness, using information in the IMF's Annual Report on Exchange Arrangements and Exchange Restrictions (AREAER). Within the AREAER, there is a category called "capital account restrictions," which researchers have used to mark complete liberalization, that is, when the restrictions go to nil.[9] Unfortunately, as Eichengreen (2001) stresses, the IMF measure is an aggregate measure of many different types of capital controls and may be too coarse. Subcategories have only become available recently (see Miniane (2000)) and improvements in the measure for previous years (in particular, see Quinn (1997)) are available only for a few recent years.

---

[9] See Mathieson and Rojaz-Suarez (1992) as well as Edwards (1998) and Rodrik (1998).

3   FINANCIAL EFFECTS OF MARKET INTEGRATION

There has been an extensive number of articles that measure the effects of the liberalization process on financial variables. We split the discussion into five parts. The first part focuses on the equity return generating process: moments of equity returns (mean, volatility, beta with respect to world returns, etc.). The second part addresses capital flows, in particular equity flows. The third part focuses on political risk. The fourth part focuses on diversification benefits. We end this section evaluating the actual investment performance of U.S. investors in emerging markets.

Before we begin, it is important to realize that our analysis, from a historical perspective, is based only on the liberalizations that occurred over the last 20 years. Some emerging markets were thriving markets earlier in the 20th century (e.g., Argentina, see Taylor, 1998) and re-emerged. Goetzmann and Jorion (1999) study the bias in returns and betas that re-emergence might cause. For studies of the late 19th century globalization, see Taylor and Williamson (1994) and Williamson (1996).

3.1   Liberalization and Returns

Bekaert and Harvey (2000a) measure how liberalization has affected the equity return-generating process in 20 emerging markets, focusing primarily on the cost of equity capital.[10] Given the complexity of the liberalization process, they define capital market liberalization using three alternative measures: official regulatory liberalization, the earliest date of either an ADR issue, country fund launch, or an official liberalization date, and the date denoting a structural break in capital flows (leading to increased flows). To measure the cost of capital, they use dividend yields. The integration process should lead to a positive return-to-integration (as foreign investors bid up local prices), but to lower post-liberalization returns. Given high return volatility and considerable uncertainty in timing equity market liberalization, average returns cannot be used to measure changes in the cost of capital. Dividend yields capture the permanent price effects of a change in the cost of capital better than noisy returns.

With a surprising robustness across specifications, they find that dividend yields decline after liberalizations, but that the effect is always less than 1% on average. The results are somewhat stronger when they use the liberalization dates from Bekaert, Harvey, and Lumsdaine (2002b) discussed earlier. Edison and Warnock (2003) find that the decrease in dividend yields is much sharper for those countries that experienced more complete liberalizations. Henry (2000a) finds similar, albeit somewhat stronger, results using a different methodology and a slightly different sample of countries.

The impact of equity market liberalization on returns is presented in Figures 2–7. First, consistent with Bekaert and Harvey (2000a) and Henry (2000a), Figure 2 shows that average returns decrease after financial liberalizations. This is consistent with finance theory depicted in Figure 1. Also it is possible that the pre-liberalization returns are upwardly biased from the effects of integration with the world market (the return to integration).[11]

---

[10] Kawakatsu and Morey (1999) focus on market efficiency. Jain-Chandra (2002) examines efficiency after liberalizations.

[11] See also Errunza (2001) who shows that there is significant growth in market capitalization divided by GDP, trading volume divided by GDP, the turnover ratio and the number of listings after liberalization.

FIGURE 2   Average Annual Geometric Returns (Pre- and Post-Bekaert–Harvey Official Liberalization Dates)

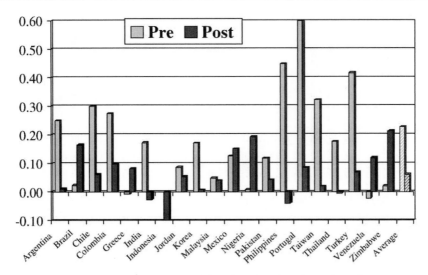

Data through April 2002. There are no pre-liberalization data for Indonesia.

Consistent with Bekaert and Harvey (1997), Figure 3 shows that there is no significant impact on unconditional volatility. Indeed, it is not obvious from finance theory that volatility should increase or decrease when markets are opened. On the one hand, markets may become informationally more efficient, leading to higher volatility as prices quickly react to relevant information or hot speculative capital may induce excess volatility. On the other hand, in the

FIGURE 3   Average Annualized Standard Deviation (Pre- and Post-Bekaert–Harvey Official Liberalization Dates)

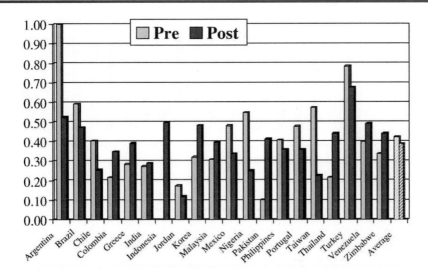

Data through April 2002. There are no pre-liberalization data for Indonesia.

FIGURE 4   Correlation with World (Pre- and Post-Bekaert–Harvey Official Liberalization Dates)

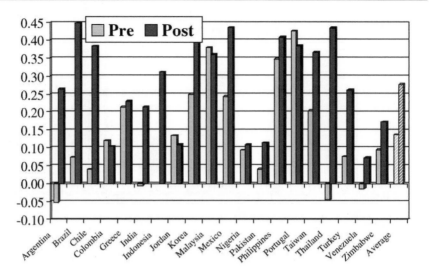

Data through April 2002. There are no pre-liberalization data for Indonesia.

pre-liberalized market, there may be large swings from fundamental values leading to higher volatility. In the long run, the gradual development and diversification of the market should lead to lower volatility.[12]

Bekaert and Harvey (2000a) argue that correlation and beta with the world market increase after equity market liberalizations. Figures 4 and 5 show that

FIGURE 5   Beta with World (Pre- and Post-Bekaert–Harvey Official Liberalization Dates)

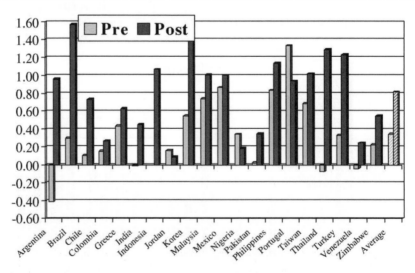

Data through April 2002. There are no pre-liberalization data for Indonesia.

_____

[12] See also Richards (1996), De Santis and Imrohoroglu (1997), Aggarwal et al. (1999) and Kim and Singal (2000) for studies of the effects of liberalization on stock market volatility.

FIGURE 6   Evolution of World Correlation (Five-Year Rolling Window: 20 Countries)

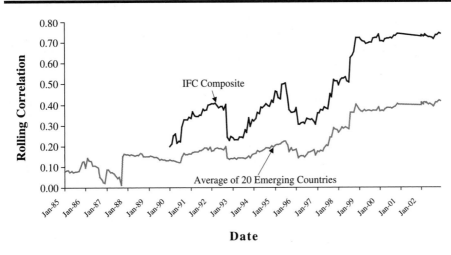

Data through April 2002.

unconditional correlations and betas both increase after liberalization. Indeed, of the 20 countries, only 3 countries experience a decrease in their correlations and betas—and the decrease is small. Figures 6 and 7 present the time-series of rolling unconditional correlations and betas. Around the time of a clustering of equity market liberalizations in the late 1980s and early 1990s, both the average correlations and betas with the world increase. There is an even larger increase at the end of the 1990s, which may reflect further integration and overall higher market volatility (see Section 5), or the increase may be temporary, brought about by a potential bubble in global technology stocks (see Brooks and Del Negro, 2002). These results are corroborated in a recent study by Carrieri et al. (2002).

FIGURE 7   Evolution of World Beta Risk (Five-Year Rolling Window: 20 Countries)

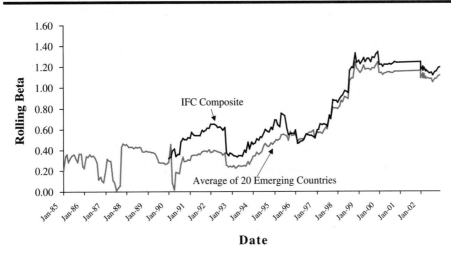

Data through April 2002.

The analysis in Figures 2–7 is unconditional. That is, we look at simple averages before and after liberalization. However, this type of analysis does not control for other financial and economic events that may coincide with equity market liberalization. Bekaert and Harvey (2000a) estimate panel regressions with a set of variables that are designed to control for coincidental financial and economic events. Interestingly, the message is similar to the unconditional analysis after liberalizations: expected returns decrease, correlations and betas increase, and there is no particular impact on volatility.

There exists interesting corroborating evidence from the firm-level price effects of ADRs. An ADR from a country with investment restrictions can be viewed as investment liberalization. For example, when Chile had repatriation restrictions in place, it had to lift them for companies listing their shares overseas to make cross-market arbitrage possible. When the ADR is announced, we expect positive abnormal returns and presumably expost under performance indicating lower expected returns after the liberalization. Of course, benchmarking ADR firms may be difficult, especially because the local market may experience significant spillover effects (see Urias, 1994). Overall, these predictions are borne out by the data and the announcement effect of ADR issuance is significant, being typically larger than 1% (see Miller, 1999; Foerster and Karolyi, 1999). Using a sample of 126 ADRs from 32 countries, Errunza and Miller (2000) document a very significant decline in the cost of capital. In addition, they show that the decline is driven by the inability of U.S. investors to span the foreign security with domestic securities prior to cross-listing. Of course, there are many reasons, apart from liberalization, why ADR issues may induce a positive price effect, including additional liquidity and the relaxation of capital constraints (Lins et al., 2001 for example). For further details, we refer to the excellent survey by Karolyi (1998). Recent studies by Chari and Henry (2001) and Patro and Wald (2002) also generally confirm the liberalization effects documented above using firm-specific data.

3.2 Liberalization and Capital Flows

With the emerging markets crises in the second half of the 1990s, the role of foreign capital in developing countries once again came under intense scrutiny. One country, Malaysia, imposed severe capital controls on October 1, 1998, in an effort to thwart the perceived destabilizing actions of foreign speculators. After a decade of capital market liberalizations and increased portfolio flows into developing countries, the process seemed to stall or even reverse. It is, therefore, important to develop an understanding of the dynamics, causes and consequences of capital flows in emerging markets. In particular, we need to understand the role of financial liberalization in these dynamics.

There is a growing body of research that studies the joint dynamics of capital flows and equity returns (see, for example, Warther, 1995; Choe et al., 1999; Froot et al., 2001; Clark and Berko, 1997; Edelen and Warner, 2001; Stulz, 1999; Edison and Warnock, 2001; Richards, 2002; Griffin et al., 2002). The first hypothesis of interest is whether foreign investors are "return chasers;" in the terms of Bohn and Tesar (1996), that is, are flows caused by changes in expected returns? A related hypothesis is that international investors are momentum investors, leading to a positive relation between past returns and flows. A second set of hypotheses focuses on the effect of flows on returns. Both Froot et al. (2001) (focusing on 28 emerging markets) and Clark and Berko (focusing on Mexico) find that increases in capital flows raise stock market prices, but the studies disagree on whether the effect is temporary or permanent. If the increase in prices is temporary, it may be just a reflection of "price pressure," which has also been documented in developed markets for mutual fund flows and stock indices (Warther, 1995; Shleifer, 1986). If the price increase is permanent, it may reflect a long-lasting decrease in the cost of equity capital associated with the risk-sharing benefits of capital market openings in emerging markets.

When focusing on emerging markets, the structural changes associated with capital market liberalization complicate any empirical analysis of capital flows, since these changes can cause permanent or at least long-lasting changes in the data-generating processes. Bekaert, Harvey and Lumsdaine (2002a) investigate the joint dynamics of returns and net U.S. equity flows acknowledging the important effects capital market liberalization may have. They precede their analysis with a detailed endogenous breakpoint analysis that helps define the relevant time-period over which to conduct the analysis. In general, they find sharply different results if their models are estimated over the entire sample—which ignores a fundamental nonstationarity in the data—versus a post-break (liberalization) sample. They find that net capital flows to emerging markets increase rapidly after liberalization as investors rebalance their portfolios, but that they level out after 3 years. As Figure 1 indicates, if capital market liberalizations induce one-time portfolio rebalancing on the part of global investors, one may expect net flows to increase substantially after a liberalization and then to decrease again (see Bacchetta and Wincoop, 2000 for a formal model generating such dynamics). The empirical pattern appears consistent with this conclusion.

Furthermore, Bekaert, Harvey and Lumsdaine (2002a) add two variables to the bivariate vector autoregression set-up of returns and equity flows in Froot et al. (2001): the world interest rate and local dividend yields. The low level of U.S. interest rates has often been cited as one of the major reasons for increased capital flows to emerging markets in 1993 (see World Bank, 1997 as well as Calvo et al., 1993, 1994; Fernandez-Arias, 1996). However, Bekaert, Harvey and Lumsdaine (2002a) do not find a significant effect on capital flows to emerging markets from an unexpected reduction in world interest rates.

Other main findings include that unexpected equity flows are indeed associated with strong short-lived increases in returns. However, they also find that they lead to permanent reductions in dividend yields, which may reflect a change in the cost of capital. Hence, the reduction in the dividend yield suggests that additional flows reduce the cost of capital, and that the actual return effect is not a pure price pressure effect because it is partially permanent.

In more recent work, the focus has shifted towards detailed studies of the trading behavior of foreign investors in an effort to detect herding behavior and other behavioral biases. Two such studies, focusing on Korea before and during the currency crisis in 1997, are Choe et al. (1999) and Kim and Wei (2002a). Choe et al. find evidence of positive feedback trading and herding by foreign investors before the crisis, but not during the crisis period. They find no evidence that trades by foreign investors had a destabilizing effect on Korea's stock market and found the market to adjust quickly and efficiently to large sales by foreign investors. Kim and Wei find that foreign investors outside Korea are more likely to engage in positive feedback trading strategies and in herding than the branches and subsidiaries of foreign institutions in Korea or foreign individuals living in Korea. This difference in trading behavior is possibly related to the difference in possessed information by the two types of investors.

One problem that such studies face is that it is quite difficult to distinguish between irrational and rational trading in a country that is still liberalizing, has stocks trading with and without associated ADRs, and is hit with an enormous economic crisis. Another problem is that however detailed the data, some foreign transactions are bound to be undetected and may undermine testing behavioral hypotheses. For example, hedge funds may hold Korean equity exposure through an asset swap with a local company, which will not be detected by the usual capital flow statistics. Apart from trades executed through derivatives, 1998 was also a very active ADR issue year for Korea, again making the determination of net positions difficult. Of course, such problems also complicate the interpretation of the more aggregate studies discussed earlier.

There is another related and rapidly growing literature that investigates the behavior of mutual funds investing in emerging markets. These include Borensztein and Gelos (2001), Kim and Wei (2002b), and Frankel and Schmukler (2000). Given that there already exists a survey article on this topic (Kaminsky et al., 2001), we do not discuss these articles further.

Much has been made about the increased volatility of capital flows post liberalization (see Stiglitz, 2000). This discussion strikes us, in many ways, as odd. The emerging countries start with little or no capital flows and move to an environment (post liberalization) with significant capital flows which are, as expected, subject to portfolio rebalancing. Consequently, it is no mystery that the volatility of capital flows increases. In fact, if we revisit Fig. 1, the segmentation model predicts that volatility should spike around the time of market liberalization, but should then subside once the large capital inflow has occurred. Of course, there is always the worry that portfolio flows are not as "sticky" as foreign direct investment (FDI) and may disappear at a whim causing a crisis in the process (see Claessens et al., (1995) for an attempt to distinguish between hot and other forms of capital).

In Figure 8, we provide a very simple measure of the evolution of capital flow volatility over time. We computed the coefficient of variation (volatility over mean) of the U.S. holdings measure previously referenced above for 16 emerging countries. Figure 8 graphs the 3-year rolling window coefficient of variation for the aggregate U.S. holdings in these markets over time. Note that, the volatility measure starts to increase sharply in the early 1990s when many liberalizations take place and continues to increase, reaching its peak in 1995 at the time of the Mexican peso crisis. After falling sharply the volatility measure reaches another, but much lower peak at the end of 1997 around the time of the Asian crisis. Interestingly, 2000 was also a rather volatile year, but volatility in

FIGURE 8   Three-Year Rolling Coefficient of Variation of U.S. Emerging and Developed Market Equity Holdings

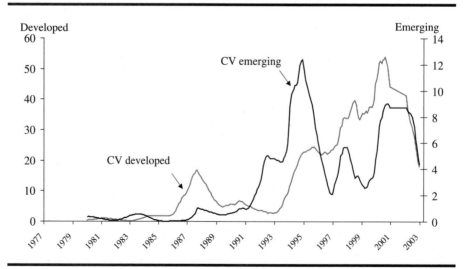

2001 fell back to levels observed in the very early 1990s. It is very difficult to establish whether this volatility is excessive. Indeed, for comparison, we also consider the 3-year coefficient of variation of U.S. holdings in developed markets.[13] There is an even more substantial increase in the mid- to late-1990s in capital flows volatility for developed markets. In fact, both measures show similar patterns and capital flows to developed countries were more volatile than flows to emerging markets.

3.3 Liberalization and Political Risk

What is the relation between equity market liberalizations and political risk? Bekaert and Harvey (2000a) present some evidence that country ratings significantly increase (lower risk) with one of their measures of equity market liberalization. This is important because Erb et al. (1996a,b) show a significant cross-sectional relation between country rating and future equity returns and Bekaert Erb, Harvey and Viscanta (1997) make the case that political risk is a priced risk in emerging markets. That is, increased ratings lead to lower costs of capital.

Table 2 summarizes the behavior around liberalizations in 20 emerging markets studied in Bekaert and Harvey (2000a) with respect to the International Country Risk Guide's (ICRG's) measures of political, economic, and financial risk ratings. We report the rating at time t, which is the month of the official liberalization, reported in Bekaert and Harvey. We also report 1 year earlier, $t - 1$, as well as 1 and 2 years after the liberalization $t + 1$, and $t + 2$. The results are striking. The ICRG measure of political risk rating increases by 10.8% from $t - 1$ to $t + 2$ (indicating lower political risk). During this same period, the largest change is with the financial risk rating measure, which increases by 26.8%, while the composite risk rating measure, which combines the three components, increases by 15.8%. This evidence is consistent with political risk and the cost of capital decreasing after equity market liberalizations. One market measure of political risk is the yield spread on dollar-denominated emerging market bonds, relative to dollar yields. Adler and Qi (2002) study market integration between the U.S. and Mexico using Brady bond spreads as an indicator of effective market integration and find that the spread significantly affects expected returns. Country risk measures may reflect the credibility of the government's market-oriented reforms and its commitment to open capital markets. Perotti and van Oijen (2001) show that privatizations (see below) are significantly associated with lower political risk over time. Perotti (1995) presents the theoretical framework that links credible privatization and political risk.

3.4 Liberalization and Diversification Benefits

Although emerging market equity returns are highly volatile, they are relatively less correlated with equity returns in the developed world, making it possible to construct low-risk portfolios. Whereas the pioneering study of Errunza (1977) was largely ignored by both the academic and practitioner communities, interest in emerging market investments re-surfaced in the early 1990s. Early studies show very significant diversification benefits for emerging market investments, (Divecha et al., 1992; De Santis, 1993; Harvey, 1995). However, these studies used

---

[13] The set of developed countries follows Harvey (1991). We omit Hong Kong and Singapore/Malaysia from the set of MSCI developed markets. We also omit New Zealand because of lack of holdings data.

TABLE 2　Equity Market Liberalization and Political Risk

(A) Political Risk	$t-1$	t	$t+1$	$t+2$	(B) Financial Risk	$t-1$	t	$t+1$	$t+2$
Argentina	56.0	61.0	64.0	66.0	Argentina	19.0	20.0	23.0	31.0
Brazil	69.0	64.0	69.0	66.0	Brazil	28.0	33.0	37.0	35.0
Chile	64.0	66.0	67.0	69.0	Chile	40.0	42.0	42.0	43.0
Colombia	54.0	59.0	61.0	58.0	Colombia	28.0	37.0	41.0	41.0
Greece	58.0	63.0	62.0	61.0	Greece	26.0	31.0	30.0	30.0
India	43.0	51.0	62.0	65.0	India	29.0	35.0	36.0	36.0
Indonesia	39.0	41.0	51.0	57.0	Indonesia	18.0	28.0	41.0	44.0
Jordan	73.0	76.0	70.0	73.0	Jordan	35.0	37.0	38.0	38.0
Korea	64.0	75.0	75.0	75.0	Korea	47.0	47.0	47.0	47.0
Malaysia	62.0	58.0	59.0	70.0	Malaysia	26.0	31.0	38.0	45.0
Mexico	69.0	68.0	70.0	71.0	Mexico	28.0	29.0	32.0	38.0
Nigeria	53.0	53.0	53.0	45.0	Nigeria	27.0	26.0	24.0	28.0
Pakistan	33.0	27.0	34.0	40.0	Pakistan	22.0	17.0	28.0	30.0
Philippines	37.0	41.0	44.0	55.0	Philippines	24.0	22.0	27.0	34.0
Portugal	70.0	71.0	67.0	76.0	Portugal	35.0	38.0	37.0	43.0
Taiwan	75.0	71.0	76.0	77.0	Taiwan	49.0	49.0	49.0	48.0
Thailand	54.0	55.0	60.0	59.0	Thailand	29.0	29.0	36.0	40.0
Turkey	48.0	45.0	45.0	52.0	Turkey	23.0	20.0	20.0	19.0
Venezuela	69.0	65.0	74.0	75.0	Venezuela	29.0	27.0	39.0	40.0
Zimbabwe	63.0	66.0	66.0	67.0	Zimbabwe	24.0	30.0	30.0	33.0
Average	57.7	58.8	61.5	63.9	Average	29.3	31.4	34.8	37.2
Increase from $t-1$		2.0%	6.6%	10.8%	Increase from $t-1$		7.2%	18.6%	26.8%

(C) Economic Risk	$t-1$	t	$t+1$	$t+2$	(D) Composite Risk	$t-1$	t	$t+1$	$t+2$
Argentina	18.0	14.0	25.5	24.5	Argentina	48.0	47.5	56.5	61.5
Brazil	20.0	23.5	26.5	25.0	Brazil	58.5	60.0	66.5	63.0
Chile	30.5	32.0	38.0	39.0	Chile	67.5	70.0	73.5	75.5
Colombia	29.5	34.0	35.0	38.0	Colombia	56.0	65.0	68.5	68.5
Greece	28.5	31.0	29.5	32.5	Greece	56.5	62.5	61.0	62.0
India	26.0	28.5	31.5	35.5	India	49.0	57.5	65.0	68.5
Indonesia	33.5	34.5	35.0	36.0	Indonesia	45.5	52.0	63.5	68.5
Jordan	38.5	38.0	38.0	39.5	Jordan	73.5	75.5	73.0	75.3
Korea	37.0	36.5	40.0	41.0	Korea	74.0	79.5	81.0	81.5
Malaysia	37.5	41.0	39.0	40.0	Malaysia	63.0	65.0	68.0	77.5
Mexico	27.5	27.5	25.5	29.0	Mexico	62.5	62.5	64.0	69.0
Nigeria	26.0	26.0	23.0	29.0	Nigeria	53.0	52.5	50.0	51.0
Pakistan	31.5	32.0	31.5	31.5	Pakistan	43.5	38.0	47.0	51.0
Philippines	29.5	29.0	31.0	34.0	Philippines	45.5	46.0	51.0	61.5
Portugal	34.0	34.5	36.0	38.0	Portugal	69.5	72.0	70.0	78.5

(Table continued on next page . . .)

TABLE 2 (continued)								
(C) Economic Risk	*t* − 1	*t*	*t* + 1	*t* + 2	**(D) Composite Risk**	*t* − 1	*t*	*t* + 1	*t* + 2
Taiwan	42.5	43.0	43.0	44.5	Taiwan	83.5	81.5	84.0	85.0
Thailand	33.0	36.5	35.5	36.0	Thailand	58.0	60.5	66.0	67.5
Turkey	26.0	28.0	28.0	27.5	Turkey	48.5	46.5	46.5	49.5
Venezuela	25.0	27.0	32.5	35.5	Venezuela	61.0	59.5	73.0	75.5
Zimbabwe	22.5	25.0	29.0	32.5	Zimbabwe	55.0	60.5	62.5	66.5
Average	29.8	31.1	32.7	34.4	Average	58.6	60.7	64.5	67.8
Increase from *t* − 1		4.2%	9.5%	15.4%	Increase from *t* − 1		3.6%	10.2%	15.8%

Notes: 100 = maximum; 0 = minimum. *t* = Official Liberalization date from Bekaert and Harvey (2000a,b). We also report the ratings 1 year before as well as 1 and 2 years after the Official Liberalization.

Source: All ratings from International Country Risk Guide.

market indexes compiled by the (IFC) that generally ignore the high transaction costs, low liquidity, and investment constraints associated with emerging market investments.

Bekaert and Urias (1996, 1999) measure the diversification benefits from emerging equity markets using data on closed-end funds (country and regional funds), and (ADRs).[14] Unlike the IFC indexes, these assets are easily accessible to retail investors, and transaction costs are comparable to those for U.S.-traded stocks. The distinguishing feature of closed-end funds is that fund share prices generally deviate from the market value of all securities in the portfolio (known as "net asset value"); they may trade at a premium when the assets are invested in closed or restricted markets, or at a discount when the foreign market has unusual political risk. Historically, they provided access to restricted markets, while open-end funds and ADRs were relatively unimportant before 1993.

Bekaert and Urias (1996, 1999) generally find that investors give up a substantial part of the diversification benefits of investing in foreign markets when they do so by holding closed-end funds. Other studies, such as Bailey and Stulz (1990), Bailey and Lim (1992) and Chang et al. (1995) found larger diversification benefits but had not taken small sample biases in the statistical tests into account. Open-end funds, on the other hand, track the underlying IFC indices much better than other investment vehicles and prove to be the best diversification instrument in the Bekaert and Urias sample.

De Roon et al. (2001) and Li et al. (2003) take the transactions costs that investors in emerging markets face directly into account when measuring diversification benefits. De Roon et al. find that the diversification benefits of investing in emerging markets are eliminated when transactions costs and, in particular, short-sale constraints are introduced. However, they admit that there is some evidence of bias in their asymptotic spanning analysis. Unlike the asymptotic mean variance tests, Li et al. use a Bayesian approach, that incorporates the uncertainty of finite samples into their analysis. They argue that the diversification benefits to investing in emerging markets remain substantial even in the presence of short-sale constraints. These two articles use the IFC indices to test for diversification benefits. Errunza et al. (1999) show that most of these diversification benefits can be obtained using domestically traded assets (ADRs and country funds).

---

[14] Also see Diwan et al. (1995).

By removing price segmentation, liberalizations may increase correlations and hence reduce diversification benefits. Using a model in which conditional correlations depend on world volatility and variables tracking the degree of integration, Bekaert and Harvey (1997) measure the time-variation in correlations for 17 emerging markets. For some countries, for example, Thailand, correlations increase markedly around the time of liberalization. The average response of these conditional correlations to liberalizations in 17 emerging markets is a small but statistically significant increase of 0.08 at most.

3.5 How Well Have Emerging Market Portfolios Done?

As we outlined before, there is some discussion in the literature suggesting that those who invest in emerging markets are subject to herding and other irrational behavior. Rather than focusing on one emerging market, we carry out two simple exercises to assess the overall performance of portfolio investment in emerging markets.

Our first exercise examines the performance of actual portfolio investments by U.S. investors in emerging countries. That is, the definition of U.S. investor is comprehensive, including all U.S. investments covered by the aggregate equity flow statistics, in contrast to studies such as Froot et al. (2001), who only focus on institutional investors. We compare their actual emerging market holdings through time to both an equally weighted and a value-weighted benchmark investment strategy as well as to the IFC Composite return. The difference between the U.S. portfolio weights and the benchmark investment weights represents U.S. investors "over" or "under" weighting in these markets. We compute these weights using the accumulated capital flow data from the U.S. Treasury and from Warnock and Cleaver (2002).

The results in Table 3 suggest that U.S. investors' country allocation led to substantially higher returns than all three benchmarks. For example, in the 1990s, the U.S. portfolio return was 11.4% compared to only 4.4% for the

TABLE 3 Performance of U.S. Investments in Emerging Equity Markets				
	IFC Composite (%)	Value-Weighted IFC 16 Countries (%)	Equally Weighted IFC 16 Countries (%)	U.S. Country Allocation Performance (%)
Mean from 1977		12.0	9.1	17.3
Std. dev. from 1977		22.6	19.2	25.9
Mean from 1981		11.2	7.0	14.2
Std. dev. from 1981		23.8	20.1	27.0
Mean from 1985	8.3	14.2	11.6	21.8
Std. dev. from 1985	23.9	25.2	21.1	28.0
Mean from 1990	0.1	4.4	2.6	11.4
Std. dev. from 1990	23.1	24.6	22.1	26.0

Data through December 2001. Mean represents the average compound return which is annualized in percent. Std. dev. is the annualized standard deviation in percent. The 16 country portfolios exclude: Jordan, Nigeria, Pakistan and Zimbabwe where holdings estimates are not available.

value-weighted benchmark of the 16 countries where we have U.S. holdings.[15] It is unlikely that this out performance would be overturned if additional countries were considered. During this period, the broader IFC Composite index returned only 0.1% on average.

The second exercise looks at aggregate investment in emerging markets versus developed markets. We conduct the following experiment. Using holdings data for both developed and emerging markets, we calculate the total U.S. foreign holdings. We determine the proportion of U.S. holdings in emerging markets versus developed markets (not including the U.S.). Using the same countries for which we have holdings data, we then calculate market capitalization weighted indices for both emerging and developed markets. Again, we can determine the proportion of total capitalization in emerging and developed markets.

The results are in Table 4. The first two columns provide summary statistics for the U.S. holdings weight times both value and equally weighted developed and emerging market indices. That is, the portfolio mimics the actual allocation between emerging and developed markets but uses market indices within these broad groups. In the next two columns, we replace the holdings weights with market capitalization weights. The difference in performance is due to the difference in U.S. allocation to emerging markets relative to developed markets— rather than any particular country selection. That is, the weights, whether holdings-based or capitalization-based are multiplied by the same return indices. The results suggest that there is not much difference between the capitalization weights and the holdings weights in terms of the returns. For example, since 1990, the returns to the holdings-based weights and the market capitalization weights are both 4.4% per annum. The volatility is also very similar. Interestingly, even a fixed 90% weight in developed markets and 10% weight in emerging markets (see the last column) produces similar results. Hence, the overall U.S. allocation performance is quite similar to the performance that would have been obtained from market capitalization weighting.

While the previous exercise is necessary for comparison, the analysis does not fairly represent the U.S. investor performance. We use the holdings to determine the aggregate weights in developed and emerging markets and then allocate to passive market capitalization benchmarks for these two groups of markets (that is, we ignore the country selection). But the results in Table 3 have already demonstrated some ability to choose the right countries. The fifth column of Table 4 allows for country selection. We use the weights in developed and emerging markets and create a developed and emerging market benchmark that reflects the country weighting chosen by U.S. investors. Consistent with the emerging market analysis, U.S. investors substantially outperform the market capitalization benchmark. For example, from 1990, the U.S. return is 7.6% per annum compared to a value-weighted benchmark return of 4.4%. The volatility of the U.S. strategy is 130 basis points lower than the volatility of the value weighted benchmark. Indeed, the U.S. global return is even higher than the MSCI world market composite return—which includes a substantial weight for U.S. equity (which we know has done well over the past 12 years). All in all, the overall investment performance of U.S. investors is much rosier than the country-by-country results, which focus on behavioral biases. Disyatat and Gelos (2001) study the asset allocation of emerging market funds and find that it is not inconsistent with mean-variance optimizing

---

[15] Holdings data are not available for Jordan, Nigeria and Zimbabwe. The revised data from Warnock and Cleaver (2002) also do not include data for Pakistan.

TABLE 4   Performance of U.S. Investment in Developed and Emerging Equity Markets

	EM/Developed Holdings Weights Times Market Cap Weighted Country Indices (%)	EM/Developed Holdings Weights Times Equally Weighted Country Indices (%)	EM/Developed Market Cap Weights Times Market Cap Weighted Country Indices (%)	EM/Developed Market Cap Weights Times Equally Weighted Country Indices (%)	EM/Developed Holdings Weights Times Holdings Weighted Country Indices (%)	MSCI World Composite (%)	10% EM 90% Developed (%)
Mean from 1977	13.0	12.1	13.1	12.1	14.4	12.2	12.9
Std. dev. from 1977	16.0	14.7	16.1	14.9	15.4	14.1	15.8
Mean from 1981	11.7	11.5	11.9	11.6	12.5	11.9	11.7
Std. dev. from 1981	16.7	15.3	16.7	15.2	15.7	14.5	16.5
Mean from 1985	12.8	13.6	12.8	13.7	14.3	12.7	12.8
Std. dev. from 1985	17.1	15.8	17.0	15.7	15.8	14.9	16.9
Mean from 1990	4.4	6.7	4.4	6.8	7.6	7.5	4.3
Std. dev. from 1990	16.5	15.0	16.4	14.9	15.1	14.5	16.5

Data through December 2001. Mean represents the average compound return which is annualized in percent. Std. dev. is the annualized standard deviation in percent.

behavior. Their results are similar in spirit to ours. However, Frankel and Schmukler's (2000) study on country funds suggests that the holders of the underlying assets (the portfolio managers) have more information than the country fund holders (the investors).

REAL EFFECTS OF FINANCIAL MARKET INTEGRATION

4

From 1980 to 1997, Chile experienced average real GDP growth of 3.8% per year while the Ivory Coast had negative real growth of 2.4% per year. Why? Attempts to explain differences in economic growth across countries have again taken center stage in the macroeconomic literature. Although there is no agreement on what determines economic growth, most of the literature finds evidence of conditional convergence. Poorer countries grow faster than rich countries, once it is taken into account that poor countries tend to have lower long-run per capita GDPs, for example, because of the poor quality of their capital stock (both physical and human). Sachs and Warner (1995) have argued that policy choices, such as respect for property rights and open international trade, are important determinants of the long-run capacity for growth. Williamson (1996) has already argued that fast growth, globalization and convergence are positively correlated from the historical perspective of the end of the 19th century until now. Here, we focus on the real effects of the most recent wave of liberalizations.

There are some interesting differences between the two countries we mentioned. First, the Ivory Coast has a larger trade sector than Chile, but the role of trade openness remains hotly debated. Second, Chile liberalized its capital markets, in particular its equity market, to foreign investment in 1992. After the liberalization, the Chilean economy grew by 6.3% per year.

4.1 Why Would Financial Liberalization Affect Economic Growth?

There are a number of channels through which financial liberalization may affect growth. First, foreign investors, enjoying improved benefits of diversification, will drive up local equity prices permanently, thereby reducing the cost of equity capital. Consequently, the real variable most sensitive to the cost of capital should be real investment. Bekaert and Harvey (2000a), Bekaert, Harvey and Lundblad (2002c), and Henry (2000b) all find that investment increases post equity market liberalization. If this additional investment is efficient, then economic growth should increase. However, in the aftermath of the recent crises, some economists feel that foreign capital has been wasted on frivolous consumption and inefficient investment, undermining the benefits of financial liberalization. Bekaert, Harvey and Lundblad (2002c) show that not only does the ratio of investment to GDP actually increase, but also that the ratio of consumption to GDP does not increase after liberalization. The additional investment appears to be financed by foreign capital as the trade balance significantly decreases.

Second, there is now a large literature on how more developed financial markets and intermediation can enhance growth and how well-functioning equity markets may promote financial development [see, for example, Levine (1991); King and Levine (1993); Levine and Zervos (1996, 1998a,b); Levine et al.

(2000)]. Furthermore, foreign investors may also demand better corporate governance to protect their investments, reducing the wedge between the costs of external and internal financial capital, and further increasing investment. There is, in fact, a large and growing literature on how the relaxation of financing constraints improves the allocation of capital and promotes growth [see Rajan and Zingales (1998); Love [in press]; Wurgler (2000)). Lins et al. (2001)] show that firms in emerging markets listing on the U.S. exchanges are able to relax financing constraints. Since ADRs can be viewed as firm-specific investment liberalizations, this research directly establishes a link between liberalization and financing constraints. Galindo et al. (2001) show that financial liberalization improves the efficiency of capital allocation for individual firms in 12 developing countries. Laeven (2001) has examined the role of banking liberalization in relaxing financing constraints for emerging markets. Forbes (2002) finds that Chilean capital controls significantly increased financial constraints for smaller firms. The interplay between economic growth, financial development and corporate finance is likely to be an important area for future research, and is a topic we return to in Section 5.

4.2 Measuring the Liberalization Effect on Economic Growth

Bekaert, Harvey and Lundblad (2001) propose a time series panel methodology that fully exploits all the available data to measure how much an equity market liberalization increases growth. They regress future growth (in logarithmic form), averaged over periods ranging from 3 to 7 years, on a number of predetermined determinants of long-run steady state per capita GDP, including secondary school enrollment, the size of the government sector, inflation, trade openness, and on initial GDP (measured in logarithms) in 1980. The right-hand side variables also include an indicator of liberalization based primarily on an analysis of regulatory reforms in Bekaert and Harvey (2000a). To maximize the time-series content in their regressions, they use overlapping data. For example, they use growth from 1981 to 1986 and from 1982 to 1987 in the same regression. They correct for the resulting correlation in the model's residuals in the standard errors. Estimating the model by the Generalized Method of Moments, they can also adjust for the correlation of residuals across countries and different variances of residuals both across countries and over time (heteroskedasticity).

Bekaert, Harvey and Lundblad (2001) consider the liberalization effect in a small sample of 30 emerging and frontier markets as defined by the IFC and found that economic growth increased by 0.7% to 1.4% per year post liberalization.

Bekaert, Harvey and Lundblad (2002c) expand the sample to 95 countries, including to countries that may not even have financial markets, as well as to developed countries. The liberalization effect now has a cross-sectional component that measures the difference in growth between segmented and financially open countries, as well as a temporal component (countries before and after liberalization). It is this cross-sectional dimension that has been the main focus of the trade openness literature.

Expanding the sample of countries strengthens the results. Taken by itself, financial liberalization leads to an increase in average annual per capita GDP growth of 1.5 to 2.3 percent per year. When they factor in a host of other variables that might also boost economic performance, improvements associated with financial liberalization still remain strong, 0.7% to 1.4% per year. In examining a number of different samples (whose size depends on the availability of control variables), the financial liberalization effect seems robust. They also consider an alternative set of liberalization dates. The main results are robust to these alternative dates. Further, they carry out a Monte Carlo experiment whereby one country's liberalization date is assigned randomly to another country. This allows them to test whether these results primarily reflect overall economic growth in the late 1980s and early 1990s (when the liberalization dates are concentrated). The Monte Carlo exercise shows that the liberalization dates do not really explain economic growth when they are decoupled from the specific country to which they apply, showing that the effect is not related to the world business cycle during these years.

4.3 Intensity and Simultaneity Problems in Measuring Real Liberalization Effects

4.3.1 Intensity of the Reforms

There is a heated debate about the effect of capital account openness on economic growth and economic welfare, especially in developing countries [see, for example, Rodrik (1998); Edwards (2001); Arteta et al. (2001)]. Eichengreen (2001) suggests that the weak and inconsistent results might be due to the fact that the IMF's AREAER was used as a measure of capital account restrictions. Because this measure does not differentiate between capital account restrictions, it is too coarse to yield meaningful results. When capital account restrictions are more finely measured, as in Quinn (1997), Quinn et al. (2001), and Edwards (2001), there does appear to be a growth effect, although it is fragile (see Arteta et al., 2001). Bekaert, Harvey and Lundblad (2001, 2002c), focusing on equity liberalization only, find a robust growth effect. Moreover, they also employ a measure that captures the intensity of the liberalization by taking the ratio of the market capitalization of the IFCs investable index versus the IFCs global index (see also Bekaert, 1995; Edison and Warnock, 2003) or the number of investable securities compared to the total number of securities. These measures also point to a strong positive growth effect from liberalization.

4.3.2 Financial Liberalization and Macroeconomic Reforms

It is possible that financial liberalizations typically coincide with other more macro-oriented reforms which are the source of increased growth and not the financial liberalizations. However, when Bekaert, Harvey and Lundblad (2002c) add variables capturing macroeconomic reforms, such as inflation, trade openness, fiscal deficits and the black market premium, the liberalization effect remains intact. In some specifications, it does weaken somewhat suggesting that macroeconomic reforms may, indeed, account for some of the liberalization effect.

4.3.3 Financial Liberalization and Financial Market Development

Another possibility is that financial liberalization is the natural outcome of a financial development process, and that, consistent with many endogenous growth theories, it is financial development that leads to increased growth. When Bekaert, Harvey and Lundblad (2002c) add a number of banking and stock market development indicators to their regressions, the liberalization effect is reduced only marginally in most specifications but more substantially in a specification excluding the poorest countries. Moreover, they find that financial liberalization predicts additional financial development, but that the decision to liberalize does not seem to be affected by the degree of financial development. Hence, it is likely that one channel through which financial liberalization increases growth is by its impact on financial development.[16]

4.3.4 *Functional Capital Markets*

A final possibility acknowledges the imperfection of capital markets, which drives a wedge between the cost of internal and external capital and makes investment sensitive to the presence of internally generated cash flows. Foreigners may demand better corporate governance and financial liberalization, which may coincide with security law reforms that enforce better corporate governance. Improved corporate governance may lead to lower costs of capital and increased investment (see Dahlquist et al., 2002). To capture this, Bekaert, Harvey and Lundblad (2002c) use a variable constructed by Bhattacharya and Daouk (2002), who trace the implementation and enforcement of insider trading laws in a large number of countries. Bekaert, Harvey and Lundblad (2003a) find that the enforcement of insider trading laws has a positive effect on growth and is statistically significant in three of their four samples. Importantly, it does not diminish the impact of financial liberalizations on economic growth. Another reason to suspect that corporate governance matters for growth prospects is that Bekaert, Harvey and Lundblad (2001) find larger liberalization effects for countries with an Anglo-Saxon legal system, which are thought to have better corporate governance systems (see Shleifer and Vishny, 1997). On a more basic level, it appears that more secure property rights lead to better capital accumulation and higher growth (see Claessens and Laeven, 2003).

4.4 Other Real Effects of Financial Liberalization

The positive growth effects are very surprising from the perspective of a large literature focusing on the detrimental effects of financial liberalization. Figure 9 is taken from a World Bank document on private capital flows to emerging markets. The consensus view is simple. Financial integration naturally leads to increased capital inflows. This, in turn, increases asset prices (either rationally or irrationally), improves liquidity, and triggers a rapid expansion in bank credit. The lending boom then leads to a consumption binge, and potentially a real estate bubble. Apart from the appreciation in asset prices, the real exchange rate appreciates as well, aggravating macroeconomic vulnerability. A weak and inadequately regulated banking sector may aggravate this process by lending for speculative purposes, consumption and frivolous investments, including the fueling of a construction boom. When inflated assets are used as collateral to justify further borrowing, a boom–bust cycle is clearly in the making. The consensus view appears to be that liberalization dramatically increases financial sector vulnerability in many countries and that a weak banking sector played a large role in both the Mexican and Asian crises.

While this interpretation of how foreign capital can wreak havoc in the real economy of developing countries is widely accepted, it is surprising that empirical evidence for this view is very scarce. Bekaert, and Harvey (2000b) conduct a very simple exercise. First, they find the date at which foreign investors may have become marginal investors in the local equity market by using structural break tests applied to empirical measures of U.S. holdings of local market capitalization

---

[16] See Beck et al. (2000a,b), Demirgüç-Kunt and Levine (1996), Demirgüç-Kunt and Maksimovic (1996) and Rajan and Zingales (2001), for work on financial development and growth.

**FIGURE 9   Capital Inflows Can Lead to a Vicious Circle
that Increases Economic Vulnerabilities**

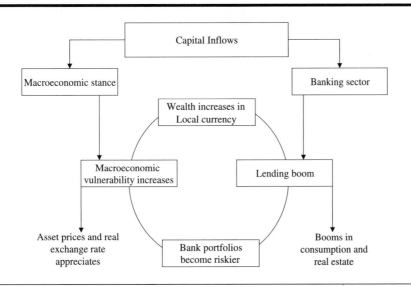

Source: World Bank (1997).

(see also, above). Second, they test for changes in a number of real variables, finding a larger trade sector, less long-term country debt, lower inflation and lower foreign exchange volatility. They also test whether the real exchange rate appreciates after the equity flow breaks and find that it does in 9 of 16 countries. However, there is a significant depreciation in four countries. Overall, panel estimates reveal a real appreciation of 5–10% that is statistically significant in about half of the specifications. Hence, the empirical evidence for the real appreciation story is not as strong as typically believed.

Finally, there is a clear sense that increased volatility in financial markets post liberalization (for which the empirical evidence is tenuous) also translates into real variability. Bekaert, Harvey and Lundblad (2002d) test this prediction directly. Investigating a large cross-section of liberalized and segmented markets and using information before and after liberalization for a large number of emerging market economies, they establish that the volatility of consumption and GDP growth did not significantly increase post-liberalization. When they focus on the years preceding the recent Asian crisis, volatility actually decreases, which is especially true for the volatility of consumption growth. When they include the crises years (1997–2000) and focus on a subset of developing economies, this strong result is weakened. However, even with the crises' years, in no case does volatility significantly increase.

Bekaert, Harvey and Lundblad also strip out predictable consumption growth and focus on idiosyncratic consumption growth variability as in Athanasoulis and van Wincoop (2000, 2001).[17] They find that consumption growth volatility mostly significantly decreases post-liberalization. The analysis indicates that the drop in idiosyncratic volatility is economically large. The assertion that globalization has gone too far for emerging economies is not supported by their empirical analysis. Nevertheless, the crises that did occur do suggest that financial integration is best accompanied by vigorous reforms of the domestic financial sector.

---

[17] Lewis (1996, 2000) provides an analysis of risk sharing in developed markets.

5

CONTAGION

5.1 Currency Crises and Contagion

In the mid to late 1990s, a number of emerging markets experienced spectacular currency crises, first Mexico in 1994 (the "Tequila Crisis"), then Southeast Asia in 1997 (the "Asian Flu" crisis), and Russia in 1998 (the "Russian Virus" crisis). These crises not only rejuvenated research on speculative currency attacks, but also created a new buzzword: "contagion." We divide this literature roughly into two components. First, there is the work that explores why crises occur in the first place. Second, there is a large body of work on why crises spread. The literature is too vast to cover here adequately. For many more references, we refer to the survey articles of Claessens et al. (2001), Claessens and Forbes (2001), De Bandt and Hartmann (2000) and Krugman (2001). Of course, some articles examine both what causes currency crises and how they spread across countries.

5.1.1 Predictable Currency Crises?

There are two main explanations for why a currency may experience speculative pressures that can lead to a crisis and devaluation (or the floating of the currency).

The first explanation, building on the seminal work of Krugman (1979) and Flood and Garber (1984), simply argues that if governments follow policies inconsistent with the currency peg, a speculative attack is unavoidable. Speculators will sell the local currency and buy foreign currency. The central bank will lose foreign reserves defending the peg until a critical level of low reserves is reached, at which point the central bank will give up. Whereas initial models focused on expansionary fiscal policies, expansionary monetary policies can also lead to speculative attacks. Of course, this model has the strong implication that speculative attacks should be partially predictable. In fact, growing budget deficits, fast money growth and rising wages and prices should precede speculative attacks. If prices rise while the nominal exchange rate remains unchanged, the real exchange rate will appreciate. Hence, real exchange rate over-valuations should also signal an imminent crisis. The combination of budget deficits and real exchange rate overvaluation may also lead to excessive current account deficits. Consequently, if Krugman is correct, speculative pressures should be predictable from economic data.

The second explanation recognizes that, sometimes, speculative attacks seem to come out of the blue. That is, the crises are self-fulfilling, caused by "animal spirits," as Keynes once phrased it. A significant group of investors simply starts speculating against the currency, provoking a large capital outflow that leads to the eventual collapse of the exchange rate, thereby validating the negative expectations regarding the survival chances of the peg. The authorities have no choice but to change their policies and accept the devalued currency, even though there are ex ante no fundamental reasons for dropping the peg.[18] The empirical prediction of these models is very strong, in that a currency crisis is

---

[18] Technically, such self-fulfilling attacks are possible in models with multiple equilibriums. There is a stable equilibrium, in which the government follows the right policies consistent with the peg, but there is also another equilibrium in which speculators attack the currency and the government accommodates the lower exchange rate; see, for example, Obstfeld (1986) or Masson (1999). Drazen (1998) provides a different approach in studying political contagion.

essentially unpredictable; government policies will only become expansionary after the currency has been attacked and devalued.

More recent contributions to this literature (see Ozkan and Sutherland, 1998; Bensaid and Jeanne, 1997) introduce interaction with fundamental variables in this class of models. Basically, a deterioration of fundamentals (for instance in unemployment) may make defending the currency more costly (for instance, by raising interest rates) eventually leading to a crisis. However, the actual occurrence and timing of the crisis is still determined by the animal spirits of speculators.

Krugman (2001) distinguishes third-generation models in which currency crises lead to severe short-term real output declines. Inspired by the Asian crisis, these models may stress moral hazard driven excessive investment (Corsetti et al., 1999) or bank runs in a fragile banking system (Chang and Velasco, 2001) as the source of an eventual exchange rate collapse.

Because we have competing theories, with different empirical predictions, it would be nice if the data would provide a clear indication of which theory is correct, and definitively establish whether devaluations are predictable or not. Unfortunately, this is not the case. Although there have been many empirical studies, they differ in the countries and sample periods covered, as well as in the questions addressed. For example, it may be that a currency experiences speculative pressure but that the government successfully defends the currency and that no devaluation occurs. Some studies focus on predicting this kind of speculative pressure, (see, e.g., Eichengreen et al., 1995). One could also distinguish between actual devaluations, and regime transitions, like flotations.

Overall, there appear to be macro-economic signals that predict currency crises. Eichengreen et al. focusing on devaluations in OECD (developed) countries, find that monetary factors, current account deficits and inflation matter, but fiscal deficits do not matter. Past crises matter for current ones indicating that credibility is important. Esquivel and Larrain (2000) include also developing countries in their sample and find that real exchange rate misalignment, high monetary growth rates, low foreign exchange reserves and current account imbalances predict currency crises.

Klein and Marion (1997) and Goldfajn and Valdes (1997) also confirm that real exchange rate over-valuation is an important factor in predicting currency crises. Kaminsky et al. (1998) claim that a currency crisis is imminent when variables such as exports, output, the money/international reserves ratio and equity prices cross threshold levels. The empirical results therefore, fall somewhere between the first two models; there is some but rather weak, predictive power. The evidence on currency crisis predictability seems inconclusive.

5.1.2 Currency Crisis Contagion

It is from the perspective of the self-fulfilling attack literature that contagion seems easiest to understand. This literature defines contagion, in the context of currency crises, as the effect on the probability of a speculative attack, which stems from attacks on other currencies (see also De Gregorio and Valdés, 2001). When speculators attack one currency successfully, they may well try another. However, it is important to realize that contagion may also be truly rational and, perhaps, predictable, for a variety of reasons. For example, trade is a strong linkage between countries that has an obvious currency component (see Gerlach and Smets, 1994). When the British pound leaves the European Monetary System (EMS) in 1992 and depreciates, but the Irish punt remains in the EMS and does not devalue, it is likely that the Irish punt experiences a real exchange rate appreciation relative to the pound (unless inflation rapidly reacts to the changes in exchange rates, which, in 1992, it did not). Hence, the real exchange rate appreciation adversely affects the competitive position of Irish exporters, eventually causing economic and political pressure to devalue. A related channel of apparent contagion is an income effect—reduced growth and lower income levels after a crisis reduce the demand for imports from other countries. A third channel is the "wake up call." It may be that the second country experienced similar negative macroeconomic conditions or followed similar inconsistent policies.

In addition to these channels, Forbes (2000) analyzes two other channels by which crises spread: a credit crunch (banks affected by a crisis in one country reduce lending to other countries) and a forced-portfolio recomposition or liquidity effect (investors that suffer losses from a crisis in one country sell assets in other countries). Forbes uses data from over 10,000 firms to test for the relative importance of each of these five channels of "contagion" during the Asian and Russian crises and finds that the first two channels (based largely on trade) are the most important.

Esquivel and Larrain (2000) document some evidence of regional contagion, in that a currency is more likely to devalue if a neighboring country has experienced a devaluation even controlling for other determinants of devaluation. Eichengreen et al. (1996) also find that contagion is primarily due to trade links. More research seems warranted on the channels through which contagion may occur.

5.2 Contagion and Equity Markets

Contagion in equity markets refers to the notion that markets move more closely together during periods of crisis. A first problem in the literature is then to define what constitutes a crisis, especially given the extreme volatility of many emerging equity markets. Consider the simple exercise in Table 5 that details the five most severe negative returns in 17 emerging markets. In 9 of 17 markets, August 1998 (Russian default) was among one of the five poorest performing months. For the Asian Crisis of July 1997 to May 1998, Indonesia, Korea, Malaysia and Thailand each have four representatives in the five worst returns during these months. On the other hand, none of the Latin American countries have any of their five worst return months during the Asian Crisis. Finally, the Mexican crisis of December 1994 shows up in a large negative return for Mexico. Interestingly, this month does not appear in any of the other Latin American or Asian worst return months. It should also be noted that October 1987 which is the date of a sharp drop in the U.S. stock market, shows up in the list for Mexico, Portugal, Taiwan and Thailand.[19]

The analysis in Table 5 is related to the recent work of Bae et al. (in press) who, using daily returns data in a number of emerging markets, look for the coincidences of extreme movements. Interestingly, they attempt to characterize (predict) the degree of coincidence using fundamental economic variables such as interest rates, exchange rate changes and conditional volatility (also see Karolyi and Stulz (1996) and Hartmann et al., 2001). The coincidence of extreme equity return movements may be one definition of contagion but Forbes and Rigobon (2002) declare, "there is no consensus on exactly what constitutes contagion or how it should be defined." Rigobon (in press) states, "paradoxically, . . . there is no accordance on what contagion means."

---

[19] There is also some evidence that equity markets anticipate some currency crises (see Harvey and Roper, 1999; Becker et al., 2000; Glen, 2002).

TABLE 5	The Five Largest Negative Log Returns				
	Largest	**2nd Largest**	**3rd Largest**	**4th Largest**	**5th Largest**
Argentina	Jul-89	Jan-90	Apr-81	Apr-84	Jan-82
	−104.8%	−77.6%	−59.8%	−52.7%	−46.2%
Brazil	Mar-90	Jun-89	**Aug-98**	Jun-92	Jan-99
	−84.2%	−56.3%	**−46.7%**	−36.7%	−34.5%
Chile	Jan-83	**Aug-98**	Sep-81	Oct-87	Sep-84
	−32.9%	**−30.9%**	−21.2%	−21.2%	−18.6%
Colombia	**Aug-98**	Jan-99	Feb-92	Jun-99	May-00
	−22.2%	−20.5%	−19.2%	−19.0%	−15.2%
Greece	Jan-88	**Aug-98**	Jan-83	Oct-92	Oct-85
	−36.8%	**−27.6%**	−20.5%	−18.9%	−18.5%
India	May-92	Mar-93	Mar-01	Nov-86	Sep-01
	−27.9%	−19.6%	−19.0%	−17.6%	−16.6%
Indonesia	**Aug-97**	**May-98**	**Dec-97**	**Jan-98**	Sep-98
	−51.2%	**−49.0%**	**−44.8%**	**−43.0%**	−27.6%
Korea	**Dec-97**	**Oct-97**	**Nov-97**	**May-98**	Oct-00
	−40.9%	**−35.3%**	**−32.7%**	**−26.4%**	−23.3%
Malaysia	**Aug-97**	Oct-87	**Aug-98**	**Nov-97**	**Jun-98**
	−37.4%	−36.5%	**−30.9%**	**−27.2%**	**−24.4%**
Mexico	Nov-87	Dec-82	Oct-87	**Dec-94**	**Aug-98**
	−89.9%	−62.8%	−55.3%	**−43.1%**	**−41.0%**
Pakistan	May-98	Oct-98	Jun-98	May-00	Jul-96
	−43.3%	−30.8%	−29.1%	−24.3%	−17.5%
Philippines	Sep-90	**Aug-98**	**Aug-97**	Sep-87	Oct-00
	−34.7%	**−31.9%**	**−28.2%**	−27.5%	−22.1%
Portugal	Nov-87	Dec-87	Oct-87	Feb-88	Oct-92
	−34.7%	−27.8%	−23.2%	−16.0%	−15.3%
Taiwan	Oct-87	Aug-90	Jun-90	Oct-88	Dec-88
	−43.9%	−41.8%	−30.7%	−28.8%	−28.7%
Thailand	Oct-87	**Aug-97**	**Oct-97**	**May-98**	**Dec-97**
	−41.3%	**−39.3%**	**−38.1%**	**−33.1%**	**−29.1%**
Turkey	**Aug-98**	Feb-01	Nov-00	Sep-01	Nov-90
	−52.2%	−52.0%	−43.2%	−40.6%	−37.8%
Venezuela	Dec-85	Nov-95	**Aug-98**	Mar-92	Jun-94
	−68.9%	−62.0%	**−50.5%**	−30.3%	−29.2%
Composite	**Aug-98**	Oct-87	Aug-90	Sep-01	**Oct-97**
	−29.3%	−28.9%	−19.0%	−16.8%	**−16.5%**

Note: Bolded dates and log returns represent crisis periods.

Importantly, contagion is not simply increased correlation during a crisis period. From a completely statistical perspective, one would expect higher correlations during periods of high volatility.[20] Forbes and Rigobon (2002) present a statistical correction for this conditioning bias and argue that there was no contagion during the three most recent crises.[21]

Bekaert, Harvey and Ng (2003b) and Tang (2002) define contagion as excess correlation—correlation over and above what one would expect from economic fundamentals and take an asset pricing perspective to studying contagion. For a given factor model, increased correlation is expected if the volatility of a factor increases. The size of the increased correlation will depend on the factor loadings. Contagion, therefore, is simply defined by the correlation of the model residuals. Tang restricts the underlying asset pricing model to a world capital asset pricing model (CAPM) whereas Bekaert et al. examine a more general factor model.

By defining the factor model, they effectively take a stand on the global, regional and country specific fundamentals as well as the mechanism that transfers fundamentals into correlation. Concretely, they apply a two-factor model with time-varying loadings to "small" stock markets in three different regions, Europe, Southeast Asia and Latin America. The two factors are the U.S. equity market return and a regional equity portfolio return. Their framework nests three models: a world capital asset pricing model (CAPM), a world CAPM with the U.S. equity return as the benchmark asset and a regional CAPM with a regional portfolio as the benchmark. They also add local factors to allow for the possibility of segmented markets. If the countries in a particular region are globally integrated for most of the sample period, but suddenly see their intra-regional correlations rise dramatically during a regional crisis, their contagion test would reject the null hypothesis of no contagion. On the other hand, if these countries' expected returns are not well described by a global CAPM, but rather by a regional CAPM, the increased correlations may simply be a consequence of increased factor volatility.

Equity return volatilities in the Bekaert, Harvey and Ng (2003b) model follow univariate generalized autoregressive conditional heteroskedasticity (GARCH) processes with asymmetry as in Bekaert, and Harvey (1997) and Ng (2000). Hence, negative news regarding the world or regional market may increase the volatility of the factor more than positive news and hence lead to increased correlations between stock markets.[22] Moreover, their model incorporates time-varying betas where the betas are influenced by trade patterns as in Chen and Zhang (1997). The results in Bekaert, Harvey and Ng (2003b) indicate the presence of contagion around the Southeast Asian crisis, but not during the Mexican crisis. This contagion is not limited to Southeast Asian, but extends to Latin America. These conclusions are broadly consistent with Rigobon (in press (b)) and Dungey and Martin (2001) who use a different methodology.

Finally, there are a number of recent papers that link contagion to liquidity and financial frictions (see Calvo, 1999; Calvo and Mendoza, 2000a,b; Kodres

---

[20] See Stambaugh (1995), Boyer et al. (1999), Loretan and English (2000), Forbes and Rigobon (2002), and early work by Pindyck and Rotemberg (1990, 1993). Work linking news, volatility and correlation includes King and Wadhwani (1990), Hamao et al. (1990) and King et al. (1994).

[21] As Forbes and Rigobon (2002) note, their methodology only works under a restrictive set of circumstances. An alternative is the test in Rigobon (in press (a)).

[22] Longin and Solnik (1995) report an increase in cross-country correlation during volatile periods. Other empirical studies (for example, Erb et al., 1994; De Santis and Gerard, 1997) find different correlations in up and down markets while Longin and Solnik (2001), Ang and Bekaert (2002) and Das and Uppal (2001) document higher correlations in bear markets. Erb et al. (1995) document higher correlations during U.S. recessions.

and Pritsker, 2002; Rigobon, 2002b; Yuan, 2002). Kyle and Xiong (2001) show how wealth effects can lead to contagion.

OTHER IMPORTANT ISSUES   6

6.1 Corporate Finance

Corporations in emerging markets provide an ideal testing ground for some important theories in corporate finance. For example, Lombardo and Pagano (2000) examine how legal institutions affect the return on equity. The cross-sectional variation in such institutions is particularly large for emerging markets. Similarly, it is often argued that the existence of a sufficient amount of debt helps mitigate the agency problems that arise as a result of the separation of ownership and control. In a number of emerging markets, the existence of multilevel ownership provides an environment where there is an acute separation of cash flow and voting rights. Given the possibility of severe agency problems, emerging markets provide an ideal venue to test these theories. That is, powerful tests of these theories can be conducted in samples that have large variation in agency problems.

In order to compete in world capital markets, a number of countries are grappling with setting rules or formal laws with respect to corporate governance. There is a growing realization that inadequate corporate governance mechanisms will increase the cost of equity capital for emerging market corporations as they find it more difficult to obtain equity investors.

Overall, research has characterized the degree of external corporate governance in emerging markets as weak (Johnson et al. (2000b); Denis and Connell, 2002; Klapper and Love, 2002). Both shareholder rights and the legal enforcement of the rights that do exist are generally lacking in emerging markets (La Porta et al., 1998), and the use of corporate takeovers as a disciplining mechanism is almost nonexistent. Further, as mentioned above, it is frequently the case that insiders possess control rights in excess of their proportional ownership. This is usually achieved through pyramid structures in which one firm is controlled by another firm, which may itself be controlled by some other entity, and so forth (Shleifer and Vishny, 1997; La Porta et al., 1998, 1999; Claessens et al., 2000; Lins, 2003). Finally, irrespective of pyramid structures, managers of emerging market firms sometimes issue and own shares with superior voting rights to achieve control rights that exceed their cash flow rights in the firm (Nenova, in press; Lins, 2003). Taken together, the net result is that a great number of firms in emerging markets have managers who possess control rights that exceed their cash flow rights in the firm, which, fundamentally, gives rise to potentially extreme managerial agency problems.

When external country-level corporate governance is weak, it is possible that internal governance in the form of concentrated ownership will step in to fill the void (see Himmelberg et al., 2002). Lins (2003) investigates whether management ownership structures and large non-management blockholders are related to firm value across a sample of 143 firms from 18 emerging markets. He finds that firm values are lower when a management group's control rights exceed its cash flow rights. Lins also finds that large non-management control rights blockholdings are positively related to firm value. Both of these effects are significantly more pronounced in countries with low shareholder protection. One interpretation of these results is that, in emerging markets, large non-management blockholders can act as a partial substitute for missing institutional governance mechanisms.

Lemmon and Lins (2003) use a sample of 800 firms in eight East Asian emerging markets to study the effect of ownership structure on value during the region's financial crisis. The crisis negatively impacted firms' investment opportunities, raising the incentives of controlling shareholders to expropriate minority investors. Further, because the crisis was for the most part unanticipated, it provides a "natural experiment" for the study of ownership and shareholder value that is less subject to endogeneity concerns. During the crisis, cumulative stock returns of firms in which managers have high levels of control rights, but have separated their control and cash flow ownership, are 10 to 20 percentage points lower than those of other firms. The evidence is consistent with the view that ownership structure plays an important role in determining the incentives of insiders to expropriate minority shareholders.

A related issue is the relation between the ownership structure and local authority. Johnson and Mitton (2003) examine Malaysian firms before and after the imposition of capital controls and find that firms with stronger ties to Prime Minister Mahatir benefited from the imposition of the capital controls. They interpret this as evidence that the capital controls provided a screen behind which favorable firms could be supported, as evidence of crony capitalism.

Claessens et al. (2003) examine the incidence of bankruptcy filings during the Asian crisis. They find after controlling for firm characteristics that bank-owned or group-affiliated firms were much less likely to file for bankruptcy. They also find that those countries with stronger creditor rights and better judicial systems have increased likelihood of bankruptcy filings. Johnson et al. (2000a) show that countries with lower quality corporate governance were hit harder during the Asian crisis.

Gibson (2000) examines the relation between CEO turnover and firm performance in emerging markets. In general, he finds a high turnover after poor performance, which is consistent with good corporate governance. However, when he isolates firms with a large domestic shareholder, such as a group-affiliated firm, there is no relation between performance and CEO turnover. This suggests that these ownership structures impede good corporate governance in emerging markets.

Lins and Servaes (2002) use a sample of over 1000 firms from seven emerging markets to study the effect of corporate diversification on firm value. They find that diversified firms trade at a discount of approximately 7% to single-segment firms. From a corporate governance perspective, Lins and Servaes find a discount only for those firms that are part of industrial groups, and for diversified firms with management ownership concentration between 10% and 30%. Further, the discount is most severe when management control rights substantially exceed management cash flow rights. Their results do not support internal capital market efficiency in economies with severe capital market imperfections.

Since management control and a separation of management ownership and control are associated with lower firm value in emerging markets, a question arises as to whether alternative external firm-level governance mechanisms exist that might improve the situation for minority shareholders. Several alternate governance mechanisms have the potential to lessen real or perceived agency problems between a firm's controlling shareholders and managers and its minority shareholders. Harvey et al. (2002) examine whether debt contracts can alleviate problems with potentially misaligned incentives that result when managers of emerging market firms have control rights in excess of their proportional ownership. Harvey et al. provide evidence that higher debt levels lessen the loss in value attributed to these managerial agency problems. When the authors investigate specific debt issues, they find that internationally syndicated term loans, which arguably provide the highest degree of firm-level monitoring, enhance value the most when issued by firms with high levels of expected managerial agency problems.[23]

Another potential firm-level governance mechanism that has received considerable research attention is a firm's decision to issue a cross-listed security, such as an ADR. For firms in emerging markets and those with poor external governance environments, this allows the firm to "opt in" to a better external governance regime and to commit to a higher level of disclosure, both of which should increase shareholder value. Along this line of reasoning, Doidge et al. (2002) present evidence that non-U.S. firms with exchange-listed ADRs have higher Tobin's Q values and that this effect is most pronounced for firms from countries with the worst investor rights. Lang et al. (2002a) find that firms from emerging markets or non-English legal origin countries that have exchange-listed ADRs show a greater improvement in their information environment (as measured by stock market analyst coverage and analyst forecast accuracy) than do developed markets firms with English legal origins that have exchange-listed ADRs. Lang et al. also show that improvements in the information environment for firms with listed ADRs are positively related to firm valuations.

Lins et al. (2001) test directly whether improved access to capital is an important motivation for emerging market firms to issue an ADR. They find that, following a U.S. listing, the sensitivity of investment to free cash flow decreases significantly for emerging market firms, but does not change for developed market firms. Also, emerging market firms explicitly mention a need for capital in their filing documentation and annual reports more frequently than do developed market firms, whereas, in the post-ADR period, emerging market firms tout their liquidity rather than a need for capital access. Further, Lins et al. find that the increase in access to external capital markets following a U.S. listing is more pronounced for firms from emerging markets. Overall, these findings suggest that greater access to external capital markets is an important benefit of the U.S. stock market listing, especially for emerging market firms.

Research analysts have the potential to increase the scrutiny of controlling management groups endowed with private benefits of control, which should improve firm values. Controlling managers have incentives to hide information from the investing public in order to facilitate consumption of these private control benefits. Lang et al. (2002b) find that analyst coverage positively impacts Tobin's Q values and that there is an incremental valuation benefit to additional analysts coverage when the management/family group controls a firm. Further, these benefits of analysts' coverage are significantly more pronounced for firms from countries with poor shareholder rights and with non-English origin legal systems.

The private benefits of control are also studied in Dyck and Zingales (2002a). They find that the private benefits of control are higher when the buyer comes from a country that protects investors less (and, thus, is more willing or able to extract private benefits). In countries where private benefits of control are larger capital markets that are less developed, ownership is more concentrated, and privatizations are less likely to take place as public offerings. Dyck and Zingales (2002a,b) show that one important mechanism to minimize the negative impact of the private benefit of control and to enforce good corporate governance is the local media (as represented by the ratio of newspaper circulation to total population).

---

[23] Booth et al. (2001) find that the choice of debt ratios in emerging markets is more sensitive to country-specific factors than in developed markets. This is consistent with the existence of greater information asymmetries in developing markets. Demirgüç-Kunt and Maksimovic (1996) examine the link between firm financing and stock market development.

6.2 Fixed Income

Emerging market equities have garnered a great deal more research attention than emerging market bonds. This is probably due to the availability of equity data versus bond data.[24] Although much of the research on emerging market bonds applies only to the last 15 years, global bond investing has a long and storied history. Through the First World War, London was the center of global finance. Indeed, the U.S. was for much of the 19th century considered as an emerging market. Not only was it emerging, but it also went through periodic eras of default. According to Chernow (1990), "During the depression of the 1840s—a decade dubbed the Hungry Forties—state debt plunged to 50 cents on the dollar. The worst came when five American states—Pennsylvania, Mississippi, Indiana, Arkansas and Michigan—and the Florida Territory defaulted on their interest payments."

Latin American lending had already become quite widespread in the 19th century. Chernow states that ". . . as early as 1825 nearly every borrower in Latin America had defaulted on interest payments. In the 19th century, South America was already known for wild borrowing sprees, followed by waves of default." By the 1920s, foreign lending in the U.S. had once again become widespread. In fact, the sale of repackaged foreign bonds to individual investors, and the subsequent losses, was an impetus to the passage of the Glass-Steagall Act in 1933, (see Chernow, 1990).

Erb et al. (2000) provide a historical analysis of emerging market bonds, using data from 1859 for Argentina, Brazil and the U.S. They find a similar level of volatility in emerging market bond and equity returns. Indeed, their correlation analysis (using more recent data) suggests that the correlation between emerging market bond returns and emerging market equity returns is over 0.70. Perhaps this is not surprising. Emerging market bonds are high-risk bonds, and often these types of bonds act like equity.

Considerable theoretical and empirical research has focused on understanding sovereign yield spreads (the spread between foreign government bond yields denominated in U.S. dollars and a similar maturity U.S. Treasury bond). The first branch of research tries to capture the strategic aspects of when a country should borrow and default (see Eaton and Gersovitz, 1981; Bulow and Rogoff, 1989a,b; Chowdhry, 1991). For example, the Bulow and Rogoff (1989b) model suggests that the threat of political and economic sanctions enforces the debt contracts between developing and developed nations. However, these models do not take a stand on what the sovereign credit spread should be. A second branch of research is cast in continuous-time, and focuses on the likelihood of default and the determination of credit spreads in particular countries (see Kuilatilaka and Marcus, 1987; Claessens and Pennachi, 1996; Gibson and Sundaresan, 2001; Duffie et al., 2003). Gibson and Sundaresan derive a relation between sovereign yield spreads and the cost of sanctions. They show that the ability to punish the sovereign borrower leads to a lower sovereign spread. Duffie et al. show how to incorporate default, restructuring as well as illiquidity into a model of sovereign yield spreads. The final branch of research examines the cross-sectional relationship between fundamental variables in the economy and the size of the sovereign spreads (see Eichengreen and Mody, 2000; Cantor and Packer, 1996; Erb et al., 1997). For example, Erb et al. show that country risk ratings are positively associated with real per capita GDP, real per capita GDP growth, and the investment to

---

[24] A historical analysis of the U.S. as an emerging market is found in Rousseau and Sylla (1999). Rousseau and Sylla (2001) examine the financial development of a number of countries.

GDP ratio. They find that ratings are negatively related to population growth. Given the strong negative correlation between ratings and sovereign spreads, these models provide a way to link the fundamental characteristics of an economy to the sovereign spread.

6.3 Market Microstructure

The particular trading arrangements in an equity market may directly affect two key functions of that country's secondary stock market: price discovery and liquidity. First, the trading process should lead to "fair" and correct prices; in other words, no investor should be able to manipulate market prices in his or her favor. Second, trading should occur at a low transaction cost, high speed, and large quantities should trade without affecting the price. These issues are the topic of the field of market microstructure. It is clear that the large cross-sectional heterogeneity of emerging markets and the formidable changes they have undergone over time should make them an interesting laboratory for market microstructure research.

While a number of academics have looked at the issue of market segmentation using detailed data from one country (see, for example, Domowitz et al., 1997; Bailey and Chung, 1995 for Mexico, and Bailey and Jagtiani, 1994 for Thailand), there is surprisingly little genuine microstructure research on emerging markets, perhaps because accurate and detailed data are difficult to obtain. There are a few exceptions though, which we now discuss.

Domowitz et al. (1998) use detailed data on Mexican stocks to investigate whether the cross-listing of securities, although beneficial from a market integration perspective, may lead to order flow migration to the more liquid international (often U.S.) market. Cho et al. (2003) use the Taiwanese market, with its unique price limits, to test the well-known magnet effect. The magnet effect postulates that prices accelerate towards the limits when getting closer to them. Cho et al. find strong evidence of a magnet effect, especially for the ceiling price.

Eventually, microstructure research is especially interested in transaction costs and liquidity, which differ greatly across emerging markets (see Glen, 2000 for an introduction to microstructure in emerging markets). Ghysels and Cherkaoui (2003) provide a detailed study of the Casablanca Stock Exchange in Morocco (CSE). The CSE is a typical emerging financial market that has gone through momentous change in the last 10 years. In the 1980s, the CSE in many ways was a backwater. It was a state institution, on which very few stocks were listed and with almost no participation of individual investors. Institutional investors would often trade on the large "upstairs." The upstairs market was a negotiated market where trades were based on mutual agreements, and where transactions were established under circumstances that were neither transparent nor standardized. During this period, the number of Moroccan shareholders was probably less than 10,000. The exchange was extremely illiquid and most stocks did not trade for weeks. In 1989, Morocco announced an ambitious privatization and economic liberalization program, which also included financial market reforms that would greatly alter the operation of the stock exchange starting in 1993. The CSE was both privatized and reformed. The market reforms created a dealer/market maker structure under which more disclosure was required from both listing companies and market makers. Whereas Morocco never prevented foreign investors from buying Moroccan stock, CSE's pre-reform the archaic structure and low trading volume effectively kept foreigners from participating in the market. The new reforms changed this, and in 1996, the CSE was included in the IFC Emerging Market database. Even before then, the number of individual investors had increased considerably, reaching 300,000 in 1996. These reforms had a profound effect on the stock market. Trading volume and liquidity exploded. Finally, on December 17, 1996, the CSE adopted the screen-driven trading system used by the Bourse de Paris.

It is generally believed that such microstructural changes should greatly affect the quality of the market, which can best be approximated by the cost of trading. There is no doubt that reforms immediately increased turnover and liquidity in the Moroccan Market, but did that also mean lower trading costs for the average trader on the market? Unfortunately, we do not have bid-ask spread data for the CSE. However, Ghysels and Cherkaoui (2003) obtained transactions data before and after the reforms for several stocks, and tried to infer the trading costs based on these data. Surprisingly, they find that, at least up until 1996, trading costs increased after the reforms. There are multiple interpretations of these results. First, on an absolute basis, although liquidity improved, the CSE remained a very thin, illiquid market with little trading. Second, foreign investors (especially new arrivals) may be among the least informed market participants. Possibly, CSE dealers possessed a tremendous amount of market power relative to foreign traders. This would imply that the high spreads were not a competitive equilibrium phenomenon, but rather indicated a fleecing opportunity, which disappeared as foreign investors became more informed and the market developed. A third possibility is that the model used by Ghysels and Cherkaoui mis-estimates true trading costs. On the other hand, if the results are accurate a few important lessons may be drawn from this detailed study. First, jumps in turnover and trading need not necessarily be associated with lower trading costs (although they typically are). Second, microstructure reforms may be an important signal to foreign investors of the local stock exchange's genuine integration into the world financial markets. However, by themselves, such reforms do not seem to contribute to bringing down the effective costs of trading. Only after screen-driven trading was introduced in late 1996 did transaction costs CSE fall (see Derrabi et al., 2000).

Obtaining estimates of liquidity and transaction costs is important because illiquid assets and assets with high transaction costs trade at low prices relative to their expected cash flows. It follows that liquidity and trading costs may contribute both to the average equity premium in stocks and to the time-variation in expected returns if there is systematic variation in liquidity. Some recent research, most notably Amihud (2002) and Jones (2001), attempts to quantify the role of liquidity in U.S. expected stock returns. Using 100 years of annual data, Jones finds that bid-ask spreads and turnover predict U.S. stock returns one period ahead, whereas the decline in transaction costs may have contributed to a fall of about 1% in the equity premium. Amihud (2002), using a 1964–1997 NYSE sample, finds that expected market illiquidity has a positive effect on the ex ante excess return and unexpected illiquidity has a negative effect on the contemporaneous stock return.

Liquidity effects may be particularly acute in emerging markets. In a survey by Chuhan (1992), poor liquidity was mentioned as one of the main reasons for foreign institutional investors not investing in emerging markets. If the liquidity premium is an important feature of the data, emerging markets should yield particularly powerful tests and useful independent evidence. Moreover, the recent equity market liberalizations provide an additional verification of the importance of liquidity for expected returns, since, all else equal (including the price of liquidity risk), the importance of liquidity for expected returns should decline post liberalization. This is important, since when focusing on the U.S. alone, the finding of expected return variation due to liquidity can always be ascribed to an omitted variable correlated with liquidity. Another important question is whether improved liquidity contributes to the decline in the cost of capital post-liberalization which is documented by Bekaert and Harvey (2000a) and Henry (2000a).

Bekaert, Harvey and Lundblad (2002e) address these questions in a recent article using a measure that relies on the incidence of observed zero daily returns in these markets. Lesmond et al. (1999) and Lesmond (2002) argue that if the value of an information signal is insufficient to outweigh associated transaction costs, market participants will elect not to trade, resulting in an observed zero return. They propose zero returns as evidence of transaction costs. Using a simple empirical pricing model and limited dependent variable estimation techniques, they infer estimates of transaction and price impact costs. Lesmond (2002) applies this indirect approach to estimate the costs of equity trading in emerging markets. The advantage of this measure is that it requires only a time-series of daily equity returns.

Bekaert, Harvey and Lundblad (2002e) use the zero return measure as a proxy for illiquidity. They find that higher illiquidity is indeed associated with higher expected returns. Whereas liberalization overall improves liquidity, its effect on the relation between illiquidity and expected returns is somewhat inconsistent. However, it is invariably the case that the effect of illiquidity on expected returns is larger post-liberalization.

6.4 Stock Selection

Most work on emerging market stock returns has focused on the IFC global index of IFC investible indices. However, there are a few papers that examine the characteristics of individual securities.

Stock selection is complicated by potentially extreme information asymmetry problems. Bhattacharya et al. (2000) provide evidence that Mexican stocks do not react contemporaneously to the usual types of news announcements. However, they find that the stocks react before such announcements, which is consistent with information leakage. In addition, they find that the price reaction of shares traded by foreigners lag those traded by nationals. This is consistent with information asymmetry.[25]

Fama and French (1998) collect information on size, book to market value, and price earnings ratios for 16 emerging markets. They find strong evidence of a value premium in these markets in both in-sample and out-of-sample tests. Rouwenhorst (1999) examines the characteristics of over 1700 firms in 20 emerging markets and finds that the cross-section of stock returns in emerging markets is driven by factors that also drive the cross-section in developed markets: size, momentum, and value.

Achour et al. (1999) examine a comprehensive list of 27 firm-specific factors to try to explain the cross-section of returns in three representative emerging markets. In contrast to previous work, Achour et al. examine both ex post and expectational firm characteristics. They find that measures, such as prospective earnings to price ratios, and analyst revision ratios, can differentiate between high and low expected return securities. While they document that some characteristics impact each market, there are considerable asymmetries across different markets. In addition, Achour et al. show that traditional measures of risk are unable to account for the differences in expected returns.

---

[25] Also see Choe et al. (2002) and Frankel and Schmukler (2000).

Van Der Hart et al. (2003) provide the most comprehensive analysis of individual stock returns in emerging markets by studying almost 3000 securities in 32 countries. Similar to Achour et al. (1999), Van Der Hart et al. look at both ex post and expectational characteristics. They confirm the profitability of strategies based on value and momentum and show that the returns cannot be explained with traditional asset pricing models. In contrast to previous work, Van Der Hart et al. examine the ability to implement these strategies. They show that the profitability of these strategies is robust to the assumed transactions cost of a large institutional investor.

6.5 Privatization

In most emerging markets, privatization was intended to increase the productivity of state-owned economic enterprises (SOEs), and to help reduce government budget deficits. In some cases, governments actively sought to promote capital market development through privatization. Many governments intended to create a class of people with a stake in the new economy, thereby making it more difficult for political changes to be reversed. Regardless of the goal, privatization was not initiated, in order to divest fully the government's interest in the real economy. Nevertheless, even the partial divestment under consideration was economically substantial.

Consider the evidence presented in Table 6. Between 1978 and 1991, SOEs in emerging markets controlled a significant proportion of (GDP). In our sample of 16 emerging economies, SOEs contributed to 10.9% of GDP during this time period. SOEs in developed economies contributed significantly less, 7.8%. Individual countries displayed significant cross-sectional variation in terms of the size of each country's SOE economic activity as a percent of GDP. For example, in the Philippines this figure was quite low, averaging 1.9% over the 14-year period. At the other extreme, SOEs in Venezuela contributed to just over 23% of GDP during the same period. Regardless of the country in question, the transfer of resources considered under any privatization program amounts to a non-trivial proportion of the wealth of the economy. Despite its importance, we provide only a short summary of the vast research on the topic because there already exists an extensive and excellent survey; see Megginson and Netter (2001).

Privatization programs impact emerging capital markets through various mechanisms. For instance, share issued privatizations (SIPs) increase the market capitalization and the value traded on local exchanges. Moreover, SIPs can change the investment opportunity set of portfolio investors. Public offers of SOEs whose cash flows are not perfectly correlated with pre-existing companies help investors to achieve gains through diversification. Under this scenario, SIPs may help to lower the risk premium investors require for holding the market portfolio of publicly traded equity.

Other methods of privatization, including the direct sale of former SOEs, the direct sale of an SOE assets, or concessions of public sector monopolies, alter the dynamics of local capital markets in less obvious ways. Consider the direct sale of an SOE to a private investor. This sale does not increase the market capitalization or value traded on the local exchange. However, the sale may alter the real investment opportunity set of the private investor.

As viewed from this perspective, all forms of privatization can impact local capital market dynamics. The common component of privatization that impacts capital markets is the transfer of productive resources from the public sector to the private sector. This transfer may allow investors to achieve benefits through diversification and may affect the cost of capital in emerging markets.

Country	SOE Economic Activity as % of GDP (1978–1991)[a]	Trade as % of GDP (1978–1991)[b]	Stock Market Capitalization as % of GDP (1978–1991)[c]
Argentina	4.7	15.4	1.8
Brazil	6.5	15.7	3.0
Chile	13.3	42.6	15.6
China	n.a.	n.a.	n.a.
Colombia	6.8	24.7	2.5
India	12.1	12.6	2.3
Indonesia	14.8	38.9	5.0
Jordan	n.a.	72.9	25.5
Malaysia	17.0	129.1	51.0
Mexico	11.6	21.5	4.3
Pakistan	10.3	29.4	2.5
Philippines	1.9	39.9	7.7
Portugal	18.2	53.0	8.4
Thailand	5.4	49.6	6.3
Turkey	7.5	22.2	3.5
Venezuela	23.1	40.9	4.0
Latin American average	11.0	26.8	5.2
Asian average	9.9	46.0	11.2
Average	10.9	40.6	9.6
United States[a]	1.2		

TABLE 6 The Role of State-Owned Enterprises in Emerging Economies (1978–1991)

[a] *Bureaucrats in Business: The Economics and Politics of Government Ownership* (1995).

[b] Time series average of data available from World Development Indicators 1999 CD-ROM.

[c] Time series average of data available from IFC Emerging Markets Database. Sample size dependent upon data availability.

Even if private investors do not benefit from the transfer of resources, i.e. their investment opportunity set does not change, privatization programs may still influence capital markets. Privatization programs can help the government signal its commitment to free market policies (see also Perotti, 1995; Biais and Perotti, 2002). For most emerging market governments, the implementation of a privatization program reverses decades of state-led economic development. Successful privatization of politically sensitive industries may convince investors to reduce the ex ante perceived risk of government interference in investment decisions and expropriation of productive assets. As a result of sustained privatization efforts, the sovereign risk premium inherent in the government's fixed income liabilities may be reduced. As this chain of events ripples through the economy, local market entrepreneurs eventually benefit in their ability to obtain debt financing at lower cost.

Bekaert, Harvey and Roper (2002f) find that the privatization of SOEs has increased local stock market capitalization and the value traded on these exchanges. They also find that privatization leads to a reduction in the dividend yield, which likely indicates a reduction in the cost of capital.

7   CONCLUSION

Most of our research on emerging equity markets has tried to draw inferences from a somewhat reluctant data set. Emerging market returns are highly non-normal (see Bekaert, Erb, Harvey and Viskanta, 1998; Susmel, 2001) and highly volatile, and the samples are short. Moreover, a dominating characteristic of the data is a potentially gradual, structural break. Although it is generally difficult to make inferences in such a setting, a few robust findings emerge: the liberalization process has led to a very small increase in correlations with the world market and a small decrease in dividend yields. This decrease could represent a decrease in the cost of capital or an improvement in growth opportunities; Bekaert, Harvey and Lundblad (2001, 2002c) find that economic growth increases post liberalization by about 1% per year on average over a 5-year period. Bekaert and Harvey (2000a), Henry (2000a), and Bekaert, Harvey and Lundblad (2002c) all find that aggregate investment increases significantly after liberalizations, providing one channel for this increased growth. Das and Mohapatra (2003) not only confirm the growth effect, but also investigate whether and how the reforms shifted the income distribution. They find an upward shift in the income share accruing to the top quintile of the income distribution at the expense of the middle class. The lowest income share remained unchanged. Such research counsels against drawing hasty inferences between economic growth and economic welfare.

Moreover, with a number of recent crises in emerging markets, the role of foreign capital in developing countries is again under intense scrutiny. Malaysia temporarily re-imposed capital controls, which deemed successful by some (see Kaplan and Rodrik, 2002). Thus, it is remarkable that we have so far failed to find negative effects of foreign investment on emerging markets. For example, although policy makers often complain about foreigners inducing excess volatility in local markets, our empirical tests never reveal a robust increase in volatility after liberalization. In other words, we cannot confirm the often-heard argument that foreign capital consistently drives up real exchange rates. We cannot even find increased real variability, that is, evidence of the variability of GDP and consumption growth rates increasing post liberalization (see Bekaert, Harvey and Lundblad). Despite very real problems in the financial and corporate sectors of the crisis countries in Southeast Asia, the current literature on the effects of capital flows on emerging markets reveals little reason for rich developed countries to discontinue their financing of emerging market country development. After all, one potential reason for the disappointingly small effect of the cost of capital that Bekaert, and Harvey (2000a) find, may be a combination of "segmentation risk"—foreign investors anticipating future policy reversals of foreign investment restrictions—and "home bias." "Home bias" refers to the fact that investors across the world have fairly small proportions of their assets allocated to foreign markets, and the proportion allocated to emerging markets is miniscule.[26] Portes and Rey (2002) find that the most important determinant of global equity transactions between two countries is geographical proximity.[27] We cannot help but wonder whether a world blessed with a vast pool of private, internationally active, speculative capital would have faced the kind of liquidity crises we have seen in recent years, and in the wake of these crises the many proposals to limit capital flows.

There remain a number of important caveats, however. Most of our research has focused on equity market liberalization. Few dispute the beneficial effects of foreign direct investment (see Borensztein et al., 1998), and most of the work critical of foreign capital flows focuses on the banking sector and short-term bond flows (see, e.g., Kaminsky and Reinhart, 1999, 2000). For example, liberalizing debt flows in a weak institutional environment, including a poorly developed and supervised banking sector, may have negative consequences. Portfolio equity flows are somewhere in between and seem to have beneficial effects. Contrasting the real effects of equity market liberalizations and banking sector liberalizations appears to be an important topic for future research.[28] This, then, also naturally leads back to an old international economics and developmental economics question (see Edwards, 1987): what is the optimal sequencing of economic and financial liberalizations in developing countries?

---

[26] See Lewis (1999) for a survey of the vast literature on this topic.

[27] Also see Ahearne et al. (in press).

[28] Bekaert and Harvey (2003) provide a list of possible directions for future research in emerging markets finance.

4⅝			
5½	5½	−	⅜
5½	213/16	−	¼
20⅝	213/16	−	⅞
	17⅜	18⅛	+ ⅞
13½	6½	6½	− ½
7¼	6½	31/32	− ⅛
	15/16		
1		9/16	
	9/16	9/16	
1 15/32	713/16	715/16	
7 15/16	713/16	7 15/16	
	2⅝	211/32	2½ +
	2¾	2¼	2¼
5⅛	12 1/16	11⅜	11¾ +
87	33¾	33	33⅛ −
602	25⅝	24 9/16	25⅝ +
833	12	11⅝	11⅞ +
16	10½	10½	10⅞ −
78	15⅞	15 13/16	15⅞ −
4508	9 1/16	8¼	8⅞ +
430	11¼	10⅝	
463	5	4⅞	

Absolute return objective   A return objective that is independent of a reference or benchmark level of return.

Absolute-return vehicles   Investments that have no direct benchmark portfolios.

Accounting risk   The risk associated with accounting standards that vary from country to country or with any uncertainty about how certain transactions should be recorded.

Accreting swap   A swap where the notional amount increases over the life of the swap.

Accrual equivalent after-tax return   The tax-free return that, if accrued annually, produces the same after-tax accumulation as the taxable portfolio.

Accrual equivalent tax rate   A method of measuring tax drag that finds the annual accrual tax rate that would produce the same after-tax accumulation as a tax system based in whole or in part on deferred realized gains.

Accrual taxes   Taxes that are levied and paid on a periodic basis, usually annually.

Accumulated benefit obligation (ABO)   The present value of pension benefits, assuming the pension plan terminated immediately such that it had to provide retirement income to all beneficiaries for their years of service up to that date.

Accumulated service   Years of service of a pension plan participant as of a specified date.

Active investment approach   An approach to portfolio construction in which portfolio composition responds to changes in the portfolio manager's expectations concerning asset returns.

Active management   An approach to investing in which the portfolio manager seeks to outperform a given benchmark portfolio.

Active return   The portfolio's return in excess of the return on the portfolio's benchmark.

Active risk   A synonym for tracking risk.

Active/immunization combination   A portfolio with two component portfolios: an immunized portfolio which provides an assured return over the planning horizon and a second portfolio that uses an active high-return/high-risk strategy.

Active/passive combination   Allocation of the core component of a portfolio to a passive strategy and the balance to an active component.

Active-lives   The portion of a pension fund's liabilities associated with active workers.

Actual extreme events   A type of scenario analysis used in stress testing. It involves evaluating how a portfolio would have performed given movements in interest rates, exchange rates, stock prices, or commodity prices at magnitudes such as occurred during past extreme market events (e.g., the stock market crash of October 1987).

Ad valorem fees   Fees that are calculated by multiplying a percentage by the value of assets managed; also called assets under management (AUM) fees.

Add-on interest   A procedure for determining the interest on a bond or loan in which the interest is added onto the face value of a contract.

Adverse selection risk   The risk associated with information asymmetry; in the context of trading, the risk of trading with a more informed trader.

After-tax asset allocation   The distribution of asset classes in a portfolio measured on an after-tax basis.

Algorithmic trading   Automated electronic trading subject to quantitative rules and user-specified benchmarks and constraints.

Allocation/selection interaction return   A measure of the joint effect of weights assigned to both sectors and individual securities; the difference between the weight of the portfolio in a given sector and the portfolio's benchmark for that sector, times the difference between the portfolio's and the benchmark's returns in that sector, summed across all sectors.

Alpha   Excess risk-adjusted return.

Alpha and beta separation   An approach to portfolio construction that views investing to earn alpha and investing to establish systematic risk exposures as tasks that can and should be pursued separately.

Alpha research   Research related to capturing excess risk-adjusted returns by a particular strategy; a way investment research is organized in some investment management firms.

Alternative investments   Groups of investments with risk and return characteristics that differ markedly from those of traditional stock and bond investments.

American option   An option that can be exercised on any day through the expiration day. Also referred to as *American-style exercise.*

Amortizing and **accreting swaps**   A swap in which the notional principal changes according to a formula related to changes in the underlying.

Amortizing swap   A swap where the notional amount declines over the life of the swap.

G-1

Anchoring trap The tendency of the mind to give disproportionate weight to the first information it receives on a topic.

Angel investor An accredited individual investing chiefly in seed and early-stage companies.

Appraisal data Valuation data based on appraised rather than market values.

Arbitrage The condition in a financial market in which equivalent assets or combinations of assets sell for two different prices, creating an opportunity to profit at no risk with no commitment of money. In a well-functioning financial market, few arbitrage opportunities are possible. Equivalent to the *law of one price.*

Arrears swap A type of interest rate swap in which the floating payment is set at the end of the period and the interest is paid at that same time.

Ask price (or ask, offer price, offer) The price at which a dealer will sell a specified quantity of a security.

Ask size The quantity associated with the ask price.

Asset allocation reviews A periodic review of the appropriateness of a portfolio's asset allocation.

Asset covariance matrix The covariance matrix for the asset classes or markets under consideration.

Asset location The choice of accounts in which specific assets are placed.

Asset swap A swap, typically involving a bond, in which fixed bond payments are swapped for payments based on a floating rate.

Asset/liability management The management of financial risks created by the interaction of assets and liabilities.

Asset/liability management approach In the context of determining a strategic asset allocation, an asset/liability management approach involves explicitly modeling liabilities and adopting the allocation of assets that is optimal in relationship to funding liabilities.

Asset-only approach In the context of determining a strategic asset allocation, an approach that focuses on the characteristics of the assets without explicitly modeling the liabilities.

Assurity of completion In the context of trading, confidence that trades will settle without problems under all market conditions.

Assurity of the contract In the context of trading, confidence that the parties to trades will be held to fulfilling their obligations.

Asynchronism A discrepancy in the dating of observations that occurs because stale (out-of-date) data may be used in the absence of current data.

At the money An option in which the underlying value equals the exercise price.

AUM fee A fee based on assets under management; an ad valorem fee.

Automated trading Any form of trading that is not manual, including trading based on algorithms.

Average effective spread A measure of the liquidity of a security's market. The mean effective spread (sometimes dollar weighted) over all transactions in the stock in the period under study.

Back office Administrative functions at an investment firm such as those pertaining to transaction processing, record keeping, and regulatory compliance.

Backtesting A method for gaining information about a model using past data. As used in reference to VAR, it is the process of comparing the number of violations of VAR thresholds over a time period with the figure implied by the user-selected probability level.

Back-to-back transaction A transaction where a dealer enters into offsetting transactions with different parties, effectively serving as a go-between.

Backwardation A condition in the futures markets in which the benefits of holding an asset exceed the costs, leaving the futures price less than the spot price.

Balance of payments An accounting of all cash flows between residents and nonresidents of a country.

Bancassurance The sale of insurance by banks.

Barbell portfolio A portfolio made up of short and long maturities relative to the investment horizon date and interim coupon payments.

Basis The difference between the cash price and the futures price.

Basis point value (BPV) Also called *present value of a basis point* or *price value of a basis point* (PVBP), the change in the bond price for a 1 basis point change in yield.

Basis risk The risk that the basis will change in an unpredictable way.

Basis swap A swap in which both parties pay a floating rate.

Bear spread An option strategy that involves selling a put with a lower exercise price and buying a put with a higher exercise price. It can also be executed with calls.

Behavioral finance An approach to finance based on the observation that psychological variables affect and often distort individuals' investment decision making.

Benchmark Something taken as a standard of comparison; a comparison portfolio; a collection of securities or risk factors and associated weights that represents the persistent and prominent investment characteristics of an asset category or manager's investment process.

Best efforts order   A type of order that gives the trader's agent discretion to execute the order only when the agent judges market conditions to be favorable.

Beta   A measure of the sensitivity of a given investment or portfolio to movements in the overall market.

Beta research   Research related to systematic (market) risk and return; a way investment research is organized in some investment management firms.

Bid price (or bid)   The price at which a dealer will buy a specified quantity of a security.

Bid size   The quantity associated with the bid price.

Bid–ask spread   The difference between the current bid price and the current ask price of a security.

Binary credit options   Options that provide payoffs contingent on the occurrence of a specified negative credit event.

Binomial model   A model for pricing options in which the underlying price can move to only one of two possible new prices.

Binomial tree   A diagram representing price movements of the underlying in a binomial model.

Block order   An order to sell or buy in a quantity that is large relative to the liquidity ordinarily available from dealers in the security or in other markets.

Bond option   An option in which the underlying is a bond; primarily traded in over-the-counter markets.

Bond-yield-plus-risk-premium method   An approach to estimating the required return on equity which specifies that required return as a bond yield plus a risk premium.

Bottom-up   Focusing on company-specific fundamentals or factors such as revenues, earnings, cash flow, or new product development.

Box spread   An option strategy that combines a bull spread and a bear spread having two different exercise prices, which produces a risk-free payoff of the difference in the exercise prices.

Broad market indexes   An index that is intended to measure the performance of an entire asset class. For example, the S&P 500 Index, Wilshire 5000, and Russell 3000 indexes for U.S. common stocks.

Broker   An agent of a trader in executing trades.

Brokered markets   Markets in which transactions are largely effected through a search-brokerage mechanism away from public markets.

Brokers   See *futures commission merchants.*

Bubbles   Episodes in which asset market prices move to extremely high levels in relation to estimated intrinsic value.

Buffering   With respect to style index construction, rules for maintaining the style assignment of a stock consistent with a previous assignment when the stock has not clearly moved to a new style.

Build-up approach   Synonym for the risk premium approach.

Bull spread   An option strategy that involves buying a call with a lower exercise price and selling a call with a higher exercise price. It can also be executed with puts.

Bullet portfolio   A portfolio made up of maturities that are very close to the investment horizon.

Business cycle   Fluctuations in GDP in relation to long-term trend growth, usually lasting 9–11 years.

Business risk   The equity risk that comes from the nature of the firm's operating activities.

Butterfly spread   An option strategy that combines two bull or bear spreads and has three exercise prices.

Buy side   Investment management companies and other investors that use the services of brokerages.

Buy-side analysts   Analysts employed by an investment manager or institutional investor.

Buy-side traders   Professional traders that are employed by investment managers and institutional investors.

Calendar rebalancing   Rebalancing a portfolio to target weights on a periodic basis; for example, monthly, quarterly, semiannually, or annually.

Calendar-and-percentage-of-portfolio rebalancing   Monitoring a portfolio at regular frequencies, such as quarterly. Rebalancing decisions are then made based upon percentage-of-portfolio principles.

Call   An option that gives the holder the right to buy an underlying asset from another party at a fixed price over a specific period of time.

Calmar ratio   The compound annualized rate of return over a specified time period divided by the absolute value of maximum drawdown over the same time period.

Cap   A combination of interest rate call options designed to hedge a borrower against rate increases on a floating-rate loan.

Cap rate   With respect to options, the exercise interest rate for a cap.

Capital adequacy ratio   A measure of the adequacy of capital in relation to assets.

Capital allocation line   A graph line that describes the combinations of expected return and standard deviation of return available to an investor from combining an optimal portfolio of risky assets with a risk-free asset.

Capital flows forecasting approach An exchange rate forecasting approach that focuses on expected capital flows, particularly long-term flows such as equity investment and foreign direct investment.

Capital market expectations (CME) Expectations concerning the risk and return prospects of asset classes.

Caplet Each component call option in a cap.

Capped swap A swap in which the floating payments have an upper limit.

Carried interest A private equity fund manager's incentive fee; the share of the private equity fund's profits that the fund manager is due once the fund has returned the outside investors' capital.

Carry Another term for owning an asset, typically used to refer to commodities. (See also *Carry market*).

Carry market A situation where the forward price is such that the return on a cash-and-carry is the risk-free rate.

Cash balance plan A defined-benefit plan whose benefits are displayed in individual recordkeeping accounts.

Cash flow at risk A variation of VAR that measures the risk to a company's cash flow, instead of its market value; the minimum cash flow loss expected to be exceeded with a given probability over a specified time period.

Cash flow matching An asset/liability management approach that provides the future funding of a liability stream from the coupon and matured principal payments of the portfolio. A type of dedication strategy.

Cash price or **spot price** The price for immediate purchase of the underlying asset.

Cash settlement A procedure used in certain derivative transactions that specifies that the long and short parties engage in the equivalent cash value of a delivery transaction.

Cause-and-effect relationship A relationship in which the occurrence of one event brings about the occurrence of another event.

Cautious investors Investors who are generally averse to potential losses.

Cell-matching technique (stratified sampling) A portfolio construction technique used in indexing that divides the benchmark index into cells related to the risk factors affecting the index and samples from index securities belonging to those cells.

Centralized risk management or **companywide risk management** When a company has a single risk management group that monitors and controls all of the risk-taking activities of the organization. Centralization permits economies of scale and allows a company to use some of its risks to offset other risks. See also *enterprise risk management*.

Chain-linking A process for combining periodic returns to produce an overall time-weighted rate of return.

Cheapest to deliver A bond in which the amount received for delivering the bond is largest compared with the amount paid in the market for the bond.

Cherry-picking When a bankrupt company is allowed to enforce contracts that are favorable to it while walking away from contracts that are unfavorable to it.

Civil law A legal system derived from Roman law, in which judges apply general, abstract rules or concepts to particular cases. In civil systems, law is developed primarily through legislative statutes or executive action.

Claw-back provision With respect to the compensation of private equity fund managers, a provision that specifies that money from the fund manager be returned to investors if, at the end of a fund's life, investors have not received back their capital contributions and contractual share of profits.

Clearinghouse An entity associated with a futures market that acts as middleman between the contracting parties and guarantees to each party the performance of the other.

Closed-book markets Markets in which a trader does not have real-time access to all quotes in a security.

Closeout netting In a bankruptcy, a process by which multiple obligations between two counterparties are consolidated into a single overall value owed by one of the counterparties to the other.

Coincident economic indicators Economic indicators that correlate with current economic activity; a set of economic variables whose values reach peaks and troughs at about the same time as the aggregate economy.

Collar An option strategy involving the purchase of a put and sale of a call in which the holder of an asset gains protection below a certain level, the exercise price of the put, and pays for it by giving up gains above a certain level, the exercise price of the call. Collars also can be used to provide protection against rising interest rates on a floating-rate loan by giving up gains from lower interest rates.

Collateral return (or collateral yield) The component of the return on a commodity futures contract that comes from the assumption that the full value of the underlying futures contract is invested to earn the risk-free interest rate.

Collateralized debt obligation A securitized pool of fixed-income assets.

Combination matching (or horizon matching) A cash flow matching technique; a portfolio is duration-matched with a set of liabilities with the added constraint that it also be cash-flow matched in the first few years, usually the first five years.

Commingled real estate funds (CREFs) Professionally managed vehicles for substantial commingled (i.e., pooled) investment in real estate properties.

Commitment period The period of time over which committed funds are advanced to a private equity fund.

Commodities Articles of commerce such as agricultural goods, metals, and petroleum; tangible assets that are typically relatively homogeneous in nature.

Commodity forward A contract in which the underlying asset is oil, a precious metal, or some other commodity.

Commodity futures Futures contracts in which the underlying is a traditional agricultural, metal, or petroleum product.

Commodity option An option in which the asset underlying the futures is a commodity, such as oil, gold, wheat, or soybeans.

Commodity spread Offsetting long and short positions in closely related commodities. (See also *Crack spread* and *Crush spread.*)

Commodity swap A swap in which the underlying is a commodity such as oil, gold, or an agricultural product.

Commodity trading advisors Registered advisors to managed futures funds.

Common law A legal system which draws abstract rules from specific cases. In common law systems, law is developed primarily through decisions of the courts.

Community property regime A marital property regime under which each spouse has an indivisible one-half interest in property received during marriage.

Completeness fund A portfolio that, when added to active managers' positions, establishes an overall portfolio with approximately the same risk exposures as the investor's overall equity benchmark.

Confidence band With reference to a quality control chart for performance evaluation, a range in which the manager's value-added returns are anticipated to fall a specified percentage of the time.

Confidence interval An interval that has a given probability of containing the parameter it is intended to estimate.

Confirming evidence trap The bias that leads individuals to give greater weight to information that supports an existing or preferred point of view than to evidence that contradicts it.

Consistent growth A growth investment substyle that focuses on companies with consistent growth having a long history of unit-sales growth, superior profitability, and predictable earnings.

Constant maturity swap or **CMT swap** A swap in which the floating rate is the rate on a security known as a constant maturity treasury or CMT security.

Constant maturity treasury or **CMT** A hypothetical U.S. Treasury note with a constant maturity. A CMT exists for various years in the range of 2 to 10.

Constraints 1) Restricting conditions; 2) Relating to an investment policy statement, limitations on the investor's ability to take full or partial advantage of particular investments. Such constraints are either internal (such as a client's specific liquidity needs, time horizon, and unique circumstances) or external (such as tax issues and legal and regulatory requirements).

Contango A condition in the futures markets in which the costs of holding an asset exceed the benefits, leaving the futures price more than the spot price.

Contingent claims Derivatives in which the payoffs occur if a specific event occurs; generally referred to as options.

Contingent immunization A fixed-income strategy in which immunization serves as a fall-back strategy if the actively managed portfolio does not grow at a certain rate.

Continuous auction markets Auction markets where orders can be executed at any time during the trading day.

Continuous time Time thought of as advancing in extremely small increments.

Contrarian A value investment substyle focusing on stocks that have been beset by problems.

Controlled foreign corporation A company located outside a taxpayer's home country and in which the taxpayer has a controlling interest as defined under the home country law.

Convenience yield The nonmonetary return offered by an asset when the asset is in short supply, often associated with assets with seasonal production processes.

Conversion factor   An adjustment used to facilitate delivery on bond futures contracts in which any of a number of bonds with different characteristics are eligible for delivery.

Convexity   A measure of how interest rate sensitivity changes with a change in interest rates.

Convexity adjustment   An estimate of the change in price that is not explained by duration.

Cooling degree day   The greater of i) 65 degrees Fahrenheit minus the average daily temperature, and ii) zero.

Core capital   The amount of capital required to fund spending to maintain a given lifestyle, fund goals, and provide adequate reserves for unexpected commitments.

Core-plus   A fixed-income mandate that permits the portfolio manager to add instruments with relatively high return potential to core holdings of investment-grade debt.

Core-satellite   A way of thinking about allocating money that seeks to define each investment's place in the portfolio in relation to specific investment goals or roles.

Core-satellite portfolio   A portfolio in which certain investments (often indexed or semiactive) are viewed as the core and the balance are viewed as satellite investments fulfilling specific roles.

Corner portfolio   Adjacent corner portfolios define a segment of the minimum-variance frontier within which portfolios hold identical assets and the rate of change of asset weights in moving from one portfolio to another is constant.

Corner portfolio theorem   In a sign-constrained mean–variance optimization, the result that the asset weights of any minimum-variance portfolio are a positive linear combination of the corresponding weights in the two adjacent corner portfolios that bracket it in terms of expected return (or standard deviation of return).

Corporate governance   The system of internal controls and procedures used to define and protect the rights and responsibilities of various stakeholders.

Corporate venturing   Investments by companies in promising young companies in the same or a related industry.

Cost basis   The amount paid to acquire an asset.

Cost of carry   The costs of holding an asset.

Cost of carry model   A model for pricing futures contracts in which the futures price is determined by adding the cost of carry to the spot price.

Country beta   A measure of the sensitivity of a specified variable (e.g., yield) to a change in the comparable variable in another country.

Covariance   A measure of the extent to which the returns on two assets move together.

Coverage   Benchmark coverage is defined as the proportion of a portfolio's market value that is contained in the benchmark.

Covered call   An option strategy involving the holding of an asset and sale of a call on the asset.

Covered interest arbitrage   A transaction executed in the foreign exchange market in which a currency is purchased (sold) and a forward contract is sold (purchased) to lock in the exchange rate for future delivery of the currency. This transaction should earn the risk-free rate of the investor's home country.

Crack spread   The difference between the price of crude oil futures and that of equivalent amounts of heating oil and gasoline.

Credit default swap   A swap used to transfer credit risk to another party. A protection buyer pays the protection seller in return for the right to receive a payment from the seller in the event of a specified credit event.

Credit derivative   A contract in which one party has the right to claim a payment from another party in the event that a specific credit event occurs over the life of the contract.

Credit event   An event affecting the credit risk of a security or counterparty.

Credit forwards   A type of credit derivative with payoffs based on bond values or credit spreads.

Credit method   When the residence country reduces its taxpayers' domestic tax liability by the amount of taxes paid to a foreign country that exercises source jurisdiction.

Credit protection seller   With respect to a credit derivative, the party that accepts the credit risk of the underlying financial asset.

Credit risk or **default risk**   The risk of loss caused by a counterparty's or debtor's failure to make a timely payment or by the change in value of a financial instrument based on changes in default risk.

Credit spread forward   A forward contract used to transfer credit risk to another party; a forward contract on a yield spread.

Credit spread option   An option based on the yield spread between two securities that is used to transfer credit risk.

Credit spread risk   The risk that the spread between the rate for a risky bond and the rate for a default risk-free bond may vary after the purchase of the risky bond.

Credit swap   A type of swap transaction used as a credit derivative in which one party makes periodic payments to the other and receives the promise of a payoff if a third party defaults.

Credit VAR   A variation of VAR related to credit risk; it reflects the minimum loss due to credit exposure with a given probability during a period of time.

Credited rates   Rates of interest credited to a policyholder's reserve account.

Credit-linked notes   Fixed-income securities in which the holder of the security has the right to withhold payment of the full amount due at maturity if a credit event occurs.

Cross hedging   With respect to hedging bond investments using futures, hedging when the bond to be hedged is not identical to the bond underlying the futures contract. With respect to currency hedging, a hedging technique that uses two currencies other than the home currency.

Cross-default provision   A provision stipulating that if a borrower defaults on any outstanding credit obligations, the borrower is considered to be in default on all obligations.

Cross-product netting   Netting the market values of all contracts, not just derivatives, between parties.

Crush spread   The difference between the price of a quantity of soybeans and that of the soybean meal and oil that can be produced by those soybeans.

Currency forward   A forward contract in which the underlying is a foreign currency.

Currency option   An option that allows the holder to buy (if a call) or sell (if a put) an underlying currency at a fixed exercise rate, expressed as an exchange rate.

Currency return   The percentage change in the spot exchange rate stated in terms of home currency per unit of foreign currency.

Currency risk   The risk associated with the uncertainty about the exchange rate at which proceeds in the foreign currency can be converted into the investor's home currency.

Currency swap   A swap in which the parties make payments based on the difference in debt payments in different currencies.

Currency-hedged instruments   Investment in nondomestic assets in which currency exposures are neutralized.

Current credit risk (or jump-to-default risk)   The risk of credit-related events happening in the immediate future; it relates to the risk that a payment currently due will not be paid.

Cushion spread   The difference between the minimum acceptable return and the higher possible immunized rate.

Custom security-based benchmark   A custom benchmark created by weighting a manager's research universe using the manager's unique weighting approach.

Cyclical stocks   The shares of companies whose earnings have above-average sensitivity to the business cycle.

Daily settlement   See *marking to market*.

Data-mining bias   Bias that results from repeatedly "drilling" or searching a dataset until some statistically significant pattern is found.

Day traders   Traders that rapidly buy and sell stocks in the hope that the stocks will continue to rise or fall in value for the seconds or minutes they are prepared to hold a position. Day traders hold a position open somewhat longer than a scalper but closing all positions at the end of the day.

Dealer (or market maker)   A business entity that is ready to buy an asset for inventory or sell an asset from inventory to provide the other side of an order.

Decentralized risk management   A system that allows individual units within an organization to manage risk. Decentralization results in duplication of effort but has the advantage of having people closer to the risk be more directly involved in its management.

Decision price (also called arrival price or strike price)   The prevailing price when the decision to trade is made.

Decision risk   The risk of changing strategies at the point of maximum loss.

Dedication strategies   Specialized fixed-income strategies designed to accommodate specific funding needs of the investor.

Deduction method   When the residence country allows taxpayers to reduce their taxable income by the amount of taxes paid to foreign governments in respect of foreign-source income.

Deemed dispositions   Tax treatment that assumes property is sold. It is sometimes seen as an alternative to estate or inheritance tax.

Deemed distribution   When shareholders of a controlled foreign corporation are taxed as if the earnings were distributed to shareholders, even though no distribution has been made.

Deep in the money   Options that are far in-the-money.

Deep out of the money   Options that are far out-of-the-money.

Default risk   The risk of loss if an issuer or counterparty does not fulfill its contractual obligations.

Default risk premium   Compensation for the possibility that the issue of a debt instrument will fail to make a promised payment at the contracted time and in the contracted amount.

Default swap   A contract in which the swap buyer pays a regular premium; in exchange, if a default in a specified bond occurs, the swap seller pays the buyer the loss due to the default.

Defaultable debt   Debt with some meaningful amount of credit risk.

Deferred swap   A swap with terms specified today, but for which swap payments begin at a later date than for an ordinary swap.

Deferred taxes   Taxes that are postponed until some future date.

Defined-benefit plan   A pension plan that specifies the plan sponsor's obligations in terms of the benefit to plan participants.

Defined-contribution plan   A pension plan that specifies the sponsor's obligations in terms of contributions to the pension fund rather than benefits to plan participants.

Deflation   A decrease in the general level of prices; an increase in the purchasing power of a unit of currency.

Delay costs (or slippage)   Implicit trading costs that arise from the inability to complete desired trades immediately due to order size or market liquidity.

Delivery   A process used in a deliverable forward contract in which the long pays the agreed-upon price to the short, which in turn delivers the underlying asset to the long.

Delivery option   The feature of a futures contract giving the short the right to make decisions about what, when, and where to deliver.

Delta   The relationship between the option price and the underlying price, which reflects the sensitivity of the price of the option to changes in the price of the underlying.

Delta hedge   An option strategy in which a position in an asset is converted to a risk-free position with a position in a specific number of options. The number of options per unit of the underlying changes through time, and the position must be revised to maintain the hedge.

Delta-normal method   A measure of VAR equivalent to the analytical method but that refers to the use of delta to estimate the option's price sensitivity.

Demand deposit   A deposit that can be drawn upon without prior notice, such as a checking account.

Demutualizing   The process of converting an insurance company from mutual form to stock.

Derivative   A financial instrument that offers a return based on the return of some other underlying asset.

Derivatives dealers   The commercial and investment banks that make markets in derivatives. Also referred to as market makers.

Descriptive statistics   Methods for effectively summarizing data to describe important aspects of a dataset.

Deteriorating fundamentals sell discipline   A sell discipline involving ongoing review of holdings in which a share issue is sold or reduced if the portfolio manager believes that the company's business prospects will deteriorate.

Diff swap   A swap in which payments are based on the difference in floating interest rates on a given notional amount denominated in a single currency.

Differential returns   Returns that deviate from a manager's benchmark.

Diffusion index   An index that measures how many indicators are pointing up and how many are pointing down.

Diffusion index for stocks   An indicator of the number of stocks rising during a specified period of time relative to the number of stocks declining and not changing price.

Direct commodity investment   Commodity investment that involves cash market purchase of physical commodities or exposure to changes in spot market values via derivatives, such as futures.

Direct market access   Platforms sponsored by brokers that permit buy-side traders to directly access equities, fixed income, futures, and foreign exchange markets, clearing via the broker.

Direct quotation   Quotation in terms of domestic currency/foreign currency.

Discount interest   A procedure for determining the interest on a loan or bond in which the interest is deducted from the face value in advance.

Discounted cash flow (DCF) models   Valuation models that express the idea that an asset's value is the present value of its (expected) cash flows.

Discrete time   Time thought of as advancing in distinct finite increments.

Discretionary trust   A trust structure in which the trustee determines whether and how much to distribute in the sole discretion of the trustee.

Disintermediation   To withdraw funds from financial intermediaries for placement with other financial intermediaries offering a higher return or yield. Or, to withdraw funds from a financial intermediary for the purposes of direct investment, such as withdrawing from a mutual fund to make direct stock investments.

Distressed debt arbitrage   A distressed securities investment discipline that involves purchasing the traded bonds of bankrupt companies and selling the common equity short.

Distressed securities Securities of companies that are in financial distress or near bankruptcy; the name given to various investment disciplines employing securities of companies in distress.

Diversification effect In reference to VAR across several portfolios (for example, across an entire firm), this effect equals the difference between the sum of the individual VARs and total VAR.

Dividend recapitalization A method by which a buyout fund can realize the value of a holding; involves the issuance of debt by the holding to finance a special dividend to owners.

Dollar duration A measure of the change in portfolio value for a 100 bps change in market yields.

Downgrade risk The risk that one of the major rating agencies will lower its rating for an issuer, based on its specified rating criteria.

Downside deviation A measure of volatility using only rate of return data points below the investor's minimum acceptable return.

Downside risk Risk of loss or negative return.

Due diligence Investigation and analysis in support of an investment action or recommendation, such as the scrutiny of operations and management and the verification of material facts.

Duration A measure of the approximate sensitivity of a security to a change in interest rates (i.e., a measure of interest rate risk).

Dynamic approach With respect to strategic asset allocation, an approach that accounts for links between optimal decisions at different points in time.

Dynamic hedging A strategy in which a position is hedged by making frequent adjustments to the quantity of the instrument used for hedging in relation to the instrument being hedged.

Earnings at risk (EAR) A variation of VAR that reflects the risk of a company's earnings instead of its market value.

Earnings momentum A growth investment substyle that focuses on companies with earnings momentum (high quarterly year-over-year earnings growth).

Econometrics The application of quantitative modeling and analysis grounded in economic theory to the analysis of economic data.

Economic exposure The risk associated with changes in the relative attractiveness of products and services offered for sale, arising out of the competitive effects of changes in exchange rates.

Economic indicators Economic statistics provided by government and established private organizations that contain information on an economy's recent past activity or its current or future position in the business cycle.

Economic surplus The market value of assets minus the present value of liabilities.

Effective capital gain tax rate A rate that adjusts the capital gains tax rate to reflect previously taxed dividends, income, or realized capital gains.

Effective duration Duration adjusted to account for embedded options.

Effective spread Two times the distance between the actual execution price and the midpoint of the market quote at the time an order is entered; a measure of execution costs that captures the effects of price improvement and market impact.

Efficient frontier The graph of the set of portfolios that maximize expected return for their level of risk (standard deviation of return); the part of the minimum-variance frontier beginning with the global minimum-variance portfolio and continuing above it.

Electronic communications networks (ECNs) Computer-based auctions that operate continuously within the day using a specified set of rules to execute orders.

Emerging market debt The sovereign debt of nondeveloped countries.

Endogenous variable A variable whose values are determined within the system.

Endowments Long-term funds generally owned by operating non-profit institutions such as universities and colleges, museums, hospitals, and other organizations involved in charitable activities.

Enhanced derivatives products companies (or special purpose vehicles) A type of subsidiary separate from an entity's other activities and not liable for the parent's debts. They are often used by derivatives dealers to control exposure to ratings downgrades.

Enterprise risk management An overall assessment of a company's risk position. A centralized approach to risk management sometimes called firmwide risk management.

Equal probability rebalancing Rebalancing in which the manager specifies a corridor for each asset class as a common multiple of the standard deviation of the asset class's returns. Rebalancing to the target proportions occurs when any asset class weight moves outside its corridor.

Equal weighted In an equal-weighted index, each stock in the index is weighted equally.

Equitized Given equity market systematic risk exposure.

Equitizing cash A strategy used to replicate an index. It is also used to take a given amount of cash and turn it into an equity position while maintaining the liquidity provided by the cash.

Equity forward A contract calling for the purchase of an individual stock, a stock portfolio, or a stock index at a later date at an agreed-upon price.

Equity-indexed annuity A type of life annuity that provides a guarantee of a minimum fixed payment plus some participation in stock market gains, if any.

Equity options Options on individual stocks; also known as stock options.

Equity risk premium Compensation for the additional risk of equity compared with debt.

Equity swap A swap in which the rate is the return on a stock or stock index.

ESG risk The risk to a company's market valuation resulting from environmental, social, and governance factors.

Estate All of the property a person owns or controls; may consist of financial assets, tangible personal assets, immovable property, or intellectual property.

Estate planning The process of preparing for the disposition of one's estate (e.g., the transfer of property) upon death and during one's lifetime.

Eurodollar A dollar deposited outside the United States.

European option An option that can be exercised only at expiration. Also referred to as *European-style exercise*.

Eurozone The region of countries using the euro as a currency.

Ex post alpha (or Jensen's alpha) The average return achieved in a portfolio in excess of what would have been predicted by CAPM given the portfolio's risk level; an after-the-fact measure of excess risk-adjusted return.

Excess capital An investor's capital over and above that which is necessary to fund their lifestyle and reserves.

Excess currency return The expected currency return in excess of the forward premium or discount.

Exchange A regulated venue for the trading of investment instruments.

Exchange fund A fund into which several investors place their different share holdings in exchange for shares in the diversified fund itself.

Exchange for physicals (EFP) A permissible delivery procedure used by futures market participants, in which the long and short arrange a delivery procedure other than the normal procedures stipulated by the futures exchange.

Execution uncertainty Uncertainty pertaining to the timing of execution, or if execution will even occur at all.

Exemption method When the residence country imposes no tax on foreign-source income by providing taxpayers with an exemption, in effect having only one jurisdiction impose tax.

Exercise or **exercising the option** The process of using an option to buy or sell the underlying.

Exercise rate or **strike rate** The fixed rate at which the holder of an interest rate option can buy or sell the underlying.

Exogenous shocks Events from outside the economic system that affect its course. These could be short-lived political events, changes in government policy, or natural disasters, for example.

Exogenous variable A variable whose values are determined outside the system.

Expiration date The date on which a derivative contract expires.

Explicit transaction costs The direct costs of trading such as broker commission costs, taxes, stamp duties, and fees paid to exchanges; costs for which the trader could be given a receipt.

Externality Those consequences of a transaction (or process) that do not fall on the parties to the transaction (or process).

Factor covariance matrix The covariance matrix of factors.

Factor push A simple stress test that involves pushing prices and risk factors of an underlying model in the most disadvantageous way to estimate the impact of factor extremes on the portfolio's value.

Factor sensitivities (also called factor betas or factor loadings) In a multifactor model, the responsiveness of the dependent variable to factor movements.

Factor-model-based benchmark A benchmark that is created by relating one or more systematic sources of returns (factors or exposures) to returns of the benchmark.

Fallen angels Debt that has crossed the threshold from investment grade to high yield.

Family offices Entities, typically organized and owned by a family for its benefit, that assume responsibility for services such as financial planning, estate planning, and asset management.

Federal funds rate The interest rate on overnight loans of reserves (deposits) between U.S. Federal Reserve System member banks.

Fee cap A limit on the total fee paid regardless of performance.

Fiduciary A person or entity standing in a special relation of trust and responsibility with respect to other parties.

Fiduciary call A combination of a European call and a risk-free bond that matures on the option expiration day and has a face value equal to the exercise price of the call.

Financial capital As used in the text, an individual investor's investable wealth; total wealth minus human capital. Consists of assets that can be traded such as cash, stocks, bonds, and real estate.

Financial equilibrium models Models describing relationships between expected return and risk in which supply and demand are in balance.

Financial futures Futures contracts in which the underlying is a stock, bond, or currency.

Financial risk Risks derived from events in the external financial markets, such as changes in equity prices, interest rates, or currency exchange rates.

Fiscal policy Government activity concerning taxation and governmental spending.

Fixed annuity A type of life annuity in which periodic payments are fixed in amount.

Fixed trust A trust structure in which distributions to beneficiaries are prescribed in the trust document to occur at certain times or in certain amounts.

Fixed-income forward A forward contract in which the underlying is a bond.

Fixed-rate payer The party to an interest rate swap that is obligated to make periodic payments at a fixed rate.

Floating supply of shares (or free float) The number of shares outstanding that are actually available to investors.

Floating-rate loan A loan in which the interest rate is reset at least once after the starting date.

Floating-rate payer The party to an interest rate swap that is obligated to make periodic payments based on a benchmark floating rate.

Floor A combination of interest rate options designed to provide protection against interest rate decreases.

Floor broker An agent of the broker who, for certain exchanges, physically represents the trade on the exchange floor.

Floor traders or **locals** Market makers that buy and sell by quoting a bid and an ask price. They are the primary providers of liquidity to the market.

Floored swap A swap in which the floating payments have a lower limit.

Floorlet Each component put option in a floor.

Forced heirship rules Legal ownership principles whereby children have the right to a fixed share of a parent's estate.

Formal tools Established research methods amenable to precise definition and independent replication of results.

Forward contract An agreement between two parties in which one party, the buyer, agrees to buy from the other party, the seller, an underlying asset at a later date for a price established at the start of the contract.

Forward curve The set of forward or futures prices with different expiration dates on a given date for a given asset.

Forward discount (or forward premium) The forward rate less the spot rate, divided by the spot rate; called the forward discount if negative, and forward premium if positive.

Forward hedging Hedging that involves the use of a forward contract between the foreign asset's currency and the home currency.

Forward price or **forward rate** The fixed price or rate at which the transaction scheduled to occur at the expiration of a forward contract will take place. This price is agreed on at the initiation date of the contract.

Forward rate agreement (FRA) A forward contract calling for one party to make a fixed interest payment and the other to make an interest payment at a rate to be determined at the contract expiration.

Forward strip Another name for the *forward curve.*

Forward swap A forward contract to enter into a swap.

Foundations Typically, grant-making institutions funded by gifts and investment assets.

Fourth market A term occasionally used for direct trading of securities between institutional investors; the fourth market would include trading on electronic crossing networks.

Front office The revenue generating functions at an investment firm such as those pertaining to trading and sales.

Front-run To trade ahead of the initiator, exploiting privileged information about the initiator's trading intentions.

Full replication When every issue in an index is represented in the portfolio, and each portfolio position has approximately the same weight in the fund as in the index.

Fully funded plan A pension plan in which the ratio of the value of plan assets to the present value of plan liabilities is 100 percent or greater.

Functional (or multifunctional) **duration**   The key rate duration.

Fund of funds   A fund that invests in a number of underlying funds.

Fundamental law of active management   The relation that the information ratio of a portfolio manager is approximately equal to the information coefficient multiplied by the square root of the investment discipline's breadth (the number of independent, active investment decisions made each year).

Funded status   The relationship between the value of a plan's assets and the present value of its liabilities.

Funding ratio   A measure of the relative size of pension assets compared to the present value of pension liabilities. Calculated by dividing the value of pension assets by the present value of pension liabilities. Also referred to as the funded ratio or funded status.

Funding risk   The risk that liabilities funding long asset positions cannot be rolled over at reasonable cost.

Futures commission merchants (FCMs)   Individuals or companies that execute futures transactions for other parties off the exchange.

Futures contract   An enforceable contract between a buyer (seller) and an established exchange or its clearinghouse in which the buyer (seller) agrees to take (make) delivery of something at a specified price at the end of a designated period of time.

Futures exchange   A legal corporate entity whose shareholders are its members. The members of the exchange have the privilege of executing transactions directly on the exchange.

Futures price   The price at which the parties to a futures contract agree to exchange the underlying.

Gain-to-loss ratio   The ratio of positive returns to negative returns over a specified period of time.

Gamma   A numerical measure of the sensitivity of delta to a change in the underlying's value.

Global custodian   An entity that effects trade settlement, safekeeping of assets, and the allocation of trades to individual custody accounts.

Global investable market   A practical proxy for the world market portfolio consisting of traditional and alternative asset classes with sufficient capacity to absorb meaningful investment.

Global minimum-variance portfolio   The portfolio on the minimum-variance frontier with smallest variance of return.

Gold standard currency system   A currency regime under which currency could be freely converted into gold at established rates.

Gordon (constant) **growth model**   A version of the dividend discount model for common share value that assumes a constant growth rate in dividends.

Government structural policies   Government policies that affect the limits of economic growth and incentives within the private sector.

Grinold–Kroner model   An expression for the expected return on a share as the sum of an expected income return, an expected nominal earnings growth return, and an expected repricing return.

Gross domestic product (GDP)   The total value of final goods and services produced in the economy during a year.

Growth in total factor productivity   A component of trend growth in GDP that results from increased efficiency in using capital inputs; also known as technical progress.

Growth investment style   With reference to equity investing, an investment style focused on investing in high-earnings-growth companies.

Guaranteed investment contract   A debt instrument issued by insurers, usually in large denominations, that pays a guaranteed, generally fixed interest rate for a specified time period.

Hague Conference on Private International Law   An intergovernmental organization working toward the convergence of private international law. Its 69 members consist of countries and regional economic integration organizations.

Heating degree day   The greater of i) the average daily temperature minus 65 degree Fahrenheit, and ii) zero.

Hedge funds   A historically loosely regulated, pooled investment vehicle that may implement various investment strategies.

Hedge ratio   The relationship of the quantity of an asset being hedged to the quantity of the derivative used for hedging.

Hedged return   The foreign asset return in local currency terms plus the forward discount (premium).

Hedging   A general strategy usually thought of as reducing, if not eliminating, risk.

High yield   A value investment substyle that focuses on stocks offering high dividend yield with prospects of maintaining or increasing the dividend.

High-water mark   A specified net asset value level that a fund must exceed before performance fees are paid to the hedge fund manager.

High-yield investing A distressed securities investment discipline that involves investment in high-yield bonds perceived to be undervalued.

Highest-in, first-out (HIFO) A concept related to tax loss harvesting in which investors are allowed to sell the highest cost basis lots first, which defers realizing the tax liability associated with lots having a lower cost basis.

Historical method A method of estimating VAR that uses data from the returns of the portfolio over a recent past period and compiles this data in the form of a histogram.

Historical simulation method The application of historical price changes to the current portfolio.

Holdings-based style analysis An approach to style analysis that categorizes individual securities by their characteristics and aggregates results to reach a conclusion about the overall style of the portfolio at a given point in time.

Homogenization Creating a contract with standard and generally accepted terms, which makes it more acceptable to a broader group of participants.

Human capital or **net employment capital** An implied asset; the present value of expected future labor income.

Hybrid markets Combinations of market types, which offer elements of batch auction markets and continuous auction markets, as well as quote-driven markets.

Hypothetical events A type of scenario analysis used in stress testing that involves the evaluation of performance given events that have never happened in the markets or market outcomes to which we attach a small probability.

Illiquidity premium Compensation for the risk of loss relative to an investment's fair value if an investment needs to be converted to cash quickly.

Immunization An asset/liability management approach that structures investments in bonds to match (offset) liabilities' weighted-average duration; a type of dedication strategy.

Immunization target rate of return The assured rate of return of an immunized portfolio, equal to the total return of the portfolio assuming no change in the term structure.

Immunized time horizon The time horizon over which a portfolio's value is immunized; equal to the portfolio duration.

Implementation shortfall The difference between the money return on a notional or paper portfolio and the actual portfolio return.

Implementation shortfall strategy (or arrival price strategy) A strategy that attempts to minimize trading costs as measured by the implementation shortfall method.

Implicit transaction costs The indirect costs of trading including bid–ask spreads, the market price impacts of large trades, missed trade opportunity costs, and delay costs.

Implied repo rate The rate of return from a cash-and-carry transaction implied by the futures price relative to the spot price.

Implied volatility The volatility that option traders use to price an option, implied by the price of the option and a particular option-pricing model.

Implied yield A measure of the yield on the underlying bond of a futures contract implied by pricing it as though the underlying will be delivered at the futures expiration.

Income tax structure How and when different types of income are taxed.

Incremental VAR A measure of the incremental effect of an asset on the VAR of a portfolio by measuring the difference between the portfolio's VAR while including a specified asset and the portfolio's VAR with that asset eliminated.

Index amortizing swap An interest rate swap in which the notional principal is indexed to the level of interest rates and declines with the level of interest rates according to a predefined schedule. This type of swap is frequently used to hedge securities that are prepaid as interest rates decline, such as mortgage-backed securities.

Index option An option in which the underlying is a stock index.

Indexing A common passive approach to investing that involves holding a portfolio of securities designed to replicate the returns on a specified index of securities.

Indirect commodity investment Commodity investment that involves the acquisition of indirect claims on commodities, such as equity in companies specializing in commodity production.

Individualist investors Investors who have a self-assured approach to investing and investment decision making.

Inferential statistics Methods for making estimates or forecasts about a larger group from a smaller group actually observed.

Inflation An increase in the general level of prices; a decrease in the purchasing power of a unit of currency.

Inflation hedge An asset whose returns are sufficient on average to preserve purchasing power during periods of inflation.

Inflation premium Compensation for expected inflation.

Information coefficient The correlation between forecast and actual returns.

Information ratio The mean excess return of the account over the benchmark (i.e., mean active return) relative to the variability of that excess return (i.e., tracking risk); a measure of risk-adjusted performance.

Information-motivated traders Traders that seek to trade on information that has limited value if not quickly acted upon.

Infrastructure funds Funds that make private investment in public infrastructure projects in return for rights to specified revenue streams over a contracted period.

Initial margin requirement The margin requirement on the first day of a transaction as well as on any day in which additional margin funds must be deposited.

Initial public offering The initial issuance of common stock registered for public trading by a formerly private corporation.

Input uncertainty Uncertainty concerning whether the inputs are correct.

Inside ask (or market ask) The lowest available ask price.

Inside bid (or market bid) The highest available bid price.

Inside bid–ask spread (also called market bid–ask spread, inside spread, or market spread) Market ask price minus market bid price.

Inside quote (or market quote) Combination of the highest available bid price with the lowest available ask price.

Institutional investors Corporations or other legal entities that ultimately serve as financial intermediaries between individuals and investment markets.

Interest rate call An option in which the holder has the right to make a known interest payment and receive an unknown interest payment.

Interest rate cap or **cap** A series of call options on an interest rate, with each option expiring at the date on which the floating loan rate will be reset, and with each option having the same exercise rate. A cap in general can have an underlying other than an interest rate.

Interest rate collar A combination of a long cap and a short floor, or a short cap and a long floor. A collar in general can have an underlying other than an interest rate.

Interest rate floor or **floor** A series of put options on an interest rate, with each option expiring at the date on which the floating loan rate will be reset, and with each option having the same exercise rate. A floor in general can have an underlying other than the interest rate.

Interest rate forward (See *forward rate agreement*)

Interest rate management effect With respect to fixed-income attribution analysis, a return component reflecting how well a manager predicts interest rate changes.

Interest rate option An option in which the underlying is an interest rate.

Interest rate parity A formula that expresses the equivalence or parity of spot and forward rates, after adjusting for differences in the interest rates.

Interest rate put An option in which the holder has the right to make an unknown interest payment and receive a known interest payment.

Interest rate risk Risk related to changes in the level of interest rates.

Interest rate swap A contract between two parties (counterparties) to exchange periodic interest payments based on a specified notional amount of principal.

Interest spread With respect to banks, the average yield on earning assets minus the average percent cost of interest-bearing liabilities.

Internal rate of return The growth rate that will link the ending value of the account to its beginning value plus all intermediate cash flows; money-weighted rate of return is a synonym.

Intestate Having made no valid will; a decedent without a valid will or with a will that does not dispose of their property is considered to have died intestate.

In-the-money Options that, if exercised, would result in the value received being worth more than the payment required to exercise.

Intrinsic value or **exercise value** The value obtained if an option is exercised based on current conditions.

Inventory cycle A cycle measured in terms of fluctuations in inventories, typically lasting 2–4 years.

Inverse floater A floating-rate note or bond in which the coupon is adjusted to move opposite to a benchmark interest rate.

Investment objectives Desired investment outcomes, chiefly pertaining to return and risk.

Investment policy statement (IPS) A written document that sets out a client's return objectives and risk tolerance over a relevant time horizon, along with applicable constraints such as liquidity needs, tax considerations, regulatory requirements, and unique circumstances.

Investment skill   The ability to outperform an appropriate benchmark consistently over time.

Investment strategy   An investor's approach to investment analysis and security selection.

Investment style   A natural grouping of investment disciplines that has some predictive power in explaining the future dispersion in returns across portfolios.

Investment style indices   Indices that represent specific portions of an asset category. For example, subgroups within the U.S. common stock asset category such as large-capitalization growth stocks.

Investor's benchmark   The benchmark an investor uses to evaluate performance of a given portfolio or asset class.

Irrevocable trust   A trust arrangement wherein the settlor has no ability to revoke the trust relationship.

J factor risk   The risk associated with a judge's track record in adjudicating bankruptcies and restructuring.

J-curve   The expected pattern of interim returns over the life of a successful venture capital fund in which early returns are negative as the portfolio of companies burns cash but later returns accelerate as companies are exited.

Joint ownership with right of survivorship   Jointly owned; assets held in joint ownership with right of survivorship automatically transfer to the surviving joint owner or owners outside the probate process.

Key rate duration   A method of measuring the interest rate sensitivities of a fixed-income instrument or portfolio to shifts in key points along the yield curve.

Lagging economic indicators   Economic indicators that correlate with recent past economic activity; a set of economic variables whose values reach peaks and troughs after the aggregate economy.

Law of one price   The condition in a financial market in which two financial instruments or combinations of financial instruments can sell for only one price. Equivalent to the principle that no arbitrage opportunities are possible.

Leading economic indicators   A variable that varies with the business cycle but at a fairly consistent time interval before a turn in the business cycle; a set of economic variables whose values reach peaks and troughs in advance of the aggregate economy.

Legal and regulatory factors   External factors imposed by governmental, regulatory, or oversight authorities that constrain investment decision-making.

Legal/contract risk   The possibility of loss arising from the legal system's failure to enforce a contract in which an enterprise has a financial stake; for example, if a contract is voided through litigation.

Leverage-adjusted duration gap   A leverage-adjusted measure of the difference between the durations of assets and liabilities which measures a bank's overall interest rate exposure.

Leveraged floating-rate note or **leveraged floater**   A floating-rate note or bond in which the coupon is adjusted at a multiple of a benchmark interest rate.

Liability   As used in the text, a financial obligation.

Life annuity   An annuity that guarantees a monthly income to the annuitant for life.

Lifetime gratuitous transfer   A lifetime gift made during the lifetime of the donor; also known as *inter vivos* transfers.

Limit down   A limit move in the futures market in which the price at which a transaction would be made is at or below the lower limit.

Limit move   A condition in the futures markets in which the price at which a transaction would be made is at or beyond the price limits.

Limit order   An instruction to execute an order when the best price available is at least as good as the limit price specified in the order.

Limit up   A limit move in the futures market in which the price at which a transaction would be made is at or above the upper limit.

Linear programming   Optimization in which the objective function and constraints are linear.

Liquidity   The ability to trade without delay at relatively low cost and in relatively large quantities.

Liquidity event   An event giving rise to a need for cash.

Liquidity requirement   A need for cash in excess of new contributions (for pension plans and endowments, for example) or savings (for individuals) at a specified point in time.

Liquidity risk   Any risk of economic loss because of the need to sell relatively less liquid assets to meet liquidity requirements; the risk that a financial instrument cannot be purchased or sold without a significant concession in price because of the market's potential inability to efficiently accommodate the desired trading size.

Liquidity-motivated traders   Traders that are motivated to trade based upon reasons other than an information advantage. For example, to release cash proceeds to facilitate the purchase of another security, adjust market exposure, or fund cash needs.

Locked limit   A condition in the futures markets in which a transaction cannot take place because the price would be beyond the limits.

Locked up   Said of investments that cannot be traded at all for some time.

Lock-up period   A minimum initial holding period for investments during which no part of the investment can be withdrawn.

Logical participation strategies   Protocols for breaking up an order for execution over time. Typically used by institutional traders to participate in overall market volumes without being unduly visible.

London Interbank Offer Rate (LIBOR)   The Eurodollar rate at which London banks lend dollars to other London banks; considered to be the best representative rate on a dollar borrowed by a private, high-quality borrower.

Long   The buyer of a derivative contract. Also refers to the position of owning a derivative.

Longevity risk   The risk of outliving one's financial resources.

Long-term equity anticipatory securities (LEAPS)   Options originally created with expirations of several years.

Low P/E   A value investment substyle that focuses on shares selling at low prices relative to current or normal earnings.

Lower bound   The lowest possible value of an option.

M²   A measure of what a portfolio would have returned if it had taken on the same total risk as the market index.

Macaulay duration   The percentage change in price for a percentage change in yield. The term, named for one of the economists who first derived it, is used to distinguish the calculation from modified duration. See also *modified duration*.

Macro attribution   Performance attribution analysis conducted on the fund sponsor level.

Macro expectations   Expectations concerning classes of assets.

Maintenance margin requirement   The margin requirement on any day other than the first day of a transaction.

Managed futures   Pooled investment vehicles, frequently structured as limited partnerships, that invest in futures and options on futures and other instruments.

Manager continuation policies   Policies adopted to guide the manager evaluations conducted by fund sponsors. The goal of manager continuation policies is to reduce the costs of manager turnover while systematically acting on indications of future poor performance.

Manager monitoring   A formal, documented procedure that assists fund sponsors in consistently collecting information relevant to evaluating the state of their managers' operations; used to identify warning signs of adverse changes in existing managers' organizations.

Manager review   A detailed examination of a manager that currently exists within a plan sponsor's program. The manager review closely resembles the manager selection process, in both the information considered and the comprehensiveness of the analysis. The staff should review all phases of the manager's operations, just as if the manager were being initially hired.

Mandate   A set of instructions detailing the investment manager's task and how his performance will be evaluated.

Margin   The amount of money that a trader deposits in a margin account. The term is derived from the stock market practice in which an investor borrows a portion of the money required to purchase a certain amount of stock. In futures markets, there is no borrowing so the margin is more of a down payment or performance bond.

Market bid   The best available bid; highest price any buyer is currently willing to pay.

Market fragmentation   A condition whereby a market contains no dominant group of sellers (or buyers) that are large enough to unduly influence the market.

Market impact (or price impact)   The effect of the trade on transaction prices.

Market integration   The degree to which there are no impediments or barriers to capital mobility across markets.

Market microstructure   The market structures and processes that affect how the manager's interest in buying or selling an asset is translated into executed trades (represented by trade prices and volumes).

Market model   A regression equation that specifies a linear relationship between the return on a security (or portfolio) and the return on a broad market index.

Market on open (close) order   A market order to be executed at the opening (closing) of the market.

Market order   An instruction to execute an order as soon as possible in the public markets at the best price available.

Market oriented   With reference to equity investing, an intermediate grouping for investment disciplines that cannot be clearly categorized as value or growth.

Market resilience Condition where discrepancies between market prices and intrinsic values tend to be small and corrected quickly.

Market risk The risk associated with interest rates, exchange rates, and equity prices.

Market segmentation The degree to which there are some meaningful impediments to capital movement across markets.

Market timing Increasing or decreasing exposure to a market or asset class based on predictions of its performance; with reference to performance attribution, returns attributable to shorter-term tactical deviations from the strategic asset allocation.

Market-adjusted implementation shortfall The difference between the money return on a notional or paper portfolio and the actual portfolio return, adjusted using beta to remove the effect of the return on the market.

Market-not-held order A variation of the market order designed to give the agent greater discretion than a simple market order would allow. "Not held" means that the floor broker is not required to trade at any specific price or in any specific time interval.

Marking to market A procedure used primarily in futures markets in which the parties to a contract settle the amount owed daily. Also known as the *daily settlement.*

Mass affluent An industry term for a segment of the private wealth marketplace that is not sufficiently wealthy to command certain individualized services.

Matrix prices Prices determined by comparisons to other securities of similar credit risk and maturity; the result of matrix pricing.

Matrix pricing An approach for estimating the prices of thinly traded securities based on the prices of securities with similar attributions, such as similar credit rating, maturity, or economic sector.

Maturity premium Compensation for the increased sensitivity of the market value of debt to a change in market interest rates as maturity is extended.

Maturity variance A measure of how much a given immunized portfolio differs from the ideal immunized portfolio consisting of a single pure discount instrument with maturity equal to the time horizon.

Maximum loss optimization A stress test in which we would try to optimize mathematically the risk variable that would produce the maximum loss.

Mega-cap buy-out funds A class of buyout funds that take public companies private.

Methodical investors Investors who rely on "hard facts."

Micro attribution Performance attribution analysis carried out on the investment manager level.

Micro expectations Expectations concerning individual assets.

Middle-market buy-out funds A class of buyout funds that purchase private companies whose revenues and profits are too small to access capital from the public equity markets.

Midquote The halfway point between the market bid and ask prices.

Minimum-variance frontier The graph of the set of portfolios with smallest variances of return for their levels of expected return.

Missed trade opportunity costs Unrealized profit/loss arising from the failure to execute a trade in a timely manner.

Model risk The risk that a model is incorrect or misapplied; in investments, it often refers to valuation models.

Model uncertainty Uncertainty concerning whether a selected model is correct.

Modern portfolio theory (MPT) The analysis of rational portfolio choices based on the efficient use of risk.

Modified duration An adjustment of the duration for the level of the yield. Contrast with *Macaulay duration.*

Monetary policy Government activity concerning interest rates and the money supply.

Money markets Markets for fixed-income securities with maturities of one year or less.

Moneyness The relationship between the price of the underlying and an option's exercise price.

Money-weighted rate of return Same as the internal rate of return; the growth rate that will link the ending value of the account to its beginning value plus all intermediate cash flows.

Monitoring To systematically keep watch over investor circumstances (including wealth and constraints), market and economic changes, and the portfolio itself so that the client's current objectives and constraints continue to be satisfied.

Monte Carlo simulation method An approach to estimating VAR that produces random outcomes to examine what might happen if a particular risk is faced. This method is widely used in the sciences as well as in business to study a variety of problems.

Mortality risk The risk of loss of human capital in the event of premature death.

Multifactor model A model that explains a variable in terms of the values of a set of factors.

Multifactor model technique With respect to construction of an indexed portfolio, a technique that attempts to match the primary risk exposures of the indexed portfolio to those of the index.

Multiperiod Sharpe ratio A Sharpe ratio based on the investment's multiperiod wealth in excess of the wealth generated by the risk-free investment.

Mutuals With respect to insurance companies, companies that are owned by their policyholders, who share in the company's surplus earnings.

Natural liquidity An extensive pool of investors who are aware of and have a potential interest in buying and/or selling a security.

Net interest margin With respect to banks, net interest income (interest income minus interest expense) divided by average earning assets.

Net interest spread With respect to the operations of insurers, the difference between interest earned and interest credited to policyholders.

Net worth The difference between the market value of assets and liabilities.

Net worth tax or **net wealth tax** A tax based on a person's assets, less liabilities.

Netting When parties agree to exchange only the net amount owed from one party to the other.

Nominal default-free bonds Conventional bonds that have no (or minimal) default risk.

Nominal gross domestic product (nominal GDP) A money measure of the goods and services produced within a country's borders.

Nominal risk-free interest rate The sum of the real risk-free interest rate and the inflation premium.

Nominal spread The spread of a bond or portfolio above the yield of a Treasury of equal maturity.

Nondeliverable forwards (NDFs) Cash-settled forward contracts, used predominately with respect to foreign exchange forwards.

Nonfinancial risk Risks that arise from sources other than the external financial markets, such as changes in accounting rules, legal environment, or tax rates.

Nonparametric Involving minimal probability-distribution assumptions.

Nonstationarity A property of a data series that reflects more than one set of underlying statistical properties.

Normal backwardation The condition in futures markets in which futures prices are lower than expected spot prices.

Normal contango The condition in futures markets in which futures prices are higher than expected spot prices.

Normal portfolio A portfolio with exposure to sources of systematic risk that are typical for a manager, using the manager's past portfolios as a guide.

Notional amount The dollar amount used as a scale factor in calculating payments for a forward contract, futures contract, or swap.

Notional principal amount The amount specified in a swap that forms the basis for calculating payment streams.

Objective function A quantitative expression of the objective or goal of a process.

Off-market FRA A contract in which the initial value is intentionally set at a value other than zero and therefore requires a cash payment at the start from one party to the other.

Offsetting A transaction in exchange-listed derivative markets in which a party re-enters the market to close out a position.

Open market operations The purchase or sale by a central bank of government securities, which are settled using reserves, to influence interest rates and the supply of credit by banks.

Open outcry auction market Public auction where representatives of buyers and sellers meet at a specified location and place verbal bids and offers.

Operations risk or **operational risk** The risk of loss from failures in a company's systems and procedures (for example, due to computer failures or human failures) or events completely outside of the control of organizations (which would include "acts of God" and terrorist actions).

Opportunistic participation strategies Passive trading combined with the opportunistic seizing of liquidity.

Opportunity cost sell discipline A sell discipline in which the investor is constantly looking at potential stocks to include in the portfolio and will replace an existing holding whenever a better opportunity presents itself.

Optimization With respect to portfolio construction, a procedure for determining the best portfolios according to some criterion.

Optimizer A heuristic, formula, algorithm, or program that uses risk, return, correlation, or other variables to determine the most appropriate asset allocation or asset mix for a portfolio.

Option A financial instrument that gives one party the right, but not the obligation, to buy or sell an underlying asset from or to another party at a fixed price over a specific period of time. Also referred to as contingent claims.

Option price, option premium, or **premium** The amount of money a buyer pays and seller receives to engage in an option transaction.

Option-adjusted spread (OAS) The current spread over the benchmark yield minus that component of the spread that is attributable to any embedded optionality in the instrument.

Options on futures (futures options) Options on a designated futures contract.

Options on physicals With respect to options, exchange-traded option contracts that have cash instruments rather than futures contracts on cash instruments as the underlying.

Order-driven markets Markets in which transaction prices are established by public limit orders to buy or sell a security at specified prices.

Ordinary income Earnings from employment.

Ordinary life insurance (also whole life insurance) A type of life insurance policy that involves coverage for the whole of the insured's life.

Orphan equities investing A distressed securities investment discipline that involves investment in orphan equities that are perceived to be undervalued.

Orphan equity Investment in the newly issued equity of a company emerging from reorganization.

Out-of-the-money Options that, if exercised, would require the payment of more money than the value received and therefore would not be currently exercised.

Output gap The difference between the value of GDP estimated as if the economy were on its trend growth path (potential output) and the actual value of GDP.

Overall trade balance The sum of the current account (reflecting exports and imports) and the financial account (consisting of portfolio flows).

Overconfidence trap The tendency of individuals to overestimate the accuracy of their forecasts.

Overnight index swap (OIS) A swap in which the floating rate is the cumulative value of a single unit of currency invested at an overnight rate during the settlement period.

Pairs trade (or pairs arbitrage) A basic long–short trade in which an investor is long and short equal currency amounts of two common stocks in a single industry.

Panel method A method of capital market expectations setting that involves using the viewpoints of a panel of experts.

Partial correlation In multivariate problems, the correlation between two variables after controlling for the effects of the other variables in the system.

Partial fill Execution of a purchase or sale for fewer shares than was stipulated in the order.

Participate (do not initiate) **order** A variant of the market-not-held order. The broker is deliberately low-key and waits for and responds to the initiatives of more active traders.

Passive investment approach An approach to portfolio construction in which portfolio composition does not react to changes in capital market expectations; includes indexing and buy-and-hold investing.

Passive management A buy-and-hold approach to investing in which an investor does not make portfolio changes based upon short-term expectations of changing market or security performance.

Passive traders Traders that seek liquidity in their rebalancing transactions, but are much more concerned with the cost of trading.

Payer swaption A swaption that allows the holder to enter into a swap as the fixed-rate payer and floating-rate receiver.

Payment netting A means of settling payments in which the amount owed by the first party to the second is netted with the amount owed by the second party to the first; only the net difference is paid.

Payoff The value of an option at expiration.

Pension funds Funds consisting of assets set aside to support a promise of retirement income.

Pension surplus Pension assets at market value minus the present value of pension liabilities.

Percentage-of-portfolio rebalancing Rebalancing is triggered based on set thresholds stated as a percentage of the portfolio's value.

Percentage-of-volume strategy A logical participation strategy in which trading takes place in proportion to overall market volume (typically at a rate of 5–20 percent) until the order is completed.

Perfect markets Markets without any frictional costs.

Performance appraisal The evaluation of portfolio performance; a quantitative assessment of a manager's investment skill.

Performance attribution A comparison of an account's performance with that of a designated benchmark and the identification and quantification of sources of differential returns.

Performance evaluation The measurement and assessment of the outcomes of investment management decisions.

Performance guarantee A guarantee from the clearinghouse that if one party makes money on a transaction, the clearinghouse ensures it will be paid.

Performance measurement A component of performance evaluation; the relatively simple procedure of calculating an asset's or portfolio's rate of return.

Performance netting risk For entities that fund more than one strategy and have asymmetric incentive fee arrangements with the portfolio managers, the potential for loss in cases where the net performance of the group of managers generates insufficient fee revenue to fully cover contractual payout obligations to all portfolio managers with positive performance.

Performance-based fee Fees specified by a combination of a base fee plus an incentive fee for performance in excess of a benchmark's.

Periodic (or batch) **auction markets** Auction markets where multilateral trading occurs at a single price at a prespecified point in time.

Permanent income hypothesis The hypothesis that consumers' spending behavior is largely determined by their long-run income expectations.

Personality typing The determination of an investor's personality type.

Plain vanilla swap An interest rate swap in which one party pays a fixed rate and the other pays a floating rate, with both sets of payments in the same currency.

Plan sponsor An enterprise or organization—such as a business, labor union, municipal or state government, or not-for-profit organization—that sets up a pension plan.

Pledging requirement With respect to banks, a required collateral use of assets.

Point estimate A single-valued estimate of a quantity, as opposed to an estimate in terms of a range of values.

Policy portfolio A synonym of strategic asset allocation; the portfolio resulting from strategic asset allocation considered as a process.

Policyholder reserves With respect to an insurance company, an amount representing the estimated payments to policyholders, as determined by actuaries, based on the types and terms of the various insurance policies issued by the company.

Political risk (or geopolitical risk) The risk of war, government collapse, political instability, expropriation, confiscation, or adverse changes in taxation.

Portable Moveable. With reference to a pension plan, one in which a plan participant can move his or her share of plan assets to a new plan, subject to certain rules, vesting schedules, and possible tax penalties and payments.

Portable alpha A strategy involving the combining of multiple positions (e.g., long and short positions) so as to separate the alpha (unsystematic risk) from beta (systematic risk) in an investment.

Portfolio implementation decision The decision on how to execute the buy and sell orders of portfolio managers.

Portfolio management process An integrated set of steps undertaken in a consistent manner to create and maintain an appropriate portfolio (combination of assets) to meet clients' stated goals.

Portfolio optimization The combining of assets to efficiently achieve a set of return and risk objectives.

Portfolio segmentation The creation of subportfolios according to the product mix for individual segments or lines of business.

Portfolio selection/composition decision The decision in which the manager integrates investment strategies with capital market expectations to select the specific assets for the portfolio.

Portfolio trade (also known as program trade or basket trade) A trade in which a number of securities are traded as a single unit.

Position a trade To take the other side of a trade, acting as a principal with capital at risk.

Position trader A trader who typically holds positions open overnight.

Positive active position An active position for which the account's allocation to a security is greater than the corresponding weight of the same security in the benchmark.

Post-trade transparency Degree to which completed trades are quickly and accurately reported to the public.

Potential credit risk The risk associated with the possibility that a payment due at a later date will not be made.

Potential output The value of GDP if the economy were on its trend growth path.

Preferred return With respect to the compensation of private equity fund managers, a hurdle rate.

Pre-investing The strategy of using futures contracts to enter the market without an immediate outlay of cash.

Premium Regarding life insurance, the asset paid by the policy holder to an insurer who, in turn, has a contractual obligation to pay death benefit proceeds to the beneficiary named in the policy.

Prepackaged bankruptcy A bankruptcy in which the debtor seeks agreement from creditors on the terms of a reorganization before the reorganization filing.

Prepaid swap A contract calling for payment today and delivery of the asset or commodity at multiple specified times in the future.

Present (price) value of a basis point (PVBP) The change in the bond price for a 1 basis point change in yield. Also called *basis point value* (BPV).

Present value distribution of cash flows A list showing what proportion of a portfolio's duration is attributable to each future cash flow.

Pretrade transparency Ability of individuals to quickly, easily, and inexpensively obtain accurate information about quotes and trades.

Price discovery Adjustment of transaction prices to balance supply and demand.

Price improvement Execution at a price that is better than the price quoted at the time of order placement.

Price limits Limits imposed by a futures exchange on the price change that can occur from one day to the next.

Price risk The risk of fluctuations in market price.

Price uncertainty Uncertainty about the price at which an order will execute.

Price weighted With respect to index construction, an index in which each security in the index is weighted according to its absolute share price.

Priced risk Risk for which investors demand compensation.

Primary risk factors With respect to valuation, the major influences on pricing.

Prime brokerage A suite of services that is often specified to include support in accounting and reporting, leveraged trade execution, financing, securities lending (related to short-selling activities), and start-up advice (for new entities).

Principal trade A trade with a broker in which the broker commits capital to facilitate the prompt execution of the trader's order to buy or sell.

Private equity Ownership interests in non-publicly-traded companies.

Private equity funds Pooled investment vehicles investing in generally highly illiquid assets; includes venture capital funds and buyout funds.

Private exchange A method for handling undiversified positions with built-in capital gains in which shares that are a component of an index are exchanged for shares of an index mutual fund in a privately arranged transaction with the fund.

Private placement memorandum A document used to raise venture capital financing when funds are raised through an agent.

Probate The legal process to confirm the validity of a will so that executors, heirs, and other interested parties can rely on its authenticity.

Profit-sharing plans A defined-contribution plan in which contributions are based, at least in part, on the plan sponsor's profits.

Projected benefit obligation (PBO) A measure of a pension plan's liability that reflects accumulated service in the same manner as the ABO but also projects future variables, such as compensation increases.

Prospect theory The analysis of decision making under risk in terms of choices among prospects.

Protective put An option strategy in which a long position in an asset is combined with a long position in a put.

Proxy hedging Hedging that involves the use of a forward contract between the home currency and a currency that is highly correlated with the foreign asset's currency.

Prudence trap The tendency to temper forecasts so that they do not appear extreme; the tendency to be overly cautious in forecasting.

Psychological profiling The determination of an investor's psychological characteristics relevant to investing, such as his or her personality type.

Public good A good that is not divisible and not excludable (a consumer cannot be denied it).

Purchasing power parity The theory that movements in an exchange rate should offset any difference in the inflation rates between two countries.

Pure sector allocation return A component of attribution analysis that relates relative returns to the manager's sector-weighting decisions. Calculated as the difference between the allocation (weight) of the portfolio to a given sector and the portfolio's benchmark weight for that sector, multiplied by the difference between the sector benchmark's return and the overall portfolio's benchmark return, summed across all sectors.

Put An option that gives the holder the right to sell an underlying asset to another party at a fixed price over a specific period of time.

Put–call parity An equation expressing the equivalence (parity) of a portfolio of a call and a bond with a portfolio of a put and the underlying, which leads to the relationship between put and call prices.

Put–call–forward parity The relationship among puts, calls, and forward contracts.

Quality control charts A graphical means of presenting performance appraisal data; charts illustrating the performance of an actively managed account versus a selected benchmark.

Quality option (or swap option) With respect to Treasury futures, the option of which acceptable Treasury issue to deliver.

Quoted depth The number of shares available for purchase or sale at the quoted bid and ask prices.

Quote-driven markets (dealer markets) Markets that rely on dealers to establish firm prices at which securities can be bought and sold.

Rate duration A fixed-income instrument's or portfolio's sensitivity to a change in key maturity, holding constant all other points along the yield curve.

Ratio spread An option strategy in which a long position in a certain number of options is offset by a short position in a certain number of other options on the same underlying, resulting in a risk-free position.

Real estate Interests in land or structures attached to land.

Real estate investment trusts (REITs) Publicly traded equities representing pools of money invested in real estate properties and/or real estate debt.

Real option An option involving decisions related to tangible assets or processes.

Real risk-free interest rate The single-period interest rate for a completely risk-free security if no inflation were expected.

Rebalancing Adjusting the actual portfolio to the current strategic asset allocation because of price changes in portfolio holdings. Also: revisions to an investor's target asset class weights because of changes in the investor's investment objectives or constraints, or because of changes in capital market expectations; or to mean tactical asset allocation.

Rebalancing ratio A quantity involved in reestablishing the dollar duration of a portfolio to a desired level, equal to the original dollar duration divided by the new dollar duration.

Re-base With reference to index construction, to change the time period used as the base of the index.

Recallability trap The tendency of forecasts to be overly influenced by events that have left a strong impression on a person's memory.

Receiver swaption A swaption that allows the holder to enter into a swap as the fixed-rate receiver and floating-rate payer.

Recession A broad-based economic downturn, conventionally defined as two successive quarterly declines in GDP.

Reference entity An entity, such as a bond issuer, specified in a derivatives contract.

Regime A distinct governing set of relationships.

Regulatory risk The risk associated with the uncertainty of how a transaction will be regulated or with the potential for regulations to change.

Reinvestment risk The risk of reinvesting coupon income or principal at a rate less than the original coupon or purchase rate.

Relative economic strength forecasting approach An exchange rate forecasting approach that suggests that a strong pace of economic growth in a country creates attractive investment opportunities, increasing the demand for the country's currency and causing it to appreciate.

Relative return objective A return objective stated as a return relative to the portfolio benchmark's total return.

Relative strength indicators A price momentum indicator that involves comparing a stock's performance during a specific period either to its own past performance or to the performance of some group of stocks.

Remaindermen Beneficiaries of a trust; having a claim on the residue.

Replacement value The market value of a swap.

Repurchase agreement A contract involving the sale of securities such as Treasury instruments coupled with an agreement to repurchase the same securities at a later date.

Repurchase yield The negative of the expected percent change in number of shares outstanding, in the Grinold–Kroner model.

Required return (or return requirement) With reference to the investment policy statement, a return objective relating to the level of return that will be adequate to satisfy a need.

Resampled efficient frontier The set of resampled efficient portfolios.

Resampled efficient portfolio An efficient portfolio based on simulation.

Residence jurisdiction A framework used by a country to determine the basis for taxing income, based on residency.

Residence–residence conflict When two countries claim residence of the same individual, subjecting the individual's income to taxation by both countries.

Residence–source conflict When tax jurisdiction is claimed by an individual's country of residence and the country where some of their assets are sourced; the most common source of double taxation.

Residue With respect to trusts, the funds remaining in a trust when the last income beneficiary dies.

Retired-lives The portion of a pension fund's liabilities associated with retired workers.

Return objective An investor objective that addresses the required or desired level of returns.

Returns-based benchmarks Benchmarks that are constructed using 1) a series of a manager's account returns and 2) the series of returns on several investment style indexes over the same period. These return series are then submitted to an allocation algorithm that solves for the combination of investment style indexes that most closely tracks the account's returns.

Returns-based style analysis An approach to style analysis that focuses on characteristics of the overall portfolio as revealed by a portfolio's realized returns.

Reverse optimization A technique for reverse engineering the expected returns implicit in a diversified market portfolio.

Revocable trust A trust arrangement wherein the settlor (who originally transfers assets to fund the trust) retains the right to rescind the trust relationship and regain title to the trust assets.

Rho The sensitivity of the option price to the risk-free rate.

Risk aversion The degree of an investor's inability and unwillingness to take risk.

Risk budget The desired total quantity of risk; the result of risk budgeting.

Risk budgeting The establishment of objectives for individuals, groups, or divisions of an organization that takes into account the allocation of an acceptable level of risk.

Risk exposure A source of risk. Also, the state of being exposed or vulnerable to a risk.

Risk governance The process of setting overall policies and standards in risk management.

Risk management The process of identifying the level of risk an entity wants, measuring the level of risk the entity currently has, taking actions that bring the actual level of risk to the desired level of risk, and monitoring the new actual level of risk so that it continues to be aligned with the desired level of risk.

Risk objective An investor objective that addresses risk.

Risk premium approach An approach to forecasting the return of a risky asset that views its expected return as the sum of the risk-free rate of interest and one or more risk premiums.

Risk profile A detailed tabulation of the index's risk exposures.

Risk tolerance The capacity to accept risk; the level of risk an investor (or organization) is willing and able to bear.

Risk tolerance function An assessment of an investor's tolerance to risk over various levels of portfolio outcomes.

Risk-neutral probabilities Weights that are used to compute a binomial option price. They are the probabilities that would apply if a risk-neutral investor valued an option.

Risk-neutral valuation The process by which options and other derivatives are priced by treating investors as though they were risk neutral.

Roll return (or roll yield) The component of the return on a commodity futures contract that comes from rolling long futures positions forward through time.

Rolling return The moving average of the holding-period returns for a specified period (e.g., a calendar year) that matches the investor's time horizon.

Sample estimator A formula for assigning a unique value (a point estimate) to a population parameter.

Sandwich spread An option strategy that is equivalent to a short butterfly spread.

Savings–investment imbalances forecasting approach An exchange rate forecasting approach that explains currency movements in terms of the effects of domestic savings–investment imbalances on the exchange rate.

Scalper A trader who offers to buy or sell futures contracts, holding the position for only a brief period of time. Scalpers attempt to profit by buying at the bid price and selling at the higher ask price.

Scenario analysis A risk management technique involving the examination of the performance of a portfolio under specified situations. Closely related to *stress testing*.

Seats Memberships in a derivatives exchange.

Secondary offering An offering after the initial public offering of securities.

Sector/quality effect In a fixed-income attribution analysis, a measure of a manager's ability to select the "right" issuing sector and quality group.

Security selection Skill in selecting individual securities within an asset class.

Security selection effect In a fixed-income attribution analysis, the residual of the security's total return after other effects are accounted for; a measure of the return due to ability in security selection.

Segmentation With respect to the management of insurance company portfolios, the notional subdivision of the overall portfolio into sub-portfolios each of which is associated with a specified group of insurance contracts.

Sell side Broker/dealers that sell securities and make recommendations for various customers, such as investment managers and institutional investors.

Sell-side analysts   Analysts employed by brokerages.

Semiactive management (also called enhanced indexing or risk-controlled active management)   A variant of active management. In a semiactive portfolio, the manager seeks to outperform a given benchmark with tightly controlled risk relative to the benchmark.

Semiactive, risk-controlled active, or **enhanced index approach**   An investment approach that seeks positive alpha while keeping tight control over risk relative to the portfolio's benchmark.

Semivariance   A measure of downside risk. The average of squared deviations that fall below the mean.

Separate property regime   A marital property regime under which each spouse is able to own and control property as an individual.

Settlement date or **payment date**   The designated date at which the parties to a trade must transact.

Settlement netting risk   The risk that a liquidator of a counterparty in default could challenge a netting arrangement so that profitable transactions are realized for the benefit of creditors.

Settlement period   The time between settlement dates.

Settlement price   The official price, designated by the clearinghouse, from which daily gains and losses will be determined and marked to market.

Settlement risk   When settling a contract, the risk that one party could be in the process of paying the counterparty while the counterparty is declaring bankruptcy.

Settlor (or **grantor**)   An entity that transfers assets to a trustee, to be held and managed for the benefit of the trust beneficiaries.

Shari'a   The law of Islam. In addition to the law of the land, some follow guidance provided by Shari'a or Islamic law.

Sharpe ratio (or reward-to-variability)   A measure of risk-adjusted performance that compares excess returns to the total risk of the account, where total risk is measured by the account's standard deviation of returns.

Short   The seller of a derivative contract. Also refers to the position of being short a derivative.

Shortfall risk   The risk that portfolio value will fall below some minimum acceptable level during a stated time horizon; the risk of not achieving a specified return target.

Shrinkage estimation   Estimation that involves taking a weighted average of a historical estimate of a parameter and some other parameter estimate, where the weights reflect the analyst's relative belief in the estimates.

Shrinkage estimator   The formula used in shrinkage estimation of a parameter.

Sign-constrained optimization   An optimization that constrains asset class weights to be nonnegative and to sum to 1.

Single-payment loan   A loan in which the borrower receives a sum of money at the start and pays back the entire amount with interest in a single payment at maturity.

Situational profiling   The categorization of individual investors by stage of life or by economic circumstance.

Smart routing   The use of algorithms to intelligently route an order to the most liquid venue.

Smoothing rule   With respect to spending rates, a rule that averages asset values over a period of time in order to dampen the spending rate's response to asset value fluctuation.

Socially responsible investing (ethical investing)   An approach to investing that integrates ethical values and societal concerns with investment decisions.

Soft dollars (also called soft dollar arrangements or soft commissions)   The use of commissions to buy services other than execution services.

Sole ownership   Owned by one person; assets held in sole ownership are typically considered part of a decedent's estate. The transfer of their ownership is dictated by the decedent's will through the probate process.

Sortino ratio   A performance appraisal ratio that replaces standard deviation in the Sharpe ratio with downside deviation.

Source jurisdiction or **territorial tax system**   A framework used by a country to determine the basis for taxing income or transfers. A country that taxes income as a source within its borders imposes source jurisdiction.

Source–source conflict   When two countries claim source jurisdiction of the same asset; both countries may claim that the income is derived from their jurisdiction.

Sovereign risk   A form of credit risk in which the borrower is the government of a sovereign nation.

Spontaneous investors   Investors who constantly readjust their portfolio allocations and holdings.

Spot return (or price return)   The component of the return on a commodity futures contract that comes from changes in the underlying spot prices via the cost-of-carry model.

Spread   An option strategy involving the purchase of one option and sale of another option that is identical to the first in all respects except either exercise price or expiration.

Spread duration The sensitivity of a non-Treasury security's price to a widening or narrowing of the spread over Treasuries.

Spread risk Risk related to changes in the spread between Treasuries and non-Treasuries.

Stack and roll A hedging strategy in which an existing stack hedge with maturing futures contracts is replaced by a new stack hedge with longer dated futures contracts.

Stack hedge Hedging a stream of obligations by entering futures contracts with a *single* maturity, with the number of contracts selected so that changes in the *present value* of the future obligations are offset by changes in the value of this "stack" of futures contracts.

Stale price bias Bias that arises from using prices that are stale because of infrequent trading.

Standard deviation The positive square root of variance.

Stated return desire A stated desired level of returns.

Static approach With respect to strategic asset allocation, an approach that does not account for links between optimal decisions in future time periods.

Static spread (or zero-volatility spread) The constant spread above the Treasury spot curve that equates the calculated price of the security to the market price.

Stationary A series of data for which the parameters that describe a return-generating process are stable.

Status quo trap The tendency for forecasts to perpetuate recent observations—that is, to predict no change from the recent past.

Sterling ratio The compound annualized rate of return over a specified time period divided by the average yearly maximum drawdown over the same time period less an arbitrary 10 percent.

Stock companies With respect to insurance companies, companies that have issued common equity shares.

Stock index futures Futures contracts on a specified stock index.

Storage costs or **carrying costs** The costs of holding an asset, generally a function of the physical characteristics of the underlying asset.

Straddle An option strategy involving the purchase of a put and a call with the same exercise price. A straddle is based on the expectation of high volatility of the underlying.

Straight-through processing Systems that simplify transaction processing through the minimization of manual and/or duplicative intervention in the process from trade placement to settlement.

Strangle A variation of a straddle in which the put and call have different exercise prices.

Strap An option strategy involving the purchase of two calls and one put.

Strategic asset allocation 1) The process of allocating money to IPS-permissible asset classes that integrates the investor's return objectives, risk tolerance, and investment constraints with long-run capital market expectations. 2) The result of the above process, also known as the policy portfolio.

Stratified sampling (representative sampling) A sampling method that guarantees that subpopulations of interest are represented in the sample.

Stress testing A risk management technique in which the risk manager examines the performance of the portfolio under market conditions involving high risk and usually high correlations across markets. Closely related to *scenario analysis.*

Strike spread A spread used to determine the strike price for the payoff of a credit option.

Strip An option strategy involving the purchase of two puts and one call.

Strip hedge Hedging a stream of obligations by offsetting each individual obligation with a futures contract matching the maturity and quantity of the obligation.

Structural level of unemployment The level of unemployment resulting from scarcity of a factor of production.

Structured note A variation of a floating-rate note that has some type of unusual characteristic such as a leverage factor or in which the rate moves opposite to interest rates.

Style drift Inconsistency in style.

Style index A securities index intended to reflect the average returns to a given style.

Stylized scenario A type of analysis often used in stress testing. It involves simulating the movement in at least one interest rate, exchange rate, stock price, or commodity price relevant to the portfolio.

Sunshine trades Public display of a transaction (usually high-volume) in advance of the actual order.

Surplus The difference between the value of assets and the present value of liabilities. With respect to an insurance company, the net difference between the total assets and total liabilities (equivalent to policyholders' surplus for a mutual insurance company and stockholders' equity for a stock company).

Surplus efficient frontier   The graph of the set of portfolios that maximize expected surplus for given levels of standard deviation of surplus.

Survey method   A method of capital market expectations setting that involves surveying experts.

Survival probability   The probability an individual survives in a given year; used to determine expected cash flow required in retirement.

Survivorship bias   Bias that arises in a data series when managers with poor track records exit the business and are dropped from the database whereas managers with good records remain; when a data series as of a given date reflects only entities that have survived to that date.

Swap   A contract calling for the exchange of payments over time. Often one payment is fixed in advance and the other is floating, based upon the realization of a price or interest rate.

Swap rate   The interest rate applicable to the pay-fixed-rate side of an interest rate swap.

Swap spread   The difference between the fixed rate on an interest rate swap and the rate on a Treasury note with equivalent maturity; it reflects the general level of credit risk in the market.

Swap tenor   The lifetime of a swap.

Swap term   Another name for *swap tenor*.

Swaption   An option to enter into a swap.

Symmetric cash flow matching   A cash flow matching technique that allows cash flows occurring both before and after the liability date to be used to meet a liability; allows for the short-term borrowing of funds to satisfy a liability prior to the liability due date.

Synthetic call   The combination of puts, the underlying, and risk-free bonds that replicates a call option.

Synthetic forward contract   The combination of the underlying, puts, calls, and risk-free bonds that replicates a forward contract.

Synthetic index fund   An index fund position created by combining risk-free bonds and futures on the desired index.

Synthetic put   The combination of calls, the underlying, and risk-free bonds that replicates a put option.

Tactical asset allocation   Asset allocation that involves making short-term adjustments to asset class weights based on short-term predictions of relative performance among asset classes.

Tactical rebalancing   A variation of calendar rebalancing that specifies less frequent rebalancing when markets appear to be trending and more frequent rebalancing when they are characterized by reversals.

Tail value at risk (or conditional tail expectation)   The VAR plus the expected loss in excess of VAR, when such excess loss occurs.

Target covariance matrix   A component of shrinkage estimation; allows the analyst to model factors that are believed to influence the data over periods longer than observed in the historical sample.

Target semivariance   The average squared deviation below a target value.

Target value   The value that the portfolio manager seeks to ensure; the value that the life insurance company has guaranteed the policyholder.

Tax alpha   The value created by using investment techniques that effectively manage tax liabilities.

Tax avoidance   Developing strategies that minimize tax, while conforming to both the spirit and the letter of the tax codes of jurisdictions with taxing authority.

Tax concerns   Concerns related to an investor's tax position.

Tax drag   The negative effect of taxes on after-tax returns.

Tax efficiency   The proportion of the expected pre-tax total return that will be retained after taxes.

Tax evasion   The practice of circumventing tax obligations by illegal means such as misreporting or not reporting relevant information to tax authorities.

Tax loss harvesting   The practice of realizing a loss to offset a gain or income, thereby reducing the current year's tax obligation.

Tax premium   Compensation for the effect of taxes on the after-tax return of an asset.

Tax risk   The uncertainty associated with tax laws.

Tax structures   The specifics of how governments collect taxes.

Taylor rule   A rule linking a central bank's target short-term interest rate to the rate of growth of the economy and inflation.

Tenor   The original time to maturity on a swap.

Term life insurance   A type of life insurance policy that provides coverage for a specified length of time and accumulates little or no cash values.

Termination date   The date of the final payment on a swap; also, the swap's expiration date.

Testamentary gratuitous transfer   The bequeathing or transfer of assets upon one's death. From a recipient's perspective, it is called an inheritance.

Testator   A person who makes a will.

Theta   The change in price of an option associated with a one-day reduction in its time to expiration; the rate at which an option's time value decays.

Tick   The smallest possible price movement of a security.

Time deposit A deposit requiring advance notice prior to a withdrawal.

Time horizon The time period associated with an investment objective.

Time to expiration The time remaining in the life of a derivative, typically expressed in years.

Time value or **speculative value** The difference between the market price of the option and its intrinsic value, determined by the uncertainty of the underlying over the remaining life of the option.

Time value decay The loss in the value of an option resulting from movement of the option price toward its payoff value as the expiration day approaches.

Time-period bias Bias that occurs when results are time-period specific.

Time-series estimators Estimators that are based on lagged values of the variable being forecast; often consist of lagged values of other selected variables.

Time-weighted average price (TWAP) strategy A logical participation strategy that assumes a flat volume profile and trades in proportion to time.

Time-weighted rate of return The compound rate of growth over a stated evaluation period of one unit of money initially invested in the account.

Timing option With respect to certain futures contracts, the option that results from the ability of the short position to decide when in the delivery month actual delivery will take place.

Top-down Proceeding from the macroeconomy, to the economic sector level, to the industry level, to the firm level.

Total future liability With respect to defined-benefit pension plans, the present value of accumulated and projected future service benefits, including the effects of projected future compensation increases.

Total rate of return A measure of the increase in the investor's wealth due to both investment income (for example, dividends and interest) and capital gains (both realized and unrealized).

Total return The rate of return taking into account capital appreciation/depreciation and income. Often qualified as follows: **Nominal** returns are unadjusted for inflation; **real** returns are adjusted for inflation; **pretax** returns are returns before taxes; **post-tax** returns are returns after taxes are paid on investment income and realized capital gains.

Total return analysis Analysis of the expected effect of a trade on the portfolio's total return, given an interest rate forecast.

Total return swap A swap in which one party agrees to pay the total return on a security. Often used as a credit derivative, in which the underlying is a bond.

Tracking risk (also called tracking error, tracking error volatility, or active risk) The condition in which the performance of a portfolio does not match the performance of an index that serves as the portfolio's benchmark.

Trade blotter A device for entering and tracking trade executions and orders to trade.

Trade settlement Completion of a trade wherein purchased financial instruments are transferred to the buyer and the buyer transfers money to the seller.

Trading activity In fixed-income attribution analysis, the effect of sales and purchases of bonds over a given period; the total portfolio return minus the other components determining the management effect in an attribution analysis.

Transaction exposure The risk associated with a foreign exchange rate on a specific business transaction such as a purchase or sale.

Transcription errors Errors in gathering and recording data.

Translation exposure The risk associated with the conversion of foreign financial statements into domestic currency.

Transparency Availability of timely and accurate market and trade information.

Treasury spot curve The term structure of Treasury zero coupon bonds.

Treynor ratio (or reward-to-volatility) A measure of risk-adjusted performance that relates an account's excess returns to the systematic risk assumed by the account.

Turnover A measure of the rate of trading activity in a portfolio.

Twist With respect to the yield curve, a movement in contrary directions of interest rates at two maturities; a nonparallel movement in the yield curve.

Type I error With respect to manager selection, keeping (or hiring) managers with zero value-added. (Rejecting the null hypothesis when it is correct.)

Type II error With respect to manager selection, firing (or not hiring) managers with positive value-added. (Not rejecting the null hypothesis when it is incorrect.)

Unconstrained optimization Optimization that places no constraints on asset class weights except that they sum to 1. May produce negative asset weights, which implies borrowing or shorting of assets.

Underfunded plan   A pension plan in which the ratio of the value of plan assets to the present value of plan liabilities is less than 100 percent.

Underlying   An asset that trades in a market in which buyers and sellers meet, decide on a price, and the seller then delivers the asset to the buyer and receives payment. The underlying is the asset or other derivative on which a particular derivative is based. The market for the underlying is also referred to as the spot market.

Underwriting (profitability) **cycle**   A cycle affecting the profitability of insurance companies' underwriting operations.

Undisclosed limit order (reserve, hidden, or iceberg order)   A limit order that includes an instruction not to show more than some maximum quantity of the unfilled order to the public at any one time.

Unhedged return   A foreign asset return stated in terms of the investor's home currency.

Unique circumstances   Internal factors (other than a liquidity requirement, time horizon, or tax concern) that may constrain portfolio choices.

Universal life insurance   A type of life insurance policy that provides for premium flexibility, an adjustable face amount of death benefits, and current market interest rates on the savings element.

Unrelated business income   With respect to the U.S. tax code, income that is not substantially related to a foundation's charitable purposes.

Unstructured modeling   Modeling without a theory on the underlying structure.

Uptick rules   Trading rules that specify that a short sale must not be on a downtick relative to the last trade at a different price.

Urgency of the trade   The importance of certainty of execution.

Valuation   The process of determining the value of an asset or service.

Valuation reserve   With respect to insurance companies, an allowance, created by a charge against earnings, to provide for losses in the value of the assets.

Value   The amount for which one can sell something, or the amount one must pay to acquire something.

Value at risk (VAR)   A probability-based measure of loss potential for a company, a fund, a portfolio, a transaction, or a strategy over a specified period of time.

Value investment style   With reference to equity investing, an investment style focused on paying a relatively low share price in relation to earnings or assets per share.

Value weighted (or market-capitalization weighted)   With respect to index construction, an index in which each security in the index is weighted according to its market capitalization.

Value-motivated traders   Traders that act on value judgments based on careful, sometimes painstaking research. They trade only when the price moves into their value range.

Variable annuity   A life annuity in which the periodic payment varies depending on stock prices.

Variable life insurance (unit-linked life insurance)   A type of ordinary life insurance in which death benefits and cash values are linked to the investment performance of a policyholder-selected pool of investments held in a so-called separate account.

Variable prepaid forward   A monetization strategy that involves the combination of a collar with a loan against the value of the underlying shares. When the loan comes due, shares are sold to pay off the loan and part of any appreciation is shared with the lender.

Variable universal life (or flexible-premium variable life)   A type of life insurance policy that combines the flexibility of universal life with the investment choice flexibility of variable life.

Variance   The expected value of squared deviations from the random variable's mean; often referred to as volatility.

Variation margin   Additional margin that must be deposited in an amount sufficient to bring the balance up to the initial margin requirement.

Vega   A measure of the sensitivity of an option's price to changes in the underlying's volatility.

Venture capital   The equity financing of new or growing private companies.

Venture capital firms   Firms representing dedicated pools of capital for providing equity or equity-linked financing to privately held companies.

Venture capital fund   A pooled investment vehicle for venture capital investing.

Venture capital trusts   An exchange-traded, closed-end vehicle for venture capital investing.

Venture capitalists   Specialists who seek to identify companies that have good business opportunities but need financial, managerial, and strategic support.

Vested   With respect to pension benefits or assets, said of an unconditional ownership interest.

Vintage year   With reference to a private equity fund, the year it closed.

Vintage year effects The effects on returns shared by private equity funds closed in the same year.

Volatility Represented by the Greek letter sigma (σ), the standard deviation of price outcomes associated with an underlying asset.

Volatility clustering The tendency for large (small) swings in prices to be followed by large (small) swings of random direction.

Volume-weighted average price (VWAP) The average price at which a security is traded during the day, where each trade price is weighted by the fraction of the day's volume associated with the trade.

Volume-weighted average price strategy A logical participation strategy that involves breaking up an order over time according to a prespecified volume profile.

Wealth relative The ending value of one unit of money invested at specified rates of return.

Weather derivative A derivative contract with a payment based on a weather-related measurement, such as heating or cooling degree days.

Wild card option A provision allowing a short futures contract holder to delay delivery of the underlying.

Will (or testament) A document associated with estate planning that outlines the rights others will have over one's property after death.

Within-sector selection return In attribution analysis, a measure of the impact of a manager's security selection decisions relative to the holdings of the sector benchmark.

Worst-case scenario analysis A stress test in which we examine the worst case that we actually expect to occur.

Yield beta A measure of the sensitivity of a bond's yield to a general measure of bond yields in the market that is used to refine the hedge ratio.

Yield curve The relationship between yield and time to maturity.

Yield curve risk Risk related to changes in the shape of the yield curve.

Yield spread The difference between the yield on a bond and the yield on a default-free security, usually a government note, of the same maturity. The yield spread is primarily determined by the market's perception of the credit risk on the bond.

Yield to worst The yield on a callable bond that assumes a bond is called at the earliest opportunity.

Zero-cost collar A transaction in which a position in the underlying is protected by buying a put and selling a call with the premium from the sale of the call offsetting the premium from the purchase of the put. It can also be used to protect a floating-rate borrower against interest rate increases with the premium on a long cap offsetting the premium on a short floor.

Zero-premium collar A hedging strategy involving the simultaneous purchase of puts and sale of call options on a stock. The puts are struck below and the calls are struck above the underlying's market price.

$4\frac{5}{8}$ $4\frac{11}{16}$ $-\frac{3}{8}$

$5\frac{1}{2}$ $5\frac{1}{2}$ $-\frac{3}{8}$

$5\frac{1}{2}$ $21\frac{3}{16}$ $-\frac{1}{8}$

$20\frac{5}{8}$ $21\frac{3}{16}$ $+\frac{7}{8}$

$17\frac{3}{8}$ $18\frac{1}{8}$ $+$

$6\frac{1}{2}$ $6\frac{1}{2}$ $-\frac{1}{2}$

$7\frac{1}{4}$ $6\frac{1}{2}$ $-\frac{1}{8}$

$\frac{15}{16}$ $\frac{31}{32}$ $-\frac{1}{8}$

$\frac{9}{16}$ $\frac{9}{16}$

$\frac{9}{16}$ $7\frac{15}{16}$

$7\frac{13}{16}$ $7\frac{15}{16}$

$7\frac{15}{16}$

$2\frac{5}{8}$ $2\frac{11}{32}$ $2\frac{1}{2}$ $+$

$2\frac{3}{4}$ $2\frac{1}{4}$ $2\frac{1}{4}$

$12\frac{1}{16}$ $11\frac{3}{8}$ $11\frac{3}{4}$ $+$

$6\frac{1}{2}$ $33\frac{3}{4}$ 33 $33\frac{1}{8}$ $-$

87

$25\frac{5}{8}$ $24\frac{9}{16}$ $25\frac{3}{8}$ $+$

602 12 $11\frac{5}{8}$ $11\frac{7}{8}$ $+$

833

$10\frac{1}{2}$ $10\frac{1}{2}$ $10\frac{1}{2}$ $-$

16

$15\frac{7}{8}$ $15\frac{13}{16}$ $15\frac{7}{8}$ $-$

78

$9\frac{1}{16}$ $8\frac{1}{4}$ $8\frac{1}{2}$ $+$

808

$11\frac{1}{4}$ $10\frac{1}{8}$

430

default value at risk. *See* credit value at
  risk (VAR)
defaultable debt, V3: 94
deferred capital gains, V2: 179–182
deferred swaps, V5: 155
deficits. *See also* debt
  affecting economic growth, V3: 74
  manipulating, V3: 69 (*see also* fiscal
    policy)
  ratio of GDP to, V3: 80–81
defined benefit (DB) pension plans.
    See also pension plans; retirement
    portfolios
  about, V2: 368–369
  allocating shareholder capital
    accounting for value mismatch
      and risk, V2: 478–481
    alternative pension policies, V2:
      484–486
    asset allocation changes, effects
      on optimal capital structure,
      V2: 486
    conclusions about, V2: 489–490
    funding shortfalls (underfunding),
      V2: 475–476, 488
    illustrations, V2: 481, 483–484
    implementation of changes,
      V2: 488
    introduction to, V2: 473–475
    moving from a DB plan to a DC
      plan, V2: 489
    overfunding, V2: 488
    pension liabilities, immunization
      of, V2: 487, 487n13
    recognizing risk, V2: 477–478
    risk budgets, V2: 475, 482
    risk mismatch between assets and
      liabilities, V2: 476–477
    risks and capital, cushioning, V2:
      487–488
    strategic analysis and policy
      development, V2: 482–488
    underfunding (funding
      shortfalls), V2: 475–476, 488
    weighted average cost of capital
      (WACC) and risk, V2: 479–480
  corporate risk management and
    investment of assets, V2: 381–382
  definitions, V2: 367, 369
  discussed, V2: 49–50
  distinguished from defined
    contribution plans, V2: 367–368
  investment policy statements
    example of, V2: 378–381
    legal and regulatory factors, V2:
      377–378
    liquidity requirements, V2:
      375–376
    return objectives, V2: 373–375

  risk objectives, V2: 369–373
  tax concerns, V2: 377
  time horizon, V2: 376–377
  unique circumstances, V2: 378
  longevity risk and, V2: 346–347
defined contribution (DC) pension
    plans. *See also* employee share
    ownership plans (ESOPs);
    employee stock ownership plans
    (ESOPs)
  about, V2: 382–383
  defined, V2: 367
  discussed, V2: 50
  distinguished from defined benefit
    plans, V2: 367–368
  investment decision making in
    conclusions about, V2: 61
    education of participants and
      pension scheme design, V2:
      56–58
    introduction to, V2: 49–51
    knowledge, confidence, and
      investment choices of
      participants, V2: 51–53
    portfolio diversification and
      investor perceptions of risk, V2:
      53–55
    U.K. comparisons, V2: 58–61
  investment policy statements
    example of, V2: 384–388
    objectives and constraints
      framework, V2: 383–384
  longevity risk and, V2: 347
  moving from a DB plan to a DC
    plan, V2: 489
deflation, in business cycle, V3: 58–62
delay costs, V6: 24, 26
delivery options, V4: 116
delivery requirements, in repurchase
  agreements, V4: 111
Dell, Inc., V4: 226
Deloitte Touche Thomatsu
  International Business Guides,
  V2: 171, 171n1
delta, V5: 230, 465–467
delta hedging, V5: 309, 456–457. *See also*
  option portfolio risk management
delta-normal method, V5: 238. *See also*
  value at risk (VAR)
demand
  bond yield affected by, V3: 95
  in BRICs forecasts, V3: 194
  electricity price linked to, V5: 175
  season affecting (*see* seasonality)
  for venture capital, V5: 30–31
demand deposits, V2: 428n30
demographics, in BRICs forecasts, V3:
  193, 198, 209, 221
demutualizing, V2: 406

Denmark, V2: 185n5, 200n18, V3: 84
depreciation expense, in EPS estimates,
  V3: 165–166, 167–168, 171
depth, liquid markets and, V6: 20
derivative trades, V6: 101–102
derivatives. *See also* credit derivatives
  about, V4: 111
  accounting risk in, V5: 226–227
  bond variance vs. bond duration,
    V4: 114
  credit risk in, V5: 220n7, 256,
    266–267
  credit risk instruments, V4: 123–128
  currency management and, V6:
    217–219
  dealer ratings in, V5: 266
  interest rate futures, V4: 114–120
  interest rate options, V4: 121–123
  interest rate risk, V4: 111–113
  interest rate swaps, V4: 120–121
  other risk measures, V4: 113–114
  products used in, V4: 115
  weather-related, V5: 200–201
  zero sum nature of, V5: 96n126
derivatives-based semiactive equity
  strategies, V4: 250–253
descriptive statistics, V3: 25
Deutsche Bank, V5: 10
Deutsche Telekom, V4: 301
developed market equity, V3: 245
developed market fixed income,
  V3: 245
developed markets, equity indexes for.
  See international equity indexes
developing countries. *See* Brazil,
  Russia, India, and China (BRICs);
  emerging markets; international
  interactions
Diamond, Peter, V2: 20
Dietz, Peter O., V6: 134, 267, 341
diff swaps, V5: 160–161
differential returns, V6: 149
differential voting rights, V4: 329
diffusion indexes, V3: 84, 137–138. *See
  also* economic indicators
diligence
  Code of Ethics requirements, V1: 156
  defined, V1: 156
  Standards of Professional
    Conduct V.A
    about, V1: 80, 171–173
    application of standard, V1: 82–84
    case study, V1: 211, 213
    compliance procedures, V1: 81–82
    group research and decision
      making, V1: 81, 172–173
    secondary or third-party research,
      use of, V1: 81, 172
    text of standard, V1: 13

LIRR method. *See* linked internal rate of return (LIRR) method
litigation, as corporate takeover defense, V4: 329
Litterman, Robert, V3: 274, 282. *See also* Black-Litterman approach
lives, V2: 369
Livingston, Joseph, V3: 51
Livingston Survey, V3: 51
LLCs. *See* limited liability companies (LLCs)
loans. *See also* floating-rate loans
    converting currencies of, V5: 493–497
    FRA in risk management on, V5: 336–339
    interest rate calls on, V5: 433–439
    interest rate puts on, V5: 439–444
local currency, calculating multicurrency returns in, V6: 207
local law, relationship with Code of Ethics and Standards of Professional Conduct, V1: 16
local market return, V5: 379
lock-up period, V5: 64–65, 80–81
locked-up investments, V3: 46
Loews Cineplex Entertainment Corporation, V5: 107
logical participation algorithmic strategies, V6: 46–49
London, off-shore banking services, V2: 258
London Interbank Offered Rate (LIBOR), V4: 221, V5: 152n2, 165, 494n14
London International Financial Futures Exchange (LIFFE), V5: 293
London Stock Exchange, V6: 12
Long-Leading Index, V3: 139
long–short investing
    about, V4: 244–245
    equitizing a market-neutral long–short portfolio, V4: 246–247
    example of, V4: 249
    long-only constraint, V4: 247
    price inefficiency on the short side, V4: 245–246
    short extension strategies, V4: 247–248
long tail, V2: 419n26
long-term bonds, in asset allocation, V3: 245
Long-Term Capital Management (LTCM) fund, V2: 11, 23–24, 30, V3: 76–77, V5: 74, 257
longevity risk
    in asset allocation, V3: 303–304
    defined, V2: 343
    lifetime-payout annuities and, V2: 316–318

Monte Carlo simulation, V2: 343
    probability of living to age 100, V2: 317
    retirement portfolio and, V2: 343–345
Lopes, Lola, V2: 34, 35, 37, 38, 40, 44
"loser's game," V2: 83
loss aversion
    defined, V2: 14, 14n2
    discussed, V2: 107
    frame dependence and, V2: 14–15
    investor goals and, V2: 291–292, 291n2
low-basis, V2: 269
low-basis stocks
    acquisition methods, V2: 270
    basis, about, V2: 269–270
    case studies, V2: 283
    dealing with low-basis holdings, V2: 270–271
    diversification stages, V2: 273–275
    introduction to, V2: 269
    reducing concentrated exposure, V2: 276–282
    summary and implications, V2: 282–285
low P/E investors, V4: 225
Lowenstein, George, V2: 36
lower cost enhancements, benchmark bond indexes and, V4: 21
loyalty to clients
    Asset Manager Code of Professional Conduct, V1: 221, 224–225
    Standards of Professional Conduct III.A
        about, V1: 48–50, 164–165
        application of standard, V1: 51–53
        case studies, V1: 181–183, 189–191, 206, 208
        compliance procedures, V1: 50–51
        soft dollar arrangement provisions, V6: 30
        text of standard, V1: 12
loyalty to employers, Standards of Professional Conduct IV.A
    about, V1: 69, 169–170
    application of standard, V1: 71–74
    case studies, V1: 186–188, 206
    definitions, V1: 70
    independent practice, V1: 70
    leaving an employer, V1: 70–71
    nature of employment, V1: 71
    text of standard, V1: 13
    whistleblowing, V1: 71, 170
LR model. *See* Levine-Renelt (LR) model
LTCM fund. *See* Long-Term Capital Management (LTCM) fund
Luxembourg, V2: 200n18, 258

M
M², V6: 174
Macaulay duration, V4: 30n19, V5: 340, 341n7
macro attribution in portfolio performance evaluation
    analysis of, V6: 154–158
    defined, V6: 150
    inputs for, V6: 152–153
    overview of, V6: 151
macro expectations, V3: 6
Macroeconomic Asset Management (case study), V1: 184–186
macroeconomic stability, as growth factor, V3: 205, 206–208
macromarket analysis. *See also* cyclical indicator approach; microvaluation analysis
    business cycle/stock price connection in, V3: 135
    economy and security market linked in, V3: 134–135
    interest rates in, V3: 142–145
    international interactions in, V3: 77
    money supply in, V3: 140–142
    for non-U.S. markets, V3: 145
    role of, V3: 133–134
    web resources for, V3: 184–186
Mahathir Mohamad, V4: 406
maintenance phase of life, investor characteristics, V2: 104
Malaysia
    Asian currency crisis, V4: 402
    capital flow in, V3: 387
    currency pegging in, V3: 77
    emerging market benchmarks for, V4: 368n10
    foreign capital controls, V4: 386
    impact of benchmarking, V4: 369–371
    stock ownership patterns, V4: 406
Malkiel, Burton, V4: 203
managed futures investment
    benchmarks and historical performance of, V5: 93–95
    characteristics of, V5: 96–97
    classification of, V5: 61, 92
    defined, V5: 7–8, 91
    example of, V5: 99–101
    interpretation of, V5: 95–96
    market opportunities for, V5: 92–93
    overview, V5: 91–92
    past performance and due diligence in, V5: 99
    portfolio role of, V5: 97–99
management buyout (MBO), V4: 330, 332
management fees, V1: 235, V3: 378

straddles, as equity portfolio strategy, V5: 427–430

straight through processing (STP), V6: 10

straight-through processing (STP) systems, V5: 217

strangles, V5: 429

straps, V5: 429

strategic analysis, in DB pension plans, V2: 482–488

strategic asset allocation. *See also* asset allocation
AO vs. ALM approach to, V3: 232–234
defined, V3: 227, 229
implementing, V3: 295–297
return objectives in, V3: 234–237
risk objectives in, V3: 237–241
role of, V3: 228–229
TAA vs., V3: 229–230

Strategic Asset Allocation: Portfolio Choice for Long-Term Investors (Campbell and Viceira), V3: 300, 301

strategic hedge ratio. *See* benchmark hedge ratio

strategic partners, V5: 33

stratified sampling, V4: 217, 218. *See also* cell-matching technique

stress testing, V5: 247–249

strike spread, V4: 124

strip hedges, V5: 198

strips, V5: 172, 198, 340n4, 429

structural level of unemployment, V3: 75

structure trades, V4: 73–74

structured notes
defined, V5: 482, 488
swaps in risk management for, V5: 488–490, 490–493

style analysis, of portfolio managers, V4: 142

style drift, V4: 242, 243

style exposures, V6: 83–84

stylized scenario approach, V5: 247–248

success, evaluating private equity prospects for, V5: 45

success, private equity prospects and, V5: 44

suitability, Standards of Professional Conduct III.C
about, V1: 60–62, 166–168
application of standard, V1: 63–64
case study, V1: 179–181, 181–184
compliance procedures, V1: 62
text of standard, V1: 12–13

Sultanate of Oman, V3: 77

supermajority rule, corporate takeovers and, V4: 328

supervisors
Code of Ethics requirements, V1: 157–158
responsibilities of (Standards of Professional Conduct IV.C)
about, V1: 76, 171
adequate compliance procedures defined, V1: 76
application of standard, V1: 78–80
case studies, V1: 181–184, 189–191, 205
compliance procedures, V1: 76–78
text of standard, V1: 13

supply, V5: 175. *See also* seasonality

surety companies. *See* casualty insurance companies

surplus
in ALM process, V3: 285 (*see also* mean-variance surplus optimization)
casualty insurance companies, V2: 422
defined, V2: 408n21
in pension fund analysis, V5: 244–245

surplus at risk, V5: 244–245

surplus beta decision, V3: 285. *See also* mean-variance surplus optimization

surplus efficient frontier, V3: 285. *See also* mean-variance surplus optimization

survey methods, V3: 51–52, 65

Survey of Consumer Finances, V2: 45, V3: 300

Survey of Professional Forecasters, V2: 64

surveys, V3: 140, V5: 10

survivorship bias
in CME development, V3: 15
global performance appraisal and, V6: 235
hedge fund analysis affected by, V5: 74
managed futures analysis affected by, V5: 95–96

Swaminathan, Bhaskaran, V2: 30

swap counterparties, V5: 144–145, 149–150

swap curves, V5: 152–153, 162

swap markets, V5: 47

swap rates, V5: 150–151, 220n7

swap spreads, V4: 77–78, V5: 153

swap tenor, V5: 148

swap terms, V5: 148

swaps
commodities in (*see* commodity swaps)
credit risk in, V5: 253–254
currencies in (*see* currency swaps)

defined, V5: 141, 479
equities in (*see* equity swaps)
equity total return swaps, V4: 221
as exchange rate strategy
dual-currency bonds in, V5: 499–502
foreign cash conversions in, V5: 497–499
loan conversions in, V5: 493–497
forward contracts on, V5: 526
as interest rate strategy (*see also* interest rate swaps)
duration adjustments in, V5: 485–488
fixed-rate vs. floating-rate loans in, V5: 482–485
introduction to, V5: 481–482
inverse floaters in, V5: 490–493
leveraged floating-rate notes in, V5: 488–490
introduction to, V5: 141–142
option to enter into (*see* swaptions)
risk management overview, V5: 479–481
total return, V5: 164–166

swaptions. *See also* swaps
for callable debt adjustments
adding calls in, V5: 522–526
removing calls in, V5: 520–522
in future borrowing plans, V5: 513–516
risk management overview, V5: 512–513
in swap terminations, V5: 516–520
types of, V5: 163–164, 481, 512

Sweden
economic flexibility in, V3: 369–370
economic indicators for, V3: 84
exit taxes, V2: 254
stock ownership patterns, V4: 320

Swensen, Dave, V2: 83

Switzerland
economic indicators for, V3: 84
gift taxes, V2: 240
in global market correlation, V3: 360, 361
pension plan assets in, V3: 307–308
stock ownership patterns, V4: 319
wealth and wealth transfer taxes, V2: 253

symmetric cash flow matching, V4: 47

synthetic cash, V5: 360–364

synthetic index fund, V5: 355–358

systematic biases, V6: 145–146

systematic risk, V2: 271, V5: 229n21, 350

systematic trading strategies
for hedging currency risk, V5: 303–304
for managed futures, V5: 92